A Great Feat of Improvisation

Logistics and the British Expeditionary Force in France 1939-1940

Clem Maginniss

Helion & Company Limited

Helion & Company Limited
Unit 8 Amherst Business Centre
Budbrooke Road
Warwick
CV34 5WE
England
Tel. 01926 499 619
Email: info@helion.co.uk
Website: www.helion.co.uk
Twitter: @helionbooks
Visit our blog at blog.helion.co.uk

Published by Helion & Company 2021
Designed and typeset by Mary Woolley (www.battlefield-design.co.uk)
Cover designed by Paul Hewitt, Battlefield Design (www.battlefield-design.co.uk)

ISBN 978-1-913336-15-8

British Library Cataloguing-in-Publication Data.
A catalogue record for this book is available from the British Library.

In Memory of:

5114497 Private Fred Gilbert Royal Warwickshire Regiment[1]

5114456 Private Hugh Maginniss Royal Warwickshire Regiment[2]

Signalman John Yeomans Royal Corps of Signals[3]

Three Warwickshire Citizen Soldiers for whom logistics in the BEF were all too real

and

Vincent Charles Sorge

1956-1982

Leader and Logistician

1 Wounded three times and then captured whilst fighting with 8th Warwicks on the Ypres-Comines Canal on 27 May 1940.

2 Evacuated from Rouen, transferred to 2nd Norfolk Regiment and Killed In Action near Saye in Burma 19 February 1945.

3 Evacuated from the East Mole Dunkirk, released to industry and joined the Stoneleigh Home Guard.

Contents

List of Abbreviations

AA - Anti-Aircraft
AAA - Anti-Aircraft Artillery
AAD - Advanced Ammunition Depot
AA & QMG - Assistant Adjutant & Quartermaster-General
AASF - Advanced Air Striking Force
ABA - Advanced Base Area
ABC - Armoured Brigade Company
ADAPS - Assistant Director Army Postal Services
ADGB - Air Defence Great Britain
ADGW - Aerially Delivered Gas Weapon
ADOS - Assistant Director Ordnance Services
AF - Army Form
AFV - Armoured Fighting Vehicle
AFW - Army Field Workshop
AG - Adjutant General
AGE - Anti-Gas Equipment
AGM - Anti-Gas Measures
AMOH - Air Ministry Official History
AMPC - Auxiliary Military Pioneer Corps
AOC - Air Officer Commanding
AOD - Advanced Ordnance Depot
AOW - Advanced Ordnance Workshops
AP - Ammunition Point or Armour Piercing
APO - Army Post Office
AQ - Adjutant & Quartermaster-General
AQMG - Assistant Quartermaster-General
ARH - Ammunition Railhead
ARP - Ammunition Refilling Point
ASD - Ammunition Sub-Depot
ASP - Air Stores Park
A/T - Anti-Tank
AT - Animal Transport
ATN - Ambulance Train
ATR - Ambulance Train Railhead
ATS - Auxiliary Territorial Service

BAD - Base Ammunition Depot
BAFF - British Air Forces France
BCV - Bulk Contamination Vehicle
BEF - British Expeditionary Force
BOD - Base Ordnance Depot
BOH - British Official History
BOW - Base Ordnance Workshop
BPFC - Base Petrol Filling Centre
BSA - Base Sub-Area
BSD - Base Supply Depot
CAD - Central Ammunition Depot
CAP - Corps Ammunition Park
C^3 - Command, Control & Communications
CCS - Casualty Clearing Station
CIGS - Chief of the Imperial General Staff
C-in-C - Commander-in-Chief
CPP - Corps Petrol Park
CRAOC - Commander Royal Army Ordnance Corps
CRASC - Commander Royal Army Service Corps
CRE - Commander Royal Engineers
CW - Chemical Warfare
CWGC - Commonwealth War Graves Commission
DAA & QMG - Deputy Assistant Adjutant & Quartermaster-General
DAC - Divisional Ammunition Company
DAER - Daily Ammunition Expenditure Rate
DAQMG - Deputy Assistant Quartermaster-General
DDMO - Deputy Director Military Operations
DDOS - Deputy Director Ordnance Services
DDST - Deputy Director Supplies & Transport
DID - Detail Issue Depot
DMI - Director Military Intelligence
DMO - Director Military Operations
DMT - Director Military Training
DOS - Days of Supply or Director Ordnance Services
DPC - Divisional Petrol Company
DQUAD - Destination, Demand, Distance and Duration
DSC - Divisional Supply Column
ECM - *En-Cas Mobile*
FSPB - Field Service Pocket Book.
FSR - Field Service Regulations
GBAD - Ground Based Air Defence
GHQ - General Headquarters
GLOC - Ground Line of Communication
GOC - General Officer Commanding
GRT - Gross Registered Tonnage

GS - General Staff (or General Service)
GSO - General Staff Officer
GSU - GHQ Salvage Unit
GW - Gas Warfare
GWR - Great Western Railway
HE - High Explosive
HMF - His Majesty's Factory
HMG - Heavy Machine Gun
HMS - His Majesty's Ship
HQ - Headquarters
HRS - Heavy Repair Shop
IGS - Indian General Staff
IPE - Individual Protective Equipment
IWM - Imperial War Museum
KIA - Killed in Action
LMG - Light Machine Gun
LMR - Longmoor Military Railway
LMS - London Midland & Scottish (Railway)
LNER - London & North Eastern Railway
LOC - Line of Communication
MBA - Main Base Area
MBU - Mobile Bath Unit
MEDLOC - Mediterranean Line of Communication
MHE - Material Handling Equipment
MMG - Medium Machine Gun
MOD - Ministry of Defence
MPP - Maintenance Project Plan
MRW - Mobile Railway Workshop
MSBA - Medical Sub-Base Area
MSR - Main Supply Route
MT - Mechanical (or Motor) Transport
MTSD - Motor Transport Stores Depot
MV - Motor Vessel
NAAFI - Navy Army & Air Force Institutes
NBI - Non-Battle Injury
NCP - Northern Channel Ports
NGR - Narrow Gauge Railway
nm - nautical mile
OC - Officer Commanding
OIC - Officer-in-Charge
OR - Other Rank(s)
ORB - Operations Record Book (RAF)
ORBAT - Order of Battle
PAD - Passive Air Defence
POL - Petroleum Oils & Lubricants

POLD - Petroleum Oils & Lubricants Depot
POW - Prisoner of War
PP - Petroleum Point
PRH - Petrol Railhead
PRP - Petrol Refilling Point
psc – Passed Staff College
PW - Permanent Way
PWD - Port Workshop Detachment
QAIMNS - Queen Alexandra's Imperial Military Nursing Service
QMG - Quartermaster-General
RAF - Royal Air Force
RAOC - Royal Army Ordnance Corps
RASC - Royal Army Service Corps
RCC - Railway Construction Company
RCO - Railway Construction & Operating Company
RE - Royal Engineers
REC - Railway Executive Committee
RFF - Royal Filling Factory
RHQ - Regimental Headquarters
RLCM - Royal Logistic Corps Museum
RMTC - Reserve Motor Transport Company
RN - Royal Navy
ROC - Railway Operating Company
ROF - Royal Ordnance Factory
rpg - rounds per gun
rpgpd - rounds per gun per day
RPI - Retail Price Index
RTA - Road Traffic Accident
RTC - Rail Tank Car or Railway Training Centre
RTO - Railway Traffic Officer
RUSI - Royal United Services Institution
RVP - Rendezvous Point
RWC - Railway Workshop Company
SAA - Small Arms Ammunition
SAT - Standard Ammunition Train
SCI - Smoke Curtain Installation or Spray Container Installation
SEP - South East Ports
SGR - Standard Gauge Railway
SLOC - Sea Line of Communication
SNCF - *Société Nationale des Chemins de Fer Francais*
SPOD - Sea Port of Disembarkation
SPOE - Sea Port of Embarkation
SR - Supplementary Reserve
SRD - Supply Reserve Depot
SRH - Supply Railhead

SS - Steam Ship
TA - Territorial Army
TCC - Troop Carrying Company
TML - Tank Museum Library
TNA - The National Archives (UK)
TSC - Transportation Stores Company
TSD - Transportation Stores Depot
VRD - Vehicle Reserve Depot
WD - War Diary (Army)
WE - War Establishment
WET - War Establishment Table
WMT - Wheeled Motor Transport
WO - War Office
WOOH - War Office Official History

List of Diagrams

List of Maps

List of Photographs & Illustrations

Notes:

WDLMRC: War Department Longmoor Military Railway Collection (courtesy of Colonel David Ronald (DR) and Mike Christensen (MC) OBE).
MT: Motor Transport
NOR: No Object Reference.
RLCM: Royal Logistic Corps Museum.
SRB: Supply Rations Bakeries.

List of Tables

BEF Divisions & Types
France 1940

Nomenclature	Type	Initial Allocation	Remarks
1st	Armoured	IV Corps	
1st	Infantry	IV Corps	Canadian - Brigade Group only
1st	Infantry	I Corps	
2nd	Infantry	I Corps	
3rd	Infantry	II Corps	
4th	Infantry	II Corps	
5th	Infantry	GHQ Reserve	
12th	Infantry (TA)	LOC	Eastern
23rd	Infantry (TA)	LOC	Northumbrian
42nd	Infantry (TA)	III Corps	East Lancashire
44th	Infantry (TA)	III Corps	Home Counties
46th	Infantry (TA)	LOC	North Midland & West Riding
48th	Infantry (TA)	I Corps	South Midland
50th	Motorised (TA)	II Corps	Northumbrian
51st	Infantry (TA)	Saar Force & 10th French Army	Highland
52nd	Infantry (TA)	IV Corps	Lowland
Beauman	Infantry	LOC	*Ad Hoc* – mostly TA

BEF
Senior & Key Q Appointments

Appointment	Incumbent	Corps~	Remarks
Quartermaster-General	Lieutenant-General W G Lindsell	RA	DSO OBE MC
Deputy QMG	T/Brigadier R H R Parminter DSO MC	Late	Manchester Regiment
Maintenance	Brigadier G H Gill CMG DSO	Late	R Munster Fusiliers
Movements AQMG	Colonel A K Grant DSO	Late	R West Kent Regiment
Director-General Transportation	A/Brigadier D J McMullen DSO OBE	RE	
DDG Transportation	Colonel L H Woodhouse MC	RE	Rail, Docks & IWT
DDG Transportation	Colonel J R Roberts	RE	Construction & Stores
Director Works	Brigadier W Cave-Brown CBE DSO MC	RE	
Director Tptn Construction	Colonel R D Waghorn	RE	WEF February 1940
Director Docks	Colonel J R Sadler	RE	
Director Railways	Colonel E A Johnstone CBE	RE	
Director Railway Operating	Colonel F A Pope	RE	
Director Supplies & Transport	Brigadier G K Archibald DSO	RASC	
Director Supplies & Petrol	A/Brigadier G C G Blunt DSO OBE	RASC	WEF December 1939

ADST <	Colonel A H Maude CMG DSO TD	RASC	
Deputy Director Transport	Colonel A P B Pereira DSO	RASC	
Deputy Director Supplies	Colonel A E Holbrook DSO	RASC	
Director Ordnance Services	Brigadier A C V Gibson OBE	RAOC	
Deputy Director Ordnance Services	Colonel C Cansdale OBE	RAOC	4 x Assistant Directors
POME+	T/Brigadier J D White DSO MC	RAOC	
Engineer 1st Class	Colonel J H Graham	RAOC	
Director Labour	T/Brigadier E A Cox-Field MBE		
Assistant Director Postal	Lieutenant-Colonel W R Roberts	^RE	
DA & QMG I Corps	A/Brigadier J G Halsted CBE MC	Late	Loyal (North) Lancs
AQMG I Corps	Lieutenant-Colonel T J W Winterton	^	^ Ox & Bucks LI
DDST* I Corps	T/Brigadier C le B Goldney MC	RASC	May 1940 – III Corps
DA & QMG II Corps	A/Brigadier G E Mansergh MC	RSIGS	
AQMG	Colonel A E F Q Perkins MC	RE	KIA 10 May 1940
DDST II Corps	A/Brigadier V O Beuttler CBE DSO	RASC	
DA & QMG III Corps	A/Brigadier H M Gale MC	RASC	
DDST* III Corps	Brigadier L G Humphries	RASC	
GOC LOC	Major-General P de Fonblanque	RE	Died 2 July 1940
DDST LOC	Colonel C L St J Tudor OBE MC	RASC	

Notes:

~ Late Regiment or Corps. ^ denotes still badged.
< ADST: Assistant Director Supplies & Transport
DDG: Deputy Director-General
* DDST: Deputy Director Supplies & Transport
+ POME: Principal Ordnance Mechanical Engineer

BEF Logistics Notes

To set the scene for logistics in 1939, it is useful to briefly describe how the key functions were enacted. Combat Supplies (ammunition, petrol and rations) were a Royal Army Service Corps (RASC) responsibility, as was the Expeditionary Forces Institute (EFI), whilst technical and Motor Transport (MT) spares were the prerogative of the Royal Army Ordnance Corps (RAOC). The Corps of Royal Engineers (RE) were responsible for the construction and maintenance of logistic infrastructure and the Postal Services, and the Auxiliary Military Pioneer Corps (AMPC) provided Pioneer and Labour capability.

Transportation, conducted by the Royal Engineers, included rail operation, construction and maintenance, plus Ports and Docks, Inland Water Transport (IWT) and Movement Control (MC). Road transport at 2nd and 3rd Line was, for the most part, the responsibility of the RASC. The RE, RASC and RAOC deployed a wide variety of units to France in the period 1939-1940 and their scope and scale gives a clear impression of the complexity and depth of logistic operations. Equipment Support was the least coherent capability within the logistic matrix because the responsibility for it was split between the RE, RASC, RAOC and in specific instances, regimental specialists. As the motorization and mechanization of the Army progressed, the centralization of the vehicle repair and stores systems was a natural corollary, but the concept was overrun by the complexities and dynamics of the rearmament and expansion programmes, thus delaying the formation of the Royal Electrical and Mechanical Engineers (REME) until 1942. Corps, GHQ and Base units included:

Corps:

RASC: Ammunition Company, Ammunition Park, Petrol Park, Supply Column and Pack Transport Company.
RAOC: Army Field Workshop and Ordnance Field Park.
General: Corps Postal Unit and Corps Salvage Unit.

GHQ:

RASC: Army Tank Brigade Company, Artillery Company, Bridging Company, Anti-Aircraft Company, Artillery Regiment Section, HQ GHQ Troops RASC, GHQ Troops Company, Supply Personnel Company, Supply Personnel Section, Line of Communication Railhead Company, Troop Carrying Company, MT Works Services Company, Petrol Depot and Ambulance Car Company.
RAOC: AA Brigade Workshop and AA Regiment Section.

General: GHQ Postal Unit, Advanced Stationery Depot, Printing Press, Graves Registration & Enquiry, AMPC Group Headquarters, AMPC Company HQ, Labour Section, GHQ Section Salvage Corps and Mobile Bath Unit.

Base:

RE: Railway Construction Company, Railway Operating Company, Railway Survey Company, Railway Workshops, Port Postal Regulation Centre, Base Postal Office, Line of Communication Postal Unit, Advanced Air Striking Force Postal Unit.

RASC: Supply Depot, Field Bakery, Field Butchery, Petrol Filling Centre, Bulk Petrol Company, Bulk Petrol Storage Company, Heavy Repair Shop, Vehicle Reception Depot, Motor Transport Stores Depot, Ambulance Car Company, and Line of Communication MT Company.

RAOC: Advanced Base Ordnance Depot, Base Ordnance Depot, Ordnance Stores Company, Advanced Ordnance Workshop, Base Ordnance Workshop, Ordnance Workshop Company, Port Workshop Detachment, Base Ammunition Depot, Ordnance Ammunition Company, Armoured Corps Ordnance Field Park and Armoured Corps Workshop.

General: Foreign Labour Training Centre, "*Prestataire*" Labour Company, Palestinian Company AMPC and Palestinian Section AMPC.

Glossary

Adjutant & Quartermaster-General. The overarching term, usually abbreviated to A&Q, or AQ, used by the British Army in the Second World War, to define those activities, which provided support to combat forces in the fields of administration and logistics.

Ammunition Point. A forward detachment of an ammunition company to facilitate the replacement of ammunition expended.

Air Interdiction. Air Interdiction (AI) is an air operation conducted to destroy, neutralize or delay the enemy's military potential, before it can be brought to bear effectively against friendly forces at such a distance from friendly forces, that detailed integration of each air mission with the fire and movement of friendly forces is not required.[1]

Base. A place where the Line of Communication originates, Theatre *materiel* is held and where the principal business of supplying the forces in the field is located.

Battlefield Air Interdiction. Battlefield Air Interdiction (BAI) is an air operation conducted to destroy, neutralize or delay the enemy's military potential, which is in a position, to directly affect friendly forces such that detailed integration of air missions with the fire and movement of friendly forces is required.[2]

Canned Fuel. Liquid fuel in a returnable and reusable container. In the BEF this was usually a 2 or 4-gallon can, although French 5 litre cans, 50 litre drums and 200 litre barrels were also used.

Cased Fuel. Liquid fuel in a 4-gallon non-returnable tin, colloquially known as a 'flimsy', with two tins 'cased' in a wooden, cardboard or three-ply box for protection.

Chemical Warfare. Chemical Warfare (CW) was defined as those aspects concerned with the offensive and defensive use of gas, incendiary and smoke munitions, and those defence measures required to protect British Forces.

Close Air Support. Close Air Support (CAS) is air action against hostile targets, which are in close proximity to friendly forces, and which, require detailed integration of each air mission with the fire and movement of those forces.[3]

Combat Supplies. Combat Supplies are ammunition, POL and rations. Although the term combat supplies was not current in the British Army during 1940, it neatly summarizes

1 Air Publication *3000, British Air Power Doctrine*, 3rd Edn, Directorate of Air Staff (UK MOD, 1999), p.3.13.2.
2 Air Publication *3000, British Air Power Doctrine*, 2nd Edn, Directorate of Air Staff (UK MOD, 1993), pp.62-63.
3 Air Publication *3000, British Air Power Doctrine*, 3rd Edn, p.3.13.1.

the items that were the most important in delivering direct military effect in the front-line. Ammunition included, in the BEF context, small arms and artillery ammunition, specialized infantry natures, Gas Warfare munitions and explosives. POL covered all liquids fuels, lubricants (oils and greases) and antifreeze. Rations included food for personnel and forage for animals, plus disinfectants and water purification chemicals.

Consist. The composition of a train, by wagon or coach, with the designation starting at the locomotive and ending at the brake van.

Cross-load. To transfer a consignment of *materiel* or material from one asset to another, within the same transportation mode.

Delivery Point. The place where 2nd Line RASC transport hands over loads to 1st Line transport of the unit.

Dump. A temporary storage area, usually in the open, for munitions, equipment, or supplies. A dump had minimal security assets and possibly no dedicated technical manpower presence.

En-Cas Mobile (movable if necessary). A group of railway wagons, a barge, or other conveyance, kept permanently under load ready for immediate despatch on an emergency.

Equipment Support. Equipment Support (ES) includes the preparation and repair of equipment for battle and the repair and recovery of equipment battle casualties and failures. The ES staffs have a vital role in monitoring the serviceability of critical equipments in a formation to ensure that combat power is maintained.[4]

Equipment Support Management. A key component of ES is Equipment Support Management (ESM) which is the process of controlling the allocation, repair policy, refurbishment, redesign and replacement of, and re-supply of material for, equipment throughout its service life.[5]

Gas Warfare. Gas Warfare (GW) related specifically to the employment, in military operations, by any nation of any chemical substance, solid, liquid or gas, designed to have a poisonous or irritant affect, upon the human body, and this included tear gases.

Ground Lines of Communication. The system of communication on land by rail, road and navigable waterways between the army and its base or bases, including the district through, which they pass, within allocated boundaries. There were also Air and Sea Lines of Communication from the Home Bases of the United Kingdom and the Empire to the Theatres of Operations.

Ground-Loading. On field operations, ground-loading refers to temporarily un-loading stocks from combat or logistic vehicles, which would normally be held on them, in order to rest or maintain vehicles or to undertake other support tasks. Ground-loaded stocks do not constitute a dump.

Lines of Support. Lines of Support are used to describe the boundaries of specific elements of logistic functions. Lines of Support was not a term that was in use during 1940 appearing in various publications and is a simple method of assigning capability to units and formations.

1st Line - organic to a unit.

4 *Army Field Manual* Vol 1, *Combined Arms Operations*, Part 6, *Combat Service Support*, DGD&D 18/34/44, Army Code No 71344 (UK MOD, 1998), p.viii.

5 Ar*my Doctrine Publication* Vol 3, Logistics, DGD&D/18/34/63, Army Code No 71566 (UK MOD, 1996), p.xiii.

2nd Line - organic to a brigade or division.
3rd Line - allocated to a Corps or Army.
4th Line - provided by the Base. For the BEF, 4th Line was delivered in-Theatre and from the United Kingdom, although some supplies for Force K6 were delivered from India.

Maintain. To take supply and repair action, in order to keep a force in a condition to conduct its mission.

Manoeuvre. The British Army describes 'Manoeuvre' as the employment of forces on the battlefield (using movement) in combination with fire or fire potential, to achieve a position of advantage in respect to the opposition in order to accomplish the mission.[6]

Material. Raw or semi-finished products required by the military forces in the field to conduct operations.

Materiel. From the French, *materiel* is a generic term applied to finished military products such as ammunition, equipment, stores, supplies and vehicles, although sometimes used to cover materials.

Mechanical Transport. Wheeled, tracked, or semi-tracked land vehicle utilised in a logistic context to move men and material to, on or from the battlefield and powered by the Internal Combustion Engine (ICE) either Spark Ignition or Compression Ignition fuelled by petroleum spirit or diesel oil respectively. Often abbreviated to MT, it does not include combat vehicles, such as tanks, Armoured Personnel Carriers or Self-Propelled Guns. Motor Transport (MT) included Wheeled or tracked or semi-tracked land logistic vehicle powered by the ICE but to provide specific clarification for wheeled vehicles, the term Wheeled Motor Transport (WMT) is employed.

Permanent Way. Permanent Way (PW) is a 19th Century term, often abbreviated to PWay, which encapsulates all the guidance and support systems for the railway. This includes the rails, sleepers, ballast, blanketing and drainage.

Petrol Point. A forward detachment of a Petrol Company or Park to facilitate the replenishment of POL to units and to which, demands are sent.

Railhead. A place on a railway, where transhipment to another mode of transport, usually WMT, takes place. In 1940, a railhead was defined as a point on the railway along the line of advance or withdrawal that was deemed to be the terminus for rail operations and at which transhipment to another mode of transportation was enacted. By doctrinal definition therefore, points along the railway at which units drew personnel, material, supplies and ammunition were not railheads.[7]

Rail Regulating Station. A place on the Rail Line of Communication at which the forward dispatch of trains is regulated to ensure their arrival at the correct railheads at convenient times. The composition of trains may also be adjusted at the Rail Regulating Station if this is required and such action is usually the result of changes in demand by corps or divisions.

Rake. A group of coupled wagons, not necessarily of the same type, deemed either to be ready for movement or for future tasking.

6 *Army Doctrine Publication*, Vol 1, *Operations*, HQDT/18/34/46, Army Code No 71565 (UK MOD, 1994), pp.3-17 to 3-19.

7 Army Council, *Military Engineering*, Vol VIII, *Railways*, 26/Manuals/103, War Office (London: HMSO, 1929), p.97.

Re-clothing Point. A forward detachment of a Petrol Company, consisting of one or more WMT vehicles from which units may draw reserve clothing to replace items contaminated by chemical agents.

Refilling Point. The point where ammunition or petrol loads are transferred from 3rd to 2nd Line transport.

Rendezvous. A place where supply columns or ammunition columns are met by representatives of the headquarters concerned and directed to Refilling Points.

Reverse Logistics. Operations related to the reuse of products and materials, by moving them from their typical final destination of use for the purpose of capturing value or proper disposal.

Set. Usually a complete train, including locomotive and wagons or coaching stock, or a mix of both, assembled to undertake a rail movement task. A 'Set' was usually associated with a recurring task.

Standard Gauge Railway (SGR). A railway which, had a track gauge of 4 feet 8½ inches (1435mm). In 2018, Standard Gauge is rated between 1432 mm and 1435mm to account for those SGRs, which have been reduced in gauge by 3 mm, to improve the ride of high-speed trains.

Supplies. Rations, forage, liquid fuels, solid fuels, lubricants, disinfectants and medical consumables. Whilst not a Supply item, mail was normally delivered through the Supply system.

Sustain. Maintain the necessary levels of combat power for the duration required to achieve assigned objectives.

Theatre of Operations. The whole area of land or sea in which, fighting may be expected, or in which, the movements of troops and *materiel* are liable to interruption or interference by the enemy.

Tranship. To transfer a consignment of *materiel* from one mode of transportation to another.

Transportation. In the context of the BEF, transport by SGR rail, Inland Water Transport (IWT) docks and the supporting movement control organizations.

Nomenclature

Armed Services. The Armed Services are always spelt thus, Royal Navy (RN), Army and Royal Air Force (RAF).

Army Forms. Army Forms are abbreviated to AF, followed by a letter descriptor and a numeric, for example, AF G1098. The spacing of the form designator in publications and forms varies, so to create consistency references to Army Forms are shown thus, eg AFG 1098.

British Expeditionary Force Organization and Order of Battle. The six volume series by Alan Philson has been abbreviated in the footnotes to BEFORBAT, quoting the relevant volume.

Capitalization. Capitalization has been applied to named units, for example 5 Divisional Ammunition Company and types of unit that are abbreviated in the text, for instance, Army Field Workshops (AFW). Generic units not in these categories, such as infantry battalion, field regiment, ordnance company or ammunition park use lower case, unless confusion might result, for example, divisional train, a RASC unit and not a railway asset, thus shown as Divisional Train.

Dunkerque. The French spelling of 'Dunkerque' is used in preference to the English 'Dunkirk', which is a village between Canterbury and Faversham in Kent. The exception to this descriptor is where 'Dunkirk' is quoted from documents and books or is used by organizations in titles, for example Dunkirk Veterans Association and the Dunkirk Memorial.

Formations and Units. In the text formations are described in full, for example 5th Division. In the tables and maps, symbology is used to create clarity. The BEF as an Army is shown as XXXX; Corps, XXX; Division, XX and Brigade, X. Base is always spelt uppercase, whilst corps and divisions use lowercase unless specified, for example II Corps or Royal Army Service Corps, or are a title, for example Divisional Ammunition Company or are shown thus in an original document. The following nomenclature has been utilized throughout the work, except where contemporary document references are quoted and are different. Examples shown:

Army – by number: Third.

Corps – Roman numerals: III Corps.

Division – number and where appropriate role: 1st Armoured Division.

Brigade – number and where appropriate role or title: 4th Infantry Brigade.

Units (Cavalry & Infantry) – by number and abbreviated title: 10th Hussars or 5th Norfolks.

Units (Artillery) – by number and title: 7th Field Regiment.

Units – (Engineer & Logistics) – number and title: 522 Ammunition Company RASC.

RAF Wings and Squadrons – Number and title: 12 (Bomber) Squadron.
RAF logistic units – by number and title: 28 Maintenance Unit.
Nationality – assumed to be British unless noted: 1st (Canadian) Division.

Field Service Pocket Book. After introduction, the Field Service Pocket Book, 1938, is abbreviated to FSPB. Although the base document publication is date 1938, the supporting pamphlets were issued dated 1939 or 1940.

Gort. John Standish Surtees Prendergast Vereker, 6th Viscount VC GCB CBE DSO & Two Bars MVO MC (1886-1946) is referred to as Viscount or General Gort unless referenced documents use Lord.

Gross Vehicle Weight. The term 'Gross Vehicle Weight' which was used in 1939-40 has now been replaced by 'Maximum Authorised Mass' but to ensure continuity of historical accuracy, the former terminology is used throughout the manuscript.

History of the Second World War. The British Official History of the Second World Word published for sale by HMSO is abbreviated after introduction to the series to BOH (British Official History).

Line of Communication. When reference is made to the Line of Communication in the main text or footnotes, the abbreviation LOC is used, except where it is in reference to a contemporary document eg HQ L of C Q Movements 22/4 dated 5 May 1940. To provide clarity GLOC is used to describe the Ground Line of Communication and SLOC, the Sea Line of Communication.

Logistic Units. Logistic units, including Royal Engineer units undertaking logistic tasks, are shown initially in full but are then abbreviated. For example, 8 Railway & Construction Company is 8 RCO and 3 Base Ammunition Depot, 3 BAD. The Divisional RASC units, eg 5th Divisional RASC are shown as units without the 'th', thus 5 Division RASC. BEF Corps logistic units are identified thus eg II CAP rather than 2 CAP, to prevent confusion with Divisional elements.

Numerics. Numbers are written from Zero to Nine in letters and then 10 in numbers. The exception is where confusion might result. For example, 55 divisions might be interpreted as 55 Division and thus is written as fifty-five divisions and to provide clarity, for distance a decimal is used eg 2.5 miles, whilst for time, a fraction, eg 2½ days.

Operations Record Book. In the footnotes, the Operations Record Book of RAF headquarters, organizations and squadrons is abbreviated to ORB. The ORB comprises two parts. RAF Form 540: 'Summary of Events' and Form 541: 'Details of work carried out.' In addition, appendices may also be present including operational orders, administrative instructions, miscellaneous reports and telegraphic messages.

Publication location. Official Publications that were not intended for public purchase or access are not ascribed a Place of Publication. These documents were almost exclusively published under the auspices of HMSO, Air Ministry or the War Office.

Ranks. Upper case is used for ranks referring to individuals, for example Corporal Smith or appointments, thus Major-General Administration but lower case for non-specific references. To conform to the convention of the period, hyphens are used in specific ranks, for example, lieutenant-colonel, except in relation to modern authors or where the contemporary document differs from it.

Ships. The names of ships, whether naval or merchant are shown in italics, eg HMS *Rochester* or SS *Clewbay*.

Staff. 'Staff' with an upper case S denotes officers holding a Staff officer appointment or role, whilst staff with a lower case s refers either to personnel in a team or organization, whether military or civilian, or to the process of raising, progressing and resolving problems.

The Second World War, 1939-1945, Army. The War Office monographs often known as the 'Red Book Series', have, in the footnotes, after an initial introduction to the relevant title, been abbreviated to WOOH (War Office Official History), followed by the specific subject.

The Second World War, 1939-1945, Royal Air Force. The Air Ministry monographs often known as the 'Blue Book Series', have, in the footnotes, after an initial introduction to the relevant title, been abbreviated to AMOH, followed by the specific subject.

War Diary. In the footnotes, War Diary (AFC 2118) is abbreviated to WD when referring to the reference.

Weights & Measures

The official Weights and Measures of the British Army of 1939-1940 were Imperial and not Metric, although in France, the logisticians were often accounting in Metric, especially in the procurement of goods and services from French sources or if they were relaxing in an *estaminet.* Whilst logistics in the British Army of the 21st Century is almost entirely enacted in Metric, I have chosen to retain the historical Imperial because the contemporary publications and references use the system and referral to them requires no conversion. For those who prefer a Metric output, the following conversions may be used:

Pounds to Kilogrammes: x 0.453592
Tons to Tonnes: x 1.01605
Gallons to Litres: x 4.54609
Yards to Metres: x 0.914
Miles to Kilometres: x 1.60934
Acres to Hectares: x 0.405
Fahrenheit to Celsius: -32 then multiply by 5 then divide by 9.
A hundred-weight (cwt) was a common measure of the time and is 112 pounds.
Time is denoted within the 24 hour clock, for example 2000 (8 pm).

Foreword

It is strange that we have had to wait until 2020 for a detailed study of the logistics of the British Expeditionary Force (BEF) in 1939-40 to be published. Strange, because logistics underpins all military operations: without the ability to move and supply troops, nothing can happen – or nothing good, anyway. History is replete with examples of what happens when logistics are neglected or go wrong, Napoleon's retreat from Moscow in 1812 and the German Ardennes Offensive of December 1944 (the 'Battle of the Bulge') among them. It is scarcely a startling insight for a military historian to proclaim the importance of logistics, but all too often as a subject it is treated to lip service at best. Sometimes it is worse than this. I can think of an article on British operations in the First World War in which the authors state that they have ignored the logistic implications of their argument – yet logistics should have been central to their case. Logistics, in short, remains a deeply unfashionable subject to research.

Clem Maginniss, thankfully, is one of the few authors to buck this trend. As a British Army officer and career 'loggie', who is also a skilled historian, he is admirably qualified to write this book. It is not going too far to say that he has cast the BEF's experience in a new light. Even for someone like me, who thought they had a decent grasp of the subject, *A Great Feat of Improvisation* is a revelation. Popular authors understandably concentrate their attention on the teeth arms, especially the infantry and tank crew. Even the best scholarly study, Edward Smalley's *The British Expeditionary Force, 1939-40* (2015) did not include logistics as one of its major themes. So much of what is in this book will be new to almost all readers.

The detail includes the low-level and mundane; a fire in a garage which destroyed five motorcycles was the BEF's first loss of logistic equipment on the day the balloon went up on 10 May 1940. This was not caused by hostile action, but as the author comments it 'was hardly an auspicious start to the campaign'. Far from mundane is his account of the evacuation of lines of communication troops from Dunkirk and other ports, and of course his detailed description and analysis of how logistics actually worked – or in some cases did not work – during the Phoney War and the fighting in May-June 1940. One particularly obscure but fascinating story that is told here is this the BEF's preparations for chemical warfare. We know that gas was not used in 1940; but given the experience of the First World War, which had a huge influence on the inter-war Army, it is not surprising that the BEF was prepared to fight in a chemical environment and, indeed, use gas offensively. Perhaps the most compelling part of this story is the strenuous and mostly successful efforts made to bring supplies of chemical weapons back to the UK when it was clear that the campaign was going badly. As Maginniss notes, logisticians thus performed a role that was strategically important, as the stock of gas weapons were a 'significant military and political asset'.

Clem Maginniss also paints on a much broader canvas. Although at first sight it might seem that he has written a rather narrow study, in fact it fits into a much wider context and sheds light on larger issues. David Edgerton's work, for instance, has turned conventional wisdom about Britain in the era of the Second World War on its head. Professor Edgerton argues persuasively that Britain was a 'warfare state', militarily strong, not weak, and the roots of this power predated the outbreak of war in 1939, not least in British preparations for total war. The Chamberlain government, popularly regarded as hapless because of its appeasement policy, in reality did much to put the British economy on a sound footing for war. This book offers some powerful support for this thesis. Take, for instance, Maginniss's discussion of the construction of new Royal Ordnance Factories in the late 1930s. 'Each of these new facilities, titled Royal Filling Factories (RFF) using prodigious amounts of labour and material funded entirely by the taxpayer took three years to complete, with limited and phased production being started whilst building continued'. This broad view of logistics, from 'Factory to Fire Trench' to quote the title of one of the chapters, is one of the things that makes this book so valuable.

Of course, much more could have been done in the 1930s to ready the British armed forces for war. That was particularly true of the Army, which generally stood behind the Royal Air Force and the Royal Navy in the queue for resources. As this book shows the logistic corps were not exempt from the shortages and problems that beset the BEF in 1939-40; the case study of logistic support to 1st Armoured Division makes that clear. That these problems were mostly overcome was down to the quality of the people who made the BEF's logistic system work. It is inevitable that a book on the history of logistics offers relatively few opportunities for individuals to emerge from the khaki mass. On occasion they do and give the story a human face. Two stories which stuck in my mind concerned the two officers who, under enormous pressure to evacuate chemical weapons, fell out so badly as to have a fight; and the five men of 153 Railway Operating Company who were killed in action in the course of bringing back trains from advanced locations. Clem Maginniss concludes that 'The foundations of logistic support to the BEF were, given the circumstances, remarkably sound, although there was a high level of improvisation required'. Fortunately for the BEF, sufficient men at a variety of levels rose to the challenge of departing from the script, and improvised, with a great deal of success.

Clem Maginniss has carried out a formidable amount of archival work and the result, *A Great Feat of Improvisation,* is an important book. It brings out into daylight much about the history of the BEF which has hitherto been in shadow. No future historians of the BEF of 1939-40, or indeed the British Army of the Second World War, will be able to ignore it. It sets the bar for military logistic history very high indeed.

Gary Sheffield
Professor of War Studies, University of Wolverhampton,
and Honorary President of the Western Front Association
Wantage and Wolverhampton, July 2020

A Personal Introduction
Dennis R O'Callaghan

My Father, Private William (Bill) O'Callaghan, was a pre-war regular soldier and Signaller in the 2nd Battalion the Norfolk Regiment (2nd Norfolks), which was the first infantry battalion to be complete in France landing at Cherbourg on 21 September 1939, with its MT party consisting of 78 vehicles disembarking at Saint Nazaire. As a Battalion HQ Signaller, my Father was witness to the successes and failures of the BEF's logistics at unit level, especially during the period of engagement with German forces in May 1940.

If the reader can imagine, for one moment, what it was like to manage the logistics of battalions such as 2nd Norfolks, which were constantly moving to new positions and often out of communication with their brigade HQs and Royal Army Service Corps supporting units. Delivering to these battalions which were in defence, yet counter attacking both under artillery and air attack, whilst travelling along roads teeming with refugees and Allied soldiers redeploying must have been as the cliche says, a logistical nightmare.

My father was embroiled with these events, enjoying some of the logistic largesse and suffering the many shortages described in this book, whilst conducting his duties as a Signaller, a sentry and a sniper, whilst being witness to the ultimate sacrifice of his comrades in the defence of freedom. In this respect, I am privileged to have been asked to write a personal introduction to *A Great Feat of Improvisation* and thus remember my Father, who was only one of two survivors of the massacre at Le Paradis on 27 May 1940, in which 97 men, many from 2nd Norfolks, were murdered having surrendered to the enemy according to the Laws of War. May they Rest In Peace.

Grimston
Norfolk
February 2021

Acknowledgements

I have many acknowledgements to all those who have laid the foundations for this book. Foremost, I must thank my Mother and late Father and their parents, whose experiences of the First and Second World Wars were indelibly marked upon their lives. I am in great debt to those whose personal experiences have added colour to events during the British Expeditionary Force's (BEF) deployment and operations in France, although sadly all of them have 'Marched off the Square': John Yeomans of GHQ BEF Signals, John Carpenter[1] of 522 Company Royal Army Service Corps (RASC), Frank Nunez of 50th (Northumbrian) Infantry Division Column RASC and Lionel Woodhead of 6 (Line of Communication) Provost Company of the North-Western Expeditionary Force. I am indebted to Elaine Schafer and Rosemary Duxbury for their access to the memoirs and letters of their Father, the late Fred Gilbert of 8th Battalion Royal Warwickshire Regiment.

I must acknowledge the 'quiet' contribution of the many logisticians from the three Armed Services, whom I have had the privilege of serving with over five decades, and in particular the late Lieutenant Colonel David Russett, a regimental Quartermaster whose professional knowledge and astute observations on the importance of supporting the 'Soldier' and the 'Mission' have been a guiding light. Equally, I thank the many commercial logisticians I have had the pleasure of working with, especially from the railway, road transport, distribution and civil engineering industries, whose perspectives have added value to the historical assessments of events which occurred 80 years ago.

My thanks are certainly due to the many staff at the National Archives at Kew who so efficiently deliver a wealth of research material to one's 'bird-box', the operation is indeed a logistic marvel, and also the Department of Documents at the Imperial War Museum for access to relevant documents. I am indebted to the Trustees of the Royal Logistic Corps Museum at Deepcut[2] and its Director, Simon Walmsley, for their constant support, including the kind offer of photographs to assist in the illustration of this book. My thanks are also due to the Senior Librarian, John Pearce and his team at the Royal Military Academy Sandhurst, for their dedication in meeting my stream of requests for information and to the late Professor Alex Danchev, fellow Cadet at RMAS in 1978, for his illuminating work on Lord Alanbrooke.[3]

1 A Second Lieutenant and platoon commander in 1940, he served in the post-war army and was promoted to Major-General in 1971 and appointed Transport Officer-in-Chief (Army), retiring in 1975 as Director of Movements (Army) having been awarded the CB and MBE. He died in 2009.
2 Located at Worthy Down Hampshire.
3 Alex Danchev & Dan Todman, Dan (eds.), *War Diaries, 1939-1945, Field Marshal Lord Alanbrooke* (London: Weidenfeld & Nicolson, 2001).

The staff of the Tank Museum at Bovington, particularly Jonathon Holt, extended every courtesy in selecting supporting illustrations from the Collection and I am immensely grateful for the constructive assistance of that doyen of historical tank knowledge, David Fletcher MBE. The staff at the Defence CBRN Centre Winterbourne Gunner were most helpful in searching for period documents relating to Gas Warfare equipment, storage and training. Major (Retired) Jim Salisbury and Dave Hargreaves of Swynnerton Training Area were enthusiastic in their support in enabling me to study the physical history and remains of the Royal Ordnance Factory, which once occupied the site.

I owe a great debt to the regimental committees, authors, editors and researchers of the Second World War histories of the Corps of Royal Engineers, Royal Army Service Corps, Royal Army Ordnance Corps and Royal Pioneer Corps, whose industry has enabled future authors to access not only the professional deeds of their logisticians but also some of the colourful characters and personal contributions to the events in France and Belgium in 1939 and 1940.

My thanks are also due to Dennis O'Callaghan, the Son of Private William O'Callaghan, of the 2nd Norfolks, and one of only two survivors of the massacre at Le Paradis on 27 May 1940, for writing a Personal Introduction to *A Great Feat of Improvisation* and to Professor Gary Sheffield for his courtesy, time and analysis in scribing the Foreword. My thanks must go to John Head and the members of the 2nd Norfolks' Pilgrimage Group, many of whose direct relations fought in the campaign, for the opportunity to visit some of the sites of the BEF's key actions and to hear of their relatives' service.

I must pay special thanks to Major (Retired) Stephen Pope for not only his 43 years of Army comradeship but also his assistance with tank material, which has been invaluable, whilst his fascinating and comprehensive book, the *The First Tank Crews*,[4] encouraged me to write *A Great Feat of Improvisation*. My grateful thanks are also due to Hollie Barrett, whose scientific qualifications have been so well applied in the creation of the excellent maps and diagrams and her contribution to the cover graphics. I must thank the dedicated team at Helion, especially Duncan Rogers, the industrious members of which, have turned the script on my hard-drive into a book on the shelf.

My greatest gratitude of debt though, is to my wife Edwina, who has, in addition to her demanding career, acted as researcher and sounding board, which she informs me, has been a positive experience. Although a retired officer of the Queen Alexander's Royal Army Nursing Corps (Volunteers) she has proved herself to be a true logistician, who has sustained me day and night, morally and physically, whilst I have been head down researching and writing. She has done so much to ensure that our A&Q arrangements have never failed whilst I have been writing this book, but her especial contribution has been, without doubt, the delivery, without fail, of outstanding Food Services and she has therefore, fully met the motto of the Royal Logistic Corps, *We Sustain*; thank you.

4 Stephen Pope, *The First Tank Crews, The Lives of the Tankmen Who Fought at the Battle of Flers-Courcelette*, 15 September 1916 (Solihull: Helion, 2016).

Author's Preface

A Great Feat of Improvisation refers frequently to A&Q, the period abbreviation for Adjutant & Quartermaster-General, which in 21st Century parlance is Personnel and Logistics. Whilst the latter term may be more familiar to the contemporary reader, I have chosen to retain the A&Q nomenclature, not only to sustain the historical thread but also to maintain coherence with the documents from the period. *A Great Feat of Improvisation* focuses upon the 'Q' capability provided by the Royal Engineers, the Royal Army Service Corps, the Royal Army Ordnance Corps and the Auxiliary Military Pioneer Corps. There is a dip into the 'A' arena, particularly in the areas of leave and welfare, which required substantial Q resources to function effectively, but I have not analysed the operations of the Army Medical Services,[1] which in 1940 were the responsibility of the Adjutant-General, with the exception of the 'Q' interface in relation to the evacuation of patients by ambulance train[2] and the supply and transportation of supporting ordnance equipment, medical stores and consumables. Also omitted, is the work of the Provost, except in relation to its key logistic task of road traffic control.

The headquarters and unit war diaries held in the National Archives (TNA) Kew have been fundamental to researching the operations and performance of the British Expeditionary Force's logisticians, but the documents have limitations. In some instances, the use of security code-words and numbers, some of which, 80 years on, are difficult to match to specific tasks or locations, whilst the use of 'veiled' words require some deduction to tease out the meaning. Some records do not exist in the TNA having been destroyed during the evacuation of the BEF,[3] whilst others were lost or damaged in transit, and over the years, it is obvious that some

1 For details of the Army's medical units, structures and capabilities of the period, see, Lieutenant-Colonel T B Nicholls MB CHB RAMC (Retd), *Organization, Strategy and Tactics of the Army Medical Services in War*, 2nd Edn (London: Bailliere, Tindall & Cox, 1941). For a description of the operations of the Army Medical Services in the British Expeditionary Force, see, F A E Crew FRS, *History of the Second World War* (BOH) *The Army Medical Services, Campaigns*, Vol 1 (London: HMSO, 1956), pp.1-113.

2 The lead Corps for the technical operation of the ambulance trains was the Royal Engineers. Road ambulances, operated by various organizations in the BEF including units, the Royal Army Medical Corps (Field Ambulances and Motor Ambulance Convoys) and Ambulance Car Companies (Royal Army Service Corps), also moved patients. Whilst the deployment of the ambulance trains is examined as a component of the BEF's railway operations, the movement of patients by road has not been assessed because without describing the medical evacuation chain, its context would be lost.

3 5 Division Ammunition Company for example, recorded on 31 May 1940 that: 'Appendix and record of issues and receipts of ammunition were lost in the general destruction of records on 29th May 1940'. TNA WO 167/250: 5 DAC, WD.

files have been extensively weeded. The *RAF Narrative of the Campaign* summarized the fate of some of the records: 'The one big gap in the British records of the campaign, from the air aspect, relates to the RAF Component......and the historian in search of fuller documentary material in this direction is regretfully referred to an indeterminate spot at the bottom of Boulogne harbour'.[4] This regrettably also applies conceptually to some of the Army's logistic records.

The war diaries can pose a challenge. Entries should have been made on the AFC 2118 but in some instances, especially in *ad hoc* units, blank or lined note-paper has been utilized. Some war diaries, and those of HQs in particular, are in typescript, whilst those in manuscript have varying levels of legibility, with pencil entries susceptible to fading, and inevitably in all records, the content is variable. War diaries were kept in different ways by units, subject to direction by Commanding Officers and Adjutants, or reflected the whim of their scribes and compilers. HQs with clerical support and experienced Staff officers were much better placed to record and analyse events, with the content and composition generally subject to over-sight and scrutiny, although sometimes those diaries without close supervision are often most revealing in their honesty and frustrations. In addition, some war diaries were compiled or completed after the campaign, either from notes or memory, with all the possibilities of error, inaccuracy, forgotten detail and added colour.[5] Some war diaries lucidly expose controversial or unpalatable issues, whilst others, in remaining silent on such matters, leave the researcher in the position of never knowing, unless information comes from another reasonably reliable source, of whether a contentious issue has been intentionally omitted.

Logistic units usually had a much greater test in detailing events than infantry battalions and artillery regiments. In some cases, the geographical spread made it difficult to receive and collate timely information, in others the deployment of small detachments created a complex matrix of activity, which was challenging to summarize. Conversely, some authors were assiduous in their work and conscientiously recorded matters of routine detail sometimes at the expense of the wider picture. In this respect, the orders of the Officer Commanding 5 Divisional Ammunition Company RASC is most unusual in directing the compilation of RASC Section (ie platoon) war diaries, which contain much interesting information on 5 DAC operations, tasks, administration and soldiers, with detail in some cases down to individual vehicles and drivers.[6] Historians though, have a huge debt of gratitude to those who laboured, often under the most trying of circumstances, to capture the events of the day and in the broader sense, there is more than enough information across the spectrum to offer a strong flavour of their trials and tribulations.

One indispensable secondary publication based upon detailed research at the TNA is Alan Philson's, *The British Army, 1939-1945, Tables of Organization and Equipment, British Expeditionary Force, Organization and Order of Battle, 10 May 1940*, referred hereon in the book

4 TNA AIR 41/21: The Campaign in France and the Low Countries, September 1939 - June 1940, RAF Narrative (TOP SECRET) Air Historical Branch, 1944, Foreword.

5 A letter from War Office Records to OC 2 Division Petrol Company in late December 1940 took note of the fact that the unit war diary for May 1940 was 'in the course of compilation' and 'With regards to the war diary for June, it will suffice if it commences on the date of the re-assembly of the unit'. TNA WO 167/212: 2 DPC, WO Records 26/Records/3804 (C7) dated 28 December 1940. In this instance it appears that the 'compilation' probably refers to all the supporting documents because the AFC 2118, which is mostly in pencil, has all the hall-marks of being completed contemporaneously.

6 TNA WO 167/250: 5 DAC RASC, WD.

as BEFORBAT, Volumes 1-6 (Milton Keynes: Military Press, 2005-2007). BEFORBAT contains all the known War Establishment Tables (WET) of every type of unit within the BEF and is an outstanding reference. Most of the information in BEFORBAT has been carefully mined from the myriad of relevant War Office files and can only be described as a Labour of Love. Alan Philson is to be commended upon an exemplary piece of work, which has delivered these most useful documents to historians in a coherent and structured manner. The other key reference is John de S Winser, *BEF Ships, Before at and after Dunkirk* (Gravesend: World Ship Society, 1999), which is the shipping equivalent BEFORBAT. BEFORBAT and BEF Ships deserve wider exposure and accolade in the military history community because it is works such as these that provide the fundamental foundations of comprehending the BEF's structure and capability.

Last but not least, I have where possible, tried to bring colour to the process of military history by introducing the names of various logisticians from Private to General. Their names and actions have, for far too long, been consigned, for good or bad, to the memories of their families or those who served with them and it is timely to bring them and their contribution to the BEF and the defence of the Nation to life. Many will inevitably remain anonymous, their names never receiving a mention in the records, but I believe that those that appear on the pages of the book offer a fair reflection of the courage, competence, industry, initiative, innovation and dedication of the BEF's logisticians but equally the frustrations, fears and failures of ordinary soldiers immersed in extraordinary events.

Clem Maginniss
East Dereham
Norfolk
February 2021

Author's Note

In the course of research for this book, it has been a privilege to discover a direct military BEF connection which joined my paternal and maternal families nearly 10 years before my Mother and Father met. Fred Gilbert, a commercial artist and one of my Mother's cousins and Hugh Maginniss, an insurance agent and one of my Father's brothers, both joined the Royal Warwickshire Regiment at Budbrooke Barracks as 'Citizen Soldiers' on 16 October 1939, subsequently serving in France with the BEF, although their wartime experiences were very different. Fred was wounded three times before being captured, spending five hard years as a POW, whilst Hugh was evacuated under Operation CYCLE, being transferred to 2nd Norfolk Regiment and serving in India, before being Killed in Action in Burma in February 1945. That he was a combat logistician in the battalion quartermaster platoon and distributing rations when he was killed by enemy fire, is a timely, although sad reminder that whilst being a 'loggie' is a not a glamourous or safe military occupation, it was and remains, an important one.

Reviews of *An Unappreciated Field of Endeavour*,[1] highlighted an issue with the over-use of abbreviations, a problem compounded by the arrangement of the book, which was structured so chapters did not have to be read sequentially. *A Great Feat of Improvisation* is similar in this respect and although I have sought to adjust the use of abbreviations, inevitably in a book of this scope on military logistics, which assesses a wide range of complex and inter-locking operations, tasks, capabilities, units and installations, abbreviations are arguably all but inescapable. Indeed, research of contemporary documents reveals long lists of military abbreviations, which far exceed those in the book and in this respect the reader has been sheltered from the onslaught experienced by those serving in the BEF. The use for example, of POL rather than Petroleum, Oils and Lubricants, or WMT in lieu of Wheeled Motor Transport to take two of many, I trust creates clarity and fluency than confusion and distraction. I apologize if the arrangement does otherwise.

Finally, the Royal Logistic Corps Museum has kindly provided a number of photographs, many of which have not been published before, to illustrate *A Great Feat of Improvisation*. Regrettably, some of those depicting officers and men do not record their names, so the Museum and the author would be grateful to receive, through the Publisher, any information appertaining to them.

1 Clem Maginniss, *An Unappreciated Field of Endeavour, Logistics and the British Expeditionary Force on the Western Front 1914-1918* (Warwick: Helion, 2018).

Introduction

In the 1971 film *'Dad's Army'*, those two astute observers of military strategy, Captain Mainwaring and Sergeant Wilson are conversing in Mainwaring's bank office about the war news in June 1940.

> Captain Mainwaring: "Bringing our lads back to Blighty like that was a glorious achievement; it was a great example of British improvisation getting them out of France."
>
> Sergeant Wilson: "Pity they couldn't have improvised some way of keeping them there!"[1]

Mainwaring's observation has stood the test of time, whilst Wilson's comment was embedded in the concept of the 2nd British Expeditionary Force (BEF), which too had to be recovered in short order. Rather less obviously but equally true, the logistic organization of the BEF was a great feat of improvisation and the light, which illuminates the story has, for far too long, been held behind a bushel, although not so the operational aspects, which received a public airing in the *Journal of the Royal United Service Institution* not two months after the BEF had departed from France.[2] Clearly seeking to put a positive tactical spin on an otherwise unmitigated strategic disaster, the author, in the only association with logistics in the article, boldly suggested that the BEF could have 'continued to offer prolonged resistance on its own front',[3] which from a logistic perspective was probably a fair assessment. Whilst the exploits of the combat elements of the BEF in 1940 have been analysed in depth, the contribution of the logisticians who kept the BEF in the fight has marched, or perhaps rather driven, into the mists of time. Much has been written on the BEF's strategic, operational and tactical activities but almost nothing, with the exception of the medical aspects[4] and one book on the critical railway support,[5] has been publicly published upon its logistics. In this respect, Dr Rob Thompson's

1 *Dad's Army* - The Film, Columbia (British) Productions, 1971.
2 na, 'The Operations of the British Expeditionary Force in Belgium and Northern France', *The Journal of the Royal United Service Institution*, Vol LXXXV, August 1940, No 539, p.393.
3 Ibid.
4 *The Army Medical Services, Campaigns*, Vol 1.
5 William A T Aves, *Supporting the British Expeditionary Force, The Royal Engineer Railway Units in France, 1939-1940*, (Donington: Shaun Tyas, 2012). This book, written by a retired naval officer, examines in detail, the technical aspects of the units and their railway tasks rather than the wider

observation that historically 'logistics is not forgotten so much as ignored'[6] is absolutely true in the case of the BEF because the logisticians as a group have been completely overshadowed by the wider events in May and June 1940. In analysing the numerous works on the BEF's operations in France, the words of the then General Wavell, also appear particularly apposite:

> In most military books strategy and tactics are emphasized at the expense of the administrative factors.........Bear in mind when you study military history or military events the importance of the administrative factor, because it is where most critics and many generals go wrong.[7]

Since 1939, this pertinent observation has remained a fundamental reminder to historians that whilst logistics have a cardinal, and sometimes defining influence on the support to, and shape of, military operations, logistics is, historically, probably the least examined and understood element of conflict, omissions which unquestionably apply to the BEF. In a more soldierly observation of the problem, the lack of interest in the subject has been brilliantly summarized by a British Army regimental Quartermaster who succinctly stated, 'that nobody gives a s**t about logistics until the toilet paper runs out'.[8] The logistic services were however, a fundamental component of the BEF and their contribution is worthy of much greater exposure than they have received hitherto, which to date in the public domain has relied almost exclusively on the authors and editors of the Second World War Corps histories[9] of the Corps of Royal Engineers (RE),[10] Royal Army Service Corps (RASC),[11] the Royal Army Ordnance Corps (RAOC)[12] and the Royal Pioneer Corps (RPC).[13] Whilst illuminating and interesting, these histories, per force of space, devote relatively little coverage and analysis to the BEF, whilst also inevitably by definition, focusing upon the individual Corps' contribution to the deployment and campaign.

operational issues but is a comprehensive narrative of the subject. Its focus however, supported by a wealth of amazing research and not a little deduction, is the operations and fates of the locomotives deployed to France. Frustratingly, there is no index.

6 *The Douglas Haig Fellowship Records* Issue No 2/18, p.61.

7 Archibald Wavell, 'Generals and Generalship': *The Lees Knowles Lectures Delivered at Trinity College Cambridge in 1939*, (London: Macmillan, 1941), p.11.

8 The late Lieutenant Colonel David Russett RLC, RQM 150 (Northumbrian) Transport Regiment, 1998.

9 The Corps of Royal Electrical and Mechanical Engineers was not formed until 1942. See, Brigadier B B Kennedy CBE & Colonel J A Tatman (Comp.) *Craftsmen of the Army, The Story of the Royal Electrical and Mechanical Engineers*, (London: Leo Cooper, 1970).

10 Major-General R P Pakenham-Walsh CB MC, *The History of the Corps of The Royal Engineers*, Vol VIII, 1938-1948 (Chatham: The Institution of Royal Engineers, 1958).

11 Regimental Committee, *The Story of the Royal Army Service Corps, 1939-1945* (Aldershot: Institution of the RASC, Bell & Sons, 1955).

12 Brigadier H A Fernyhough CBE MC & Major H E D Harris, *History of the Royal Army Ordnance Corps, 1939-1945* (London & Beccles: William Clowes, nd but 1967).

13 Major E H Rhodes-Wood, *A War History of the Royal Pioneer Corps, 1939-1945* (Aldershot: Gale & Polden, 1960).

The exception, although by default rather than design, is the excellent material in the War Office histories[14] published in limited copy in the early 1950s.[15] These historical monographs,[16] the archival basis of which are held in The National Archives (TNA) at Kew comprise the War Official Official History (WOOH) and are often collectively known as the 'Red Book Series' and were for internal use[17] by the Armed Forces, being classified as RESTRICTED, CONFIDENTIAL or SECRET under the lead title: *The Second World War, 1939-1945, Army*. These documents, have over the decades, been declassified and occasionally appear for sale,[18] whilst the Military Library Research Service Ltd has reprinted several logistic volumes, including *Movements* and *Ordnance Services*. The WOOH is based upon official documents and contains a mine of information but that on the BEF, as for other campaigns, is spread over many volumes, which are, for the most part, difficult to acquire.[19] The WOOH foreword however, not only neatly summarizes the works but also offers a taste of the fine menu: 'This book is one of a series, compiled by the authority of the Army Council, the object of which is to preserve the experience gained during the Second World War, in selected fields of military staff work and administration'.[20]

Despite the impressive individual contributions from the logistic Corps histories and the WOOH, none of the works offer any coherency to, or analysis of, the BEF's complex logistic diaspora, which, apart from the paucity of academic or general publications on the subject, is the most serious omission in the comprehension of a core capability that underpinned every aspect of the BEF's combat effectiveness. *A Great Feat of Improvisation* seeks therefore, to redress some of the lacuna in the logistic historiography of the BEF in order to demonstrate not

14 These publications are not be confused with the Official Histories which were published by the HMSO for public sale.

15 Details of the definitive print run must sit in a dusty file somewhere. *Maintenance in the Field*, Vol 1, a RESTRICTED document, ran to 500 copies and other volumes had similar numbers depending upon the subject matter. CONFIDENTIAL and SECRET volumes were generally not so numerous, and the latter were copy numbered. An undated and un-referenced War Office memorandum states in paragraph 3: 'The number of copies available for issue is restricted and the initial distribution is being confined to Divisional Commanders and above and to schools and training establishments likely to be concerned with the subject'. Memorandum held by the author. Volumes of the WOOH were also issued to the Royal Navy and the Royal Air Force, as the library stamps of the ones in Defence and private ownership attest.

16 Documents on the policy for the War Office histories and Historical Monographs are held in TNA WO 366/4, whilst production costs and staffing requirements are at WO 366/3, with the series 277 and 366 covering the details. QMG subjects are in WO 366/8.

17 War Office memorandum paragraph 2: 'No general announcement of the publication of the books in the series has been, or will be, nor will they be included in the Catalogue of War Office Publications'.

18 The rare volumes are being exchanged at prices in excess of £300.

19 The key volumes, by year of publication, containing coverage of BEF logistics, are: *Transportation*, Brigadier R Micklem CMG CBE (War Office, 1950); *Ordnance Services*, Officers of the Ordnance Directorate (War Office, 1950); *Fighting, Support and Transport Vehicles and the War Office Organization for their Provision*, Part II - *Unarmoured Vehicles*, Major R Campagnac RASC and Major P E C Hayman 15/19 KRH (War Office, 1951); *Administrative Planning*, Colonel H W Wilson OBE TD (War Office, 1952); *Maintenance in the Field*, Vol 1, Lieutenant-Colonel J A H Carter OBE KORR and Major D N Kann MBE RASC (War Office, 1952); *Supplies and Transport*, Vol I, Colonel D W Boileau late RASC (War Office, 1954) and *Movements*, Major J B Higham RE & E A Knighton MBE (Comps.), (War Office, 1955).

20 WOOH volume Foreword.

only its importance to military operations during the campaign but also record and highlight the incredible contribution of a significant number of men and women to the deployment, sustainment, operations and evacuation of the BEF in the period 1939-1940. In this respect, it is wide-ranging in its reach, and except for pertinent logistic matters, does not focus upon the evacuation from Dunkerque.

The greatest challenge in researching the logistic aspects of the BEF is the scope and scale of its many facets. Whilst as an organization its lifespan was not quite 10 months, the planning and industry involved in supporting it was remarkable and deserves exposure. *A Great Feat of Improvisation* is not a comprehensive examination of every aspect of BEF logistics, although it covers much ground, or a short history. To achieve the former would involve more than one volume and the latter would omit much fascinating detail. It does however, bring a new and fresh perspective by analysing in a series of engaging essays, the critical contribution of particular components of military logistics through the lens of specific elements and themes, each of which, cast penetrating light into dark corners of an important, yet mainly forgotten and ignored story.

A Great Feat of Improvisation touches upon how pre-war strategic, economic, political and defence dynamics influenced the plans to generate and deploy the BEF and concomitantly create an enormous challenge to an initially significantly under-resourced logistic organization that inevitably struggled to retain professional coherence during its rapid expansion, whilst also delivering operational capability to the BEF. *A Great Feat of Improvisation* explores the success of the BEF's Quartermaster-General, Lieutenant-General W G Lindsell,[21] in utilizing the skills of his logistic planners and soldiers to deliver the operational logistic capability that was the salvation of the BEF during its deployment, advance, withdrawal and evacuation. Logistic operations in France and Flanders are analysed to highlight the military 'logistic learning steps',[22] including the impact but not the detail of supporting the Advanced Air Striking Force (AASF).[23] The development of the BEF's Wheeled Motor Transport (WMT) component is reviewed, including its influence upon the deployment and employment of armour, infantry, artillery and air components, which were all affected by the expanding use of WMT, creating a requirement to improve its efficiency and effectiveness, which, with a rapidly expanding force was a clear challenge. The organization and capability of logistics at divisional level is explained, supported by an analysis of the BEF's ammunition supply system and a review of the logistics which, under-pinned the BEF's growing offensive Gas Warfare (GW) capability.

Rarely studied, the logisticians played a crucial role in the preparations for the evacuation of material from the Main Base Areas and the Ground Line of Communication (GLOC) after Dunkerque, whilst logistic support to the 1st Armoured Division is examined from the

21 Major (Temporary Lieutenant-Colonel) W G Lindsell DSO OBE MC psc RA, wrote a most interesting article, 'Administrative Lessons of the Great War', *JRUSI*, Vol LXXI, February 1926, pp.712-719. Lindsell was also the author of the manual entitled *Military Organization and Administration* published in 1923 (Aldershot: Gale & Polden, 23rd Edn, 1941) which ran, in various editions, until the 1960s, which lucidly illustrates its resilience. He also wrote, *A & Q or Military Administration in War*, 3rd Edn (Aldershot: Gale & Polden, 1933). Lindsell held several senior QMG posts during the Second War World, including the BEF in France, and appointments in the Middle East and India.

22 Whilst this process is often referred to as a learning curve, the reality is that as a result of various factors, regressive activity sometimes occurs, and the outputs are often more like steps than a smooth curve.

23 The logistic operations of the AASF are fascinating and deserve a singleton study.

division's formation to its evacuation from France. Elements of the soldiers' administration, directed by the Adjutant-General's (AG) Branch in GHQ BEF is examined, and to complete the A&Q coherence, the 'A' is embedded with an assessment of the logistic 'Q' contribution to managing and delivering the BEF's leave policy. Also explained, is the planning and delivery of the 'Quartering' requirement within the United Kingdom for the returning units of the BEF. *A Great Feat of Improvisation* draws these threads from the bobbins to weave a colourful pattern of achievement, whilst illustrating how logistics evolved to overcome complex challenges and in doing so, transformed operations, creating a legacy that remains relevant to the British Army's logistics in the 21st Century.[24] Logistics however, do not swim alone in the military pond. At the operational level, the role of logistics is to develop, sustain and regenerate combat power to ensure that the tempo and effectiveness of the operations maintains momentum. Equally, logistics placed constraints on strategy and tactics, a critical point concisely summarized by a future field force QMG: 'Strategy and tactics are now tied hand and foot by administration'.[25] The BEF's logistics, never perceived as racy, has been all but forgotten, and its practitioners, from General to Private, are mostly long gone and the experiences they recorded and the lessons they learnt, many still relevant in the 21st Century, lie in dusty volumes and files in archives and libraries.[26] I trust that *A Great Feat of Improvisation* brings their fascinating achievements to life.

24 See, William G T Tuttle, *Defense Logistics for the 21st Century*, Jr (Annapolis: Naval Institute Press, 2005).
25 Lindsell, 'Administrative Lessons of the Great War', *JRUSI*, Vol LXXI, February 1926, p.713.
26 For 'dusty' read un-opened because I am sure that the TNA in particular does not have any dusty files!

Part I

Plans and Preparations

1

Cinderella and the Pumpkin
The influences of Experience, Empire, Politics and Finance in shaping BEF logistics 1919-1939

Influencing Factors

In setting the scene, it is illuminating to briefly outline the key factors in the development, planning, preparation and enactment of the logistic lay-down of the BEF in France. First and foremost was the influence of the imperial defence mission upon the organization of the Army.[1] In particular, formations and units primarily established, equipped and trained for colonial operations were by the early 1930s, increasingly unsuitable for operations against a peer enemy on the Continent, whilst armoured manoeuvre forces were not optimised, nor indeed easily adapted for colonial deployment, especially for internal security and counter insurgency missions.[2] From the logistic perspective, whilst the majority of the Royal Army Service Corps (RASC)[3] and Royal Army Ordnance Corps (RAOC)[4] units were based in the

1 In 1937, 50% of the Army's infantry battalions were deployed overseas and 54% of the total British Army Regular personnel. Calculations based on N H Gibbs, BOH, *Grand Strategy*, Vol I, *Rearmament Policy* (London: HMSO, 1976), p.450, Table 13, Distribution of the Army At Home and Overseas at the End of 1937.

2 Harold R Winton, *To Change an Army: General Sir John Burnett-Stuart and British Armoured Doctrine, 1927-1938* (Kansas: University of Kansas Press, 1988), pp.229-231.

3 In 1935 the RASC consisted of 5,552, All Ranks, a figure down from 6,536 in 1926, with a TA establishment of 3,384 and a strength of 1,511. The Army Reserve Sections consisted of 180 Other Ranks in A, 2,226 in B and 2,017 in D, totalling 4,423 and the Supplementary Reserve establishment of 9,385 and a strength of 8,749 All Ranks. Cmd 5104, *The General Annual Report on the British Army for the Year ending 30 September 1935* (London: HMSO, 1936). These figures confirm the relative stability of logistic Regular and Army Reserve numbers, the relative buoyancy of the Supplementary Reserve numbers but the challenges of TA recruiting.

4 In 1935 the RAOC consisted of 3,353 All Ranks, a figure, which was the result of an annual increase from 1927 when it was 2,850, with a TA establishment of 457 and a strength of 299. The Army Reserve Sections consisted of 18 Other Ranks in A, 518 in B and 867 in D, totalling 1,403 and a Supplementary Reserve establishment of 2,910 and strength of 2,279 All Ranks. See, Cmd 5104. For some reason, *The Second World War, 1939-1945, Army* (WOOH), *Ordnance Services*, Officers of the

UK,[5] there was little opportunity to develop and practice on any substantial scale, potential future options for delivering capability in support of major operations at corps level or greater, which expeditionary warfare on the Continent demanded.[6]

The second factor was the relatively recent operational large-scale war-fighting experience of the logistic services, which was based upon the organizations determined by the Great War. Perhaps inevitably, the Western Front was the driver for most of the lessons,[7] a reflective that became more pronounced as attention turned to the possibility of a significant Land Force Continental commitment. It was unfortunate therefore, at this juncture, that two issues blunted the potential for greater intellectual rigour in assessing for the shape and lay-down of future logistic support in this environment. The first, was the perception that the initial strategic start-point would be similar to 1914 and the second that lessons identified from operations out-with the Western Front during the Great War had little or nothing to contribute to future deployments to Europe. As it transpired, whilst there were differences, especially in resources and terrain, mobile operations in the Eastern Desert,[8] Palestine and Mesopotamia generated a number, of very pertinent outcomes, particularly in relation to the security of the Ground Lines of Communication (GLOC). The inevitable inter-war evaporation of the coherent corporate knowledge of logistics 'at scale', which was so hard-won in 1914-1918 was another aspect of the post-Great War period. The thousands of soldiers who had created this capability were demobilized and the British Army effectively returned to the pre-Great War focus of colonial operations, although in some cases, the deployments involved appreciable numbers and intense actions. There were of course, military logisticians who continued to serve in the Regular and Territorial Army and shared their Great War knowledge skills with the fresh blood, whilst others who retired returned to the fold in 1939. Whilst perhaps no longer in their professional military prime, their experience of scale was a positive contribution to managing the logistic support to what was a rapidly expanding organization by early 1940.

The experience of the Great War certainly influenced the leadership and the planners in their response to emerging issues, sometimes positively and occasionally negatively, but equally this

Ordnance Directorate (War Office, 1950), p.x, states for 1939 a figure of 2,500 All Ranks, reinforced upon mobilization of a smaller group within the Territorial Army.

5 In 1935, 80% of the RASC units were in the UK and 92% of the RAOC. This does not reflect in detail the deployment of personnel but clearly indicates the focus on the Home Base; percentages calculated from information in Cmd 5104, pp.32-33. The disparity, with, for example infantry battalions, is explained by the logistic arrangements overseas. In India, where 45 infantry battalions were deployed, the Royal Indian Army Service Corps (RIASC) delivered much of the capability, whilst locally engaged logistic units and contractors usually supported static garrisons in colonial stations.

6 The outline global distribution of the British Army on 1 January 1938 was 106,704 troops based in the UK; 55,498 in India, including Burma; 21,187 in the Middle East and Mediterranean; 12,143 in the Far East and 1,806 in the West Indies. TNA WO 33/1502: Memorandum by Secretary of State for War, 10 February 1938.

7 The term 'lessons' in the military environment requires clarification. 'Lessons Identified' are those lessons from an exercise, operation or campaign, which are assessed to have relevance to the future but have not been executed. 'Lessons Learned' are those lessons, which have resulted in changes in policy, organization, structures, establishments, planning, training, procedures, drills or equipment.

8 Operationally, the Northern part of the Sinai to the East of the Suez Canal. See, Lieutenant-General Sir George MacMunn KCB KCSI DSO psc & Captain Cyril Falls (Comps.), *Official History of the Great War, Military Operations, Egypt and Palestine,* Vol I (London: HMSO, 1928).

should not detract from a growing comprehension of the emergence of new threats and military systems, the concerns of which, in certain instances, and the risk of aerial attack against Home Base munitions sites is a good example, became almost a phobia in the minds of some Defence planners in all three Armed Services.[9] Indeed, in the period 1936-1938, Home Defence became such an acute issue that the delivery of Ground Based Air Defence (GBAD) capability in the UK started to bend, albeit relatively briefly, the Army's organizational, logistic and equipment programme out of shape,[10] General Ironside recording in his diary: 'The decision to form six AA divisions seals the fate of the Territorial Army as an Army able to go into the field. All our guns and money and energy will be expended in making these divisions.'[11]

The third factor was the influence of colonial operations, which were a feature of the inter-war period.[12] Mainly small in scale, imperial deployments did however, provide officers and soldiers alike, plenty of opportunity for field service, not a little action, and a raft of lessons, not all of them relevant for every deployment in the future, in much the same way as Afghanistan has done in the early 21st Century. These operations reminded the Army that no matter how small a task, careful logistic planning and execution were essential in enabling successful outcomes but some of the lessons from these interventions were not fully applicable to substantial force deployments on the Continent of Europe. Mass however, was critical but not utilized to support colonial operations, resulting in an erosion of logistic capacity 'at scale' to deploy and sustain a Field Force of two plus divisions. Fortunately, the Royal Engineers, the Corps responsible for delivering the Army's rail operating and movement capability, not only retained appropriate Regular assets but were forward leaning in expanding Reserve units.[13] The RE also invested in developing and improving a central training facility at Longmoor in Hampshire,[14] which included the Woolmer Instructional Military Railway (WIMR),[15] thereby enabling All Arms

9 For a senior logistic officer perspective on this issue, see, TNA WO 32/4612: Future Army Organization - 1935, QMG Response dated 16 December 1936 to CIGS SECRET Paper, 'Future Reorganization of the British Army' dated 9 September 1935. Remarkably, the documents in this file remain in the original cream War Office folder from 1935.

10 See, Gibbs, BOH *Grand Strategy*, Vol I, *Rearmament Policy*, pp.460-464.

11 Entry 29 May 1938. Colonel Roderick Macleod and Denis Kelly (eds.), *The Ironside Diaries, 1937-1940* (London: Constable, 1962), pp.46-47.

12 The locations of these operations included Iraq, Kurdistan, Palestine, Persia, and the NW Frontier of India. See for example, the following Indian Official Histories: Indian General Staff (IGS), *The Third Afghan War, 1919, Official Account* (Calcutta: Government of India, 1926) and *Operations in Waziristan, 1919-1920*, 2nd Edn (Delhi: Government Central Press, 1923). For a comprehensive recent study of these campaigns, see, the excellent Brian Robson, *Crisis on the Frontier: The Third Afghan War and the Campaigns in Waziristan, 1919-1920* (Staplehurst: Spellmount, 2004).

13 In 1932, the RE had seven Supplementary Reserve railway companies; three construction, two operating, one workshop and one stores, plus an HQ Railway Operating Group.

14 Longmoor remains in MOD ownership in 2020 as a training and accommodation facility. Whilst the RTC ceased operating in 1969 and the rails have long since gone, some of the track-beds can be traced on the ground.

15 From 1935, the Longmoor Military Railway. The WIMR title ensured that wags described it as the 'Will It Move Railway'. For an early 1930s account see, 'The Woolmer Instructional Military Railway', *The Railway Gazette*, 25 November 1932 and for a one volume history, D W Ronald & R J Carter, *The Longmoor Military Railway* (Newton Abbot: David & Charles, 1974).

P1.1 Colonial Experience. Operations across the Empire and in particular the NW Frontier of India, tested various components of the British Army's logistic capability. (RLCM: A1/MT/RLCAB/000163)

rail movement training and practice, activities also undertaken by the RAF.[16] Off the rails, the RASC was at the forefront of military logistic vehicle innovation.

The fourth factor was continuing logistic doctrinal development, which looked beyond the colonial focus and examined the future challenges in a Continental manoeuvre environment. The RASC sought to capitalize upon emerging mechanical transport capability, which offered more capacity, and with the production of more capable cross-country vehicles,[17] greater mobility. The RASC Training College at Aldershot has been described in the period as a 'hotbed of innovation'[18] and RASC studies, supported by trials at the Mechanical Warfare Experimental Establishment at Farnborough, identified a series of issues in relation to effective support to divisional level operations, including traffic control, defence against air attack, vehicle maintenance, recovery and repair, ammunition supply and the distribution of Petrol, Oils and Lubricants (POL).[19] Liquid fuel supply for the motorized and increasingly mechanized future

16 'The Woolmer Instructional Military Railway', *The Railway Gazette*, p.4.

17 The British Army was not the only military organization to recognize the opportunities as French use of WMT in South Morocco in 1934 and Italian operations in Abyssinia from 1935, lucidly demonstrated. See, Brevet Lieutenant-Colonel G C Shaw RAOC, *Supply in Modern War* (London: Faber & Faber, nd but 1938), p.150.

18 David Fletcher, *British Military Transport, 1829-1956* (London: The Stationery Office, 1998), p.56.

19 Major General Patrick G Turpin CB OBE MA FCIT, *The Turn of the Wheel, The History of the RASC, 1919-1939*, Institution of the Royal Corps of Transport (Buckingham: Barracuda Books, 1988), pp.130-131.

Army was not however, solely RASC business and in 1935, the QMG to the Forces,[20] responding to a paper by the Chief of the Imperial General Staff (CIGS)[21] outlining the future options for the reorganization of the British Army, incisively articulated its importance: 'Petrol ... is the life-blood of the 1st Contingent we propose to put in the field'.[22] All of this conceptual work, reinforced by trials and exercises in the UK and abroad, combined with a new divisional RASC structure created a robust and resilient organization[23] that proved capable of modification to meet the greater dispersion and mobility of tracked armoured forces, although the deployment and recovery of tanks at the operational level was not resolved and remained in limbo before becoming a hard lesson of 1940. From 1928, the RASC was also a key player in a series of Wheeled Motor Transport (WMT) experiments, trials and exercises in Egypt to test and improve logistic support in desert operations, resulting in a series of not only Lessons Identified but also Lessons Learned, with particular emphasis on passive and active defence against air and ground threats.[24] This work was essential to refining RASC support to the developing Mobile Division in Egypt and culminated in early 1939 with the formation being allocated four WMT companies, directed by a Commander RASC.[25] Colonel D C Cameron OBE RASC, Commandant of the RASC Training College in the late 1920s, initiated much of this work and his innovation and industry was a key driver in integrating operational RASC units to all combat formations.[26]

The last and indeed, defining factor in the deployment, sustainment and redeployment of any British expeditionary force was the critical role of the maritime dimension, which not only was effectively out-with the control of the War Office, but also was on a strategic scale that dwarfed the Army's influence in its provision, although equally the scale of the logistic lift it could provide in relation to the proposed expeditionary force suggested that this was the one aspect that the

20 Lieutenant-General Sir Reginald May KCB KBE CMG DSO (1879-1958) late Royal Fusiliers. May served in the 2nd Battalion during the Second Boer War, and after the Great War as a senior officer in the appointments of Director of Movements (1919-1923) and the Senior Administrative Officer of Northern Command (1927-1930). He commanded 49th (West Riding) Division (1930-1931) and was the Commandant of the Royal Military College Sandhurst before being appointed to the post of QMG in 1935, retiring in 1939.

21 Field-Marshal Sir Archibald Armar Montgomery-Massingberd GCB GCVO KCMG (1871-1947), late Royal Artillery.

22 Montgomery-Massingberd served in India from 1892 before serving in South Africa during the Second Boer War. Arriving in France as a major in 1914, he served in a series of General Staff appointments being promoted to substantive major-general on 1 January 1917 effectively becoming Deputy Commander of Fourth Army during the last months of the Great War. Post-war he was Chief of Staff (COS) of the British Army of the Rhine before being appointed as Deputy COS in India, returning to command 53rd (Welsh) Division in 1922 and 1st Infantry Division in 1923. After two years on half-pay he was appointed as GOC Southern Command in 1928, Adjutant-General to the Forces in 1931 and CIGS in 1933, retiring from the Army in 1936. TNA WO 32/4612: Future Army Organization - 1935, QMG Response dated 16 December 1936 to CIGS SECRET Paper, 'Future Reorganization of the British Army' dated 9 September 1935.

23 In 1931, when these structures were embedded to the 1st and 2nd Infantry Divisions, they were in cadre form, with the Peace Establishment of each company consisting of two officers, 56 Other Ranks, 15 WMT vehicles and three motor-cycles. Turpin, *The Turn of the Wheel*, p.132.

24 Ibid, pp.109-112. Fletcher, *British Military Transport*, p.62 and Winton, *To Change an Army*, p.154.

25 Turpin, *The Turn of the Wheel*, p.111.

26 Ibid.

War Office planners could rely upon being delivered to effect.[27] Whilst the role of sea-power in its broadest sense was embedded in supporting expeditionary forces in the context of the Empire and the Colonies, its application in a European continental environment has tended to be overlooked, despite its vital role in the Great War, which reinforced the simple adage that if an Army is going to be in the fight, it must get to the fight. Indeed, the role of sea-power during the Second World War is increasingly often marginalized or compartmentalized in the historiography[28] and in this respect, its role in enabling British Land and Air Forces to be deployed and sustained on the Continent is no exception.

The Logistic Revolutionaries

Whilst the corporate body of the RASC led by Cameron and supported by senior officers, focused upon an evolutionary practical approach to nurture logistic development, he was also at the forefront of a more revolutionary solution in solving the conundrum of supplying mechanized forces in the field, particularly in an adverse air environment. At a Royal United Services Institution lecture in February 1929, with the QMG to the Forces, Lieutenant-General Sir W Hastings KCB in the Chair,[29] he exposed the necessity of taking a completely new approach to the problem, with an emphasis, upon reducing the size and scope of the Administrative Base. His concept included the wide dispersion of logistic stocks, the 3rd Line movement of material by WMT rather than the railway[30] and the replacement of failed vehicles rather than conducting major repairs, thereby improving protection, enhancing flexibility, improving mobility and maintaining momentum. Whilst providing innovative proposals as a component of his paper, his attack upon the logistic *status quo* can only be described as ferocious, which must have brought some of the orthodox members of the audience to the point of apoplexy. He had some particularly harsh words on the culture of the Base installations and Service Directorates that supported the concept:

> Once these establishments had sprung into being they came to be regarded as natural and inevitable, as part of experience. So they have imposed themselves on our regulations,[31] and reproduce themselves in every Administrative Staff exercise. One struggles to cut them down in vain. The reason is that we are dealing with Directorates,

27 John de S Winser, *BEF Ships, Before at and after Dunkirk* (Gravesend: World Ship Society, 1999), describes the types and numbers of ships taken up from trade to service the BEF's expanding requirements, some of which were not fully employed.

28 One exception to this trend is Phillips Payson O'Brien, *How the War was Won* (Cambridge: Cambridge University Press, 2015).

29 Held on Wednesday 27 February 1929 at 1500 and published as 'The Supply of Mechanized Forces in the Field', *Royal United Services Institution* (RUSI), Vol LXXIV November 1929, No 496, pp.744-758.

30 A particular point raised by Colonel Cameron was the potential vulnerability of railheads to enemy air action, a concern that matured in May 1940, although the results were to some extent mitigated by quickly re-locating the railheads to small country stations rather than larger yards or sidings. This action lucidly demonstrated that the BEF's logisticians were able to learn and improvise.

31 Army Council, *Field Service Regulations* (FSR), Vol I, *Organization and Administration*, 26/Regulations/189, War Office (London: HMSO, 1930).

> very difficult people to treat, since they wrap themselves up in technical mystery like a hedgehog in its spikes.[32]

Post-lecture, there was, unsurprisingly, some lively debate, including discussion on the challenges of Command, Control and Communications (C^3) of dispersed logistic sites, the provision of air transport to enable urgent support to small armoured forces[33] and the role of the RAF in protecting Army logistic capability.[34] Whilst the group was at one in agreeing the problems, there was general caution on the proposed solutions, with the QMG in his summary, perhaps not unexpectedly, proffering an evolutionary roll-out, the absolute need to protect logistic capability whatever the lay-down and a more constructive assessment of the role and professional capabilities of the 'the Directors'.[35] In particular, the suggestion to eliminate the railway as a mode of transport was greeted with scepticism, although this was based upon its significant practical lift capability rather than any inherent cultural objection,[36] whilst the proposal to rely solely upon WMT brought observations from RE officers in relation to bridge weights and road maintenance, exposing that a saving in one area created a resource requirement in another. Major-General Davies late RE also highlighted the importance of the combat logisticians maintaining a close relationship with the infrastructure engineers to ensure that the critical synergy between the two was synchronised to best effect.[37] What is especially interesting is that the debate encapsulated nearly everything that British Army logisticians were to manage during the course of the Second World War, and in this respect it reflected the breath and depth of intellect and experience of its officers in 1929.

Cameron was not the only officer proposing new ideas to create logistic agility and resilience. In 1938, an officer of the RAOC[38] was suggesting similar revolutionary solutions to not only seize the opportunities offered by new WMT engineering but also to mitigate the risks posed by emerging threats created by more mobile ground manoeuvre forces and Air Interdiction

32 Colonel D C Cameron OBE, 'The Supply of Mechanized Forces in the Field', *Royal United Services Institution* (RUSI), Vol LXXIV November 1929, No 496, p.745.

33 Whilst not viewed by the RAF as a key task, the movement and support of light infantry and artillery forces were embedded in the War Office document on the subject, although there was a cautionary caveat: 'It must be realized, however, that troops may suffer considerably from air sickness during a long journey, and their fighting value immediately after arrival might be impaired.' It is difficult to judge whether the Air Ministry inserted this sentence as a practical warning or to persuade the Army to avoid the air transport option. Army Council, *The Employment of Air Forces with the Army in the Field*, 26/Manuals/1076, War Office (London: HMSO, 1932), pp.22-23.

34 Cameron, 'The Supply of Mechanized Forces in the Field', RUSI Vol LXXIV November 1929, No 496, p.745.

35 Ibid, p.757, QMG Summary. In relation to the Directors, Warder Barraclough in the BBC TV comedy series *Porridge* would no doubt have observed that Colonel Cameron was being 'rather unfair upon a well-meaning body of men'.

36 Major-General Davies, late RE, responded, 'With the large volume of supplies to be carried (using "supplies" in a very broad sense), I consider that railways must continue to play a dominant part in war, especially in countries where the roads are not so good as they are in Europe'. Ibid, p.755.

37 Ibid, p.755.

38 Brevet Lieutenant-Colonel George Cumberland Shaw, who was regular contributor to military journals, and in particular RUSI, including the articles 'Supply and Transportation' and 'The Language of Authority'.

(AI) capability.[39] His proposals, exposed in *Supply in Modern War*, were, in a word, radical. He wrote:

> There must be a clean sweep of all from, and including, the main base in its present form, forwards: all the accumulated administrative ritual of all but a century; all the fixed cumbersomeness of Regulating Stations, Railheads, and Advanced Bases; the standardized and scheduled movement of Ammunition and Petrol Parks, and of Divisional Ammunition and Petrol Companies; the stereotyped functioning of Refilling Points, Rendezvous, and Delivery Points; and the holy rites of the Corps and Divisional administrative area.[40]

Given the resources and rigour that had been embedded by the RASC in particular, into assessing how to best utilize future capabilities and match emerging threats, senior logistic officers must have read these words with some unease and probably not a little frustration, especially as Shaw suggested that: 'The umbilical cord of administrative movement must be broken, to give freedom of movement to war's new mechanized offspring, which can largely carry the substance of its lines of communication within itself'.[41] Whilst an interesting concept and certainly one to generate lively debate in a Q syndicate at the Army Staff College at Camberley, the practicalities of delivery were beyond the realms of supporting operations 'at scale' with mechanized armoured forces,[42] although by 1938 increasing use of air transport to support forces on the North-West Frontier was embedded in a Joint-Service doctrinal publication[43] and airborne and infantry forces would be supplied by air during the Second World War in Europe and Burma,[44] albeit with the application of very substantial air transport resources.[45] The theory was however, supported by practice in that a division was capable of operating from its assigned resources for a number of days, although the length of the period was dependent on the type and intensity of the task and the reaction of the enemy but beyond those boundaries, replenishment was an inevitable requirement if the division was to remain combat effective. Indeed, one of the activities rarely practised on pre-war exercises was formation level refuelling either because the

39 Air Interdiction (AI) is an air operation conducted to destroy, neutralize or delay the enemy's military potential, before it can be brought to bear effectively against friendly forces at such a distance from friendly forces, that detailed integration of each air mission with the fire and movement of friendly forces is not required. *Air Publication 3000, British Air Power Doctrine*, 3rd Ed, p.3.13.2.

40 Shaw, *Supply in Modern War*, p.218.

41 Ibid.

42 In the 21st Century, even armies equipped with High Mobility Load Carriers and supported by heavy-lift helicopters and air-drop can only support relatively small armoured formations in this manner.

43 See, a most interesting publication, Government of India Defence Department, *Frontier Warfare – India* (Army and Royal Air Force), MGS-M121 (N) 20000 (New Delhi: Government of India Press, 1939), which noted that, 'In an emergency, provided sufficient suitable aircraft can be made available for the purpose, it may be possible to maintain a force wholly or largely by air'; p.143, para 9.

44 For Burma, see, WOOH, *Supplies and Transport*, Vol II, Colonel D W Boileau late RASC (London: War Office, 1954), pp.75-77 and p.93.

45 For an examination of the logistic and air transport aspects of the airborne support to Operation OVERLORD, see, WOOH, *Airborne Forces*, Lieutenant-Colonel T B H Otway DSO, The Royal Ulster Rifles (Comp.) (London: War Office, 1951), pp.162-167 and pp.192-197. The administrative lessons from other airborne operations are also discussed in the volume.

movement during the schemes did not exceed the range of the vehicles or replenishment was conducted outside the tactical training envelope,[46] a point reinforced by a War Office logistic history, which observed: 'Realistic administrative exercises in the British Army are regrettably conspicuous by their absence'.[47]

Shaw did however raise several very important points in relation to flexibility, dispersion, decentralization and communications, aspects the RASC had identified as key to successfully supporting mobile operations in a dynamic ground and air environment, whilst in stating that 'Supply ... forms the basis on which rests the whole structure of war; it is the very foundation of Tactics and Strategy',[48] he absolutely reinforced its importance to military operations. He also made the astute observation that mechanized forces would require increased support, thereby altering the 'teeth to tail' ratio in favour of the logisticians,[49] although his view was based upon an analysis that this would occur through default rather than need, as machines replaced man-power in combat units and the personnel so released, effectively moved rearwards.[50] Shaw's proposal to abandon the use of rail as a 3rd Line transportation force multiplier[51] must though, have exercised, if only briefly, the minds of the Transportation Staff in the Corps of Royal Engineers, who responsible for enabling, in conjunction with commercial or nationalized railway systems,[52] effective military movement of *materiel* and personnel and at a time when plans were being developed to increase the numbers of specialist Supplementary Reserve railway units to meet perceived future commitments.[53] Indeed, this work was an example of a Lesson Learned from the Great War, when GHQ BEF realised that the deploying force had an emerging capability gap.[54] Of especial note, was Shaw's failure to explain how armour, which moved by rail, was to be otherwise positioned in an operational Theatre. In the areas of provisioning, supply and Material Handling Equipment (MHE) however, he was on stronger professional ground. MHE certainly had the capability to be a logistic multiplier and given the commercial interest in the late 1930s and the constraints on manpower during the Second World War, it is surprising that that the Army continued to rely so much on manual labour,[55]

46 Brigadier John Sutton (ed.), *Wait for the Waggon, The Story of the Royal Corps of Transport and its Predecessors, 1794-1993* (Barnsley: Leo Cooper, 1998), p.103.
47 WOOH, *Maintenance in the Field,* Vol 1, Lieutenant-Colonel J A H Carter OBE KORR and Major D N Kann MBE RASC, (War Office, 1952), p 57.
48 Shaw, *Supply in Modern War*, p.216.
49 Ibid, p.332.
50 His conceptual assessment appears to be based upon the work of an American economist and social theorist, Stuart Chase, *Men and Machines* (New York: Macmillan, 1929).
51 Shaw, *Supply in Modern War*, p.219.
52 The importance and interconnectivity of the railways for the movement of freight is lucidly illustrated by reference to private internal company publications, such as *Great Western Railway: Miscellaneous Instructions covering the Conveyance of Merchandise and Live Stock Traffic* (Paddington: Great Western Railway, 1930).
53 Major-General R P Pakenham-Walsh CB MC, *The History of the Corps of The Royal Engineers*, Vol VIII (Chatham: Institution of Royal Engineers, 1958), pp.21-22.
54 Colonel A M Henniker CBE (Comp.) *Official History of the Great War: Transportation on the Western Front, 1914-1918* (London: HMSO, 1937), pp.53-57.
55 At the unit level, the regimental history of 208 Field Company RE TA brilliantly summarizes the amount of muscle that was needed just to move the unit from A to B, noting that soldiers were constantly required to handle *materiel* and equipment, 'From store to vehicle, vehicle to train, train to vehicle, vehicle to ship, ship to train, train to vehicle and vehicle to destination'. Sussex Colonel L F

although the Royal Engineers had started to utilize an increasing amount of mechanical plant for construction, and in conjunction with contractors and port authorities, for dock operations.[56]

Politics and Money

In December 1937, the Cabinet agreed the priorities for the re-equipment of the Armed Services: Royal Navy, Royal Air Force, Air Defence of Great Britain (ADGB)[57] and the Army's Field Force.[58] CIGS was thus channelled by the politics of the hour to place GBAD of the United Kingdom at the top of its priorities[59] and a European deployment under the Western Plan at the bottom. War Office expenditure on equipment was therefore, prioritised on Anti-Aircraft (AA) guns and ammunition, gun tractors, searchlights and ancillary items,[60] whilst to decrease costs, the supporting logistic vehicles were to be provided by emergency impressments from the civil sector, which given the plan to utilize most of them in the UK Home Base reduced the operating risks to this solution. The changing dynamics of the Army's role had a clear influence upon logistics in terms of units, war reserves and equipment, and the ability of industry to deliver to meet emerging and then sometimes evaporating requirements.[61] The agreement to form a Field Force regardless of its shape and size was logistically shaped by its potential deployment Theatre. The Eastern Plan, which included India and the Middle East, and within the latter a focus upon Egypt,[62] had priority over the Continental Western Plan, generating specific equipment needs for hot desert operations[63] but wider logistic issues also emerged including the provision of tentage for Territorial Army Field Hospitals and the production of petrol tins.[64]

The initial pre-occupation of the War Office with the Eastern Plan and especially desert operations, affected not only the provision of nearly every type of equipment and store but also

Morling DSO OBE TD (Comp.), *Sussex Sappers: A History of the Sussex Volunteer and Territorial Army Royal Engineers from 1890 to 1967*, (208th Field Coy RE Committee, nd but 1973), p.58.

56 Army Council, *Military Engineering*, Vol VII, *Accommodation and Installations*, 26/Manuals/1062, War Office (London: HMSO: 1934), pp.263-275, Mechanical Handling of Materials and pp.288-300, Constructional Plant.

57 At an *ad hoc* meeting of ministers on 8 November 1937, it was agreed that: 'The Secretary of State for War should be authorised to instruct the War Office that the provision of anti-aircraft defences is to have absolute priority over all other forms of war material'. Quoted in Gibbs, BOH, *Grand Strategy*, Vol I, *Rearmament Policy*, p.467.

58 CP 316 (37). Memorandum by Minister for Co-ordination of Defence dated 15 December 1937, subsequently confirmed by the Cabinet. See, WOOH, *Fighting, Support and Transport Vehicles and the War Office Organization for their Provision*, Part I, *Common Problems*, Major R Campagnac RASC & Major P E C Hayman, 15/19 KRH (Comps.), (War Office, 1951) p.11.

59 For a summary, see, Gibbs, BOH, *Grand Strategy*, Vol I, *Rearmament Policy*, pp.460-464.

60 The frustrations within the Army were clear, General Ironside, the General Officer Commanding-in-Chief of Eastern Command, recording in his diary of 3 February 1938: 'The Air Defence of Great Britain is absorbing all the money which was intended for the Field Force. 'The Air Ministry dictates what it wants and the Army estimates bear the cost'; Macleod & Kelly, *The Ironside Diaries, 1937-1940*, p.47.

61 For a description, see, Gibbs, BOH, *Grand Strategy*, Vol I, *Rearmament Policy*, pp.465-482.

62 See, Ibid, pp.483-486.

63 WOOH, *Fighting, Support and Transport Vehicles*, Part I, *Common Problems*, p.3.

64 Ibid, p.8.

P1.2 Colonial Logistics. Colonial operations often required specialist or modified equipment incurring increased expense, whilst sometimes reducing capability for combat in Europe. An example is a Ford B Van with SDF body fitted with headlamp sun reflectors, water condenser and additional petrol and water can fitments for duties in the Sudan. (RLCM: RAOC/WTB1/NNA/0481/1)

the quantities and specifications.[65] The subsequent change of priority to the Western Plan resulted in equipping an increasingly motorized and mechanized Army to Continental war scales, a decision requiring a major uplift in industrial production. Whilst these two demands were not mutually exclusive, they established creative tensions within the Army's organizational and equipment programmes, which generated increasing frictions in initiating industrial production, especially in relation to a very substantial proposed need for logistic WMT.[66] The maturing plan expanded exponentially between December 1938 when War Office requirements were based upon meeting the approved five division deficiency programme, and April 1940, when schedules for supporting a thirty-six division Army were assessed, although only thirty-two had been authorised by this date.[67] The industrial base in the UK fundamentally underpinned future military logistic resilience, a point expressed by the Secretary of State for War:[68] "I recognize, no

65 Ibid, p.6.
66 See Table 1.1.
67 In December 1939, the War Office collated the requirements for sixty principal stores to support, by mid-1941, a fifty-five division Army. These figures were indicative and also arguably speculative, although the Treasury and the Ministry of Supply interpreted them to mean they should plan but not act upon them. See, M M Postan, BOH, *British War Production* (London: HMSO, 1952), p.73, Table 8.
68 Few people remember Hore-Belisha's time as the Secretary of State for War (28 May 1937 - 4 January 1940). His memory lives on though, through his efforts, during an earlier period as Minister of Transport, to improve road safety, when he gave his name to the 'Belisha Beacon', provided to highlight the presence of the zebra pedestrian crossings. For his time as Secretary of State for War, see, R J

man more, that the essence of our effort depends on production.[69] The strength of the British Army is not only in Aldershot and on Salisbury Plain; it is in Woolwich and Nottingham"[70] The Master-General of the Ordnance (MGO) was of the same opinion: 'We cannot get away from the fact that the possibilities of munitions supply really govern the whole problem'.[71] Whilst production was focused upon UK capacity, design was not and the War Office sought solutions from abroad and built the weapon systems or modified designs under licence. One example is the Ordnance SBML 2-inch Light Mortar Launcher, which was developed from a 50 mm design by the Spanish company *Esperanza y Cia*. Others included the 0.303 inch Bren Light Machine Gun (LMG) from Czechoslovakia and the 40 mm LAA gun from Sweden.[72]

Table 1.1
Selected War Office Equipment Future Requirements December 1938 and April 1940[73]

Material	December 1938	April 1940	Remarks
Tanks	5,025	7,096	
Tracked Carriers		11,647	
WMT & Motorcycles	25,545	376,299	
Field Artillery & AA guns	2,226	12,677	Including conversions
2 pdr Tank & Anti-Tank guns	Nil[74]	13,561	
Artillery & Tank ammunition	14.8 million	64.4 million	Excluding AA ammunition

Minney, *The Private Papers of Hore-Belisha* (London: Collins, 1950). Of interest, is that in the Great War, Hore-Belisha held a commission in the Army Service Corps, although he attempted to transfer to the Royal Flying Corps but was unsuccessful. He served on the Western Front, in Salonkia and in Egypt, returning to Oxford in 1919 to complete his studies.

69 For a comprehensive critical assessment of the military-industrial complex, see the incisive David Edgerton, *Warfare State Britain 1920-1970*, (Cambridge: Cambridge University Press, 2006), pp.15-58.

70 Minney, *The Private Papers of Hore-Belisha*, p.179. Hore-Belisha was in this instance referring to the Woolwich Arsenal and Royal Ordnance Factory (ROF) Nottingham but the point had a broader context. The Nottingham factory site was purchased for £94,475 (£5.925 million in 2018 based on RPI) by the War Office from the Metropolitan Cammell Carriage & Wagon Company for conversion to the production of the 3.7-inch Heavy and the 40 mm Bofors Light Anti-Aircraft (LAA) guns.

71 MGO War Office 57/Gen/7477 quoted in WOOH, *Fighting, Support and Transport Vehicles*, Part I, *Common Problems*, p.3.

72 All three of these weapons were so capable that they or their upgrades remained in the British Armed Forces inventory for nearly 50 years.

73 Postan, BOH, *British War Production*, pp.74-75.

74 By December 1938 the five-division deficiency programme was planned to have been completed. Production however, continued in 1939, with 114 weapons in Q1 and 248 in Q2 totalling 1,000 by the end of the year; Ibid, p.103, Table 10.

P1.3 Colonial Logistic Innovation. A Crossley Light 6 Wheel Low Profile truck for tactical operations. (RLCM: A1/MT/VR/NOR)

In the Spring of 1939, the Government policy took a massive change in strategic direction, when the Cabinet reluctantly accepted that a major continental deployment[75] was not only inevitable should war with Germany break out but was now an essential element of an alliance with France, and a potentially important insurance against German seizure of airfields in the Low Countries. The Cabinet thus promised the French Government that four infantry divisions would be sent to France within 33 days of mobilization, with the first of two armoured divisions arriving seven months after the main deployment.[76] In April 1939, the Cabinet also approved the expansion of the Army, Regular and Territorial, to thirty-two divisions,[77] completely overturning previous positions, whilst sanctioning the concomitant expenditure. The War Office was tasked with planning the dispatch of these forces to France after the start of mobilization, called Z Day. This was a significant task because some of the formations had yet to be established and there

75 For an erudite explanation, see, Michael Howard, *The Continental Commitment, The Dilemma of British Defence Policy in the Era of Two World Wars* (London: Temple Smith, 1972), pp.123-130.

76 Only 14 months before, in February 1938, the BEF's future commander, Viscount Gort, had informed the Committee of Imperial Defence (CID) whilst CIGS, that: '... if the Field Force were sent abroad it would have no guns which could compare with those of foreign armies ... [and] ... in these circumstances it would be murder to send our Field Force overseas to fight against a world class power'. BOH, *Rearmament Policy*, p.478. Viscount Gort's prediction proved all too accurate, although as it transpired the equipment was not the defining weakness.

77 Seven of which were TA Anti-Aircraft Divisions for Home Defence.

were large deficiencies of specific equipment and *materiel* for the standing formations. The four regular divisions would be deployed in two corps and there would be two RAF elements,[78] for which the Army would have some logistic responsibility.[79] This new policy had, as one might expect, a massive impact upon the logistic planning for operations[80] and the structure of Treasury defence financing.[81] As an illustration of the immense cost this involved, the Army Defence Programme,[82] which had begun in 1934 with a budget of £39.5 million, was, in June 1939, funded to £700 million.[83]

78 The British Air Forces in France (BAFF) comprised two elements: the Air Component of the BEF, which was under Viscount Gort's operational control, and the Advanced Air Striking Force (AASF) which was a forward based element of Bomber Command. In January 1940, the command arrangements, especially in relation to logistics, changed with the appointment of an Air Officer Commanding (AOC) BAFF. In addition, the establishment of HQ BAFF removed the anomalous requirement for GHQ BEF to request air support from the AASF through HQ Bomber Command, and although GHQ had no exclusive right to support, the arrangement created a more effective means of applying for it. TNA WO 277/34: Air Support in the Battle of France.

79 There was much confusion on the ground about these responsibilities, especially because the RAF was to provide support to specified Army units in defined Areas of Responsibility. The AASF was not provisioned for in-Theatre operational movement and relied heavily on Host Nation Support, a decision that Great War experience firmly indicated was flawed and a risk that matured in 1940. See, *The Second World War, 1939-1945, Royal Air Force* (AMOH), Air Publication 3397 (CONFIDENTIAL downgraded UNCLASSIFIED, March 1966), *Maintenance*, CD 1131 (Air Ministry, 1954), pp.63-66.

80 By September 1939 the process had matured to deploy the forces to a timeline shown in the table below.

Table 1.2
BEF
Planned Deployment Timelines – September 1939

In-Theatre Timeline	Divisions	Army Tank Brigades	Remarks
Z + 33 days	4 x Regular Infantry	1	1st, 2nd, 3rd & 4th XX
Z + 4 months	2 x TA Infantry		
Z + 5 months	1 x Territorial Motor	1	50th (Northumbrian) XX
Z + 5 months	3 x Territorial Infantry	1	
Z + 8 months	1 x Armoured	1	1st Armoured XX
Z+ 12 months?	1 x Armoured	1	Not deployed
	Total: 12	Total: 5	

81 For an examination of the influence, from the Treasury perspective, upon the Army programme, see, G C Peden, *British Rearmament and the Treasury, 1932-1939* (Edinburgh: Scottish Academic Press, 1979), pp.167-178.

82 The creative tension generated with the consumer economy by rising defence expenditure was encapsulated by the question 'guns or butter?', which had entered the public lexicon by 1937 to the point where young children remembered the challenge being discussed at the Sunday lunch table. Memory of Mary Maginniss (nee Palmer, aged 7 in 1937), in October 2019. It is of interest that Mary Palmer lived in Coventry, the productive capacity of which was crucial to the British rearmament programme.

83 WOOH, *Fighting, Support and Transport Vehicles*, Part I, *Common Problems*, p.13. At 2018 values, calculated using Measuring Worth GDP share of the economy, this equates to £18.92 billion and

Old Chestnuts and New Threats

The deployment to Shanghai in China of a division[84] of three infantry brigades[85] in early 1927, lucidly demonstrated that the British Army was capable of mobilizing[86] and transporting such a force[87] across the Globe in support of an international coalition of nations,[88] which indicated a continuing capability in movements planning, logistic out-load and the acquisition of shipping.[89] The logistic components were relatively small for a division but this was driven by the internal geography of the deployment.[90] Of greater longevity, were operations on the North-West Frontier of India, a location, which not infrequently, reminded those involved of the fragility of logistics in counter insurgency operations and the need for logisticians to be combat capable[91] but also generated innovative procedures such as mobile vehicle maintenance

£146.30 billion respectively.

84 TNA WO 191/1: General Staff, Peacetime Operations Abroad, 'Shanghai Defence Force'. It is of interest that the Army HQ General Staff Officer 1 was Colonel Viscount Gort VC DSO MVO MC and the Assistant Adjutant & Quartermaster-General, Colonel W D S Brownrigg DSO; respectively 12 years later, the Commander-in-Chief and Adjutant-General of the BEF.

85 13th & 14th Infantry Brigades from the UK and 20th (Indian) Infantry Brigade from the sub-continent; 27th Infantry Brigade was also dispatched from the UK but held in reserve in Hong Kong. TNA FO 371/63436: Dispatch of Shanghai Defence Force to Shanghai, 1927.

86 1,581 A Section Regular Reservists were mobilized to complete unit personnel establishments; only four failed to respond. See, Hansard HC (16 March 1927), Vol 203, c2112-2113. The total number of Section A Reserves mobilized in 1927 was 2,912. See, Cmd 5104, p.29.

87 There were RN and RAF components, including naval aircraft, embarked on HMS *Argus* and HMS *Hermes* and No 1 Squadron RAF.

88 Known as the Shanghai Defence Force or SHAFORCE, it consisted of Dutch, French, Italian, Japanese, Portuguese, Spanish, UK and US units totalling 40,000 personnel. The UK force comprising 20,000 personnel, had a Land element strength of 15,000 personnel and was entitled Duncan Force after its GOC Major-General and later Sir, John Duncan (1872-1948) CB CMG CVO DSO, late Royal Scots Fusiliers. Duncan had considerable experience as a GOC, commanding 22nd Division in Macedonia (1917-1918), 54th (East Anglian) Division in 1923 and immediately before his retirement, 1st Infantry Division in 1928.

89 The logistic requirements for an infantry division of this type engaged on combat operations 20 miles in advance of a railhead with a LOC 200 miles in length were planned to be comparatively light, with the daily tonnage totalling 270-300 tons *per diem*, depending upon the location and mission. The composition was: Supplies: 100 tons; local supplies, 35 tons; petrol, 33 tons; locomotive coal 33 tons; ammunition, 32 tons; engineer stores, 20 tons; ordnance *materiel*, 10 tons and mail and EFI, 7 tons. Army Council, *Military Engineering*, Vol VIII, *Railways*, 26/Manuals/103, War Office (London: HMSO, 1929), p.23.

90 RASC units included 12 MT Company, a supply depot and a bakery detachment. 3 (Indian) MT Company (Motor Ambulance Convoy) with 20 Fiat ambulances and 18 Divisional Troops Transport Company RIASC with 400 mules were dispatched from India to support 20th (Indian) Brigade. Of interest though, was 38 MT Company, equipped with the latest Morris 6 wheeled 30 cwt lorries. Turpin, *The Turn of the Wheel*, pp.64-65.

91 On 9 April 1937, a convoy commanded by Major T Z Waters MC RIASC consisting of four armoured cars, 31 x 3-ton Thornycroft 6x4 military lorries and 16 contracted civilian lorries and two private cars, was ambushed in the *Shahur Tangi* defile, with the loss of 47 killed and 50 wounded, the latter including Major Waters. The dead consisted of seven British officers, two British Other Ranks, 27 Indian Other Ranks, seven *Waziristan* Scouts, one Follower and three civilian drivers. For details of this action, see, IGS, *Official History of Operations on the NW Frontier of India, 1936-37* (New Delhi: Government of India Press, 1943), pp.55-65.

squads on the Line of Communication.[92] The deployment to Palestine in the period 1936-1939 reinforced the need to mitigate ground based threats to logistics in such environments[93] but equally exposed the vital importance of ensuring appropriate levels of Equipment Support (ES)[94] in an Army that was increasingly reliant upon WMT and tracked armoured vehicles for logistic and combat capability.[95] The exercises conducted by the newly formed Mobile Division in the harsh environment of the Egyptian desert reinforced not only this lesson but also the significance of well trained soldiers who were able to operate and maintain wheeled and tracked vehicles in hostile conditions to deliver operational effect.

The shape, size, composition and logistic capability of the BEF had been subject to much turbulence in the 1930s with the equipment programme an especial issue. The Cabinet position was founded upon the Treaties of Locarno,[96] which substantiated a basic tenet of British policy in Europe, namely, 'Limited Liability'.[97] British military deployments to the Continent, if there were to be any, were to be small and more of a gesture than of militarily significance, whilst the whole concept of engagement and subsequently appeasement, sought to eliminate the need for any deployments.[98] From the War Office perspective, the period between 1935 and 1939 was one of immense turmoil for the British Army as emerging threats began to crystallize

92 Government of India Defence Department, *Frontier Warfare – India*, p.144, para 6. These 'Service Squads', comprising one NCO and six soldiers, were deployed to assist, during intense periods of operation, LOC WMT units to complete 1st Line vehicle maintenance, thus enhancing reliability and output. A Service Squad could complete the schedule for a section of vehicles in five hours of daylight and seven in artificial lighting conditions.

93 Turpin, *The Turn of the Wheel*, pp.117-122.

94 Equipment Support (ES) includes the preparation and repair of equipment for battle and the repair and recovery of battle casualties and non-combat related failures. HQ ES staffs have a vital role in monitoring the serviceability of critical equipments in a formation to ensure that combat power is maintained. See, *Army Field Manual* Vol 1, *Combined Arms Operations*, Part 6, *Combat Service Support*, DGD&D 18/34/44, Army Code No 71344 (UK MOD, 1998), p.viii.

95 Brigadier H A Fernyhough CBE MC & Major H E D Harris, *History of the Royal Army Ordnance Corps, 1939-1945* (London & Beccles: William Clowes, nd but 1967), p.50.

96 The Treaties of Locarno were seven agreements negotiated in Switzerland between Belgium, Czechoslovakia, France, Germany, Great Britain, Italy and Poland in the period 5-16 October 1925 and formally signed in London on 1 December 1925. The treaties were essentially mutual guarantees of frontiers, but there were hidden agendas and perspectives behind the negotiations, which were to have unfortunate repercussions in the mid-1930s. Not least of these, was the belief by the then Foreign Secretary, Sir Austen Chamberlain, that the treaties reduced not extended Britain's continental liabilities. For further details see: Gibbs, BOH, *Grand Strategy*, Vol I, *Rearmament Policy*, Chp 2. Sally Marks, *The Illusion of Peace: International Relations in Europe, 1918-1933* (Basingstoke: Palgrave Macmillan, 2003), p.89, notes that, 'A few men knew that the spirit of Locarno was a fragile foundation on which to build a lasting peace'. See also, Gaynor Johnson (ed.) *Locarno Revisited: European Diplomacy Revisited, 1920-1929*, (London & New York: Routledge, 2004).

97 A term used to describe the policy of the British Governments of the 1930s, which focused on keeping the military Land force commitment to any future continental conflict as small as possible. See, Howard, *The Continental Commitment*, pp.96-120.

98 Nearly 90 years on, appeasement remains a topic for academic study, with arguments in support or otherwise, hotly debated. The bibliography is certainly lengthy. Engaging is Tim Bouverie, *Appeasing Hitler, Chamberlain, Churchill and the Road to War* (London: The Bodley Head, 2019), whilst Andrew David Stedman, *Alternatives to Appeasement, Neville Chamberlain and Hitler's Germany* (London: I B Tauris, 2011), examines the wider issues and options.

and old ones maintained traction.[99] In this respect, the re-armament of the British Army was conducted in two main phases: the first was designed to make good the deficiencies within the Army, with no increase in its size, whilst the second sought to equip a rapidly expanding force to meet a developing threat.[100] The end of the first phase merged with the beginning of the second, creating stresses on the War Office munitions organization that not only led to a significant expansion but also its separation into an independent government body, the Ministry of Supply.[101] Whilst defence planners wrestled with the potential problems that a resurgent Germany might present,[102] with all the issues relating to a potential continental Land force commitment, others in the War Office were more concerned with responding to more immediate threats.[103] Italian actions in the Mediterranean littoral of North Africa, in Abyssinia[104] and the Horn of Africa were a perpetual cause of concern because of the potential impact upon the security of Egypt and the Suez Canal,[105] both of which, were deemed vital to Britain's economic, imperial and defence interests in India and the Far East. The increasingly complex security issues in Palestine generated not only a counter insurgency operation but also rising concerns within the corridors of the Admiralty and War Office about the fragility of the country's potential role in supporting the development of a Middle East base.[106] The security and stability of the North-Western Frontier[107] of India was almost incessantly dynamic in the period and operations at brigade plus level, supported by the Royal Air Force,[108] were a feature of the military Diaspora, generating Air-Land and logistic lessons that regrettably were not

99 For an assessment of the European dynamics, see Williamson Murray, *The Change in the European Balance of Power, 1938-1939* (Yale: Yale University Press, 1975).

100 For a brief analysis of the dynamics of industrial capacity for aircraft and tanks, see, Edgerton, *Warfare State Britain*, pp.42-44.

101 For a survey of this issue and the creative tensions therein, see, Robert Paul Shay Jr, *British Rearmament in the Thirties, Politics and Profits* (Guildford: Princeton University Press, 1977), Chp III, 'Industrial Mobilization for Rearmament'.

102 For an engaging analysis, see, Wesley K Wark, *The Ultimate Enemy, British Intelligence and Nazi Germany, 1933-1939* (London: I B Tauris, 1985).

103 In a minute to CIGS, Director-General Territorial Army observed: 'The commitments away from the Western Front come and go with every change in the political situation - the Western Front is with us always and we cannot escape from it'. DGTA War Office 79/Gen3292 dated 25 April 1938 quoted in WOOH, *Fighting, Support and Transport Vehicles*, Part I - *Common Problems*, p.7.

104 The employment of gas by the Italians in Abyssinia was a pre-cursor to the deployment of British gas weapons to Egypt and France in 1939, and thus, concomitantly, additional logistic tasks. WOOH, *Special Weapons and Types of Warfare*, Vol I, *Gas Warfare* (War Office, 1951), (SECRET), p.4.

105 See, Major-General I S O Playfair CB DSO MC, BOH, *The Mediterranean and Middle East*, Vol I, *The Early Successes against Italy (to May 1941)*, (London: HMSO, 1954), pp.9-11 & pp.35-37 and Steven Morehead, *The British Defence of Egypt 1936-1940, Conflict and Crisis in the Eastern Mediterranean* (London & New York: Frank Cass, 2005).

106 Playfair, BOH, *The Mediterranean and Middle East*, Vol I, pp.13-16.

107 IGS, *Official History of Operations on the NW Frontier of India*, 1936-37.

108 For the official military histories, see, Ibid and IGS, *Official History of Operations on the NW Frontier of India, 1920-35* (New Delhi: Government of India Press, 1945). For a wider perspective, also see, Alan Warren, *Waziristan, The Faqir of Ipi and the Indian Army, The North West Frontier Revolt of 1936-37* (Bangalore: Oxford University Press, 2000).

transferred to the European Joint Service environment,[109] whilst the increasing vulnerability of British possessions on the Chinese coast to Japanese aggression, were lucidly exposed in 1937.[110]

Towards France

The massive expansion of the Army and the deployment, to France, of the Field Force, involved a extensive equipment programme that had an increasingly significant impact upon the economy, and the automotive industry in particular because of the large demand for WMT. The exponential growth in the requirement for WMT reinforced its significance to continental and desert warfare and load-carrying vehicles were of especial importance although the need for the BEF's deployment to France was moderated by the availability of the railway as a logistic multiplier. The plan to use equipment impressed from the civil sector to fill the capability gap,[111] whilst apparently a sound one given the difficulty both from the planning and financial perspectives to create an immediate industrial production base for military cargo vehicles, sat uncomfortably with the suggestion that the British Army was properly prepared for expeditionary operations 'at scale'. In the longer term, this arrangement had the potential to unbalance parts of the war economy and in 1939 introduced a series of supply, maintenance and repair issues for the War Office.

The quest for WMT was not however the only logistic issue which was created by the proposal to expand an Army without a resourced plan to underpin it and given the constraints, extemporization became a key feature of logistic planning in the pre-war period. Even these imperatives though, did not drive the process as fast as one might have expected because as late as December 1939, arguments were put forward that suggested the BEF required less, not more road transport. The substance of this debate was generated partly by the 'Maginot Complex', which focused some military minds on the prospects of static warfare, and partially by the view that the French Railways provided an admirable service; on both counts, those who held these views failed to comprehend the criticality of WMT at the operational level, a lesson writ large by the experience of the BEF in Great War.[112]

The personnel component imposed equally demanding challenges upon the logistic services because the expanding numbers of soldiers had to be equipped, clothed, fed, accommodated, cared for, transported and trained. Most recruits had not only to grasp the realities of soldiering, but also had to learn new trades in an alien organization and then apply them in a demanding environment, often learning 'On the Job'. This was especially true of the logistic services and a factor that should be considered when assessing their performance during the deployment in France. The military capability of Territorial officers was a contemporary concern, an issue

109 Had the doctrinal and practical Joint-co-operation between the Army and the RAF on the NW Frontier been developed in the UK and European Theatres during the 1930s, the capability of the Land component in France in 1940 would undoubtedly have been the better for it. See, Government of India Defence Department, *Frontier Warfare – India.* The logistic aspects are covered in pp.139-154.

110 Martin H Brice, *The Royal Navy and the Sino-Japanese Incident 1937-41* (London: Ian Allan, 1973).

111 Explored in Chapter 2, 'Everybody's Trucking'.

112 Clem Maginniss, 'Four Wheels on My Wagon, The influence of Wheeled Motor Transport upon British Army operations on the Western Front, 1914-1918', *An Unappreciated Field of Endeavour, Logistics and the British Expeditionary Force on the Western Front, 1914-1918* (Warwick: Helion, 2018), pp.267-293.

P1.4 Inter-war Logistic Recruiting. The RASC invested in recruiting for the Regular and Reserve components of the Corps during the 1930s, publishing some wonderful period material, including this iconic postcard. (RLCM: A1/MT/RLCA/20550)

explored by Alexander Jones,[113] and although the focus is upon command and leadership in infantry battalions, similar fragilities certainly existed in TA logistic units. General Gort, the C-in-C BEF was exposed to the vagaries of this rapidly expanding Army when he met a captain and a subaltern from 48th (South Midland) Division at a dump. Engaging them in conversation neither officer recognized him or his rank, and after he moved on, the captain asked Gort's Personal Assistant, the Earl of Munster, who the major was.[114] An exposure of the differentials and the influences of these cultural elements upon the logistic outputs is a thread within the logistic story but the aspect is worthy of more detailed academic study. For all its limitations however, in May 1940 the BEF was a product of remarkable improvisation, and the logistic support, despite the many demands placed upon it, impressive. Indeed in 1939, the British Army was the only completely motorized force to take to the field in North West Europe;[115]

113 Alexander David Jones, 'Pinchbeck Regulars? The Role and Organisation of the Territorial Army, 1919-1940' (Balliol College University of Oxford, PhD Thesis, 2016).

114 Colville described Gort's response to this incident as 'half-amused indignation'. J R Colville, *Man of Valour* (London: Collins 1972), p.178.

115 With the exception of an Animal Transport (AT) component imported from India in late 1939 specifically to assist in providing 1st Line transport support to units located in areas which, were not conducive to operations by WMT. TNA WO 167/1433: Headquarters Force K6, Indian Contingent, WD, 1939-1940.

in comparison, an infantry division of the German Army had 4,800 horses on establishment, whilst relying on an equally complex array of WMT impressed from the civil sector.[116]

Whilst the Army may have been deficient in equipment, there was no shortage of competent planners capable of applying logistic military principles to the problem, although perforce of circumstances, they were not always able to 'square the circle', so in examining the tasks and outputs of the BEF's logisticians it is useful to remember, as a bench-mark, the current Principles of Logistics,[117] which are part of the British Army's operational planning: foresight, efficiency, simplicity, co-operation and flexibility. Whilst not described in this manner in the period 1939-1940, their importance would have been readily understood by the logisticians of the day. Through the application of a process of what is now called DQUAD: Destination, Demand, Distance and Duration,[118] planners were able to quantify, within working limits, future logistic requirements, in Time and Space, activities which are examined in the following chapters. In delivering the outputs to support combat capability, the logisticians of the BEF faced several substantial challenges. A key issue was the rapid expansion of the British Army, with the attendant issues of sustaining the growing numbers of formations, units and personnel and doing so with competent and qualified logisticians. In this respect, the BEF faced many of the same issues as its predecessor in 1914-1916,[119] although in 1940 was blessed with senior planning and unit logistic commanders who had learned the hard way in the Great War, especially but not exclusively on the Western Front, and despite the down-sizing and re-shaping of the Army during the inter-war period and a focus upon colonial operations, had precious experience of operations 'at scale'. The lacuna in the skills arena was the knowledge to deliver logistic support to a motorized and mechanized force conducting mobile operations against a peer enemy.

If there was a key flaw in the planning for the deployment of the BEF, it was the inherent constraints in the structure, organization and manning of the Base and the GLOC. Whilst the divisions were formed of Regular units reinforced with Regular Reservists, the Base consisted of a mix of Regular, Territorial Army, Supplementary Reserve and Militiamen,[120] and latterly volunteers, each group having varying levels of military life, technical knowledge and operational experience. The Militiamen were conscripts initially aged 20-21 called up through

116 For an examination of the role of horses in the Germany Army during the Second World War, see R L Dinardo, *Mechanized Juggernaut or Military Anachronism? Horses and the German Army of WWII* (Mechanicsburg: Stackpole Books, 2008).

117 The Principles of Logistics are defined in *Army Doctrine Publication* Vol 3, *Logistics* (UK MOD, 1996), pp.1-4 to 1-6, paras 0108-0113 and *Army Field Manual* Vol 1, *The Fundamentals*, Part 6, *Combat Service Support*, Chp 1, pp.1-3 to 1-5. See also, *The Royal Logistic Corps*, Vol 1, Pamphlet 1, *Logistic Support Doctrine* (UK MOD, 1997), p.1-2 and p. 4-3.

118 For an explanation of the application of DQUAD, see *Army Doctrine Publication* Vol 3, pp.2-3 to 2-5, paras 0207-0211. See also *The Royal Logistic Corps*, Vol 1, Pamphlet 1, pp.3-4 to 3-5. A key point relating to Demand is not just the quantity but the timings, with requirements for a force of fixed size and composition being a mix of Steady State, for example rations; Cyclic, such as different clothing for changing seasons and Surge, for instance, ammunition and fuel for an offensive.

119 See, Maginniss, *An Unappreciated Field of Endeavour*, pp.46-52.

120 For an analysis of the issues relating to conscription in the inter-war period, see, Peter Dennis, *Decision by Default: Peacetime Conscription and British Defence 1919-1939* (London: Routledge & Kegan Paul, 1972).

the Military Training Act of May 1939[121] and were titled thus to distinguish them from soldiers in the Regular Army. To emphasise this distinction, each man was issued with a civilian suit in addition to a military uniform. The intention was for the first intake to undergo six months of basic and trade training before being discharged into an Active Reserve, being recalled for short training periods and annual camps, although there was considerable discussion as to how militarily effective this solution would be.[122] The RASC was fortunate in relation to the Militia, obtaining priority for men who were qualified drivers and tradesmen. Of the six months of Militia service, soldiers served two in the RASC Militia Training Battalion and four months in a field force unit. Of the 4,000 militiamen allocated to the Corps in 1939, 2,856 were WMT drivers, 450 Supply Clerks, 348 MT Artificers, 270 MT clerks, 42 Bakers and 30 Butchers. In the event, the RASC only received two intakes of Militiamen, one of 659 in July and another of 586 in the middle of September, although a further 3,000 were later transferred from Royal Artillery units in France.[123]

The RAOC, in particular, relied on improvised units,[124] which had to be formed upon mobilization to deliver the Ordnance Services[125] component, an arrangement that would never generate the critical coherency and effectiveness required to ensure support to a deploying expeditionary force. The dispersion of logistic nodes on the 500 miles of GLOC, an outfall of the air threat assessment, exacerbated this issue because more personnel were required, often in small detachments, to man it, which diluted an already inexperienced, although in many cases, able, pool of people. In these respects, not only was the Army the Cinderella of the Services but also military logistics, a capability upon which so much was to depend, remained in many respects a pumpkin. This situation caused many issues in France, not least of which, was that the deployment was the first time the logisticians had supported an operational mechanized force at a corps level, a factor complicated by the scale of deployment. The following chapters tell the story of their challenges, strengths, limitations and achievements.

121 The Act was superseded upon the outbreak of war in September 1939 by the National Service (Armed Forces) Act 1939.

122 This discussion was not confined to the War Office. On 4 June 1939, the school Literary Society of Ratcliffe College near Leicester, held a debate titled 'Britain's half-hearted attempt at conscription will prove ineffective'. *The Ratcliffian*, Vol XIX No 162, September 1939, p.583. The author's uncle Nicholas Maginniss contributed to the debate, whilst his brother Hugh, an Old Ratcliffian, was shortly to become a Militiaman in the Royal Warwickshire Regiment before serving in the BEF.

123 WOOH, *Supplies and Transport*, Vol I, Colonel D W Boileau late RASC (War Office, 1954), p.38. The progress and proof editing reports for this volume are in TNA WO 366/44.

124 Other Ranks in the RAOC served in two branches, Workshops and Stores Branch, the latter employing initially, clerks, storemen and ammunition examiners. There were later sub-divisions in the storeman trades including ammunition, armaments, small arms, MT stores, packing, traffic, rubber, gas production, laundry, signals, wireless, radar and general. WOOH, *Ordnance Services*, p.x.

125 Ordnances Services included the provision, storage and repair of Army equipment including ammunition and clothing. In the Base areas, RAOC units included Base Ammunition Depots, Base Ordnance Depots, Base Ordnance Workshops and laundries.

2

Everybody's Trucking
The expansion of the logistic task vehicle fleet in the British Army in the period 1935-1940

Introduction

The British Army of late 1918 was an immensely capable force, equipped with State of the Art weapons and beginning to seize the opportunities offered by the internal combustion engine for mobile warfare, and logistic support. 20 years on, one could have been forgiven for thinking that time had stood still because in 1938, most commanders and defence planners, perceived that any future campaign would be similar to late 1917, with periods of static warfare and some limited mobile operations. Such an approach seems at odds with the wide debate during the 1930s, on the strengths of mobile forces, and the supporting experimentation with them in the field,[1] but given the force structure, which remained based on the infantry division, there could only be one conclusion as to the British Army's perspective of warfare. The story is therefore a complex, yet thoroughly interesting one, in which Grand strategic policy, defence finance, government taxation, military technical requirements, inter-Service rivalry, regimental prejudices, commercial initiatives and vehicle engineering, all combined to influence the outcome. To support a massive expansion programme and the expeditionary force in France, some quite remarkable improvisation had to be enacted, in order to procure the necessary logistic load-carriers.[2] How this was achieved, and the lessons that were learned from executing it, is the subject of this chapter.

1 For the combat aspects, see, See, Harold R Winton, *To Change an Army, General Sir John Burnett-Stuart and British Armoured Doctrine, 1927-1938* (Kansas: University of Kansas Press, 1988) and for logistics, Colonel D C Cameron OBE, 'The Supply of Mechanized Forces in the Field', *Royal United Services Institution* (RUSI) Vol LXXIV November 1929, No 496.

2 In this chapter, load-carrier also includes specialist types, such as vehicles for tankers, technical stores, workshops, recovery and Heavy Equipment Transporters (HET).

Despite the travails of the inter-war period, the BEF was, in 1939, the only motorized force to deploy in the European Theatre,[3] although there were no specialized military logistic task vehicles in quantity production in the United Kingdom, with which to support such formations, so many units were equipped partially or wholly, with vehicles impressed from the civilian sector. Given the vibrancy of the British motor industry, this may appear surprising but was a product of British Government and War Office policy in the 1930s, which sought for financial and economic reasons to rely on commercial trends rather than a military lead in the design of military Wheeled Motor Transport (WMT). By the time it was motorized in 1930, the RASC became the largest single user of WMT and logistic load-carriers, resulting in three classifications of Army vehicles. 'A' vehicles sponsored by Master-General of the Ordnance (MGO) 5 included tanks, Dragon tracked artillery tractors, all tracked and semi-tracks, armoured cars and specialist combat unit WMT. 'B' vehicles, sponsored by MGO 6 covered all Army WMT with the exception of RASC equipments, which were sponsored by QMG 3, including all load or passenger WMT on RASC unit establishments or driven by RASC personnel, including all ambulances and fire engines.[4] The RAOC was responsible for the storage, issue and repair of all 'A' and 'B' vehicles, whilst the RASC had its own systems for the vehicles it sponsored.[5]

RASC officers employed in the Motor Transport (MT) arena were a mix of WMT operators and mechanical engineers, who sought to forge resilience professional interfaces with the automotive engineering and production industries, thereby generating constructive relationships between the military and commercial spheres. This arrangement created a pool of expertise and reinforced the fact that WMT was an adjunct of Supply, which meant there was less emphasis on maturing the components of future Army capability. In 1925, MGO split the staff of the Director of Artillery, with Branch II being formed to manage the development of Armoured Fighting Vehicles (AFV) and WMT,[6] although the transfer of responsibility from the QMG and RASC was not effective until 1927 and Director of Artillery II was re-titled Director Mechanization.[7] Even then, the RASC remained the largest user of WMT and QMG remained predominately responsible for the first stage in the provision of RASC vehicles

3 The British Army was not however, fully motorized because upon mobilization, the TA yeomanry regiments of the 1st Cavalry Division retained their horses. See, Dennis C Bateman, 'Goodbye to Boots and Saddles, The Twilight of the British Cavalry', *British Army Review*, No 114 (UK MOD, December 1996), pp.75-89.

4 For a description of RASC vehicle trials and experiments in the inter-war period, see, Major General Patrick G Turpin CB OBE MA FCIT, *The Turn of the Wheel: The History of the RASC, 1919-1939*, Institution of the Royal Corps of Transport (Buckingham: Barracuda Books, 1988), pp.169-179.

5 This arrangement continued until 1942, when, as a result of the recommendations of the War Office Beveridge and Sinclair Committees, the RAOC absorbed the storage and issue functions of the RASC, and the REME the repair responsibilities. See WOOH, *Fighting, Support and Transport Vehicles*, Part I, *Common Problems*, p.100.

6 Ibid, pp.51-52.

7 As Campagnac and Hayman observe, Director of Artillery II had good justification in adhering to his appointment title in the intervening two years because it was only in December 1926 that the War Office formally changed the terminology from 'mechanicalize' and 'mechanicalization' to 'mechanize' and 'mechanization'. The title of Director of Mechanicalization was hardly one to inspire future developments. Ibid, p.52.

P2.1 Testing & Trialling. 6x4 WMT undergoing trials in UK. (RLCM: A1b/MT/ RLCA/30007)

and consequently the 'Supply' focus remained.[8] One important outfall from this change was the failure to analyse the future opportunities for the coherent integration of the compression ignition power-plants fuelled by diesel oil,[9] to military vehicle design, with the Mechanical Warfare Board only reporting, if often comprehensively, on commercial developments, rather than driving potential military specifications and applications.[10] This situation was compounded by civil vehicle taxation and road haulage legislation,[11] which was influenced by the politics of rail transportation.[12]

8 Ibid, p.52.
9 The War Office was however, presumably expecting the introduction of some CI vehicles because there is a 16-page section on the engine and its supporting systems in the 1937 MT handbook. See, Army Council, *Manual of Driving and Maintenance for Mechanical Vehicles (Wheeled)*, 1937, War Office (London: HMSO, 1938), pp.209-224.
10 Fletcher, *British Military Transport*, p.58.
11 See, C I Savage, BOH, Inland *Transport* (London: HMSO & Longmans, Green & Co, 1957), pp.15-16.
12 For an analysis, see, H J Dyos and D H Aldcroft, *British Transport: An Economic Survey from the Seventeenth Century to the Twentieth* (Leicester: Leicester University Press, 1971), pp.342-345 and Phillip S Bagwell, *The Transport Revolution from 1770* (New York: Barnes & Noble, 1974), pp.222-235.

Mechanization and Motorization

The General Staff in the War Office remained a compact body until 1937 and the lines of responsibility for the three directorates, Director Military Operations & Intelligence (DMO & I), Director Staff of Duties (DSD) and Director Military Training (DMT) in relation to vehicle procurement was for the most part, clear. DMO & I forecast the type of operations for which, provision was required and evidence of the threat against which, equipment should be designed. DSD issued general vehicle specifications, although in effect DSD only monitored this for WMT and defined future populations against the ORBAT from DMO & I. DMT directed tactical and employment training through several Arm and Service Directors, based upon the RASC model established in 1907, although this lapsed during the Great War. Mechanization was however, well underway by 1934, a memorandum prepared for the 1935 Estimates Committee[13] lucidly explained the problem in defining 'mechanization' under two headings:

(1) The employment of the internal combustion engine as a substitute for the horse.
(2) The employment of the internal combustion engine to obtain tactical advantages on the battlefield by means of armoured fighting vehicles.

The former might be more effectively described as motorization and the latter, mechanization. The term 'mechanization' described the introduction of Mechanical Transport to the British Army, both wheels and tracks. In the pre-Second World War period, the term 'mechanize' was used to describe the equipping of horsed Regular cavalry regiments with light or cruiser tanks[14] and infantry battalions with tracked carriers. 'Motorization' usually referred to WMT both for logistic carriers and for the carriage of combat troops, and infantry battalions so equipped were termed motor-battalions.[15] The motorization of the Army, whilst an increasingly pressing requirement militarily, was also driven by the decreasing availability of light draught horses in the commercial sector as they were replaced by vehicles powered by internal combustion engine. A 1935 War Office memorandum summarized the problem: 'the increasing difficulty of obtaining light draught horses[16] makes progress in mechanization increasingly urgent apart from any other advantages to be gained thereby.......... mainly (sic) for this reason, it has been decided that the Territorial Army will go to war on a fully mechanized basis'.[17]

13 Appx 2 to a Memorandum by the PUS on the Special Programme dated 1 January 1935. See, WOOH, *Fighting, Support and Transport Vehicles*, Part I, *Common Problems*, p.13.
14 For details, see, Roger Salmon, *Everything Worked Like Clockwork, The Mechanization of the British Regular and Household Cavalry, 1918-1942* (Solihull: Helion, 2016).
15 *Army Training Memorandum* No 15 of 1935 proposed for example, that a 'lorry' was sufficient to replace a light draught horse and an infantry battalion should have a 12-cwt van for the Regimental Medical Officer, and eight 30-cwt commercial lorries for their G1098.
16 At the end of 1935, the British Army had 12,563 horses on strength at public expense in the UK and 2,966 horses and mules in Colonies, totalling 15,529. Cmd 5104, *The General Annual Report on the British Army for the Year ending 30 September* 1935 (London: HMSO, 1936), pp.70-72. The thousands of animals in the Indian Army were not funded by the British taxpayer.
17 WOOH, *Fighting, Support and Transport Vehicles*, Part I, Common Problems, p.13.

Motorization and mechanization did not however, result in soldiers no longer marching. 208 (Sussex) Field Company RE (TA) discovered that having arrived at Orchies railway station[18] near the Franco-Belgian border in late September 1939, the available WMT was dedicated solely to move unit stores and the soldiers had to march 14 miles on *pave*[19] to the unit location at Templeuve.[20] In much more demanding circumstances, 2nd Durham Light Infantry, amongst many other units, combat, technical and logistic, discovered a similar problem during the withdrawal from the River Dyle in 1940. Having marched for 28 miles in 24 hours they rested in a village near Elinghen in Belgium, but the troop-carrying lorries failed to parade, and the battalion had to march another 16 miles before the WMT arrived to take the soldiers off their weary feet.[21]

The motorization of the Army was a slow process, which had effectively commenced during the Great War[22] and continued until 1937 when the Army declared that its Regular units had completed the programme, although some yeomanry regiments of the TA retained their horses and were deployed to Palestine in 1940 as part of 1st Cavalry Division.[23] The RASC was the first element of the British Army to be motorized, a process almost complete by 1929 and the Corps, directed by QMG 3 in the War Office, initiated supporting structures to ensure that the developing WMT capability was effective. As the motorization and mechanization of the Army progressed, the centralization of the vehicle repair and stores systems was a natural corollary but the concept was overrun by the complexities and dynamics of the rearmament and expansion programmes, thus delaying the formation of the Royal Electrical and Mechanical Engineers until 1942.[24] The RASC retained its integral Equipment Support units and kept under Corps control, the Heavy Repair Workshop (HRS), the Vehicle Reserve Depot (VRD), and the MT Stores Depot (MTSD) at Feltham. This enabled the RASC to ensure that its reserves of vehicles and spares were fit for mobilization in 1939, although as military load-carrier production increased to meet the plan of the thirty-two division Army, a new rail-served VRD had to be constructed at Ashchurch[25] in Gloucestershire.

18 Orchies is approximately 15 miles SE of Lille.

19 A cobblestone road, which was especially wearing upon the feet to march on.

20 Morling, *Sussex Sappers*, p.59. The regimental historian recorded: 'It is doubtful if anyone who made that march will forget the discomfort of marching on "Pave'…

21 David Rissik, *The DLI at War: The History of the Durham Light Infantry, 1939-1945* (Durham: The Depot, nd but 1952), p.17.

22 For its impact in the Great War, see, Maginniss, *An Unappreciated Field of Endeavour*, Chp 10. Warwick: Helion, 2018).

23 TNA WO 106/2042: Plan MCD: Move of 1st Cavalry Division to Palestine from UK and WO 169/486: 550 Company RASC, WD, 1940.

24 See, WOOH, *Royal Electrical and Mechanical Engineers*, Vol 1, *Organization and Operations*, Major-General Sir E Bertram Rowcroft KBE CB (Comp.), (War Office, 1951).

25 The requirement for a second VRD had been articulated by the QMG to CIGS in December 1935: 'I am inclined to think that we may have to establish in peace, elsewhere than at Feltham, a second Vehicle Reserve Depot supplementary to the existing one'. TNA WO 32/4612: Future Army Organization – 1935, QMG Response dated 16 December 1936 to CIGS SECRET Paper, 'Future Reorganization of the British Army' dated 9 September 1935. In 2020, the site is still in use by the MOD for the storage of vehicles.

P2.2 Vehicle storage enhancement. VRD Ashchurch was constructed during 1938-1940 to supplement VRD Feltham. Located in the West of England, 2.5 miles to the East of Tewkesbury, to reduce the possibility of aerial attack, it was connected to the LMS Evesham to Tewkesbury railway line and operated by the RASC, although between 1942-1945 it was a US Army depot. It remains in MOD hands for military vehicle storage, and rail-served, although the sheds no longer have internal rail loading platforms. (Steve Cheetham)

Inter-war Blues

The profile of military operations and the shortage of funding during the early 1930s was not conducive to the purchase of large numbers of military specials so substantial orders were rarely forthcoming. In the late 1920s and early 1930s, a range of 30-cwt and 3-ton 6x4 chassis[26] was developed by the War Office, in conjunction with the motor industry and these equipment models became the foundation of the Army's military logistic vehicle fleet until the War Office adopted the 3- ton lorry as the standard load carrier in 1940.[27] Nonetheless, prototypes of some

26 The 6x4 chassis was the result of Great War experience.

27 The terminology for load-carriers requires explanation. The rating of, for example, 3 tons, referred to the operational planning lift of the vehicle, although the plated load was often in excess of this figure. For example, the operational lift of the Bedford OYD was 3 tons (6,720 lbs) but the plated load was 3.61 tons (8,092 lbs). The Bedford QLD also had a rating of 3 tons but was plated to lift a load of 3.675 tons (8,232 lbs). Tank Museum, *Data Book of Wheeled Vehicles, Army Transport, 1939-1945* (London: HMSO, 1983), p.53 (43) & p.58 (51). Vehicles were sometimes loaded in excess of the plated figure but inevitably this degraded performance and caused increased wear on components, including brakes,

P2.3 Empire Experience. 6x4 WMT in India. The 6x4 configuration with twin wheels was mainly superseded for mass production with 4x2 and later 4x4, using single tyres. (RLCM: A1b/MT/RLCA/20717)

very capable vehicles were built and the Colonies provided a sound market for small numbers of cross-country equipments. The Indian Army operated in some especially demanding terrain and being independent of the War Office for vehicle procurement, adopted a different approach. By the early 1930s, American manufacturers had established a commercial market on the Sub-Continent and GHQ India purchased Chevrolet and Ford trucks with six cylinder engines, which were more capable of handling the steep gradients on the mountain roads.[28] GHQ India also sought cross-country haulage capability for artillery, a demand which, resulted in some magnificent lorries,[29] such as the Guy CA 8x8 of 1931.[30] These minor orders appealed mainly to small firms specializing in high quality equipments but they were unable to deliver mass production to meet the demands of a Continental war.

suspensions and power trains. The Bedford MWD was an anomaly in this respect because the rate was 15-cwt (1,680 lbs) but the plated load was 1.225 tons (2,744 lbs). Ibid, p.40 (18A).

28 Fletcher, *British Military Transport*, p.61.

29 Load-carrying vehicles had two generic variants. The term 'truck' described load-carrying vehicles of 1 ton or less, whilst 'lorries' were load-carriers of 30-cwt or more.

30 For illustrations and more detail of this fine piece of engineering, see: Philip Ventham and David Fletcher, *Moving The Guns: The Mechanization of the Royal Artillery 1854-1939* (London: HMSO, 1990), pp.99-100.

The mixture of vehicles in the British Army of 1939-1940[31] was influenced by the Crosland Committee,[32] which was formed in 1934 to consider to what extent the 3-ton 6x4 lorry could be replaced by a civilian 4x2 model. It exceeded though, its initial Terms of Reference (TOR) by degrading the influence of the Eastern Plan and enhancing the importance of the Western Plan for deployment to the Continent, which was to undergo many revisions before it was enacted as W4 in the autumn of 1939, and thus unhinged the future deployable capability requirements of the Army. In assessing the balance between Six and Four wheelers, the Committee was guided by a set of employment principles, which were accepted by the War Office, two of which were of particular significance. First, where cross-country capability was essential, for instance some 1st Line transport, 6x4 equipments must be retained. Secondly, RASC Divisional Ammunition Companies (DAC) were to have a proportion of six-wheelers to support artillery units in locations incapable of being reached by 4x2 vehicles. The Committee thus recommended that over 50 per cent of military 6x4 vehicles should be replaced by 4x2 civilian types, on the basis that as an expeditionary force would deploy to an operational theatre with good roads and railways, the importance of capable military specials had declined, except for niche tasks such as gun tractors and specialist recovery vehicles.[33] One key assumption the committee made, which no doubt enhanced this perspective, was that the Army would not require to operate in terrain which matched that of the trench areas on the Western Front, during the Great War,[34] thus providing a strong argument against those proposing a requirement for tracked logistic vehicles.

Hiring and Firing

To supplement the in-service military specials, the War Office sought the assistance of the civilian sector through four sources: the Subsidy Scheme, hiring, impressments and production. Vehicles with a military specification usually came via the War Office Vehicle Subsidy Scheme, through which, the War Office paid an annual sum to transport companies to purchase and operate suitable equipments on the understanding that they would be available for military use.[35] There were a series of standards and specifications to which, vehicles had to conform covering the transmission, chassis, radiator, axles, wheels, brakes, bodywork, and lubrication. Operating criteria for a 30-cwt Subsidy 4x2 vehicle for example, included the capability to travel with its maximum approved load at 30 mph for one mile and at 22 mph for two hours, whilst being able to climb an average incline of 1 in 10 at 8 mph. The fuel tank had to have a minimum capacity of 15 gallons, creating a range with its reserve supply in reusable cans of at least 200 miles with the maximum load. Of especial significance, was the requirement to quantify the spares provision for each type of Subsidy vehicle.[36] Managing this process in the detail was a

31 For a comprehensive review, see, Les Freathy, *British Military Trucks of World War Two: Manufacturers, Types, Variants and Service of Trucks in British Army and Royal Air Force Service, 1939-1945* (Erlangen: Tankograd Publishing, 2013).

32 Report of Crosland Committee in War Office file 57/Vehs/6060 quoted in WOOH, *Fighting, Support and Transport Vehicles*, Part II, *Unarmoured Vehicles*, Major R Campagnac RASC and Major P E C Hayman 15/19 KRH (Comp.), (War Office, 1951), p.8.

33 Ibid, p.8.

34 Ibid, p.8.

35 The Subsidy Scheme was initiated in 1911. For enactment and operation particulars, see Ibid, pp.9-39.

36 Ibid, pp.35-36.

time consuming task because the numbers of licensed commercial vehicles continued to grow and by 1939 there were approximately 200,000 goods vehicle operators in the UK with a fleet average of 2.5 vehicles.[37] Changes, however, were inevitable as the motor industry introduced new designs. In 1932, a general performance specification was introduced to replace the more restrictive construction specifications, the vehicles being tested in an annual trial on a road circuit in the Welsh hills.[38]

The trend in the commercial sector was however, moving away from the preferred military 6x4 medium mobility configuration towards lighter 4x2 lower mobility vehicles with a higher payload and this process and the findings of the Crosland Committee, resulted in the Subsidy scheme being withdrawn in 1935. With its demise, the War Office found it difficult to sway civil design to meet military needs and thus sought to keep niche production capability alive by placing small orders for specialist vehicles such as gun-tractors and recovery vehicles. Hiring, which was usually conducted by Command HQs to support temporary local needs was expanded to support specific activities, many of which were linked to mobilization, especially of the Anti-Aircraft Divisions, [39] although the planning was not always carefully co-ordinated because in 1939 some of the dormant contracts failed as the transport companies had their vehicles impressed. Another concern to the War Office was the growing number of government departments seeking to acquire, through hiring or requisition, road haulage assets from the commercial sector during mobilization. With the perceived threat of air attack upon the civil infrastructure growing, the Home Office began planning support for Air Raid Precautions (ARP) and the Fire Services, whilst the Ministry of Transport focused on the distribution of essential supplies.[40] The Food (Defence Plans) Department of the Board of Trade and the forerunner of the Ministry of Food, was one government organization keen to quantify its road transport needs and in so doing during September 1938 discovered that the War Office had impressed some cold storage vans it required to distribute food.[41] Inevitably, these competing requirements demanded more coherency and the topic was of sufficient import for the Committee of Imperial Defence (CID) to have directed on 23 November 1937 that the Ministry of Transport should be responsible for the provision, allocation and co-ordination of all civil road haulage resources and transport services, including those required by Defence, although the Services had the power to impress vehicles in peace, whereas the Ministry of Transport could only do so after a state of emergency had been declared. Despite this direction from the CID, collating the requirements, identifying the assets and producing an effective plan

37 Savage, BOH, *Inland Transport*, p.53 notes 218,186 operators and 513,147 vehicles.

38 WOOH, *Fighting, Support and Transport Vehicles*, Part II, *Unarmoured Vehicles*, p.7.

39 Some of the hiring was planned, through a dormant contract, to support mobilization. Other hiring was enacted *ad hoc*.

40 In early 1938, the Ministry of Transport recorded 465,000 licensed goods vehicles and tractor prime-movers in the United Kingdom; *Fourth Annual Report of the Licensing Authorities, 1937-1938*. Government needs were assessed as follows. The Armed Services: 20,000; ARP: 30,000; Fire Services: 20,000. An un-quantified number were identified as potentially being required to sustain the flow of essential supplies if parts of the railway system were disrupted and to relocate key government and industrial assets to improve resilience. See, Savage, BOH, *Inland Transport*, p.54.

41 TNA MAF 72/703: Protests against earmarking and impressments of food trade vehicles for War Office purposes.

took time and to highlight but one example, the problem of managing vehicle hiring for the Services mobilization needs was never satisfactorily resolved.

An Impressive Failure?

Meanwhile, the War Office continued to craft its mobilization impressment planning, developing a scheme, which appeared to have many advantages, with financial savings being a key imperative. This work had commenced by mid-1935, the QMG Staff at the War Office identifying that 'at least 12,000 vehicles' would need to be impressed to enable the proposed Expeditionary Force to deploy.[42] Utilizing suitable vehicles from the commercial sector reduced the resources and costs required to operate VRDs, whilst enabling the rapid provision of vehicles for Home and Overseas service, although as it transpired this solution certainly came with a series of problems. Nearly all the vehicles required modification for field service, which included painting, a task usually completed by the unit.[43] Additional types and makes were included, creating un-planned complexity, whilst there was a shortage of spares and a subsequent necessity to procure, hold and distribute a vast range of them. The regimental history of 208 Field Company RE noted: 'The stores situation was somewhat aggravated because the vehicles which had been issued were all of different makes, types and dates of manufacture. The spares to be carried were thus multiplied by the need for a provision to be made for each vehicle rather than a percentage to cover all vehicles of one make'.[44] In addition, workshop tradesmen were not familiar with most of the equipment and some vehicles required special tools to service them.

The maintenance and repair issues of this varied collection of WMT certainly became unwieldy and the spares issue almost unmanageable, two outcomes the professional military road transport operators and engineers had, from the Great War experience, sought to avoid. An officer of 2nd Lincolns summarized the initial outcome: '....the spare-part problem for so many types was beyond us. When we landed in France and drove to the Belgian border the roads of France were littered with these broken down vehicles'.[45] There was little improvement by the end of October, with 4 Division Commander Royal Army Service Corps (CRASC) reporting that the response to a demand on the MT Stores Depot for spares was a letter inviting the unit to re-submit the request in 14 days, a solution which of course, further extended the receipt of any available items.[46] Whilst this was perhaps understandable given that the logistic

42 TNA WO 32/4612: Future Army Organization – 1935, QMG Response dated 16 December 1936 to CIGS SECRET Paper, 'Future Reorganization of the British Army' dated 9 September 1935.

43 2nd Lincolns noted that one van arrived in the unit lines at Verne Citadel Portland with 'Swindon Steam Laundry' on the sides. Nigel Hamilton, *The Full Monty: Montgomery of Alamein, 1887-1942* (London: Allen Lane, 2001), p.301. This advert, however, fails to match the style of a vehicle allocated to 5 Squadron RFC in 1914, which used it as the ammunition lorry. Painted a brilliant scarlet, with the legend 'The World's Appetiser' on the sides emblazoned in gold, it belonged to Elizabeth Lazenby & Son, sauce soup and pickle manufacturers of London. During the withdrawal from Mons, the pilots of 5 Squadron were thus able to identify from the air, their munitions transport. See, Walter Raleigh, *The War in the Air: Being the Story of The part played in the Great War by the Royal Air Force*, Vol I (Oxford: Clarendon Press, 1922), p.287 and *Whitaker's Red Book or Who's Who in Business 1914* (London: J Whitaker & Sons, 1914).

44 Morling, *Sussex Sappers*, p.57.

45 Record of Captain J G M B Gough, quoted in Hamilton, *The Full Monty*, p.300.

46 TNA WO 167/235: 4 Division CRASC, WD, entry 27 October 1939.

services were still establishing facilities, 2 Division CRASC clearly identified in mid-December 1939 that there was an unresolved inherent failure in the planning and delivery of MT spares. By this date demands for vehicle spares and tool kits were still not being met to the point that some WMT had been 'Vehicle Off the Road awaiting spares' for three months.[47] To illustrate some of the frustrations from this debacle, OC 1 LOC Railhead Company noted that not only did 40 percent of the unit vehicles not have a foot-pump for tyre inflation but also that the equipment was woefully inadequate, it taking a soldier 30 minutes to pump to 20 pounds per square inch (psi). As most of the unit WMT had 10 - 12 tyres of seven different types operating between 78-100 psi, the logistics of maintaining the correct pressures became an appreciable challenge, although as a measure of mitigation seven percent of the vehicles had mechanical inflators.[48] To complete this sorry tale, there was a shortage of tilts[49] and tarpaulins, issues, which in the severe winter of 1939-40 generated a deleterious effect upon the condition of the transported material.[50]

In January 1938, the requirement was approximately 10,000 vehicles[51] for the Field Force including a new need, recommended by the Carr Committee[52] for 3,693 vehicles in the 3-ton 4x2 category, of which only 1,900 were assessed to be available. Impressment policy was the responsibility of the QMG whilst the staff of Director Supplies & Transport exercised control of its implementation. Task delivery was conducted by the RASC through the HQ of Inspectorate of Supplementary Transport based at Regents Park Barracks in London, who was assisted by 35 inspectors covering four districts across the UK. This work bore fruit, rapidly generating large numbers of equipments, although the last-minute decision to accelerate the deployment of the BEF's First Contingent caused a recasting of the programme, much of which had to be 'hot-planned' with orders issued by telephone. Fortunately plans were in place to purchase spares for the impressed equipments, except for those additional types introduced at the last minute, although as the logisticians were to discover, the quantity and scope of the inventory failed to meet the demand, partly because there was insufficient information relating to reliability of the impressed vehicles upon which to generate an accurate mean distance between failure for each type and thus procure the relevant quantities and types of spares. This was a 'Lesson Learned', the hard way in the Great War, and then apparently forgotten, with Marcosson, in *The Business of War*, attributing much of the BEF's WMT operational success on the Western Front to what he describes as 'Vehicle Intelligence' and in particular, its excellent inventory control, repair

47 TNA WO 167/210: 2 Division CRASC, 18 December 1939, OC 2 Division Supply Column report.
48 TNA WO 167/1095: 1 LOC Railhead Company RASC, 'Report on 12 ton Oil Engined Vehicles', nd but late October 1939.
49 The tilt is the load-bed cover, usually of canvas, fitted over a metal frame, to protect the load from view, the weather, pilferage and to a limited extent, liquid chemical agents.
50 WOOH, *Supplies and Transport*, Vol I, p.118.
51 War Office 57/Vehs/6238 Minute QMG to Secretary of State dated 21 January 1938 quoted in WOOH, *Fighting, Support and Transport Vehicles*, Part II, *Unarmoured Vehicles*, p.10, fn 3. The 10,000 requirement was 2,000 less than the 'at least 12,000' guideline exposed to CIGS by QMG in December 1935, the shifting sands of logistic planning and operational dynamics influencing the numbers on a regular basis. TNA WO 32/4612: Future Army Organization - 1935, QMG Response dated 16 December 1936 to CIGS SECRET Paper, 'Future Reorganization of the British Army' dated 9 September 1935.
52 The Carr Committee was responsible for recommending the shape and size of vehicle war reserves. WOOH, *Fighting, Support and Transport Vehicles*, Part II, *Unarmoured Vehicles*, p.10.

and registration recording systems and noted that its database, the 'Motor Census of the Army Mechanical Transport' was a 'notable industrial document', which 'would be worth its weight in gold to any motor manufacturer'.[53]

A greater challenge came from the Ministry of Transport, which revoked the pre-mobilization agreement with the War Office and requisitioned 7,000 vehicles earmarked for Army use, whilst other Departments chose to retain some vehicles for essential civil services.[54] Nonetheless by the end of September 1939, the War Office had acquired 26,312 vehicles[55] of which 6,354 were motor-cycles, 4,285 were cars[56] and 15,305 were load-carrying vehicles[57] with the selection being made by RASC officers under the direction of the Chief Inspector of Supplementary Transport (CIST), an organization, which had been maturing under the direction of the QMG since early 1935. The efficiency and effectiveness of CIST was critical to the mobilization and deployment of the Army, a factor cogently articulated by the QMG in late 1935, and an output that he compared to the capability of the Remount system in 1914.[58] The Impressment Scheme was for the most part effective, in spite of the fact that it was designed to acquire a considerably smaller number of vehicles than occurred but standards had to be sacrificed to meet demand, as the BEF quickly discovered upon its arrival in France. There were, moreover, issues relating to its management. The additional officers required for impressments at scale during mobilization should have been subject to closer pre-war scrutiny because it became clear that a few were unscrupulous and others incompetent, which led to the acquisition of unsuitable and unreliable equipments, both of which were detrimental to operational capability.[59] Fortunately most of the CIST personnel conducted their duties with diligence as the rejection of 40 vehicles out of 86 processed for 1st London Division at Woolwich, illustrates.[60] In addition, documentation was not always completed correctly and pilfering of ancillaries was another irritation. The BEF's dependence on civilian equipments is lucidly illustrated by the fact that of the 25,000 WMT vehicles deployed to France in September and October 1939, only 2,000 had been in military service before mobilization.[61] Even with the introduction of growing numbers of military vehicles from production in the period November 1939 to May 1940, 46 percent of the losses in the 1-10 ton range were impressed.[62]

53 Issac F Marcosson, *The Business of War* (London: John Lane, The Bodley Head, 1918), pp.165-166.

54 See, WOOH, *Fighting, Support and Transport Vehicles*, Part II, *Unarmoured Vehicles*, p.44.

55 See, Ibid, p.60. Between 2-11 September 1939, 1,200 vehicles per day were being impressed.

56 Motorcycles and cars were impressed from agents and factories. Ibid, p.44.

57 Military load-carriers and specialist types, such as technical stores, workshops and signals vehicles were also included for the purposes of statistical record.

58 TNA WO 32/4612: Future Army Organization – 1935, QMG Response dated 16 December 1936 to CIGS SECRET Paper, 'Future Reorganization of the British Army' dated 9 September 1935.

59 See, WOOH, *Fighting, Support and Transport Vehicles*, Part II, *Unarmoured Vehicles*, p.45.

60 IWM Dunlop MSS 74/164/8 'Report No.10 Visits made to London 17th, 18th and 19th November 1939', quoted in Alexander David Jones, 'Pinchbeck Regulars? The Role and Organisation of the Territorial Army, 1919-1940' (Balliol College University of Oxford, PhD Thesis, 2016).

61 WOOH, *Maintenance in the Field* Vol I, p.37. The revision of the drafts for this volume is in TNA WO 366/45: Maintenance in the Field - Revision of Drafts.

62 Calculated from tables in WOOH, *Fighting, Support and Transport Vehicles*, Part II, *Unarmoured Vehicles*, p.61.

Commercial Conversions and Military Specials

The motor industry provided the Army with many new builds, some of which were civilian designs with production militarization delivered through various modifications including increased ground clearance, enhanced fuel capacity, more robust springs and upgraded power-plant cooling systems. In addition, dual rear wheels were often replaced with singles, cross-country tyres fitted, and a range of military fitments added such as tilts, extra tool bins and carriers for petrol, oil and water cans. The 3-ton 4x2 types were particularly well suited to military adaptations, with the most common, the Austin K3,[63] the Bedford OY[64] and the Commer Q4.[65] The Austin was based on a civilian vehicle which the company had started to produce in 1939 as part of its return to truck manufacture. It had a 3,462 cc spark ignition 60 bhp engine, a four-speed constant-mesh gearbox and hydraulic brakes. The military version sported an open cab and twin 3.4 x 17 rear tyres on the early models, later versions having a slit top closed cab and single 10.50 x 16 tyres. The Bedford OY was mechanically similar to its civilian brother the OL but featured the wide flat fronted bonnet of the MW. Powered by a 3,519 cc spark ignition engine, it had a fuel tank capacity of 32 gallons and hydraulic brakes with vacuum servo assistance. The early models had 32 x 6 dual rear tyres, but these were replaced by 10.50 x 16 singles all round in later builds. There were many variants of the basic chassis: the OYD was the GS version and the OYC tanker for fuel or water, carrying 800 or 350 gallons respectively.[66] The Rootes Group Commer Q4 was closely related to the civilian Superpoise, which entered production in 1939. Powered by a 4,086 cc 81 bhp SI engine it was initially fitted with twin 3.4 x 17 tyres on the rear axle, although these were soon replaced by 10.50 x 16s singles all round.

There were however, limits on the capability of civilian vehicles pressed into military service. Government road transport taxation policies during the inter-war period had an impact on the size and power of some of these commercial vehicles; high taxes and a speed limit of 20 mph on lorries over 2.5 tons un-laden resulted in volume production being concentrated on smaller classes,[67] which tempted vehicle manufacturers to use the largest of their car engines in the smaller commercial vehicles. For instance, all the Bedford series, MW (15-cwt),[68] OX (30-cwt),[69] OY (3-ton)[70] and QL (3- ton) [71] all had a 6-cylinder 3,519 cc SI engine, giving 72 bhp at 3,000 rpm, which meant that the 3-ton lorry was under powered, especially for cross-country work.[72] This focus on small load-carriers stunted the development of the CI engine,

63 Tank Museum, *Data Book of Wheeled Vehicles, Army Transport*, p.49 (36).
64 Ibid, p.50 (37).
65 Ibid, p.50 (38).
66 Ibid, pp.83 (118) - 84 (119).
67 The un-laden weight of the Bedford OY was 2.65 tons and the Gross Vehicle Weight 6.45 tons. Bart Vanderveen, *Historic Military Vehicles Directory* (London: Battle of Britain International Prints Ltd, 1989), p.166.
68 Tank Museum, *Data Book of Wheeled Vehicles, Army Transport,* p.38 (14).
69 Ibid, p.45 (28).
70 Ibid, p.53 (43).
71 Ibid, p.55 (48).
72 The GS 15-cwt MWD offered 22.0 bhp per ton, whilst the GS 3-ton QLD was rated at less than half this figure at 10.6 tons. Ibid, p.38 (14) and p.55 (48).

P2.4 New Capability. Bedford 4x4 QL. The BEF had few 4x4 WMT variants but operations in France demonstrated their utility. (RLCM: A1b/MT/RLCA/20547)

fuelled with diesel, which because of its size and weight, was usually confined to vehicles with a load capability of 6 tons and above. In the round, the trend of commercial design was towards vehicles of low weight, power and ground clearance, all characteristics in direct contradiction to military requirements. Whilst there was some utility for these equipments in France, the Middle East was a very different proposition.

The Army's greatest problem was that despite the recognition of the importance of the military special, so well learned from the Great War and inter-war colonial operations, there was no capability to place these vehicles into mass production, so the shortcomings of the Defence Requirements Programmes, lay not so much in the failure to equip the Regular Army, as in the inability to provide, until it was to late to be effective, the war potential to support the expanding Territorial Army.[73] At a tactical level, whilst the War Office had discussions with Vauxhall Motors they did not mature to any immediate orders; the Bedford MW 15-cwt truck[74] for example was first produced in 1937 but by the outbreak of war, only 50 had been ordered for the British Army. The potential production capacity of Austin and Ford, two of the three

73 TNA WO 163/49: OS11, 'Memorandum by the CIGS on the Training of III Corps,' 6 February 1940.

74 The Bedford MW was the first British truck to have built in headlamps. *Data Book of Wheeled Vehicles*, p.38 (14).

largest commercial vehicle manufacturers, also lay militarily dormant until 1939. In this respect, the War Office had not approached the future need for logistic load-carriers from a strategic perspective, relying upon impressments and hiring for immediate and short-term needs and an assumption that the motor industry had surplus capacity and could fill the production gap if required.[75] Unfortunately, the failure of the War Office to cogently identify its future industrial need in this arena resulted in the factories being re-allocated to other munitions manufacture and in particular, aircraft production.

During the Munich Crisis, with the Army's major vehicle deficiencies clearly in the minds of the War Office planners, they seized upon an offer by the General Motors Corporation (GMC) to hold the sale of all their load-carriers in global stock, in order to give the British Government first refusal on their purchase. The proposal was not taken up, but as a mark of appreciation, Treasury approval was obtained for the purchase of 500 GMC load-carriers for the Middle East. With an eye to the future, the Director of Mechanization had held meetings in the Spring of 1939 with Vauxhall, to establish MW production rates, and was informed that 2,000 might be built in the first 6 months, rising to 3,000 per month in the long term. By the end of September 1939, Vauxhall had orders for 27,000 vehicles, 11,000 of them the MW.[76]

As rearmament gathered pace, there was increasing competition for industrial capacity and strategic resources, and by early 1938, the War Office supply organization was struggling to keep pace with the changing demands. Various proposals examined how the War Office might improve their systems but during the year, the Centre of Gravity in the debate shifted, and the argument was no longer about what steps the War Office should take to put its supply organization on a rearmament basis but whether supplies for the Army should be handled by the War Office.[77] There was much inter-departmental discussion over the merits or otherwise of a Ministry of Supply,[78] with both the Admiralty and the Air Ministry opposed to inclusion in the

75 How this matured is difficult to understand, given that the analysis of the Middle East options suggested that military vehicle war reserves would need to be enhanced. WOOH, *Fighting, Support and Transport Vehicles*, Part II, *Unarmoured Vehicles*, p.13.

76 By the end of the war nearly 66,000 MWs had been built in several different models, of which the following were the most important:

Table 2.1
Bedford MW Variants

Model	Role	Remarks
MWD	GS Truck	
MWC	Water Bowser	200 gallons
MWG	AA gun carrier	20 mm Polsten
MWR	Radio Vehicle	Fitted For Wireless (FFW)
MWT	Anti-tank gun carrier	2 pdr portee
MWV	Enclosed van	

77 When Sir Hugh Elles' term as the Master-General of the Ordnance ended, the appointment lapsed and his department, under a newly established Deputy Master-General, passed, on 1 January 1938, to the control of the Director of Munitions Production.

78 For an explanation of the background to the formation of the Ministry of Supply and its organization, see: J D Scott & R Hughes, BOH, *The Administration of War Production* (London: HMSO 1955), pp.68-78 and Chp 10.

new body. The Army though, had little choice, and the relevant elements of the Staff, inclusive of the Contracts Branch, were transferred *en bloc* to the new ministry on 1 August 1939. One of the positive effects, was to end the cumbersome system of 'parts contracts', in which up to ten separate agreements were required for each vehicle covering the chassis, body, cab, tilt and in some cases, the tow hook.

The rapidly changing profile of rearmament and the political perspective which supported it, left the planners with no opportunity to create a balanced vehicle fleet, resulting in the British Army employing a mixture of types,[79] both military and civilian, built by a number of manufacturers, although the 3-ton (4x2) was the predominant load-carrier, making up 53 percent of the fleet by quantity. The balance included older military specials, such as the Leyland Retriever 3 ton 6x4 lorry,[80] dating from 1933, whilst others, like the Bedford 15-cwt 4x2 MW did not come into service until 1939. By May 1940, there were eight generic types of military specification WMT vehicles in the 1-10 ton range in field service with the BEF, produced by 16 manufacturers and the list below summarizes the range and diversity of the types.[81]

79 The load capacities of the 15-cwt - 3-ton generic vehicle systems are shown below:

Table 2.2
15 cwt - 3-ton
Generic Load-Carriers - Rated Capacity

Type	Personnel	Load (tons)	Remarks
Truck 15-cwt 4x2 GS	7	1.0	Bedford MW, Ford WOT2, Guy Ant, Morris CS8
Truck 3-cwt 4x2 GS	22	1.5	Bedford OX, Morris CS11, Thornycroft
Truck 30-cwt 6x4 GS			Morris (CD series)
Lorry 3-ton 4x2 GS	28	3.0	Austin K3, Bedford OY, Commer Q4, Leyland Lynx
Lorry 3-ton 4x4 GS			AEC Matador, Albion FT11, Bedford QL, Thornycroft Nubian
Lorry 3-ton 6x4 GS			AEC Marshal, Karrier CK6, Leyland Retriever, Thornycroft Tartar

80 Tank Museum, *Data Book of Wheeled Vehicles, Army Transport,* p.67 (67).
81 For a resume of technical details, see, *Data Book of Wheeled Vehicles* and Vanderveen, *Historic Military Vehicles Directory.*

Table 2.3
BEF – WMT Military Marques: 1-10 tons[82]

Generic Type	Manufacturer & Nomenclature	Remarks
Truck 15-cwt 4x2 GS	Austin BYD Bedford MW Commer Beetle Ford WOT2 Guy Ant Morris Commercial CS8	350 made in 1940 Wide range of body types 400 ordered in 1935 4x4 also produced Production commenced in 1934
Truck 30-cwt 4x2 GS	Bedford OX Morris Commercial CS11/30 Thornycroft GF/TC4 Thornycroft HF/TC4	Production started mid-1939 Produced 1935-1939 50 delivered to RASC in 1939 150 delivered to RASC in 1939
Truck 30-cwt 6x4 GS	Crossley Morris Commercial CD & FW Thornycroft Valiant	Produced 1933-1939
Lorry 3-ton 4x2 GS	Austin K3 Bedford OY Commer Q4 Leyland Lynx	500 GS Open Cab built in 1940 Based on civilian OL Based on Superpoise 1,497 produced 1939-1940
Lorry 3-ton 4x4 GS	AEC Matador Albion FT11 Bedford QL Thornycroft Nubian	Medium Artillery Tractor 500 GS ordered in 1940 3 prototypes built in 1940 Production from June 1940
Lorry 3-ton 6x4 GS	AEC Marshal Karrier CK6 Leyland Retriever Thornycroft Tartar	1,000 built 1935-1940 December 1939 onwards Production commenced 1933
Lorry 6-ton 4x2 GS	Dennis Max Mk 1 ERF Foden DG4/6	500 built 1940-1941 423 built 1939-1941 150 built 1940-1941
Lorry 10-ton 6x4 GS	Foden DG6/10 Leyland Hippo Mk 1	Production 1939-1941 330 supplied to RASC 1939-1940

82 Ibid.

One interesting major omission, given its long history, was the 4x4 load carrier. In 1903 Austro-Daimler built a 4x4 armoured car, whilst in the United States, FWD and Jeffery had produced nearly 55,000 vehicles during the Great War, with the FWD Corporation continuing the process with 4x4 and 6x6 in the 1920s and 1930s. Commer, Guy and Morris-Commercial produced experimental 4x4 Field Artillery Tractors to the specifications issued by the Mechanization Board, and the Guy and Morris vehicles were approved in late 1938, for Army service, thereby confirming a position for the 4x4 vehicle in the military environment, although not in the load-carrying role.[83] In Britain, the 6x4[84] was preferred to the 4x4 for this task and although several prototypes were built, by Commer, Garner, Guy and Karrier, there were no commercial manufacturers producing the 4x4 load-carrying chassis until 1938 when the Associated Equipment Company (AEC) introduced the Matador,[85] the first heavy 4x4 lorry[86] to be made in quantity in the United Kingdom, approximately 8,600 being produced by 1945, with small additional runs until 1953.[87] Purchased as a Medium Artillery Tractor rather than a load-carrier, the Matador[88] was based on an AEC commercial 4x4, the 4 ton Hardy, which was produced in small numbers, mainly for the export market. Also purchased as a FAT but fitted with a GS body was a small buy of 23 Garner 4x4 G3 lorries.[89] Designed by Nicholas Straussler and prototyped in 1937-38, it was manufactured by Garner mainly from Ford parts. The War Office ordered 45 in November 1939 but apparently only purchased 23,[90] although there is no record of the G3 serving with the BEF.[91] The Thornycroft Nubian[92] was too late into service to serve with the BEF, entering production in June 1940, and the RAF took most of the 4,000 plus output.[93]

At a meeting on 23 December 1938, Vauxhall suggested to the War Office that the company could produce a 4x4 vehicle but it was not until 12 September 1939 that they were requested to proceed with a prototype, this being completed on 1 February 1940; two more were ready for

83 WOOH, *Fighting, Support and Transport Vehicles,* Part II, *Unarmoured Vehicles*, p.10 and Tank Museum, *Data Book of Wheeled Vehicles, Army Transport*, pp.74 (82) - 75 (84).
84 The 3-ton 6x4 provided 11% of the BEF's transport.
85 The first models had SI engines of 7.41 litres producing 92 bhp but later variants had a 6-cylinder CI engine of 95 bhp. The focus on the Matador as an artillery tractor almost certainly delayed its introduction as a load-carrier. Tank Museum, *Data Book of Wheeled Vehicles, Army Transport*, pp.76 (86) - 77 (87).
86 Gross Vehicle Weight was 10 tons 17-cwt. Ibid, p.77 (87).
87 The Matador remained in British military service until the 1960s, being replaced by the AEC Martian and Militant Mk I lorries, vehicles, which remained in the inventory until the mid 1980s.
88 The abbreviation MAT may have influenced its renaming from Forward Model 0853 to Matador. The Matador was famous for its pulling capability, which endeared it to forestry operators, show-grounds, heavy-duty recovery companies and commercial garages long after the war.
89 See, Vanderveen, *Historic Military Vehicles Directory*, p.189.
90 'Straussler Trucks and Tractors', *Wheels & Tracks Magazine No 37* (Plaistow: Battle of Britain Prints International Ltd, 1991).
91 The Garner G3 is not recorded in the *Data Book of Wheeled Vehicles*. The total build is believed to have been 53, with 30 being exported to Turkey.
92 Ibid, p.57 (50).
93 The Nubian was the only wartime British 4x4 to be in consistently in production post-war and elements of the design lasted into the early 1970s, mainly for fire tenders. Vanderveen, *Historic Military Vehicles Directory*, p.172.

trials by mid-April.[94] The Army tested these two vehicles thoroughly, before placing an order in mid-1940, for an initial batch of 4,272, and the legend of the QL series[95] was born. Production was delayed until February 1941 because of the need to focus on the main effort, which was the maintenance of high levels of Bedford OY and MW production, not only replace the losses from operations in France, but also to meet the demands of the expanding Army. In addition, it took 30 percent more manpower to build a 4x4 over a 4x2 and skilled labour was at a premium but once production gained momentum 52,245 QLs[96] were built during the war in addition to the three prototypes. The designation QL probably stemmed from the fact that it was a 4x4, and Quad was a common name for these vehicles, and that it was a full-length lorry, as opposed to an artillery tractor, hence L, for 'Long'. The following 4x4 load-carriers were being trialled, in production, or on issue in 1939-1940; the Albion FN 11 4x4 was in the same class as the QL but only 500 were produced, mainly as mobile workshops.[97]

Table 2.4
WMT 4x4 Load-Carriers 1940[98]

Vehicle	Production Start	Remarks
AEC Matador	1938	Medium Artillery Tractor
Albion FT 11N	February 1940	Mainly used for mobile workshops
Bedford QL	February 1941	3 prototypes produced in 1940
Garner G3	January 1940?	Only 23 procured - used as an artillery tractor
Karrier K6	December 1940	Developed pre-1940
Thornycroft Nubian	June 1940	Production continued post war

94 For a detailed review of the QL series, see, Robert Coates, *Bedford to Berlin and Beyond, QL: The Forces Favourite 4x4* (Croydon: Fitzjames Press, 1994), p.25.
95 For a detailed review of the QL series, see, Ibid.
96 Ibid, p.31. The QL was produced in several different variants, which are listed below:

Table 2.5
Bedford QL Variants

Model	Role	Remarks
QLB	40 mm AA gun tractor	Crew of 8 plus driver
QLC	Tractor with 6.0-ton semi-trailer	Trailer permanently attached
QLD	GS cargo with tilt	1,500 battery storage and office trucks produced
QLR	Signals vehicle	Remained in service until the 1970s
QLT	Troop Carrying Vehicle (TCV)	29 men plus kit. 3,373 built
QLW	Tipper	1,000 made including 600 air-portable models

97 Tank Museum, *Data Book of Wheeled Vehicles, Army Transport,* p.54 (46).
98 There was no QL lorry produced because the letters formed a prefix to the specific vehicle designators. For a resume of technical details, see, Tank Museum, *Data Book of Wheeled Vehicles, Army Transport* and Vanderveen, *Historic Military Vehicles Directory*.

A particular shortfall in logistic vehicle capability, was the availability of sufficient Heavy Equipment Transporters (HET) capable of moving tanks and other armoured vehicles in excess of 10 tons. The BEF only had around 25 HETs[99] capable of lifting 20-40 tons, nearly all impressed, and a significant number of 10-ton variants, although few were designed to move tracked vehicles.[100]

Vehicle Off the Road

The variation of military types compounded the spares, maintenance and repair issues created by impressment of commercial marques. Equally challenging was the training and mentoring of vehicle operators, many of who had no driving licence before they joined the Army and were now expected to handle an array of equipment, for which there was little and on occasions, no training, especially in respect of cross-country driving.[101] Road Traffic Accidents (RTA)[102] were an increasing problem and the subject of a note in *Army Training Memorandum* 32 in May 1940, which stated that: 'The majority of these accidents are due to negligence or carelessness and reflect directly on the unit's standard of discipline and training.'[103] Apart from the personnel casualties,[104] vehicles were either written off to the detriment of the vehicle reserve or unavailable for tasking until repaired, which given the shortage of spares and trained workshop personnel in the BEF not only adversely affected modification and overhaul projects but also transport capability, a point lucidly highlighted in the note: 'Military vehicles carry important loads and their…..non-arrival may seriously affect the success of an operation'.[105]

The operators were not however, the only ones to receive preventative censure from the chain of command: 'It appears that many officers who have mechanical vehicles on charge are inclined to regard all driving accidents as errors of judgement on the part of the drivers……. An avoidable accident is an offence and disciplinary action should be taken if the matter is not being dealt with by the Civil Power'.[106] Whilst this direction may have been deliverable in combat formations, Base logistic units, many of them *ad hoc* and recently formed, and under pressure to perform, had a much greater challenge, often having low-levels of technical training, dispersed command and control arrangements and sometimes limited experience of the Army's

99 At the outbreak of war, there were only two Scammell 6x4 Pioneer Transporters in service, both of which had been purchased to move the Vickers Mk II Medium Tank. See, G N Georgano, *World War Two Military Vehicles (Transport and Half-Tracks)*, (London: Osprey Automotive, 1994), p.49.

100 The BEF lost 100 military and 350 civilian 10-ton variants in France. Many of these equipments appear to have been drawbar systems rather than semi-trailers. See, WOOH, *Fighting, Support and Transport Vehicles*, Part II, *Unarmoured Vehicles*, p.61.

101 Army Council, *Army Training Memorandum* No 31, April 1940 (War Office, 1940), pp.18-120, Appx C, Cross-Country Driving of Wheeled Vehicles.

102 See, *Manual of Driving and Maintenance for Mechanical Vehicles (Wheeled)*, pp.103-109, Sect 13, Prevention of Accidents.

103 Army Council, ATM No 32, May 1940, Sect 10, Negligent Driving.

104 Military personnel were not the only casualties. Binnie Hale, Violet Loraine and Jack Payne, entertainers contracted by the Entertainments National Service Association (ENSA) were all injured in RTAs whilst travelling to perform for the troops in France. Dave Thurlow, *Building the Gort Line: The BEF and its Defences in France, 1939-40* (Warwick: Helion, 2019), p.220.

105 Ibid.

106 Ibid.

disciplinary system, all of which, meant that the processes were probably too much of a burden to pursue in the detail. In this respect, the perspective of the Commanding Officer of 2 Petrol Oil & Lubricants Depot (POLD) at Morlaix offers an excellent example of the challenges because both RASC transport sections allocated to it in March 1940 had more than their fair share of accidents on the country lanes and tracks that connected the sub-depots, a problem exacerbated by the use of six-wheeled articulated vehicles attached from 2 BSD, which were unsuitable for operations in the site and were thus returned.[107] This decision however, did not solve the RTA problem. F Section of 7 Reserve MT Company[108] arriving with 'all new vehicles in excellent condition [and] extremely new and inexperienced drivers' had eight accidents in five days, with two occurring on the first day,[109] whilst the section from 5 Reserve MT Company[110] that replaced them, equipped with impressed vehicles and yet more inexperienced drivers continued the motion, the depot commander observing; 'An ordinary day's work – no particular event beyond daily report of accident to the MT'.[111] As the RASC prided itself as the lead WMT professionals of the Army, such a situation lucidly exposes the low level of technical training in these rapidly formed organizations,[112] an issue which in this case, spilled outside the unit causing additional clerical action for the staff of 2 POLD, and a frustration with the War Office firmly expressed in the war diary,[113] although in the case of F Section, personal relations with the commander were not compromised.[114]

Motor-cycles, then as now, were not the safest form of transport, with inadequate head protection being a fundamental issue. A RASC officer in 1 POLD, Second-Lieutenant Pickering met 'with an accident' whilst riding a motor-cycle on 14 March 1940, his injuries detaining him in 4 British General Hospital until 24 April when he returned to the unit.[115] An intriguing mystery started on 22 May 1940 when the motor-cycle ridden by Despatch Rider Driver Fuller aged 21 also from 1 POLD and a soldier with a Private Pilot's Licence, was discovered on the side of the road two miles from Blain, with no clue as to his whereabouts,

107 TNA WO 167/1149: 2 POLD RASC, WD, 9 March 1940.

108 TNA WO 167/1091: 7 Reserve MT Company. The war diary does not commence until April 1940 but the 2 POLD WD specifically states F Section deployed to the depot on 8 March 1940, replacing A Section from 1 Reserve MT Company, which moved to Rennes.

109 TNA WO 167/1149: 2 POLD RASC, WD, 9 March 1940.

110 TNA WO 167/1089: 5 Reserve MT Company file only contains Field Returns (AFW 3008 (Officers) & AFW 3007 (Other Ranks) and Casualty Returns (AFW 3010 (Officers), AFW 3011 (Other Ranks) & AFW 3012 (Attached Personnel). In this instance, the record of one unit, sheds light upon the activities of another. It is frustrating though, not to be able to compare the perspectives of the two units.

111 TNA WO 167/1149: 2 POLD RASC, WD, 12 March 1940.

112 The RASC took MT standards very seriously. Even in 1940 the Corps MT Instructor's Course was four weeks in length, but the rapid expansion diluted the the skill-set pool. See, General Staff, *Royal Army Service Corps*, Training Pamphlet No 1, *Training System in War*, Part III: *Training of NCOs*, (War Office 1940), p.8.

113 The war diary asked, 'Why on earth does England not prepare her men better?' TNA WO 167/1149: 2 POLD, WD, 14 March 1940.

114 The war diary recorded F Section's departure from the depot with the comment that the commander, Captain Leycester was 'one of nature's gentlemen'. TNA WO 167/1149: 2 POLD RASC, WD, 16 March 1940.

115 TNA WO 167/1148/: 1 POLD RASC, WD, entries March-April 1940.

P2.5 WMT Operator Training. Key to logistic capability but challenging to deliver in the expanding BEF. The numbers of accidents and equipment failures in France was testament to the difficulties in overcoming the problem. (RLCM: A1/MT/RLCA/20716).

until he was found dead on 4 June 1940.[116] Not all accidents involving WMT however, occurred on approved operational or support tasks. A Park of 1 MT VRD suffered a fatality when on 20 May, a corporal and two soldiers removed a staff car without permission to enable them to enjoy the local nightlife, crashing the vehicle near the Gnome-Rhone works.[117] Driver Franks died of his injuries in 9 General Hospital on 25 May,[118] Driver Finklestone was very seriously injured and Corporal Killen evacuated to the UK.[119] As the Germans had cut the GLOC on the day

116 TNA WO 167/1148/: 1 POLD RASC, WD, entries May-June 1940. A Graves Registration Report dated 24 January 1956 records T/121164 Driver Richard Alfred Fuller RASC being buried at Escoublac-La-Baule War Cemetery but does not describe the circumstances of his death recording the date as 4 June 1940, although it could have been as early as 21 May. One conclusion is that having fallen from his motor-cycle and been injured, he collapsed in woodland and died. His sister, Cynthia Evelyn, served in the Women's Royal Naval Service, dying of an illness in RN Hospital Woolton whilst in service in March 1946, aged 23; see *Repton Village* <www.reptonvillage.org.uk>

117 TNA WO 167/1153: 1 MT VRD A Park, WD, 20 May 1940.

118 T/16552 Driver William Raymond Franks, aged 39, was buried on 26 May 1940 and lies in Le Grand-Luce War Cemetery, which is 17 miles SE of Le Mans.

119 TNA WO 167/1153: 1 MT VRD A Park, WD, 20 May 1940. The war diary notes the intention to hold a Board of Enquiry into the circumstances but does not mention the name of the driver. Corporal Killen would almost certainly however, been demoted as the NCO in charge.

of the accident, such incidents not only diverted time and resources from the main effort but also reduced logistic capability. British soldiers were not however, the only casualties of such accidents. The commander of the First French Army Group, General Gaston-Henri Billotte, was seriously injured on 21 May, when his driver crashed into a lorry at night. He remained in a coma for two days before dying on 23 May, the RTA causing even more disruption to the Allied command arrangements.[120]

The rapid introduction of WMT across the expanding Army had a deleterious effect upon equipment care standards and the severe winter of 1939-1940 posed substantial challenges in this regard, a point recognized by the Worcestershire Yeomanry, a TA anti-tank regiment, equipped with the 2-pounder, as it prepared to embark for France:

> However much the Regiment had improved in gunnery, in its maintenance of vehicles it was woefully weak; there was still a great lack of experienced drivers and the hard winter was soon to spotlight these deficiencies. During the night of January 2/3, two of every three vehicles to be used by the Road Party the next day, had to be started up every hour; despite these precautions many of them had to be taken in tow when the party set off at seven in the morning for Southampton.[121]

This issue was clearly recognized by GHQ BEF and corps MT Maintenance Schools were established, a decision which, rightly attracted the interest of the Commander II Corps, Lieutenant-General Alan Brooke,[122] although the cultural and technical influence of this training took time to produce effect, an issue exacerbated by the cold meteorological conditions. The procedures for frost-precautions for vehicles without anti-freeze in the coolant systems, whilst not complex, were certainly onerous to conduct in the cold and the dark,[123] a point firmly made to the chain of command by numerous logistic commanders including 4 Division CRASC[124] and OC 1 LOC Railhead Company.[125] The widespread introduction of anti-freeze additives therefore improved not only soldiers' morale but also operational capability, although the logistic system was slow to distribute the relevant quantities in a timely manner, even to divisional units.[126] Even when anti-freeze was available, the supervision of driver maintenance was key to ensure procedures were correctly conducted, the failure of which could have serious

120 TNA CAB 44/67: The BEF in Belgium and Artois, 10 May-3 June 1940, entry 22 May 1940.

121 D R Guttery, *The Queen's Own Worcestershire Hussars, 1922-1956* (Stourbridge: Mark & Moody, 1958), p.10. The regiment was probably equally embarrassed by an incident in which one of the 2-pdr guns was sufficiently damaged during the move to render it immobile, although another unit recovered it and the Worcestershire Yeomanry received it in France three days later.

122 Brooke visited the recently established facility at Sainghin on 18 December 1939. Danchev & Todman, *War Diaries, 1939-1945,* p.26.

123 The procedure involved draining down the whole cooling system and then refilling it with hot but not boiling water to re-start the engine. Whilst this task could be conducted in barracks doing so in the field was not a meaningful act of war. See, *Manual of Driving and Maintenance for Mechanical Vehicles (Wheeled)*, pp.270-271, Sect 66, Frost Precautions.

124 The 4 Division CRASC WD noted that it 'was not a practical solution to empty radiators at night'. TNA WO 167/235, entry 23 October 1939.

125 TNA WO 167/1095: 1 LOC Railhead Company RASC, WD, entries October 1939.

126 TNA WO 167/235: 4 Division CRASC, WD, entry 23 October 1939, which noted that none of the sub-units held any anti-freeze.

P2.6 New Heavies. Convoy of Foden 6x4 DG6/12 10 ton lorries. (RLCM: A1/MT/RLCA/20504)

consequences, especially in winter conditions. In November 1939 1 Base Ordnance Depot (BOD) identified that vehicles were arriving from the UK with no anti-freeze in the radiators,[127] whilst during one February 1940 night, a Royal Artillery unit suffered 13 cracked engine blocks when drivers failed to ensure that the anti-freeze levels and concentrations were correct.

The withdrawal from France focused the minds of the logistic planners in a whole series of areas and one of their major concerns was the regeneration of a task vehicle fleet. First and foremost, was the requirement to make good the considerable losses, which amounted to 84,427 vehicles of all types, of which 52,859 were load-carriers in the 15-cwt to 10-ton range.[128] The Wehrmacht benefited from the British WMT abandoned in France. 6,500 vehicles were recovered just from the Dunkerque area, of which 4,500 were salved and placed into service, deploying across Continental Europe and the Soviet Union during the war.[129] The estimated losses of the load-carrying fleet in France are summarized in the table below:

127 TNA WO 167/1168: 1 BOD RAOC, WD, entry 4 November 1939.

128 All figures calculated from tables in WOOH, *Fighting, Support and Transport Vehicles*, Part II, *Unarmoured Vehicles*, p.61.

129 See, Frank, Reinhard, *Trucks of the Wehrmacht: German Vehicles in World War II* (Atglen PA: Schiffer Publishing Ltd, 1994), pp.151-163 and Jochen Vollert, *British Military Trucks in Wehrmacht Service*

Table 2.6
BEF – Estimated Losses of Load-Carriers in France[130]

Type	Rate	Configuration	War Department	Impressed
Truck	8-cwt	4x2	4,588	322
	15-cwt	4x2	11,442	26
Lorry	1-ton	4x2	705	281
	30-cwt	4x2	5,125	3,971
	30-cwt	6x4	1,326	4
	3-ton	4x2	11,782	14,009
	3-ton	4x4	57	0
	3-ton	6x2	329	212
	3 ton	6x4	2,435	0
	6-ton	6x4	122	454
	10-ton	6x4	195	384
Transporter	10-ton	6x4	95	336
	20-ton	6x4	0	5
	30-ton	6x4	0	5
	40-ton	6x4	0	12
Total			38,201	20,021
Trailers			1,251	300

One of the unforeseen advantages of these losses was the elimination, almost overnight, of the extensive type range of the 20,000 impressed vehicles. This created an opportunity to standardize equipments, although because of the experience of operations on the Continent, and the need to replace the losses, there was a view, quickly dispelled by the war in the Western Desert, that vehicles manufactured to civilian specification were acceptable to support manoeuvre warfare. The War Office selected the 3-ton lorry as the standard load-carrier, and although several

(Erlangen: Tankograd Publishing, 2012).

130 The table has been calculated from information in WOOH, *Fighting, Support and Transport Vehicles*, Part II, *Unarmoured Vehicles*, p.61, Appx B (1), Approximate Losses of B Vehicles by Types in the Evacuation of France, which gives a clear indication of the balance between the generic vehicle types. There is a health warning in that the figures generated by Central Ordnance Depot Chilwell upon which the table is based, lists a total of 100,458 WMT vehicles, including 25,778 motor-cycles lost in France, whereas other War Office sources suggest that only 89,699 were shipped with 5,272 returning thus the total loss was 84,427 but there may be a differential in counting RAF equipment from the AASF.

different manufacturers produced their own type,[131] there was some standardization. As the war moved into 1941, there was an increasing emphasis on the 4x4 vehicle but because many of the bodies built for the 6x4 system during the 1930s were still in use, this chassis continued in production until the end of the war.

Conclusion

The British Army had been through a very challenging period but some of the lessons identified from the French campaign relating to military specifications were not learned until operations in the Western Desert made the need absolutely clear. Impressment met a remit beyond its original concept, which at least motorized the BEF and enabled it to deploy to France with some mobility. The ES outfall was in effect unsustainable and had the BEF not been evacuated in June 1940 there would have come a time when the impressed vehicles would have to have been replaced by military specification types and the civilian vehicles returned to their owners.

In this respect, the losses sustained in France created an opportunity to re-balance the fleet and although the solution had imperfections, it was far better than the alternative of retaining the commercial impressments. As industrial production increased, military specification WMT began to flow from the factories, although having greater standardization of types would have improved operating availability through more efficient ES systems and driven down the spares inventory, whilst also reducing the requirement for logistic lift across the transportation spectrum. The failure to ensure that there were sufficient HETs to support the expanding armoured formations was a lucid indication that the G and the Q Staff were out of kilter, and unlike the load-carrier, the planners and vehicle manufacturers were unable to provide a quick solution, although the BEF was not alone in failing to properly plan for field vehicle recovery operations.[132]

131 The five key vehicles, with production numbers, were:
Austin K3 (4x2): 17,000
Austin K5 (4x4): 12,280
Bedford QL (4x4): 52,248
Bedford OY (4x2): 72,385
Fordson WOT6 (4x4): 30,000

132 The Germans too failed to place enough emphasis on this key logistic task. See Robert Forczyk, *Case White: The Invasion of Poland, 1939* (Oxford: Osprey, 2019), p.331.

3

Horseshoes to Sparkplugs
Infantry division organic logistic organization in the BEF

Outline Organization

The divisions that deployed to France during 1939-1940 were a mixed bag in organization, task, equipment and structure.[1] The infantry division establishments[2] were broadly similar but strengths differed daily, whilst the type and quantity of equipment varied considerably.[3] In addition, the scope of deployment, geographic spread and span of command that included divisions being transferred between corps in the BEF and those under French command, all generated interesting logistic challenges and resulted in ORBATs and structures being adjusted to suit the dynamics. The ORBAT and equipment of the infantry divisions varied but most of them had three brigades, each with three battalions plus a divisional cavalry regiment. Artillery support consisted of three field regiments[4] and an anti-tank regiment. Engineer support was provided through three field companies and one field park company,[5] whilst medical support consisted of three field ambulances and one field hygiene section. The divisional signals unit,

1 Details of the establishments, scaling and equipment of divisional units are in Philson, BEFORBAT, Vol 2.
2 For example, the personnel War Establishment (WE) of 2nd Infantry Division (Regular) was 13,934, and 4th Infantry Division 13,928, whilst that of 42nd (East Lancashire) was 13,123. 50th (Northumbrian) Motor Division was 11,234. The standard infantry division is shown as 14,737 in Philson, BEFORBAT, Vol 2, p.124.
3 The Line of Communication divisions, 12th (Eastern), 23rd (Northumbrian) and 46th (North Midland & West Riding) were, for various reasons, inadequately trained, lightly scaled and had reduced logistic support in comparison to other divisions.
4 Field regiments were planned to be equipped with the 25 pdr but because production was behind requirements, three gun types were issued: 18 pdr, 25 pdr on an 18 pdr carriage and the 4.5-inch howitzer
5 The Corps of Royal Engineers also generated logistic output, especially with regard to infrastructure and utilities, especially water, but the focus of the divisional field company and field park company was combat engineering in the form of mobility and counter-mobility. For establishments, manpower and equipment, see, Philson, BEFORBAT, Vol 2, pp.98-101.

P3.1 Inter-war UK divisional logistic capability. An unidentified RASC company at Eelmoor Plain near Aldershot. Note the respirator haversacks. (RLCM: A1/MT/RASC/NOR)

employment platoon, chemical warfare section and provost company were also integral to the establishment.

Within the division, logistic policy was controlled through the AQ Staff headed by the Assistant Adjutant & Quartermaster-General (AA & QMG), a lieutenant-colonel, supported by the Deputy Assistant Adjutant General (DAAG) and the Deputy Assistant Quartermaster-General (DAQMG). In the logistic arena, the AA & QMG led on Medical Services, the production and authorization of administrative instructions and policies regarding ammunition, Ordnance Services and Supplies, including POL, leaving the DAQMG to manage, with the Service Directors in the HQ,[6] the daily issues relating to movements, railways, ammunition,

6 These officers were not Staff officers but technical advisors and included, Assistant Director Medical Services (ADMS), Commander RASC (CRASC), Deputy Assistant Director Ordnance Services (DADOS), Senior Ordnance Mechanical Engineer (SOME), Deputy Assistant Provost Marshal (DAPM) and the Senior Chaplain.

Ordnance Services, equipment, clothing, Salvage, Postal Services and the provision of water.[7] The two logistic tasks the DAAG was responsible for was cookery and billeting.[8]

In supporting combat power, logistics was focused at divisional level, with no formed units organic to the brigade. Whilst this solution concentrated resources at the appropriate level, inevitably there were occasions when by design or default, brigades operated outside of the divisional umbrella, which was an appreciable support challenge because the Q construct was not organized to meet this requirement in dynamic manoeuvre environments, although in planned deployments such as Force W to the Saarland, the Q Staffs were able to create the necessary logistic 3rd and 2nd Line ORBAT, with the provision of the 3rd Line corps slice the most complex problem. The organic divisional 2nd Line logistic component was common across nearly all of the divisions, although the armoured formations had differentials driven by the dispersion of combat formations. A fundamental arrangement of the divisional logistic structure was the key role played by the RASC, with only the Light Aid Detachments (LAD)[9] and Mobile Bath Unit (MBU) of the RAOC and the Divisional Postal Unit (DPU) of the Corps of Royal Engineers (RE) not being cap-badged to it.

Table 3.1
Infantry Division – Organic Logistic Units

Unit	Number per Division	Total Personnel	Remarks
HQ RASC	1	35[10]	Total divisional RASC 1185
Divisional Ammunition Company RASC	1	390	
Divisional Petrol Company RASC	1	301	
Divisional Supply Column RASC	1	458	
Light Aid Detachment (Light) RAOC	4	52	13 personnel per LAD
Light Aid Detachment (Heavy) RAOC	7	91	
Divisional Postal Unit RE	1	25	
Mobile Bath Unit RAOC	1	20	
Total		1,372	

7 Major-General Sir W G Lindsell DSO OBE MC idc psc, *Military Organization and Administration* (Aldershot: Gale & Polden, 23rd Edn, 1941), pp.40-41.

8 The DAAG's main effort was people. He was thus responsible for discipline, courts-martial, POWs, battlefield clearance of personnel and burials, Provost, ceremonial, leave, casualties, reinforcements, claims, working parties and the war diary. Ibid, p.40.

9 Gun Buster, rather understating their role, noted, 'In a mechanised army, their importance and utility is considerable', *Return via Dunkirk*, p.67.

10 The WE was 36 inclusive of the medical officer RAMC, thus 35 x RASC. See, Philson, BEFORBAT, Vol 2, p.110, HQ RASC WE II/1931/5/2.

Organic divisional logistic capability was supported by corps 3rd Line RASC assets including the Corps Ammunition Park (CAP)[11] and Corps Petrol Park (CPP),[12] and three Army Field Workshops (AFW) and an Ordnance Field Park (OFP) from the RAOC. This meant that only 9.3 per cent of the personnel in the division served in logistic units, with the majority, 1,185, 86.3 percent, serving in the divisional RASC.[13] In addition, there were another 245 logistic personnel, nearly all badged to the RASC, serving in the division undertaking support tasks in the brigade HQs, field ambulances or AQ technical appointments in the divisional HQ.[14] These figures do not include logistic personnel integral to units at 1st Line and badged to the regiment such as drivers and cooks in infantry battalions,[15] which as the table below illustrates, were not insignificant, representing 14.8 percent of the battalion manpower establishment.

Table 3.2
Infantry Battalion – Logistic Tradesmen and Non-Tradesmen[16]

Tradesmen		Non-Tradesmen		Remarks
Qualification	No	Qualification	No	
Blacksmith	1	Butcher	1	
Bricklayer	1	Cooks	14	
Carpenter	6	Drivers IC*	55	*Internal Combustion[17]
Driver Mechanic	14	Postal	1	
Equipment Repairer	1	Quartermaster	8	Including QM and RQMS
Mason	1	Transport Control	1	Sergeant
Motor Mechanic	2	Storeman	6	
Technical Storeman	2	Water Duties	2	
Total	28		88	Total personnel: 116

11 The CAP, consisting of an HQ, two divisional sub-parks and one corps troops sub-park, carried the 3rd Line ammunition for all units in a corps of two divisions. See Philson, BEFORBAT, Vol 2, p.59, WE III/1931/37A/2.

12 The corps troops ammunition company and corps troops supply column were 2nd Line assets operating at corps level to support corps units and were not usually tasked to directly support divisional operations.

13 Percentage calculated from figures in Philson, BEFORBAT, Vol 2, p.124.

14 The RASC provided 59 personnel for each field ambulance, thus totalling 177, plus 40 drivers for the divisional HQ and two Fitters. In the HQ the RAOC filled two technical officer posts and eight clerical ones, whilst the RASC provided a catering advisor and a RASC clerk. The three AQ Staff officer posts were any Arm or Service. The RASC also provided five posts in brigade HQs and the RAOC, six, thus totalling 33 in a division. The AQ Staff Captain was found from any Arm or Service. Total logistic personnel in HQ appointments and units thus 1,642; 11.1 percent of the divisional WE.

15 Based upon an Infantry Battalion (Higher Establishment) authorized by WE II/1931/12F/1. Philson, BEFORBAT, Vol 2, p.104.

16 Table compiled from information in Ibid, p.106.

17 The term Driver IC referred to the WMT drivers in the Administration Platoon, 35 of which were allocated to the rifle companies. IC was an Army term to identify the soldier as a Driver, Motor Transport rather than Driver, Horse Transport or Animal Transport.

P3.2 BEF Divisional WMT. The complex mix of RASC WMT in BEF divisions complicated logistic planning, load lifts, MT training and Equipment Support. (RLCM: A1/MT/RLCA/30015)

Whilst there were some limitations to the divisional logistic organization, it also had its merits, although inevitably, after the withdrawal in June 1940, there were adjustments as a result of the campaign lessons identified study.

A key point is that whilst the War Equipment Tables (WET) reflected a fixed capability, the outputs on the ground depended on strength rather than establishment and additionally, the capabilities of the equipment, which in France did not always fully meet the military requirement. How logistic assets were utilized also depended upon planning by the Staff officers in the divisional HQ, the influence of unit commanders and the skill sets of the soldiers. The operational aspects were equally important because offensive and defensive tasks required a different balance of logistic activity, with the former requiring more fuel and latter great quantities of ammunition and defence stores. An advance to contact usually required more WMT to support troop lift, whilst 'breaking clean' from the enemy often generated the need for significant quantities of explosives for demolitions.[18]

18 In this respect, the RASC Load and Vehicle Allocation Lists in the appx to this chapter are but an example of the logistic planning detail required to support an infantry division with ammunition, fuel and supplies.

RAOC deployment was focused at corps level, with each division being allocated a section[19] from a OFP.[20] An OFP consisted of two corps sections and two divisional sections plus a reserve section, the latter holding for emergency issue to units, 2.5 percent of the vehicles in the corps. There were however, two constraints with this arrangement. First, if a third division came under the command of a corps, there were insufficient OFP resources to support all the divisions, unless a third section was allocated. Secondly, whilst the divisional sections were tasked to support a division, there was a mobility issue because these organizations had insufficient WMT to move all the boxed stores and vehicle assemblies in one lift.[21] The RAOC also provided a LAD, detached from an AFW,[22] to assist the Divisional HQ & Signals unit in delivering its Equipment Support tasks, whilst each infantry brigade, divisional cavalry regiment and artillery regiment was also permanently assigned a LAD.[23] The RAOC was also responsible for the provision of the divisional MBU,[24] although the WET[25] indicates that it was effectively an All Arms unit. Capable, in theory, of bathing 120-140 men per hour it was as important to morale as it was to health and hygiene,[26] whilst it was also designed to support the provision of chemical decontamination capability, but the scaled equipment of the day was

19 In 1940, the RASC used the term 'Section' to describe what was a platoon sized organization and 'sub-section' for the smallest RASC grouping..
20 Authorised by WE III/1931/54/3. Philson, BEFORBAT, Vol 2, p.73.
21 Ibid, p.71..
22 Ibid, p.71. The AFW was authorised by WE III/1931/53/3 and was established for main workshop, three recovery sections and 15 LADs.
23 Ibid, p.71.
24 The MBU was transported in 2 x 3-ton lorries and consisted of 20 personnel commanded by a subaltern, including 1 x barber and 1 x plumber. Ibid, p.77.

Table 3.3
Divisional Mobile Bath Unit - Manning

Appointment or Trade	Establishment	Corps	Remarks
OIC	1	All Arms	Lieutenant or Second-Lieutenant
2IC	1	All Arms	Sergeant
OIC General Duties	1	All Arms	Corporal
Barber	1	All Arms	
Carpenter	1	Usually RE	
Clerk	1	Usually RASC	
Driver	4	RASC	
General Duty	8	All Arms	
Plumber	1	RE	
Sanitary Assistant	1	RAMC	
Total	20		

25 WE II/1931/26/1. Philson BEFORBAT, Vol 2, p.71.
26 In his letters home, Private Fred Gilbert, a Militia soldier of 8th Warwicks, describes the frustration of rarely having access to bathing facilities, writing in one letter on 20 March 1940 'Baths are few are far between' but more positively on 19 April, 'going to the pithead for a bath'. Obviously, access to the 48th Division MBU was, at best, limited. Gilbert letters, March - May 1940.

inadequate for the task. In the early months of the BEF's deployment, MBU capability was constrained by resources, whilst once operations had commenced, the tactical situation often limited or prevented their use.

Whilst centralization at corps level brought some advantages, there was dissonance with other Services, including the RASC, which had 'divisionalised' to use the contemporary term, their assets, in order to create greater mobility. This problem was compounded because RAOC training was separated from that controlled by Director Military Training (DMT), which meant that the RAOC found it more difficult to develop supporting doctrine and influence emerging logistic concepts. The RE manned the DPU,[27] responsible for the sorting of all mail to and from units within the formation. None of the one hundred and six Auxiliary Military Pioneer Corps (AMPC) companies deployed to France were organic to the division[28] most being employed in the Base, with the depots being reliant on them to deliver outputs, whilst others were engaged in fierce action during combat operations.[29] Some AMPC units were attached to divisions to support specific tasks and these had a vital role in supporting engineer projects, defence works and dumping programmes. The provision of logistics at divisional level thus devolved mainly upon the RASC, which, with its emphasis on the delivery of combat supplies[30] was the major player.

New Concepts and Old Chestnuts

The organization of the divisional RASC had changed considerably in scope and equipment, if not in concept, during the inter-war period.[31] In 1918, the Divisional Train consisted of four Horse Transport (HT) companies, whose function was to sustain units with supplies. One of these sub-units, the Divisional Ammunition Company (DAC) was a Royal Artillery asset and it was not until 1921 that the RASC assumed responsibility for the supply of common user ammunition natures in the divisional area. Motorization generated more changes, and the 1923 edition of *Field Service Regulations* (FSR), Volume I, shows a train headquarters, two Mechanical Transport (MT) companies and one HT company. Between 1924 and 1927, the arguments for and against commodity companies or composite infantry brigade companies continued, with

27 The DPU personnel establishment under WE II/1931/21/2 was 25, and this platoon sized unit was equipped with a Boys A/T rifle. Philson, BEFORBAT, Vol 2, p.77.

28 The one exception to this during the campaign, was the three *ad hoc* light infantry battalions formed from eleven AMPC companies that formed Z Brigade, then Digforce, then lastly C Brigade of Beauman Division. For manpower and equipment, see, Philson, BEFORBAT, Vol 3, pp. 39-40. For details of the operations, see, Major E H Rhodes-Woods, *A War History of the Royal Pioneer Corps, 1939-1945* (Aldershot: Gale & Polden, 1960), pp.49-59.

29 HQ 10 Group with eight companies was deployed to support the RAF AASF.

30 Combat supplies are ammunition, POL and rations. Although the modern term 'combat supplies' was not current in the British Army during the period, it neatly summarizes the items that were the most important in delivering direct military effect in the front-line. Ammunition included, in the BEF context, small arms and artillery ammunition, specialized infantry natures, explosives and gas munitions. POL covered all liquids fuels, lubricants (oils and greases) and antifreeze. Rations included food for personnel and forage for animals, plus disinfectants and water purification chemicals.

31 For a review of the changes to the Divisional RASC in the inter-war period, see, Major General P Turpin CB OBE MA FCIT, *The Turn of the Wheel: The History of the RASC 1919-1939* (Buckingham: Barracuda Books, 1988), pp.130-133.

the former concept gaining ground. The Regular RASC was declared motorized in 1930, when 4 HT Company, the last operational sub-unit was disbanded at Catterick on 31 December 1929, although the HT Training Company in Aldershot was retained until HT was withdrawn from the TA divisional trains in 1932. Whatever the organizational arrangements however, RASC divisional logistic support doctrine retained a clear focus on delivering stocks to units, and to give divisions greater mobility by holding stocks on wheels. Generating this capability was a key task in the 1930s and is neatly summarized by Lieutenant-Colonel Shaw RAOC is his book, *Supply in Modern War*: 'From the foregoing it is clear that the salient features of mechanized operations will be the dispersion of forces and their speed. Dispersion implies decentralization, and this-from a supply angle-connotes some measure of self-containment in both unit and formation'.[32]

By 1940, most of the infantry divisions in the BEF were supported by three RASC units commanded by a Commander RASC (CRASC) from divisional headquarters; there was no Regimental Headquarters (RHQ).

Table 3.4
BEF Infantry Division 1940
Organic RASC Units

Unit	Personnel	Task Vehicles	Remarks
Ammunition Company	390*	76	*2 x Royal Artillery personnel
Petrol Company	301	62	
Supply Column	458	89	

The CRASC, a lieutenant-colonel, was responsible to the divisional commander for all executive duties in connection with the supply and transport services. He reported to Director Supplies & Transport (DST) at corps headquarters to ensure that RASC policy was enacted in accordance with the regulations. The team consisted of a major responsible for supply operations, an adjutant and three captains covering ammunition, local resources and requisitioning, and divisional supplies, supported by a medical officer and 29 Other Ranks.[33] His spectrum of responsibility was though, extensive, a situation eruditely observed in a contemporary publication, *Britain's Modern Army*: 'On his efficiency depends the lifeblood (petrol) the endurance (food) and striking power (ammunition) of the division, and this efficiency has to be maintained under all conditions of climate, locality and actual battle'.[34] One of the key concerns of a divisional CRASC was the technical competence of the RASC officers in a rapidly expanding army, a matter partially addressed by the formation of the RASC Officer Producing Centre at Saint Lawrence Ramsgate, where the training of RASC officers had been centralized.[35]

32 Brevet Lieutenant-Colonel G C Shaw RAOC, *Supply in Modern War* (London: Faber & Faber, nd but 1938), p.188.

33 Philson, BEFORBAT, Vol 2, p.110, HQ Divisional RASC, WE II/1931/5/2.

34 na, *Britain's Modern Army* (London: Oldhams Press, 1941), p.249.

35 Each of the key courses ran monthly. Two-week courses were: ammunition and company commanders, whilst supply, Brigade RASC officers and workshop officers' courses were one week. Army Council,

Divisional Ammunition Company

The Divisional Ammunition Company (DAC)[36] was organized into a headquarters, a workshop and support section,[37] and three transport sections,[38] the latter with a mixture of equipment and tasks established so each section, ALPHA, BRAVO and CHARLIE carried ammunition for an infantry brigade within the division and one third for divisional troops. In addition, each section had two unallocated vehicles, equating to 10 percent of the tasked strength, as an operational reserve, generating a total task[39] vehicle establishment of 76 within the company.[40] The BEF possessed a limited number of wheeled medium mobility load-carriers and this was reflected in the ORBAT of the DAC. Only ALPHA section had this equipment, in the form of four 6x4 lorries, to support the 4x4 tractor drawn 18/25 and 25 pounder guns, whilst CHARLIE section was a replica of BRAVO.[41] There were a number of different types of Small Arms Ammunition (SAA) that were carried including 0.50-inch for the Vickers Heavy Machine Gun (HMG) mounted on the Light Tank Mk VI and 7.92 mm for the Besa Medium Machine Gun (MMG) mounted on the Light Tank Mk VIC and the Cruiser Mk II (A10). The DAC ammunition one-time lift is shown in the table below.[42]

Army Training Memorandum No 30, March 1940 (War Office, 1940), p.17. The title, 'Producing Centre', has more than a touch of an industrial solution to the shortage. For details of the syllabus and programmes for these courses, see, General Staff, *Royal Army Service Corps*, Training Pamphlet No 1, *Training System in War*, Part IV: *Collective Training* (War Office 1940).

36 WE II/1931/13/3. Philson, BEFORBAT, Vol 2, pp.115-118.

37 Shown in the WET as D Section.

38 AFG 1098 domestic vehicle per section provided a centralized feeding facility, and the section defence detachment moved in a 1-ton lorry, equipped with 1 x 0.303-inch LMG (Bren) on a Motley Mount for AA action and a Boys 0.55-inch A/T rifle.

39 Load carrying vehicles had two generic variants. The term 'truck' described a load carrying vehicle of 1 ton or less, whilst 'lorries' were load-carriers of 30 cwt or more.

40 Philson, BEFORBAT, Vol 2, p.117

41 See Appx to Chp 3, Table 3A.1 - DAC Ammunition Load List.

42 The vehicle types and loads do not fully reflect the detail shown in the WET in Philson, BEFORBAT, Vol 2, p.117 because there were variations created by vehicle type availability and load plans. The table has been composed from various documents held in the RLC Museum and BEFORBAT and illustrates one possible organization.

Table 3.5
Divisional Ammunition Company
Holdings on Wheels

Nature[43]	Wpn Pop	Scale per wpn	Rounds	WMT Lift	Remarks
25 pdr HE	72	53	3,816	27 x 3 ton 3 x 30 cwt	
25 pdr Smk		17	1,224		
25 pdr AP		5	360		
18 pdr HE	12	32	384	9 x 3 ton 1 x 30 cwt	
18 pdr Shrapnel		26	312		
18 pdr Smk		4	48		
4.5-inch HE*	12	63	756		*35 lbs
4.5-inch Smk*		21	252		*& Starshell
2 pdr AP[44]	48	48	2,304	3 x 3 ton 3 x 30 cwt	
0.55-inch A/T Rifle[45]	360	50	18,000		
0.380-inch Pistol[46]	1,400	6	8,400	9 x 3 ton 3 x 30 cwt	
0.303-inch Rifle Ball	8,000	40	320,000		
0.303-inch LMG SAA	460	600	276,000		
0.303-inch LMG AA	190	600	114,000		
0.303-inch MMG	28	1,500	42,000		
0.5-inch HMG	28	250	7,000		
3-inch Mortar HE	18	42	756	3 x 3 ton	
3-inch Mortar Smk		30	540		
2-inch Mortar HE[47]	18	12	1,298	6 x 3 ton	
2-inch Mortar Smk		36	3,888		

43 For an explanation of the weapon systems see, na, *The British Army in WWII* (London: Greenhill Books 1990), pp.153-155. For details of the ammunition, see, War Office, *Textbook on Ammunition*, 26/ Manuals/1543 (HMSO, 1936).

44 Some units were equipped with the French Hotchkiss 25 mm Anti-Tank gun.

45 Whilst receiving in many publications a bad press for its poor anti-tank performance, *Infantry Section Leading* (War Office, HMSO, 1938), p.9 clearly states that purpose of the Boys Anti-Tank Rifle was defence against *lightly* (author's italics) armoured vehicles. The tungsten carbide 0.55 inch round could penetrate 24 mm of armour at 100 yards, 13 mm of armour at 300 yards and 9 mm at 500 yards. The Boys was the first infantry weapon in the British Army requiring the mandatory wearing of ear-plugs by the firer.

46 0.455-inch ammunition was also issued for the Webley Mk VI service revolver.

47 The 2-inch mortar had an HE and a smoke round. When the BEF deployed to France in September 1939, there were no HE rounds available for issue.

Grenades[48]			1,620	3 x 30 cwt	
Very, Signal[49]	300	6	1,800	3 x 3 ton	
Explosives[50]*			5 tons		*Mainly RE
A/T Mines			1,000	2 x 3 ton	
A/T Mines, Dummy			1,000		

A complication for the DAC was preparing to support offensive Gas Warfare (GW). The key issue at divisional level was the distribution of gas artillery rounds, 'Grey Shell' in the colloquial of the day, for 4.5-inch howitzers. Whilst never deployed from 21 Base Ammunition Depot (BAD) at Fecamp to field units, 18,000 were held in-Theatre in mid-April 1940[51] and DAC that supported field regiments of the Royal Artillery holding the 4.5-inch piece were expected to handle the gas munitions, which were all filled with Mustard, coded Y.[52] 'Grey Shell' was distributed in the same manner as conventional munitions, although subject to special control and handling measures.[53] Whilst the supply of other gas munitions was conducted through GHQ,[54] the system for chemical mines and contamination bombs had by April 1940, not been refined and the War Office guidance expected the Q Staff within a divisional HQ to resolve the problem on the ground, the directive stating: 'Special provision, must therefore be made'.[55] To date, no documentary evidence has been identified from the BEF's files, which would indicate how these munitions were to be distributed but it is probable that the DAC would have been tasked, although these weapons were never deployed to France, for which, the Q Staff were no doubt grateful.

The DAC provided 2nd Line road transport for the supply of ammunition within the division, with reserve munitions being held for the division within the corps area in the divisional ammunition sub-park (DAP) of the 3rd Line CAP. Vehicles of the CAP ran stocks forward, via a Rendezvous Point (RVP) to an Ammunition Refilling Point (ARP). The DAC was responsible for covering the gap between the ARP and the unit echelons, which doctrinally was expected to be 10-12 miles but operationally was usually longer. When corps units were attached to a division, sections or sub-sections of the corps troops ammunition company would be detached to the DAC to deliver the necessary level of support; this type of flexible 'Task Organization' was a common feature of logistic operations of the period. HQ DAC was

48 For details, see, War Office, *Text Book of Ammunition*, Chp X.
49 Pyrotechnics. For details, see, Ibid, Chp XII.
50 For details, see, Ibid, Chp XI.
51 The 25 pdr also had a gas shell but production problems delayed the issue to the Army until September 1940. WOOH, *Special Weapons and Types of Warfare*, Vol I, *Gas Warfare* (War Office, 1951), (SECRET), Appx II.
52 Ibid.
53 A Corps Troops Ammunition Company (CTAC) was responsible for the delivery of the 6-inch Grey Shell.
54 When a CW Company RE was detached from GHQ Troops, an element of the GHQ RASC Company was attached to the relevant formation RASC Company, which at divisional level would have been the DAC. General Staff, *The Tactical and Technical Employment of Chemical Weapons*, Military Training Pamphlet (MTP) No 32, Part I, *Chemical Warfare Units, Organization, Employment and Training* (War Office, April 1940), p.3.
55 Ibid.

normally located mid-way between the ARP and the unit ammunition echelon. At the ARP, which was an exchange point (XP) where ammunition was transferred, by hand, to vehicles of the DAC, which then moved forward, sometimes via the HQ DAC location, to Ammunition Points (AP).[56] Motorcycle Despatch Riders were used to maintain communications, bring ammunition demands from the unit to HQ DAC, control packet movement and guide the DAC lorries from the AP to unit locations.

The threat from enemy ground and air forces, combined with the German GW capability, created an imperative for dispersion, and the DAC rarely operated from a company hide; the devastation created by the sympathetic detonation of a full company load of explosives would have been catastrophic. The section AP could either move forward, or unit transport could move back and collect stocks from the delivery point, which was the ammunition interface with the combat unit. The system was however, flexible and RASC vehicles often went forward to replenish unit reserves, or deliver artillery ammunition to the gun lines. This procedure had though, disadvantages because the RASC drivers were usually less familiar with the tactical situation, some of the DAC lorries were larger, and command and control was more difficult, but its major advantage was the consequential reduction in manual stock handling thus decreasing delivery time.

Dumping[57] was widely used, particularly to support artillery fire plans. In May 1940, 3 DAC[58] was tasked, for example, with executing, in 24 hours, a divisional dumping programme of 200 rounds per gun, as part of the BEF's advance to contact onto the River Dyle.[59] This was a major task for 3 DAC because the 3rd Division's artillery consisted of three field regiments (7th, 33rd and 76th) with a mixed gun inventory, making a total of 72 guns.[60] The DAC had therefore, to dump 14,400 rounds, which were soon in demand, 7th Field Regiment firing 700 rounds on 14 May in support of operations in defence of the River Dyle around Louvain.[61]

Divisional Petrol Company

The nomenclature of the Divisional Petrol Company (DPC) was perhaps inappropriate because Petroleum, Oils and Lubricants (POL) were not the only materials conveyed by the sub-unit, although it described the key task. Organized into a HQ, a workshop, [62] and three transport sections, the latter with a mixture of equipment and tasks, each transport section had two

56 In 1940, the term 'Ammunition Point', was a forward detachment of the DAC. Army Council, Field Service Pocket Book (FSPB), Pamphlet No 1, *Glossary of Military Terms and Organization in the Field, 1940* (London: HMSO, 1940), p.1.

57 *Army Field Manual* (AFM) Vol 1, *Combined Arms Operations*, Part 6, *Combat Service Support*, defines a 'dump' as a temporary storage area, usually in the open, for bombs, ammunition, equipment or supplies. A dump has minimal C^3, security and bulk handling resources; it requires activation before use.

58 TNA WO 167/224: 3 DAC RASC, WD, April 1940.

59 Known as Plan D. There was also a Plan E, which referred to a move to the River Escaut. GHQ's Operational Instruction No 36 and Administrative Instruction No 10 were the base planning documents. See, WO 197/57: Forward Move of the BEF (Plan D) - Administrative instructions and correspondence.

60 7th and 33rd Field Regiments were equipped with 24 x 25 pdrs each, whilst 76th Field Regiment had 12 x 18/25 pdrs and 12 x 4.5-inch howitzers. Philson, BEFORBAT, Vol 2, p.14, 3rd Infantry Division.

61 TNA WO 167/468: 7th Field Regiment RA, WD, May 1940.

62 Shown in the WET as D Section. Philson, BEFORBAT, Vol 2, p.119, WE II/1931/13A/2.

unallocated vehicles, equating to 10 percent of the tasked strength, as an operational reserve, generating a total task vehicle establishment of 57 within the company and a personnel strength of 301.[63] An AFG 1098 domestic vehicle per section provided a centralized feeding facility, and the section defence detachment moved in a 1-ton lorry. The DPC had four tasks. The DPC provided 2nd Line transport for the supply of POL within the division, the two petrol sections, ALPHA and BRAVO each carrying enough fuel for every divisional unit to travel 25 miles by road, thus totalling 50 miles. Each 3-ton truck was planned to carry 160 x 4-gallon tins (cased), 640 gallons, or 190 x 4-gallon cans (uncased) totalling 760 gallons, thus allowing capacity for the drums of the six percent quota of lubricants to complete the load.[64] Vehicles of the CPP brought POL forward to an exchange point in the divisional area called a Petrol Refilling Point (PRP). At the PRP, the cans were transferred to lorries from ALPHA and BRAVO sections of the DPC and the vehicles then moved forward, often via the DPC location, to up to four Petrol Points (PP).

Most vehicles in the BEF were powered by spark ignition engines, although compression ignition power-plants fuelled by petroleum spirit were fitted to some equipments, most notably the Infantry Tank Mark II,[65] and most production versions of the AEC 4x4 Matador Medium Artillery Tractor, so there was a small requirement for diesel fuel, and whilst not a major problem in France, the increase in the numbers of vehicles powered by compression ignition engines, created a complication for the distribution of fuel by the DPC. The distribution of oils and lubricants using drums and cans was relatively simple consisting mainly of Oil Mineral 220 for engines, an Oil Compound (OC 600), some simple mineral oils, and a general purpose, lime-based grease.[66] Oils and lubricants were distributed on a planning quota of six percent of the volume of the fuel,[67] although the usage varied between vehicle types.

CHARLIE section was responsible for the movement of blankets[68] and greatcoats[69] in bulk for all units of the division, less the artillery. The reason for this rather bizarre arrangement was

63 Ibid.

64 Army Council, FSPB, Pamphlet No 9, *Supply and Replenishment of Material in the Field, 1939*, p.13. Recovering the empty tins, a 3 ton lorry could lift 204 cased tins or 272 uncased. The 'case' weighed 12 lbs and each full 4-gallon tin, 33 lbs.

65 Only 23 x A12, the Infantry Tank Mark II, were deployed to France. Armed with a 2 pdr 40mm gun, the A12 had frontal armour of 78mm, weighed 26.3 tons, was powered by diesel and had a maximum speed of 15 mph; with these characteristics, the A12 was probably the most capable tank possessed by any of the combatants in 1940, with perhaps the exception of the French Somua 35. All the A12s were on the establishment of 7 RTR and were lost in France. For more details, read, David Fletcher, *The Great Tank Scandal: British Armour in the Second World War* Part 1 (London: HMSO, 1989), Chp 2.

66 By 1945, the types of Allied Oils and Lubes inventory had expanded to the point that a Joint Associated Services Lubricant Panel was established to recommend rationalization of American, British and Canadian grades; the Panel succeeded in reducing the product range from 361 to 118.

67 The ratios for standard vehicle types are shown in Army Council, FSPB, Pamphlet No 9, *Supply and Replenishment of Material in the Field*, pp.15-16, daily Consumption of Petrol and Lubricants. A Cruiser tank used oil at 15% of the fuel requirement and a 3 ton lorry, 4.5%.

68 In the days before the issued military sleeping bag, the humble blanket was an essential item of equipment for the soldier, although some purchased civilian bags.

69 A 3 ton lorry could lift 825 x damp blankets in bales of 25 or 800 in bundles of 10, or 800 loose damp greatcoats or 2,000 ground sheets in bundles of five. If the blankets and greatcoats were dry more could be carried. Army Council, FSPB, Pamphlet No 9, *Supply and Replenishment of Material in the Field*, p.12.

that the mechanization of 1st Line transport in units created sufficient lift for soldiers' baggage and greatcoats but not their blankets. The DPC thus became, for administrative reasons, responsible for the carriage of unit blankets, although from an operational perspective it was not the most inspired decision, especially as it required 10 x 3 ton lorries to conduct the carriage.[70] Equally importantly, CHARLIE section was responsible for the carriage and delivery of the division's Anti-Gas Equipment (AGE), which included a reserve of clothing, equal to 25 percent of unit scales and for the Cape, Anti-Gas[71], equating to two percent of divisional personnel establishment, tasks which matured from a decision by the Taylor Committee to divorce AGE and reserve clothing from the Supply chain the DPC became the convenient choice.[72]

Vehicles of the CPP brought AGE forward to the PRP where it was transferred to lorries from CHARLIE Section of the DPC and the vehicles then moved forward, often via the DPC location, to potentially four Petrol Points (PP). CHARLIE section was also responsible for back-loading this clothing, in gas-proof bags to the PRP. Finally, the DPC was responsible for the technical supervision and maintenance of the affiliated RASC operated transport in the divisional and brigade headquarters, the three field ambulances and the field hygiene section, so the workshop section was therefore, larger than the vehicle establishment of the DPC required.[73]

Divisional Supply Column

The Divisional Supply Column (DSC) was organized into a headquarters, a workshop and two echelons. The echelons were identical, comprising a headquarters and four sections. Each echelon was designed to carry one Day of Supply (DOS) for the division consisting of rations, which, included forage if appropriate, ordnance, and engineer stores, plus the delivery of mail to the DPU. An echelon was also responsible for the back loading of items for repair and salvage, and the return mail. To enact these tasks, the DSC was established for 458 personnel[74] and a mix of task vehicles, which were 26 x 12 cwt vans, 10 x 1 ton, 15 x 30 cwt and 48 x 3 ton lorries.[75] The function of the DSC was to provide 2nd Line road transport for food and stores from the Supply Railhead (SRH) in the corps area to divisional units, over a distance of 40 miles, with each echelon delivering on alternate days. Pack trains for supply items[76] usually consisted of 38 wagons,[77] and were dispatched daily from the in-Theatre Base. These trains ran to a SRH at

70 Philson, BEFORBAT, Vol 2, p.119, WE II/1931/13A/2.
71 Not on individual issue but available to decontamination teams, was the Suit, Anti-Gas, Light, consisting of over-boots, trousers, jacket, gloves and a hood.
72 This task required 8 x 3 ton lorries. Philson, BEFORBAT, Vol 2, p.119, WE II/1931/13A/2.
73 Ibid.
74 Philson, BEFORBAT, Vol 2, p.111, WE II/1931/15/3.
75 Ibid, p.113.
76 Supply items included: food, forage, POL, solid fuels, disinfectants and hospital supplies. Army Council, FSPB, Pamphlet No 1, *Glossary of Military Terms and Organization in the Field*, p.11.
77 A 10 ton railway wagon could transport 430 cases (each case of two 1-gallon jar) of rum jars, or 283 x 50 lb biscuit cases, or 210 x 25 lb sacks of bread, or 407 x 36 lb preserved meat cases or 224 x 80 lb bags of oats. A 3 ton lorry could carry respectively, 52, 79, 52, 55 and 82. A refrigerated rail van could usually lift nine tons of frozen meat, which thus required three x 3 ton lorries for onward movement. Army Council, FSPB, Pamphlet No 9, *Supply and Replenishment of Material in the Field*, Sect 4, Transport Load Tables, pp.12-14.

the front of the GLOC area or the rear of the corps areas, on a scale of one train per day per two divisions.

The DSC could support a gap of 80 miles for short periods, but such activity levels soon impinged upon efficiency because vehicle maintenance was curtailed, and driver fatigue mounted. The operation of the system was simple but effective because the two-echelon system enabled one echelon to work the railhead, whilst the other was delivering supplies. On Day One, bulk supplies were loaded to echelon vehicles at the SRH and then moved to a 'break bulk' area, where the *materiel* was redistributed in accordance with the requirements of units, usually utilizing, in a wooded area, a 'Horse-Shoe' circuit. Vehicles would enter an outer circuit and dump their bulk loads, before proceeding to an inner one and collecting their unit loads that had been built from stocks held in the dumps that had been created on the outer circuit. On the second day, the WMT would move forward into the divisional area and one of two methods of re-supply would be enacted.

The first system involved the vehicles moving, via Meeting Points to Delivery Points. Brigade HQ selected the Meeting Points where the DSC echelon met unit guides who took them forward to Delivery Points where the supplies would be transferred to unit vehicles. To create flexibility during mobile operations, the divisional headquarters sometimes allocated a RVP. This was a hide to which an echelon could be directed, and if necessary, supplies re-organized, whilst the Meeting and Delivery Points were confirmed. The second system required the selection, by the divisional staff, of Supply Points where unit vehicles would collect stocks. This system had several advantages. It kept the DSC WMT out of unit lines, afforded an echelon greater control of its assets, generated flexibility for collecting units and left the option of the RASC echelon going forward to unit B echelons.

Reserve MT Companies

The organic RASC 2nd Line resources in the BEF were reinforced, by what were in effect 4th Line Reserve MT Companies (RMTC),[78] which were planned for an expeditionary force on a scale of one per division, although because of the need to deploy Works MT companies, only seven were sent to France.[79] These units were a significant size, comprising 482 personnel and 144 x 3 ton lorries capable of moving in a one-time lift either 2,480 soldiers equating to the marching strength of four rifle battalions, or 396 tons of stores, ammunition or fuel, or 66,000 gallons of canned water.[80] The creation of the RMTC was essentially a product of the restructuring of the infantry battalions and Liddell-Hart argued that had the 'truck' establishments of the infantry battalions been increased, the RMTC would not have been required in the troop transport role.[81] There is little argument about this but there were insufficient vehicles available in 1940 for it to be enacted. As it transpired, the formation of the RMTC generated much greater operational capability than retaining all the WMT at battalion level, although the battles of

78 For details of the WET, see, WE IV/1931/44/2 in Philson, BEFORBAT, Vol 3, p.99.

79 The initial allocation of the RMTC to the First Contingent of the BEF was as follows: 1st Division (19 Company), 2nd Division (15 Company), 3rd Division (51 Company) and 4th Division (50 Company). WOOH, *Supplies and Transport*, Vol II, p.365, Appx VA.

80 Philson, BEFORBAT, Vol 3, p.99.

81 See, Basil Liddell-Hart, *The Defence of Britain* (London: Faber & Faber 1939), pp.373-374.

May and June 1940 lucidly exposed that the tactical penalties were far higher than had been initially assumed. Infantry battalion establishments were reviewed and WMT lift increased but the debate concerning the balance of transport allocation had a long history and was to surface again during operations in France during 1944.

Conclusion

Divisional logistic support to the BEF of 1939-1940 is a fascinating period of military history. For the first time in warfare, motorized logistic corps took to the field to support a mechanized force, and did so against a backdrop of rapid expansion and improvisation. Divisional logistic units, although not always to establishment in manpower and equipment, and often suffering from an initial lack of individual technical and tactical skills on which to build, were, for the most part, combat ready by May 1940, and generally acquitted themselves well in battle. The two most serious limitations in the structures were enabling support to independent brigade operations and the fragility created by the RASC 'commodity' sub-units being divorced from the division.

The DSCs were usually the most practised at their art because their services were required on a daily basis, whilst the DPCs also had an opportunity to hone their field skills. The DACs achieved the least live practice, although the drivers became familiar in identifying their loads and dumping programmes were exercised in some divisions. The shape, size, composition and role of the logistic divisional units were not always in accordance with doctrine and establishments and there was much frustration relating to training and tasking, but most units were able to deliver sufficient capability to support operations. The RMTC, whilst not allocated to every division, provided a very significant increase in road transport capability and played a key logistic role throughout the BEF's operations in France.

Perforce of organization, the RASC was the major logistic cap-badge at the divisional level but the integral components from the RE that provided the DPU, and the RAOC, which sponsored the MBU, both played important supplementary supporting roles. The effective operation of the DPU, especially in its interface with the DSC, was essential to ensuring the swift arrival of the mail, a process that certainly under-pinned morale. Equally, a fully functioning MBU was welcomed on an individual basis from everyone from the divisional commander to the most junior soldier, whilst it served a key military purpose in sustaining hygiene and preventing the spread of disease and infection. The least co-ordinated and coherent component of the divisional logistic matrix was Equipment Support. Whilst a RAOC officer acted as the Senior Ordnance Mechanical Engineer (SOME) in the HQ, most of the activity was executed at unit level through RAOC LADs, which were not directly controlled by the SOME and the RASC workshops were out-with his responsibilities.[82]

82 The logistic and operational impact of these arrangements during the campaign are worthy of further study, although the outcomes were an imperative to the formation of the Royal Electrical Mechanical Engineers (REME) in 1942. See, WOOH, *Royal Electrical and Mechanical Engineers*, Vol 1, *Organization and Operations*.

Appendix to Chapter 3
Divisional RASC Example Load Lists

Notes:

The example load-lists have been compiled from several sources to offer an indication of the planning required to deliver ammunition, fuel and supplies for an infantry division. In particular, the numbers of vehicles shown in the tables are at variance to the WETs shown in Philson, BEFORBAT, Vol 2.

Table 3A.1
Divisional Ammunition Company
Ammunition Load List

Section	Nature	Vehicles	Qty	Lift (tons)
ALPHA	18 & 25 pdr	3 ton - 6x4	4	12.0
		30 cwt - 6x4	2	3.0
	4.5-inch howitzer (HE)	3 ton - 4x2	4	12.0
	Small Arms - mainly 0.303-inch	3 ton - 4x2	4	12.0
	2 pdr & 25mm A/T AP	3 ton - 4x2	1	3.0
	Grenades	3 ton - 4x2	1	3.0
	Mortars - 2 & 3-inch	3 ton - 4x2	2	6.0
	Fireworks & explosives	3 ton - 4x2	1	3.0
	A/T mines	3 ton - 4x2	2	6.0
	0.55-inch A/T	30 cwt - 4x2	1	1.5
	Operational Reserve	3 ton - 4x2	1	3.0
	Operational Reserve	30 cwt - 4x2	1	1.5
		Task Vehicles	24	66.0
BRAVO	18 & 25 pdr	3 ton - 4x2	4	12.0
		30 cwt - 4x2	2	3.0
	4.5-inch howitzer	3 ton - 4x2	4	12.0
	Small Arms - mainly 0.303-inch	3 ton - 4x2	4	12.0
	Grenades	3 ton - 4x2	1	3.00
	Mortars - 2 & 3-inch	3 ton - 4x2	2	6.0
	Fireworks & explosives	30 cwt - 4x2	2	3.0
	0.55-inch A/T	30 cwt - 4x2	2	3.0
	Operational Reserve	3 ton - 4x2	1	3.0
	Operational Reserve	30 cwt - 4x2	1	1.5
		Task Vehicles	**23**	58.5
CHARLIE	Replica of BRAVO Section	Task Vehicles	**23**	58.5
Company	Three Sections	Task Vehicles	**70**	183.0

Table 3A.2
Divisional Petrol Company
Vehicle Allocation List

Section	Nature	Vehicles	Quantity
ALPHA	POL POL Operational Reserve	3 ton - 4x2 30 cwt - 4x2 One of above Total Task Vehicles	6 6 1 13
BRAVO	Replica of BRAVO Section	Total Task Vehicles	13
CHARLIE	Blankets AGE & Reserve Clothing Operational Reserve	3 ton - 4x2 3 ton - 4x2 3 ton - 4x2 Total Task Vehicles	17 2 2 21
Company	POL, Blankets & Clothing	Total Task Vehicles	47

Table 3A.3
Divisional Supply Column
Vehicle Allocation

Section	Commodity	Vehicles	Qty	Lift tons	Lift 2 Echs
ALPHA Divisional Troops	Supplies Supplies Supplies Engineer Stores Ordnance Stores	3 ton - 4x2 30 cwt - 4x2 12 cwt van 3 ton - 4x2 3 ton - 4x2 Task Vehicles	4 4 3 1 1 13	26	52
BRAVO Brigade Support	Supplies - 3 x Infantry Battalions Supplies - Field Regiment RA Ordnance Stores Supplies - Infantry Brigade HQ Supplies - Field Company RE Supplies - Field Ambulance	3 ton - 4x2 3 ton - 4x2 3 ton - 4x2 12 cwt van 12 cwt van 12 cwt van Task Vehicles	3 1 1 1 1 1 8	17	34
CHARLIE Brigade Support	Identical to BRAVO	Task Vehicles	8	17	34
DELTA Brigade Support	Identical to BRAVO	Task Vehicles	8	17	34
Echelon	Four Sections	Task Vehicles	37	77	
Echelon I & II	Eight Sections	Task Vehicles	74	154	154

Part II

Early Days

4

Marrying the Driver
Logistics and the deployment of the BEF to France

At War with Germany

On 2 September 1939, under Plan W4[1] Movement Table A4811,[2] the first four Movement Control (MC) officers[3] and 18 officers and 31 Other Ranks of the initial Advance Parties of the BEF arrived in France by air,[4] the spearhead of a major expedition by the British Army and the RAF onto the Continent.[5] In a demonstration of logistic modernity, the BEF's QMG, Lieutenant-General W G Lindsell,[6] followed them, leaving for Paris by air at 2300 on 3

1 TNA WO 197/1: Movement Control Instruction Plan W4.
2 Held in Copy No 32 of Plan W4.
3 Two each from No 1 and No 2 Movement Control Groups based at the Royal Engineer Transportation Centre Longmoor in Hampshire.
4 Even in 1933, the guidance was that where possible, such parties should be dispatched by air. Army Council, *Manual of Movement (War)* (London: HMSO, 1933), p.55, Sect 54.
5 Key planning documents included B354 General Instructions (Security) and the following, all classified SECRET, A4812 - Advanced Parties by Destroyer, A4799 - Movement of Personnel and MT and normal Advanced Parties and A4813 - Stores Movement Tables. TNA WO 191/1: Movement Control Instruction Plan W4.
6 Lieutenant-General Sir Wilfrid Gordon Lindsell GBE KCB DSO MC (1884-1973) was commissioned into the Royal Artillery in 1903, serving in France during the Great War. He was an instructor at the School of Military Administration (1921-1923) and on the Directing Staff at the Army Staff College (1925-1928), attending the Imperial Defence College in 1929. Posted to the War Office (1930-1933), he was Commandant of the Senior Officers' School Sheerness (1934-1935), then Deputy Military Secretary at the War Office. Commander Royal Artillery 4th Division in (1937-1939), he promoted to major-general in 1939 to assume the appointment of Major-General Administration Southern Command. Appointed as QMG to the BEF in September 1939, 'Tommy' Lindsell was knighted after the evacuation from France. He served in several senior logistic appointments during the war, including Lieutenant-General Administration Home Forces and then the Middle East and was the Principal Administrative Officer in the Indian Command from 1943, retiring from the Army in 1945. The Adjutant-General of the BEF, Lieutenant-General Sir Douglas Brownrigg described Lindsell as 'master of his craft'. For additional details, see, Nick Smart, *Biographical Dictionary of the British Generals of the Second World War* (Barnsley: Pen & Sword, 2005), p.191.

P4.1 The Far Bank. Carrier & Light Tank Mark VIB of 2nd RTR being off-loaded at Cherbourg. Before the introduction of Roll-On Roll-Off MT shipping during the Second World War, discharge required ships' derricks or dockside cranes, although the first modern Roll On-Roll Off train ferry service commenced in 1850. (Tank Museum: 0015/A4)

September 1939.[7] By 27 September, the First Contingent was in France and the move to the corps sectors via the Assembly and Concentration Areas had commenced. The deployment of the first echelon of the BEF consisting of GHQ,[8] corps troops, four infantry divisions in two corps and the GLOC including the Base, involved the move of 20,000 tons of ammunition, 20,000 tons of motor spirit and 10,000 tons of supplies,[9] including 1,600 tons of frozen meat.[10]

7 TNA CAB 106/211: 'Notes on the 'Q' Organization of the BEF' dated 16 January 1942, para 2.

8 GHQ was initially based in the Chateau de la Blanchardiere on the NE edge of Le Mans. TNA CAB 120/247: British Expeditionary Force: Lord Gort's First Despatch, para 5. It was not Gort's style however to live in luxury. The chateau at Arras was described by the Prime-Minister Neville Chamberlain as 'fairly large but sadly lacking in comforts', whilst observing that 'the C-in-C is said to be completely indifferent to cold, dirt, or fatigue so he doesn't mind'. J R Colville, *Man of Valour: Field-Marshal Gort VC* (London: Collins, 1972), p.163. This engaging book is the sole biography of Gort, who died of liver cancer in 1946 and in contrast to many senior generals, never published his memories to place his position on public record. For an examination of his time in command of the BEF, see pp.147-182.

9 WOOH, *Maintenance in the Field*, Vol I, p.30.

10 Ibid, p.39.

The QMG to the BEF was effusive, noting that, 'The original plans for movement of the BEF to France and for its initial maintenance were worked out in great detail by the War Office before the outbreak of war, and after reconnaissance in France'.[11] Given that the BEF's formation and deployment[12] was the result of five years of political dithering, incoherent defence policy,[13] rapid expansion, military improvisation and scrambling modernization,[14] its dispatch was indeed the result of an impressive feat of planning and execution, although in some areas under-pinned by considerable and sometimes uncalculated risks. Of especial note was the reliance upon Volunteers from the Supplementary Reserves to man the Docks Groups and the Movement Control organization, both which were vital to effective and efficient deployment and yet were not well practised, a fragility which had it matured, could have so easily proved embarrassing at best and catastrophic at worst.[15]

Both the planning and execution phases had inherent fragilities and limitations caused by several factors including time restrictions, excessive security and insufficient attention to key aspects of logistic detail, including Host Nation infrastructure capability, rail transportation agility, French mobilization requirements and unit 1st Line integrity but by the end of September 1939,[16] 152,031 Army personnel and 9,392 RAF were in France and the size of the Force grew almost daily, reaching 438,686 by mid-May 1940.[17] The regimental historian of the 13th/18th Royal Hussars noted the move of the BEF to France as having 'worked perfectly', which in the Regiment's case appears to have been the case, but it was not an observation that could be applied to every aspect of the deployment.[18] By mid-June 1940 however, the equivalent of fifteen infantry divisions, plus the 1st Armoured Division, had moved to Theatre, a remarkable achievement,[19] although there were deficiencies in equipment, training, coherency and logistics, flaws which industry and commanders sought to resolve as quickly as possible.[20]

11 TNA WO 197/112: Movement and Maintenance in the BEF.

12 For a concise resume of the British Army in the 1939-1940 period, see, Mark Nicholls and Linda Washington (eds.), *Against All Odds, The British Army of 1939-1940*, (London: National Army Museum, 1989).

13 For an analysis of the issues, see, Howard, *The Continental Commitment* and Shay, *British Rearmament in the Thirties: Politics and Profit.*

14 For an explanation of the rearmament process, see, Gibbs, BOH, *Grand Strategy*, Vol 1, *Rearmament Policy* and for the military aspects, the erudite Brian Bond, *British Military Policy between the Two World Wars* (Oxford: Clarendon Press, 1980).

15 The Movement Control organization was, with the exception, of 11 Regular officers, manned by the Supplementary Reserve. TNA CAB 120/247: British Expeditionary Force: Lord Gort's First Despatch, para 7.

16 WOOH, *Maintenance in the Field*, Vol I, p.30.

17 AG Statistical Return 3/944/40 dated 2 August 1940, quoted in F A E Crew FRS, BOH, *The Army Medical Services, Campaigns*, Vol I, p.112. Inclusive of this figure are 4,370 soldiers of the 1st (Canadian) Division who did not arrive in France until June 1940.

18 Major-General Charles H Miller CB CBE DSO psc, *History of the 13th/18th Royal Hussars (Queen Mary's Own), 1922-1947* (London: Chisman, Bradshaw Ltd, 1949), p.34.

19 The BEF was organized into three corps, supported by GHQ Troops and the Base. Prevented by the German invasion in May 1940, the intention, in June, was to form a fourth corps, with a concomitant restructuring to an Army Group, with two Armies, each of two corps. For a detailed exposure of the Order of Battle (ORBAT) and establishments, see, Philson, BEFORBAT, Vols 1-6.

20 Industrial production of military equipment, whilst not always in balance with Defence requirements, showed clear increases in the period September 1939 - June 1940. See, Central Statistical Office,

A Degree of Mobility

The planning and execution of the operation though, followed, for the most part, the logistic guidelines in the 1933 *Manual of Movement (War)*:[21] mobilization, formation of a field force, organization of a Base, dispatch of units to UK ports, sea voyage, dis-embarkation, move to a concentration area, provision of maintenance and subsequent movement, the importance of the last task to operational capability being firmly reinforced:

> The degree of mobility possessed by a force in the field is governed by the facilities for adequate maintenance of personnel and material, which cannot be effected without ample facilities for movement … A study of the resources available for movement in a theatre of war is therefore a primary consideration when a plan of campaign is being formulated and remains the first importance in every phase of subsequent operations.[22]

The BEF was to occupy a defence line of 55 miles along the Franco-Belgian frontier called the *Secteur Defensive De Lille*[23] from Maulde in the East, to Halluin in the North and thence South-West to Armentieres, later extended to Bailleul.[24] The shortest and fastest deployment route, using the least shipping, would have been to use the South East Ports (SEP), Dover, Folkestone and Ramsgate, for embarkation, to the French North Channel Ports (NCP) of Boulogne, Calais and Dunkerque, a distance of approximately 70 miles by road to the BEF Concentration Area, which would have been the most efficient use of logistic resources but required the conceptual acceptance that the BEF's Base would be in the UK. The perceived threat of air attack however,[25] an outcome which almost became obsession in the minds of some of the operational and logistic planners,[26] precluded this solution, although given the political imperatives to enter the line as quickly as possible to demonstrate solidarity with the French, which emerged whilst the BEF was deploying, the SEP-NCP solution would have been less disruptive and considerably more effective and efficient.

The concern about the effect of air attack upon the Base and the GLOC, especially during the deployment phase had been raised by the QMG to the Forces in September 1935, when he wrote to CIGS, 'I am quite convinced that two Air Defence Brigades are inadequate to protect ports of disembarkation, the re-mobilizing area and the concentration area in France',[27] although in 1939, only one brigade was assigned to this task. As it transpired, it was the Admiralty, reinforced by Merchant Marine logistics that influenced the War Office to change

BOH, *Statistical Digest of the War* (London: HMSO, 1951), p.139, Table 117, Munitions, Index of Ministry of Supply Munitions Production.

21 Army Council, *Manual of Movement (War)*, pp.5-9, Sects 4-12.
22 Ibid, p.1.
23 For a detailed analysis of the BEF's defence plans, see the comprehensive Thurlow, *Building the Gort Line*, pp.58-114.
24 Major L F Ellis, BOH, *The War in France and Flanders, 1939-1940*, (London: HMSO, 1953), Situation Map facing p.34.
25 TNA CAB 106/211: 'Notes on the 'Q' Organization of the BEF' dated 16 January 1942, para 3.
26 WOOH, *Ordnance Services, Officers of the Ordnance Directorate* (War Office, 1950), p.134.
27 TNA WO 32/4612: Future Army Organization – 1935, QMG Response dated 16 December 1936 to CIGS SECRET Paper, 'Future Reorganization of the British Army' dated 9 September 1935.

its stance and eventually nearly all the French ports from Saint Nazaire to Dunkerque were being utilized in some capacity.[28] Lieutenant-General Lindsell, QMG to the BEF recorded: 'It soon became apparent that the shipping of stores to the western ports of France threw a heavy strain upon shipping and the convoy escorts. For this reason the Admiralty pressed for an early transfer of the Base to Northern France'.[29] Whilst the War Office accepted the argument about transferring some port operations to the Channel, GHQ would not agree to transferring the Base *en-masse* because of the continuing concern about the air threat but it did create, after protracted discussions with the Host Nation, an Advanced Base located in the area between the Rivers Somme and Seine, in order to reduce the need for merchant shipping and railway rolling stock by making greater use of Cherbourg, Fecamp, Le Harve and Saint Malo.[30]

The outline plan drafted in 1938,[31] utilized ports in South Wales and South-Western England to load for sailings to French ports shown in the table below, with Cherbourg being the main Sea Port of Disembarkation (SPOD) for personnel and no BEF port being further East than Le Harve,[32] with the exception of Dieppe, which was used for medication evacuation to Newhaven.

Table 4.1
BEF – Initial Deployment Ports[33]

Brest	Cherbourg	Le Harve	Nantes	St Nazaire
AFV & WMT Ammunition Canned Petrol Stores Supplies	Personnel Unit WMT	Personnel Unit WMT	AFVs & WMT Canned Petrol Stores Supplies	AFVs & WMT Ammunition Stores

The initial deployment involved several shipping convoys departing over three days 9-11 September. The first convoy consisted of four personnel ships departing from Southampton for Cherbourg, then on 10 September, a mixed convoy of six personnel, two MT and one stores ships on the same route. On 11 September, the sea movement was in full swing, with 33 ships departing from Avonmouth, Barry, Newport and Southampton embarked with ammunition,

28 Captain S W Roskill DSC RN, BOH, *The War at Sea, 1939-1945*, Vol I, *The Defensive* (London: HMSO, 1954), p.64.
29 TNA WO 197/112: Movement and Maintenance in the BEF.
30 TNA WO 197/112: Movement and Maintenance in the BEF.
31 TNA CAB 106/218: Plan W4: Notes on the preparation of the plan for the First Contingent of the British Field Force.
32 One important series of moves through Le Harve was the deployment of the ten TA Engineer Field Companies and two Engineer Field Parks that comprised the two groups of X Force, tasked to assist in the construction of BEF defence works. WOOH, *Military Engineering (Field)*, Major-General R P Pakenham-Walsh CB MC (Comp.), (War Office, 1952), p.5. This important organization was not a solely military concept because the idea was driven by the Secretary of State for War, Leslie Hore-Belisha. See, Thurlow, *Building the Gort Line*, p.19.
33 Information from TNA CAB 106/218: Plan W4 and WOOH, *Movements*, Major J B Higham RE & E A Knighton MBE (Comp.) (War Office, 1955).

cased petrol, personnel, stores and vehicles to Brest, Nantes and Saint Nazaire.[34] Whilst the Base was established in a Northern location around Brest and a Southern one in the Nantes and Saint Nazaire area, the BEF would deploy along a 500 mile GLOC,[35] which for those personnel in Motor Transport (MT) parties disembarking at Cherbourg to collect vehicles from Brest was effectively 650 miles.[36] The plan envisaged personnel from Cherbourg travelling by rail to the BEF Assembly Area in the areas of Le Mans-Laval to rendezvous with the WMT road convoys and the tracked vehicles on rail from Brest before moving by road[37] and rail[38] to the Concentration Area near the Franco-Belgian border. A reconnaissance of the proposed Base and Assembly areas was completed in September 1938 by a British Military Mission in conjunction with the French authorities but because of security concerns its members did not study the detail in sufficient depth, nor were any of the officers who conducted it posted to the QMG's staff in GHQ BEF, flaws, which were exposed when the deployment commenced.[39] This frustration was cogently expressed by the Deputy Assistant Quartermaster-General (DAQMG) of War Office General Staff (Plans):[40] 'We had no accurate information about the conditions in France, the port facilities and the railways……A great deal of information was in fact available but none of it had been obtained by an officer trained in administrative matters, and it was all too vague to be of any use'.[41] This comment is of interest because according to the War Office history of Movements, QMG Staff officers were attached to the GS Plans Branch and conducted several visits to France under its auspices to conduct discussions with the *Quatrieme Bureau* of the *Ministere de la Guerre*, inspect ports and identify sites for potential BEF logistic facilities.[42] Perhaps the fixation in the War Office with security,[43] negated this

34 For vessel details, see Winser, *BEF Ships*, p.7.
35 Map 4: BEF - Transportation and Rail Line of Communication.
36 MT parties travelled by rail from Cherbourg to Brest, a distance of 150 miles.
37 Map 5: BEF - Road Routes from Ports to Assembly Area.
38 Troops trains for the BEF were planned to lift 800 - 2000 soldiers plus stores and baggage, with *halte-repas en-route* for light refreshments. WOOH, *Transportation*, Brigadier R Micklem CMG CBE (War Office, 1950), p.27. Whilst Plan W4 notes that trains were granted rail paths, the feeding of the troops was for some reason, not embedded in the Maintenance Project Plan (MPP). WOOH, *Supplies and Transport*, Vol I, p.109.
39 TNA CAB 106/211: 'Notes on the 'Q' Organization of the BEF' dated 16 January 1942, para 2.
40 War Office GS (Plans), formed in June 1938, consisted of two majors, one a GSO 2 and the other a DAQMG headed by a Royal Artillery Lieutenant-Colonel, L A Hawes. GS (Plans) was responsible for co-ordinating all Army contingency planning, including that for France, the Middle East, India and the Far East, which was a very tall order for such a small Branch, although it appears that officers from the QMG Branch were seconded to support the planning. See, Major-General L A Hawes CBE DSO MC, 'The Story of the "W" Plan, The Move of Our Forces to France in 1939', *The Army Quarterly*, July 1971, pp.445-456.
41 Ibid, p.446.
42 WOOH, *Movements*, pp.26-27.
43 As a security measure, nearly all the documents relating to Plan W4 identify the ports using a code number but the document listing them is not in the relevant TNA file, WO 197/1: Movement Control Instruction Plan W4. Other papers reveal the ports but not the codes. Fortunately, a postal distribution diagram dated 26 September 1939 shows both, although interestingly, despite this very sensitive information, it was not classified. The codes were: Brest (052), Cherbourg (046), Nantes (042) and Saint Nazaire (041). Dieppe, Le Harve and Marseilles are not coded in the document; Dieppe was the medical evacuation port, whilst Le Harve and Marseilles were not included in Plan W4. Key

work to the point where senior logistic commanders, nor their Staffs, were permitted access to the broader plan, which made it impossible for the specialist experts to offer professional assessments of the logistic implications of the General Staff's directives and instructions, the issues only becoming clearly apparent to them as the deployment started. At the very least, coherent staffing communication appears to have evaporated and during the initial movement to France, these dysfunctional arrangements certainly generated significant disruption to the flow of consignments beyond the ports, with Movement Control,[44] Ordnance Services and the Army Postal Service[45] initially in the dark as to the locations and future dispositions of units. Oddly, the post-campaign notes from QMG BEF make no mention of security being an issue in this respect,[46] although the Lessons Identified document from GHQ Transportation Services lucidly articulates it as a feature, whilst it is evident from some of the Base installation war diaries that it was more than a nagging irritation until it was resolved, creating consequential interruption to outputs and considerable additional corrective work.[47] To compound this mistake, the failure to ensure a professionally qualified Works Services officer from the Corps of Royal Engineers was embedded in the pre-war reconnaissance team resulted in serious errors of judgement in site selection, resource requirements and project timeline analysis.[48]

Plan W4

The 1939 Plan W4 prepared by the War Office GS (Plans) Branch[49] intended that the First Contingent of the BEF should be deployed in three phases, shown in the table:

GLOC sites were also listed: Rennes (052), Le Mans (053) and Amiens (113). TNA WO 167/1379: GHQ BEF Assistant Director Postal Services (ADAPS), diagram dated 26 September 1939, Appx 30.

44 Whilst the *Manual of Movement (War)* observed that 'security is usually of paramount importance, especially in concentrations and strategic moves', its overzealous application during the deployment of the BEF caused more problems than it solved. An additional complication was that five letter codes for formations, railheads and depots were not permitted to prevent confusion with code names for operations. See, Army Council, *Manual of Movement (War)*, p.39, Sect 35 and p.40, Sect 35.

45 TNA WO 167/1379: GHQ BEF, ADAPS SS/39 dated 26 September 1939.'

46 TNA CAB 106/211: 'Notes on the 'Q' Organization of the BEF dated 16 January 1942.

47 TNA WO 167/51: GHQ Transportation Services, DG (Tn) dated 11 October 1939.

48 WOOH, *Works Services and Engineer Stores*, Major-General A G B Buchanan MICE (War Office, 1953), p.103. The reference highlights that a Works Services officer had been included but was removed from the reconnaissance party in order to reduce the numbers on the basis that the General Staff and Transportation representatives could conduct the work and that the French had agreed to provide all the accommodation required. Neither of these promises matured.

49 See, Hawes, 'The Story of the "W" Plan', pp.445-456.

Table 4.2
BEF First Contingent Deployment

Phase	Grouping	Remarks
I	Advance Parties	
	Base and GLOC units	
	Anti-Aircraft units	
	Air Component[50]	Fighter Wing (Hurricanes)
	AASF – 1st Echelon[51]	Bomber Command
II	GHQ BEF	
	I Corps	1st & 2nd Divisions plus Corps Troops
	RAF Component	Main Body
	AASF – 2nd Echelon	1st Flight
III	II Corps	3rd & 4th Divisions plus Corps Troops
	RAF Component	Balance
	AASF – 2nd Echelon	2nd Flight

The RAF Component[52] was under command of GHQ and consisted of two bomber squadrons, four Hurricane fighter squadrons commanded by 60 Wing and six army co-operation squadrons. The AASF[53] was the forward based element of Bomber Command comprising ten light bomber squadrons in five wings, equipped with the Fairey Battle[54] with a mission, 'to assist the FRENCH in resisting a German advance into France, Belgium and Luxembourg'.[55] Whilst GHQ did not control the AASF, the Army was responsible for delivering significant transportation and infrastructure support for it, thereby exposing the paucity of pre-war financing, programming and planning in this arena because the Army was not resourced to support the outputs. To

50 Upon the formation of HQ British Air Forces France (BAFF) in January 1940, the Air Component BEF was renamed Royal Air Force Component British Expeditionary Force (RAFCBEF).

51 Movement plans for the 1st Echelon are contained in TNA AIR 14/444.

52 Army Council, *The Employment of Air Forces with the Army in the Field* (War Office, 1938) refers to the 'Air' Component. The Air Staff but however, were not content to use the term 'air' in the title as it might offer the impression the Army had a 'green' air arm and it was substituted by the nomenclature 'RAF'.

53 For details of the deployment and operations, of the RAF Component and the AASF, see, Victor F Bingham, *Blitzed: The Battle of France, May-June 1940* (New Malden: Air Research Publications, 1990), pp.15-26.

54 The contemporary observations relating to the combat capability of the Fairey Battle are exposed in TNA AIR 35/115: Operational Roles of Aircraft. For a recent analysis, see Greg Baughen, *The Fairey Battle, A Reassessment of its RAF Career* (Stroud: Fonthill, 2017).

55 TNA AIR 35/244: AASF Operation Instruction No 7, 'Employment of AASF Bomber Units and Units of Bomber Command, which may be attached to AASF in event of an attempted land invasion by Germany' dated 21 March 1940. Three types of operation were listed in the instruction: support to land operations, dis-organization of the German Line of Communication West of the Rhine and neutralization of enemy air capability by attacking bases and airfields.

achieve a solution, the GHQ BEF utilized a combination of Host Nation resources reinforced by diverted military logistic assets, although the demand always lagged behind availability.[56] Another issue that the Host Nation assisted the BEF to overcome during the initial deployment was the provision of rationing by the extensive use of local purchase of food through the French Army *Intendance* Service. In addition, as a contingency to mitigate the interruption of movement schedules, the War Office issued three days of emergency rations to the soldiers, which created a perhaps not entirely unforeseen consequence. As the official report noted, 'it was found that even well-disciplined troops find it difficult to eke out their rations over three days and cases came to light of men consuming the bulk of their rations the first day and/or giving food away to FRENCH civilians. A lesson from this is that it is important for Commanders to ensure that the men do not eat or give away their rations without the orders of their officers.' [57]

The War Office plan to use the French Western Ports only came to fruition as a result of a development in the mid-1930s of the leisure industry because the key rail line Rennes to Nantes and Saint Nazaire via Masserae and Redon had been single, only being doubled in order to promote greater holiday traffic to the Brittany coastal resorts. Without this additional rail capacity, the proposed GLOC would have been incapable of delivering the required levels of traffic to support either the deployment or the consequent sustainment. As it transpired, the GLOC struggled from the start of the operation to meet the planned outputs, a problem created by restricted access to port capacity at Nantes and Saint Nazaire. Placing the SPODs so far to the West to mitigate the effects of the assessed air threat also created two transportation constraints. The first was the additional distance from the Sea Ports of Embarkation (SPOE) in the UK, which increased the shipping loop times, thereby generating a need for more ships, whilst also creating complexities in convoy routing and protection. The second was a GLOC nearly 500 miles in length, which meant that the BEF had to place more reliance on rail at 3rd Line from the Base to the corps and divisional areas. The British base marshalling yard for both areas was at Rennes, which is around 140 miles from Brest and 70 miles from St Nazaire. From the rail Centre of Gravity at Rennes, the GLOC ran 220 miles through Alencon and Rouen to the BEF Rail Regulating Station at Abancourt and thence another 50 miles to the various corps railheads in the Arras area.[58] Given that in 1940, railways were vulnerable to attack from the air, this arguably laid the BEF open to the very danger than the planners had hoped to avoid by placing the Main Base far to the West, although in the event the French railway system was much more resilient than had been expected.

Allied Forces had used some of the selected sites during the Great War but many buildings were by 1939 unavailable and the deterioration or removal of railway track decreased their operational value.[59] The proposed site for the Engineer Base Depot at Nantes for example had been an American hospital in 1918 but now consisted of a few concrete roads and several dilapidated huts with the nearest railway 0.75 miles distant, a problem compounded by the impracticality of constructing effective rail facilities in the location.[60] Such failures were

56 See, AMOH, Air Publication 3397 (CONFIDENTIAL downgraded UNCLASSIFIED, March 1966), *Maintenance*, CD 1131 (Air Ministry, 1954), pp.54-70.
57 TNA CAB 106/211: 'Notes on the 'Q' Organization of the BEF' dated 16 January 1942, para 3.
58 For details of these rail facilities, see, Aves, *Supporting the British Expeditionary Force*.
59 TNA CAB 106/211: 'Notes on the 'Q' Organization of the BEF' dated 16 January 1942, para 5d.
60 WOOH, *Works Services and Engineer Stores*, p.103.

inevitably reflected in the effectiveness of the Maintenance Project Plan (MPP)[61] and the Key Plans (KP).[62] Four issues in particular, were to cause frustration to the logisticians. The first was effectively a strategic one because whilst the aerial assault did not materialize in the timeframe they had expected, the mitigation of the risk, particularly through distance and dispersion, created as many problems as it solved because the consequential length and fragmentation of the GLOC, compounded by fragile communications, generated the need for assets to be deployed to operate the increasing number of logistic nodes, whilst an insufficiency of suitably qualified and experienced personnel to execute the tasks exacerbated the problem.

The second was at an operational level, which involved a fundamental mis-appreciation of the importance of appropriate covered storage with supporting transportation access for the Base Supply and Ordnance depots. Thirdly, were two tactical level issues. The landing of troops, ahead of supplies, was an issue resolved through the good services of the French Army *Intendant-General* department at Brest and Cherbourg, which placed at the BEF's disposal, sufficient reserves to cover the shortfall as well as assisting in the purchase of local produce including fresh vegetables, potatoes, fresh milk, eggs, coal and wood.[63] The separation of drivers from vehicles, which in the view of many logisticians a fundamental mistake, was compounded by a miscomprehension of the practical effects of French mobilization upon the railway timetable from Cherbourg to Brest, which was planned to take seven hours to cover 150 miles but sometimes took 30, most of which was not a relaxing event. 2 Docks Group summarized the experience of many soldiers, the war diary recording that its advance party arrived at Brest 'after passing a grim 26 hours on the train'.[64]

With Untiring Energy

Logistics were fundamental to the mobilization of units in the UK, with regimental quartermasters at the centre of activity, the QM of the 13th/18th Royal Hussars being accorded especial praise: 'August was a time of feverish activity for the Regiment. Stores and equipment came pouring in and work fell particularly hard on Lieutenant-Colonel and Quartermaster A G Ellery[65] and his team, who worked with untiring energy'. The 15th/19th Royal Hussars dispatched 21 officers' chargers to the Remount Depot at Melton Mowbray but still retained its full complement of horsed cavalry equipment on charge a year after it had been mechanized.[66]

61 TNA WO 197/2: First Maintenance Project: Reception of Forces in France and system of maintenance in the initial stages.
62 The KPs were contained in appendices to the main document. The 1st KP showed the proposed allotment of the installations and depots of the Base on a large-scale map. The 2nd KP defined the requirement by logistic Service, whilst the 3rd KP focused upon permanent detailed arrangements for the logistic lay-down. Army Council, *Manual of Movement (War)*, pp.57-58, Sect 55.
63 WOOH, *Supplies and Transport*, Vol I, p.105.
64 The 2 Docks Group RE, WD, entry 11 September 1939.
65 Lieutenant-Colonel Ellery was 56 which precluded him from serving in an active theatre of operations overseas and he handed over to a newly commissioned QM, ex-RSM Burder, the only member of the regiment who had embarked with the 13th Hussars in India for service in France in 1914. Miller, *History of the 13th/18th Royal Hussars*, p.33.
66 Major G Courage DSO, *The History of the 15/19 The King's Royal Hussars, 1939-1945* (Aldershot: Gale & Polden, 1949), p.4.

As Reservists[67] and Militiamen arrived in barracks, additional accommodation and rations were required, whilst mobilization stores were inspected for quantity and performance. 1st Line ammunition, except smoke rounds for mortars and artillery, was drawn upon orders for embarkation.[68]

An important task was the receipt of military vehicles[69] and WMT impressed from the commercial sector, sometimes the day before embarkation, caused much additional work, especially as units were tasked with painting ex-commercial vehicles khaki-green.[70] A vital issue was the management of the AFG 1098 equipment for units forming upon mobilization, many of which were 'War Establishment only' Base organizations, yet essential to the sustainment of the deployed BEF. 76 Company RASC, assigned as No 1 Works MT Company, was informed in mid-October that it was unlikely that all of its mobilization stores would be issued before its deployment to France[71] and such arrangements meant that instead of AFG 1098 stores being received and inspected by the unit in the UK, they were dispatched to the relevant overseas port care of the Docks Directorate, which of course did not allow for ships being diverted to an alternative destination, or the fact that such consignments had to be held in store at the port, an installation military doctrine assigned as a transit facility and not a depot.[72] To compound this failure there were no allocated resources to manage the task, creating unnecessary congestion and confusion. The result was chaos, with some equipment disappearing from the accounting regime and thus resulting in a full re-issue, whilst other units received items that added little to their operational capability, one example being the delivery of several dental chairs to a Royal Artillery regiment.[73]

In between the many military activities, a key logistic task was to store the regimental silver. 2nd Essex dispatched its precious history enshrined in metal to the local Lloyds Bank for safekeeping escorted by six soldiers with fixed bayonets. The next day the regimental Second-in-Command was horrified to see the boxes being transferred to other storage by an elderly driver

67 The 15th/19th Royal Hussars received over 600 reservists in the first 10 days of September 1939, but few of them had been trained as mechanized cavalry and they were rather bizarrely equipped as horsed cavalry, probably because this was the only clothing available before dispatch to France to serve in Labour or Docks companies. Ibid, p.4.

68 TNA CAB 106/235: BEF Ammunition Supply (Gibson Report), p.1.

69 The 15th /19th Royal Hussars deploying the vehicle party to Avonmouth on 29 September 1939, received, during the evening before, its last consignment of vehicles: four light tanks, six lorries and some motorcycles. Courage, *The History of the 15/19 The King's Royal Hussars*, p.5.

70 The 13th/18th Hussars received all manner of WMT, including bakers' vans and grocers' lorries painted green, red and blue. Miller, *History of the 13th/18th Royal Hussars*, p.34.

71 TNA WO 167/1158: 1 Works Transport Company (76 Company RASC), WD, 15 October 1939.

72 Army Council, *Manual of Movement (War)*, p.59, Sect 56.

73 WOOH, *Maintenance in the Field*, Vol I, p.26.

in a Carter Paterson[74] van.[75] Being displaced within or from their barracks to accommodate other activities disrupted some units' mobilization. The 15th/19th Royal Hussars had 1,000 Supplementary Reservists from 1 Docks Group RE arrive at the Cavalry Barracks in York and thus decamped into tents established on the lawns,[76] whilst 2nd Essex vacated Warley Barracks at Brentwood to enable the expansion of the regimental depot, a task which was in addition to a deployment to assist Anti-Aircraft (AA) Command.[77] 2nd Northumberland Fusiliers had completed mobilization at Connaught Barracks Dover by 10 September, transferring to tented accommodation at Dibgate Camp near Folkestone[78] until the unit departed for Southampton on 1 October,[79] whilst on 7 September, 2nd East Yorkshires entrained at Plymouth for Bridport in Dorset for three weeks training with 3rd Division.[80] All these battalion and regimental tasks and activities, which were spread across the whole of the United Kingdom, required the appropriate level of logistic support to sustain them and is a forgotten component of the deployment to France.

Movement to the two main Sea Ports of Embarkation (SPOE) at Avonmouth for vehicles and Southampton for personnel from unit lines was by rail and road, so the length of the journey greatly depended upon the location of the unit. Most regimental histories record little of the mobilization period and others even less in relation to movement in the UK. A regimental history of the 2nd Royal Fusiliers[81] succinctly summarized, without comment, the battalion's travels from their peace station in Dover to the SPOEs, an experience, which is typical of many units but regrettably does not expose the planning and industry required to enable the battalion to undertake its moves:

> Our next move, on 25th September, was to Talavera Barracks, Aldershot, where we remained until 5th October, and where officers and men were equipped with further mobilization equipment and other requirements prior to our embarkation for France. The Mechanical Transport and Bren Carriers under the command of Lieutenant L V

74 The road haulage company of Carter Paterson was founded in 1860 and formed into a private company, Carter, Paterson & Co Ltd, in 1887, expanding its business until the Big Four railway companies purchased control of it in equal shares in the mid-1930s enabling Carter Paterson to operate a countrywide service from 1936. By 1946, Carter Paterson was operating a fleet of over 1,000 motor vans and delivering 34 million parcels a year. Ownership passed upon railway nationalisation to the British Transport Commission and Carter Paterson was subsequently absorbed into British Road Services. Whitaker, *Whitaker's Almanack* (London: J. Whitaker & Sons, Ltd, 1944).

75 Colonel T A Martin MBE, *The Essex Regiment, 1929-1950* (Brentwood: The Essex Regiment Association, 1952), p.131. The battalion was perhaps fortunate that the van had not been impressed for service with the BEF, but all the silver was returned in good order after the end of the war.

76 Courage, *The History of the 15/19 The King's Royal Hussars*, pp.3-4.

77 Martin, *The Essex Regiment*, p.130.

78 Dibgate Camp, 2 miles NW of Folkestone, is retained by the UK MOD as a training area. The concrete bases for the canvas marques are *in situ*.

79 Brigadier C N Barclay CBE DSO, *The History of the Northumberland Fusiliers in the Second World War* (London: William Clowes, 1952), p.27.

80 Lieutenant-Colonel P R Nightingale OBE, *The East Yorkshire Regiment (Duke of York's Own) in the War, 1939-45* (York & London: William Sessions Ltd, 1952), p.7.

81 12th Infantry Brigade, 4th Division, II Corps: BOH, *The War in France and Flanders*, p.362.

> Fane-Gladwin embarked at Bristol[82] on 27th September, and the Battalion embarked at Southampton on 5th October.[83]

WMT usually travelled by road and tracked vehicles whether Armoured Fighting Vehicle (AFV) or engineer plant, moved by rail.[84] One flaw in this plan was that the unit MT parties were responsible for assisting in the loading of the equipment to the ship but in some cases delays to the arrival of the ship meant they had departed to meet the schedule of unit personnel ship, leaving other parties to undertake the task.[85] Other issues included the failure to have access to all the ships' plans resulting in vehicles being 'shut-out' because there was insufficient space for the assigned loads, derricks not being rigged for embarkation thus creating delays[86] and net slings being to narrow for the vehicles. In addition, many of the ships' crews were inexperienced in vehicle slinging which created more friction, but the significant time burglar was handling the impressed commercial cargo vehicles. Some lorries were too long to be lowered into the hold and were dispatched to Dover for movement by train ferry, whilst others had cabs that were too high and these had to be removed, often resulting in a day's delay in the ship's departure.[87]

Some units were fortunate in travelling with their vehicles in the same shipping convoy from Avonmouth or Southampton, thereby retaining cohesion, but this was the exception rather than the rule.[88] Successful vehicle loading in accordance with the schedule did not always guarantee timely arrival in France. The SS *City of Florence* embarked 300 vehicles at Newport and was proceeding to Barry Roads to meet the convoy when a shore battery, believing her to be an enemy vessel, placed an artillery round through the bow one foot above the waterline, resulting in several days delay whilst the cargo was transferred to another ship.[89] Other failures were not so rapidly resolved. The SS *Nailsea Lass*[90] having loaded 7,000 tons of transportation stores, mostly rails and bridging *materiel*, at Barry, suffered a catastrophic failure of her boiler plates after the furnaces were lit under empty boilers,[91] entailing a four week delay in the delivery of the cargo to France, which had to be transferred to the SS *Llanarth*.[92] The SS *Marwarri* sailing

82 This was Avonmouth, to the North-West of Bristol.

83 na, *A Short History of the 2nd Battalion Royal Fusiliers (City of London Regiment) during the First Year of the War* (Aldershot: Gale & Polden, 1941), p.5.

84 Army Council, *Manual of Movement (War)*, p.67, Sect 63.

85 WOOH, *Movements*, p.176.

86 Planning procedures directed that ships' derricks should be used to embark cargo to ensure that whatever was loaded in a UK port could be off-loaded at the port of disembarkation. Ibid, p.138.

87 Ibid, p.138.

88 An artillery officer described the unnerving experience of the soldiers being divorced from its equipment: 'An artillery regiment separated from its guns is like a fond mother parted from her children. She isn't happy till she gets them back'. Gun Buster, *Return via Dunkirk* (London: Hodder & Stoughton, 1940), p.13. Gun Buster was the pseudonym of Captain Richard Austin.

89 Ibid, p.141.

90 The SS *Nailsea Lass* was sunk by a torpedo from U-48 on 24 February 1941, 60 nm SW of Fastnet sailing with a cargo of 1,301 tons of charcoal, 1,031 tons of pig iron and 300 tons of iron ore; the crew of 44 was saved. Admiralty, *British Merchant Vessels Lost or Damaged by Enemy Action during the Second World War* (London: HMSO, 1957), p.17.

91 WOOH, *Movements*, p.141.

92 The *SS Llanarth*, loaded with 7,980 tons of flour from Melbourne to Leith and Aberdeen, was sunk on 27 June 1940 by a torpedo from U-30; the crew of 35 was saved. Admiralty, *British Merchant Vessels Lost or Damaged by Enemy Action*, p.7.

with a cargo of two batteries of AA guns and supporting specialist equipment, was sunk in shallow water by a magnetic mine laid by U-32, 3.5 nautical miles from the Scarweather Light Vessel in Swansea Bay on 5 October 1939.[93] Whilst the local authorities pondered upon the best salvage solution, the RE Movement Control officer engaged a Trinity House cutter and a diver to conduct the urgent recovery of the important range predictors and height finders so the equipment could be refurbished at Woolwich.[94]

The railways in the UK ran hundreds of ammunition, freight, vehicle and passenger trains to support the mobilization of the Armed Services and the deployment of the BEF and AASF to France.[95] Whilst not on the scale of 1914,[96] 261 trains were scheduled to arrive at the Southern Railway's Docks at Southampton between 9 September and 5 October 1939, whilst 34 special trains were run in the period 12-19 September bringing 14,000 soldiers to Aldershot Command.[97] Despite this military railway activity most units considered the mundane process of a railway journey unworthy of comment but some regimental scribes took more interest. 1st Berkshires' record of the battalion's departure from Farnborough North Station was more poetic than martial noting that:

> On the surface it has the appearance of a casual military move made for a prosaic purpose; beneath, the organization ran smoothly, without fuss or bother of any sort, just as it had been planned. The troops arrived and entrained; the whistle blew; officers from the Depot waved from the platform; the jolting on the points of the rail ceased; and the battalion settled down to its journey'.[98]

2nd Essex noted the circuitous journey from Brentwood and Warley Station, with the train running North to Cambridge, then travelling South-West through Bedford, Bletchley and Bicester before heading South to Reading and then Southampton.[99] 2nd Cameronians were fortunate to travel by a more direct route from Richmond in Yorkshire but were delayed for several hours when the train they were in was struck in the rear between Nottingham and Leicester on the London & North Eastern Railway Great Central Line by a locomotive hauling another troop train at around 0600 on 11 September.[100] Fortunately, the collision and the

93 WOOH, *Movements*, p.142, records this ship as the SS *Marwari*. She was salvaged and survived the war. Admiralty, *British Merchant Vessels Lost or Damaged by Enemy Action*, p.63.
94 The SS *City of Florence* survived the war.
95 Rail movement to the ports was controlled by the staff of Directorate of Movements at the War Office. See, WOOH, *Movements*, Appx 2 to Chp 2 and Army Council, *Manual of Movement (War)*, p.67, Sect 62.
96 In 1914, there were 711 special trains accepted into Southampton Docks involving 1,422 train movements. TNA WO 106/49B/4 contains a neatly scribed handwritten SECRET Staff Table for Southampton Port export arrivals, with rail traffic in blue and listing: Train Number, Time of Arrival, Departing Station, Army Division allocation, Unit, Passengers, Vehicles, Artillery pieces, Stores Tonnage and Telegraph Codes.
97 O S Nock, *Britain's Railways at War, 1939-1945* (London: Ian Allan, 1971), p.51.
98 Brigadier Gordon Blight, *The History of the Berkshire Regiment, 1920-1947* (London & New York: Staples Press, 1953), p.179.
99 Martin, *The Essex Regiment*, p.131; 16 September 1939.
100 The Ministry of Transport accident records are silent on the circumstances of this incident, which may have been the result of a mis-judged shunting move or the relatively fortunate outcome of a much more

damage were both minor and the train arrived in Southampton 16½ hours after it left Richmond but with the advantage that the battalion detrained in swift order, embarking on the SS *City of Paris* at 1830, two hours after arrival.[101]

One of the key limitations to the deployment plan was separating the MT parties from the vehicle ships because there was usually insufficient suitable accommodation on the available vessels. Whilst 'bedding down on the decks' was an acceptable solution on the short sea crossing from the South East Ports to Boulogne, Calais and Dunkerque, the War Office decided that as ships in convoy from the Western Ports might be at sea for several days, the troops should, for the most part, not accompany the vehicles, a decision which undoubtedly caused delays in executing Plan W4 because the MT parties had a 30 hour rail journey to Brest and then a 250 mile plus drive to the Assembly Area centred on Le Mans to meet the unit main body groups travelling from Cherbourg by rail.[102] Indeed, the BEF QMG Staff noted that the first problem that had to be overcome in delivering the deployment of the BEF in France was that of 'marrying the driver who landed in Cherbourg with the vehicle that was landed at Brest'.[103] Some units were fortunate in this respect. As examples, the 13th/18th Royal Hussars sailed complete from Southampton to Brest, the 15th/19th Royal Hussars from Avonmouth to Saint Nazaire, the 3rd Medium Artillery Regiment from Avonmouth to Brest and 208 Field Company RE from Southampton to Cherbourg. 2nd Cameronians were also relieved not to be split but rather less enthused as a Line of Communication battalion to detach B Company for dock security and labouring duties at Cherbourg and A and C Companies for the same at Brest.[104]

Lost at Brest

The docks at Brest, Nantes and Saint Nazaire were a hive of activity, although not all of it was constructive. Pilfering of stocks on the dockside and of equipment from vehicles was rife, a problem not confined to France. The *Manual of Movement* summarized the challenge in securing military equipment in a commercial environment: 'The safe custody of consignments in transit is the responsibility of the technical transport agency, but is often difficult to effect without considerable assistance from other authorities'.[105] Whilst collecting 2nd Lincolns' vehicles from the dockside at Brest, officers and drivers discovered that all the locked car and van boots had been rifled.[106] The MT party of 1st Berkshires was 'shocked and angered' by the open

serious failure of a signal passed at danger. In October 1939 there were six accidents on the National Rail Network that were of sufficient severity to require notification, although only the two involving fatalities at Bletchley and Hindley have a published report.

101 Brigadier C N Barclay CBE DSO, *The History of the Cameronians (Scottish Rifles)*, Vol III (London: Sifton Praed, nd but 1947), p.30.

102 This was raised by Director-General Transportation (DGT) BEF (Brigadier D J McMullen) in a deployment After Action Review, in which this was a noted as a 'lesson identified', although the document specifically noted that it related to short sea voyages, which presumably covered sailings from Southampton to Cherbourg and Le Harve but not the Western British and French ports. TNA WO 167/51: GHQ Services, Transportation, DG (Tn) dated 11 October 1939, 'Lessons'.

103 TNA CAB 106/211: 'Notes on the 'Q' Organization of the BEF' dated 16 January 1942, para 3.

104 Barclay, *The History of the Cameronians*, Vol III, p.30.

105 Army Council, *Manual of Movement (War)*, p.42, Sect 40.

106 Hamilton, p.300.

theft occurring at Avonmouth,[107] whilst 208 Field Company RE discovered at Cherbourg that essential stores had been removed from vehicles.[108] The staff car of Lieutenant-General Barker, Commander I Corps was another target with the dashboard clock and vehicle tools stolen[109] and even GHQ was not immune with stationery boxes from Ordnance Services disappearing *en-route* to France.[110] The historian of 3rd Medium Regiment RA observed that none of the thefts were surprising, given that at the time 'it was so easy to walk into the docks and drive off in a very nice Ford V8 Saloon Staff car, which obviously could not have belonged to anybody'.[111] The Regiment 'lost' a water trailer from the dockside at Brest but this may have been towed away in error by another unit.[112]

Safety was a key dockside issue. A trooper from the 15th /19th Royal Hussars fell off the quay at Saint Nazaire having, remarkably, suffered the same misfortune at Avonmouth when he spent 20 minutes in the water.[113] 3rd Medium Artillery Regiment suffered the loss of an 8 cwt vehicle on the dock through fire,[114] which led, inevitably, to 2/11th Battery attempting to seek the write-off of a quantity of stores considerably in excess of the load capacity of the truck, whilst the response of unit personnel accused of having been negligent in the accounting of *materiel* sought to claim it was 'Lost at Brest'.[115] One key issue was the slow unloading rate for the stores ships, which averaged only 450-500 tons per ship daily,[116] caused by insufficient military and civilian skilled stevedore labour, an issue which attenuated shipping turn-round schedules. Stores ships took 2-5 days to unload with a turn-round of 4-7 days, not inclusive of the requirement to form the departing convoy.[117] The *Manual of Movement* was clear about the importance of maintaining momentum in this arena: 'The quantity of stores that can be imported into the theatre of war is limited by the capacity of the ports and the facilities for the clearance from these ports. Any attempt to import a greater quantity will result in congestion at the docks and consequent slowing down of the whole process of maintenance.[118] The BEF was in a hurry to in-load its *materiel* but a combination of circumstances, not least a shortage of skilled labour, the challenges of sorting the mixed cargoes from the ships on the dockside[119] and a shortage of suitable rail wagons for the loads, thwarted the plan.[120] The Base ports of Nantes and Saint Nazaire were expected to handle 3,000 tons per week each but output was half this

107 Blight, *The History of the Berkshire Regiment*, p.175.
108 TNA WO 167/51: GHQ Services, Transportation, DG Tn dated 11 October 1939, 'Lessons'.
109 Morling, *Sussex Sappers*, p.58.
110 WOOH, *Ordnance Services*, Officers of the Ordnance Directorate (War Office, 1950), p.135.
111 na, *The History of the 3rd Medium Artillery Regiment Royal Artillery, 1939-1945* (Liverpool & London: The Northern Publishing Company, nd but 1945), p.27.
112 Ibid, p.27.
113 Courage, *The History of the 15/19 The King's Royal Hussars*, p.5.
114 The regimental history is silent as to the cause, which could have been the result of a soldier smoking, but equally likely was leaking petrol vaporizing on a hot engine manifold. na, *The History of the 3rd Medium Artillery Regiment*, p.26.
115 Ibid, p.26.
116 TNA WO 167/51: GHQ Services, Transportation, DG (Tn) dated 11 October 1939, 'Lessons'.
117 TNA CAB 106/211: 'Notes on the 'Q' Organization of the BEF' dated 16 January 1942, para 4b.
118 Army Council, *Manual of Movement (War)*, p.79, Sect 71.
119 TNA WO 167/51: GHQ, Transportation, DG (Tn) dated 11 October 1939, 'Lessons'.
120 TNA WO 167/51: GHQ, Transportation, DG (Tn), R/47 dated 11 October 1939, 'Supply of suitable Open Wagons'.

figure, which immediately unbalanced the War Office intention to import 8,000 tons weekly in order to meet daily requirements and build the planned reserves.

At Brest the reduced imports were the product of a number of factors including poorly stowed mixed cargoes, unmarked consignments, incomplete documentation, insufficient rail wagons, labour shortages and unrest,[121] strong Easterly winds and tidal flooding of some of the berths[122] and to complete a rather negative report there was a 'severe epidemic of sore throats and colds' amongst the personnel of 2 Docks Group.[123] One irritating issue was the 'long *dejeuner*' taken by the French locomotive crews operating the dock shunters, but this was overcome when the operators agreed, in a fine gesture of co-operation and goodwill, to allow the Docks Group military railwaymen to take over the task whilst they were enjoying lunch.[124] The initial arrival of the key combat supplies of ammunition and fuel were also delayed. The first two ammunition ships loading at Newport were late arriving, with the second having to be replaced.[125] This outcome was exacerbated by the late arrival of the second pair of ammunition ships, although fortunately the munitions trains with the cargo, were stabled, at some risk, in Newport Docks and were available in short order.

50 percent of the initial sailings of canned petrol had to be curtailed because of leaking cans, which had a ripple effect in France in building the planned fuel reserve to schedule.[126] Initially, the flow of petrol was so slow that effectively the BEF was being refuelled from UK daily with no reserve to build a working margin on the GLOC. By M+32,[127] the BEF was still 4,000 tons short of its planned allocation, which meant the BEF was consuming each day what was being imported, a particularly fragile arrangement for an Army commencing a 500 mile drive by road to its Concentration Area. An often-forgotten element of petrol consumption in the BEF was the fuel required for cooking,[128] which was based upon 1.5 gallons per month per man,[129] so with the First Contingent deployed, a remarkable 7,890 gallons per day were assigned for this purpose. Another logistic wrinkle to resolve was the provision of petrol for BEF vehicles hired in France; that it was quickly arranged with the Host Nation was no doubt a relief to the GHQ Supply Directorate officer tasked with a delivering a solution.[130]

121 TNA WO 167/876: 2 Docks Group RE, WD, 5 October 1939 notes, 'Labour trouble all day'.
122 According to the 2 Docks Group RE WD, this was caused by very high equinoctial spring tides. See TNA WO 167/876: 2 Docks Group RE, WD, entry 13 October 1939.
123 TNA WO 167/876: 2 Docks Group RE, WD, 3 October 1939. There was also a minor outbreak of what the war diary described as 'dysentery' but may have been an undiagnosed gastric illness. Poor hygiene was an uncommon problem during the early part of the deployment, especially in Base units because of weak drills and poor indquate living conditions.
124 TNA WO 167/51: GHQ, Transportation, DG (Tn) dated 11 October 1939, 'Lessons'.
125 WOOH, *Movements*, p.176.
126 Ibid.
127 On 8 October 1939.
128 In 1939, the Army had three types of field portable cookers, of which the Cooker, Portable, No 1, is probably the best known and an equipment that remained in service until the late 1980s. Each cook-set came with ancillaries and the No 1 Set was especially well served in this respect. See, Army Council Instructions, *Vocabulary of Army Ordnance Stores*, Section J2, *Portable Cookers* (War Office, 7 June 1939).
129 Figures calculated from information in WOOH, *Supplies and Transport*, Vol II, Appx XA, p.509.
130 TNA WO 167/1076: GHQ Supply Directorate (Petrol) RASC, WD, 11 September 1939.

Manure Heaps and Battered Barns

Many units had a relatively benign experience during the deployment, 2nd Royal Fusiliers recorded that:

> After a very rough crossing to Cherbourg, and several hours spent in a French train, we arrived in the early hours of the morning of 7th October at the small village of Asnieres,[131] where we were later joined by our MT. The Battalion spent several happy days in this French village and the friendliness and hospitality extended to us by the villagers knew no limits.[132] About the middle of October we reached our concentration area, at Henin Lietard, a small industrial village in Northern France.[133]

The movement of 1st Royal Welch Fusiliers (RWF)[134] was typical of many units. Disembarking at Cherbourg on 24 September, the battalion moved by train that night to Noyen-sur-Sarthe, 16 miles South-West of Le Mans, detraining to march six miles to Parce-sur-Sarthe, with the MT party joining the main body three days later. On 29 September, the battalion entrained to Achiet-le-Grand 13 miles South of Arras before conducting a night march of 14 miles to Hendecourt-les-Cagnicourt nine miles South-East of Arras arriving at 0500 on 1 October.[135]

Inevitably, no matter how meticulous the planning to marry unit MT bodies with the personnel parties in the Assembly Area, the outcomes of some of the unit *rendezvous* were not quite what many soldiers expected, or the planners had intended. 2nd Durham Light Infantry[136] of 6th Infantry Brigade spent a day on the docks at Cherbourg 'hanging about waiting for a train',[137] something which did not accord with the concept of a swift arrival to the field of battle. The expectations of the main body of 1st Berkshires,[138] also in 6th Brigade, were definitively not met in September 1939, when, having travelled by rail from Cherbourg to the BEF Assembly Area to join the battalion vehicle parties, they alighted at a rural wayside station approximately 20 miles South-West of Le Mans to be met by the advance party equipped with French horse transport for the baggage and no WMT for the troops.[139] The RAF ground parties suffered from similar problems, created by poor planning, a failure in logistic support and the incorrect routing of convoys, which resulted in details travelling by rail arriving ahead of the WMT convoys carrying the unit equipment. Whether this scenario was created by a confusion of responsibilities between the War Office and the Air Ministry or at the operational level in France

131 Asnieres-sur-Vegre, which is approximately 25 miles by road, SW of Le Mans.

132 The villagers must have been especially hospitable because the village had hosted 1st Berkshires, 25-28 September 1939. Blight, *The History of the Berkshire Regiment, 1920-1947*, pp.181-182.

133 na, *A Short History of the 2nd Battalion Royal Fusiliers (City of London Regiment) during the First Year of the War*, pp.5-6.

134 6th Infantry Brigade, 2nd Division, I Corps. Ellis, BOH, *The War in France and Flanders,* p.361.

135 TNA WO 167/843: 1 RWF, WD, 24 September-1 October 1939.

136 The 6th Infantry Brigade, 2nd Division, I Corps and Ellis, BOH, *The War in France and Flanders,* p.361.

137 David Rissik, *The DLI at War, The History of the Durham Light Infantry, 1939-1945* (Durham: The Depot, nd but 1952), p.5.

138 6th Infantry Brigade, 2nd Division, I Corps. Ellis, BOH, *The War in France and Flanders,* p.361.

139 Blight, *The History of the Berkshire Regiment, 1920-1947,* p.181.

is difficult to adjudge but it was effectively a logistic shambles. 50 (Army Co-operation) Wing was particularly unfortunate with the WMT arriving at the aerodromes 13 days after the rail parties,[140] which delayed the fly-in of 53 Blenheim (Strategic Reconnaissance) Squadron until 18 September and 4 and 13 Lysander (Tactical Reconnaissance) Squadrons until 2 October,[141] which was not only an embarrassingly poor advertisement for the swift application of air power but also a reduction of planned capability.

In the Assembly Area, the divisions and corps troops of the BEF were planned to shake-out in preparation for a move to the Concentration Area near the Franco-Belgian frontier. Political and military imperatives however, initiated an earlier move, with units and brigades deploying as they were ready,[142] a decision which disrupted the MPP,[143] but did not prevent the troops from seizing the opportunity to enjoy a little relaxation and extra rations. The 1st Berkshires recorded: 'Some of the troops visited the local *estaminets* and learnt, with some surprise, the potency of the *vin blanc*......and the cooks began to make delicious omelettes',[144] whilst some of the officers of 2nd Northamptons were entertained to a champagne reception by Comte de Courtillolles and his family.[145] From the Assembly Area, units moved the 250 miles to the Concentration Area centred on Bethune, Lens and Douai to the South-West of Lille. In this location, 3rd Medium Regiment RA had poor fortune in comparison to 1st Berkshires in the Assembly Area, being billeted in Souastre, which was described as, 'a dismal place where all the inhabitants appeared over to be over 80, where there were several funerals a day, and the village seemed to consist only of manure heaps and battered barns'.[146] Unit WMT moved by road, whilst all tracked vehicles travelled by rail as well as all personnel and the AFG 1098 stores that could not be moved by unit WMT. In addition, each sub-unit had to ensure that one domestic vehicle travelled with the rail party.[147] The move of 13th Infantry Brigade[148] from the Assembly Area to the Concentration Area on 29 November 1939[149] offers a clear insight into the task.

140 AMOH, Air Publication 3397, *Maintenance*, CD 1131, p.55.

141 See, Peter D Cornwell, *The Battle of France, Then and Now: Six Nations Locked in Aerial Combat, September 1939 - June 1940* (Old Harlow: Battle of Britain International, 2007), p.16.

142 TNA WO 197/112: Movement and Maintenance in the BEF.

143 TNA WO 197/2: First Maintenance Project: Reception of Forces in France and system of maintenance in the initial stages.

144 Blight, *The History of the Berkshire Regiment, 1920-1947*, p.181.

145 Brigadier W J Jervois MC, *The History of the Northamptonshire Regiment, 1934-1948* (The Regimental History Committee, 1953), p.52.

146 na, *The History of the 3rd Medium Artillery Regiment*, p.28. Whilst the history of the 3rd Medium Regiment may not be unique in its wit, the author certainly has a lively sense of humour.

147 By January 1940, these moves were well practised and supported by a Standing Instruction. See, for example, HQ L of C SI for Movement from Assembly area to Concentration Area (SECRET) in TNA WO 167/56: Q Branch Line of Communication.

148 5th Division, II Corps. Ellis, BOH, *The War in France and Flanders*, p.363.

149 The planned date was 30 November 1939 but was brought forward by 24 hours, thereby demonstrating the flexibility required by units.

P4.2 Strategic Enabler. Rail was critical to the deployment of the BEF from the SPODs to the corps areas on the Franco-Belgian frontier, but pre-war training was essential in delivering effective capability. A train of tracked armour, WMT and artillery is loaded at Longmoor Downs in 1933. (WDLMRC: DRMC/V1/171a)

Table 4.3
Move of 13th Infantry Brigade by Rail
Assembly Area to Concentration Area[150]

Unit	Entrainment	Officers	Other Ranks	AFV	WMT	Bicycles
2nd Cameronians	Alencon[151]	20	590	10 Carriers	6 x G1098	35[152]
2nd Wiltshires	La Hutte[153]	20	590	10 Carriers	6 x G1098	35
164 Field Ambulance	La Hutte	9	172	Nil	1 x G1098	?[154]

150 Information extracted from details in Movement Control Order No R10; TNA WO 167/57: L of C HQ 'Q' (M) Movement. The number of bicycles hardly confirms a fully operational motorized combat force, but they were useful for local administrative errands.

151 Alencon is 33 miles North of Le Mans and 10 miles North of La Hutte-Coulombiers.

152 A Higher Establishment infantry battalion on WE II/193112F/1 was established for 35 bicycles. Philson, BEFORBAT, Vol 2, p.105.

153 Although called La Hutte in the BEF MC documents the correct name for the station is La Hutte-Coulombiers, a location 23 miles North of Le Mans.

154 The original document, Movement Control Order No R10; TNA WO 167/57: L of C HQ 'Q' (M) Movement records a ?. WE III/1931/46/2 for a field ambulance does not identify bicycles on the WET. Philson, BEFORBAT, Vol 2, p.69.

P4.3 Strewn with Vehicles. Given the poor reliability of many of the impressed vehicles, recovery was a key aspect of the deployment on the GLOC routes in September and October 1939, a capability that was equally important during the advance to contact in May 1940 and the subsequent withdrawals in May and June. An AEC 850 FWD R6T recovers a Morris-Commercial 6x4 30 cwt Command Variant on a straight-bar tow; note the spare fuel cans on the rear of the casualty. The AEC 850 was originally purchased to tow the 3-inch AA gun and was capable of hauling a light tank on a trailer with a carrier behind, running on its tracks. (Tank Museum: 6508/A1)

An Apple in the Eye

From the Western French ports and by October, Cherbourg to Le Mans and from Le Harve and thence to the Concentration Area, Main Supply Routes (MSR) had been agreed with the Host Nation. Along each MSR, staging areas[155] were established at 70-100 mile intervals, this being the distance of a day's convoy movement.[156] Each staging area consisted of a group of villages in which the vehicles of a brigade group could be refuelled and repaired, and its soldiers fed, watered and rested. A Movement Control officer with a supporting staff, commanded

155 Gort noted that, 'Among the many important lessons which were learnt during the largest road movement ever undertaken with motor transport by any British Army were the need for early reconnaissance of staging areas, for control at the dispersal points, and for allowance for unforeseen delays', which for any Transportation planner must have been a frustrating statement of the obvious. TNA CAB 120/247: British Expeditionary Force: Lord Gort's First Despatch, para 10.

156 WOOH, *Movements*, p.182.

each staging area and was responsible for arranging the billeting plan, laying out vehicle parks, creating one-way traffic circuits and liasing with the French military and civil authorities.[157] From Le Mans, four routes, ALPHA, CHARLIE, DELTA and ECHO ran North-East to the Concentration Area. South of the River Somme, freedom of road movement was overseen by the *Zone Interieure*, through a series of traffic and regulating posts in each French Military Region manned by men local to the area, supported by French gendarmerie and local police who were responsible for traffic control and signposting, although in the ports, Base and staging areas, the BEF's provost companies directed UK military convoys and erected additional signage.[158] Initially, there were joint Anglo-French military traffic controls but the Host Nation re-allocated many of these resources as the BEF Provost capability grew.[159] North of the River Somme, the *Zone d'Armee* was an area of controlled road movement and whilst the BEF was responsible for its movements within allocated routes, French Army supply traffic crossed the BEF MSRs so it was important that the French Movement Control organization, HQ *Commissaire Regulateur Routiere* (CCR) in Amiens, was apprised of British movements and that schedules were strictly adhered to.[160] The CCR staff officers were punctilious in movements planning, plotting every move notified to the HQ on large road movement graphs to identify potential conflicts or congestion and initiating the relevant action to prevent it. French road movement control operations were rated by GHQ as 'exceedingly good'[161] and from the British perspective, its most remarkable achievement was the crossing of the Sixth French Army from left to right across the advance of the 5th and 50th Division during the advance to the River Dyle.[162]

One of the key issues during the road moves was the poor reliability of the thousands of vehicles impressed from the civil commercial sector in the UK, with the difficulty in the provision of spares being a particular problem.[163] An officer of 2nd Lincolns[164] summarized the initial outcome: '....the spare-part problem for so many types[165] was beyond us. When we landed in France and drove to the Belgian border the roads of France were littered with these broken down vehicles'.[166] Major-General Bernard Montgomery, GOC 3rd Division was thoroughly unimpressed by the MT arrangements:

157 Ibid, p.182.

158 Major S F Crozier MBE, *The History of The Corps of Military Police* (Aldershot: Gale & Polden, 1951), pp.30-31 and WOOH, *Maintenance in the Field*, Vol I, p.27.

159 Crozier, *Corps of Military Police*, p.31.

160 To facilitate co-ordination, GHQ BEF placed a liaison officer, Major E Beddington-Behrens MC, in HQ CRR; the CCR also co-ordinated significant or major movements. TNA WO 167/57: L of C HQ 'Q' (M) Movement briefing note.

161 TNA WO 167/57: L of C HQ 'Q' (M) Movement briefing note.

162 WOOH, *Movements*, p.183.

163 This was a key issue and 'lesson identified' by the BEF QMG Staff. TNA CAB 106/211: 'Notes on the 'Q' Organization of the BEF' dated 16 January 1942, para 8j. The document states, 'Our system of vehicle maintenance pre-supposes that we have an adequate supply of spare parts, in fact the BEF was always short of spares …'

164 9th Infantry Brigade, 3rd Division, II Corps. Ellis, BOH, *The War in France and Flanders*, p.362.

165 The BEF's dependence on civilian equipments is lucidly illustrated the fact that of the 25,000 WMT vehicles deployed to France in September and October 1939, only 2,000 had been in military service before mobilization. WOOH, *Maintenance in the Field*, Vol I, p.37.

166 Record of Captain J G M B Gough, quoted in Hamilton, *The Full Monty*, p.300.

> The transport was inadequate and completed on mobilisation by vehicles requisitioned from civilian firms. Much of the transport of my division consisted of civilian vans and lorries from the towns of England; they were in a bad state of repair and, when my division moved from the ports up to its concentration area near the French frontier, the countryside of France was strewn with broken down vehicles.[167]

Viscount Gort was regrettably rather less well informed about this failure in a critical logistic capability in his Command, writing in his despatches, 'Breakdowns and accidents were few'. [168]

The history of 208 Field Company RE summarized the logistic issue generated by the impressment solution: 'The stores situation was somewhat aggravated because the vehicles which had been issued were all of different makes, types and dates of manufacture, the spares to be carried were thus multiplied by the need for a provision to be made for each vehicle rather than a percentage to cover all vehicles of one make'.[169] Inevitably, with so many vehicles on the French roads,[170] driving on the right-hand side with inexperienced and sometimes tired drivers, accidents were inevitable. 2 Docks Group suffered an early casualty when Captain Reginald Tucker who was a commercial railway engineer was killed in a motorcycle accident,[171] whilst Driver Arthur Butler of 76 Company RASC[172] was killed near Evreux, *en-route* to the Concentration Area.[173] 3rd Medium Artillery Regiment was fortunate to avoid what could have resulted in a serious incident caused by the enthusiastic French welcome. Travelling along the MSR between Belleme and Mortagne, to the Concentration Area, flowers and fruit were showered upon the troops[174] when an apple hit a driver square between the eyes, causing him to lose control of the vehicle, which then travelled into a ditch.[175] Given the circumstances, it was surprising that the largest motorized movement that the British Army had ever undertaken[176] did not result in much greater numbers of casualties both military and civilian, Gort noting fairly

167 Bernard Law, Viscount Montgomery of Alamein, *The Memoirs of Field-Marshal Montgomery* (London: Collins, 1958), p.50.

168 TNA CAB 120/247: British Expeditionary Force: Lord Gort's First Despatch, para 10.

169 Morling, *Sussex Sappers*, p.57.

170 The British Army planning output for a single line road was the transport of 3,000 tons of material *per diem*. Army Council, *Military Engineering*, Vol V, *Roads*, 26/Manuals/1061 (War Office, 1935), p.27.

171 TNA 167/876: 2 Docks Group RE, WD entry 25 September 1939. His funeral took place on 27 September and he rests in the CWGC section of Brest (Kerfautras) Cemetery, Plot 40, Row 9, Grave 1.

172 T/16230 Driver Arthur Butler was aged 37 and married to Dorothy of Nottingham when he was killed on 30 October 1939. He rests in Evreux Communal Cemetery, Row C, Grave 22.

173 The unit held a memorial service for Driver Butler on 5 November 1939. TNA WO 167/1158: 76 Company RASC, WD. Equally poignant, was the entry for 11 November 1939: 'No commemoration service was held but all ranks wore poppies'.

174 Such was the level of hospitality along the MSRs, the Commander-in-Chief BEF recorded it in his first despatch: 'Drivers and vehicles were on the road for long periods, but their duty was lightened by the hospitality of the French inhabitants, which all ranks will recall with gratitude'. TNA CAB 120/247: British Expeditionary Force: Lord Gort's First Despatch, para 4.

175 The regimental history suggests that Driver Grewer was also distracted by the attentions of a 'sweet madamoiselle' [sic]; na, *The History of the 3rd Medium Artillery Regiment*, p.27.

176 TNA CAB 120/247: British Expeditionary Force: Lord Gort's First Despatch, para 4.

in his Despatches that the move reflected, 'great credit on the drivers, who were unaccustomed to long hours at the wheel and to driving on the right-hand side of the road.'[177]

As the GLOC was not in full operation by the time of the move from the Assembly Area to the Concentration Area, ammunition, fuel and rations were sent by rail to establish Advanced Dumps based on railheads, which was in theory a neat solution but some of the available railheads were not suitable for the task,[178] whilst command and control was not as tight as it should have been and in a classic display of regimental logistic culture the units of I Corps took full advantage of the opportunity. As an official report wryly observed, 'This was an example of the foresight of a Commander being thwarted by the acquisitive instinct of the old Regular Army Quartermaster'.[179] Such frustrations were equalled in irritation but not scale, by the attitude of a Staff officer at Orchies Railway Station who ordered 208 Field Company RE to abandon the unit stores on the platform if they could not be cleared by WMT in time for the arrival of the next train. The unit history recorded: 'What was surprising to a Territorial unit was the inefficiency of the organization, where it would have been expected to find a Regular Staff Officer handling everything with calmness and efficiency'.[180] Commander II Corps, Lieutenant-General Brooke inspected his railheads on 16 October, and was not impressed by the logistic arrangements, noting, 'Visited Supply and Ammunition railheads this morning. These not running properly yet. Rations coming up anyhow and proper pack trains not yet organized'.[181] This observation from a most capable soldier confirms that the BEF from the logistic perspective was not in fighting order but it was certainly not caused by a lack of enthusiasm or dedication by the logisticians.

Conclusion

The BEF's move to France was, given the circumstances, a successful operation but unlike its predecessor in 1914 it had the good fortune not be involved in a meeting engagement during the deployment. Conceptually and doctrinally, Plan W4 was sound and in accordance with the *Manual of Movements (War)* but the practical application was more of a challenge. The key issue was influence of the perceived threat of air attack, which created an unnecessarily long GLOC, which then by default was under-resourced, thereby diluting command, control and coherence. The reliance upon the Supplementary Reserve to deliver the Docks operation within the SPODs was inevitable given the force structure but the use of units that had to form upon mobilization so early in the deployment was mistake. Many of the specialist Supplementary Reserve units were technically competent but outputs were adversely affected by fragile command, control and coherence. The Staff mis-appreciation of the storage requirements for the Base Ordnance and Supply Depots was a fundamental error that caused considerable issues during the development phase and not a little friction with the Host Nation, although the allocation of sites that were

177 TNA CAB 120/247: British Expeditionary Force: Lord Gort's First Despatch, para 10.
178 Because of this, issues from the Ammunition Railheads (ARH) were restricted to 1st Line smoke rounds and explosives until improved arrangements were enacted. TNA CAB 106/235: BEF Ammunition Supply.
179 TNA CAB 106/211: 'Notes on the 'Q' Organization of the BEF' dated 16 January 1942, para 6d.
180 Morling, *Sussex Sappers*, p.59.
181 Danchev & Todman, *War Diaries, 1939-1945*, p.7.

assigned to the billeting of French government, defence, industrial tasks lucidly indicates that the planning was not as detailed or as clear as has been suggested by some contemporary observers and later historians.

Whilst motorization, with its fragility in training and experience, was fundamental to the mobility of the BEF, it remained, within the constraints of Plan W4, reliant upon the French railway for its 3rd Line transportation. That the corps railheads were still not effectively functioning in mid-October 1939 clearly indicates the limitations of the BEF's logistic outputs at this juncture. The challenges inherent in the operation of the commercial WMT fleet were such that they were not resolved until the vehicles were left in France as a result of the evacuation in mid-1940. The critical issue however, was the supply of canned fuel, which at points during the deployment, threatened to bring the road movement along the GLOC to a halt. That it did not, was a combination of swift action by the logistic Staff, resulting in the delivery of sufficient stocks to units and effective economies of consumption being introduced. Whilst General Lindsell's observation that the movement plans worked 'most successfully'[182] might hide a multitude of logistic sins, including Gort's limited interest or understanding of logistics, the BEF did arrive in its allotted sector in the Line and to this extent the logistic planners and operators achieved the Mission.

182 TNA WO 197/112: Movement and Maintenance in the BEF.

5

Docks and Stocks
The challenges of building the Base

Organization and ORBAT

One of the fundamental lessons from the Great War was to maintain in an operational Theatre of War, a logistic base, capable of sustaining the forces in the field and the experience from 1914-1918 greatly influenced it shape, size and composition. The 'Base' was not a single site comprising several units but a conceptual term covering the mainly static component of the GLOC, which encompassed the area of the North and North West of France. The LOC was commanded by GHQ through HQ Line of Communication (LOC),[1] which commanded two districts, North and South, each of which controlled four sub-areas, encompassing all the relevant facilities located in the Main Base Area (MBA) in the West and the Advanced Base Area (ABA) in the Dieppe-Le Harve-Rouen Triangle. There was also X (Arras) LOC Sub-Area commanded directly by GHQ, which covered the Corps Rear Areas and the GHQ Troops Area up to the Franco-Belgian frontier.[2] X Sub-Area would become 'live' upon the commencement of Plan D, the advance to the River Dyle, when HQ 23rd (Northumbrian) Division, under GHQ command for labouring and vulnerable point protection, would assume command.[3]

What is particularly instructive, given the importance of the Base and the GLOC to the sustainment of the BEF, is that remarkably, the Commander-in-Chief, Viscount Gort never

1 The GOC was Major-General Philip de Fonblanque DSO (1885-1940). Commissioned into the RE in 1905, he served in Command and Staff appointments on the Western Front during the Great War. Appointed Chief Administrative Officer of Scottish Command in 1937 he was deployed in October 1938 to head the British Mission in the Sudetenland monitoring the withdrawal of the Czech Army.

2 See also, Map 2, Ground Line of Communication: Sub-Areas.

Table 5.1
GLOC - Command & Control

HQ North District Sub-Areas	HQ South District Sub-Areas
Boulogne	Cherbourg
Dieppe (Medical)	Marseilles
Le Mans	Nantes
Rouen	Rennes

3 TNA WO 167/58: Plan D - Operational Instructions.

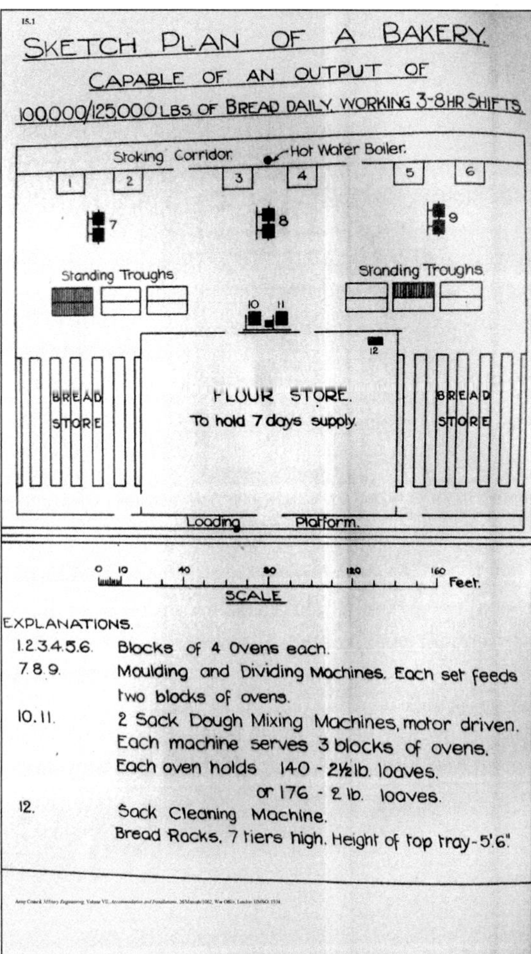

15.1 Sketch Plan of a Bakery. The Corps of Royal Engineers was capable of creating various types of logistic facilities. (Army Council, *Military Engineering*, Vol VII, *Accommodation and Installations*, 26/ Manuals/1062, War Office, London: HMSO: 1934)

undertook an inspection or visit to view its structure, issues and operations, a point forcefully made by the post-evacuation Howard Committee.[4] In this respect, whilst his appointment carried many responsibilities, his apparent failure to fully engage with the logisticians suggest that he may not have appreciated its strengths and limitations and the influence of them upon the BEF's combat capability. How much intellectual rigour was expended in relation to the fundamental issue of GLOC security is difficult to assess from the archival material. The doctrinal position was clarified by *Field Service Regulations* (FSR) but the threat assessment was almost certainly clouded by the focus upon air defence,[5] with 'raids' by mobile forces a secondary consideration.[6] The issue of the position of the GLOC in relation to the enemy was however, cogently articulated, the FSR advising that, 'Where, however, the principal communications run obliquely from the front or lie behind one flank of the army, the situation is likely to be comparatively disadvantageous, since the enemy may be enabled to attack the communications without a corresponding risk to his own'.[7] This observation, regrettably from the BEF's perspective, transpired to be to all to prescient.

4 TNA WO 33/2384: 'Report on the Committee on the Evacuation of the British Expeditionary Force from French Ports' (Howard Committee), para II, Command of Lines of Communication.

5 The concern about air defence, which was assessed to be the principal threat, was doctrinally articulated in 1935. Army Council, *Field Service Regulations* (FSR) Vol III, *Operations – Higher Formations*, 26/ Regulations/1803, War Office (London: HMSO, 1935), pp.14-15.

6 Ibid, p.15.

7 Ibid.

A reconnaissance for the establishment of the Base was conducted in 1938, which, in accordance with the guidelines in the *Manual of Movement (War)*,[8] produced the 1st Key Plan, allocating two areas around the Sea Ports of Disembarkation (SPOD) at Brest to create a Northern Base Area,[9] and at Nantes and Saint Nazaire to form a Southern Base Area. Within each of these areas, there were two components: the Docks, which were doctrinally, solely a transit facility,[10] although logistic planning and execution compromised this purist approach, and the depot facilities, which included 4th Line supply, ordnance and workshop installations, reinforcement camps, and medical facilities including hospitals and support units. One of the key aspects to the planning and development of the Base depots was the scale of the real estate that was required for each site, an issue that not only generated practical challenges in site selection but also complexities in negotiating the detail of the requirements with the Host Nation. Even in 1933, when the manual was published, the scope was extensive and grew as the Army became increasingly more reliant upon complex equipment, which required more support.

Growing concerns about the vulnerability of the depots to air attack generated creative tension between the need for appropriate Ground Based Air Defence (GBAD)[11] and the imperative for greater dispersion and thus a need for more estate, a dilemma influenced by the requirement to keep the construction of internal depot railway infrastructure to the minimum.[12] By 1939, the shortage of field and Host Nation GBAD to protect the Base resulted in dispersion being the solution, whilst the need for more Base depots to support a two corps deployment with a subsequent expansion to three then four corps generated concomitant requests to the French for more real estate, which inevitably created frictions, especially as some of the initial baseline assumptions were too conservative and had to be up-scaled.[13] That the Secretary of State for War was pressing for IV Corps, comprising four divisions, to deploy to France in Spring 1940 undoubtedly exacerbated the challenges of managing this problem.[14]

8 Army Council, *Manual of Movement (War)*, 26/Manuals/1297, War Office (London: HMSO, 1933), pp.54-64, Sects 52-58.
9 Map 6: BEF – Northern Base Area at Rennes: First Key Plan.
10 Army Council, *Manual of Movement (War)*, p.59, Sect 56.
11 FSR considered the air threat so serious that it suggested that air defence assets should precede the deployment of the main force. Army Council, FSR, Vol III, *Operations – Higher Formations*, pp.14-15.
12 Colonel W G Lindsell DSO OBE MC psc RA, *A & Q, or Military Administration in War* (Aldershot: Gale & Polden, Third Ed, 1933), p.40 is cautious on Passive Air Defence (PAD) dispersion because of the need for substantial rail infrastructure construction within the sites. By 1939 it had become a much more significant issue, with dispersed sites using external railheads to service the operations.
13 The acreage required for each site varied depending upon the perception of the air threat, availability of GBAD, the topographical conditions, covered storage availability, the application of safety distances for ammunition and POL, access to the railway network and the planned requirements for expansion.
14 R J Minney, *The Private Papers of Hore-Belisha* (London: Collins, 1950), p.254.

Table 5.2
Real Estate Required for Base Depots[15]

Base Depot[16]	Acres	Remarks
Ammunition	500 – 1000	Safety distances a key driver
Engineer Stores	100 – 200	
Ordnance	100 – 200	Covered storage required
Supplies	250 – 500	Included POL and rations
Transportation	100 – 200	Rail connection essential

As the size of the BEF and its concomitant support expanded, the type and scope of the dock areas, warehouses, accommodation, field storage sites and railheads, which, had been allocated under the original plan became by December 1939 wholly inadequate and effectively the Base remained in a constant state of development until the evacuations began in late May 1940.[17] In this month, enormous resources were dedicated to sustaining the BEF, although there were several interesting dichotomies, not least of which, was the effort expended in storing in-Theatre, 60 days rations for 400,000 men, whilst some critical Mechanical Transport (MT) spares were dues out, a situation amply illustrated by the fact that on 30 April 1940, 1 Base Ordnance Depot (BOD) had 17,000 indents unsatisfied and demands were arriving at the rate of 1,400 per day.[18] Spares for tanks were also in short supply. On 1 January 1940, the stock for the 50 Infantry tanks in France consisted of 16 pairs of tracks and no sprockets, whilst to support the 123 Light tanks there were in Base stores, 137 pairs of tracks and 136 pairs of sprockets.[19] This example illustrates the creative tension caused by the logistic services being expected to deliver outside of the envelope without the relevant industrial outputs.[20]

The different types of units in the Base lucidly illustrate the complexity of supporting an increasingly motorized and mechanized Army deployed to conduct mobile expeditionary operations.[21] Whilst most Base assets were logistic and medical, the BEF also deployed Infantry, Royal Armoured Corps and General Base Depots for personnel reinforcements, light infantry battalions for point protection and manual-handling tasks and the 3rd Anti-Aircraft Brigade in the GBAD role. For training, labouring and ground defence duties, 12th (Eastern) Division was located in the Rouen Sub-Area, whilst two brigades of 46th (North Midland & West Riding) Division were assigned to the Rennes Sub-Area and one brigade to Nantes. Most of the Royal Engineer units in the Base, except those in divisions allocated to the GLOC, generated logistic output, with a focus on transportation, including movements, docks and

15 Table compiled from information in Lindsell, *A & Q, or Military Administration in War*, p.41.
16 For the outline planning details for each type of depot, see, Ibid, pp.47-50.
17 Map 9: BEF – Base Engineer, Ordnance & Supply Depots and Workshops.
18 WOOH, *Ordnance Services*, p.153.
19 Ibid, p.151.
20 The shortage of tank track and vehicle spares was not confined to the BEF, the German Army being equally tested during the Polish campaign in this respect during autumn 1939. Forczyk, *Case White*, p.331.
21 For a detailed list of all the units and the establishments see, Philson, BEFORBAT, Vol 3.

P5.1 Racking and Stacking. The initial shortage of skilled staff, MHE and racking caused serious disruption to BOD operations and thus to the distribution of many key spares. (RLCM: RAOC/ Trades 6560/2)

railways, with the majority of the latter, covering survey, operating, construction, stores and repair. The RE also deployed an artisan works company, Base and LOC postal units, a forestry company and a camouflage factory.[22] The RASC deployed the following types of unit in the Base: Supply depot, field bakery, field butchery, petrol filling centre, bulk petrol company, bulk petrol storage company, Heavy Repair Shop (HRS), Vehicle Reserve Depot (VRD), Motor Transport Stores Depot (MTSD), ambulance car company, and Line of Communication MT company. The RAOC allocated the following capabilities: advanced Base ordnance depot, Base Ordnance Depot (BOD), ordnance stores company, Advanced Ordnance Workshop (AOW), ordnance workshop company, Port Workshop Detachment (PWD), Base Ammunition Depot (BAD), ordnance ammunition company, armoured corps Ordnance Field Park (OFP) and armoured corps workshop. The Auxiliary Military Pioneer Corps (AMPC)[23] deployed in Labour Companies,[24] the title of which, denoted the task: Depot, Docks, General, Ordnance, Railway, RASC and Works, although the nomenclature was amended in November 1939 to

22 Philson, BEFORBAT, Vol 3, p.ii.
23 For a list of AMPC Companies in the BEF, see, Major E H Rhodes-Wood, *A War History of the Royal Pioneer Corps*, pp.338-341.
24 The use of the term 'Labour' in the War Office, was greeted with little enthusiasm by Colonel J V R Jackson late Buffs, who as the AAG at AG 14 responsible for developing the capability, who fought

'Companies AMPC'.[25] The AMPC also managed the Foreign Labour Training Centre[26] and Italian, *Prestataire*[27] and Palestinian[28] Companies.

A Brewer's Drayman

Chronologically, the logisticians sought first to meet the daily maintenance demands, whilst seeking to create a working margin to mitigate failures such as contaminated fuel or transportation disruption, with the outcome being the generation of operational reserves to meet unforeseen contingencies and major kinetic combat. The greatest challenge to output on the GLOC in the deployment and initial reinforcement phases was the considerable reliance on improvised logistic units, an arrangement strongly contrasting with the Regular and its associated Reserve components in I and II Corps. Whilst authorized through a War Establishment Table (WET)[29] few of these units existed in peace and they had to be mobilized using personnel from the Regular and Territorial Armies, Supplementary Reservist and Militia, who paraded with varying standards and levels of military and technical knowledge and field operating experience. This was exacerbated by the failure to train most of these personnel in their war roles, a point concisely summarized by the experience of a Railway Traffic Officer, who described the initial capability of his team: 'A brewer's drayman, a tinsmith, a train-driver and a painter – not a semblance of clerical experience among them'.[30] Director-General Transportation (DGT) BEF, Brigadier D J McMullen[31] was scathing in his post deployment report, writing that the Docks Groups were 'thrown together' at the outbreak of war and were consequently unorganised, a damning comment on such a critical asset.[32] Some Regulars were aware of their mobilization tasks and conducted pre-deployment preparation but this work became nugatory when allotments to posts were amended. In addition, many of the logistic

for the title 'Pioneer Corps'. He won his campaign, although initially the departmental process added Auxiliary Military to the name. Ibid, p.6.

25 Ibid, pp.13-15.

26 Including 1,776 recruits, the Training Centre had an establishment of 2,055. Philson, BEFORBAT, Vol 3, p.125.

27 Consisting of Austrian, Czech, German and Polish personnel. Rhodes-Wood, *A War History of the Royal Pioneer Corps*, p.24.

28 650 strong and comprised of 26 nationalities recruited from Palestine. Ibid, p.25.

29 See, Philson, BEFORBAT, Vol 3.

30 WOOH, *Movements*, p.87. No doubt the RTO was in a dilemma over the assignment of the train driver, who was probably the only one of the team who understood at least part of the technical work but whose skills would have been much more effective in a Railway Operating Company.

31 Brigadier D J McMullen DSO (1891-1967) was appointed to the post having been seconded to the Egyptian Government for railway duties (1920-1929) and served as the Assistant Director of Transportation in Egypt (1936-1937). Commissioned into the RE in 1911, he served on the Western Front and Palestine during the Great War and upon his evacuation from France in 1940 was appointed first Inspector and then Director-General of Transportation at the War Office. Promoted to substantive Major-General in 1943, he was awarded the CB, then knighted in 1946. McMullen Barracks near Marchwood Military Port is named after him. See also, Smart, *Biographical Dictionary of the British Generals of the Second World War*, p.204.

32 TNA WO 167/51: GHQ Services, Transportation, DG (Tn) dated 11 October 1939, 'Lessons'.

Base units that formed only on mobilization were planned to receive AFG 1098[33] equipment upon arrival in France, a solution almost surely doomed to fail and, when it did, had a direct and adverse impact upon unit operational outputs.[34] Inevitably therefore, logistic coherence in Base and GLOC units was initially low, and in some cases non-existent, which manifestly conflicted with the need for a swift crafted entry to France, supported by a resilient GLOC capable of delivering combat support to the infantry divisions. In this respect, it was fortunate that logisticians had time to bring order to the organization.

Defence of the Base and the GLOC was embedded in the plan, with the Host Nation leading on the provision of capability to protect vulnerable points on railways and roads.[35] The War Office also provided two infantry battalions for port defence duties at Brest, Cherbourg, Nantes and Saint Nazaire.[36] Given that the establishment of the Base in the West was driven by the concern about the perceived effects of air attack,[37] the British allocated few assets to active air defence, preferring to rely upon the passive aspects of distance and dispersion to achieve the effect.[38] For active GBAD the BEF deployed the 3rd Anti-Aircraft (AA) Brigade[39] but otherwise initially relied upon Host Nation ground and aerial assets,[40] with the French guaranteeing AA units to defend Brest and Saint Nazaire,[41] although the seaward flank of ports on the coast posed a serious challenge for GBAD because of the lack of depth in deploying AA guns and balloons.[42] One aspect that has not been generally considered is the influence of Gas Warfare (GW)[43] on the location and operation of the Bases. In April 1940, the BEF GHQ Chemical Warfare (CW) Staff drafted a paper entitled 'Scale of Gas Attack to which the

33 The AFG 1098 was the Mobilization Stores Table for each type of unit and was suffixed with a code number and letter (eg 33C) to identify each organization.
34 TNA WO 167/51: GHQ Services, Transportation, DG (Tn) dated 11 October 1939, 'Lessons'.
35 Plan W4 First Maintenance Project, p.3, para 8. TNA WO 197/2: First Maintenance Project: Reception of Forces in France and system of maintenance in the initial stages.
36 One battalion was assigned to Brest, with one company detached to Brest. The second battalion was detailed to Nantes and Saint Nazaire. TNA WO 197/2: Plan W4 First Maintenance Project, p.20, para 24.
37 TNA CAB 106/21: 'Notes on the 'Q' Organization of the BEF' dated 16 January 1942, para 3.
38 An official record summarized the position: 'The anti-aircraft defences of the base areas was negligible. The FRENCH originally undertook it, but we had to take it over ultimately and there was very little protection'. See TNA CAB 106/211: 'Notes on the 'Q' Organization of the BEF' dated 16 January 1942, para 14 (ii).
39 TNA WO 197/2: Plan W4 First Maintenance Project, p.3, para 9 and Ellis, BOH, *The War in France and Flanders*, p.366.
40 For a resume of RAF and French air operations in the period, see, Robert Jackson, *Air War over France, 1939-40* (London: Ian Allan, 1974) and in detail, Cornwell, *The Battle of France.*
41 Army Council, TNA WO 197/2: Plan W4 First Maintenance Project, p.3, para 9.
42 FSR, Vol III, *Operations - Higher Formations*, p.15.
43 In 1939, Chemical Warfare (CW) was defined as those aspects concerned with the offensive and defensive use of gas, incendiary and smoke munitions, and those defence measures required to protect British Forces. GW related specifically to the employment, in military operations, by any nation of any chemical substance, solid, liquid or gas that was designed to have a poisonous or irritant affect, upon the human body, and this included tear gases. For details, see, WOOH, *Special Weapons and Types of Warfare*, Vol I, *Gas Warfare*, Lieutenant-Colonel D J C Wiseman (Comp.) (War Office, 1951) and Home Office, *Air Raid Precautions*, Handbook No 1, *Personal Protection Against Gas* (London: HMSO, 1938), p.2.

BEF may be subjected'.[44] The assessment was based on the Germans using, as their offensive GW main effort, air delivered gas weapons consisting of spray and bombs. Air delivered gas weapons, and in particular high and low level spray, were assessed to be the greatest threat to the BEF's operations, although this analysis was based less on hard evidence of German capability and more upon what the British perceived the Germans might be able to achieve.[45] The GHQ CW Staff assessed that although the SPODs and Base areas were excellent targets, especially for a persistent agent such as blister, the enemy's ability to deliver a concentrated attack would be degraded by the distances, dispersion, air defence assets, pre-attack measures and the weather. The key concern was GW attacks on the ports, which were relatively easy to find and had little overhead protection for stocks. Base areas were generally dispersed and more difficult to identify but initially the shortage of covered accommodation for *materiel* made them vulnerable to contamination with blister agents, with rations, especially fresh food, an particular problem.

The initial Base ports of Nantes and Saint Nazaire were each expected to handle 3,000 tons per week but the output was half this figure, which immediately unbalanced the War Office intention to import 8,000 tons weekly in order to meet daily requirements and build the planned reserves.[46] As it transpired, developing the Base proved to be a much greater challenge than had been assessed, with insufficient rail facilities, shortage of covered accommodation and a dearth of labour being the key issues. Suitable buildings for the Base Supply Depots (BSD) were essential for the preservation of stocks but only 33 percent of the need could be provisioned, the French civil sector opposing the requisition of additional premises. The formation of an ABA was the obvious solution to this problem and the key initiator to do so rapidly was the pressing need to resolve the Supply situation, which even by mid-September 1939 had become increasingly precarious.[47] Such a solution was fully supported doctrinally by *Field Service Regulations*, which noted that 'If the line of communications is very long, it may sometimes become necessary to establish the base nearer to the scene of operations'.[48]

There was precedent in that a Medical ABA had been established at Dieppe,[49] from the beginning of the deployment and the port was used for berthing the hospital ships, whilst Le Harve had been used to a limited extent to import personnel and vehicles. The French however, were keen to avoid attracting the attention of the *Luftwaffe* by greater use of the Northern Channel Ports and it was October 1939 before the air defence issues were sufficiently resolved for authority to be granted, although in anticipation of a positive response from the Host Nation work was begun to establish an ABA in the Le Harve-Rouen-Dieppe Triangle,

44 TNA WO 193/717: Scale of Gas Attack to which the British Expeditionary Force may be subjected.

45 Part of this assessment was driven by British work on High Level Spray (HLS) and latterly on Low Level Spray (LLS). In 1939, the RAF's Air Delivered Gas Weapons (ADGW) consisted of two generic types. Iron bombs of 250 or 30 lb capacity, and a spray system, using containers of three sizes. All the ADGW were charged with one agent, a persistent vesicant, Mustard, although there were several variants. Mustard was the chemical of choice for the creation of casualties and the contamination of ground, equipment and buildings. See, Report on Trials in Algeria (VERY SECRET) in TNA AVIA 15/254: Chemical Warfare: Research and Development, 'Reports on Gas Spraying Trials'.

46 Map 3: BEF - Deployment & Sustainment: Key Ports and Import of *Materiel*.

47 WOOH, *Supplies and Transport*, Vol I, pp.110-111.

48 Army Council FSR, Vol III, *Operations – Higher Formations*, p.14.

49 This was titled 1 Medical Sub-Base Area (MSBA). TNA WO 167/93.

with an Advanced Base Supply Depot at Rouen operating by 27 September and capable of receiving 3,000 tons per week by 10 October.

The ABA concept also became a component of the long-term expansion of the GLOC, designed to potentially sustain up to fifty-five divisions with a strength of approximately 2.25 million men.[50] Another ABA, to support the in-Theatre training of the incoming armoured divisions, was also planned for Pacy, 35 miles South-South-East of Rouen but the German attack on 10 May 1940 prevented the progression of this project.[51] As the deployment of the BEF continued, nearly every major port on the North coast of France was involved in supporting British Ground and Air Forces in France, including Dieppe for medical evacuation, Le Harve and Rouen for general stores and Fecamp for ammunition, which comprised some conventional stocks but the key import was GW munitions in the form of gas shells for artillery and RAF aerial weapons.[52] In addition, Boulogne was used by personnel travelling on leave, whilst Calais[53] was the SPOD for locomotives, wagons, heavy tracked plant and material transported on the London & North Eastern Railway (LNER) train ferry from Harwich. The alternative train ferry route was the Southern Railway's Dover to Dunkerque service, although its capacity was greatly reduced by the conversion of two of the three ferries[54] to Royal Navy minelayers an arrangement, which not only failed to effectively utilize a critical logistic asset, but also lucidly demonstrated the planning dissonance between the Admiralty and the War Office.[55] Some of these movements were complex, with rail wagons loaded with equipment direct from various contractors marshalled at Harwich Docks by the LNER being joined by engineer plant arriving by road on low-loaders.[56] The table below illustrates the geographical spread of the ports in BEF use, the allocation of commodities to them and the tonnage imports.

50 WOOH, *Administrative Planning*, Colonel H W Wilson OBE TD (War Office, 1952), p.3. In December 1939, the War Office collated the requirements for 60 principal stores to support, by mid-1941, a fifty-five division Army. These figures were indicative, although the Treasury and the Ministry of Supply interpreted them to mean they should plan but not act upon them. This was effectively a planning aspiration, its achievement within two years potentially unlikely based upon manpower availability and industrial production. See, Postan, BOH, *British War Production,* pp.74-75.

51 The Base Ordnance Depot (BOD) and the Base Ordnance Workshop (BOW) within the Base AFV Area were planned to be capable of supporting ten armoured divisions, with expansion to twelve if required. See, WOOH, *Ordnance Services*, p.155.

52 Fecamp was selected as the main SPOD for GW munitions but to lessen German GW interest in the port, it was decided to import conventional ammunition to assist in disguising the more sensitive activity. TNA WO 193/716: Despatch of Gas and Equipment to the BEF, Note in MO4 B/M 1/182 dated 14 November 1939.

53 Staff officers and some soldiers from BEF GHQ at Arras used the civil ferry services to Dover, which were relatively frequent and convenient, for trains to London for War Office meetings. As the BEF expanded, so many personnel were using this route that it become a financial issue and the Finance Branch in GHQ sought to greatly restrict its use. 'Minutes of Leave Meeting held in AG's Office on 16 February 1940, GHQ (A) A2971/4/65 (PS) dated 18 February 1940' para 5a, in TNA WO 167/11: GHQ AG, WD refers.

54 The two ferries were the MV *Hampton Ferry* and MV *Shepperton Ferry*. A J Mullay, *For the King's Service: Railway Ships at War* (Easingwold: Pendragon Publishing, 2008), p.64.

55 Roskill, BOH, *The War at Sea, 1939-1945*, Vol I, *The Defensive,* p.64.

56 The rail component of this consignment arrived on 17-20 wagons and included 26 bulldozers, scrapers, ditchers and excavators for 135 Excavator Company RE and a commercial road element of 10 plant equipments plus a military convoy, the low-loaders of which were planned to carry eight

Table 5.3
BEF – Key Ports and Tonnage Imports
September 1939 – June 1940[57]

UK Port	Commodity	Tons	France	Remarks
Avonmouth	Petrol	13,000	Nantes	Cased petrol
		31,000	Brest	
Barry	General Stores	205,000	Nantes	
Dover	Personnel	NA	Boulogne	Leave traffic
		NA	Calais	GHQ traffic
	Train Ferry*	NA	Dunkerque	*Southern Railway service
Fowey	Ammunition	21,000	Brest	
		8,000	St Malo	
Harwich	Train Ferry*	24,000	Calais	*LNER service
Newhaven	Ammunition*	18,000	Fecamp	*Including gas munitions
	Medical evacuation	NA	Dieppe*	*Advanced Medical Base
Newport	Ammunition	48,000	St Nazaire	
Newport	Ammunition	14,000	Brest	
Poole	Petrol	55,000	Caen	Cased petrol
Southampton	General Stores	103,000	Le Harve	
		126,000	Brest	
		15,000	Rouen*	*Mainly Supply items
Swansea	Petrol	10,000	Brest	Cased petrol
		57,000	Nantes	
	Total	**748,000**		

With a resume of the outline logistic capabilities complete, it is timely to explore the deployment and operations of the Services of Transportation, Supply and Ordnance, each which delivered key outputs within the Base.

Transportation

The Corps of Royal Engineers (RE) were responsible for what was described in 1939 as 'Transportation', which included Movement Control,[58] railway construction and operating,

of the plant vehicles that arrived on civilian WMT. TNA WO 167/57: L of C HQ'Q'(M) Movement, 'War Office Movement Instruction No 28 (Stores), Q14A/17/3 dated 17 October 1939 (SECRET)'.

57 WOOH, *Movements*, p.201, Appx D to Chp 10.

58 In later campaigns, Movement Control was the responsibility of the Q (Movements) Staff and not Director-General Transportation. The Movement Control organization in France was not replicated

P5.2 Stevedore Training. Supplementary RE Reservists of 1 Docks Group RE conducting 'dry' training in the 'hold' of SS *Apple Pie* at the Transportation Centre Longmoor in the summer of 1938. The importance of the Docks Groups to effective logistic operations was reinforced during the deployment of the BEF but so was the significance of training and C^3, all of which required much improvement. (WDLMRC: DRMC/ V1/181c)

docks, Inland Water Transport (IWT) and all aspects of in-Theatre surface transportation except for road operations. DGT BEF, assisted by two deputies and their supporting Staff, was responsible for these services with the efficiency of the British contribution in these areas being enhanced because the British military railway component was controlled through one Corps, the RE, which was responsible for infrastructure construction and repair, railway operating and signalling, and locomotive and rolling stock maintenance. The initial task of the 'Transportation Service' as the capability was known, was the reception, unloading and onward movement of BEF units and *materiel* as they arrived at the SPODs. Plan W4 deployed the first two Docks Groups to Le Harve, thereby creating the need for a rail move to their assigned locations at Cherbourg, Nantes and Saint Nazaire.[59] Why this indirect solution was chosen is not explained by information in the documents but was presumably driven by the availability and allocation of shipping. By April 1940, there were three Docks Groups in France. No 1 was working the allocated British dock areas of Nantes, Marseilles and Saint Nazaire,[60] No 2, Brest, Cherbourg, Caen and Saint Malo and No 3, Boulogne, Le Harve and Rouen, with other ports being operated by the French civil authorities.[61] The duties of a Docks Group were technical and supervisory, with the

in other Theatres. WOOH, *Transportation*, p.40.

59 Moving under the authority of Plan W4 A4812 - Advanced Parties by Destroyer, the 2 Docks Group Advance Party of five, left Hounslow by coach for Portsmouth on 4 September 1939, transferring to the W Class destroyer HMS *Wren* to Cherbourg, where the members were accommodated in the Hotel Moderne. TNA WO 191/1: Movement Control Instruction Plan W4 and TNA WO 167/876: 2 Works Group RE, WD. HMS *Wren* was sunk by aerial bombing on 27 July 1940 approximately 20 nautical miles East of Aldeburgh Suffolk. The 37 fatalities included the Captain, Lieutenant-Commander Frederick Harker RN. Richard & Bridget Larn, *Shipwreck Index of the British Isles*, Vol 3, *The East Coast*, (London: Lloyd's Register of Shipping, 1998), Sect 2, Suffolk.

60 TNA WO 167/875: 1 Docks Group RE, WD.

61 WOOH, *Transportation*, p.51.

HQ being a multi-disciplinary logistic team containing a number of specialists from the RE, plus the RASC and RAOC, including supply and ordnance officers respectively, and a RAOC Sergeant Ammunition Examiner. RE technical personnel included three locomotive drivers and two firemen, four brakesmen and shunters and 15 railway clerks.[62]

There were a series of issues during the first six months of the deployment relating to ship loading in the UK. Many ships had mixed cargoes, a measure designed to spread the loss of material in a fire or a sinking, whilst others were loaded directly from trains without considering the discharge requirement, particularly in relation to destination. Consigning *materiel* to 1 BOD was inefficient because the time saved in UK by full ship loading was certainly off-set by that lost in France, a problem compounded by inadequate marking and documentation, which led to a reduction in the pace of ship unloading and subsequent clearance from the docks.[63] Dock labour was either civilian provided by the French port authorities, or military controlled through the AMPC. The latter, whilst under military command, was not generally skilled, consisting mainly of older cavalry and other military Reservists, although with a leavening of professional dockers in the original dock labour companies.[64] This arrangement was not particularly efficient and a decision was taken to form permanent stevedore battalions,[65] of which three were operating in France by the end of 1939. Another issue was the split responsibility at the SPOD between the Sea Transport Service of the Ministry of Shipping in charge on-board and the Docks Group having authority on the quay. QMG BEF took up the cudgel with the Deputy QMG at the War Office[66] to clarify the arrangements and an agreement was reached with the Ministry of Shipping that the discharge of ships would be the task of the Military Docks Service subject to the ship's Captain retaining full responsibility for the berthing and safety of the vessel.[67] The French allotted specific priority berths to the UK in each port as shown in the table below, although they could be used by non-BEF ships when vacant. Depending upon French military and civil shipping, additional berths could be assigned to the BEF for specific tasks.

62 Philson, BEFORBAT, Vol 3, p.61.

63 TNA WO 167/51: GHQ Services, Transportation, DG (Tn) dated 11 October 1939, 'Lessons'.

64 Only 30% of the personnel in these companies were assessed to be skilled in docks work. TNA WO 167/51: GHQ Services, Transportation, DG (Tn) dated 11 October 1939, 'Lessons'.

65 Philson, BEFORBAT, Vol 3, p.60. A stevedore battalion had a WE of 1,030 personnel.

66 Major-General T A Riddell-Webster DSO (1886-1974) was commissioned into the Cameronians (Scottish Rifles) in 1905 and served on the Western Front in the Great War being admitted to the DSO in 1915. Attending Staff College (1924-1925), he was CO 2nd Cameronians (1930-1933), Assistant Adjutant & QMG at the War Office (1933-1934), Commander Poona (Independent) Brigade Area (1935-1938) before his appointment as a Major-General as Director Movements & Quartering at the War Office (1938-1939) and then Deputy QMG (1939-1940). Chief Administrative Officer Middle East Command (1940-1941), he was GOC-in-C Southern India (1941) before being knighted and promoted to General to assume the post of QMG to the Forces (1942-1946). Smart, *Biographical Dictionary of the British Generals of the Second World War*, p.271.

67 WOOH, *Transportation*, pp.50-51, Chp IV, Appx B, War Office 79/Mob/3250 (DQMG (A)) dated 15 March 1940 from DQMG to QMG BEF.

Table 5.4
BEF – Berth Allocation and Working at French Ports[68]

Port	Task or Cargo	No of Berths	Docks Group	Stevedore Battalion	Remarks
Boulogne	General & Personnel*	3	3	Civil	*GHQ & leave
Brest	Ammunition MT & Petrol	3*	2	1	* Plus MT berths if required
Caen	Petrol*	2	2	Civil	*Cased fuel
Calais	Train Ferry*	1	Civil	Civil	*LNER ex-Harwich
Cherbourg	MT	4	2	1	
	Personnel*	2	2	1	*Including leave
Dieppe	Medical	3*	NA	NA	*Hospital carriers
Donges	Bulk Petrol*	1	Civil	Civil	*Ocean Oil Terminal
Dunkerque	Bulk Petrol*	1	Civil	Civil	*Ocean Oil Terminal
	Train Ferry*	1	Civil	Civil	*Southern Railway ex-Dover
Fecamp	General & Ammunition*	2	3	2	*Gas munitions SPOD
Honfleur	Bulk Petrol*	1	Civil	Civil	
Le Harve	Cargo*	12	3	2	*Including Mail
Marseilles	General & Personnel	7	1	Civil	Supporting MEDLOC
Nantes	General & Petrol	6*	1	3	* Plus MT berths if required
Rouen	General	3-5	3	Civil	
St Malo	General & Ammunition	2	2	Civil	
St Nazaire	General & MT	4*	1	1	* Plus MT berths if required

IWT had been a consistent feature of the Transportation Service on the Western Front during the Great War[69] but played a much smaller part in supporting the BEF in 1940. Whilst the GHQ WET listed a Directorate of IWT with a Director in the rank of lieutenant-colonel under the DGT, Brigadier McMullen had to request the War Office, through the QMG BEF,

68 Date as at 30 April 1940. Information collated from WOOH, *Transportation*, p.51, Chp IV, Appx C.
69 For an academic examination, see, Christopher Phillips, 'Logistics and the BEF: The Development of Waterborne Transport on the Western Front, 1914-1916', *British Journal of Military History*, Vol 2, No 2 (2016).

P5.3 Detail Issue Depot. DID operations were an essential component of the BEF's logistic matrix during the initial deployment. (RLCM: B3/SRB/NOR)

to approve the formation of it, describing the increase of personnel as a 'small show'.[70] He was clear however, that the incoming Director IWT (DIWT) should be 'an expert canal officer (such as a Grand Union Canal Coy Official) who really knows the snags of canal work: I do not want a Shipping or Docks man who has a smattering of IWT Knowledge [sic] but need the real expert Canal Operator……..The Captain RE on the staff should also be a true canal official'.[71] This approach was absolutely in the mould of Field-Marshal Sir Douglas Haig during the Great War, who sought to place appropriate civilian expertise in specific logistic posts to create the most effective outputs.[72]

The DIWT post was not filled until January 1940 but the incumbent quickly proceeded to create some order and coherency to IWT contracts, several of which had been let by Service directorates. DIWT rapidly created a positive working relationship with the *Director des Voies Navigables* at the French *Grand Quartier General* (GQC) which assigned a lieutenant from the *Sapeurs du Navigation* as a liaison officer to the BEF's IWT Directorate. DIWT also wasted no time to co-operating with the *IVme Bureau* in Paris, which was the controlling authority

70 TNA WO 167/51: GHQ Services, Transportation, DG (Tn) IW/1 dated 14 October 1939.
71 TNA WO 167/51: GHQ Services, Transportation, DG (Tn) IW/1 dated 14 October 1939.
72 See, Maginniss, *An Unappreciated Field of Endeavour*, pp.261-262.

for the movement of bulk petrol by barge and coastal tanker.[73] DGT recognized that railway capacity was at a premium and sought to find alternatives and IWT was certainly well suited to the carriage of aggregate, ammunition, bulk petrol, construction materials, cased supplies, coal, crated items and defence stores. DIWT thus drafted a circular for distribution by the BEF QMG Staff, which highlighted the new procedures for bidding for IWT,[74] with a specific note that all consignments were to be a minimum of 80 tons. Medical evacuation and the carriage of frozen meat were two other IWT tasks under consideration by May 1940.

Supply Services

The RASC was responsible for Supply and the following units were a component of the First Contingent deployment: two Base Supply Depots (BSD), each having a petrol sub-depot, two field butchery and Cold Storage Depots (CSD)[75] and two field bakeries.[76] Initially Petroleum Oils and Lubricants (POL) and rations were, in accordance with the contemporary doctrine, treated as parallel items of Supply to be handled by the same unit, a fallacy, which was quickly exposed by the realities of the deployment,[77] with the petrol sub-depots being broken out of the BSD structure as independent units.[78] One supply personnel company with a HQ and sixteen sections holding an initial 200,000 field rations was also deployed, establishing, then operating, Detail Issue Depots (DID),[79] which were located at the ports and along the GLOC, including the Assembly, Staging and AASF areas and providing the railhead supply detachments.[80] The DIDs held small working stocks of rations and POL and were a small but essential cog in the effective operation of the GLOC. Some of them did an outstanding job in the circumstances, the DID at Le Mans for example, issuing 40,000 rations in one day in addition to thousands of petrol tins,[81] but fundamentally the BSDs and DIDs were not properly, trained, manned or sufficiently experienced to execute the work with which they were tasked, and it took time and the strong hand of the Supply Investigation Department (SID) to bring professional order.[82]

73 WOOH, *Transportation*, p.45.
74 New contracts were not to be initiated by Services, but existing ones were to run to expiration. Ibid.
75 For details, see, Army Council, *Military Engineering*, Vol VII, *Accommodation and Installations*, pp.123-133, Cold Storage Installations.
76 The RASC was equipped with hand-operated field bakeries but the RE were capable of improvising or constructing power bakery facilities. See, Ibid, pp.202-203, Bakeries and Plate 115, Layout for a Bakery for 100,000-125,000 lb Bread Daily.
77 WOOH, *Transportation*, p.40.
78 The supply of petroleum products is examined in Chp 6, 'Leakers and Fillers'.
79 Deputy Director Supplies & Transport (DDST) BEF believed the best type of officer to command a DID was a late ASC Supply officer with Great War experience, who had the professional knowledge and grip to ensure receipts, issues and storage were correctly conducted but these officers were in much demand elsewhere, whilst others were deemed to be over age for operational service abroad. WOOH, *Supplies and Transport*, Vol I, p.108.
80 WOOH, Vol I, p.38.
81 WOOH, *Supplies and Transport*, Vol I, p.108.
82 The SID was a very effective organization within GHQ BEF during the Great War and sought to drive down loss, theft, fraud and waste but is now forgotten even by logisticians. Whilst initially focused on the Base areas, the work of the SID extended to Armies. One of the key tasks was to ensure the efficiency of distribution, one successful example in July 1917, being the recovery of 199 loaded railway wagons that had disappeared from the tracking process whilst in transit. See, Colonel R H Beadon,

P5.4 Logistic Lesson Learnt. One of the post campaign 'logistic lessons learnt', was the provision of integrated mobile field bakeries. (RLCM: B3/SRB/RLCAB/000853)

The original plan to ship from UK daily pack train loads so they were ready to store and then issue in France was thwarted by the rations being loaded to ships as mixed cargoes, priority of unloading being given to ammunition, insufficient trained Supply staff, and inappropriate buildings for the BSDs. The ration supply system thus quickly crumbled, only being saved from complete failure by the provision of locally purchased items through the assistance of the French Army *Intendant-General* department,[83] with the DIDs in isolated locations being almost completely dependent upon this system during the initial deployment period. Tea, sugar and jam were purchased in Paris but the quantities were so significant that they generated concerns from the French authorities.[84] It thus soon became clear that effective action was required to resolve the mounting problems, a point focused by the fact that by mid-September, HQ AASF had received so few rations that supplies were being dispatched by air, prompting an

CBE psc, *The Royal Army Service Corps: A History of Transport and Supply in the British Army*, Vol II (Cambridge: Cambridge University Press, 1931), pp.101-102 and Issac F Marcosson, *The Business of War* (London: John Lane, The Bodley Head, 1918), p.118. The activities and effectiveness of the SID in delivering logistic capability in the BEF in the Great War is worthy of academic study.

83 WOOH, *Supplies and Transport*, Vol I, p.105.

84 Ibid, p.111.

P5.5 Cold Storage. The acquisition of commercial refrigerated facilities was essential to the BEF's cold chain capability for the distribution of meat and an example of the significance of the civil economy in supporting military operations in France. (RLCM: B3/SRB/RLCAB/000823).

on-the-ground investigation by the Assistant Director Supplies & Transport from QMG 6 at the War Office. This exposed the on-going turmoil and initiated solutions,[85] not least of which, was a central purchasing office for the BEF to prevent different Services bidding against each other for material and contracted services.

Planning for rationing the BEF effectively commenced in 1937 when work was initiated to develop a new Field Service Ration Scale (FSRS). A draft daily scale was created, of approximately 3,800 calories, which consisted of two options, fresh and tinned. The Fresh Ration included 16 oz bread, 14 oz frozen meat, 8 oz potatoes, 3 oz bacon and 1 oz cheese plus 3½ oz, 2 oz milk, sugar, ¾ oz tea, ¼ oz salt and weekly supplements of flour, dried fruit, oatmeal, rice, mustard and peppered ham, supported by tinned tongue, ham, herring and

85 Ibid, p.107.

salmon.[86] The Tinned Scale introduced 12 oz of biscuit in lieu of bread and 12 oz of preserved meat instead of frozen product and utilized tinned items such as 6 oz potatoes, 4 oz tomatoes, 2½ oz of bacon or ham, 8 oz cheese, 2 oz fruit and 1 oz chocolate, all of which could also be used as alternatives to fresh items when these could not be obtained locally or transported without special arrangements.[87] The ration also included extras such as 2 oz cigarettes and two boxes of matches per week, and at the discretion of a brigadier or above, on the recommendation of the senior medical officer with the authority of the C-in-C BEF, thrice weekly ½ gill of rum or ¼ oz cocoa, 1/6 oz tea and ¼ oz marmite.[88] The FSRS was, with minor adjustments, utilized for the BEF in 1939. No sooner had it been approved and in operational service, experience in France reinforced the fact that the ration was too complex to be managed by untrained or inexperienced Supply personnel and there should be a focus on the essential rather than the luxury until such times that the ration Supply chain was operating effectively.[89] Indeed, the logic driving this issue was so compelling that the QMG to the Forces, General Sir Walter Venning[90] decided that a simple boxed ration was the solution, which initiated the BEF Special Ration Scale E, the ancestor of the 21st Century Composite Ration Pack. Scale E consisted of 12 oz preserved meat, 12 oz biscuit, and in tins, 2 oz sugar, 2 oz condensed milk, 2 oz cheese, 2 oz jam and 2 oz eating chocolate with alternatives of salmon and meat loaf plus cigarettes, matches and rum.[91]

Supplying the BEF with rations, forage,[92] liquid and solid fuels, lubricants, disinfectants and medical consumables was a vital task, with 101,000 tons being shipped from UK Supply

86 WOOH, *Supplies and Transport*, Vol II, p.436, Appx IX/3. The weekly supplements allowed for one of the following to be issued daily: 4 oz dried fruit, 3 oz tinned salmon, 5 oz tinned herring, 4 oz flour, 3 oz ham or tongue, 1½ oz oatmeal and together, 1 ½ oz rice and 1/8 oz curry powder.

87 WOOH, *Supplies and Transport*, Vol II, Appx IX/3, p.436.

88 Ibid.

89 WOOH, *Supplies and Transport*, Vol I, p.109.

90 General Sir Walter King Venning (1882-1964) GCB CMG CBE MC was commissioned into the Duke of Cornwall's Light Infantry in 1901, being attached to the West African Frontier Force before Western Front experience in the Great War in regimental and GHQ posts. An instructor at the Army Staff College (1919-1921), he served in the War Office (1922-1927), as AQMG of 1st Division at Aldershot (1927-1929) and DA & QMG of Eastern Command India (1929-1931) before assuming command of 2nd (Rawalpindi) Infantry Brigade (1931-1934). Promoting to major-general, he served as Director of Movements & Quartering at the War Office (1934-1938) before promotion to lieutenant-general in 1938 to assume the appointment of QMG to the Forces until 1942. He was knighted in 1939. He retired from the Army aged 60 to serve as the Director-General of the British Supply Mission to Washington until 1946. For additional details, see, Nick Smart, *Biographical Dictionary of the British Generals of the Second World War*, pp.315-316.

91 WOOH, *Supplies and Transport*, Vol II, Appx IX/4, p.436.

92 For a motorized Army it may seem strange that 5,500 tons of forage was imported. These supplies were for Force K6 from the RIASC. With a strength of 1,723 personnel, 1,996 mules, 68 horses and 528 carts in four Animal Transport (AT) Companies, with supporting units, Force K6 was brought to France to deliver 1st Line transport capability to units in areas where WMT or tracked vehicles, were unable to operate, although as it transpired, the deployment did not for the most part, reflect the original concept, with 22 AT Company for example, spending most of its time in the Base Area and others supporting RE construction activity. See, TNA WO 167/1433: HQ Force K6, Table 'Arrival of Force K6 at Marseilles from India', nd but probably 26 December 1939 and WOOH, *Maintenance in the Field*, Vol I, p.39.

Reserve Depots (SRD), plus 25,000 tons of frozen meat,[93] 9,000 tons of coal and coke, 5,500 tons of forage and 3,500 tons of potatoes.[94] The inclusion of frozen meat in the FSRS generated the requirement to emplace a cold chain to move and stock it. Contractors held 2,300 tons in UK commercial stores representing 40 days consumption for the First Contingent of which, 1,600 tons was shipped as part of the initial deployment.[95] To move frozen meat in France, DGT requested 140 insulated ice cooled rail vans be provided, either from production or from the UK railways, but as a temporary measure GHQ BEF hired 200 vans in the 6–15 ton range through the *Société Francais de Transport et Entrepots Frigerifiques*. As plans matured, the UK ordered an additional 60 cool vans and hired a further 70.[96] Of the first two field butcheries, No 1 was deployed to Saint Nazaire[97] and No 2 to Le Harve[98] within the ABA and of the two subsequent units, No 3 went to Boulogne[99] and No 4 was earmarked for a potential facility at Dunkerque.[100] In November 1939, an agreement with the *Intendant-General* Department confirmed the current and future allocations of cold storage facilities to the BEF,[101] which emphasizes the trend of moving the storage of some of the MBA stocks into the ABA.

Table 5.5
BEF – Cold Storage Allocation[102]

Location	November 1939 (Tons)	Future Storage (Tons)
Boulogne	Nil	2,200
Le Harve	2,000	6,200
Le Mans	Nil	240
Lille	Nil	300
Saint Nazaire	1,500	1,000
Total	3,500	9,940

93 WOOH, *Maintenance in the Field*, Vol I, p.39. The figure of 60,000, equating to a reserve of 840 lbs per person, quoted in Ellis, BOH, *The War in France and Flanders*, p.15, would therefore, appear to be incorrect.
94 WOOH, *Maintenance in the Field*, Vol I, p.40.
95 Ibid, p.105.
96 GHQ DGT Loose Minute dated 10 November 1939, 'Memorandum of the Meeting held in the General Manager's Office of the SNCF, 88 Rue Saint Lazare on 27 October 1939'. TNA WO 167/51: GHQ Services, Transportation.
97 TNA WO 167/1119: 1 Field Butchery RASC, WD, September 1939.
98 TNA WO 167/1120: 2 Field Butchery RASC, WD, September 1939.
99 TNA WO 167/1121: 3 Field Butchery RASC, WD, February 1940.
100 TNA WO 167/1122: 4 Field Butchery RASC, WD, February 1940.
101 TNA WO 167/51: GHQ Services, Transportation, 'No 1 Sub Committee - Personnel and Accommodation, Notes of Second Meeting held on 3 November 1939'.
102 Table collated from information in TNA WO 167/51: GHQ Services, Transportation, 'No 1 Sub Committee - Personnel and Accommodation, Notes of Second Meeting held on 3 November 1939'.

P5.6 RASC Bakery Operations. RASC Bakers working an established bakery, although many of the BEF's facilities were improvised. (RLCM: SRB/RLCAB/000880)

In common with many of the Base units, the tardy dispatch and movement of unit AFG 1098 stores by rail disrupted the establishment of the BSDs, which also left the soldiers of 1 BSD without their blankets and cooking kit for a week and by 20 September there was still no stationery and no access to a medical officer for the 800 plus soldiers on strength.[103] 1 BSD was located in the rail-served Baccarat factory, which was capable of storing 3,000 tons of rations on two floors but was under constant threat of recovery by the Host Nation to utilize it for glass production.[104] By 25 September, the depot was becoming increasingly busy, although the arrival of ration lorries with no protective tarpaulins interrupted issues. Receipts of rations from the UK were rapidly growing, although the bills of lading made for mixed reading, the war diary recording, 'Supplies of pork and beans arriving in huge quantities and other luxuries but no bully beef or biscuits and no tea'.[105]

Having received its equipment at Redon[106] by 17 September, 1 Field Bakery was bereft of flour and the bakers laboured in the petrol sub-depot until bread baking commenced on 22 September and by 24 September it was issuing 14,000 lb of bread to Nantes daily and 6,000 lb

103 TNA WO 167/1115: 1 BSD RASC, WD, September 1939. The depot commander was Lieutenant-Colonel H J C Hawkins OBE RASC.
104 TNA WO 167/1115: 1 BSD RASC, WD, September 1939.
105 TNA WO 167/1115: 1 BSD RASC, WD, 25 September 1939.
106 Redon is 45 miles to the NW of Nantes by road.

to Saint Nazaire,[107] although there were later interruptions to production when wet batches of flour arrived, having being left in the open on the dockside.[108] Sometimes however, the industry of the bakers, often working in austere field conditions, was not supported by the distribution system, with bread arriving at the Supply Railheads (SRH) in poor condition, 4 Division CRASC reporting that stocks received at Doullens were 'crushed, sodden and in some cases in burnt condition'[109] and on another occasion, the division only received 7,000 lb of its daily 11,000 lb allocation, the discrepancy only being discovered when the pack train was unloaded, leaving the divisional Supply Staff Officer insufficient time to supplement the shortage through local purchase.[110] The shortage of bread was however, not the only ration problem in February 1940 because fresh meat was arriving in 'a very a dirty and filthy condition' caused by an acute shortage of protective brown hessian wrappers in the UK.[111]

Ordnance Services

Ordnance Services within the Base were a critical component of the BEF's logistic capability, and the deployment plan allocated the following assets to it, although during the first three to four months of months of the operation, the improvised nature of the units did not generate the military efficiency and effectiveness required to prosecute resilient operations.

Table 5.6
BEF Base – Initial Deployment of Ordnance Assets

Assets	Quantity	Remarks
Advanced Ordnance Depot (AOD)	1	Arras - St Pol area
Advanced Ordnance Workshop (AOW)	1	Nantes then Arras in late October 1939
Base Ammunition Depot (BAD)	2	No 1 (Nantes) & 2 (Brest) BAD[112]
Base Ordnance Depot (BOD)	2	No 1 (Nantes) & No 2 (Le Harve)
Base Ordnance Workshop (BOW)	1	Nantes
Port Workshop Detachment (PWD)	4	Assigned to Docks Group RE

For security reasons, neither the Deployment Plan W4 nor the MPP were made available before mobilization to the designates appointed to the GHQ BEF posts of Director Ordnance Services (DOS) and Principal Ordnance Mechanical Engineer,[113] so the relevant technical Staff officers were unable to study the plans nor the potential issues before they embarked for France. This hindrance however, was just the start of an uphill struggle the Ordnance Directorate within

107 TNA WO 167/1123: 1 Field Bakery RASC, WD, September 1939.
108 TNA WO 167/1123: 1 Field Bakery RASC, WD, September 1939.
109 TNA WO 167/235: 4 Division CRASC, WD, 23 October 1939.
110 TNA WO 167/235: 4 Division CRASC, WD, 3 February 1940.
111 TNA WO 167/235: 4 Division CRASC, WD, 3 February 1940.
112 The establishment and operations of the BADs are covered in the Chp 7, 'Factory to Fire Trench'.
113 Respectively, late RAOC, Brigadiers A C V Gibson and J D White; WOOH, *Ordnance Services*. p.134.

P5.7 Mobile Equipment Support. 3 Port Workshop Detachment RAOC working on the Atlantic Quay Cherbourg in October 1939. Left to Right: Staff Sergeant D McGilroy, Private R H Woodward, Sergeant W G Combe (s?) MM. (RLCM: RAOC/WTB1/RAO/388)

GHQ faced in bringing order to the delivery of Ordnance Services to the BEF. The movement of the GHQ mobilization equipment to France was a complete shambles, with stores in transit for more than two weeks compounded by considerable pilfering, which was a headache for many units. Of the 16 stationery boxes dispatched from Aldershot for the Ordnance Directorate, only four arrived in the BEF Assembly Area and each of these was filled with millboards. Inevitably planning was disrupted whilst office machinery, such as typewriters and copiers were hired, furniture borrowed and stationery purchased, whilst the inadequate office accommodation was never properly resolved.[114]

There were however, much greater challenges to be overcome, which had been created by a combination of weak pre-war planning, a failure to ensure the existence of coherent co-ordination with the Host Nation and unstructured deployment. It became rapidly clear to Director Ordnance Services that the covered storage space required for a BOD[115] supporting the maintenance of a twelve division motorized force had been significantly underestimated,

114 WOOH, *Ordnance Services*, p.135.

115 For a generic layout, see, Army Council, *Military Engineering*, Vol VII, *Accommodation and Installations*, Plate 83, Base Ordnance Depot Layout.

P5.5 Rummy Tummy. Many of the logistic sites in the Base initially had poor restaurant facilities leading to issues with health, hygiene and morale and thus, inevitably, to a reduction in capability. (RLCM: RAOC/WTB1/RAO/373/3)

with crated MT items such as engines and major assemblies and large stocks of searchlights and ancillaries, being a particular initial problem, whilst the challenge of storing and maintaining the increasing reserves of Anti-Gas Equipment (AGE) became a constant headache for the Ordnance Directorate. The need for additional accommodation was exacerbated by its restricted availability. French government departments, or contractors working on their behalf, occupied some of the allocated BOD buildings in Nantes, whilst others proved to be unsuitable for storage, either because floor strengths were inadequate, access restricted or the fabric poor. The Chief Ordnance Officer (COO) of 1 BOD summarized this unsatisfactory situation:[116] 'Without additional space the Base Ordnance Depot cannot be operated beyond a few weeks'.[117] Requirements for covered accommodation rose from a pre-war estimate of 300,000 square feet to 1,050,000 in December 1939, whilst acquisitions by the end of October had reached 566,000 square feet in 28 buildings and tents, with 2,100,000 square feet of uncovered space, scattered over an area of 20 square miles. Whilst this met the need for dispersion, command and control became a fundamental challenge, creating even greater inefficiencies. Many of the buildings required repair, especially the roofs, which led to stock damage, whilst the restricted floor area to stack height ratios reduced planned storage space, with rail and road access also being generally

116 Colonel M R Neale MC. TNA WO 167/1168: 1 BOD RAOC, WD, September 1939.
117 TNA WO 167/1168: 1 BOD/2 dated 22 September 1939.

P5.8 A Lighter Logistic Moment. Note the RASC Suppliers jacket and the anti-gas eye-shield tucked into the service dress hat chip-strap. (RLCM: B3/SRB/RLCAB/000876)

poor. Congestion was so acute that consignments from the UK had to be temporarily curtailed whilst barges were used as storage at Nantes and 200 were allocated but not utilized at Rouen.[110]

A key failure however, was the poor synchronization of the 1 BOD deployment, which meant that stocks were arriving before the depot could be established. Eventually, 1 BOD occupied two major sites comprising two sub-depots; one at Savenay,[119] 25 miles to the North-West of Nantes and another at Bruz,[120] 10 miles to the South-West of Rennes. Reflecting the GHQ deployment, the movement of the BOD AFG 1098 stores, which totalled for a HQ and two sub-depots on 'light' scales, 600 tons, was another shambles, the stores arriving two weeks after the personnel, yet these stores, including key equipment such as racking, storehouse trucks, mobile cranes, crate tools and office equipment,[121] were essential for effective depot operations. This failure exacerbated the fundamental skills issue within the BOD because many soldiers were from the TA and Supplementary Reserve and had limited military training, whilst those from the Militia often had no or few relevant technical qualifications, although upon mobilization individuals' abilities were assessed and they were allocated, where possible, to appropriate tasks.[122] 2 BOD had similar issues, with the dearth of steel racking being an especial concern.[123] Security created yet another problem because the GHQ Staff initially refused to supply the Ordnance Directorate the BEF ORBAT and location lists. To compound this bizarre situation, *materiel* distribution

118 WOOH, *Ordnance Services*, p.136.
119 TNA WO 167/51: GHQ Services, Transportation, 'Northern Base - List of Proposed Permanent Depots'.
120 TNA WO 167/51: GHQ Services, Transportation, 'Southern Base - List of Proposed Permanent Depots'.
121 TNA WO 167/1168: 1 BOD RAOC, WD, October 1939.
122 WOOH, *Ordnance Services*, p.136.
123 TNA WO 167/1168: 1 BOD RAOC, WD, October 1939.

relied upon serial numbers, code addresses and special markings, some of which were out of date and others unrecognised by Movement Control, which not only led to much irritation but also to considerable delays in dispatching stores.[124] 1 BOD thus struggled to sustain the outputs, a difficulty aggravated by an inappropriate unit War Establishment. Indeed, given that the opening stock account was recorded on locally adapted stationery, the soldiers had no accommodation and catering facilities had to be arranged, it is a wonder that any order was brought.

Lessons however, were quickly learned, at least at unit level. 2 BOD was initially planned to be located around Rennes in new construction but the need to reduce the length of the GLOC suggested a site North of the River Seine and the French, keen on ensuring that 2 BOD was not in Le Harve, duly obliged with 800,000 square feet of covered accommodation around Yvetot, approximately 30 miles East-North-East of Le Harve, which also, conveniently, had rail access.[125] A detailed reconnaissance however, revealed that the buildings were mainly isolated barns across 600 square miles of rural France. At this juncture, personal relationships intervened. The COO of 2 BOD,[126] Colonel W W Richards MC,[127] with characteristic initiative, made direct contact with the President of the *Compagnie Generale Transatlantique* (CGT) and using his powers of persuasion secured some of the best storage facilities in Le Harve, totalling 1,000,000 square feet, including 520,000 square feet of CGT warehousing at the Gare Maritime.[128] No doubt the French authorities and GHQ BEF Contracts & Finance Branch was unimpressed by this private arrangement, which cut swiftly through all the 'red tape' but Colonel Richards had delivered an effective solution to the Ordnance storage problem.

1 BOD however, was plagued by a constant flow of failure emanating from the UK, with November 1939 being a particularly challenging month.[129] The arrival of *materiel* without supporting documentation was a constant headache, although at least the identification of items such as vehicles, weapons and medical stores was relatively easy. The arrival at Brest Docks of '10 x Coulters, Steel Frames on Steel Wheels',[130] was of a different order and neither the equipment nor its intended recipient had been identified by the end of the month.[131] Some vehicles arrived with no anti-freeze in the radiators, which with winter arriving meant urgent additional checks and correctional action.[132] The AFG 1098 and medical equipment for 3 General Hospital, which had been discharged at Brest, was 'dispersed' from the port having arrived without the consignment documentation and labelling but after much clerical industry and time, 16 of the rail wagons were traced, some in the MSBA Dieppe and others in Vertou; the location of the

124 WOOH, *Ordnance Services*, p.140.
125 Ibid, p.146.
126 The Deputy Chief Ordnance Officer was none other than Lieutenant-Colonel G C Shaw RAOC, author of the controversial, *Supply in Modern War*.
127 Perhaps unsurprisingly, Colonel Richards was a Major-General by 1945, having been awarded the CBE and CB. See, Fernyhough, & Harris, *History of the RAOC, 1939-1945*, p.489.
128 WOOH, *Ordnance Services*, p.146.
129 TNA WO 167/1168: 1BOD RAOC, WD, November 1939.
130 A 'coulter' is a cutting blade attached to the beam of a plough. It is possible that it was commercial equipment that had been loaded in error to a BEF vessel.
131 TNA WO 167/1168: 1BOD RAOC, WD, 2 November 1939.
132 TNA WO 167/1168: 1BOD RAOC, WD, 4 November 1939.

balance remained a mystery.[133] In mid-November, a consignment of two wheeled 'Carriage Ambulance Stretcher' equipments were sent to 1 BOD but without the inner tubes or outer covers for the wheels, the war diary thus wryly observing the effect of of 'rendering the carriage useless for its purpose',[134] a problem resolved through local purchase. On a more positive note, 1 BOD issued by rail, battalion mobilization stores to 1st Welsh Guards arriving from Gibraltar via Marseilles, and dispatching also by rail, the AFVs and WMT to an OFP for collection by the receiving units.[135] The visit of the 1940 Army Staff College Course in mid-December 1939, whilst involving extra work, did give the opportunity for 1 BOD to show off its organization consisting of three sub-depots, each with a workshops and a store,[136] plus three parks for AA guns and searchlights.

Equipment Support

As the BEF expanded, whilst also increasing its WMT and AFV fleets, Equipment Support became ever more important, in the same way that in the past Veterinary and Remount Services had been crucial to the operational capability of the Army when its logistics and fighting arms depended upon animal transport. As the Regular cavalry was mechanized various types of Cruiser and Light tanks began flowing into the Army's inventory.[137] New guns were also equipping Royal Artillery regiments, including the 25 pounder field pieces and the 3.7-inch Heavy AA gun and the 40 mm Light AA Bofors. The greatest change however, was the modernization of the infantry battalion's equipment inventory. Units had 1st Line WMT, tracked Universal Carriers, towed anti-tank guns and a growing selection of mortars, anti-tank rifles, Light Machine Guns (LMG), whilst to communicate, new telecommunications equipment was being introduced.[138] The ability to maintain and repair this growing and increasingly complex inventory required the appropriate equipment such as recovery vehicles and transporters, a wide range of mechanical, electrical, electronic and optical workshop facilities, a bewildering array of spares and most importantly, the skilled engineers, artificers and tradesmen to execute the work.

In 1939, there was no one Corps responsible for Equipment Support because the tasks were shared across many parts of the Regimental system, although the task of infantry Equipment Support fell on the RAOC. In the Base and the ABA, the RE deployed workshop capability,

133 TNA WO 167/1168: 1BOD RAOC, WD, 7 November 1939.

134 TNA WO 167/1168: 1BOD RAOC WD, 11 November 1939.

135 TNA WO 167/1168: 1BOD RAOC, WD, 29 November 1939.

136 No 1 Sub-Depot, MT; No 2, General Stores, less clothing; No 3, Artillery and Signals equipment. TNA WO 167/1168: 1BOD RAOC, WD, entry 12 December 1939.

137 For details of this process, see, Roger Salmon, *Everything Worked Like Clockwork: The Mechanization of the British Regular and Household Cavalry, 1918-1942* (Solihull: Helion, 2016).

138 For details of British Army communications and equipment in the 1930s and their use in the BEF, see, WOOH, *Signal Communications*, Colonel T B Gravely OBE (War Office, 1950) and Major-General R F H Nalder CB OBE, *The History of British Army Signals in the Second World War, General Survey* (London: Royal Signals Institution, 1953), pp.1-35. The complexities brought into the logistic system during this period by the introduction of electronic communications systems, is certainly an area worthy of study.

whilst the RASC fielded a Heavy Repair Shop (HRS)[139] and the RAOC, Base Ordnance Workshops (BOW)[140] and Advanced Base Workshops.[141] The establishment of 2 BOW at Nantes was almost as dysfunctional as that of 1 BOD, with an Advanced Ordnance Workshop (AOW) being initially deployed to cover the task.[142] An ordnance workshop company was detached from 2 BOW in support and fortunately, the garage facility that had been allotted was available and the equipment arrived to plan, so a capability was operational from 19 September. Reconnaissance identified suitable buildings to expand to a BOW but the *Comite des forges*[143] was reluctant to offer the sites stating they were allocated to the French Army. Eventually six buildings, with a floor space of 266,000 square feet were assigned to enable 2 BOW to install its machinery and commence operations.[144]

Port Workshop Detachments (PWD) were assigned to Brest, Cherbourg, Nantes and St Nazaire[145] tasked with effecting repairs to wheeled and tracked vehicles thus speeding unloading from ships and ensuring swift dock clearance. This was a wise decision because during embarkation in the UK several procedures had, in many circumstances, not been adhered to, the consequence of which, required PWD intervention. For example, ignition keys were not attached to the steering column or instrument panel, resulting in PWD personnel having to 'hot-wire' the vehicles. Some WMT had been improperly stowed in holds resulting in damage to mirrors, mudguards, radiators, headlamps and tracks rods, whilst other vehicles had been manoeuvred using the starter motors thus discharging the battery, resulting in delays in departure from the docks whilst re-charging was conducted.[146] The impressed civilian vehicles were more susceptible to damage than the military ones and repairs were often delayed because of a shortage of the appropriate spares.

Some of these issues were created by the rules appertaining to the carriage of fuel in vehicle tanks during sea movement, which meant that all fuel from WMT had to be drained before loading,[147] with subsequent positioning in the hold being undertaken manually, but using the starter motors to 'bump' the WMT, especially the heavier types, into the correct slot was just too tempting for tired soldiers under pressure to complete loading. Tracked vehicles were to have sufficient fuel for manoeuvring in the hold, with any remnants being drained, which was an additional risk in confined spaces but had to be weighed against the hazard of petrol leaking onto the deck or the fumes into the hold,[148] both of which posed a serious menace to the health

139 For a diagram of HRS lay-down, see, Army Council, *Military Engineering*, Vol VII, *Accommodation and Installations*, Plate 106, Heavy Repair Shop Layout.
140 For a diagram of a BOW lay-down, see, Ibid, Plate 107, Base Ordnance Workshops Layout.
141 For a diagram of an Advanced BOW lay-down, see, Ibid, Plate 109, Advanced Ordnance Depot Workshops Layout.
142 TNA WO 167/1196: Advanced Base Workshop RAOC, WD.
143 The *Comite des forges* or Foundry Committee was the French organization responsible for the allocation of real estate suitable for workshops.
144 WOOH, *Ordnance Services*, p.140.
145 1 PWD was assigned to Nantes, 2 PWD to Brest, later transferring to Rennes, 3 PWD to Cherbourg and 4 PWD to Le Harve and Rouen
146 WOOH, *Ordnance Services*, p.142.
147 Army Council, FSPB, Pamphlet No 7, 1939, *Movement by Sea, Rail and Air*, p.9.
148 Seals and connectors for vehicle fuel lines and tanks were sufficiently unreliable for the War Office WMT manual to state: 'Before garaging a vehicle, the driver will examine the fuel system in detail for leaks … No vehicle with such leakage of fuel will be garaged until the leakage has been rectified or the

of personnel and the safety of the ship.[149] The vehicles then required refilling, which was a post disembarkation task that exposed another logistic wrinkle because some of the petrol cans marked for the fuel had, in UK, been filled with diesel or water, these liquids being poured into the vehicle tanks in error, which meant the fuel systems had to be drained, flushed and refilled.[150] To prevent further damage and to improve efficiency, 1 PWD at Nantes was tasked with conducting all vehicle movement within the ships' holds, a system that was then adopted at all SPODs with a PWD, although arguably, given their skills, technical personnel would have been more gainfully employed repairing vehicles rather than preventing failure, but it was step in the right direction in delivering more effective and efficient logistic outputs by placing the task in the hands of specialists. Despite the designation, the PWDs were also tasked to repair bicycles, typewriters, other AFG 1098 equipment, and rather more bizarrely, to recover crashed aircraft.[151]

Conclusion

The development of the Base had a fragile start. The failure of the War Office General Staff to take the technical logisticians into the planning operational circuit resulted in several dilemmas, which were only solved through the due process of time and practical experience. The under-estimation of the ordnance storage requirement was combination of a mis-appreciation of the demand and the constant expansion of the BEF and was complicated by the issues over the availability of appropriate Host Nation real estate. The deployment of Base units, especially from the RAOC, revealed an inherent mis-judgement concerning the effective readiness and operational capability of 'War Establishment only' organizations, whilst the manner of their movement, separating units from their mobilization stores, was a concept waiting to fail.

The insatiable appetite for rail construction to support emerging logistic demands and infrastructure development was a surprise to the General Staff but not to the logisticians and engineers. It was fortunate that the RE had foreseen the need and matured a rail capability that could be phased and flowed to the task. The professionalism of the Corps in managing this work, especially given the winter weather and the dynamic environment, was one of the key inputs to the enlargement of the Base. The RASC was generally well found in terms of output, although the rapid expansion of the BEF led to a scarcity of trained technical personnel, generating issues with standards and accounting both of which, were an inevitable consequence of pre-war decisions. The Corps utilized its ex-Regular Reservists to effect in the Supply arena and was quick to recognize that the doctrine of streaming the distribution of fuel with rations was a fundamental error, moving swiftly to correct it.

defective portion of the system drained or isolated from the main supply tank'. Army Council, *Manual of Driving and Maintenance for Mechanical Vehicles (Wheeled)*, 1937, MT, pp.125-126.

149 The Army clearly comprehended the threat posed by petrol and to a lesser extent diesel fuels and the War Office WMT manual devoted four pages to the prevention of fire in relation to the use of MT. Ibid, pp.124-127.

150 WOOH, *Ordnance Services*, p.142.

151 3 PWD was the lead in this activity, recovering in November 1939 an aircraft that had landed in a field 15 miles from Cherbourg before nosing over onto its back. Ibid, p.148.

Split Equipment Support responsibilities were a feature of the pre-war Army, although it was obvious to many logisticians that with an increasingly technical Army, radical reforms would be necessary to ensure combat capability. In this respect, 'Cap-Badge politics' had an adverse effect in delivering a different approach, with for example, the RASC, a mature Corps in the forefront of combat logistics that had refined its machinery, understandably reluctant to handover its internal Equipment Support capability to another organization. Equally, the Corps of Royal Engineers was determined to retain the specialist integrated railway Equipment Support assets, and unlike the RASC, successfully defended its corner, although different imperatives influenced the outcomes. As the motorization and mechanization of the Army progressed, the centralization of the vehicle repair and stores systems was a natural corollary, but the concept was overrun by the complexities and dynamics of the rearmament and expansion programmes, thus delaying the formation of the Royal Electrical and Mechanical Engineers (REME) until 1942. From the BEF perspective, a transformation of the Equipment Support arrangements would certainly have been of benefit, but the timing of the delivery would have been crucial to minimize disruption to output.

In summary, given the hand, which they were dealt, the logisticians proved to be remarkably adept in delivering the requirement, although the inadequate production of spares from industry proved to be consistent complication. Base structures and systems, whilst sometimes roughly hewn, gradually became more robust as constant daily practise ironed out the wrinkles, soldiers gained 'On the Job' experience and innovation started to emerge. As time progressed, logisticians began to feel confident with 'Scale', whilst relearning the importance of detail and delivering 'right first time'. By early May 1940, the Base was ready to effectively support combat operations and did so, although had the Germans not invaded, it is probable that senior logistic officers would have progressively turned their attention from effectiveness to efficiency to ensure that resources were not squandered,[152] but it took manoeuvre operations to reinforce the point that the Base had to integrate agility with capacity.

152 The importance of the 'War on Waste' is brilliantly exposed in an Open Circular entitled 'Economy' to All Ranks signed by Brigadier J G Halsted OBE MC, the DA & QMG I Corps. TNA WO 167/144: I Corps ADOS, I Corps CRO 30 dated 5 December 1939.

6

Leakers and Fillers
The supply of Petrol Oil and Lubricants to the BEF

Inter-War Developments

A critical, if not the defining task, in the supply of the BEF was the provision of Petroleum, Oil and Lubricants (POL) for its motorized and mechanized army, without which, the capital invested to create mobility was effectively worthless.[1] In comparison to ammunition, in which there was an increasingly strong Defence investment in industrial production and military storage infrastructure, the War Office was able to utilize commercial facilities in UK to deliver the storage and turnover of POL stocks and reserves,[2] thereby driving down costs, whilst delivering capability. Indeed, in creating what was thought to be a cheap, effective and tactically flexible fuel distribution based upon the non-returnable disposal tin can, excessive parsimony led to the introduction of one that that was logistically fragile, fraught with safety issues, created a major requirement for manual labour and upon the deployment of the BEF, required the employment of new capital equipment to ensure resilience.

The logistics of providing petroleum support for motorized and mechanized forces was the subject of many debates during the late 1920s and early 1930s, with the RASC at the forefront of the process, although the RE played an increasingly significant role in constructing and maintaining, sometimes in conjunction with contractors, bulk fuel installations in the Base and at Rear Aerodromes, and to a lesser extent in the corps areas.[3] Of particular significance, was the growing demand for petroleum products as cavalry regiments and infantry battalions were mechanized during the 1930s, the dynamism being highlighted by a 1934 Royal Engineer manual highlighting that the acreage and tonnage quoted in it for a bulk petrol depot might 'be inadequate in any particular case'.[4] In 1930, an infantry division required 6,400 gallons

1 QMG 6 (b) in the War Office was also responsible for planning the acquisition, transportation and storage of RAF POL products for the Air Component of the BEF and RAF assets from Fighter Command, and Bomber Command, which supported the deployment of the AASF.

2 For a summary of the Armed Services outline plans for War Reserves storage, see, D J Payton-Smith, BOH, *Oil: A Study in War-time Policy and Administration* (London: HMSO, 1971), pp.61-64.

3 Army Council, *Military Engineering*, Vol VII, *Accommodation and Installations*, pp.116-120 and Plate 77, Base Bulk Petrol Depot Layout.

4 Army Council, *Military Engineering*, Vol VII, *Accommodation and Installations*, p.21.

of petrol per day and a cavalry division, 7,900 gallons. By 1936, with the mechanization and motorization of the Army in full swing, these quantities had risen to nearly 21,000 for the former and 26,000 for the latter.

In 1928, a logistic Staff exercise was held at the RASC Training College, which examined many of the potential problems inherent in distributing fuel for a future motorized and mechanized Army, and this in turn led to a debate between two schools of thought: 'Can' and 'Bulk'. The former won the day, on four premises. First, that the Army relied heavily on the impressment of civilian vehicles to support expeditionary operations 'at scale',[5] and that although the commercial sector was moving towards distribution in bulk, civilian tankers would be unsuitable for field service, particularly regarding mobility and the purchase of a military 'special' would be necessary. Secondly, 3rd Line transport of fuel relied, for the most part, on Rail Tank Cars (RTC) and it was foreseen that these might be in short supply in an operational theatre, thereby reducing the effectiveness of bulk distribution at 2nd Line. Thirdly, the can provided a method of field storage, which, if the transport of bulk fuel was not to be disrupted, the road tanker could not. Fourthly, the tactical re-fuelling of vehicles was assessed to be more flexible, quieter and often quicker with cans.

Given these strong arguments, it is not surprising that the 'Can' school won the day but it is important to recognize that the decision was made at a period when it was perceived that the most likely deployments would be to demanding locations with relatively poor infrastructure in support of Imperial defence or trade protection, such as China, Egypt or India, and it is instructive that in early 1927 a three brigade force had to deployed to Shanghai after the British concession in Hankou was invaded by Chinese Nationalist forces.[6] The logistic emphasis in these environments focused upon the simple rather than the complex, but the deployment to France was of a different order and the humble can became a serious logistic issue as the broader implications of the distribution requirements for a thirty-two division motorized and mechanized force became fully apparent.

A Flimsy Solution?

The decision to focus upon 'packed' fuel[7] initially relied upon 'canned' fuel[8] using the robust in-service 2-gallon steel can, which was effectively the same as the civilian one, an item that was in quantity production and circulation during the 1920s. As roadside fuel-filling stations became more common and cars began to be fitted with internal 'reserve' tanks, the imperative to carry spare canned fuel to reach a filling point declined and the numbers of commercial cans with it. From the Defence perspective, the 2-gallon can thus became more expensive to produce and of course, required an in-Theatre filling plant and a Reverse Logistics chain to support

5 TNA WO 32/4612: Future Army Organization – 1935, QMG Response dated 16 December 1936 to CIGS SECRET Paper, 'Future Reorganization of the British Army' dated 9 September 1935.
6 13th and 14th Infantry Brigades from the UK and 20th (Indian) Infantry Brigade from the sub-continent. 27th Infantry Brigade was also dispatched from the UK but held in reserve in Hong Kong. TNA FO 371/63436: Dispatch of Shanghai Defence Force to Shanghai, 1927.
7 Liquid fuel in either a returnable and reusable can or in a non-returnable tin.
8 Liquid fuel in a returnable and reusable container. In the BEF this was usually a 2 or 4-gallon can, although French 5 litre cans, 50 litre drums and 200 litre barrels were also used.

it. It was therefore, retained as the vehicle reserve fuel carrier but replaced in the fuel supply chain by the much cheaper, tin-plate disposable 4-gallon tin, commonly called a 'flimsy',[9] which was 'cased' at two tins per wooden, cardboard or three-ply box[10] and filled at a factory thereby introducing the economies of scale to drive down cost.[11] In conjunction with the Anglo-Iranian Oil Company and Shell, two filling factories were established for the War Office[12] at the oil ports of Avonmouth and Llandarcy, and for the RAF, at Ardrossan and Stanlow.[13] At this point however, parsimony intervened because insufficient tin-plate and paint were purchased, or labour hired and trained, to fully test the manufacturing lines for quality and quantity and as a result, these plants were never fully run up to work them to efficiency with proficient staff. Inevitably, when mobilization was initiated there were issues with production out-turn, safety and the standard and resilience of the cans.[14] The War Office thus invested limited capital in UK industrial capacity and even less in deployable military capability but events in France clearly exposed the fragility of this decision and it was therefore, fortunate that the members of the 'Bulk' school did not completely lose their case. The Army exercises of 1935, involving the equivalent of two small corps, reinforced the advantages of using cans in the divisional and corps areas but enabled the RASC to experiment with bulk refuelling by hiring civilian tankers that provided the key evidence in late 1939 to adopt a different approach to fuel distribution in France, which, whilst requiring greater capital investment in expeditionary logistics, reduced not only the fragility in fuel distribution, but also the size of the expanding demand for manual handling of fuel cans and tins in the supply chain.

In September 1939, the administration of British Army POL was vested in QMG 6 (b) consisting of three RASC Staff officers, whose key pre-war planning assessments for the BEF were based upon six divisions in two corps operating offensively and supported by the allocated GLOC units. Liquid fuel requirements[15] were calculated to be 192,000

9 The 'flimsy' is certainly an early example of a recyclable but non-reusable container, and this at a time, when most glass bottles had a deposit on them. It was, however, a costly failure and was replaced partly by the reusable 2-gallon can, then a 4-gallon can and finally by a copy of the jerrycan, the RASC spelling of which, was 'jerrican'. Interestingly, the first batch brought back from North Africa for assessment was probably Italian.

10 The 'flimsy' was notorious for leaking, creating un-necessary fuel loss and a major fire hazard, especially on ships.

11 WOOH, *Supplies and Transport*, Vol I, p.43.

12 The QMG formally expounded this concept in 1935. TNA WO 32/4612: Future Army Organization - 1935, QMG Response dated 16 December 1936 to CIGS SECRET Paper, 'Future Reorganization of the British Army' dated 9 September 1935.

13 For an examination of the national petroleum product preparations for the Second World War, see, BOH, *Oil*, pp.52-59.

14 WOOH, *Supplies and Transport*, Vol I, p.33.

15 The documents, primary and secondary, use both Imperial tons and gallons for the Definition of Quantity of liquid fuels. Bulk petrol, although the Specific Gravity varies slightly depending upon type, was planned at 300 gallons per ton. The gross weight of canned petrol in a returnable container equated to 242 gallons per ton to account for the weight of the can. The gross weight of cased petrol in non-returnable tins equated to 224 gallons per ton to account for the weight of the tins and the case. A figure of say 100 tons may therefore, unless specifically noted, refer to gross tonnage including the containers or just the fuel weight.

gallons[16] per day, which was principally petrol[17] because there were relatively few compression ignition vehicles in BEF service. Each corps was expected to consume approximately 80,000 gallons daily, whilst the daily consumption rate for an armoured division in offensive operations was 26,000 gallons per day. Of interest, was petrol for cooking, estimated to be 1.5 gallons per man per month, and thus for a force of 400,000, a total of 19,726 gallons daily.[18] Given that the distribution of liquid fuel in the BEF was focused upon the 4-gallon disposable tin, the logistic challenge of provisioning, transporting, storing and accounting for the BEF's fuel, a task, which grew as the BEF expanded, is lucidly exposed. The initial Maintenance Project Plan (MPP)[19] covered the requirement to M+32[20] involving the shipment of 1,937,500 filled tins to France and suitable shipping was identified to meet the task and the timeframe. The most significant pressing concern was increasing the flow to France. The Board of Trade, rightly as it transpired, sought for safety reasons, to limit the size of vessels for the carriage of cased petrol to a load of 300 tons, which meant that many small ships would be required to conduct the movement, with a bottleneck of berths in UK and France impeding the acceleration of the schedule. As it transpired, the issue became academic because can manufacture and thus the filling factory output from Avonmouth and Llandarcy was initially under 50 percent of the planned target, whilst there were also issues with the resilience and quality of the tins.[21] So instead of having to hire more ships, QMG 6 had to withdraw some from the out-load programme, which quickly disrupted the build of stocks in France.

Priming the Pump

Pre-war fuel distribution policy was based upon cased petrol in 4-gallon disposal tins but as the scale of the future deployment of the BEF became clear, a different approach was adopted, which sought to introduce some bulk stocks at the three to sixth month point, and after 12 months, supplying the RAF, Base and the GLOC using bulk fuel, with the combat formations remaining on cased.[22] As it transpired, acquiring Ocean Terminal and Inland bulk storage in France was not a significant issue but exploiting bulk stocks by moving the fuel to the consumer required either specialist road and rail transportation assets and transfer equipment or in-Theatre can-filling systems, operated by appropriately trained personnel, resources which took time to

16 WOOH, *Supplies and Transport*, Vol I, p.103. The petrol for spark ignition engines on overseas operations was rated at 80 octane, dyed red, the code MT 80 being used to denote it was for use by WMT or armoured vehicles including tanks.
17 Petrol for commercial WMT was rated at 68 octane whilst the British Army used 72 octane coded MT 72 and coloured yellow or orange to denote it was for use by military WMT. For overseas operations, MT 80 was standard for all ground spark ignition vehicles, which caused maintenance issues on some engines not adaptable for the higher-octane rating.
18 Figures calculated from information in WOOH, *Supplies and Transport*, Vol II, p.509, Appx XA. The daily requirement for cooking thus equated to 4,931 x 4-gallon tins per day, the transport lift being 31 x 3 ton lorries.
19 TNA WO 197/2: First Maintenance Project: Reception of Forces in France and system of maintenance in the initial stages.
20 M Day was 6 September 1939.
21 This was caused by the failure, in order to save money, to operate the plants during peace-time, thus working them to efficiency with proficient staff. WOOH, *Supplies and Transport*, Vol I, p.43.
22 Map 8: BEF – Base Petroleum Ports & Depots.

procure and deploy, factors which acted as a brake on the enthusiasm and plans of the GHQ Petrol Supply Staff.

The disruption to the cased in-load would have been critical had pre-war planning not stolen a march on the failure. Through a secret contract with the Anglo-Iranian Oil Company enabled by the *Société General de Huites de Petrole*, the War Office had imported 200,000 x 2-gallon returnable cans and hired two 5,000 ton tanks at Donges, five miles to the East of Saint Nazaire on the River Loire, for MT spirit, although a small inconvenience was that one was filled with diesel, so it had to be discharged and cleaned.[23] On 6 September 1939, using female labour, Anglo-Iranian commenced filling the returnable cans from the bulk stock of French alcoholised petrol at Donges,[24] from which, the cans could be railed to BEF locations. Filling proceeded at 300-400 cans per hour[25] and the BEF hired from the Host Nation, additional five and 50 litre cans for the Army and 200 litre barrels for the AASF.[26] Thus of the proposed total of 25,500 tons of fuel in-Theatre by M+32, 19.6 percent, 5,000 tons, were converted to bulk stocks. Of the 25,500 tons, 8,000 was allocated for the BEF to move to its Concentration Area, and 5,000 tons for 15 days of half operational rate and 20 days at operational rate.[27]

In the Base, road-served POL Depots (POLD) were established at Blain and Saint Thegonnec, with the former planned to be rail-served with a connection to the *Société Nationale des Chemins de fer Francais* (SNCF)[28] network.[29] 100 ton Detail Issue Deports (DID) stocking cased fuel were quickly established at Brest, Rennes, Laval, Le Mans and Douai using road and rail transport to support the Main Base Areas (MBA), the GLOC and its staging areas. Plans were confirmed with the French for cased fuel sites at Arras for 700 tons of packed fuel with road and IWT access and another one at Bethune for 400 tons, with a further 1,250 tons spread across sites in Beauvais, Calais, Cambrai and Dieppe using road, rail and IWT capability. Five further facilities totalling 1,750 tons located in the vicinity of Calais, Dieppe, Paris and Saint Quentin were also identified.[30] In addition, the French agreed to allow packed fuel to be shipped through the port of Caen, a solution enacted in October 1939,[31] with the subsequent

23 TNA WO 167/1076: GHQ, Supply Directorate (Petrol), WD, September 1939.

24 TNA WO 167/1076: GHQ, Supply Directorate (Petrol), WD, 6 September 1939. In 2020, Donges remains an oil terminal and refinery operated by *Total*.

25 WOOH, *Supplies and Transport*, Vol I, p.106 states that the filling capability was 25,000 cans per day but the GHQ Supply Directorate (Petrol), WD, 6 September 1939 in TNA WO 167/1076, states filling was running at 300 - 400 cans per hour, which equates to 7,200 - 9,600 based on 24 hour production. It is possible that both are correct, and the plant was not fully operational when the Supply Directorate note was issued.

26 TNA WO 167/1076: GHQ, Supply Directorate (Petrol), WD, 6 September 1939.

27 WOOH, *Supplies and Transport*, Vol I, p.106.

28 *Société Nationale des Chemins-der-Fer Francais*.

29 TNA WO 167/51: GHQ, Services, Transportation, 'List of Proposed Permanent Depots giving Order of Priority of Construction' (SECRET). Despite the importance of liquid fuel to the BEF the task was listed as Priority 4. The connection to the SNCF network was to be at the North end of Fay de Bretagne station.

30 TNA WO 167/1076: GHQ, Supply Directorate (Petrol), 'Petrol Supplies for the BEF' (SECRET) dated 28 October 1939.

31 From the Royal Navy perspective, this was of sufficient import to warrant an entry in the Official History. Roskill, BOH, *The War at Sea, 1939-1945*, Vol I, *The Defensive*, p.64.

P6.1 Ocean Terminal. Shell-Mex bulk tanker and storage on the River Tyne at Jarrow in the late 1920s. Despite the pre-war plan for fuel distribution to rely upon the disposable can, limited bulk fuel commercial capacity was introduced to provide a reserve immediately before the BEF's deployment, with the concept being slowly expanded. (RLCM: POL/RASC/NOR)

establishment of the rail-served No 4 POLD 10 miles East of Moult Argences, a town 12 miles South-East of the port.[32]

A POLD consisted of a HQ plus a number of sections, each with 54 personnel established to store 6,500 tons of packed fuel along a rail 'whisker' in 25 x 260 ton stacks; key task equipment consisted of 6 x tractors and 12 x trailers. Labour was planned to be provisioned on the basis of one man handling eight tons of packed fuel per eight hours, or if Material Handling Equipment (MHE) was not available, five tons.[33] A POLD could be deployed in the Base, the Advanced Base and corps areas and was thus an excellent example of a unit, which was based upon 'task organization',[34] it size and output being based upon the requirement. The main POLDs, holding mainly cased fuel, are shown in the table below.

32 TNA WO 167/1076: GHQ, Supply Directorate (Petrol), WD, entry 12 November 1939. The depot was established using a connection to the private Moult to Lisieux rail line that served the Tuileries de Beauvais factory.

33 Philson, BEFORBAT, Vol 1, p.158. Such MHE included portable conveyers.

34 Whilst the term 'task organization' was in use by late the 20th Century, the concept and activity has a much longer history and is focused upon organizing military resources, with the relevant Command, Control & Communications structure and assets to meet a particular mission or task.

Table 6.1
BEF Key Packed Fuel Storage and Filling Facilities

Depot	Main Access	Location	Sub Area	Remarks
1 Base POLD	Rail	Blain	Nantes	
2 Base POLD	Rail	L'Hermitage	Rennes	
3 Base POLD	Rail	Abancourt	Rouen	
4 Base POLD	Rail	Moult Argences	Cherbourg	In-load from Caen SPOD
Base Petrol Filling Centre	Rail	Donges	Nantes	Commercial operation
	Road	Lomme	Corps	Lille (Lomme)
	Rail, Road & IWT	Rouen	Rouen	Section detached to Lomme
	Rail	Vertou	Nantes	
Foret de la Traconne[35]	Road	Dump	Nantes	To support AASF
Vignacourt	Road	Dump	Rouen	To support Air Component

The challenges of storing larges quantities of cased fuel safely and protecting it from the attentions of the enemy was an issue examined before the war. Concealment in buildings removed the need for camouflage but liquid fuel, and petrol in particular, could not be stored inside closed buildings, the hazards created by the vapour from leaking tins being all too obvious. Open-side barns were one solution, offering some protection from view and the weather, but groups of them effectively generated an identifiable target. The logisticians' solution was to site most of the depots in forests, where cased and canned fuel stacks could be hidden and camouflaged under the tree canopies, with ever-green locations being the preferred options. This approach however, created additional logistic burdens, including engineer works to the forest tracks to sustain the movement of WMT and the provision of tarpaulins, which were used to break the sharp edges of the stacks, but the canvas had to be appropriately painted to blend in with the surroundings. The weather also influenced operations. In the cold and damp of winter, the engineer effort to maintain the tracks was considerable,[36] although from the safety perspective,

35 TNA AIR 35/123: Reserve stocks of aviation fuel, bombs and small arms ammunition, 1940, 'AASF Fuel Requirements,' AASF S/.3586/Org dated 7 May 1940.

36 On 31 January 1940 for example, the speed limit for all the roads and tracks within the depot sites was reduced to 5 mph because of the damage being caused by WMT during the thaw conditions. TNA 167/1148/1: 1 POLD RASC, WD.

the wet woodland greatly reduced the opportunity for the spread of fire,[37] these scenarios being reversed in dry and warm conditions.[38]

The static camouflage and concealment work were remarkably effective at some sites, but the challenge was to lower the signature of dynamic activities such as track maintenance, vehicle movement and case stacking, all three of which were generally more difficult to reduce in the winter. The logisticians were certainly well aware of the problem because CO 1 POLD[39] requested the RAF to conduct, in early January 1940, an aerial visual reconnaissance from 2,000 and 500 feet of the sites at Blain, Bouvron and Notre Dame, which resulted in the production of a concise report highlighting the key issues.[40] Unsurprisingly, it was the dynamic activities, which attracted attention, although poorly camouflaged vertical stacks on the open sides of forestry blocks were a clear indicator of a field logistic site. The report also exposed the failure to conceal bright green and blue oil drums, which were especially obvious as were the bright metal portable conveyers used for moving the cases and cans.[41] On a more positive note, appropriately camouflaged low stacks in scrubland were difficult to identify, although the site was compromised by the soldiers working at it looking up to the aeroplane, the pilot commenting, 'I should like to emphasise the much published fact, that the human face is very noticeable from the air. If a man dressed in khaki looks down and stands quite still, it is very difficult to notice him.[42] In this respect, personal drills were as equally important in protecting fuel stocks, as the use of equipment.

Bulking Out

It quickly became clear to the GHQ Petrol Supply Directorate that the pre-war plans to rely upon cased fuel were not sufficiently robust to service the needs of the BEF 'at scale' and the Staff drafted an ambitious scheme to create a solution to increase bulk storage capability across the GLOC in three phases, with a particular emphasis on ensuring access to multi-modal

37 1 POLD did not receive its three fire tenders until 22 March 1940. TNA WO 167/1148/1: 1 POLD RASC, WD, 22 March 1940. The threat of fire was ever present, with one igniting in the rubbish heap in the depot railway yard on 13 May 1940, and although the war diary does not speculate upon the cause, discarded cigarette ends were a constant hazard.

38 On 29 March 1940, the CO ordered, as a precaution against the spread of fire, the removal of all the brushwood camouflaging the sides of the stacks. TNA WO 167/1148/1: 1 POLD RASC, WD.

39 Initially, 1 POLD was assigned as 5 Section, 1 BSD but was re-designated as a depot when it became clear that the storage and issue of petroleum products required to be separated from the Supplies function. Apart from the technical entries in the war diary, there are several others of interest. On 1 December 1939, it reported that Prince George of Greece had placed his chateau and the grounds at the unit's disposal, whilst on 3 December, the unit hosted 60 Staff College students on a course visit. 1 POLD received a formal visit from Prince George on 4 May 1940, whilst a sadder entry on 27 April 1940, recorded the death by drowning in a canal, of a Private from 112 Company AMPC. TNA WO 167/1148: 1 POLD RASC, WD.

40 TNA WO 167/1148/1: 1 POLD RASC, 'Report on Flight over 5 Section', Squadron-Leader H M C Harwood RAF, dated 6 January 1940.

41 TNA WO 167/1148/1: 1 POLD RASC, 'Report on Flight over 5 Section', p.2.

42 TNA WO 167/1148/1: 1 POLD RASC, 'Report on Flight over 5 Section', p.2.

transportation.[43] Phase 1 focused upon acquiring bulk Ocean Terminal and Inland storage. Ocean Terminal requirements were 25,000 tons at Le Harve, of which 15,000 tons was MT spirit and the balance aviation fuel, whilst the British sought another 15,000 – 20,000 tons at Dunkerque and 15,000 tons at Rouen to be delivered by small coastal tankers using the River Seine. Eventually 70,000 tons of bulk storage was identified as possibly available through a contract at Rouen and Honfleur, a smaller port opposite Le Harve on the River Seine, although to achieve full effect it was necessary to construct a rail siding and dredge the berth at Honfleur. The approach to the French to use tankage at Calais was politely refused. Phase 2 identified possible sites on the Seine near Paris for 3,000 – 5,000 tons of bulk fuel accessed by Rail Tank Cars (RTC) and road tankers. Phase 3 sought to generate Ocean Terminal bulk storage of 6,000 – 7,000 tons at St Malo.[44] Accessing storage did not of course mean the tankage was filled but because most of the proposed bulk stocks were to be imported as refined products, the interface with the French commercial co-ordinating organization, *Société pour l'Importation Des Petroles and Derives* being crucial in managing conflicting priorities and resolving, with the Host Nation authorities, issues relating to customs documentation and dues.[45]

Inevitably, these proposals and plans initiated a series of concomitant supporting tasks. Whilst the dispersion mitigated the risk of loss, the challenge was in controlling and maintaining the stocks with the personnel resources to hand and a new unit, the bulk storage petrol company, consisting of some personnel with commercial technical expertise from the petroleum industry, was formed to oversee the military aspects of these ocean and inland sites.[46] Transportation, especially 3rd Line rail from the MBA and ABA to the corps Petrol Railheads (PRH) was the other key issue. Whilst sheeted open rail wagons sufficed to move canned fuel, the movement of bulk supplies required RTCs and 148 x 15 ton cars were requested from the UK.[47] To reduce reliance on rail, GHQ sought to use IWT for canned and bulk petrol, although it was identified that the French rarely carried packed petrol by barge.

By February 1940, bulk petrol traffic was developing using barges on the River Seine from Le Harve to Honfleur and Rouen, supported by occasional tanker movement from Donges and Brest to ports on the Seine. The concept was expanded to include a plan to transport daily, 600 tons of bulk petrol from Dunkerque to Douai to supply the can-filling stations in the rear of the corps, although the French, because of limited barge resources, were only able to move small quantities, so QMG BEF requested the acquisition of 12 power and 24 dumb barges from the UK. A week before the German ground offensive commenced, two power barges arrived at Dunkerque and one power and one dumb at Calais but the service never commenced.[48] In addition, it was clear that bulk delivery by road would be required and an order was placed through the War Office for the acquisition of 59 x 10 ton road tankers and 140 x 2.5 ton bulk

43 TNA WO 167/1076: GHQ, Supply Directorate (Petrol), 'Petrol Supplies for the BEF' (SECRET) dated 28 October 1939.

44 TNA WO 167/1076: GHQ, Supply Directorate (Petrol), 'Petrol Supplies for the BEF' (SECRET) dated 28 October 1939.

45 Documents in TNA WO 167/1076: GHQ, Supply Directorate (Petrol).

46 Regimental Committee, *The Story of the Royal Army Service Corps, 1939-1945* (Aldershot: Institution of the RASC, Bell & Sons, 1955), p.59. For the establishment, see, Philson, BEFORBAT, Vol 3, p.92.

47 TNA WO 167/1076: GHQ, Supply Directorate (Petrol), 'Petrol Supplies for the BEF' (SECRET) dated 28 October 1939.

48 WOOH, *Transportation*, p.46.

P6.2 Bulk Fuelling by Road. Thornycroft Road Tanker of 1930. Whilst the 'flimsy' took priority in fuel distribution, the concept of bulk refuelling using road tankers did not evaporate and was expanded to support units in the Base Areas and airfields. (RLCM: A1b/MT/ Tankers 5474)

fuel lorries. As a result of this decision, three Bulk Petrol Transport Companies (BPTC) were deployed to the BEF to move bulk petroleum products in the GLOC Area. A BPTC had a HQ, a workshop section and three operating sections.[49] Operating sections had 15 tankers, each of which was of 800 or 1,000 gallons capacity, plus an additional five held by company HQ. A BPTC had therefore, a one-time lift at 100 percent availability, of 40,000 or 50,000 gallons depending upon the size of the tankers; at divisional and corps level however, the tin remained the distribution method.

Developing a close relationship with the French Army petroleum specialists was time well invested both operational and technically. The Petroleum Supply Directorate team[50] had a most useful visit to the French *Grand Quartier General* on 27 October and were briefed upon the French Army fuel supply system, which included underground storage, pipelines, filling

49 For details of equipment, vehicles, weapons and trades, see WET WE IV/1931/34C/1, see, Philson, BEFORBAT, Vol 3, pp.91-92.

50 Lieutenant-Colonel Fuller, and Captains Crawford and Jarvis of the RASC. TNA WO 167/1076: GHQ, Supply Directorate (Petrol), WD, 27 October 1939.

systems for road tankers and rail-served bulk storage. The French also explained their *Mobite* can filling system, which used a British Tecalemit[51] hand operated multiple hose automatic cut-off system for charging 50 litre cans with MT spirit and diesel.[52] In this niche area, Tecalemit demonstrated the significant importance of small engineering companies to the logistic capabilities of mechanized armies. On 11 November, a petrol supply reconnaissance team from GHQ BEF inspected potential sites at Rouen to establish a fuel supply depot in the ABA. A location on the Quai des Colonies, within the Standard Oil terminal, was selected, which enabled the creation of a comprehensive facility. The site had a rail siding with equipment to fill RTCs, whilst the facility could also charge road tankers and petrol barges using IWT. In addition, there was sufficient space to accommodate the key processes of a can filling unit: receipt and storage of empty cans, filling operations and storage and dispatch of full cans, with a capacity of 11,000 x 4-gallon returnable cans per day.[53]

Eburite and Explosion

The 'leaker' problem quickly appeared and was a logistic feature of the deployment and the subsequent campaign, which caused a reduction in operational capability, initiated a need for additional stocks, generated a fire safety problem, especially on ships, contaminated ground and created accounting issues. 1 BSD staff estimated that 75 percent of the leaker tins were in wooden cases, whilst the cardboard Eburite case[54] was initially rated to be better than the wooden case and the most robust, a three-ply one.[55] Practical experience however, soon proved that the Eburite cases would not dry properly if they became wet, eventually losing their form and the company was requested to investigate the possibility of water-proofing them because wood and three-ply material were increasingly in short supply. This task had, according to a GHQ Petroleum meeting on 13 February 1940, been satisfactorily achieved offering, allegedly, protection for six months of field storage.[56] In addition, to provide can corrosion protection, a directive was issued to paint all the MT spirit cans green,[57] which no doubt also had a positive result in improving tactical camouflage and concealment because once out of the case the bright shiny tin was not the most welcome item in a location, especially when the Sun was shining. The concept of casing fragile tins in materials that whilst cheap, was relatively insubstantial and yet intended to be stocked in field conditions, indicates that there was insufficient intellectual rigour, common sense and practical testing applied to the detailed application of the initial concept. The external protection of the tins was not the only problem with the flimsies. In early January 1940, Q I Corps was reporting water contamination in petrol and diesel stored in

51 Tecalemit was formed in the UK in 1927, introducing high-pressure lubrication systems for vehicles in 1930 before expanding into amongst other automotive servicing areas, fuel pumping equipment.
52 TNA WO 167/1076: GHQ, Supply Directorate (Petrol), WD, October 1939.
53 TNA WO 167/1076: GHQ, Supply Directorate (Petrol), WD, 11 November 1939.
54 Eburite was a trade name for cases manufactured by the Eburite Cardboard Container Company of North Acton, London.
55 TNA WO 167/1115: 1 BSD RASC, WD, 18 September 1939.
56 TNA WO 167/1076: GHQ Supply Directorate (Petrol), 'Notes of Petroleum Meeting of 13 February 1940'.
57 TNA WO 167/1076: GHQ, Supply Directorate (Petrol), 'Notes of Petroleum Meeting of 13 February 1940'.

them,[58] a problem which, in the sub-zero temperatures being experienced led to maintenance issues and subsequent operational degradation, especially because the uncontaminated diesel tested was discovered to wax at –10°C. Standard Oil offered the Petroleum Directorate a non-waxing dieselite but after testing it, the Directorate concluded that it was 'not gas oil……. and is probably dangerous to use'.[59] Of equal concern, rust was found in tins filled with the precious 100 octane aviation spirit for Hurricane fighters,[60] a problem compounded by the poor marking of aviation spirit cans, which in the dark of winter was a recipe for a drama, either in the supply chain or worse in the air.[61]

The shipment of canned petrol was certainly a hazardous undertaking because of the risk of explosion and fire, and even after war was declared the Ministry of Shipping continued to exercise caution, a policy, which as it transpired, was well founded. Flawed manufacturing standards for the 4-gallon flimsy non-returnable tins introduced 'leakers' into the supply chain, whilst the nails securing the wooden crates were apt to pierce the tins if they were subject to rough handling, which given the numbers of transfers from one transportation medium to another was not an infrequent outcome,[62] a problem that had been incisively exposed during pre-war exercises in Egypt.[63] In addition, at one of the filling plants, a defect in the machinery caused the nails securing the case lids to penetrate the tins.[64] The failure to grip this problem came close to creating a disaster at Swansea Docks when a petrol train 'literally dripping with petrol' came to a halt in the petrol berth only for the locomotive fireman to rake out the ash-pan.[65] Quality assurance for tin production was improved and timber shoring was erected in holds to ensure that the crates and cases could be stacked vertically and securely to reduce the chance of damage. Additional precautions were taken at ports with petrol berths, orders being issued to restrict access to discharge quays and to rigidly enforce the 'No Smoking and No Naked Lights' rules. The use of steam and electric cranes was prohibited, whilst personnel were not permitted to wear hobnailed boots and horses had to wear rubber covers over the metal shoes.[66] Despite these measures however, on 9 November 1939 at Brest, the MV *Pacific Coast*, a Coast Lines diesel powered cargo vessel of 1,210 Gross Registered Tons, suffered a catastrophic internal explosion, whilst discharging at No 7 Berth East Quay.[67] Casualties were heavy and the ship severely damaged. The discharge of another vessel carrying cased tinned petrol, the MV *Coxwold*, was immediately halted and the still burning MV *Pacific Coast* was towed to mid-stream and anchored to prevent other ships and dock installations being set alight. The

58 TNA WO 167/1115: 1 BSD RASC, WD, 18 September 1939.
59 TNA WO 167/1076: GHQ Supply Directorate (Petrol), 'Notes of Petroleum Meeting of 13 February 1940'.
60 TNA WO 167/1115: 1 BSD RASC, WD, 2 January 1939.
61 TNA WO 167/1115: 1 BSD RASC, WD, 7 January 1939.
62 By rail from the filling factories to the docks, then loaded to a ship for a sea voyage, unloaded and then loaded to rail, unloaded to road and stored in a field site before more road, rail and road moves, before being dispensed to a vehicle.
63 Turpin, *Turn of the Wheel*, pp.188-189.
64 WOOH, *Movements*, p.140.
65 Ibid, p.141.
66 WOOH, *Maintenance in the Field*, Vol I, pp.41-42.
67 TNA WO 167/876: 2 Docks Group RE, WD.

next day the vessel sunk[68] leaving petrol burning on the surface of the water but it was not until 12 November that the scale of casualties was clarified: 35 dead, including the crew[69] and 21 French civilians.[70] It was fortunate that a similar event did not occur at the port of Caen, a GHQ Petroleum Supply Directorate report from an inspection on 12 November describing the operation as a 'shambles', with the public permitted access to the petrol berths, smoking next to the 'leakers' dump, including the French sentry, one of whose tasks was to prevent such activity, frayed electric cables on the dockside and poor safety procedures on board the cargo vessel.[71]

Supply and Demand

Initially, the flow of petrol was so slow that effectively the BEF was being refuelled on a daily basis with no working margin on the GLOC. By M+32, the BEF was still 4,000 tons short of its planned allocation and daily consumption rose until in part of November it was 600 tons *per diem*, which was slightly less than daily average receipts from UK. The figure of 600 tons per day equated to 40 miles daily for every vehicle in the BEF, which clearly did not match the operational output and QMG BEF initiated an investigation. The move of the corps to the Belgian frontier two weeks in advance of the planned date had eaten into fuel reserves, which were not profiled thus but there were other influencing factors. Formations and units were hoarding stocks in excess of the authorized limits, thereby increasing forward holdings, whilst the three sites in advance of the initial corps PRH became partially ineffective because there was insufficient road transport to move stocks to the corps areas once the divisions relocated to the operational positions. Weak command and control and slack MT discipline both contributed to excess use, whilst leakage from the disposable 4-gallon tins contributed to more loss. The QMG personally informed corps commanders of the grave nature of this situation and economies were quickly instituted, which, with the static dispositions of the BEF on the Franco-Belgian frontier created first stability and then improvements to the reserves by driving down daily force consumption to 350-400 tons and this figure included additional reinforcing units.

By M+116,[72] 44 days of reserves of cased MT spirit based upon a consumption rate for the Force of 500 tons per day had been accumulated despite the winter weather, although in December 1939, issues exceeded imports by 984 tons and in January 1940 by a much more significant 4,351 tons, recovering to surplus in February by 700 tons, despite an increase in daily consumption.

68 The MV *Pacific Coast* was re-floated on 1 March 1940 and a reconnaissance team was tasked to examine the feasibility of salvaging some of the cans. TNA WO 167/1076: GHQ, Supply Directorate (Petrol), WD. On 20 March 1940, 2 POLD RASC war diary recorded that 2 Bulk Storage Company RASC had been withdrawn from the depot to Brest to assist in refining the MT and aviation spirit being recovered from the hulk. TNA 167/1149: 2 POLD RASC, WD, entry 20 March 1940.

69 Nine of the crew were lost, including the Master, Humphrey Ellis Williams aged 57 and Douglas Bradley, Ordinary Seaman, aged 19; they are remembered on the Tower Hill Memorial to the Merchant Marine in London.

70 The 2 Docks Group RE war diary entry for 9 November states that 'a 2 Lt' was one of the casualties but does not state the nationality or the unit and there is no further mention thereof in the diary. TNA WO 167/876.

71 TNA WO 167/1076: GHQ, Supply Directorate (Petrol), WD.

72 31 December 1940.

Table 6.2
BEF Cased MT Spirit – Imports and Issues in Tons[73]
November 1939 – February 1940[74]

Month	**Imports**				**Issues**	**Tons per day**
Port	Brest	Caen	Nantes	Total		
November 1939	4,810	9,170	8,637	22,617	6,557	218
December 1939	1,869	3,248	1,603	6,720	7,704	248
January 1940	1,000	4,500	0000	5,500	9,851	318
February 1940	3,000	6,000	6,200	15,200	14,500*	500[75]
Total	10,679	22,918	16,440	50,037	38,612	

* Figure in the document was estimated as not all returns had been received.

Indeed, the next challenge was rather less importing fuel to France than transporting it to the BEF's divisions. The distribution of POL to the combat formations of the BEF during the winter of 1939-1940 was initially in accordance with *Field Service Regulations*[76] and BEF procedures, which directed that outside of the Base, all POL should be held on wheels, whether that be military WMT in the direct supply chain or assigned to an *En-Cas Mobile* (ECM).[77] Cased petrol was railed from the MBA or ABA to Corps PRH to be transferred to the lorries of the Corps Petrol Parks (CPP)[78] and then cross-loaded to the WMT of the Divisional Petrol

73 To convert tons to gallons for cased petrol multiply by 224 to account for the weight of the tin and the case. TNA WO 167/1076: GHQ, Supply Directorate (Petrol), 'MT Petrol Stock Return' dated 30 January 1940.
74 Figures collated from information in TNA WO 167/1076: GHQ, Supply Directorate (Petrol), 'Cased MT Petrol Position - November 1939 to February 1940'.
75 Some of the increase in consumption was due to the deployment of 50th (Northumbrian) Division, which had arrived in the Assembly Area around Le Mans in late January and early February 1940 but had been unable to move to the Concentration Area because of the road conditions of alternate freeze then thaw, which it was adjudged by GHQ to be too challenging for the movement of WMT. TNA WO 167/301: 50th Division A&Q, WD, entries February 1940.
76 Army Council, Vol I, *Organization and Administration.*
77 *En-Cas Mobile,* literally, 'movable if necessary'; a group of railway wagons, a barge, or other conveyance, kept permanently under load ready for immediate despatch on an emergency. This was a concept widely used on the Western Front by the British and French Armies. Whilst some documents indicate that the British copied the French, the pre-Great War FSR clearly articulates the conditions for forming the equivalent of ECM in the rail environment: 'This rule does not apply to such train loads of supplies or ammunition as the IGC may direct to be kept ready at certain stations for immediate despatch to the troops in case of necessity. The amount so retained will be strictly limited and should not exceed one day's supplies for the force served'. Army Council, FSR, Part II, *Organization and Administration,* War Office (London: HMSO, 1909), p.95, Chp VIII, *Transport,* Sect 63, para 6.
78 The use of the term 'Park' in the title was confusing because the CPP was established to carry all fuel on wheels to create mobility. A CPP consisted of two Sub-Parks. No 1 Sub-Park consisted of 2nd Line WMT carrying POL for 50 miles for the vehicles, and the Anti-Gas Equipment (AGE) reserves for the personnel of non-divisional units of a corps of two divisions, with an increment to support three.

Company (DPC),[79] the cans being taken forward to Petrol Points where vehicles from units collected them for distribution. In the challenging conditions of the January 1940 winter, there was interruption to petroleum train schedules to the point where a lieutenant-colonel in Supply (Petrol) wrote, referring to the fragile supply of fuel during the deployment of the BEF, 'I do not think we could endure the September/October nightmare again' before commenting upon a proposed *ad hoc* railway solution, 'When one diverts from routine with railways there is invariably a hitch', which was probably an unfair comment borne of frustration because overall SNCF had served the BEF rather well. To mitigate future failure of the 'Just in Time' fuel supply chain, POL dumps were formed 'in advance' of the PRH, either by accumulating stocks at or near the railhead or through POL being authorized by a corps HQ to be held on the ground by the DPC or units. This decision enabled the corps to have access to fuel during the bitter February of 1940 when rail disruption was more frequent and provided reserve stocks for the corps when the GLOC was cut by the German advance in May 1940, albeit it at the cost of loss and quality as stocks deteriorated in storage because there were no qualified personnel to conduct inspections.[80]

The introduction of bulk fuel stocks to a fuel supply chain predicated upon a non-returnable tin inevitably changed the dynamics of the distribution process and to facilitate the operation, QMG 6 dispatched 100,000 x 4-gallon reusable cans to Rouen, which were followed by another 1,200,000[81] before the evacuation ended. Can-filling in France had started under a commercial contract at Donges on 6 September 1939,[82] being expanded under military aegis with a Base Petrol Filling Centre (BPFC) being deployed to Rouen in the ABA and eventually one of its sections was located forward at Lomme near Lille. This deployment was vital in reducing the number of cans required in the loop and the downtime when they were empty and thus unavailable for issue, but equally the solution demanded a BPFC that was more mobile.[83] Whilst the BPFCs were viewed as an administrative convenience rather than operational capability, the one at Lomme filled cans until the town was evacuated on 26 May 1940. The slowly changing balance from an almost purely 'cased' solution to one with bulk, can and tin solutions is shown in the table below showing the holdings across the Theatre at the end January 1940.

No 2 Sub-Park consisted of 3rd Line WMT carrying POL for 25 miles for the vehicles, and the Anti-Gas Equipment (AGE) reserves for the personnel of divisional and non-divisional units of a corps of two divisions, with an increment to support three. For details of the CPP establishment authorized on WE III/1931/36A/2, see, Philson, BEFORBAT, Vol 2, pp.65-67.

79 The DPC was established to carry on wheels petrol for 50 miles for each vehicle in a division. For details, see, WE III/1931/13A/2, Ibid, pp.119-121.

80 WOOH, *Supplies and Transport*, Vol I, pp.114-115.

81 WOOH, *Supplies and Transport*, Vol I, p.113.

82 TNA WO 167/1076: GHQ, Supply Directorate (Petrol), WD, 6 September 1939.

83 The BPFC was a static unit that required engineering support to establish the heavy machinery, which greatly reduced its agility outside the Base, a lesson quickly learned from the campaign in France, the static BPFC being replaced by a mobile version.

Table 6.3
BEF Distribution of MT Spirit by Container System - 30 January 1940[84]

System	Sites	Tons	Days of Supply at 500 tons per day
Non-returnable (Tins)	GLOC POL Depots	8,890	17.78
	GLOC DID	1,542	3.00
	4 POL POLD Moult	5,154	10.30
	Corps & GHQ	700	1.40
	In Transit	1,712	3.42
	Sub-Total	17,998	35.90
Returnable Cans	GLOC POL Depots	133	0.26
	GLOC DID	80	0.16
	Donges Filling Centre	753	1.50
	Transit	50	0.10
	Sub-Total	1016	2.02
Bulk	Storage Tanks	5,986	12.0
	DID	6	0.012
	Sub-Total	5,992	12.01
Total		**25,006**	49.93

Whilst combat units continued to receive fuel in disposable tins, the importance of establishing an effective Reverse Logistics[85] system to recover the returnable cans and ensure that units followed the procedures was essential to logistic output and operational capability of the system, with a change of culture equally important as amendments to process. This challenge was explicitly exposed by the French experience of supplying liquid fuel to BEF brigades rotating through the *Maginot* Line in the Saar. Third Army issued fuel to the units of these British formations in refillable 10 litre cans and 50 litre drums, an increasing number of which, despite repeated reminders, were not returned, a problem that disrupted the fuel distribution system to the extent that the French *Grand Quartier General* issued an edict to the BEF.[86]

Whilst usable bulk fuel which had been 'packed' to cans only equated to two Days of Supply (DOS) the importation of 1,300,000 x 4-gallon returnables and the supporting filling capability to Rouen and Lomme would have given the BEF Supply staff the ability to stock 5,200,000

84 Figures collated from information in TNA WO 167/1076: GHQ, Supply Directorate (Petrol), 'MT Petrol Stock Return, 30 January 1940'.
85 Operations related to the reuse of products and materials, by moving them from their typical final place of use for the purpose of capturing value or conducting proper disposal.
86 TNA WO 197/42: Saar Force Administration, Loose Minute to Commander 1st Guards Brigade from Saar Force Area Commandant ACW 251 dated 14 February 1940.

P6.3 Bulk Refuelling by Rail. To enable bulk fuel distribution to be extended to BEF combat formations, contracts were placed to manufacture RTCs to provide the lift from the Base to the corps areas, with IWT being utilized to a limited extent. (Author)

gallons from bulk to packed equating to nearly 35 DOS at 500 tonnes per day, which would, if time had permitted, greatly reduced the reliance on cased stocks being shipped from the UK. Even with the introduction of these measures, in mid-April 1940 the delivery of fuel to formations and units continued to cause frictions and confusion, generated by the failure to meet the cased in-load programme from UK, a shortage of labour to move the fuel from and within dumps, preparations for the execution of Plan D, the move into Belgium under Operation DAVID, and planning for the redeployment of 51st (Highland) Division to the Saar. The first cased fuel ship of April 1940 only delivered 1,130 tons on 18 April instead of 2,000, although the balance of 950 arrived at Caen two days later, 350 tons of which was consigned by rail directly to the I Corps PRH.[87] This solution, whilst obviating the additional handling issue in the depots and quickly resolving the I Corps shortage, reinforced the conundrum of stock turnover. As corps HQs began to refine Plan D fuel requirements, GHQ Supply (Petrol) recognized that each corps required an additional 400 tons to conduct the move and have reserves for combat operations, which Deputy Directors Supplies & Transport (DDST) at the

87 TNA WO 167/1076: GHQ, Supply Directorate (Petrol), WD, 18 & 20 April 1940.

corps HQs chose to manage by stocking the fuel in 500 ton dumps in the Corps Rear Areas.[88] Inevitably this created more issues with real estate, concealment, labour and security, resulting in the Corps Petrol Parks (CPP) focusing as much on the control of dumped stocks, for which they were not resourced, as the primary task, the delivery of fuel held on wheels.

The fuel planning for the move of 51st (Highland) Division a distance of 250 miles by road to a concentration area near Metz resulted in an internal spat in GHQ between Q Maintenance and the Petrol Branch caused by the failure of Q III Corps to consult its DDST.[89] Q III Corps requested 500 tons[90] for the move, which required the provision of 175 tons of MT spirit fuel from an AASF dump at Rheims,[91] creating a heated discussion between Q Maintenance, which issued a distribution order and Petrol Branch, whose planning staff firmly believed the amount was excessive. This debate was only resolved when DDST III Corps entered the fray in support of the Petrol Branch. As the Branch war diary noted, the whole episode 'led to a great deal of unnecessary telephoning and taken up hours of valuable time.'[92] Despite these delays and frustrations, stocking continued until early May 1940 when the returns recorded[93] that the BEF had amassed 40,000 tons of MT spirit in tins and 32,000 tons in bulk, plus in cans, 3,000 tons of diesel and 4,000 tons of greases and lubricating oil,[94] the latter very much a forgotten but vital aspect of logistics in an Army that was reliant on mechanically powered equipment for its operational capability.[95] As the BEF prepared for combat operations, GHQ Petrol Branch calculated the BEF MT consumption would be 1,200 tons per day, giving a total of 62 DOS, 33 of which, was held as packed fuel.[96] Much of this fuel was held South of the River Somme and thus became inaccessible to the majority of the combat formations after 20 May 1940 but sufficient had been stocked forward as a result of various expedients and unofficial hoarding, to maintain the mobility of the BEF as it withdrew to the Channel coast.

Aviation Spirit

The Army was not only responsible for the provision and delivery of fuel to Land units but also to those Air Force units attached to forces in the field in accordance with *Field Service*

88 TNA WO 167/1076: GHQ, Supply Directorate (Petrol), WD, 20 April 1940.

89 It is instructive that HQ III Corps had only recently been formed and had little opportunity to 'work-up' Staff efficiency. The failure to consult with DDST confirms that the internal culture and logistic processes were yet to mature.

90 The Supply (Petrol) war diary does not clarify whether this was gross tonnage inclusive of the case and the tin, thus equating to 150,000 gallons or liquid tonnage of 112,000 gallons.

91 TNA WO 167/1076: GHQ, Supply Directorate (Petrol), WD, 19 April 1940.

92 TNA WO 167/1076: GHQ, Supply Directorate (Petrol), WD, 20 April 1940.

93 WOOH, *Supplies and Transport*, Vol I, p.123.

94 The provision of one of these products, Oil, Compound 600, was the subject of some concern in February 1940 because the two key constituents of rape seed and Western Bright Star were not available, being replaced by whale and cotton seed oils. TNA WO 167/1076: GHQ, Supply Directorate (Petrol), WD, entries February 1940.

95 The was equally true for the RAF, which calculated the requirement for its key lubricating oil, DTD 109, based on 5% of fuel totals. See, TNA AIR 35/123: Reserve stocks of aviation fuel, bombs and small arms ammunition, 1940, 'AASF Fuel Requirements', AASF S/.3586/Org dated 7 May 1940.

96 WOOH, *Supplies and Transport*, Vol I, p.123. Packed fuel consisted of cased tins, and the more robust returnable cans.

Regulations,[97] although given the scale of the task, the paucity of information relating to it in the key manuals is certainly surprising.[98] The Army's responsibility for handling fuel usually ended at the PRH from which, RAF transport delivered it to Air Stores Parks (ASP), aerodromes[99] or dumps. The one contentious issue was supply to the AASF, which was not 'attached' to the BEF in the sense detailed by *Field Service Regulations* and thus not subject to War Office planning processes,[100] although in September 1938, in conjunction with the War Office, the Air Ministry dispatched a reconnaissance team headed by the Air-Officer-Charge (Designate) for the AASF, to supplement arrangements which had been previously agreed between the British and French Air Ministries. This resulted in a decision to stock the assigned aerodromes with bombs, ammunition, fuel and oil prior to the commencement of mobilization to support the 'Quick Despatch Scheme', a task, which sat firmly within the bailiwick of the UK Air Ministry and not the War Office.[101] The scale of the fuel stocking and re-supply task for the AASF was however, effectively beyond the capability of the RAF and although the RAF remained responsible for calculating the types, quantities and specifications for fuel to support its AASF air and ground operations, it fell by default to the War Office to store the products in the Base and deliver them to the nominated railheads in accordance with the *Field Service Regulations*.

Initially, there was no direct interface between the RAF and GHQ on key logistic requirements, which presumably influenced the negative movement outcomes, that were a hallmark of the deployment of some of the RAF squadron WMT convoys, a few of which from 50 Wing arrived at the aerodromes 13 days after the rail parties,[102] although the single service RAF logistic plan to support the AASF Quick Despatch Scheme was equally fragile.[103] On 10 October 1939, a number of RAF engineer and equipment officers arrived at GHQ to establish a liaison cell known as 'Q' RAF, which was tasked with the co-ordination of fuel and ammunition demands for the Air Component BEF and the AASF, and planning, with the QMG Staff, for their storage in the Base and movement to the railheads.[104] This arrangement was reinforced by the appointment, in December 1939 of a Maintenance Officer-in-Chief, who was responsible, amongst other tasks, for 'representing air force needs to the Quartermaster-General at GHQ where their supply and movement was an Army responsibility'.[105]

97 Army Council, FSR, Vol I, *Organization and Administration*, p.146, Sect 85.
98 Neither Air Council, *Royal Air Force Pocket Book*, Air Publication 1081, Air Ministry (London: HMSO, 1937) or Army Council, *The Employment of Air Forces with the Army in the Field* (War Office, 1938), make any reference to the supply of RAF fuel or to the Army's responsibility for RAF logistics. Air Council, *Royal Air Force War Manual*, Part II - *Organization and Administration*, Air Publication 1301, Air Ministry, 1939 (reprinted June 1940) contains one paragraph on 'Reserves of Supplies and Ammunition' but makes no mention of Army responsibilities for RAF logistics. Chp XV, para 16; the document is not paginated.
99 The pre-war RAF term 'aerodrome' is used in contemporary documents to denote permanent or temporary flying stations, the word 'airfield' not entering use in the RAF lexicon until the arrival in the UK in 1942 of the United States Army Air Force (USAAF).
100 Army Council, FSR, Vol I, *Organization and Administration* p.146, Sect 85.
101 AMOH, AP 3397, *Maintenance*, p.55.
102 Ibid, p.55.
103 Ibid, p.56.
104 Ibid, p.58.
105 TNA AIR 35/125: Appointment of Maintenance Office-in-Chief; Policy, Air Ministry S.2725/ DDWO dated 23 December 1939 and TNA AIR 24/680: HQ BAFF, ORB, October 1939-June 1940.

P6.4 Can Recycling. The disposal 4-gallon can, created a appreciable handling and recycling burden, much of which, involved rail transportation. (RLCM: B6/Salvage/249/U/656/RLCA/2110)

As the size and complexity of RAF logistic tasks grew, it became increasingly clear that more effective co-ordination was required across a number of agencies out-with British headquarters in France including the War Office, Air Ministry, HQ Bomber Command, Host Nation military and civil authorities and the Ministry of Transport in UK. The Air Officer Commanding-in-Chief (AOC-in-C) Bomber Command,[106] arguably the organization with the most significant interest in a resilient solution, expressed the firm opinion that a co-ordinating HQ was needed to: 'button up the divergent or convergent requirements of the French and British Forces, the Air Component, the AASF and Bomber Command'.[107] HQ British Air Forces France (BAFF)[108] thus became operational in January 1940, reporting directly to the Air Ministry, to staff all policy, administrative and logistic matters for the RAF Component[109] and

106 Air Chief Marshal (ACM) Sir Edgar Ludlow Hewitt GCB GBE CMG DSO MC.

107 TNA AIR 41/21: The Campaign in France and the Low Countries, September 1939-June 1940, RAF Narrative (TOP SECRET) Air Historical Branch, 1944, AOC-in-C BC/ERLH/DO letter dated 28 October 1939.

108 Its first and only AOC-in-C was Air Marshal (AM) Sir Arthur 'Ugly' Barratt KCB CMG DSO. AM Barratt was aware of the many of the key issues, having been the Head of No 1 Air Mission.

109 At the same time, the ACBEF was renamed Royal Air Force Component British Expeditionary Force (RAFCBEF).

the AASF, undoubtedly improving the efficiency and effectiveness of engineering, supply and logistic outputs.[110]

The establishment of HQ BAFF came none to soon in the RAF fuel environment because by early March 1940, stocks in France had grown to considerable proportions, with nearly 2,000,000 gallons in bulk and 2,624,400 gallons cased,[111] which was in excess of the holding requirement planned for May 1940.[112] In addition to these stocks, GHQ Supply (Petrol) Branch was informed by the QMG Staff in mid-April 1940 that plans to expand RAF combat capability in France, would initiate the need for an extra 1,000,000 gallons of storage capacity.[113] Indeed, one of the maturing problems was the balance between consumption and cased stock shelf life[114] because the latter was a maximum of six months,[115] and GHQ Petrol was seeking to persuade the RAF to commence conversion to direct bulk supply in the Base area.[116] In pursuit of this outcome, the Branch appears to have had some success in changing the culture, the war diary noting: 'Air Component[117] seems more inclined now to consider bulk supply to certain rear formations, particularly six Flying Training Schools near Le Mans'.[118] Before major combat operations began on 10 May, the maximum weekly consumption by the RAF in France had been 189,000 gallons, an average daily rate of 27,000 gallons or 90 tons, giving a reserve of 97 DOS cased and 74 DOS bulk. Despite these figures, HQ BAFF was, in concert with GHQ, concerned about possibility of interruptions to supply and consequently followed the QMG BEF lead in stocking reserves between railheads and aerodromes.[119]

To support the BEF RAF Component, HQ BAFF planned to stock 324,800 gallons[120] of cased fuel on the aerodromes and Advanced Landing Grounds, and 244,000 gallons[121] in

110 There is evidence that the establishment of HQ BAFF prevented further predatory requests from the War Office to transfer Battle squadrons from the AASF to the ACBEF, and that this issue may have played a part in convincing the Air Ministry to form HQ BAFF.

111 Figures collated from information in TNA WO 167/1076: GHQ, Supply Directorate (Petrol), various documents.

112 TNA AIR 35/123: Reserve stocks of aviation fuel, bombs and small arms ammunition, 1940, 'AASF Fuel Requirements', AASF S/.3586/Org dated 7 May 1940 and 'Air Component Fuel Requirements', HQ AC/507/Admin dated 10 May 1940.

113 TNA WO 167/1076: GHQ, Supply Directorate (Petrol), WD, 18 April 1940.

114 For example, in March 1940, 2 POLD reported that in order to deliver a large order for A230, it was necessary to conduct 'hand-picking of the stacks, owing to vast majority having been condemned on account of age and condition'. TNA WO 167/1149: 2 POLD, WD, entry 21 March 1940.

115 WOOH, *Supplies and Transport*, Vol I, p.113.

116 The RAF was in advance of the Army in utilizing bulk refuellers. For a resume, see, F J Adkin, *RAF Ground Support Equipment since 1918* (Shrewsbury: Air Publishing, 1996), pp.86-88.

117 It is of note that a GHQ Staff branch was referring to the RAF element of the BEF thus, three months after the title was changed. Whilst old habits die hard, it is equally probable that it was a question of clarity and brevity, with 'Air Component' being clearly understood without the possibility of it being confused with other RAF formations.

118 TNA WO 167/1076: GHQ, Supply Directorate (Petrol), WD, 18 April 1940.

119 AMOH, AP 3397, *Maintenance*, p.59.

120 230,000 gallons 100 octane and 94,800 gallons of DTD 230. TNA AIR 35/123: Reserve stocks of aviation fuel, bombs and small arms ammunition, 1940, 'Air Component Fuel Requirements' HQ AC/507/Admin dated 10 May 1940.

121 173,000 gallons 100 octane and 71,000 gallons of DTD 230. TNA AIR 35/123: Reserve stocks of aviation fuel, bombs and small arms ammunition, 1940, 'Air Component Fuel Requirements' HQ AC/507/Admin dated 10 May 1940.

dumps in advance of the PRHs. In addition, 432,740 gallons[122] were to be stocked at the advanced petrol dump at Vignacourt,[123] which was sited in the area of the Air Component's rear aerodromes. Planning for the AASF was equally comprehensive, although as with the Air Component, the dumps allocated to the management of the ASPs over-faced the Supply & Transport sections because they were not provided with the necessary labour or WMT.[124] By early May, the planned holdings in the three ASPs supporting the AASF was a total of 483,000 gallons of packed fuel[125] and 11,350 gallons of DTD 109 oil. When the Air Stores Parks were ordered to move during the campaign, although some of the POL had been issued, the shortage of WMT only enabled the evacuation of the 100 octane with much of the DTD 230 and DTD 109 being handed over to the Host Nation authorities.[126] The withdrawal created the need for yet more aviation fuel to be dumped in new areas including 200,000 gallons to support operations from the South Champagne airfields, and for Operation HADDOCK,[127] 90,000 gallons of DTD 230 and 4,500 gallons of DTD 109 at Le Vallon and Salon-de-Provence in Southern France near Marseilles to support the two Wellington bomber squadrons[128] tasked to attack targets in Northern Italy.[129]

Conclusion

The concept of relying upon a simple fuel distribution system utilizing a cheap disposable tin, General Service WMT capability and manual labour was under-pinned by what appeared to be sound financial, technical and operational considerations. The fragility of the system however, was quickly exposed by the decision to rely on low capital investment in equipment and processes, which delivered a tin which, whilst the foundation of the output, was not fit for purpose. This in turn, resulted in a whole series of complications, including serious safety issues, loss of shipping, fuel leakage and contamination and a reduction in deliveries. The reliance upon manual labour in the supply chain, whilst saving capital investment in equipment, maintenance and training created pinch points at trans-shipment and cross-loading points. The BEF logisticians were however, quick to identify the inherent fragilities in the system and sought to create robust solutions, reaching out to UK industry and the French military in the search for effective options. The speed at which a returnable can capability, albeit small, was instituted through a French contract, lucidly proves that the military petrol supply experts,

122 266,840 gallons 100 octane and 165,900 gallons of DTD 230. TNA AIR 35/123: Reserve stocks of aviation fuel, bombs and small arms ammunition, 1940, 'Air Component Fuel Requirements' HQ AC/507/Admin dated 10 May 1940.

123 Approximately 10 miles NNW of Amiens.

124 TNA AIR 29/780: 4 ASP AASF, WD, September 1939 - June 1940.

125 256,000 gallons 100 octane and 227,000 gallons DTD 230. TNA AIR 35/123: Reserve stocks of aviation fuel, bombs and small arms ammunition, 1940, 'AASF Fuel Requirements', AASF S/.3586/Org dated 7 May 1940.

126 TNA AIR 29/781: 5 ASP AASF, WD, May - June 1940.

127 TNA AIR 35/323: Haddock Force Operations. HQ 71 Wing was dispatched on 3 June 1940 to prepare the reception and refuelling facilities, which were ready on the outbreak of war with Italy on 10 June. For a brief summary of operations, see, Jackson, *Air War over France, 1939-40*, pp.124-126.

128 99 and 149 Squadrons of 3 Bomber Group based at RAF Mildenhall and RAF Newmarket respectively.

129 TNA AIR 35/123: Reserve stocks of aviation fuel, bombs and small arms ammunition, 1940, various documents.

un-convinced by the 'flimsy' solution, had to hand, an alternative option that could be developed and expanded. This resolution, whilst having many advantages, relied upon an effective Reverse Logistics chain, a pre-condition that required a cultural change in the BEF, the soldiers of which, had been mentored to accept a uni-directional fuel supply flow based upon a disposable container.

The generation and improvisation of bulk storage and transportation capabilities drawing upon industrial technical expertise was impressive, although creating the robust military structures to make them fully effective during manoeuvre operations was a challenge of a different order. The forward dumping of stocks, whilst in direct conflict with doctrinal purity and introducing in some cases unmanageable burdens to the CPP and DPC fraternities, provided the vital fuel to keep the BEF mobile during the retreat to Dunkerque. Stock turnover became a growing problem as reserves expanded, with fuel, especially aviation spirit, 'aging out', a problem exacerbated by the dispatch of new fuel from the UK direct from ports in France to forward dumps. At the tactical level, the tin and the can had much to commend them but as operations in France were to reinforce, the effective and efficient supply of liquid fuel to an Army reliant on the internal combustion engine required to be militarily robust as well as technically competent, whilst the numbers of tins required to fill an aircraft[130] firmly suggested that the widespread introduction of a mechanized solution was urgently required.

130 The Hawker Hurricane Mk I had a fuel capacity of 97 Imperial gallons, thus requiring 25 x 4-gallon tins for a full fill, whilst the Fairey Battle Mk I required 73.

7

Factory to Fire Trench
Conventional ammunition supply for the British Expeditionary Force deployed to France 1939-1940

Industrial Dimensions

One key component of logistic operations, which was essential to the capability of the BEF, was the supply of ammunition[1] to deployed ground forces, and 'common user' munitions,[2] such as Small Arms Ammunition (SAA) to elements of the Royal Air Force. The importance of ammunition supply was clearly understood in 1940, the experience of the Great War having been enshrined in many publications. *Field Service Regulations*, Volume I, *Organization and Administration, 1930*, stated that: 'The fundamental principle of ammunition supply is that ammunition must be passed systematically and automatically from rear to front to replace that expended in battle. Troops in action should never have to turn their backs on the enemy to fetch further supplies',[3] before significantly noting that, 'A commander's power of manoeuvre is largely dependent on ability to keep his troops supplied with ammunition. Careful arrangements for ammunition supply, must therefore, form part of every plan of operations'...........[4]

In comparison to fuel planning for the BEF, there was a strong focus upon capital investment in production and storage in the United Kingdom.[5] In 1935, production facilities were located at the Royal Small Arms Factory Enfield, Royal Gunpowder Factory (RGPF) Waltham and the Royal Arsenal Woolwich Arsenal,[6] with minor activity at the Great War National Filling Factory (NFF) Hereford,[7] whilst the cartridge-case factory at Birtley and the explosives site at

1 This chapter examines the supply of conventional munitions. For an analysis of Gas Warfare (GW) munitions storage and movement, see, Chp 14, 'Operation FLANNELFOOT'.
2 'Common user' munitions were those not specific to Arm of Service and included items such as SAA and pyrotechnics.
3 Army Council, FSR, Vol I, *Organization and Administration*, p.252.
4 Ibid.
5 Map 1: Land Service Munitions - UK Munitions Production Sites and Ammunition Depots 1939 - 1940.
6 TNA SUPP 5/1260: Historical Notes on the Royal Ordnance Factories.
7 Located at Lower Bullingham and known as ROF Rotherwas. During the inter-war period it was the only one of the Great War NFF not to be decommissioned. It filled Army gas shells in the 1920s and

Irvine were both in Care & Maintenance. In 1934, the Hacking Committee examined British munitions production capability, through a strategic and military perspective, highlighting the vulnerability of the sites, and especially Woolwich, to aerial attack and proposing that any new factories should be located as far to the West and North as possible.[8] In 1936, the Robinson Committee reviewed the options through political and economic lenses, citing the importance of locating new facilities in depressed areas with high unemployment, which created additional factors in selection.[9] On a more practical note, any proposed filling factory site required an area of approximately 1,000 acres, suitable topography and geology, good drainage, a supply of water of an appropriate quantity and quality, connection to the National Rail Network and access to a suitable and sustainable labour market. Inevitably, even if an optimum site was identified there were many hurdles to be overcome in terms of opposition from vested interests, including those lobbying against compulsory purchase, the destruction of farmland and the imposition of brutalist factory architecture upon the rural landscape.[10] The preferred site for a new facility was a location near Oswestry, a proposal strongly resisted by the Ministry of Agriculture and the Council for the Protection of Rural England.[11] Thus, the Cabinet approved the construction of the first post-Great War Royal Ordnance Factory (ROF) for munitions at Chorley in Lancashire.[12] This was intended not only to replace production from Woolwich but also to increase production by a factor of 1.5 by constructing a new facility with the capacity for a wide range of munitions output in a location less vulnerable to air attack.[13] A second factory was approved in March 1936 and third in July 1937, both in South Wales, at Bridgend[14] and Glascoed,[15] although the latter was focused upon the filling of naval mines. Each of these new facilities, titled Royal Filling Factories (RFF),[16] using prodigious amounts of labour and material funded entirely by the taxpayer[17] took three years to complete,[18] with limited and phased production being started whilst building continued. By March 1940, nine RFFs[19] had

naval mines in the 1930s and was also used to store munitions. ROF Rotherwas closed in 1967 and is now an industrial estate.

8 TNA CAB 27/604: Royal Ordnance Factories - Miscellaneous Committees.

9 TNA CAB 27/604: Royal Ordnance Factories - Miscellaneous Committees.

10 Wayne D Cocroft, *Dangerous Energy, The Archaeology of Gunpowder and Military Explosives Manufacture* (Swindon: English Heritage, 2000), p.215.

11 TNA CAB 102/626: History of the Royal Filling Factory Swynnerton, D Mack.

12 See, Mike Nevell, John Roberts & Jack Smith, *A History of Royal Ordnance Factory, Chorley* (Lancaster: Carnegie Publishing, 1999).

13 TNA CAB 102/273: Munitions Factories - Location and Siting.

14 Bridgend commenced operations in early 1940, ceasing production in 1945. The factory buildings were demolished, and the site is occupied by the Bridgend Industrial Estate. The administrative site, including the original ROF HQ in *art deco moderne* block style is the HQ of South Wales Police.

15 In 2020, Glascoed is the sole ammunition filling factory in the UK.

16 For an explanation of the design, construction, operation and the archaeology of the RFFs, see, Cocroft, *Dangerous Energy*, pp.211-235.

17 Ibid. p.214.

18 This timescale had been detailed by the Planning Staff at Woolwich, which met with a cool reception from Government, which directed that the Office of Works should take over the project. Experience proved that the Woolwich assessment was correct.

19 The table below lists the development of the RRFs. Information collated from various sources, including TNA CAB 102/273: Munitions Factories - Location and Siting, and William Hornby, *Factories and Plant* (London: HMSO, 1958).

been approved with RRF No 5 at Swynnerton[20] near Stone in Staffordshire, commencing initial production in June 1940.

The scale and complexity of the sites generated by the need to conduct a wide suite of potentially hazardous tasks[21] created the need for building separation and thus nearly 1,000 acres of suitable land upon which, to locate a RFF. The construction of ROF Chorley[22] involved the excavation of three million cubic yards of earth, the laying of 30 million bricks and pouring

Table 7.1
BEF
Development of the Royal Filling Factories

RRF	Location	Area	Final Cost (£m)	2018 Equivalent (£Bn)	Approved	Initial Production	2020 Use
1	Chorley	Lancashire	13.14	4,805	1936	December 1938	Housing
2	Bridgend	Glamorgan	9.58	3,503	1937	1940	Industrial Estate
3	Glascoed	Monmouthshire	6.30	2,304	1937	April 1940	Operational
4	Hereford*	Herefordshire	00.00#	0000	Pre-war	Pre-War	Industrial Estate
5	Swynnerton	Staffordshire	13.60	4,973	May 1939	June 1940	MOD Training Area
6	Risley	Lancashire+	13.39	4,897	End 1939	September 1940	Town of Birchwood
7	Kirkby	Merseyside	8.63	3,156	End 1939	September 1940	Industrial Estate
8	Thorp Arch	West Yorkshire	5.95	2,176	March 1940	August 1941	Trading Estate
9	Aycliffe	County Durham	6.64	2,428	March 1940	August 1941	Industrial Estate
	Total		77.23	28,242~			

* Located at Lower Bullingham and known ROF Rotherwas.
+ 1939.
# Upgrade cost not identified.
~ The converted equivalent does not match the total from 1939 as there are some round offs in the calculations but the figure of plus £28 Billion gives a clear illustration of the investment.

20 ROF Swynnerton closed in 1958. Much of the site has been cleared of factory infrastructure and the land is returning to its rural roots, although the magazines, some buildings and reminders of the railway system remain. In 2020, the MOD retains use of the site as the Swynnerton Training Area and most of the administrative buildings provide accommodation and support facilities for training.

21 In addition, the ROFs had to meet the new specifications laid out in the Factories Act 1937, from which the Crown was not exempt, except where a State of Emergency justified a dispensation granted by the relevant Minister. The standards included, regular provision for cleaning, washing and painting of working areas, reasonable working temperatures and adequate ventilation and light, whether artificial or natural. Factories also had to have sanitary conveniences, with separation according to sex, appropriate washing facilities and accommodation for clothing and changing. The regulations also directed that all dangerous machinery be fenced or otherwise protected, to prevent injury to persons.

22 The investment at ROF Chorley totalled £13.14 million at 1939 prices, a project valuation, which, based upon national economic cost in *Measuring Worth UK*, equates, in 2018, to £4.805 Billion. Planned numbers of employees were expected to be 30,000. See, Hornby, BOH, *Factories and Plant*, p.101.

P7.1 Ammunition Production. Significant sums of Public money were expended to create a munitions production capability within the UK, of which ROF Swynnerton in Staffordshire was but one facility. One of the many specialized buildings with a rail platform that remain on site in 2018. (Author)

one million cubic yards of concrete to construct the 1,500 buildings, including semi-sunken magazines, 25 miles of Standard Gauge Railway (SGR), 50 miles of roads and clean-ways and nine miles of steel palisade fencing.[23] The largest concrete mixer in the World was erected on site in 1937 capable of a daily output of 5,000 tons. RFF Hereford used mainly during the inter-war period for ammunition and explosives storage was rehabilitated for production.[24] Thus, by the time the BEF deployed to France, Chorley, Hereford and Woolwich were delivering munitions, although Chorley[25] did not reach full production until mid-1940.[26] Propellants and explosive manufacturing was crucial to reinvigorating munitions production. RGPF Waltham[27] was not only deemed to be increasingly vulnerable to air attack but also in need of modernization and the Cabinet decided in July 1935 that it should be replaced, although it was not until January

23 Nevell, Roberts & Smith, *A History of Royal Ordnance Factory Chorley*, pp.24-25.
24 Hereford became RFF No 4.
25 ROF Chorley, privatised in 1985, closed in 2007. The site was used to construct Buckshaw Village, although the fine main administrative office building forms part of Runshaw College.
26 For a description of the challenges in delivering full production, especially in relation to the selection, training and reliability of labour, see, Nevell, Roberts & Smith, *A History of Royal Ordnance Factory Chorley*, pp.28-29. The first shell was filled on 4 December 1938, a 3.7-inch MKID AA with a 117 fuze.
27 For details of its operation and archaeology, see, Cocroft, *Dangerous Energy*, pp.203-204.

1937 that approval was given to build one of the three planned units at Bishopton on the South bank of the River Clyde for the production of propellants, mainly cordite, with a second unit approved in January 1939.[28] Production from ROF Bishopton[29] did not however, begin until June 1940, which meant that RGPF Waltham was the sole ROF contributor to propellant production until the evacuation of the BEF from France. To expand explosives[30] production,[31] ROF Irvine in Ayrshire was refurbished and enhanced at a cost of £2.1 million,[32] whilst a new factory was built on the Great War munitions site[33] at Pembrey,[34] for £2.90 million.[35] In addition to the immense financial cost, the efforts of the ROFs to supply the BEF with its ammunition came at some risk to those involved in the manufacturing processes. On 18 January 1940, five men were killed at RGPF Waltham in an explosion, which also destroyed four buildings and disrupted output in others to the detriment of key production[36] and another on 20 April 1940 had a similar effect with the loss of another five lives,[37] whilst at ROF Irvine there was incident

28 See, Hornby, BOH, *Factories and Plant*, p.110.

29 The complexity of the engineering tasks in constructing these factories is illustrated by the need to build, in addition to the production facilities, a power station, water, electricity and heating distribution networks, administrative, medical and welfare blocks, roads and railways. The cost of the three propellant factory sites at ROF Bishopton totalled £17.1 million at 1939 prices. Hornby, BOH, *Factories and Plant*, p.118. The national economic cost using *Measuring Worth UK*, equates, in 2018, to £6.217 Billion. For an explanation of the construction of the propellant ROFs, see, Cocroft, *Dangerous Energy*, pp.205-208.

30 For Army munitions, this was mainly Tri-Nitro-Toluene (TNT) and ammonium nitrate. See, Hornby, BOH, *Factories and Plant*, p.112.

31 Sites for the explosive factories were smaller than for propellant and filling facilities, rarely exceeding 300 acres. For a description of production processes, see, Major-General John Hay Beith CBE MC, *ROF, The Story of the Royal Ordnance Factories, 1939-1948* (London: HMSO: 1949), pp.48-56 and Cocroft, *Dangerous Energy*, pp.209-211.

32 Hornby, BOH, *Factories and Plant*, p.118. The national economic cost using *Measuring Worth UK*, equates, in 2018, to £768 million. For details of the construction and operation of the high explosive ROFs, see, Cocroft, *Dangerous Energy*, pp.209-211.

33 During the inter-war period, some of the Great War administrative buildings housed a convalescent home and a rehabilitation centre for the children of unemployed miners. See, Beith, *ROF*, p.48.

34 ROF Pembrey was sited on sand hills known as the Pembrey Burrows, eight miles to the West of Llanelli on the area occupied by the explosive and propellant factory and National Filling Factory No 18. Demolition of on-site buildings commenced in July 1938, with production commencing in November 1939. From late 1944, the ROF focused upon breaking down defective and surplus ammunition, including 200,000 rounds of 4.5-inch AA shells, although explosives and propellant production briefly resumed during the Korean War. ROF Pembrey closed in 1963 and the site is now Pembrey Country Park opened in 1980, although factory archaeology can be seen. For an academic history of the site, see Alice Pyper, 'Manufacturing Munitions at Pembrey during the Two World Wars', *The Carmarthenshire Antiquary*, Vol 53, 2017.

35 Hornby, BOH, *Factories and Plant*, p.118. The national economic cost using *Measuring Worth UK*, equates, in 2018, to £1.061 Billion.

36 Hillmans O'Hagen and Sylvester, and Trainee Hillman Sewell were all awarded the Empire Gallantry Medal, later exchanged for the GC, for their actions in preventing further explosions. Beith, *ROF*, pp.86-86 & p.104.

37 Hillmans Burns, Sollis and West were each awarded a BEM for their actions in preventing further explosions. Ibid, pp.86-87 & p.104.

that claimed the life of an Assistant Foreman, who was awarded a George Cross for fighting the fire that initiated it.[38]

Ammunition Storage

As munitions production began to slowly increase, the War Office turned its attention to developing storage facilities. The policies that were the foundation for the plans relating to the supply of ammunition for the BEF were deeply affected by the advent of offensive air power. Formal concern about the aerial threat to ammunition stocks commenced in 1913 when the War Office instituted a study to examine it.[39] The planners of the late 1930s were, to a large extent conditioned not only by the offensive air experiences in the Great War but also by their perception of its capability in a future conflict.[40] Ammunition was of course, particularly vulnerable, and the operation of large surface sites offered the enemy some attractive targets. Such assessments were not driven by theoretical speculation but by spectacular air attack events on the Western Front during the Great War. In 1918, the *Deutsche Luftstreitkrafte* did not have the capability of the *Luftwaffe* in 1939 but it had developed its Air Interdiction capability to a point where it was able to inflict some major losses on the British Army ammunition stocks and in the period 18-21 May, the BEF lost 12,500 tons to air delivered weapons.[41] In 1919, the War Office established a committee, to: 'Consider the Revisions of the Regulations for Magazines and Care of War Materiels', with a key conclusion highlighting the balance between expense and protection:

> The committee are of the opinion that the only real protection for any Magazines and Depots above ground is an adequate and efficient Anti-Aircraft defence, and that it is not practicable on account of expense to make Magazines bomb-proof without employing underground storage. They consider, however, that small magazines and dispersed buildings tend greatly to minimize the danger from aerial attack. They are further of the opinion that immunity from damage by aerial attack can only be assured by provisions of underground magazines and ammunition depots.[42]

38 Assistant Foreman McCabe was awarded the GC, Chemist Asquith, the MBE and Chargehand McLelland, the BEM. Ibid, p.88 & p.103.

39 The study concluded that explosives in sheds could be protected by steel mesh 10 feet above the roof because aerially delivered munitions of the day were light. It was as well for War Office finances that this idea was not implemented; by 1918 bombs of 500 kg and greater were being delivered.

40 For an examination of the planners' perception of the Luftwaffe's capability in the period 1936-1939, see Wesley K Wark, *The Utlimate Enemy, British Intelligence and Nazi Germany, 1933-1939* (London: I B Tauris & Co 1985), pp.59-79.

41 The Second Army lost 1,000 tons in a dump at Campagne on the night of 18-19 May, whilst in an attack on No 12 Ordnance Depot at Blarges on the night of 20-21 May 1918, aerial munitions caused the detonation of 6,000 tons out of the 27,000 tons in storage. Another attack on No 20 Ordnance Depot at Saigneville on the night of 21-22 May 1918 resulted in the destruction of 5,600 tons out of 40,000 tons in store. This conflagration was such that the flames were visible from a distance of 40 miles and the loss included the complete site stock of Small Arms Ammunition amounting to 69 million rounds. H A Jones, *History of the Great War: The War in the Air* Vol VI (London: HMSO, 1937), pp. 423-425.

42 N J McCamley, *Secret Underground Cities* (Barnsley: Leo Cooper, 1998), pp.11-12.

Assessment and some planning progressed in the 1920s but because no funds were released, construction approval was not granted. In June 1935, Master-General of the Ordnance (MGO)[43] re-commenced the formal debate with a letter to Chief of the Imperial General Staff,[44] the Quartermaster-General, the Permanent Under Secretary and the Under Secretary of State,[45] which identified two key points: space and vulnerability. On the question of depot capability, MGO noted that, 'The decision to increase our reserves of ammunition raises the question of storage accommodation available to hold them. Practically the whole of our present equipment and reserve ammunition is held at Bramley, but when the reserves have been built up to the proposed scale … the accommodation at Bramley[46] will fall short of the requirements by 116,000 square feet.' Capacity, however, was not the only issue because the MGO cogently articulated: 'I am not at all happy about storing any war requirements at Bramley ....in view of the danger of air attack it is now generally agreed that above ground storage for filled ammunition is undesirable.'[47]

The result of these experiences, concerns and committees, was that the War Office planners decided that existing surface depots should be used but only for immediate issues, whilst underground sites with good rail access should be sought for the War Reserve stocks. In late 1935, the War Office, now concerned about not only the vulnerability of Central Ammunition Depot Bramley but also its inability hold the War Reserve stocks which would be required to support future operations, committed to an expansion plan based upon dispersion by the construction of a surface depot at Longtown[48] in Cumberland and burial in underground facilities in stone quarries around Corsham in Wiltshire, although deployed overseas field ammunition sites would be reliant on aerial, GBAD, and Passive Air Defence (PAD) measures such as dispersion, concealment and camouflage.[49] The Army's decision to go underground in

43 Lieutenant-General Sir Hugh Elles KCB KCMG KVCO DSO (1880-1945).

44 Field-Marshal Sir Archibald Montgomery-Massingberd GCB GCVO KCMG (1871-1947).

45 TNA WO 32/3343: Underground Storage - Accommodation for Explosives, Minute from MGO 57/ Gen/7533 dated 11 June 1935.

46 Central Ammunition Depot (CAD) at Bramley in Hampshire was established during the Great War either side of the Great Western Railway line between Reading at Basingstoke, with German POWs assisting in its construction. Its vulnerability from air attack was the subject of several studies between the wars and whilst some remedial measures such as camouflage and tree planting had been undertaken, spacing between buildings was inadequate and there were no traverses or overhead protection for the Explosives Store Houses (ESH). TNA WO 32/3343: Underground Storage – Accommodation for Explosives. At the time of publication, Bramley remains in MOD ownership as a training area, with many of the ESH bases and a few buildings and ESHs extant, which are also offered as location sets to film companies.

47 TNA WO 32/3343: Underground Storage - Accommodation for Explosives, Minute from MGO 57/ Gen/7533 dated 11 June 1935.

48 CAD Longtown near Carlisle was deemed to be relatively safe from air attack, because of its location. In addition, the design sought to minimize the risk by dispersion and constructing the ESH as semi-sunken bunkers. Indeed, Longtown was the only UK ammunition site to employ this system, although the Germans used it extensively, with what became the British Army's 154 Forward Ammunition Depot at Wulfen, being an excellent example. Fernyhough & Harris, *History of the Royal Army Ordnance Corps, 1939-1945*, p.454. At the time of publication, Longtown remains operational as an ammunition depot.

49 A perceptive officer, Colonel Bainbridge noted in relation to the Great War: 'Concealment from hostile aircraft cannot be said to have received much consideration in determining the sites of ammunition

UK was certainly influenced by the Royal Navy and the RAF, both of which were engaged in upgrading the protection of their munitions stocks,[50] although the RAF, unlike the Army, did not articulate its requirement for subterranean storage until 1936.[51] In 1935, the Army, having commenced a detailed examination of potential sites in 1930,[52] opted for the Corsham Quarry Complex, with a plan to have three Ammunition Sub-Depots (ASD),[53] although Treasury parsimony was a constant irritation.[54] Two were operating by the summer of 1939, Tunnel Quarry[55] and Monkton Farleigh,[56] although because of ongoing construction and engineering

depots in this war. The necessity for it, will, no doubt, be clear in the next'. McCamley, *Secret Underground Cities*, p.12.

50 The Admiralty had constructed four single-cell tunnel magazines with a capacity of 1,240 tons at Ernesettle, near Plymouth in 1925, although there was a problem with water ingress that required remedial work but in 2020 the site is operational under the control of Defence Munitions. Further facilities were approved in 1937 at Crombie, Benarty Hill, Ernesettle, Milford Haven and Trecwn, totalling storage for 70,200 tons of ammunition, whilst Dean Hill was completed in 1941, closing in 2004, with a storage capacity of 36,000 tons. In addition, the Admiralty constructed, improved, extended or acquired many other sites for munitions storage including the Great Western Railway Colwall Tunnel in the Malvern Hills. For details, see, David Evans, *Arming The Fleet: The Development of the Royal Ordnance Yards, 1770-1945* (Gosport: English Heritage, 2006), pp.208-216.

51 For a description of the RAF's underground construction operations, see, AMOH, Air Publication 3236, *Works* (Air Ministry, 1956), pp.255-269. The RAF's venture into subterranean storage was not a completely successful one, and of the five underground sites, only Chilmark Quarry purchased in 1936 avoided a major catastrophe or subsequent repairs and restrictions on use. Linley was abandoned before construction was complete, whilst Llanberis suffered a major failure with two thirds of the depot collapsing on 25 January 1942, and burying 14,000 tons of bombs, which, at the time, was 20% of the RAF's stock. AIR 19/523: Accidents at Explosive Depots Llanberis and Fauld. As a result, checks at RAF Harpur Hill, built to the same design, revealed similar flaws that required remedial work to enable the continued storage of munitions in the concrete arch chambers. The biggest disaster though, was at Fauld in Staffordshire, when, on 27 November 1944, 3,670 tons of bombs exploded, leaving a crater half a mile across and 100 feet deep. It was, and remains, the biggest explosion to have occurred in the UK, with 68 people being killed. See, TNA AIR 2/6966: Explosion at 21 Maintenance Unit Fauld; John Reed, '21 Maintenance Unit RAF Fauld', *After The Battle Magazine No 18*, London: Battle of Britain Prints International Ltd, 1978, pp.35-40 and the excellent Nick McCamley, *The Fauld Disaster, 27 November 1944* (Monkton Farleigh: Folly Books, 2015).

52 The War Office surveyed 20 underground locations in Scotland, Northern England, North and South Wales and the North Midlands in addition to the 25 in the Corsham area. See, McCamley, *Subterranean Britain: Second World War Secret Bunkers*, (Monkton Farleigh: Folly Books, 2015), pp.2-5, Schedule of Underground Sites.

53 The three ASDs were: No 1 - Tunnel Quarry, No 2 - Eastlays Quarry and No 3 - Monkton Farleigh Quarry. In addition, the Army had joint storage with the RAF at Ridge Quarry. For a detailed history of their operation, see, McCamley, *Secret Underground Cities* and McCamley, *Subterranean Britain*.

54 In one example, the Treasury disputed the need to install a sub-surface electricity generation plant, arguing that power from the National Grid would suffice. The War Office cogently argued that it was essential to have an independent system to guard against technical failure, air attack and sabotage. Given that electricity was vital to operating the lighting, conveyor systems, lifts, ventilation, catering facilities, heating and ventilation, it was deemed to be operationally essential and the Treasury eventually relented. For the War Office position, see, TNA WO 32/3343: Underground Storage - Accommodation for Explosives, Letter from MGO 57/Gen/7533 dated 6 July 1936 and for Treasury approval, S.40078 dated 4 August 1936.

55 CAD Corsham No 1 ASD.

56 CAD Corsham No 3 ASD.

P7.2 Munition Production and Distribution. Transportation and especially the railway, were vital in delivering raw materials to the factories and distributing the finished products. The Ministry of Supply branch line from the GWR at Caldicot Junction Monmouthshire to RNPF Caerwent in 2008. (Author)

work to improve access and storage, and difficulties appertaining to flooding and humidity, the effective utilization of the cubic capacity remained a major challenge, whilst work to construct Ridge Quarry for the RAF delayed the Eastlays Quarry Depot for the War Office. As a component of the planning for a continental deployment and in anticipation of ammunition shipments from Southampton, in 1938 the War Office also acquired a site at Westmoors near Ferndown in Dorset and commenced construction of low profile reinforced concrete explosive storehouses[57] although as it transpired, ammunition was mostly exported from Fowey in Cornwall, Newhaven in Sussex and Newport in South Wales.

57 The three ESHs known as 'Fairfax' sheds remain on the site, testament to an association with the BEF. In June 1940, with anti-invasion preparations a priority and the site vulnerable to attack, work on expanding it as an ammunition depot ceased. The US Army was allocated the site as a Petroleum Oils and Lubricants (POL) depot under Operation BOLERO, to store 47,250 tons of packed fuel, activating it as Q-329 in July 1943. The site remained in military ownership post-war and is now the Defence Petroleum Centre. See, William F Ross & Charles F Romanus, *United States Army in World War II, The Quartermaster Corps: Operations in the War against Germany*, Office of the Chief of Military History (Washington: Department of the Army, 1965), p.267.

Underground storage, whilst creating greatly improved protection, needed much greater capital investment and resulted in higher operating costs over those for surface sites as well as sometimes generating un-expected technical and practical issues. In 1936, the plan to store the War Reserve stocks of 18 and 25 pounder and 4.5-inch artillery ammunition in Box Quarry was reviewed because of the wooden boxes, in which, the munitions were packed. Not only did they use 20 percent more space than the steel equivalents but also they posed underground, a considerably greater fire risk than at a surface depot, whilst the cost of re-boxing to steel was assessed to be £110,000.[58] In-loading ammunition to Tunnel Quarry commenced in July 1938 with the intention to eventually store 135,000 tons of mainly artillery ammunition including 2.5 million rounds of 25 pounder, 1.6 million 3 and 3.7-inch AA and 500 million rounds of SAA.[59] The in-load was however, disrupted by inadequate ventilation, which led to deterioration of stock, a problem not expected during intense active operations because the turnover would have been rapid, so more investment was required to create the conditions conducive to long-term storage.[60] In a relatively short period of time, the challenges and expense of under-ground storage became clear. After the BEF was evacuated from France, growing outputs from industry created an imperative to resolve the storage problem in UK and the War Office, whilst continuing to develop CAD Corsham, returned to the concept of surface storage by expanding Longtown and authorizing the construction of two major surface ammunition depots, both of which were rail operated,[61] at Nescliff[62] in Shropshire and Kineton[63] in Warwickshire.

Critical to the effective functioning of the expanding munitions supply chain in the UK were the railways. The new RFFs had extensive internal Standard Gauge Railway (SGR) systems connected to the National Rail Network, whilst the new ammunition depots were either rail-served or operated, thereby creating an End-to-End logistic capability to the SPODs. ROF Chorley was served by the London, Midland & Scottish Railway (LMS) but the key company supporting the supply of BEF munitions was the Great Western Railway (GWR), which served ROF Bridgend, CAD Bramley, CAD Corsham and the main ammunition SPODs of Fowey in Cornwall and Newport in South Wales, whilst traffic to Newhaven in Sussex was transferred to the Southern Railway. To service the operations of the expanding subterranean complex at

58 TNA WO 32/3343: Underground Storage – Accommodation for Explosives, 57/Gen/7533 dated 5 March 1936, Minute MGO to PUS. Based upon RPI, the re-boxing cost equates to £6.738 million.

59 TNA WO 32/3343: Underground Storage - Accommodation for Explosives, Table: Tunnel Quarry Storage.

60 The following were not stored at Tunnel Quarry: 700,000 pyrotechnics, 700,000 No 36 grenades and 2,020 tons of demolition explosives. TNA WO 32/3343: Underground Storage - Accommodation for Explosives, Table: Tunnel Quarry Storage.

61 Rail-served depots had direct access to an internal railhead or railheads from which ammunition was moved by Narrow Gauge Railway (NGR), WMT or conveyor to the storage areas. Rail operated depots had the ESHs directly served by SGR. Even Tunnel Quarry sub-depot at CAD Corsham had SGR access to the sub-surface workings, with an entrance at the Eastern end of Box Tunnel.

62 When complete, Nescliff comprised nine sub-depots covering an area of 1,800 acres and holding 200,000 tons of ammunition. Nescliff closed as an ammunition depot in 1960 and is, at the time of publication, a MOD training facility in a rural setting, whilst some of the ESHs constructed during the Second World War remain.

63 CAD Kineton had 160 ESHs storing 150,000 tons of ammunition. Kineton remains an operational ammunition depot, which was extensively rebuilt in the late 1970s, although one war-time rail operated ESH is a reminder of its previous incarnation.

Corsham, the GWR constructed, although funded at public expense by the Air Ministry and War Office, sidings at Thingley Junction South-West of Chippenham and restored the junction triangle, by building the Air Ministry Loop,[64] thus enabling more efficient train working, especially for munitions traffic.[65]

Challenges in France

The ammunition production and storage arrangements in the UK were still developing when the BEF deployed to France in 1939 resulting in appropriate infrastructure and practised processes to manage the supporting tasks of quality assurance, movement, receipt, accounting and inspection. Regrettably, the BEF was not blessed with the same capabilities, with a shortage of trained and experienced technical personnel being exacerbated by the rigours of field storage and the complexity of the BEF's ammunition inventory.[66] In September 1939, the Royal Army Ordnance Corps (RAOC) employed, on ammunition duties, only 16 Inspecting Ordnance Officers and 51 Ammunition Examiners and there was no separate ordnance ammunition branch in the War Office.[67] To compound this fragility, GHQ BEF had no Assistant Director Ordnance Services (Ammunition (ADOS (Ammn))[68] to co-ordinate the complex technical and operational munitions interfaces in France, a post that despite the full support of QMG BEF was not established until December 1939, and then because of telecommunications issues had to be located in HQ LOC in Le Mans rather than the Ordnance Directorate at Arras.[69] Qualified ammunition examiners were a precious asset and the expertise had therefore, perforce of circumstances, to be spread between 1 and 2 Base Ammunition Depots (BAD),[70] with the majority of the manpower comprising a mix of Supplementary Reservists, Militiamen and conscripts, leavened by Regular soldiers.[71] There was no time to conduct meaningful unit military and technical training before departure and the organizations had therefore, to learn

64 TNA WO 32/3343: Underground Storage - Accommodation for Explosives, Letter 57/Gen/7533 QMG 3a dated 3 January 1936. The planning for the construction of the sidings was based upon an out-load from Corsham of 2,000 tons per day.

65 R A Cooke, *Atlas of the Great Western Railway as at 1947,* Revised Edn, (Didcot: Wild Swan Publications, 1997), Map 28. Chippenham.

66 Map 7: BEF - Base Ammunition Ports & Depots.

67 In November 1939, a new War Office Branch was created within the Ordnance Directorate to take the place of the Master General of Ordnance (MGO) Branches, which had previously dealt with ammunition. The new branch was designated OS 2 (later WS 2) and its primary function was the provision, distribution and issue of ammunition.

68 The post of ADOS (Ammn) proved to be of immense value, especially once combat operations began in May 1940. TNA CAB 106/235: BEF Ammunition Supply (Gibson Report), p.8.

69 TNA CAB 106/235: BEF Ammunition Supply (Gibson Report), p.8.

70 For the outline ORBAT and War Establishment (WE) of a BAD, which usually comprised a HQ and three ordnance ammunition companies, see, Philson, BEFORBAT, Vol 3, p.118. Attached to each BAD was an AMPC Labour Company, comprising an HQ and 15 Sections, each of 26 men.

71 Of the 278 Other Ranks (OR), a deficiency of 49, posted to HQ 3 BAD and 8, 9 and 10 Ordnance Ammunition Companies, whilst it was mobilizing at Bramley in November 1939, 90% were either Militiamen or conscripts; presumably, the balance consisted of Regular soldiers or Regular Reservists. To improve this weak position, the Officer-in-Charge RAOC Records, the Corps manning Directorate, suggested that upon arrival in France, personnel from 3 BAD should be swapped with trained soldiers from 1 and 2 BAD. TNA WO 167/1144: 3 BAD RAOC, WD, entries November 1939.

'On the Job', a problem that continued after the First Contingent of the BEF had arrived in France. Had there been kinetic operations during the deployment, the weaknesses inherent in these arrangements would have been lucidly exposed.

The BEF's ammunition inventory was surprisingly complex, with artillery ammunition being the most significant logistic task by bulk and weight.[72] There was a range of 69 different natures for armoured, infantry, artillery and supporting units,[73] some of which were common user munitions such as Small Arms Ammunition (SAA) and grenades, to more complex munitions for the 3.7-inch HAA gun and in bulk, demolition explosives for the Royal Engineers. SAA included 0.38-inch and 0.455-inch rounds for revolvers and 0.303-inch ammunition for the Short Magazine Lee Enfield Rifle, Bren and Lewis Light Machine Guns (LMG) which used the same rounds, whilst the Vickers Medium Machine Gun (MMG) also used 0.303-inch but loaded to a canvas belt. Some armoured vehicles were equipped with either the 7.92 mm Besa, the 0.5-inch HMG or a 15 mm cannon. Anti-armour weapons included the Boys anti-tank rifle with a 0.55-inch armour piercing shot,[74] the French Hotchkiss 25 mm gun, and the 40 mm 2 pounder fitted to the Cruiser and Matilda II tanks. There were two mortars: 2-inch and 3-inch, firing High Explosive (HE) and smoke bombs, although there was no initially, HE for the former.[75] There were five types of anti-aircraft weapons: Hotchkiss Machine Gun, Vickers 2 pounder, 40 mm Bofors LAA, 3-inch 2-cwt and the 3.7-inch HAA[76] and eight types of artillery weapons. In addition, the ground-to-ground tube systems had a bewildering array of shell types[77] and supporting fuzes,[78] which created additional challenges to asset tracking and delivery, whilst the 13 different fuze types[79] added yet more complexity to the duties of often

72 See Table 7.9 'BEF Tube Artillery Ammunition Types' in Appx to Chp 7. For details, see War Office, *Text Book of Ammunition* (HMSO, 1936), pp.201-203.

73 21 were artillery and 12 x RE.

74 The Boys anti-tank rifle has had a bad press since 1940 on the basis that it was incapable of stopping a tank. Whilst it might have been better not to grant it the nomenclature of 'anti-tank', Army Council, *Infantry Section Leading 1938*, p.9, Sect 18, Anti-tank rifle, is specific upon its capability: 'The anti-tank rifle affords a means of protection against enemy light armoured vehicles'. The weapon training pamphlet, Army Council, *Small Arms Training*, Vol I, Pamphlet No 5, *Anti-Tank Rifle, 1942*, 26/GS Publications/702 (War Office, 1942), p.11, Appx, Table I, notes an effective penetration at 100 yards at 90° of 23.2 mm, and at 300 yards, which means that the Boys was capable of defeating in May 1940, all German tanks with a frontal or side attack, with the exception of the Pz Mk IIIE onwards. The Germans deployed 348 Mk III tanks to France, mostly E and F models with a few G. See, Peter Chamberlain and Hilary Doyle, *Encyclopaedia of German Tanks of World War Two* (London: Arms & Armour, 1999).

75 Whilst there were production and proofing issues with the 2-inch HE round, it is interesting to note that Army Council, *Infantry Section Leading 1938*, p.9, Sect 19, 2 inch mortar, states, 'It is chiefly used as a smoke producing weapon for offensive action'.

76 The 40 mm shell weighed 2.4 pounds, the 3-inch 20 cwt AA shell 16 lb and the 3.7-inch, 28 lb.

77 See Table 7A.1, 'BEF Tube Artillery Ammunition Types' in Appendix to Chp 7. For details, see War Office, *Text Book of Ammunition*, pp.201-203.

78 See Table 7A.2, 'Land Service Artillery Ammunition Fuze Matrix,' in Appx to Chp 7. For details, see War Office, *Text Book of Ammunition*, pp.201-203.

79 The fuze types are shown in Table 7A.3 in Appx to Chp 7, 'Land Service Artillery Ammunition - Fuze Types'. For details, see War Office, *Text Book of Ammunition*, pp.201-203.

in-experienced logisticians.[80] All of these points were complicated by the arrival of TA divisions equipped with a mix of 18 pounder guns and 4.5-inch howitzers, which in addition to the 18/25 pounders of the Regular divisions,[81] initially created a growing fragility in ammunition delivery and dumping, a problem resolved by the General Staff re-distributing the artillery equipment so each division was equipped with all types of divisional field piece.[82] Many personnel were not conversant with the new munitions and accidents were not infrequent. There was a particularly unpleasant incident on 16 December 1939 at the II Corps Junior Leaders School when an anti-tank mine exploded during a demonstration, killing three officers, critically injuring four, three of whom died, and seriously wounding two others.[83]

Planning for in-Theatre ammunition stocks was based upon expected expenditure rates per gun per day, the weapon population for each type and the numbers of days reserves directed by the General Staff in GHQ. The planning baseline allocated each division 6 million rounds of SAA and 1,500 anti-tank mines per month, with key daily tube consumption thus: [84]

Table 7.2
Expenditure Planning Rates – Key Weapon Systems
Rounds per gun per day (rpgpd)[85]

Artillery		Anti-Aircraft		Infantry	
25 pdr[86]	36[87]	3-inch HAA	50	3-inch mortar	13
60 pdr	30	40 mm Bofors LAA	40	2-inch mortar	10
6-inch howitzer	28			2 pdr Anti-Tank*	5

*Royal Artillery

80 All Land and Air Service ammunition, including charges and fuzes were coded. See, Army Council, FSPB Pamphlet No 9, 1939, *Supply and Replenishment of Material in the Field*, pp.17-26, Sect 6, Ammunition Code.

81 During the inter-war period, the War Office sought to replace the Great War 18-pdr field gun and the 4.5-inch howitzer with one weapon combining the high velocity of the 18-pdr and the variable propelling charges of the howitzer, firing a shell of approximately 30 lbs. The result was the 25 pdr gun-howitzer with an interim solution of a barrel modified for an 18 pdr carriage, which was the 18/25 pdr that entered service in 1937. The deployment of the 18 pdr gun and 4.5-inch howitzer combination in BEF field regiments was a solution to the capability requirement provided by the 18/25 pdr, albeit creating a logistic issue.

82 TNA CAB 106/235: BEF Ammunition Supply (Gibson Report), p.6.

83 The corps commander, Lieutenant-General Brooke wrote in his diary, 'It is shattering that our anti-tank mines should be as unsafe to handle as that!' On 17 December, he noted, 'I have got a board sitting to try and get at the bottom of the matter, but it is not easy as most of those who were near were killed'. Danchev & Todman , *War Diaries, 1939-1945, Field Marshal Lord Alanbrooke* (London: Weidenfeld & Nicolson, 2001), pp.25-26.

84 Plan W4 First Maintenance Project, p.18. TNA WO 197/2: First Maintenance Project: Reception of Forces in France and system of maintenance in the initial stages.

85 Table collated from information in TNA CAB 106/235: BEF Ammunition Supply (Gibson Report).

86 Until October 1939, this was restricted to 25 rpgpd. Plan W4 First Maintenance Project, para 20. TNA WO 197/2: First Maintenance Project.

87 30 x HE, 5 x Smoke and 1 x AP.

P7.3 Ammunition People. Experienced ammunition staff were at a premium when the BEF deployed to France, a problem exacerbated by the increasing expansion of munitions production. It was therefore surprising but most fortunate that there were very few ammunition incidents of consequence. 3 Base Ammunition Depot No 1 Sub-Depot personnel ready to deploy to France from CAD Bramley. (RLCM: RAOC/WTB1/RAO/368/1)

A summary of ammunition movement[88] from UK to France in the period September 1939 to May 1940 is shown below,[89] with the BEF ammunition flow diagram[90] lucidly illustrating the significant role of commercial transportation systems within the supply chain.

88 The ammunition movement plan for the first four regular divisions was encompassed in the Stores Movement Table (A4813) in TNA WO 197/2: First Maintenance Project.

89 Details extracted from WOOH *Movements*, p.201.

90 Diagram No 4.

Table 7.3
Conventional Ammunition
BEF Imports to France

UK Depots	UK Ports	French Ports	Tonnage	Remarks
Bramley Corsham	Fowey	Brest	21,000	
	Fowey	St Malo	8,000	
	Newhaven	Fecamp	18,000*	*Inclusive of chemical weapons
	Newport	Brest	14,000	
	Newport	St Nazaire	48,000	
		Total	109,000*+	*+32,303 tons returned 28 May – 12 July 1940

The W4 Plan directed that a reserve of 45 x Daily Ammunition Expenditure Rate (DAER) should be held In-Theatre. Two BADs were to be established, each of three ASDs holding 7,000 tons apiece, thus totalling 21,000 tons per BAD, but from the start of the deployment it was clear that as the BEF expanded more storage would be required[91] The decision of the War

91 A key driver of the increasing need for expanding the ammunition storage capability in France was the growing numbers of artillery units in the BEF, which for May 1940 is summarized in the table below. Information collated from Ellis, BOH, *The War in France and Flanders,* pp.358-371 and General Sir Martin Farndale KCB, *History of the Royal Regiment of Artillery, The Years of Defeat 1939-41* (London & Washington: Brasseys, 1996), pp.236-241.

Table 7.4
BEF Artillery
ORBAT and Equipment

Regiment Type	Number	Artillery Equipment	Remarks
Anti-Tank	14*	25 mm or 2 pdr	*Inclusive of 1 x Canadian detachment
Anti-Tank & LAA	1*	As above plus 40 mm	*101st Regiment supporting 1st Armoured Division
LAA	7*	40 mm Bofors	*Equivalent
HAA	12	3 or 3.7-inch	
Royal Horse Artillery	2	18 or 25 pdr	
Field	40	18 & 25 pdr and 4.5-inch	
Medium	16	60 pdr or 6-inch	
Heavy	2	8 or 9.2-inch	
Super Heavy	1	12-inch	
Total	95		

Office in late October 1939 to increase holdings in the BADs in France to 180 days[92] as a result of the shortage of storage in the UK also initiated the requirement to convince the French to release suitable estate for the proposed expansions and to allocate, or grant access to railheads. Apart from creating additional work for BEF ammunition specialists and logisticians, the War Office should have shouldered the burden in the Home Base but apart from the convenience of passing the work elsewhere, it is possible that the War Office identified the irritating probability of resistance from within the rural shires and from the Ministry of Agriculture, to the construction of yet more ammunition storage facilities in the UK. No doubt the War Office considered that the French would be more amenable to the requirement, whilst the continuous in-load of munitions to the Continent firmly demonstrated to Friend and Foe alike, Britain's commitment to the Alliance. Either way, the decision was operationally unsound and led to unnecessary losses of ammunition in June 1940.

Design and Deployment

The design and layout of the two BADs[93] was greatly influenced by Great War experience and particularly the lessons identified from the disaster at Audruieq[94] in July 1916, when a German

92 The table below illustrates the daily ammunition requirement in tons as the BEF expanded to 12 divisions. Table collated from various sources.

Table 7.5
BEF Expansion Plan – Daily Ammunition Requirement

Force	In-Theatre Timeline	Accumulated Ammunition Daily Tonnage Requirement
4 Regular Infantry Divisions	Z + 33 days	850
2 Territorial Infantry Divisions	Z + 4 months	1100
1 Territorial Motor Division	Z + 5 months	1480
3 Territorial Infantry Divisions	Z + 6 months	1890
1 Armoured Division	Z + 8 months	2240
1 Armoured Division	Z+ 12 months?	3200
Total Divisions -12		3200

93 For a concise explanation of the key issues relating to the design and layout of ammunition depots, see, Army Council, *Military Engineering*, Vol VII, *Accommodation and Installations*, pp.138-145, Ammunition Depots.

94 Located 11 miles NW of St Omer. The explosions were so powerful that live shells were found two miles from the depot, most of the trench mortar ammunition detonated and one oblong shaped crater was 60 feet deep. Major-General A Forbes CB CMG, *A History of the Army Ordnance Services*, Vol Three, *The Great War* (London: The Medici Society, 1929), pp.125-127.

aerial bomb caused a fire[95] that destroyed 9,000 tons of ammunition.[96] This incident, which cost an eye-watering £2.185 Billion at 2018 values,[97] had a long-lasting and fundamental effect upon the design of future ammunition depots, including those of the BEF with sites constructed away from other installations and designed to have greater internal dispersion.[98] This resulted in a depot planned to store 30,000 tons requiring at least 1,000 acres of real estate[99] and 50 miles of internal railway to serve it.[100] These points were seared into the minds of the BEF RAOC planners, the Gibson report noting of the psychology, that, 'There was an obsession as to the losses which might occur from bombing, based on memories of the Audruieq depot........ and other experiences.'[101] The BADs in 1939 were thus smaller, more dispersed and intended, despite the fire risk,[102] to be sited in woods, in order reduce the opportunities for effective enemy aerial observation.[103]

1 BAD was established in the Foret du Gavre[104] in the Southern Base Area, with the SPOD at Saint Nazaire. Stocks were cleared from the docks by rail to four railheads serving the BAD area: La Maillardais, Le Gavre, Nozay, and Coudray Plesse, from which, WMT delivered the stocks to the stacking areas. Whilst locating 1 BAD in the woods was most commendable from the tactical perspective, there was little examination of the resources required to support the process and is an excellent illustration of the balance that was required between operational security, logistic output and engineering input. The forest tracks required considerable maintenance to make them fit for high traffic levels and both of these activities could compromise the location if tight control was not exercised. This experience appears to have been tempered by the time the RAOC 'ammunition Lessons Identified' appeared in the

95 The Court of Enquiry held on 23-24 July 1916 identified that the initiation involved no more than five small aerially delivered weapons and probably only one. The immediate 'Lessons Identified' report covered the design of future depots, fire-fighting equipment, ammunition packaging, splinter protection, decoy sites and the positioning and operation of railheads within ammunition depots. The clearance of damaged munitions, many of them unstable, took months. Correspondence in TNA MUN 4/3077: Reports on Fire in France at Audruicq, including the 'Report of the Court of Enquiry' and 'Instructions in regards to Storage of Ammunition', GHQ QMG Loose Minute dated 8 August 1916. See, also Forbes, *Army Ordnance Services*, pp.126-127.

96 The loss included 500,000 rounds of 18 pdr and 10,000 rounds of 8 and 9.2-inch howitzer. Captain Wilfred Miles (Comp.), *History of the Great War* (BOH), *France and Belgium, 1916*, Vol II, and Appendices and Maps, *2nd July 1916 to the End of the Battles of the Somme* (London: Macmillan, 1938), p.112.

97 Based on the *Measuring Worth UK*, Project Economy Cost as a share of the Gross Domestic Product (GDP). The financial loss was assessed at £3.5 million in 1916 prices.

98 For the 1934 safety distances, see, Army Council, *Military Engineering*, Vol VII, *Accommodation and Installations*, Plate 85, Ammunition Depot Safety Distances.

99 1,000 acres equates to an area one third of the size of London Heathrow airport, which provides a clear illustration of the real estate required for these depots and the complexity of the staff work with the French and civilian authorities which, was required to acquire the land and to obtain the authority to store such large quantities of munitions.

100 Henniker, BOH, *Transportation on the Western Front*, pp.322-323.

101 TNA CAB 106/235: BEF Ammunition Supply (Gibson Report), p.2.

102 Army Council, *Army Training Memorandum* No 35, August 1940 (War Office, 1940), para 27 (ii) (b) p.18, RAOC Lessons from Experience, noted that whilst pine woods in particular, would always carry a fire risk, in other woodland, the risk was 'not so great as might be expected'.

103 TNA CAB 106/235: BEF Ammunition Supply (Gibson Report), p.2.

104 Foret de Gavre is 25 miles NW of Nantes.

Army Training Memorandum in August 1940, which suggested otherwise, 'Road served depots proved their worth. Little constructional work is necessary, and they are easy to conceal', which was true but only in relative terms to rail operated sites.[105] The stacking areas often needed levelling and were sometimes not next to the feeder tracks, which entailed a 'carry'[106] to and from the vehicles; all of these problems reduced in and out-loading capability. Storage materials were also required, equating for every ton of ammunition, to six feet of timber dunnage and 1.5 square yards of tarpaulin.[107]

In dry conditions, fire was a potential hazard and the Germans could have caused effective destruction by attacking the forests with incendiaries.[108] 2 BAD was located around Plouaret[109] in the Northern Base Area with the SPOD at Brest and two railheads at Plouaret and Plounerin, from which stocks were moved by WMT. Neither of the two road served BAD sites were suitable for the task, which may, despite the concern over the vulnerability of in-Theatre rail-served or operated locations, have prompted construction of three rail BADs out of the seven that were built before the evacuation. The Base storage of ammunition stocks, including aerially delivered bombs for the RAF, was the responsibility of the Army.[110] Initially, all AASF munitions were held in 1 BAD and those for the BEF Air Component at 2 BAD but these were later rebalanced and split between the sites.[111]

One of the key tasks as new depots were constructed was to ensure there was a stock balance of munition types across the different depots to ensure that the appropriate levels of ammunition were held in each site. There was however, friction between GHQ Ordnance Services and Q (Movements) because the latter Branch strongly opposed the plan on the basis that it was 'against the principles of movement.'[112] Study of the Chapter IV of the *Manual of Movement (War)* which, examines 'The Principles of Military Movement,'[113] reveals no evidence that supports this objection, although there is a comment that 'foresight and co-ordination' will minimize the adverse impact upon the capacity of transportation by constant changes to the plan.[114] The conclusion must be that Q (Movements) failed to grasp the significance of dispersion and resilience to ammunition storage above some disruption to the efficient utilization of transportation assets, which of course, could have been mitigated by better planning. Either way, Q (Movements) principles were sacrificed on the altar of operational efficiency.

In this respect, whilst it had been part of Plan W4 to ensure this balance, the initial shipping arrangements did not run in accordance with the plan. The first two ammunition ships loading

105 Army Council, *Army Training Memorandum* No 35, para 27 (ii) (a) p.18, RAOC Lessons from Experience.
106 Stacking and loading were done by hand. If a chain or portable conveyor could not be used, the ammunition also had to be carried by hand.
107 Lindsell, *A & Q, or Military Administration in War*, p.47.
108 The RAF had plans, compiled before September 1939, for Bomber Command to attack German forests with incendiaries, and these were summarized in Western Air Plan (WA) 11. See, John Terraine, *Right of the Line, The Royal Air Force in the European War 1939-1945*, (London: Hodder and Stoughton 1985), p.79 & p.690.
109 50 miles East of Brest.
110 Army Council, FSR, Vol I, *Organization and Administration*, p.146, Sect 85.
111 TNA CAB 106/235: BEF Ammunition Supply (Gibson Report), p.2.
112 Fernyhough & Harris, *History of the Royal Army Ordnance Corps, 1939-1945*, p.88.
113 Army Council, *Manual of Movement (War)*, pp.17-22.
114 Ibid, p.18.

P7.4 Ammunition Storage. The 2018 remains of rail served bomb and ammunition storage compounds at RAF Barnham Suffolk, which opened in August 1939 under the control of 94 Maintenance Unit (Author)

at Newport were late arriving, with the second having to be replaced.[115] Whilst both left to schedule, the loads were only 71 and 60 per cent respectively of the planned cargo, a differential compounded by an error in the sailing orders, which resulted in the Brest bound ship arriving at Saint Nazaire and the Saint Nazaire bound vessel docking in Brest. Adjustment to ammunition stock holdings therefore, had to be made between the Northern and Southern Bases and the AASF ammunition took longer than planned to reach the Rheims area.[116] 24 ammunition ships for the First Contingent were programmed to run from M+4 to M+41,[117] with a total of 36,000 tons flowing into Brest and Saint Nazaire, with 12 vessels unloading 1,500 tons on every voyage to each port.[118] Unloading ammunition in the docks was however, no easy task, especially as the weather turned more inclement in October and the nights drew in, with one particular issue being the difficulty in reading, using the tactical the blue light required at night, the stencilling

115 WOOH, *Movements*, p.176.
116 Ibid.
117 M Day for the W4 logistic out-load was 6 September 1939.
118 Plan W4 First Maintenance Project, Shipping Plan, Part II, Ammunition. TNA WO 197/2: First Maintenance Project: Reception of Forces in France and system of maintenance in the initial stages.

on RAF bombs and determining the whether SAA boxes were Army or RAF.[119] The separation of ammunition components to save shipping space caused additional work in France to ensure the munitions were issued in an operationally viable state. Whilst these were apparently minor issues, the despatch of munitions without fuzes or charges to incorrect locations at best caused logistic and administrative inconvenience but at worst might create an operational drama.

Proofing and production issues of ammunition also influenced stock availability. There was an initial shortage of 25 pounder smoke rounds, which meant that the approved holdings within artillery units was only five percent, instead of 25 percent, with the balance held as a central reserve. There were also very few HE rounds for the 2-inch mortar,[120] which created a reduction in platoon indirect fire capability, whilst another gap was the availability of field artillery armour-piercing rounds, which was not in accordance with authorised stock holdings. In January 1940, whilst ammunition reserves in France were increasing, there was unease in GHQ, particularly by the Staff of Major-General Royal Artillery (MGRA), concerning the rate of arrival of artillery natures and critical deficiencies, the war diary noting: 'The main subject during the past week has been the question of ammunition. Production appears to have fallen well behind the promised rate, and serious deficiencies are apparent'.[121] Much of this assessment was based upon perception and it is clear that GHQ did not have the full picture. The output of field artillery ammunition had increased from 758,000 rounds in the period September – December 1939, to 1,068,000 in the 1st Quarter of 1940, a 29 percent increase, and then to 1,516,000 in the 2nd Quarter, a total increase of 50%.[122] Medium artillery ammunition production in the same period had likewise improved respectively from 28,000 to 90,000 rounds and then to 189,000, increases of 69 and 85% respectively. LAA ammunition production had however, dropped from 160,000 in the last four months of 1939 to only 80,000 in the 1st Quarter of 1940, recovering to 542,000 in the 2nd. HAA ammunition, which had received priority in the pre-war period, reduced from 677,000 rounds in the last four months of 1939, to 574,000 in the 1st Quarter of 1940 and then 530,000 in the 2nd.[123] Of more concern, was the output of 2 and 3-inch mortar bombs, which dropped from 223,000 in the corresponding 1939 period to 155,000 in the 1st Quarter of 1940 before recovering to 278,000 in the 2nd, and the impact of the preparations in UK for operations in Scandinavia resulting in a temporary reduction of ammunition imports to the BEF from 10,836 tons in February 1940 to 5,562 tons in March.[124] By 31 March 1940 however, the BEF had an increasing inventory in-Theatre, and although some natures were short in respect of DAER, Table 7.A1 in the chapter appendix summarizes not only the stocks on hand but also the increasing demand for storage.

119 TNA WO 167/51: GHQ Services, Transportation, DG (Tn) 'Lessons' dated 11 October 1939. The document proposed that the RAF General Purpose (GP), Semi-Armour Piercing (SAP) and Armour Piercing (AP) bombs should have different coloured bands to enable easy identification in blue light. The document also suggested that the Army and RAF SAA boxes should have a definitive colour marking.

120 BEF holdings on 31 March 1940 were 14,062 rounds for 1,149 mortars.

121 TNA WO 167/13: GHQ MGRA, WD, entry 13 January 1940.

122 Central Office, BOH, *Statistical Digest of the War*, p.145, Table 123, Munitions, Filled Ammunition: Army.

123 Ibid.

124 Colville, *Man of Valour*, p.177.

P7.5 Ammunition Railhead Risks. The operation of ARHs was not without risk. Whilst the photograph shows a post-war explosion on 2 January 1946 at Savernake Ammunition Sidings in Wiltshire, in which eight soldiers were killed and 29 railway wagons destroyed, it lucidly illustrates the damage that could be caused through enemy action, poor drills or instable ammunition. (RLCM: RAOC/WTB2/NOR)

Expanding the Depots

As a result of War Office direction to increase in-Theatre holdings to 180 x DAER and the plan to have deployed eighteen divisions by August 1940, 1 and 2 BADs were expanded to four ASDs, with three holding 9,000 tons and the fourth, 7,000, thus totalling 34,000 tons, with the additional BAD to deploy on the same basis, although by February 1940 a decision was made to deploy an additional three depots, to bring the total to six inclusive of the field Advanced Ammunition Depot (AAD) listed in Plan W4 to provide forward stocks, although the AAD was never deployed because the Host Nation objected to the proposal, offering in lieu, an underground storage facility at Mery-sur-Oise, 25 miles North-North-West of Paris. This was declined on the basis that it was too far from the Base, although this was not the defining reason because there was an interesting story behind this saga.[125] The French offer to the BEF appeared at face value to be most generous, the Host Nation understanding that GHQ

125 The personnel assigned to the AAD were deployed to operate the additional ASD in 1 BAD. TNA CAB 106/235: BEF Ammunition Supply (Gibson Report).

BEF was keen on forward depots, whilst hopeful that the British Army's increasing interest in sub-surface storage in the UK would clinch the deal. An indiscretion from a French officer had however, enabled GHQ to identify that the Host Nation considered the site too far forward and had thus out-loaded the ammunition.[126] This may not though, be the whole story because whilst the documents shed no light upon the issue, it is possible that the real reason the BEF declined the French proposal of Mery is that it was unsuitable for the storage of Gas Warfare (GW) ammunition.

This decision however, left the planners with the problem of mitigating the potential disruption of ammunition along the , so another proposal was agreed with the French to operate a road-served forward site with three ASDs, each of 7,000 tons, including the capability to store GW munitions,[127] in the Foret d'Eawy to the North of Saint Saens, using a railhead at Buchy.[128] This arrangement was arguably as 'forward' as Mery-sur-Oise' but it had the advantage of being within the goose-egg of the BEF's ABA, although from the technical and security perspectives the French offer was the better solution, except of course, for GW ammunition. 3 BAD thus arrived from Bramley in December 1939,[129] the first task being to dispatch parties of soldiers to 1 BAD and 2 BAD for some technical On-The-Job training,[130] this opportunity being denied during the mobilization period at CAD Bramley by the Chief Ordnance Officer, who insisted upon the soldiers being used for labouring duties in the depot.[131] The in-load commenced on 5 January 1940 but was beset by the severe weather, with –22°C being recorded on 22 January, which caused havoc with WMT reliability, whilst the Dennis fire pump, trailer and extinguishers had to be garaged indoors to ensure operational availability.[132] On 27 January, a thaw commenced, flooding the tracks and water-logging the stack areas but the depot was able to receive 3,258 rounds of 6-inch gas shells on 3 February.[133] In the circumstances, it is perhaps not surprising that a report observed of the ammunition depots that 'No 3 BAD probably had the toughest time, being dumped in a bleak, thinly populated district at the beginning of the coldest winter for a century.'[134]

The plan to move 2 BAD from the unsuitable site in the Plouaret and Plounerin area to the Foret de Rennes was shelved, with 4 BAD exploiting the forest site from February 1940.[135] Despite the poor weather, by the third week of March, the in-load was in full swing, with 500-600 tons arriving daily from 1 and 2 BADs.[136] By early April 1940, 7,000 tons had been

126 The Gibson Report described this as a case of '*Timeo Danaos dona fereuetes*' (Beware of Greeks bearing gifts) and GHQ decided, in order to maintain relations with the French, to decline the offer on the basis the depot was too far from the Base rather than too near to the Germans. TNA CAB 106/235: BEF Ammunition Supply, p.5.

127 The reconnaissance for the storage of Land Service gas munitions was conducted on 25 December 1939. TNA WO 167/1144: 3 BAD RAOC, WD

128 TNA WO 167/1144: 3 BAD RAOC, WD, entries December 1939 and January 1940.

129 RLCM RAO/368/1.

130 TNA WO 167/1144: 3 BAD RAOC, WD, entries December 1939 and January 1940.

131 TNA CAB 106/235: BEF Ammunition Supply (Gibson Report), p.9. Fernyhough, *History of the Royal Army Ordnance Corps, 1939-1945*, makes no mention of these issues.

132 TNA WO 167/1144: 3 BAD RAOC, WD, entries January 1940.

133 TNA WO 167/1144: 3 BAD RAOC, WD, entry 7 February 1940.

134 TNA CAB 106/235: BEF Ammunition Supply (Gibson Report), p.9.

135 TNA CAB 106/235: BEF Ammunition Supply (Gibson Report), p.2.

136 TNA WO 167/1178: 4 BAD RAOC, WD, entries February and March 1940.

in-loaded to the two ASDs, which, by end of the month had stocked a total of 13,814 tons.[137] 6 BAD[138] based on 19 Ammunition Company RAOC arrived in France on 2 May to work a new depot at Blain,[139] a site close to 1 BAD, with two double ASDs. In-loading commenced on 24 May, with the arrival of 23 rail wagons of RAF Smoke Curtain Installations (SCI) containing liquid Mustard, and free-fall gas bombs, which were later evacuated to the UK from Saint Nazaire in an interesting if somewhat complex move. Over a period of two and a half days WMT transferred the weapons to a canal-side site five miles from the depot, where they were transhipped to a barge for a three day journey to Saint Nazaire.[140] By 14 June, 6 BAD had in-loaded 2,200 tons of munitions, most of which were RAF HE bombs, plus 3-inch and 3.7-inch HAA and SAA.[141] Two specialist BADs were also formed. 5 BAD, originally planned to operate a rail-served site at Blain was designated 21 BAD, to control a road-served site at Tourville-les-Ifs, four miles South of the SPOD of Fecamp, which was opened in December 1939 for the storage of RAF aerially delivered gas bombs and SCIs, although it also held Army GW artillery munitions.[142] 22 BAD,[143] a rail-served site, was opened at Chateauneuf-d'Ille-et-Vilaine,[144] eight miles South-East of SPOD Saint Malo, to service small munitions shipments through the port.[145]

137 TNA WO 167/1178: 4 BAD RAOC, WD, entries April 1940. No 1 ASD had 8,597 tons and No 2 ASD, 5,217 tons.
138 GHQ Q Maint Q/1193 (b1) dated 15 February 1940 in TNA WO 167/10: GHQ Q (Maint), suggests that 6 BAD was intended to operate a site at Yvetot, 20 miles SE of Fecamp but this was cancelled in the light of operational developments in May 1940.
139 20 miles NW of Nantes.
140 TNA WO 167/1180: 6 BAD RAOC, WD, entries May and June 1940. As the distance by road from the depot to Saint Nazaire Docks is only 35 miles, this solution must have been initiated either because of a shortage of WMT or security concerns.
141 TNA WO 167/1180: 6 BAD RAOC, WD entries June 1940.
142 See, Chp 14, 'Operation FLANNELFOOT'.
143 Originally titled 8 BAD, it was re-designated 22 BAD on 22 February 1940. The unit war diary held in TNA WO 167/1181, has an excellent selection of Part I Orders, including No 27 dated 31 May 1940, Serial 113, relating to damage caused to young trees and the possible withdrawal by the landowner of the privilege granted to the soldiers of the unit to walk in the woods and fish in the lake. Regrettably the AFC 2118 detailing the depot's operational details for May & June 1940 is missing.
144 Most documents title 22 BAD as Miniac, which is four miles to the SSE.
145 TNA CAB 106/235: BEF Ammunition Supply (Gibson Report), p.9.

Table 7.6
BEF Planned and Established Ammunition Depots – 1940[146]

BAD	Site	Location	Access	Remarks
1	Foret du Gavre	Nantes	Road	Operational September 1939
2	Plouaret	Brest	Road	Temporary site but retained as depot
3	St Saens	Rouen	Road	Operational January 1940
4	Rennes	Rennes	Rail	Operational 1 March 1940
5	Foret du Gavre	Nantes	Rail	CX and 5 BAD designated 21 BAD to operate Fecamp
6	Yvetot	Le Harve	Rail	CX and 6 BAD sent to Blain.
6	Blain	Nantes	Rail	Operational 24 May 1940
21	Fecamp	Le Harve	Road	GW munitions site; originally 5 BAD. Opened December 1939
22	Miniac	St Malo	Rail	Originally 8 BAD

Given all the challenges in mobilization, training, shortages of handling equipment and the provision of support services such as catering, it is surprising that the BADs were able to function but despite all the additional issues of accommodation, ablutions and rationing, 1 BAD, having mobilized at CAD Bramley on 2 September 1939, arrived in France on 12 September and accepted the first train to La Maillardais, one of four railheads allocated to the depot. In addition, French munitions, including anti-tank mines and 25 mm shot for the Hotchkiss anti-tank gun with which, some units of the BEF were being equipped, were taken on charge.[147] Whilst not perhaps a text-book technical solution in depot operation, it was remarkable that such an inexperienced unit, initially 'living rough' in the field without blankets[148] and sustainable catering and medical support,[149] delivered any operational output, although the 'exceptionally fine' mid-September weather was indisputably a contributory factor. Fortunately, by the time the late autumn weather arrived, several improvements had been implemented and the soldiers were also becoming accustomed to working outside. The onset though, in January 1940, of severe winter, was a challenge of a different order, which is best described by extracts from the war diary of 21 BAD.[150]

146 Table collated from information in GHQ Q Maint Q/1193 (b1) dated 15 February 1940 in TNA WO 167/10: GHQ Q (Maint).
147 TNA WO 167/1175: 1 BAD RAOC, WD, entries September 1939.
148 TNA CAB 106/235: BEF Ammunition Supply (Gibson Report), p.3.
149 There was a good deal of mild illness amongst personnel at both BADs, although the poor sanitary conditions at 2 BAD caused the greatest concern to the Deputy Director Medical Services (DDMS) because for want of tools, latrines and sumps could not be dug. TNA CAB 106/235: BEF Ammunition Supply (Gibson Report), p.3.
150 TNA WO 167/1179: 21 BAD RAOC, WD.

Date	AFC 2118 entry
16 January	Heavy snow storms made roads in the area impassable in many areas……. work was brought to a standstill at the dump.
18 January	Further blizzards resulted in one route to Fecamp being blocked to a depth of seven feet of snow in drifts. On the alternative route, transport was compelled to take to the open fields to avoid burial in the snow.
29 January	The outside temperature did not rise above freezing point…..trees, poles and pylons were hurled to the ground by the weight of ice. Telephone communications were cut off…..

Another problem, exacerbated by the demanding conditions, was the fragility of some of the manpower available for heavy labouring duties in the AMPC, a matter, which was the subject of a letter to the War Office from GHQ.[151] With many personnel aged between 35–50, the rigours of the winter were having an adverse affect upon individual performance, and the Staff were examining ways of deploying AMPC personnel to greater effect. In addition, as the deployment to France continued into 1940, GHQ also had a plan to release some male soldiers in the BADs from a range of duties and replace them with ladies from the Auxiliary Territorial Service (ATS). Both No 1 and No 2 BADs were part of this arrangement, issued by GHQ on 25 February 1940.[152] The plan included 55 ATS to replace 45 men at No 1 BAD and 43 ATS to replace 32 men at No 2 BAD, although Director ATS considered No 2 BAD as 'highly unsuitable' for the employment of ATS because of the harsh living conditions.[153] Combat operations overtook the planning for all of these activities and neither of the unit war diaries[154] have a record of ATS arriving in their locations, nor were any shown on the Field Return of Officers or Soldiers.[155]

151 TNA WO 197/72: British retaliatory position in the event of chemical warfare, GHQ (A) A/3221 (O) dated 31 January 1940.
152 TNA WO 167/11: GHQ AG, GHQ (A) 2358 (O) dated 25 February 1940.
153 Table collated from information in TNA WO 167/11: GHQ Adjutant-General, WD, GHQ (A) 2358 (O) dated 25 February 1940.

Table 7.7
ATS Plan - 1 BAD & 2 BAD

Trade	No 1 BAD	No 2 BAD
Clerk	26	14
Cook	18	4
Driver	4	15
General Duty	3	4
Orderly	4	6
Total	55	43
Replacing	45	32

154 TNA WO 167/1175: 1 BAD and WO 167/1176: 2 BAD.
155 AFW 3008 and AFW 3009 respectively.

Supporting the Divisions

The BADs were however, only one part of the ammunition supply chain. From the BADs, ammunition was moved to the corps' railheads by rail. During the deployment in September 1939 two Ammunition Railheads (ARH) were assigned in the BEF Assembly Area and one for the AASF.[156] An ARH was a GHQ Troops Ordnance unit specific to the BEF,[157] consisting of two officers and 27 Other Ranks, supported by 50 AMPC personnel for labouring duties, and its function was to manage ammunition at the railhead and control corps or other formation munitions sites in the vicinity of the ARH.[158] After the BEF deployed to the Franco-Belgian border defences, the ARH arrangements were adjusted thus:

Table 7.8
BEF Ammunition Railheads – October 1939 to April 1940[159]

Location	Code	Serving	Remarks
Ecoust-Saint-Mein	OW	I Corps & Air Component (Forward)	
Aubigny	OV	II Corps & GHQ Troops	
Pernes[160]		III Corps	Opened April 1940
Fresnay-sur-Sarthe	OY	Assembly Area	
Flixecourt	OR	Air Component (Rear)	
Harfleur	OQ	AA units in the Le Harve area	Units arriving at Le Harve
Germaine[161]	OZ	AASF	Including supporting Army units

The doctrinal position in relation to ammunition was that beyond the Base, stocks should, where possible, be held on wheels, whether that be rail or road, in order to ensure it was 'passed systematically and automatically from rear to front to replace that expended in battle'.[162] In planning to deliver this outcome, Q (Maintenance) adopted a Great War procedure, known as *En-Cas Mobile* (ECM), which involved holding ammunition on rail on Standard Ammunition

156 Evron and Noyen, although Meslay-du-Maine replaced Noyen as the deployment commenced. The AASF ARH was at Germaine. TNA CAB 106/235: BEF Ammunition Supply (Gibson Report), p.4.
157 As the ARH had not been authorised by the War Office, its establishment is not recorded in Philson, BEFORBAT.
158 BEF GHQ General Routine Order (GRO) 160, October 1939. The failure to formally establish this critical logistic capability became a significant issue.
159 Table collated from information in TNA CAB 106/235: BEF Ammunition Supply (Gibson Report).
160 Code for Pernes not identified.
161 The RAF was responsible for providing armament specialists to manage aerial munitions and to provision the relevant labour but the RAOC provided the ARH Ordnance Detachment. See, TNA WO 167/1428: No 82 Advanced Railhead Detachment RAOC, WD.
162 Army Council, FSR, Vol I, *Organization and Administration*, p.252.

Trains (SAT), although they were re-titled to Ammunition Section En-Cas Mobile (ASE), which were loaded with a standard pack of natures. In theory, this was a sound concept, but operational experience proved that in practice, natures were not always consumed at the planning rates, resulting in surplus of some ammunition and shortages of others, a problem complicated by the different weapon populations within divisions. Q (Maintenance) assessed that the time from a corps HQ making an ammunition demand to the train arriving at an ARH would be 5½ days, and thus 9 x DAER were required to be held on rail or at the ARH. For I Corps, 2 x DAER were to be held on rail within 12 hours travel of the ARH, with another 2 x DAER within 36 hours and II Corps, 2 x DAER also within 36 hours.[163]

At an ARH, ammunition would be transhipped to the WMT of the Corps Ammunition Park (CAP) for future cross-loading to the vehicles of the Divisional Ammunition Company (DAC). Growing concerns about potential disruption to the rail GLOC generated several plans in mitigation. ARHs were to hold stocks at, or in the vicinity of the railhead,[164] whilst the CAPs and DACs were to be responsible for the ammunition dumps at corps and divisional level respectively. Whilst this arrangement was doctrinally pure, *Field Service Regulations* gave specific direction as to its management, 'The formation of ammunition dumps and the quantities dumped will be carefully controlled by headquarters of formations….',[165] lessons in relation to storage[166] and transport,[167] which were learned the hard way during the Great War. It was at this point that what appeared to be a logical solution to a pressing problem parted company with reality. Doctrinally, dumps should have been authorized for a specific time to meet a specific mission to obviate the need for the full governance process to be enacted. The deposition of munitions to field sites on a semi-permanent basis generated that need, but because of the shortage of technically trained ammunition personnel the outcome was a failure to execute the appropriate levels of inspection and accounting, neither of which did anything positive for the quality or quantity of the stocks.[168] III Corps, recently formed, was by late April

163 TNA CAB 106/235: BEF Ammunition Supply (Gibson Report), p.6.

164 I Corps ARH was to hold 5 x DAER and II Corps, 7 x DAER. TNA CAB 106/235: BEF Ammunition Supply (Gibson Report), p.6.

165 Army Council, FSR, Vol I, *Organization and Administration*, pp.252-253.

166 On the Western Front, in late 1918, the Fourth Army DDST war diary contains a fair share of issues relating to unsatisfactory field storage areas, poor equipment care, improper maintenance and weak stores accounting. TNA WO 95/454/4: HQ Fourth Army, DDST, WD, entries July - November 1918. An example was a review of the Corps Reserve supply dumps in August 1918, which were described by the DDST as 'unsatisfactory', with the Canadian Corps dump being especially bad, an inspection revealing that the stocks had been dumped by the roadside with no attempt at stacking nor were there any tarpaulins to cover the *materiel* from observation or the elements. TNA WO 95/454/4, HQ Fourth Army, DDST, WD, 17 August 1918.

167 TNA WO 95/454/4: HQ Fourth Army, DDST, 'Notes on Conference at "Q" 6.45 pm, 28 August 1918': 'Situation with regard to lorries very serious in view Boche retreat behind Somme … It is not possible at present to move up any Supply Dumps as lorries not available'. This problem was still extant in October; 'Large quantities of boxed ammunition are lying about the area in various dumps. 'Q' knows of this but state that the necessity of economy in lorries makes it compulsory for ammunition to be drawn from Railheads first'. TNA WO 95/452/1, HQ Fourth Army, DDOS, WD, 19 October 1918.

168 Army Council, *Army Training Memorandum* No 35, para 27 (ii) (d) p.18, RAOC Lessons from Experience, noted the importance of exchanging officers between the BADs and ARHs to highlight the dissonance and resolve it.

1940 still struggling as a formation to bring order to its ammunition holding issues, an audit by the DDST Staff revealing that there were substantial deficiencies of stock types in the 3rd Line III CAP and the 2nd Line DACs, a situation resolved by Q Maintenance ordering a special ammunition train from the Base with the relevant munition natures.[169]

A post evacuation report identified this as a resource issue but the RASC CAPs and DACs rose to the challenge of managing large quantities of dumped stocks,[170] for which they were not established, receiving a generally positive assessment: 'On the other hand, the RASC had a useful pamphlet on the subject, which was evidently studied'.[171] The report was though, particularly scathing about the care of artillery ammunition: 'A noticeable consequence of the practice which existed between the Wars, of storing gun ammunition centrally instead of it being in unit charge was that the Royal Artillery units did not look after their ammunition properly, especially in regard to protection from damp.[172] Much had to be returned to the Base on account of damage caused by carelessness or ignorance'.[173] The problems relating to ammunition custody and care were not however, confined to the forward locations[174] because even in BADs and ARHs, proper storage arrangements were always a significant challenge, owing to the shortage of waterproof covers and dunnage, lack of space, the neglect of safety distances, a problem especially prevalent at ARHs, and guarding difficulties. To compound these issues, some of the ammunition packaging was not suitable for field storage, with, for example the boxes for AA rounds not being watertight.[175] As an aside, there also appears to have also been an obsession with the ability to stock ammunition on regimental gun-lines, sometimes to excess, which was to cause un-necessary loss of artillery ammunition during the campaign because there was rarely sufficient 1st Line transport to recover it.[176] Indeed, remarkably during operations on the night of 14-15 May 1940, a trial was conducted to assess the maximum number of rounds that could be delivered to each gun at a troop gun-line during the summer hours of darkness, a figure, which was assessed to be 500.[177]

No doubt the CAPs and DACs could have done without the task of managing these dumped ammunition stocks but there was a positive result. Unlike the Divisional Supply Columns (DSC), the Corps Petrol Parks and Divisional Petrol Companies, the CAPs and DACs were

169 TNA WO 167/180: III Corps DDST, WD, entry 25 April 1940.

170 A dump is a temporary storage area, usually in the open, for munitions, equipment, or supplies. A dump would have minimal security and possibly no dedicated technical manpower presence. The problem with the BEF's ammunition dumps was the length of time they were expected to be 'temporary'.

171 TNA CAB 106/235: BEF Ammunition Supply (Gibson Report), p.10.

172 The report could equally have observed that the chain of command failed to ensure that appropriate training was enacted in artillery units to ensure that regiments could conduct the task in the field.

173 TNA CAB 106/235: BEF Ammunition Supply (Gibson Report), p.10.

174 DDST Staff from III Corps identified that elements of both the CAP and the DACs were failing to load ammunition to lorries correctly or covering the stocks when they were dumped, the report noting, 'Supervision by Amn required'. Given the shortage of tarpaulins, the failure in protection may not have entirely been the units' fault but the loading issue was a combination of weak command, poor training and technical inexperience. TNA WO 167/180: III Corps DDST, WD, 30 April 1940.

175 TNA CAB 106/235: BEF Ammunition Supply (Gibson Report), p.10.

176 Army Council, *Army Training Memorandum* No 34, July 1940, Appx G, Lessons from Experience for the RASC, p.23.

177 Army Council, *Army Training Memorandum* No 32, May 1940, Appx B, Dumping of Field Artillery Ammunition, pp.21-22.

not practising daily operational technical logistic tasks by delivering ammunition, and although storage was not the unit role, there were opportunities to improve knowledge and exercise skills. The CAPs and DACs did not keep the all the unit WMT permanently 'bombed-up' with munitions, ground-loading[178] stocks to rest the vehicle suspensions and chassis, conduct maintenance and undertake other transport tasks. On 13 February 1940 for example, 5 DAC only had six lorries loaded with ammunition, all of which, with the exception of 480 rounds of 2 pounder anti-tank rounds[179] and one vehicle loaded with demolition explosives, was either common user SAA or infantry natures.[180] These arrangements were predicated on units being able to rapidly 're-bomb' in response to alerts. On 13 January 1940, HQ I Corps, reacting to a threat warning issued by GHQ, ordered all 1 CAP task WMT to be loaded to war scales from local dumps and the I Corps ARH at Ecoust-Saint-Mein, before all leave was cancelled the next day and the CAP placed at fours Notice To Move from 0915.[181] On 15 January, some ammunition stocks collected two days before, were ground-loaded to enable assigned WMT from 1 and 2 Ammunition Sub-Parks to be detached to the DACs from 1st and 2nd Divisions to assist in the movement of engineer demolition explosives.[182] It is also clear from unit war diaries that these units were conducting a number of out-of-role tasks in addition to ammunition field storage, which whilst not always 'doctrinally pure'[183] demonstrated flexibility and practised skills. On 14 February for example, 5 DAC had 30 lorries on engineer support tasks,[184] whilst on 1 March 1940, soldiers from 1 CAP were at the Corps ARH assisting Ordnance personnel reducing the charges on 40 mm rounds, whilst on 2 March, WMT was deployed to lift personnel and equipment of 1st Berkshires.[185] On 20 March 1 CAP was in-role again, dumping ammunition to a corps plan, the war diary noting that, 'As far as possible, the sites were located outside villages',[186] which must have brought little comfort to the inhabitants of the dumps that were not.

Conclusion

Ammunition supply to the BEF was founded upon sound principles but the delivery of the output met several practical challenges. The issues created by deploying recently mobilized *ad hoc* BADs was exacerbated by a shortage of field equipment and an inadequate number of

178 On field operations, ground-loading refers to temporarily un-loading stocks from combat or logistic vehicles, which would normally be held on them, in order to rest or maintain vehicles or to undertake other support tasks. Ground-loaded stocks do not constitute a dump.
179 One vehicle carried this ammunition, in addition to 8,040 rounds of 0.55 Boys anti-tank rifle ammunition. TNA WO 167/250: 5 DAC RASC, WD, 13 February 1940.
180 TNA WO 167/250: 5 DAC RASC, WD. These natures included mortar rounds, grenades and signal cartridges. 2-inch mortar HE was noticeable by its absence.
181 TNA WO 167/137: 1 CAP RASC, WD.
182 TNA WO 167/137: 1 CAP RASC, WD.
183 FSR directed that, 'In mobile operations however, no lorries or other vehicles provided for the transport of ammunition should be diverted from their legitimate functions, except in very exceptional circumstances'. Army Council, FSR, Vol I, *Organization and Administration*, p.252. Whilst the BEF was not engaged in January 1940, on mobile operations, the point is made.
184 TNA WO 167/250: 5 DAC RASC, WD.
185 TNA WO 167/137: 1 CAP RASC, WD.
186 TNA WO 167/137: 1 CAP RASC, WD.

technically qualified personnel, although these issues were slowly rectified over time. The shipping of munitions from the UK in separate components to save space was commendable in the administrative space but became a liability in the operational one. Both these issues would have been critical had the German offensive commenced during the initial BEF deployment period. The decision to hold additional stocks of ammunition in France because of the shortage of suitable storage in the UK whilst apparently a neat solution to the problem was undoubtedly a mistake, which led to unnecessary losses in June 1940.

Some of the ammunition packaging was not suitable for field storage and the various expedients to store ammunition on a semi-permanent basis at the ARHs and in corps and divisional dumps, without the requisite logistic and personnel resources, led to a deterioration in stock quality. Damp was a problem, sometimes caused by the failure to create appropriate foundations on wet ground and compounded by packaging that was not suitable for long-term field storage, whilst incorrect stacking often created damage to ammunition boxes. The length of the GLOC, generated by the position of the Base in Western France resulted in a reliance on rail movement that was subject to possible disruption, thus leading to mitigating solutions, many of which, were impossible to resource properly. As it transpired, the risk inherent in the forward dumping programme matured because of the speed and direction of the German advance and some stocks were lost, particularly at over-stocked regimental gun-lines. Equally, the forward stocking provided a important reserve during kinetic operations in May 1940, although the level of dumping indisputably confirmed that there was insufficient WMT ammunition lift for an Army engaging in high-intensity mobile operations.

Chapter 7 Appendix
Artillery Ammunition and Fuze

Table 7A.1
BEF Key Ammunition Stocks and Weapon Populations
31 March 1940[187]

Weapon	Pop	Nature	Stock	DAER rpgpd[188]	Authorized rpgpd[189]	Remarks
2-inch mortar	1,149	HE Smoke	14,062 247,515	1 9	Nil	Minimum use
3-inch mortar	194	HE Smoke	92,412 53,724	16 10	Nil	Minimum use
2 pdr A/T	432	AP	440,450	5	5	
25 mm A/T	282	AP	276,000	5	5	
18 pdr	216	HE Smoke Shrapnel AP	243,070 31,984 187,778 Nil	18 2 15 1	7 1 3 Nil	
25 pdr	656	HE Smoke AP	1,551,318 206,193 2,400	30 5 1	28 2 Nil	
4.5-inch howitzer	96	HE Smoke Gas	59,686 39,580 18,000	22.5 7.5 Nil	Nil Nil Nil	Minimum use Minimum use Special use
4.5-inch gun	32	HE	Nil*	25	19	*Expected April 1940
60 pdr	16	HE Shrapnel	28,800 26,300	12.5 12.5	12.5 12.5	

187 Table created from information in TNA CAB 106/235: BEF Ammunition Supply (Gibson Report), WOOH, *Special Weapons and Types of Warfare*, Vol I, *Gas Warfare*, and Thurlow, *Building the Gort Line*.

188 The DAER was based upon studies conducted as a result of the Great War on the Western Front matched to an analysis of the requirement for defensive and offensive operations over a set period including high intensity combat.

189 The authorized expenditure included ammunition planned to arrive by 30 April 1940, which explains for example, why the 12-inch howitzer stocks are Nil but there is an authorized rpgpd.

6-inch howitzer	176	HE Gas	199,600 28,000	30 Nil	Nil Nil	Minimum use Special use
6-inch gun	12	HE Shrapnel	9,996 2,994	9 6	6 6	
8-inch howitzer	12	HE	16,120	24	3.5	
9.2-inch howitzer	24	HE	28,310	20	8	
9.2-inch gun	2	HE	890	5	5	
12-inch howitzer	4	HE	Nil	7.5	3	1,000 rounds April 1940

Table 7A.2
BEF Tube Artillery Ammunition Types

Artillery Piece	Projectile Weight (lb)	Ammunition							
		AP	CP	HE	HE SL	Shot	Shrapnel	Smoke	Starshell
2 pdr A/T	2.4					x			
18 pdr	18.5	x		x	x		x	x	
25 pdr	25.0			x	x	x		x	
60 pdr	60.0			x			x		
4.5-inch howitzer	35.0			x				x	x
6-inch howitzer	86.0	x	x	x	x				x
6-inch gun	86.0		x	x			x		
8-inch howitzer Mk VIII	200.0		x	x					
9.2-inch howitzer Mk II	290.0		x	x					
12-inch howitzer	750.0		x	x					

Table 7A.3
Land Service Artillery Ammunition – Fuze Matrix

Artillery Piece	Fuzes												
	12	**16**	**44**	**80**	**88**	**101B**	**101E**	**106**	**106E**	**117**	**183**	**188**	**203**
18 pdr	AP			Shrap			HE	HE	HE/Smk	HE			
25 pdr										HE			
60 pdr				Shrap	Shrap		HE		HE				
4.5-inch howitzer			Smk				HE		HE/Smk		Star	Star	
6-inch howitzer		CP					HE		HE	HE	Star	Star	
6-inch gun		CP	HE	Shrap	Shrap				HE				
8-inch howitzer		CP				HE			HE/Smk				
9.2-inch howitzer		CP	HE	Shrap	Shrap	HE			HE				Shrap
12-inch howitzer		CP				HE			HE				

Table 7A.4
Land Service Artillery Ammunition – Fuze Types

Fuze	Type	Sub-Type
12	Percussion	Graze Action Base
16	Percussion	Graze Action Base
44	Percussion	Direct Action
80	Percussion	Time
88	Percussion	Time
101B	Percussion	Graze Action
101E	Percussion	Graze Action
106	Percussion	Direct Action
106E	Percussion	Direct Action
117	Percussion	Direct Action
183	Time	Combustion
188	Time	Combustion
203	Time	Mechanical

Abbreviations:

AP – Armour Piercing
CP – Common Pointed
HE – High Explosive
HE SL – High Explosive Streamline
Shrap – Shrapnel
Smk – Smoke

Part III

AQ Interlude

8

Mightier than the Sword
An appreciation of the achievements of the BEF's GHQ AG Personal Services Section 1939-1940

Introduction

Much has been written about the operational aspects of the BEF's deployment, a little of the logistic perspective, and almost nothing of what was then called Adjutant-General or 'A' in the currency of the time. 'A' was though, a busy and important Branch within GHQ BEF,[1] headed by Lieutenant-General Sir D W S Brownrigg[2] and focused upon what is described in 2020 as Human Resources. The spectrum of A's work was concomitantly, diverse and dynamic,[3] and to deliver the outputs, the Branch was split into two sections. The Organization Section (OS) handled collective personnel issues such as control of military reinforcement and refugee planning, casualty evacuation capability and reporting procedures, to medical and sanitary

1 For details of its responsibilities, see Army Council, FSR, Vol I, *Organization and Administration*, pp.45-58.

2 The son of a Guards general Lieutenant-General Sir Wellesley Douglas Studholme Brownrigg KCB DSO (1886-1946) was commissioned into the Sherwood Foresters in 1905. He served with distinction in Gallipoli and Mesopotamia in the Great War, being awarded the DSO and receiving six Mentions in Despatches, ending the war as a Brevet Lieutenant-Colonel. He attended the Staff College (1920-1921), was the AA & QMG to the Shanghai Defence Force in 1927 and the Senior Administration Officer in North China Command in 1928. He held two brigade commands, 159th Welsh Border and 11th Infantry (1931-1934) and was GOC 51st (Highland Division (1935-1938) before being appointed Military Secretary in 1938 and then Director-General Territorial Army in 1939. Involved in the defence of Boulogne and Calais in 1940, he was not offered employment in the post-evacuation Army, becoming a Home Guard Sector commander from 1941. For additional details, see, Smart, *Biographical Dictionary of the British Generals of the Second World War*, pp.47-48.

3 In November 1939, AG's Directorate received around 5,300 letters, and generated about 6,600. Not surprisingly, the war diary contains a succession of references, to requests for an increase in the establishment of clerks.

services,[4] burials, graves registration and the disposal of personal effects.[5] AG OS was also responsible for establishment Staffing, General Base Depots, civilian labour policy and last but not least, terms and conditions policy including pay. The Personal Services[6] Section (PSS)[7] was responsible for matters related to the individual and covered legal, discipline,[8] Courts-Martial, Provost, application of the Geneva Protocols, Prisoners of War (POW) and the compilation and publication of routine orders. The PSS also led on VIP visits,[9] commissioning, honours and awards, training attachments and Staff visits to Theatre, whilst the management of the media was another task that consumed Staff resources.[10] Attachments by officers and soldiers not in the Force, to units in the BEF, were a key element in the expansion and development of the Army, which exposed the operational environment, unit structure and tactical experimentation, all of which were essential preparation for personnel nominated to join the BEF or be posted to units training for deployment. By 31 January 1940, 850 officers and NCOs had returned to the UK to support training for incoming units, whilst the same number had been detached to the BEF to gain operational and logistic experience.[11] Military visitors included His Majesty the King, members of the Royal Family, logistic specialists, technical staff, training team personnel, senior officers and staff officers. Civilian visitors included politicians, civil servants, scientists,

4 For details, see, Crew BOH, *The Army Medical Services, Campaigns*, Vol 1, pp.1-113.

5 This subject had proved controversial at points during the Great War, with the theft of items from deceased officers' personal kits in transit to the UK being a particularly sensitive issue, the prevention of which, took a considerable time and resources to resolve. See, Captain R Bonham-Smith, 'Railway Transport Arrangements in France', *JRUSI*, Vol LXI (February 1916), pp.59-61.

6 The 2020 terminology is Personnel Services (PS).

7 The Assistant Adjutant-General, Colonel (Honorary Brigadier) James Whitehead CB CMG CBE DSO OStJ ADC late Indian Staff Corps (1880-1955) was responsible for the PSS. James Whitehead was commissioned into the Royal West Kent Regiment in 1899 but transferred to the Indian Staff Corps in 1901 attending Staff College (1911-1912). He served on the Western Front in AQ staff appointments during the Great War, being awarded the DSO and the CMG. In 1921, he became Director of Organisation at Simla and commanded 11th Indian Infantry Brigade at Abbottabad (1925-1927) Retiring from the Army, he was appointed a Chief Constable in the Metropolitan Police in October 1927, promoting to Deputy Assistant Commissioner in June 1933. He retired from the police in 1938 being recalled for service with the BEF in 1939. After returning to the UK in 1940 he commanded the Home Guard in the London District. His Private Papers are held by the IWM in Documents.6393

8 Discipline in the BEF remains a fascinating and controversial subject. For an engaging and incisive assessment, see, Edward Smalley, 'Discipline', *The British Expeditionary Force, 1939-40* (Basingstoke: Palgrave-Macmillan, 2015), pp.141-175.

9 King George VI visited the BEF 4 - 7 December 1939 before moving to the AASF and it was, unsurprisingly, a busy time for the AG. His Staff was responsible for planning and implementing the visit programme, and he accompanied His Majesty during it. The Administrative Instructions relating to His Majesty's visit are in TNA WO 167/11 and make fascinating reading. Upon AG's return from supporting this Royal visit, the files had piled up and the AG war diary of 7 December reported: 'The AG now proceeded to pull up arrears of office work'.

10 Arnold Ridley, who played Private Godfrey in the BBC TV series *Dad's Army*, was appointed as a BEF Conducting Officer for journalists having been commissioned as a second-lieutenant into the General List in October 1939. In May 1940, Ridley was evacuated from Boulogne on the destroyer HMS *Vimera*, being discharged from the Army on health grounds upon his return, his serious injuries from the Great War being a defining factor, although he subsequently joined the Home Guard in Caterham.

11 TNA CAB 120/247: Dispatches on Operations of the British Expeditionary Force, France and Belgium, September 1939 - May 1940, First Despatches, para 24.

engineers, government and industry representatives and fact finders, families visiting seriously ill soldiers, members of voluntary bodies and the media. The effective control of Staff visits by the PSS became increasingly important as senior officers in particular, sought for professional or personal reasons to spend time in France. One example was Brigadier 'Boy' Browning,[12] Commandant of the Small Arms School at Hythe, who conducted a three day visit in January 1940 and was with the BEF on 10 May, when the German attack prompted the removal of extraneous personnel from the Theatre.[13]

One of its most important tasks was the key lead on the physical and spiritual welfare of the troops, in order to underpin morale, especially for logistic soldiers. The post-war War Office monograph on morale summarized the challenges:

> The importance of maintaining morale amongst the administrative troops is not always realized. Troops in the front line are subject to danger and hardship, but those in the rear have to contend with inaction, monotony and boredom. In the front line a higher standard of morale is necessary because any lowering of morale is likely to have more serious consequences. On the other hand, under some conditions the maintenance of morale among the troops in the rear may be more difficult.[14]

Much of the output required access to logistic and financial resources and the PSS created strong links with the GHQ Q Branch and philanthropic bodies to deliver the leave policy, soldier comforts, postal facilities and the specific support enhancements for the nurses of the Queen Alexandra's Imperial Military Nursing Service (QAIMNS) and the ladies of the Auxiliary Territorial Service (ATS).[15] The daily work of the A Staff in the AG Branch was comprehensive as well as engaging but the detail of its tasks, whilst of enormous interest, and greatly deserving of wider exposure, is, unfortunately, too complex to explain in a single essay.[16]

12 Later Lieutenant-General Sir Frederick Arthur Montague Browning, GCVO, KBE, CB, DSO (1896-1965) who was the commander of I Airborne Corps and deputy commander of First Allied Airborne Army during Operation MARKET GARDEN in September 1944. He was also an Olympic bobsleigh competitor in 1928, and the husband of author Dame Daphne du Maurier.

13 Richard Mead, *General Boy: The Life of Lieutenant General Sir Frederick Browning* (Barnsley: Pen & Sword, 2010), suggests that Browning's presence, whilst officially authorized to produce an updated pamphlet on the Bren LMG for DMT GHQ, was equally driven by a desire to be close to the operational focus, although Mead notes that Boy also enjoyed the opportunity to seek out fellow officers, especially from the Grenadiers. No doubt his wish to be in France was partly driven by the disappointment of leaving command of the 2nd Grenadiers in August 1939 six weeks before the battalion deployed with the BEF.

14 TNA WO 277/16: Morale of the Army. See also, WOOH, *Morale*, Lieutenant-Colonel J H A Sparrow OBE (Comp.), (War Office, 1949), p.1.

15 The ATS was formed in September 1938, the public announcement being hastily made as a result of the Munich Crisis. For details of the organization, administration and operations of the ATS, see, WOOH, *The Auxiliary Territorial Service*, Controller J M Cowper (Comp.), (War Office, 1949) and for a contemporary personal perspective, Eileen Bigland, *Britain's Other Army* (London: Nicholson & Watson, 1946).

16 The daily activity is recorded in typescript on the loose leaves of the war diary, AFC 2118 but unfortunately, the scribe, so meticulous and succinct in his recording of events, failed to ensure his name was recorded for posterity. This is a great shame because he has a fine sense of humour; no doubt, in order to retain his sanity, he needed it.

P8.1 Supporting the Combat Soldier 1. 5114456 Private Hugh Maginniss Royal Warwickshire Regiment. Evacuated from France before service in UK and India. KIA on 19 February at Saye in Burma whilst serving with 2nd Norfolks. (Courtesy Mary Maginniss)

This chapter focuses therefore, on one area within the PSS, which, has had almost no public assessment since 1940 and yet even 80 years ago was a significant aspect of the Staff's work, and has certainly not declined in importance today: the welfare of the Soldier.

Two fundamental problems the PSS faced were the varied types of engagements upon which soldiers in the BEF were serving, their different military experiences and their diverse civilian backgrounds. There were Regulars and Territorials, Regular Reservists, the Army Officers Emergency Reserve, Supplementary Reservists,[17] Militiamen, volunteers, and the ATS. Each group had a different comprehension of military life, and the cultural, welfare and discipline process that supported it, and varying expectations of the outcomes, whilst the latter three groups in particular, brought with them an ever-expanding culture of 'civvy' street. In addition, there were the Indian troops of Force K6, comprising the Indian Army animal transport companies and supporting units,[18] of the Royal Indian Army Service Corps (RIASC). The expectations of each group were different, and the PSS Staff had to have a clear comprehension of this complex, and in some cases, roughly hewn jigsaw. If though, there was any doubt in the perception of senior staff or regimental officers, about the importance of the PSS, their minds must have been focused by the words of Leslie Hore-Belisha, Secretary of State for War, who, during his Parliamentary Introduction

17 One of them was Signalman John Yeomans (1919-2002) who served in the GHQ Complex in Arras and I am indebted to him for his knowledge of the daily routine of GHQ. One of the social military gems he highlighted, was the fact that there were no separate Officers' WCs, which meant that humble soldiers had the opportunity to mix with the Great Men, and so offer, 80 years on, a different perspective on the military commanders of the day. At the mention of Viscount Gort, his lively response, with a sparkle in his eye and in no way dulled by nearly intervening 60 years, nor the significant difference in rank, was "Oh you mean Fat Boy!" Interview, with John Yeomans in Coventry, 24 October 1999, JYIC 241099.

18 TNA WO 167/1433: HQ Force K6, table 'Arrival of Force K6 at Marseilles from India', nd but probably 26 December 1939.

to the Army Estimates on 8 March 1939, stated: 'The Army is being mechanized. I hope it is being humanized'.[19]

Home to Blighty

In terms of major projects, the formulation and implementation of the Theatre leave policy was a key activity, and one driven by the AG personally, and its profile is illustrated by the 14-page addendum on the subject in the file of the GHQ[20] AG war diary. The task was a formidable one, and the range of tasks that the Staff had to undertake, in order to bring to fruition a leave programme for members of the BEF, was amazing, and some of this work will be examined. The movements aspects were a major consideration and the average daily transport of soldiers on leave clearly illustrates the level of activity. As the Force grew, it rose from 1,700 in each direction during December 1939 to 2,200[21] in May 1940 and was projected to reach 2,500 by July. In addition, the movements system also processed RN and RAF personnel, as well as individuals on attachment to the BEF, attending courses in UK, receiving medical treatment in the Home Base, Staff visits and those posted as trickle reinforcements.

The first aspect the PSS Staff had to tackle was the creation of a clear and coherent leave policy. The G Staff generated the starting point by agreeing to 12.5 percent of the force being on privilege and compassionate leave at one time,[22] whilst the A Staff proposed that soldiers should become eligible for privilege leave after 2½ months in France. Consultations with other sections in AG, produced a basis for the length of leave, promulgated as 10 days[23] between arrival at an English port and the return to an English port for re-embarkation to France.[24] Practically, this meant soldiers were away from their units for two weeks because movement to the UK took two days each way.[25] Dispensations were granted to those domiciled in Eire or living on the distant islands of the UK, which could extend the period away from the unit to three weeks if travel was disrupted.

Leave planning was based on six monthly periods since the arrival of the BEF in France. The first leave period was October 1939 to March 1940, and the second, April – September 1940. The second period generated changes to leave policy, including a maximum of seven

19 Minney, *The Private Papers of Hore-Belisha*, p.179.
20 GHQ, based at Arras, was usually referred to by its codename: BRASSARD.
21 Leave movement had dropped to less than a 1000 personnel per day in April 1940 as most soldiers eligible for their first leave had completed it.
22 At the discretion of corps commanders, GOC LOC, OC GHQ Troops and the Heads of Services. See, Administrative Instruction (Leave) No 1 in TNA WO 167/11: GHQ AG.
23 This figure was the same as it had been in the Great War BEF in the period November 1915 to November 1917. See, Brigadier-General Sir James Edmonds CB CMG (Comp.) *History of the Great War, Military Operations, France and Belgium, 1916*, Vol I. *Sir Douglas Haig's Command to the 1st July: Battle of the Somme* (London: Macmillan, 1932), p.263.
24 Viscount Gort's first despatch noted in para 23, The Welfare of the Force, that: 'The question of leave was worked out in great detail by the Adjutant-General, Lieutenant-General Sir Douglas Brownrigg, and the members of his staff. TNA CAB 120/247: BEF First Despatches.
25 Signalman Yeomans Royal Signals was dispatched on leave from GHQ at Arras on 8 March 1940 to travel to his home in Coventry returning to Arras on Good Friday, 22 March. JYIC 241099.

percent of the Force on leave, and eligibility starting at 3 months.[26] In addition, soldiers were not permitted to have more than two periods of privilege leave within 12 months. An exception to this rule was the policy applying to senior officers, who were allowed to take five-day blocks, thereby creating greater continuity in their posts. Those who lived in, or near London, and who returned to the UK for meetings, often added an element of their leave entitlement to their duty period away. This saved time and shipping space and enabled them to see their families more frequently, although for shorter periods. Finally, the PSS arranged for 60 Indian Army personnel per month, from Force K6, to take leave in the UK, on the basis of 15 soldiers every seven days. The Staff solution to the RIASC leave arrangements appears thrifty; with 1,723 personnel in the Force it would have taken 27 months for everyone to take leave, although the British soldiers on establishment would not have been on this roster, thus reducing the cycle.

The implementation of the BEF's leave policy was promulgated in Administrative Instructions (Leave) (AI (L)), 11 of which were issued in the period December 1939 to April 1940. These publications covered a wide range of topics including movement documents, extensions to leave, clothing, Venereal Disease, travel to Eire and distant islands of the UK, rail warrants in UK, ration cards, equipment and clothing, and accommodation for members of philanthropic bodies in transit through London.[27] The AL (L) publications listing movement details, such as ports and sailing times were classified SECRET. Much effort was devoted to the leave programme and it is clear from the AG war diary that the officers of the PSS were pleased with their efforts. The first privilege leave party[28] of 134 officers and 911 Other Ranks, departed from France on 17 December 1939[29] and a member of the PSS went to the corps railheads to wish them well. He was disappointed by the response from those moving to the UK, and reported accordingly, although retaining his sense of humour, writing: 'A visit to one of the railheads gave one the impression that the thought of leave was not terribly entrancing. The entrainment was carried out in silence..........perhaps there was a large proportion of married men!'[30]

The promulgation of leave policy produced though, a raft of AG fall-out. One of the first issues was the granting of leave in France. Some officers and soldiers, mostly from the Reserves, were domiciled in France, whilst others, usually but not exclusively single personnel, were attracted to the opportunity of enjoying the experience of the country out of uniform. These requests generated much discussion, a similar amount of correspondence and a subsequent requirement for a leave pass authorised for the relevant area of France. This created some interesting problems because the C-in-C, General Gort, agreed that wives of officers could join their husbands in France from elsewhere, but they were not permitted in the military zone, which included Paris. Apart from the inconsistency involving those wives who lived there, the deletion of Paris as a leave destination no doubt dampened the enthusiasm of those couples who

26 TNA WO 167/11: GHQ AG, Minutes of a Meeting held in AG's Office GHQ on 26 January 1940: GHQ (A) A/2971/4/65 (PS) dated 26 January 1940.

27 BEF Administrative Instructions (Leave) held in TNA 167/11.

28 24 soldiers were granted compassionate leave in October 1939 and 139 in November. See, WOOH, *Movements*, p.199.

29 TNA CAB 120/247: BEF First Despatches, para 23 states that the leave programme was effective from 18 December 1939. It is possible that this date refers to the first day of leave parties arriving in UK.

30 TNA WO 167/11: GHQ AG, WD, 17 December 1939. The exclamation mark was added in pencil, although when this was done is unknown.

P8.2 Supporting the Combat Soldier 2. 5114497 Private Fred Gilbert Royal Warwickshire Regiment. Wounded three times whilst fighting with 8th Warwicks on 27 May during the Battle of the Ypres-Comines Canal and then captured, spending five tough years as a POW. (Courtesy Elaine Schafer)

yearned for a romantic break. Another issue was leave at French winter-sports resorts. The C-in-C,[31] whilst manifestly uncomfortable with the concept of officers skiing on holiday as his Command prepared for battle, felt unable to issue an order forbidding the practice, leaving the AG to issue a letter on the subject.[32] The key paragraph read: 'The C-in-C wishes officers to be informed that he will view with grave displeasure any case where an officer incurs any injury skiing, which might result in his not being at his appointed place at the appointed hour'. The result of this communication was two-fold: officers went skiing and there was a need for the administrative process and movement control organizations to enable them to do so. There must though, have been some further embarrassment and not a little confusion in GHQ, upon the receipt of a telegram, in February 1940, from the War Office, requesting the names officers and soldiers who were proficient skiers, in preparation for the formation of a winter warfare infantry unit.[33] In case some soldiers thought that this might be the opportunity for a winter holiday, the requirement stated the need

31 General Gort was a stickler for etiquette. Signalman John Yeomans relates a splendid story about walking in Arras Square with a friend from the AMPC who had been awarded the VC in the Great War. A VC holder, Viscount Gort believed that officers should salute holders of the VC regardless of their rank; the soldier was though, surprised when a General saluted him! He was even more surprised when General Gort disciplined an officer for failing to salute first. JYIC 241099.

32 TNA WO 67/11: Leave in France - Skiing, GHQ(A) A/3/8 (PS) dated 15 December 1939.

33 The telegram, War Office A/867 dated 111430Z February 1940, also stated that 'a knowledge of language', would be useful, but omitted to mention which one. Perhaps the author thought that the comment that the unit was for 'service in a country where snow prevails' offered a meaningful clue. TNA WO 167/11: GHQ AGWD.

P8.3 Freedom of the Road. The utilization of motor vehicles by soldiers on leave in the UK was made possible by the dedication of the AG Staff in GHQ BEF. Note the reusable petrol can on the running board. (Courtesy Mary Maginniss)

for 'expert skiers of good stamina & eyesight prepared to undergo severe climatic conditions'.[34] The management of this request however, was not effectively handled with 2nd Royal Fusiliers for example, temporarily losing several of its officers because of their proficiency as skiers. As the regimental history recorded: 'All this was very enterprising, but not very realistic; magnificent, but not war'.[35]

Leave in the United Kingdom created an interesting set of problems as well, from marriage to car insurance. On the former subject, the Chaplain-General was consulted so the PSS Staff could issue advice on how to be married with the least inconvenience and in the cheapest manner. No doubt the Staff were also aiming to ensure that the marriage of a soldier would create the minimum of disruption to the Army but entries in the war diary make it clear that the main effort was to enable a soldier to marry in an efficient and inexpensive way. Cars, perhaps unsurprisingly, also created a challenge for the PSS Staff. Many officers, and some soldiers, had laid their vehicles up for the duration of their service but with leave beckoning, the opportunity to utilize their personal transport, in order to maximize their activities on leave, proved most

34 TNA WO 197/210: 2 Division CRASC, WD, 1 February 1940.
35 C Northcote Parkinson, *Always a Fusilier: The War History of the Royal Fusiliers (City of London Regiment)*, (London: Sampson Low, 1949), p.18.

tempting. There were though, three problems: petrol coupons, road liability insurance and Vehicle Excise Duty. The Army solved the first one by the issue,[36] through divisional petroleum officers in the BEF, and later recruiting offices in the United Kingdom, of enough coupons for a vehicle to drive 300 miles. Road liability insurance proved more difficult to resolve because the insurance companies were reluctant to issue short-term policies but on 16 December 1939, the war diary scribe reported: 'We heard today that the insurance companies had become almost human, and had agreed to issue short-term policies for personnel using their cars on leave'.[37] Given the premiums they set though, their humanity was short-lived: one week cost 12.5 percent of the annual premium, and one month, 25 percent.[38] The Ministry of Transport was even less helpful, refusing, until August 1940,[39] to issue weekly or monthly excise licences, resulting in the drivers having to reclaim the difference; one suspects that many vehicles were run without the owners paying the road fund duty.

Comforts and Woollies

One of the first decisions made by the War Office upon the declaration of war, was the establishment, in the light of experience of the Great War, of the post of Director-General Voluntary Organizations. It was though, a misleading title, because the appointee did not direct the work of voluntary organizations but regulated the distribution of the wide range of gifts to servicemen and women from the public but not earmarked for an Armed Service and the co-ordination of the activities of the committees formed to assist in supporting those members of the public devoted to knitting clothes for the troops.[40] It is clear that many soldiers were greatly appreciative of these additional items. Private Fred Gilbert, of the Royal Warwickshire Regiment stationed in 2 Infantry Base Depot at Evreux near Rouen wrote home to record, "Actually we are very fortunate for there are some who only have the clothes they stand up in and washing shirts is unheard of and handkerchiefs don't exist."[41] The Army War Comforts Committee was responsible for the distribution of gifts offered specifically to the Army, although in both cases, the bulk of their work related to the distribution of the labours of the Woollen Comforts Scheme. From the BEF's perspective, the policy control at home was much less important than the resources required to effect the distribution of goods and in this respect,

36 The coupons were issued upon production of a Leave Pass (AFW 3145) and the vehicle registration document.
37 TNA WO 167/11: GHQ AG, WD.
38 TNA 167/11: GHQ AG, BEF AI (L) No 6 had an annex for personnel to apply for car insurance.
39 The rate for 28 days was 10s 0d for a car and 2s 0d for a motor-cycle. Based on Measuring Worth UK, this equates in 2018 to approximately £30.50 and £6.00 respectively.
40 For a resume of their wartime contribution, see, WOOH, *Army Welfare*, Brigadier M C Morgan CBE MC psc (War Office, 1953), pp.181-184.
41 Gilbert, letter dated 20 March 1939. Fortunately, upon his arrival in 8 Warwicks, the Quartermaster (QM) stores issued him with a new battle dress and a canvas suit for "dirty work," in addition to other equipment, to the point he noted, "In fact we are getting nearly as much kit as we had at the Depot." Gilbert, letter dated 9 April 1940. The Depot to which he refers, was that of the Royal Warwickshire Regiment at Budbrooke Barracks to the West of Warwick. The barracks closed in 1960 and the site has been re-developed as the village of Hampton Magna.

they were greatly assisted by the establishment of the Army Comforts Depot (ACD)[42] in a Territorial Army Drill Hall in Reading.[43]

To provide a feel for the work, on 14 February 1940, GHQ demanded from ACD, five cases of gum-boot socks, 18 cases of scarves, 18 of socks, 19 each of mittens and pullovers, and 22 of balaclavas. From a previous stock receipt, the ACD was able, on 22 February,[44] to issue 47 cases of balaclavas and 47 of scarves, to AMPC companies, units whose soldiers spent most of their time outside on construction or support tasks.[45] Tobacco supply frequently appears as an issue in unit war diaries. 1 AA Brigade Company RASC reported a shortage of cigarettes on 13 November 1939 but was fortunate to have received a gift of 1,900 on 15 November from the Overseas League Tobacco Fund.[46] The PSS officers would certainly have been delighted to learn of another positive outcome from the entry in the war diary of 2 Division CRASC, which highlighted the success of the PSS project: 'Increased quantities of comforts for the troops are now being received and include wireless sets, books and gifts of cigarettes'.[47] The co-ordination of comfort provisioning did not however, always run efficiently, which, given the rapidly expanding force was perhaps not surprising. Force K6 is an example. The PSS laboured intensively to enhance the comforts for this Indian Army contingent but was later surprised to discover that the Indian Comforts Fund was providing support on a private basis and the PSS could stand easy on the subject.[48] Whilst intended to improve soldiers' well-being, the issue of woollen comforts did not always create the harmony intended. In a report on morale from postal censorship in the period 14-28 January 1940,[49] during a particularly harsh winter in which the temperature fell to –20°C, troops in several battalions[50] complained that they were unable to wear on duty, the balaclavas that had been sent to them. Strong words were directed by soldiers at the regimental chain of command for enforcing this rule at a time of immense hardship in the field. That the AG Staff officers were able to have some direct visibility of unit morale and by implication, the decisions of the command structure, by examining mail, is an interesting subject, the effects of which are worthy of study.[51] How many commanding officers

42 The ACD was commanded by Lieutenant-Colonel R W Phillips and staffed by volunteers plus three members of the ATS. The ACD received a visit by Her Majesty the Queen in 1944 but was transferred to Didcot under RAOC control in May 1945. Phillips commanded it for the entire conflict but died in mid-1945. For a short brief on its history and operation, see, WOOH, *Army Welfare*, pp.14-16.

43 Saint Mary Butts. Part of the site remains in use as an Armed Forces Careers Information Office.

44 TNA WO 167/11: GHQ AG, GHQ (A) A/4911 dated 22 February 1940.

45 In late November 1939 there were 51 AMPC companies in the BEF. By 10 May 1940, the AMPC in France had expanded to 101 companies (not including German, Italian and Spanish ones) organized in 17 Groups. See, *A War History of the Royal Pioneer Corps, 1939-1945*, pp.13-15.

46 TNA WO 167/425: 1 AA Brigade Company RASC, WD 13 and 15 November 1939 entries.

47 TNA WO 167/210: 2 Division CRASC, WD, entry 18 January 1940.

48 TNA WO 167/11: GHQ AG, GHQ (A) A/2686 (PS) dated 9 February 1940.

49 TNA WO 167/7: BEF GHQ Intelligence, 'Report on Morale based on Postal Censorship: 14 - 28 January 1940'.

50 1st Coldstream Guards, 2nd Hampshires Regiment and 1st Green Howards were mentioned by name, whilst others were involved by inference.

51 In a letter dated 19 April 1940, Fred Gilbert reflects upon the limitations the censor places upon his writing. He is though, most careful to support the Army's operational security, omitting any detail that would be of value to the Germans. Of especial interest, is that the general tone of his letters is positive with no moaning about his situation. Indeed, he sticks to the factual, whilst making the best of it. I am grateful to his daughter, Elaine Schafer, for reading all the letters and making observations.

were aware that the C-in-C was in a position to know more about what the soldiers thought of them, and their actions, than they did?

In addition to woollens, the PSS was keen to ensure that soldiers had the opportunity for recreation. In March 1940, 145 wireless sets arrived, part of a £15,000 gift from the Nuffield Trust, and through the good services of the Army Sport Control Board, 300 chess sets, 600 domino sets and 1,698 sets of draughts.[52] Equipment for 'Sports and Games' was another issue, and initially there was little problem in obtaining the relevant items for winter activities such as football and rugby. Preparation for summer sports was however, more difficult because the Expeditionary Forces Institute (EFI) had made little profit since its arrival in France, and the purchase, from the reduced rebate, was the subject of much discussion with the PSS.[53] Books were received from the Central Book Depot (CBD),[54] which collected three million books between its inauguration in November 1939, and April 1940, and by May 1940, the BEF had 38 Field Libraries. Regimental Libraries benefited from the Penguin book scheme by which units could purchase from regimental funds, packs of 100 books, for 35s 0d.[55] The establishment of the CBD also relieved the GHQ AG PSS of its concern relating to the suitability of some of the literature reaching the troops, an element of which was described as 'undesirable'.[56]

PSS were responsible for the co-ordination and support of the eleven Volunteer Philanthropic Bodies[57] (VPB) recognized by the BEF, each of which provided a wide range of welfare services for the soldiers of the expeditionary force. PSS was cognizant of the important contribution of the VPB, whose skills and personnel were a welcome addition to the BEF's AG capability, and the deployment of their representatives was directed by the PSS, in order to ensure the most effective utilization of limited resources. Detachments were spread throughout the Theatre, but the focus was in the GLOC where the regimental structure in terms of welfare was the least robust. Another interesting task in which, the PSS was involved, was the acquisition and distribution of theatrical properties collected by the British Drama League. What the officer who was dealing with this activity thought, is not recorded but he issued a letter to formations explaining the range of items that would be available, which included: ballet skirts, peers' coronation outfits, grease paint and ostrich feather boas. Not wishing to embarrass the Staff and regimental officers who would have to deal with this matter by selecting items, he requested that any formation not requiring theatrical properties should inform GHQ AG, as soon as possible.[58] Sadly, their response is not in the files; perhaps they were, in the truest sense, unprintable. One of the most important improvements to the soldiers' comfort required

52 TNA WO 167/11: GHQ AG, GHQ (A) A/3253/PS dated 16 March 1940.

53 TNA WO 167/11: GHQ AG, Letter from GHQ (A) 3254 (PS) dated 17 March 1940.

54 Commanded by Lieutenant-Colonel Jackson, the CBD was based in Finsbury Barracks, the Headquarters of the City of London Territorial Army. The site has been modernized and is in use as an Army Reserve Centre.

55 35s in 1939 equates, using Measuring Worth RPI, to £107 in 2018.

56 See, WOOH, *Army Welfare*, p.17.

57 These were: Army Scripture Readers and Soldiers' and Airmen's Christian Association, British Red Cross, Catholic Women's League, Church Army, Church of Scotland, Lady Moore Guisberg's Leave Club in Paris, St John's Emergency Committee, Salvation Army, Toc H, YMCA - Young Men's Christian Association (YMCA) and YWCA - Young Women's Christian Association (YWCA).

58 TNA WO 167/11: GHQ AG, GHQ (A) A/4971 (PS).

the intervention of the BEF's QMG, Lieutenant-General Lindsell who wrote to the Under Secretary of State for War:

> I have to recommend that a drinking mug may be supplied to each man. At present, the men only have a mess tin, which serves both as a dinner plate and drinking vessel, besides being put to other uses e.g., boiling pan, frying pan, container for shaving water,[59] and the issue of a mug would add greatly to their amenities. [60]

The failure to issue a drinking vessel to the soldiers however, hid a much greater problem which was observed by Gort when he visited 42nd (East Lancashire) Division, when he saw men without knives and forks and eating their meat with their fingers from a corrugated iron table, commenting to Ironside the CIGS that it was 'a lamentably low standard in elementary administration'.[61]

Post and Parcels

One of the first communications processes for the welfare of soldiers that the PSS enacted was the introduction of a private telegraphic service[62] between France and the Empire, which started at 0001 on 9 February 1940, although initially, the Dominion of Canada was not included in the scheme.[63] Military telegraph forms were issued to Army Post Offices (APO), although signal message forms[64] were also acceptable, and in an emergency, plain paper. The service was designed to allow soldiers with urgent personal messages to respond to problems at home, although they were also entitled to telegraph their leave arrival details, provided they did not mention the location of the debarkation port or the sailing time of the ship, the security of cross-Channel shipping being a constant concern.[65] With an eye to the fact that many Reservists, TA personnel and Militiamen were serving in France, and in some instances, not averse to conducting their previous business, messages of a commercial nature were not permitted.[66] The

59 Whilst stationed in 2 Infantry Base Depot in the Rouen Sub-Base Area, Private Fred Gilbert noted the paucity of even this basic facility: "they have to give us hot water from the cookhouse to shave in, but we have nothing to put water in except tins which the food comes in and fruit tins have to serve as shaving mugs." Gilbert, letter dated 20 March 1940. His five years as a Prisoner of War (POW) would make these items seem like luxuries.

60 Letter from QMG to the Under Secretary of State for War: GHQ (Q) Q/2024 (b) dated October 1939 in TNA WO 167/10: GHQ BEF - QMG Maintenance (Q). The letter has no date: the document in the file is a typed copy of the original signed by the QMG.

61 Colville, *Man of Valour*, p.178.

62 TNA WO 167/11/1: GHQ AG, contains correspondence on this subject.

63 BEF GRO 540 and unit orders promulgated details. Part I orders did not though, always reflect the hard work of the PSS. For example, Part I Departmental Orders of 22 BAD, did not carry the information until 11 March 1940; it is possible though, that earlier orders are missing from the war diary. TNA WO 167/1181/2: 22 BAD, WD, refers.

64 AFC 2128.

65 The suggested GHQ method directed the soldier to give his or her Estimated Time of Arrival (ETA) at an inland railway station.

66 A survey of the service conducted shortly after it started recorded that 21% of the messages related to illness, 18% to births, 17% deaths, 17% greetings, 16% could not be classified, 7% related to personal

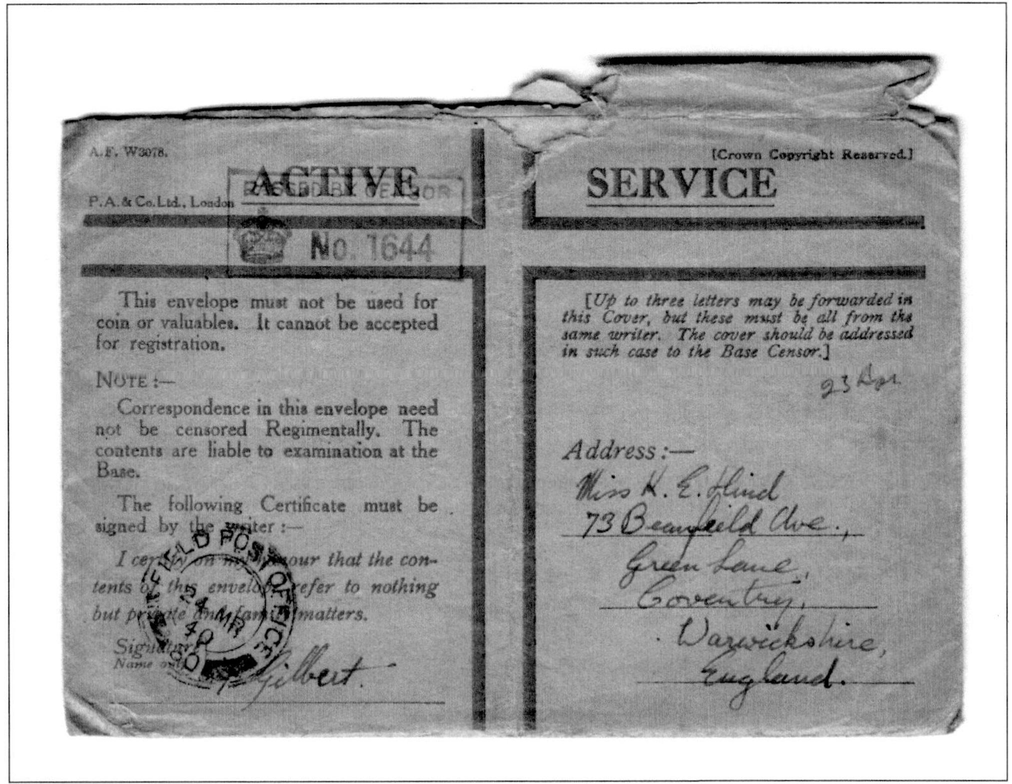

P8.4 The Letter Home. AFA 3078 - Green Envelope. (Courtesy Elaine Schafer)

service was not however, free. Charges to the UK were 2½d per word for the text and signature, with a minimum charge of 1s 3d. Other destinations were charged at 5d per word, and a minimum fee of 2s 6d.[67] Payment was in French currency.

The distribution of personal mail was the responsibility of the Royal Engineers, but the welfare element was a significant matter for the PSS. In September 1939, mail was sent from Southampton to Cherbourg on personnel ships, with mail then being dispatched from the Base by pack supply trains and civil rail services or WMT, depending upon location.[68] Mail for I and II Corps, arrived at the allocated corps railhead and, with the exception of registered mail, which was handled by the Army Postal Service, was dispatched through the RASC Divisional

enquiries and 4% were of an unauthorized commercial nature. TNA WO 167/1719: ADAPS Telegraph Survey, February 1940.

67 Using Measuring Worth UK RPI, the equivalent cost in 2018 is respectively £3.84, £1.28 and £7.68. Given prices in 2020, this clearly illustrates the massive reduction in the cost of telecommunications to the customer since 1939.

68 For a diagrammatic explanation of the BEF postal system, see Diagram 6 – BEF Postal Distribution 1940.

Supply Column chain.[69] Whilst the system was effective it introduced unnecessary delay, so in late December 1939 Postal Port Regulating Centres (PPRC) were established at Folkestone and Boulogne to manage the mail traffic between these two ports, with mail for units in the corps areas being sorted at a postal concentration and censorship office at Amiens. Mail for the Base and the GLOC continued to be handled through Cherbourg, resulting in transit times across the Theatre being reduced by 24 hours.[70] Letters from BEF military personnel to addresses in France were permitted but to conform with French regulations, all mail had to pass through the censorship office at Amiens, which inevitably created delays in delivery.[71]

Soldiers were issued with the Field Service Post Cards[72], which enabled them to give their name, military postal address, and an 'All's Well'.[73] They were also issued with the Green Envelope[74] which was free from unit censorship but subject to examination by the Censor's Office at the Base,[75] with a letter taking approximately 4-8 days to travel between recipients in the BEF and the UK.[76] There were clear regulations relating to the contents all personal mail, designed to prevent information 'useful to the enemy' circulating in an uncontrolled manner and correspondence had to be written in plain language with no use of codes, ciphers or shorthand.[77] Whilst units that deployed with the First Contingent of the BEF in 1939 were culturally embedded in censorship, with even the C-in-C reminding himself and his daughter of the rules,[78] but it was a definitive shock to later arrivals.[79] It is clear though, that some soldiers, and Private Gilbert was one of them, did not entirely comply with the regulations, and he created a code with his girl-friend, Kay Hind, which was opaque to the censor and presumably to German intelligence.[80] Letters and postcards weighing 2 oz and under sent the UK, the Empire and to British Forces abroad including His Majesty's Ships were free of postal charges and those greater than this weight were charged at 1½d for the first oz and 1d per

69 WOOH, *Miscellaneous 'Q' Services*, Brigadier A D Magnay CIE (Comp.), (War Office, 1954), p.231.
70 Ibid, p.232.
71 Ibid.
72 AFA 2042.
73 Army Council, FSPB Pamphlet No 5, 1939, *Intelligence-Information and Security* (HMSO, 1940), p.25, Sect 20.
74 The AFA 3078 was Crown Copyright and any imitation of it was deemed an infringement thereof. The Green Envelope could not be sent by registered post nor could it be used to send money. Ibid, p.26, Sect 21.
75 Ibid, p.25, Sect 21. The letters from Fred Gilbert to his girlfriend Kay Hind, whom he married after the war, in Coventry are all marked 'Passed by the Censor'.
76 Experience of the Gilbert family, residing at 10 Rochester Road, Coventry.
77 Army Council, FSPB, Pamphlet 5, pp.23-25, Sect 19, Regulations for the contents of correspondence.
78 Colville, *Man of Valour*, p.156.
79 George Blake, *Mountain and Flood, The History of the 52nd (Lowland) Division, 1939-1946* (Glasgow: Jackson, Son & Co, 1950), p,23, records that 157th Brigade battalions, 'experienced for the first time (as the unit diaries all testify with feeling) the strict censorship of letters home'.
80 From several examples, "I am having a gay time" meant he was serving 'well behind the line'; "I am having a very gay time" meant near to, or in Paris, whilst "I am doing magnificently" noted he was in the *Maginot* Line. This was not the only association Miss Hind had with codes because she was, during the war, employed at the Government Code & Cypher School Bletchley Park. I am indebted to Elaine Schafer for bringing these points to my attention.

oz[81] thereafter, with scaled rates for postage to other destinations.[82] Parcels were also greatly welcomed by the men and women of the BEF, with personal parcels under 15 pounds[83] being delivered through the General Post Office and the military postal systems. A 3 lb parcel carried by the General Post Office cost 1s 3d[84] and a 22 lb parcel 6s 0d.[85] Private Fred Gilbert estimated it took 14-26 days from dispatch from UK to receipt but he, like many soldiers, was delighted to receive 'comforts' from family and one "very battered" parcel contained manna from Heaven: handkerchiefs, aspros,[86] elastoplasts, shaving cream, Horlicks tablets, razor blades, book, sweets and chocolate.[87] Private soldiers were not however, the only members of the BEF to welcome a package from home because the C-in-C requested his daughter Jacqueline, an ATS officer serving in the War Office, to dispatch to him shaving soap, razor blades, requisites and writing paper.[88]

As soldiers and airmen of the Dominions began to arrive in Theatre, the PSS examined the requirement to establish a system that would provide a meaningful mail service for these men and airmail was assessed to be the most effective solution. With many military transport aircraft committed to operations, the GHQ decided to seek, through the War Office, the support of the civil sector. The Air Mail Scheme,[89] was therefore, based on the Empire Air Routes[90] and it applied to all members of the BEF, whether British, Indian, Dominion or Colonial. Airmail was sent surface to the Home Postal Depot at Bournemouth, for onward transit to Southampton, home of Imperial Airways flying boat operations. The one exception to these arrangements was airmail for the Indian Force K6, which had arrived in France in late December 1939. The establishment of this airmail service was initiated on 1 January 1940,[91] with mail being sent to the BEF postal censor's office in Amiens before dispatch to the Army Post Office (APO) Marseilles for movement by air to India. Unfortunately, the initial batch of mail was transferred from Amiens to the Chief Censor at Liverpool, an outcome that was not exposed to Assistant Director Army Postal Services (ADAPS) in GHQ BEF for nearly two weeks and then only by

81 Based on RPI, the 2108 equivalent cost is £0.37 and £0.24 respectively.
82 2nd Division Admin Order No 12 dated 6 October 1939, Appx A. TNA WO 167/205: HQ 2nd Division A&Q.
83 There was a reduction to the maximum postal limit, which was promulgated in October 1939 as 22 lbs. 2nd Division Admin Order No 12 dated 6 October 1939, Appx A. TNA WO 167/205: HQ 2nd Division A&Q.
84 2nd Division Admin Order No 12 dated 6 October 1939, Appx A. TNA WO 167/205: HQ 2nd Division A&Q.
85 2018 prices calculated using Measuring Worth RPI. The 1939 3 lb price (£3.84) is 29 percent higher but the 22 lb price (£18.27) is 14 percent lower than the 2018 Royal Mail prices.
86 Aspro was the Bayer trade name for aspirin.
87 Gilbert, letter dated 19 April 1940.
88 Colville, *Man of Valour*, p.156.
89 Details were promulgated on General Routine Order (GRO) 673 held in TNA WO 167/11: GHQ AG, WD.
90 The first regular weekly air-mail service between the UK and Australia commenced on 8 December 1934, and the mail took 13 days. Three airlines were involved: Imperial Airways, Indian Trans-Continental Airways and Quantas Empire Airways. Once the Short S23 Empire Flying Boats came into the service in 1937, Imperial Airways was able to handle all of the Empire, but not internal, distribution.
91 TNA WO 167/1433: HQ Force K6, GHQ Q (Maintenance), telegram No 1/1073 SC2 dated 1 January 1940.

chance through the dedicated enquiry of the NCO in charge of APO Marseilles. ADAPS, recognizing the potential sensitivity of the outcome, reacted with commendable speed to resolve the problem, arranging with the Chief Censor at Liverpool to expedite the movement of the mis-directed post by air, whilst also informing GHQ Q Branch, noting 'As there is likely to be some complaint as regards this failure it is thought that "Q" Branch should be made aware of the facts'.[92]

There was in 1940, no military 'bluey', and soldiers used surface mail envelopes, either writing AIR MAIL on the top left-hand side of the envelope or applying a blue AIR MAIL label. The service was not free, a surcharge being applied by weight. No airmail service was established for personal mail to and from the UK, although consideration was given to creating one to support the widely dispersed AASF.[93] This suggestion was not pursued because of the perceived adverse influence on morale within the BEF but had it not left the Continent in June 1940, it is possible that one might have come into operation for the whole force had suitable aircraft been made available.[94] The crucial importance of mail from home is summarized by an entry, on 18 May 1940, in the diary of Gunner Allan Barratt of 2nd Survey Regiment Royal Artillery: 'And how wonderful, that in all this chaos we had a delivery of mail so that at least some of us are able to forget the war, the bombing, the refugees, if only for a few wonderful moments as we read the letters from our families and friends'.[95] Whilst receiving a letter from family and friends, there was a rather less positive aspect in respect of its retention. Private Fred Gilbert dutifully destroyed, after he had read them, all the letters he received from family and friends, in accordance with the instructions given by his chain of command.[96] For soldiers who obeyed this directive, this must, in many cases, have been a tough call. Presumably, this order was to ensure that the authors at home did not give away operational details from UK such as the locations of AA sites, Passive Air Defence arrangements, details of munitions and aircraft factories, port activity and unit deployments,[97] which then might be accessed by the enemy should the soldier be captured, as indeed, was Private Gilbert.[98]

92 TNA WO 167/1433: HQ Force K6, GHQ ADAPS, letter APS 3/40, 'Correspondence for Indian Animal Transport Force (K6)' dated 15 January 1940.

93 It is probable that some members of the AASF and the Air Component made private arrangements for mail to carried on RAF flights returning to the UK, which were then posted to the GPO system.

94 WOOH, *Miscellaneous 'Q' Services*, p.233.

95 Quoted from Nicholls & Washington, *Against All Odds*, p.80.

96 Gilbert, letter dated 19 April 1940.

97 As the war progressed, the control of the flow of information from the UK became much more important and the relationship between Fred Gilbert and Kay Hind is a microcosm of this important issue because she went to serve at Bletchley Park, a fact unknown to the family until after she passed away in 2014 aged 93; it was a secret well kept.

98 On 27 May 1940, to the West of the village of Korentje in Belgium, whilst defending the Ypres-Comines Canal Line, a story told in his unpublished book, *For You the War is Over*. Private Gilbert was one of approximately 30 survivors of B Company 8th Warwicks which, after a gallant fight, was overwhelmed during the German assault. The Officer Commanding, Captain Burge, whom he saw being shot in the hand as he surrendered, and Second-Lieutenant Pratt, were later awarded the MC, whilst Corporal Bennett received the MM. Marcus Cucliffe, *History of the Royal Warwickshire Regiment*, 1919-1945 (London: William Clowes & Sons, 1956), p.44.

The postal service was not the only distribution service contributing to the welfare of the troops. The Military Forwarding Organization (MFO)[99] controlled by QMG 14 (a) in the War Office, and from February 1940, Q (Movements) 3 (d) was responsible for the inter-Theatre distribution of comfort items.[100] Shipping space was arranged through the Ministry of War Transport or the Government Shipping Agents, Messrs Hogg, Robinson & Capel Cure. MFO was directed to move cases between 15 pounds, the limit for the postal service, and 56 pounds. The establishment of the War Office controlled ACD, assisted the MFO in meeting this remit but comforts donations from private or regimental organizations often exceeded the MFO limit and the GHQ AG war diary highlights the difficulty the PSS had in convincing the offenders to play the game. As in the Great War, the MFO was also responsible for the movement, from Theatre to the UK, of the personal effects of deceased, injured and sick personnel. Soldiers' items were dispatched to the relevant regimental Records Offices, whilst officers' effects were stored in the Liverpool Depot of Messrs Cox and King's. The latter activity proved to be an unsatisfactory arrangement because Cox and King's, apart from suffering wartime staff shortages, did not have the facilities available to the War Office for tracing officers' relatives.

Humanized Army?

An important compassionate programme staffed and directed by the PSS was the introduction of a scheme for relatives to visit soldiers who were classed as 'very seriously ill'.[101] Given that the country was at war, and the BEF was in a military Theatre of Operations, it was a courageous decision by the War Office, and one that was prompted by PSS.[102] The concept was not unprecedented, as a similar system had been enacted during the Great War, although in that conflict, it was the YMCA[103] which was responsible for patients' relatives.[104] The scheme only provided though, for a visit, if the soldier was in a General Hospital, and it was initiated by the hospital sending a telegram to PROELICAS in London, which then made the necessary arrangements with Movement Control to move the relative to France. Visitors arrived at London Victoria railway station, were briefed by the Railway Traffic Officer's staff, and then entrained

99 For a resume of MFO operations, see, WOOH, *Movements*, pp.70-73.

100 It was also responsible for the reception and forwarding of small consignments of equipment, clothing, instruments, MT spares and medical stores. Army Council, FSPB, Pamphlet No 1, 1940, *Glossary of Military Terms and Organization in the Field*, p.8. The FSPB refers to the MFO as the Military Forwarding Service.

101 'Very seriously ill', usually abbreviated to VSI, was defined by the War Office as a condition of a patient when his or her illness was of such severity that life was imminently endangered. Correspondence on the scheme is in TNA WO 167/11/3: GHQ AG, GHQ (A) A/2449/(PS). GRO 539 promulgated the details.

102 There was also a compassionate leave scheme for soldiers whose next of kin had either died, were seriously injured or ill, to return to the UK. Not all relatives understood the correct process to make a request and this resulted in delays to returning a soldier to the UK. TNA WO 167/1096: 2 LOC Railhead Company RASC, WD, entry 13 March 1940, refers for example, to a driver whose daughter was seriously injured in an accident.

103 Young Men's Christian Association.

104 In 1916, there were, on any day, between 100 and 150 relatives in France visiting sick, injured or wounded soldiers. See, Edmonds, *History of the Great War, Military Operations, France and Belgium 1916* (London: Macmillan, 1932), p.140.

for Newhaven for the cross-Channel journey, by merchant steamer, to Dieppe. Controls were strict. Each visitor was issued with a two-page brief, a Casualty Visitor Pass, a Travel Warrant,[105] an Embarkation Card,[106] a Movement Order and three rail tickets. Hospitals and units were not responsible for hosting relatives, who were met by a member of the British Red Cross or the Saint John's Emergency Committee, who accommodated them, and made arrangements for them to travel to the hospital by car, or, if it was outside the Dieppe Medical Base Sub-Area, by rail. Visitors were not allowed to travel unaccompanied in the military zone.

Despite exceptionally low levels of combat activity, there were plenty of soldiers who became sick, or who were injured, and in the period 1 October 1939 to 30 April 1940, 10,344 soldiers were evacuated to the UK.[107] Of this total, 1,514 suffered Non-Battle Injuries (NBI)[108] in RTAs and incidents involving firearms, explosives, assaults, falls, sport and training whilst on duty or on recreation; only 9 were wounded by enemy action.[109] In addition there were 281 fatalities as a result of NBI events,[110] one of whom was the CO 1 RWF, Lieutenant-Colonel Henry Fenton Garnons-Williams, who was killed when the 13 Squadron Lysander in which he was flying, force-landed near Aix on 10 November 1939 whilst conducting a reconnaissance; the pilot, Pilot Officer B S Jones was not injured.[111] 85 percent of the 10,344 evacuated to the UK, 8,830, suffered a wide range of illnesses and disease,[112] a situation partly generated by the particularly harsh winter of 1939-1940.[113] In the period October 1939 to June 1940, 1,451 were evacuated to the UK with respiratory illnesses[114] and 297 with heart conditions.[115] Of import, was the rising

105 AB 422.

106 AF W3060.

107 Some members of the AASF were evacuated by air. See: Squadron Leader S C Rexford-Welch MA MRCS LRCP RAF, MBOH, *The Royal Air Force Medical Services*, Vol 1, *Administration*, (London: HMSO, 1954), p.481.

108 This figure does not give full visibility of the numbers of NBI because it only relates to those evacuated to the UK and does not include those admitted to BEF hospitals and discharged to units or those treated in the unit or a field ambulance. In May 1940 there were a further 1,751 NBI personnel and in June, 1,450. See, W Franklin Mellor (ed.), MBOH, *Casualties and Medical Statistics* (London: HMSO, 1972), p.182, Table 21, BEF France 1939-40, Medical Evacuations to the United Kingdom - Crude Figures.

109 Ibid.

110 Philson, BEFORBAT, Vol 5, p.108, Appx 1: Casualties. The average monthly deaths through injury October to April is 26 but doubles to 51 in May and June 1940, which is to be expected in the circumstances.

111 TNA WO 167/843: 1 RWF WD, 10 November 1939. Lieutenant-Colonel Garnons-Williams, aged 43 and husband to Katherine, lies in Douai Communal Cemetery Row K, Grave 8.

112 Mellor, MBOH, *Casualties and Medical Statistics*, p.182, Table 21.

113 47 personnel died of disease or illness in the period October - December 1939 and another 42 in January 1940, with a total of 269 from deployment to the close of the evacuation in June 1940. See, Philson, BEFORBAT, Vol 5, p.108, Appx 1: Casualties. One such was 6458157 Corporal Dennis McGillicuddy, aged 25 and married to Florence Mary, a TA soldier attached to 2nd Royal Fusiliers for active service experience, who died on Christmas Day 1939. See, na, *A Short History of the 2nd Battalion Royal Fusiliers (City of London Regiment) during the First Year of the War* (Aldershot: Gale & Polden, 1941), p.6. The CWGC records his death as 23 December 1939.

114 Mellor, MBOH, *Casualties and Medical Statistics*, p.182, Table 21.

115 Philson, BEFORBAT, Vol 5, p.108, Appx 1 suggests a total of 829 fatalities through illness or disease. The figure of 829 however, may be caused by a transposition of figures because the average monthly rate of deaths through illness shown in Appx 1 from October 1939 to April 1940 is 26 but rises to 324 for

numbers of officers and soldiers evacuated recorded as having a disease of the nervous system or a mental health condition,[116] which in part reflected the growing size of the Force, although the numbers, not unexpectedly, showed a sharp increase when combat operations commenced in May.[117]

Moral Development

Whilst the BEF may have marched on its stomach, food was not the only menu that some of the troops had on their mind.[118] An inevitable consequence of thousands of soldiers, married and single, being away from home in a foreign land and surrounded by a civilian population, was that some of them sought female company, which in many instances, especially if they were married, created a welfare issue. As a corollary, the prevention of Venereal Diseases (VD)[119] became an important operational, welfare, medical, disciplinary and political matter, with the patronization of '*maisons tolerees*'[120] by members of the BEF, becoming a particular issue.[121] In the Great War, VD had a major and adverse impact upon operational capability by hospitalizing or downgrading thousands of soldiers, and utilizing precious medical resources.[122] The handling

May and June. It is probable that the Officer figure for May and June should be three and the Other Ranks 62, with a total for the two months of 62 not 625, thus creating an average of 32.5 per month, an increase commensurate with the pressures created by a sudden and significant expansion of major combat operations. Assuming this is correct then the figures for deaths by illness should be 269 and not 829.

116 In this respect, one area that requires study, is the impact upon military decision making by those personnel suffering from Post Traumatic Stress Disorder acquired from service in the Great War and inter-war conflicts, who were deployed to the BEF in 1939-1940.

117 Approximately 1,531 personnel recorded as having a disease of the nervous system were evacuated between October 1939 and June 1940, with 48.5% of the total being in May 1940. 1,056 members of the BEF recorded as suffering from a mental health condition were evacuated in the same period, 51.4% of the total being in May and June 1940, although the 277 evacuated in June left Theatre in the first two weeks of the month. Mellor, MBOH, *Casualties and Medical Statistics*, p.181, Table 21.

118 Fred Gilbert was certainly an exception, writing that whilst in B Company, 8 Warwicks, he had four Army meals a day but "often we had and still do ... have a supper in a café of egg and chips or the like". Gilbert letter dated 23 April 1940.

119 As in the Great War, not all soldiers who contracted VD did so abroad. Particular welfare issues arose when soldiers believed they had contracted VD from their wife or girlfriend. In the Great War, BEF VD cases contracted the infections as follows: 44.74% contracted VD in France, 42.27%in UK, and 3.53% in other countries. 9.46% were from unknown sources. Not all of the admissions were first time cases. See, Major T J Mitchell, DSO MD RAMC and Miss G M Smith MBE MA, *History of the Great War*, (BOH), *Medical Services, Casualties and Medical Statistics of the Great War* (London: HMSO, 1931), p.73.

120 Licensed brothels.

121 For the influence of campaign groups seeking to place the '*maisons tolerees*' Out of Bounds to the BEF, see, the records of the Association for Moral and Social Hygiene, Enquiries and Campaigns, in the London School of Economics, Women's Library, 3 AMS/B/07/18 and 3 AMS/B/07/25 in and 3 AMS/B/07/21 for correspondence with the *'Union Temporaire' contre la Prostitution Reglementee et la Traite des Femmes.*

122 In the BEF on the Western Front, there were, from August 1914 to December 1918, 153,531 recorded hospital admissions of British and Dominion troops. In 1917, on one day, there were 8,392 soldiers in hospital for the treatment of VD, which equated to 0.55% of the BEF's ration strength. In 1918, 15.79% of admissions were due to relapses. The average hospital days per admission, was 28.6 for

of the VD issue in 1939 is therefore, an interesting one, as it is a subject involving the emotional, the practical, the moral and the operational. In 1939, commanders and Staff, regardless of their personal views, were faced with dealing with the effects of VD, and there was plenty of historical evidence and command experience to indicate that it would degrade operational capability if the spread of the diseases were not controlled. The Official History of the Medical Services in the Great War, certainly offered clear guidance: 'In the army during war men are so valuable that every possible means of successful prevention, early diagnosis and treatment should be investigated and employed if men are to be protected, the in-efficiency caused by the disease reduced and army personnel returned to their own kith and kin in good health mentally, morally and physically'.[123]

VD in the BEF 1939-1940 averaged 2.39 cases per 1000, over seven months of the deployment.[124] In October 1939 there were 384 recorded admissions, from a force of 160,000 and in April 1940, with the ration strength at 394,000, around 880, the incidence thus declining from 2.50 to 2.23 per 1000 personnel,[125] a figure 50 percent lower than the 1918 rate.[126] Much effort was therefore, devoted to preventing infection[127] in the soldiers of the BEF through education, regulation, and where necessary, early treatment. It was though, a subject that required careful handling, and for the most part it was left to the AG Branch and medical Staffs to issue policy and directives. One notable exception to this approach was that of GOC 3rd Division, Major-General Bernard Montgomery, who issued a rather more soldierly directive entitled 'Prevention of Venereal Disease'[128] to his Commanding Officers[129] than might be expected from a member of the Staff or the GOC.[130] Replete with sound military advice, it was, unfortunately, too frank for the sensitivities of the GHQ Senior Church of England and Roman Catholic Chaplains.[131]

gonorrhoea, 31.3 for non-specific VD and 37.6 for syphilis. See, Mitchell & Smith, BOH, *Medical Services, Casualties and Medical Statistics of the Great War*, p.114.

123 Ibid, p.79.

124 Mellor, BOH, *Casualties and Medical Statistics*, p.176. The figures may be subject to error because some of the BEF's medical records were lost during the evacuation of the force.

125 Ibid, p 176.

126 Mitchell & Smith, BOH, *Casualties and Medical Statistics of the Great War*, p.75.

127 According to Crew, MBOH, *The Army Medical Services, Campaigns*, Vol 1, p.79, this campaign was had a 100% success in one area because there were no recorded examples of the Indian soldiers of Force K6 contracting VD whilst serving in France.

128 HQ 3 Div 179/A dated 15 November 1939 quoted in Alun Chalfont, *Montgomery of Alamein* (London: Weidenfeld and Nicolson 1976), p.111.

129 There has been confusion as to whether the directive was a divisional order, as initially described by the II Corps Commander, Lieutenant-General Brooke, or a 'personal for subordinate commanders' letter, as noted by Montgomery. The contents of the document are reproduced in Ibid and the style is very much 'personal for'. In his diary, Alanbrooke notes it was a 'circular to his troops', which is certainly an incorrect description of the document.

130 This was not the first time that Montgomery's intercession on behalf of soldiers' sexual health had caused consternation in the chain of command because a similar incident had occurred whilst he was the CO 1st Warwicks at Alexandria in Egypt in 1932. On this occasion, Montgomery arranged for a regimental brothel to be established with medical inspections being conducted by the battalion medical officer and inevitably, this came to the attention of GHQ Cairo. For the outfall, see, Hamilton, *The Full Monty*, pp.201-203.

131 Probably the most contentious sentence was the one concerning brothels. Montgomery wrote: 'There are in Lille a number of brothels, which are properly inspected and where the risk of infection is

Their views, having reached the ears of the AG and then the C-in-C, came close to curtailing the career of a soldier who was to become one of the Nation's most famous.[132] Montgomery was saved by the intercession of Lieutenant-General Brooke, Commander II Corps, who, despite recording that he considered the language in the letter 'obscene,'[133] persuaded Gort that the matter was a chain of command issue, and that Brooke should deal with it.[134] In his diary, Brooke stated he told Montgomery that he: 'had a very high opinion of his military capabilities and an equally low one of his literary ones'.[135] It would appear that on this occasion, the pen was not mightier than the sword! Monty, despite his exemplary personal standards, took the view that operational capability outweighed in war, the absolutist moral dimension, whilst as Nigel Hamilton has identified, Brooke failed to recognize Montgomery's personal commitment to every area of his soldiers' welfare,[136] be that military, spiritual or sexual.[137]

As part of this process, GHQ was determined to ensure that the contraction of what was viewed as a self-inflicted injury did not result in soldiers having a free ticket to Blighty, either on the leave boat, or through the medical system. The PSS perspective of the problem cannot have been lightened though, by the results of the censorship work undertaken by the French *Civile Controle Postal* whose personnel at Le Harve, reported: 'Drunkenness of English troops is a plague and their attitude towards women and girls is disgraceful......some ask if there is any discipline in the English Army, others whether France is a conquered country'.[138] The importance of deterrence and of punishment was illustrated by the policy of denying soldiers diagnosed with VD their privilege of leave, although there may also have been a strong practical element to this approach with the intention of preventing married soldiers infecting their wives, which upon discovery, would bring in its train adverse domestic and medical effects. Whilst it was undoubtedly effective in reducing problems with the latter, the denial of leave also encouraged soldiers to conceal their infection. This process was unfortunately fostered by the

practically nil. These are known to the military police, and any soldier who is in need of horizontal refreshment would be well advised to ask a policeman for a suitable address.' Chalfont, *Montgomery of Alamein*, p.111.

132 The chain of events is described in: Nigel Hamilton, *Monty: The Making of a General 1887-1942* (London: Hamish Hamilton 1981), pp.334-336 and the issues surrounding it are explored in detail in Hamilton, *The Full Monty*, pp.305-310.

133 Diary entry 23 November 1939, Danchev & Todman, *War Diaries, 1939-1945*, p.19.

134 Montgomery was undoubtedly brought to book in the interview and he recorded, in an unusual written display of contrition, although matched to a considered positive output, that Alanbrooke did so 'in no uncertain manner and I received from him a proper backhander ... Anyhow it [the letter] achieved what I wanted, since the venereal disease ceased'. Viscount Montgomery KG, *The Memoirs of Field-Marshal Montgomery of Alamein* (London: Collins, 1958), p.60. No doubt, the ditty circulating within the 3rd Division describing the GOC as the 'General of Love' brought some light relief after the tensions of the episode.

135 Diary entry 23 November 1939, Danchev & Todman, *War Diaries, 1939-1945*, p.19.

136 In paragraph 5 of his letter, Montgomery wrote: 'Finally, I wish all unit commanders to keep in touch with the V.D. problem, be perfectly frank about it, and do all we can to help the soldier in this very difficult matter'. See Chalfont, *Montgomery of Alamein*, p.111.

137 Hamilton, *The Full Monty*, p.308.

138 TNA WO 167/7: BEF GHQ Intelligence, 'Report on Morale based on Postal Censorship: 14 - 28 January 1940'.

sale, over the counter at French chemists, of a drug called 'Dagenan',[139] a problem exacerbated by the refusal of the French authorities to make its sale to British personnel illegal despite a formal request by the GHQ Medical Branch.[140] Concealment was, of course, not conducive to effective treatment, and there was an additional out-fall that adversely affected medical care: soldiers who thought they had VD but were suffering, unknowingly, from another ailment, were reluctant to report sick, especially when the vision of the departing leave boat loomed.[141] As a measure to prevent soldiers using the medical chain to return to UK, the treatment of the disease in France was highly effective with only five soldiers having VD being evacuated to the UK[142] in the period October 1939 to April 1940.[143]

Equal Opportunity?

A little-known aspect of the expansion of the BEF was the deployment, to Theatre, of members of the ATS,[144] in order to release male soldiers from the Base for service in corps units. The concept was not unprecedented because women had served in the BEF during the Great War and from September 1939 Nursing Sisters had deployed[145] to general hospitals, casualty clearing stations[146] and ambulance trains, their strength reaching 1,191 by May 1940. In December 1939, Director ATS (DATS)[147] visited headquarters and units in the BEF to assess the possibility of deploying ATS to theatre. She discussed employment,[148] trades, accommodation[149] and welfare with the AG Staff, equipment with Director-General Ordnance Services and medical care with Director-General Medical Services. From this initial work, a plan was formulated to send,

139 Dagenan is a trade-name, the drug being Sulfapyridine, an anti-bacterial Sulfonamide. First produced by the UK company May & Baker, it was coded as M&B 693 and initially used to treat bacterial pneumonia, one of the successful patients being Winston Churchill in 1943.

140 Crew, BOH, *The Army Medical Services, Campaigns*, Vol 1, p.27. Dagenan has several adverse side-effects, some of them serious, which could easily be compounded by improper doses, one of which is to cause a major reduction in the white blood cells, thereby greatly reducing the capacity to fight infection.

141 BEF documents shed no light on whether there was a policy for compassionate cases that had been diagnosed with VD.

142 These cases were all gonorrhoea and were evacuated in March 1940. Mellor, *Casualties and Medical Statistics*, Table 21, p.181

143 In May and June 1940, 156 and 170 soldiers respectively, being treated in France were evacuated to UK as a consequence of the withdrawal. Ibid.

144 Army Council, *Regulations for the Auxiliary Territorial Service*, 1941 (London: HMSO, 1941).

145 The first nursing sisters of the Queen Alexandra's Imperial Military Nursing Service (QAIMNS) arrived in France on 10 September 1939, and their numbers increased, with support from the QAIMNS Reserve and the Territorial Army Nursing Service (TANS) as the force expanded.

146 During operations in May and June 1940, such was the pressure on forward medical units that some Nursing Sisters, in contravention of accepted practice, were deployed to field ambulances.

147 Dame Helen Gwynne-Vaughan was appointed DATS in July 1939 working in the War Office, initially to Director-General TA and then the Adjutant-General. WOOH, *The Auxiliary Territorial Service*, pp.5-6.

148 For operational and non-operational employment duties, see, Army Council, *Regulations for the Auxiliary Territorial Service*, p.150, Appx IV, Duties.

149 The RE were certainly forward-leaning in this arena because in 1934, four years before the formation of the ATS, plans for women's accommodation based upon wooden and Nissen Huts, during an expeditionary force deployment, had been published. See, Army Council, *Military Engineering*, Vol VII, *Accommodation and Installations*, Plate 5, & Plate 18, Women's Camps.

in the first phase, nearly 2,500 ATS[150] as Motor Transport and ambulance drivers, bi-lingual telephonists, clerks, orderlies, store-women and cooks, with other trades[151] to follow as training developed. The evacuation from France prevented the complete deployment of Phase 1, but AG's Statistical Return indicates that there were 686 ATS All Ranks, inclusive of 19 officers, deployed by early May 1940.[152] GHQ developed a matrix,[153] which detailed the deployment of 2,033 ATS personnel,[154] although it is interesting to note that the replacement was not on a one for one basis because they were replacing 1,610 men. This decision was made for operational reasons with the direction of DATS, who, by all accounts, was very clear about the capabilities and limitations of ATS soldiers.[155]

The intention to send such a large contingent to serve in, not only headquarters and hospitals but also Base post offices, ordnance, and ammunition depots,[156] created an interesting new development for the PSS. Employing so many female soldiers, most of whom knew little of the military culture, into what were in some locations, demanding field conditions,[157] generated a raft of welfare and health challenges which the officers of the PSS tackled with considerable gusto. One interesting issue, with which, the PSS was concerned was that the ATS were entitled to a china cup and saucer, whilst male soldiers were not initially scaled for a mug. Given the increasing probability of male and female soldiers serving together, at least in the Base, this was one problem PSS was keen to resolve. Most units were not structured to deliver some of the specific welfare needs of the ATS, and the VPB were therefore an essential component in the initial planning. In November 1939, the Duchess of Northumberland inaugurated a comforts

150 The policy letter, GHQ (A) A/2358 (O) was issued on 6 February 1940. TNA WO 167/11: GHQ AG.

151 By 1945 there were about 30 trades open to the ATS. For details of trades, and their supporting courses, see, WOOH, *The Auxiliary Territorial Service*, Appx IV, pp.252-257 and Army Council, *Regulations for the Auxiliary Territorial Service*, p.164, Appx X, Trade Groups.

152 AG Statistical Return 3/944/40 dated 2 August 1940, quoted in MBOH, *The Army Medical Services, Campaigns*, Vol I, p.112.

153 See: TNA WO 167/11: GHQ AG, GHQ (A) A/2358 (O) dated 25 February 1940.

154 This figure does not include the requirement for GLOC ATS signals detachments, which was being staffed in late February 1940.

155 Her energetic work in this arena, contrasts with what others have described as her anachronistic and over-militaristic approach by insisting that women should be treated the same as men, a solution which was not in keeping with the military culture of the period, although there are several examples of her decisions relating to BEF deployment where this was certainly not the case. Aged 62, Gwynne-Vaughan was retired as Director in July 1941 and Lesley Whatley, Controller ATS from October 1943, considered that her attitude and persona influenced the decision to remove her from post, being replaced by Jean Knox, a pre-war housewife of 33 who was described by the Brisbane *Courier-Mail* of 27 September 1941 as the 'youngest general in the World'. See also, Lucy Noakes, *Women in the British Army, War and the Gentler Sex, 1907-1948* (London & New York: Routledge, 2006), p.110.

156 The GHQ plan included 55 ATS to replace 45 men at 1 BAD at Le Gavre and 43 ATS to replace 32 men at 2 BAD at Plouaret. The war diaries of both units have though, no record of ATS arriving in their locations. See, TNA WO 167/1175: 1 BAD RAOC, WD and 167/1176: 2 BAD RAOC, WD respectively.

157 One location in this category was No 2 BAD at Plouaret, which although selected to have ATS deployed, was, because of the harsh living conditions, described by DATS as 'highly unsuitable' for the employment of ATS. TNA WO 167/11: GHQ AG, GHQ (A) A/2358 (O) dated 25 February 1940.

P8.5 Not Without Precedent. From the experience of the Great War, the War Office sought to generate capability enhancements in France by deploying members of the ATS to conduct specific AQ tasks to release manpower to combat roles. (RLCM: VR/NOR)

fund for the ATS, whilst the Queen Mary's Army Auxiliary Corps Old Comrades Association established a Benevolent Fund for it.

The PSS was also responsible for liasing with DATS Staff in the War Office on a range of subjects. Instructions were issued on the medico-legal aspects of female health care, toilet paper scaling, the treatment of VD and the care and future service of pregnant soldiers.[158] In addition, the Staff requested commanders to treat female homosexuality with sensitivity, believing there was little to be gained from drawing unwarranted attention to it. It was certainly a subject that had the Army's attention, as an ATS Female Medical Advisor, was tasked, in 1941, with composing a guide for unit commanders, entitled, *A Special Problem*.[159] The progression of staffing ATS long-term issues by the PSS effectively drew to a close on 10 May 1940 with the initiation of the German offensive as attention focused on more urgent operational matters.

158 Unmarried ATS officers who fell pregnant were expected to relinquish their commission. WOOH, *The Auxiliary Territorial Service*, p.227. Other Ranks were discharged. Army Council, *Regulations for the Auxiliary Territorial Service*, p.156, Appx VI, Table of Discharge.

159 WOOH, *The Auxiliary Territorial Service*, p.227.

Conclusion

The PSS had a lively and demanding period in France, and it dealt with a wide range of issues, from which, there were four key lessons. First, that nearly every aspect of improving the 'Soldier's Lot' required financial assistance and logistic support. Sometimes, and leave was an example, funding and resources were needed on a major scale, but even philanthropic activity generated a requirement for storage, transport and distribution assets. Second, the deployment of the mix of Regular personnel with Reserves of various shades and inexperienced Militia soldiers in an operational Theatre in a foreign land creating a constant flow of dynamic issues that required a comprehension of the differing military cultures and an innovative approach to generating solutions, to sometimes complex problems.

Third, the issues in deploying the ATS, whilst having precedent in the Great War, was handled with sensitivity by the PSS, despite the fact that that had no ATS officer in the Staff section, although had the German invasion not intervened, it seems likely that the establishment of a post would have only been a matter of time and with a growing ATS component, a necessary addition to the PSS team. Last, but certainly not least, the implementation of many PSS initiatives required careful co-ordination between G, A and Q, which, created an imperative to 'walk the corridors' in GHQ BEF in order to agree solutions. What is clear however, is that through dedication, industry and innovation, the officers of the PSS were committed to improving the 'Soldier's Lot'.

9

White Cliffs
The role of AQ in planning and delivering the BEF's leave programme 1939-1940

The AQ Challenge

A key GHQ AQ task was to plan, resource and manage the movement of thousands of BEF personnel travelling in France and UK who were undertaking leave, courses and meetings, in addition to the visitors, individual rotations and returnees from medical treatment in the UK. This chapter will analyse the plans and processes that supported the movements aspects of the leave programme, which was not only by far the largest task of the administrative routine movement activities but also the one that had sensitive morale and political implications, whilst requiring substantial resources, a prominent element of which, was rail and sea transport capability. In this respect, the successful delivery of the programme relied greatly upon co-ordination between the G, A and Q Branches in GHQ, especially the Finance Branch and Q (Movements). As the Force grew, leave movements rose from 1,700 personnel in each direction in December 1939 to an expected 2,200[1] in May 1940, and was projected to reach 2,500 by July.

To place this ever-increasing movements problem into perspective, the BEF expanded by 22,300 personnel in November 1939, adding another 280 soldiers per day eligible for leave in February 1940, and creating an additional daily movements task of 560 accounting for outbound and inbound travel. GHQ was also responsible for the movement of RAF personnel in the Air Component of the BEF and the AASF and all naval personnel deployed in France, although small numbers of RAF personnel sometimes flew to UK, whilst RN personnel might take passage on HM Ships. In addition to the numbers involved, there was also a cultural issue to be managed because of the different experience, comprehension and expectation of the disparate groups travelling within the BEF's leave and movements system. The movement out-fall from these policy decisions was considerable. The numerical aspects of the problem are summarized in the table below, which lucidly articulates the important role of Movement Control (MC)[2] in

1 Leave movement had dropped to less than a 1,000 personnel per day in April 1940 because most soldiers eligible for their first leave had completed it.

2 Movement Control was a joint organization comprised of personnel from the QMG Branch and the Transportation Directorate.

planning and controlling the daily transit of thousands of personnel which, on some occasions, was exceeding 5,000.

Table 9.1
Arrivals in the United Kingdom from the BEF
October 1939 – April 1940[3]

	Leave					Miscellaneous					Total	Daily
Month	RN	Army	RAF	Total	Daily	RN	Army	RAF	Total	Daily		
1939												
October	1	24	0	25	<1	3	966	9	978	31	1,002	32
November	5	139	1	145	48	85	2,550	66	2,701	90	2,846	95
December	19	23,286	2,304	25,609	1,707*	259	4,723	617	5,599	180	31,208	1,006
1940												
January	14	44,914	3,701	48,629	1,568	48	2,801	221	3,070	99	51,699	1,668
February	38	52,336	5,668	58,042	2,073	50	6,651	224	6,925	247	64,967	2,320
March	28	53,314	4,027	57,369	1,850	107	5,241	424	5,772	186	63,141	2,037
April	52	26,278	2,557	28,887	963	132	10,316	246	10,694	356	39,581	1,319
Totals	157	200,291	18,258	218,076	1,614+	684	33,248	1,807	35,739	265+	254,444	1,200#

* Based on the period 17-31 December 1939.
+ Daily average over 135 days - 17 December 1939 to 30 April 1940.
# Daily average over 212 days – 1 October 1939 to 30 April 1940. 1885 over 135 days.

The statistics expose several interesting points that bear examination. First and foremost, there was no GHQ sanctioned privilege leave before 17 December 1939, and those shown in October and November 1939 were presumably granted compassionate leave, which in November was 0.0008 percent of the Force. Secondly, there was a 107 percent increase in non-leave movement in December over November, which, although the records do not confirm it, was almost certainly caused by personnel creating or seizing the opportunity to travel to the United Kingdom on duty and take some leave. As the BEF and RAF personnel strength in France was around 190,000 by December 1939 this meant 16 percent of the force returned to the UK in December, the majority in the second two weeks, thereby placing a heavy burden upon the movement system. Thirdly, the MC staff did well to keep the leave programme rolling in January 1940. Very severe winter weather caused major disruption to rail schedules in France and the UK, whilst intelligence indicating a German invasion prompted GHQ to put the leave programme on hold on several occasions, creating additional tasks for the MC organization to return personnel to units, which not only involved 'hot-planning' but also the need to arrange accommodation and rationing. Sometimes the cancellation of leave and the bad weather occurred concurrently, causing even greater disruption to the programme. I Corps Ammunition Park RASC recorded on 14 January that all leave was cancelled and on 16 January that there was 'moderate snowfall all day'. The CAP was stood down to normal duties on 17 January but effectively four days plus

3 Table compiled from information in WOOH, *Movements*, p.199.

of the leave programme had been lost.[4] In these circumstances, it is remarkable that in January that 48,629 personnel travelled on leave plus another 3,070 on duty.[5]

Last but not least, the increasing daily personnel traffic between France and the UK was a most useful exposure to handling mass movement. This activity, whilst on occasions causing many frustrations, enabled the MC staff to gain obtain valuable experience in preparation for the momentous events during the evacuation from France in May and June 1940. The MC staff were though, planning for much greater daily activity because in accordance with War Office direction, capability was being organized and resourced to enable, by late 1941, a potential force of 2.25 million personnel Army, RN, RAF and civilian personnel to be sustained in France. From the leave perspective, this would have meant 12,500 people crossing the English Channel in each direction every day, a significant task, which was the equivalent of the personnel of nearly two infantry divisions[6]. In addition, MC had to manage the movement of reinforcements, duty personnel, visitors, casualties and families. Applying the average ratio of non-leave to leave personnel, in the period January to April 1940, which was 14.0 percent, to the 12,500, this would equate to 1,757, thereby creating a daily total of 14,257.

Command & Control

The Directorate of Movements at the War Office was responsible, through the Quartermaster-General 2 (QMG 2) Branch, for co-ordinating leave movement policy for the BEF. QMG 2 (Personnel) (a) controlled Short-sea voyages, whilst 2 (b) exercised direction over military rail movement in the UK.[7] In France, two Movement Districts controlled leave movement. Q (MC) North District, with Headquarters in Rouen, was operated by No 4 MC Group, and controlled activity in areas of Boulogne, Calais, Dieppe, Dunkerque, Fecamp, Le Harve and Rouen. Q (MC) South had its Headquarters in Vitre and had No 1 and 2 MC Groups controlling operations in the ports of Brest, Caen, Cherbourg, Marseilles, Nantes, Rennes, Saint Malo and Saint Nazaire. In the UK, MC personnel in the Home Commands were responsible for co-ordinating leave movement, with an essential component of the process being the Railway Traffic Officers (RTOs)[8] and their supporting teams. A RTO was located at every major main line station and critical railway-operating centre, yet despite their importance, they often lived in inadequate quarters with few of the requisite facilities for operating effectively. Indeed, the War Office history records that one RTO section was accommodated and rationed by the London & North Eastern Railway (LNER) for two weeks before the local garrison agreed to accept administrative responsibility for it.[9] RTO sections had a spectrum of tasks, one of which was controlling leave movement. Many RTOs and their staff were Supplementary

4 TNA WO 167/137: 1 CAP RASC, WD, entries 14-17 January 1940.
5 WOOH, *Movements*, p.199.
6 Details of the establishments, scaling and equipment of divisional units are in Philson, BEFORBAT, Vol 2. A Regular infantry division is shown as 14,737 at p.124.
7 In February 1940 there was a re-organization within the Directorate of Movements, resulting in QMG 2 being re-titled Q (M) 2 and the re-allocation of responsibilities within the Branch. WOOH, *Movements*, Chp 2, Appx A.
8 In the Great War, the abbreviation RTO described Railway Transport Officer. See, WOOH, *Movements*, p.xv.
9 Ibid, p.199.

Reservists, or Militiamen, and had much to learn about their craft, which, in some cases were the fundamentals of their trade. One RTO described the initial capability of his team: 'a brewer's drayman, a tinsmith, a train-driver and a painter – not a semblance of clerical experience among them',[10] which says little positive about the personnel selection process.

Whilst in September 1939 MC had tackled mobilization and then deployment to France, their experience of dealing with *en masse* leave personnel did not commence until 17 December 1939, and because of the nature of instituting the leave programme, there was no time to work up. 956 leave personnel arrived in UK on the first day and from then until the evacuation from France, RTOs were constantly in demand to solve a myriad of problems. Fortunately, the enemy rarely created much disruption but the severe winter of 1939-1940 and the difficulties of operating in the blackout, generated a raft of interruptions to rail movement. Thousands of servicemen were delayed, sometimes for periods of up to 48 hours and whilst all of them required food and accommodation, those proceeding on leave were particularly anxious to resume their journeys as quickly as possible. To assist them in their quest to enjoy the maximum permitted time at home, RTOs were authorized to extend the validity of leave passes depending upon the length of delays *en route*. While RTOs grappled with the daily grind of keeping soldiers on the move, at a national level, resolution of strategic or significant railway issues was managed through the Railway Executive Committee (REC)[11] formed on 24 September 1938, initially as an advisory body and then fulfilling executive functions from 1 September 1939, when the Government took over control of most of the railway companies in the UK.[12]

Internal Movements in France

Experience from the Great War indicated that the control of leave from France required careful planning. In particular, the issue of suitable travel documentation was deemed essential to the effective operation of the leave system which was administered through the AFW 3145 and AFW 3145A, held by unit staff. The W3145 books contained the unit counterfoil, an outbound embarkation ticket, which was removed at the port of embarkation, a Southern Railway warrant from the arrival port to London Victoria, railway warrants for the final destination and return and an embarkation ticket for the return sea ferry. [13]

In addition to movement documentation, there were several issues pertinent to the command and control of personnel proceeding on leave. Every soldier was supposed to take his weapon on leave, which, for the most part meant the 0.303-inch Lee Enfield rifle, although some soldiers carried a revolver, as did most officers. Personnel issued with a rifle had to carry five rounds of ammunition. Revolver bearers were not issued with ammunition, but stocks were held at the French ports to issue five rounds per man, if required, on re-entry to Theatre. Documentation

10 Ibid, p.87.

11 HQ REC was located underground at Down Street tube station, which had been closed in 1932, on the Piccadilly Line between Hyde Park Corner and Green Park. Conversion of the site began in August 1939, but the work was not complete when war was declared. Access to HQ REC was obtained, either from the surface, or by special tube train.

12 For a brief wartime account of the REC's work and a description of its HQ, see, na, *The Railway Executive Committee and its Headquarters* (London: The Railway Gazette, 1944).

13 See details in TNA WO 167/11: GHQ AG, WD, Leave Addendum.

P9.1 A Wonderful Sight. The White Cliffs of Dover. (Author)

for the carriage of firearms was by exception and soldiers were required to provide proof as to why they were not in possession of a weapon. Soldiers in France moved by unit transport to the nearest railhead to meet a train to the corps or area railhead, or if they were fortunate, they drove to it a short distance by road. The corps or area leave train would then steam to the appropriate port. Soldiers working near to the Sea Port of Embarkation (SPOE) would travel on local rail services or be taken by road to the quay. Initially, there were five railheads, one each serving GHQ and Corps Troops, I Corps, II Corps, the Air Component and the AASF but as the BEF expanded, so did the organization supporting leave movement.

In particular, the deployment of a brigade to serve with the Third French Army in the Saar created a need for additional movements resources and once 51st (Highland) Division was in place, there was requirement for two leave trains per week.[14] Each had a capacity of 500 men, which allowed flexibility in travel arrangements and space for personnel on courses. To maximize the utilization of resources, at least one ambulance coach was attached to each train to evacuate patients to a general hospital in Dieppe, or to the UK. Of great import to the soldier embarking on leave was to arrive at the correct port to sail on the steamer to the UK on time, and for the most part, this process operated efficiently. There were though problems on the return journey, with personnel arriving at the incorrect reception railheads and thereby, creating much unwanted work for the MC teams and parent units. Whilst seemingly a matter of detail, it created enough irritation for it to be raised at the AG's Leave Meeting on 16 February 1940.[15]

14 TNA WO 167/11: Minutes of Meeting in AG's Office 3 Apr 40 A/2971/PS dated 10 April 40.

15 Minutes of Leave Meeting held in AG's Office on 16 February 1940. GHQ (A) A2971/4/65 (PS) dated 18 February 1940 paragraph 5a, in TNA WO 167/11 refers.

Home to Blighty

There were two main leave sea routes to the United Kingdom. Cherbourg to Southampton was the focus for personnel serving on the GLOC, including those travelling from Marseilles on the Mediterranean Line of Communication (MEDLOC) whilst Boulogne to Dover covered the corps areas. Personnel based in or around Calais and Dieppe utilized the civil services from those ports and those at Le Harve had access to the daily duty boat to Southampton. One of the major concerns was the security of the shipping routes.[16] Accidents and global German naval operations, especially in the Western Approaches and the North Sea resulted in the loss of 312 British, Allied and Neutral ships in the period December 1939 and April 1940.[17] The Defence planners were however, determined to ensure such events did not take place in the English Channel. RN ships escorted convoys and RAF Coastal and Fighter Commands patrolled the airspace, whilst the possibility of torpedo attack and mining from U-Boats, and bombing, mining, strafing and torpedo attacks from the *Luftwaffe*, generated the need for additional defensive measures on board merchant ships carrying BEF personnel, the co-ordination of which, was a MC responsibility. These arrangements included Passive Air Defence (PAD), protection against Gas Warfare, surface and aerial action plans, and the implementation of the shipboard emergency ration policy which required each leave steamer to carry two days dry rations in case of diversion or delay.

Cherbourg sailings, controlled by the Portsmouth Naval Command, were usually late morning, with the return steamer departing on the nightly convoy from Southampton. The leave ships from Boulogne, escorted where necessary by naval forces from the Nore Command and aircraft from RAF Coastal Command, were scheduled to arrive and depart on or near High Water, and departure times were usually between 0700 and 1500,[18] with occasional days having no sailings.[19] This flexible programme was the cause of several robust discussions with SNCF because GHQ, wishing to prevent large numbers of soldiers waiting for the steamer, would have preferred a daily rail schedule which reflected the sailing times. SNCF was however, clear, that the application of special Q paths that changed each day, was not conducive to the efficient operation of a rail network, which was not only supporting the deployment of British and French forces in North Eastern France but also the civil sector. MC was though, cognizant of the problems, which would arise if there were interruptions to the flow of traffic and there were many opportunities for disruption to shipping and rail: accidents, mechanical failure, severe weather and enemy operations, so to mitigate the effects of such incidents, two transit camps were established, one was at Dover for 3,000 personnel and other at Boulogne for 2,000.

16 Administrative Instruction (Leave) No 1 in TNA WO 167/11: GHQ AG contains the details of the leave passage ports and the outline sailing times but despite the sensitive information in it, has no security classification.

17 Roskill, BOH, *The War at Sea*, Vol I, *The Defensive*, p.615.

18 TNA WO 167/205: HQ 2nd Division A&Q, Appx A to 2nd Division Admin Order, December 1939, Sailing Times - 18 December 1939 to 18 January 1940.

19 There were no planned sailings from France on Wednesday 20 December or Thursday 4 January and none from UK on Saturday 30 December and Sunday 14 January 1940. TNA WO 167/205: HQ 2nd Division A&Q, Appx A to 2nd Division Admin Order, December 1939, Sailing Times – 18 December 1939 to 18 January 1940.

The Dover–Calais commercial route, whilst offering the shortest sea crossing, was an expensive option and the records contain constant references to the concerns of the GHQ Finance Branch, which was keen to reduce the numbers of passengers and thus the cost, of using this arrangement. At the Leave meeting held in Adjutant-General's office on 16 February 1940, GHQ Finance declared a clear intent to seek the elimination of the BEF's utilization of the route, making especial reference to the numbers of senior officers who used it to visit the War Office.[20] Whilst the Finance Branch may have alighted upon colonels and above as the key offenders, senior officers were not the exclusive generators of this problem as Signalman Yeomans, under military orders, travelled on this route for leave in March 1940.[21] At the same meeting, concerns were raised by the AG representative about the movement of Queen Alexandra's Imperial Military Nursing Service (QAIMNS) nursing sisters from the Advanced Medical Base at Dieppe on the Dieppe–Newhaven sea crossing. The concept made excellent practical sense because it eliminated the need to travel to Boulogne, thus saving money and time but another key advantage was that the medical staff could also travel to UK on hospital ships, easing the burden on commercial costs, whilst assisting, if necessary, with the care of casualties and offering additional options for travel. There were however, no military transit facilities at Newhaven, which meant that nursing sisters would, if steamers were delayed on the outbound journey from England, have to be accommodated in local hotels, some of which, were not deemed by GHQ to be suitable establishments for such ladies to frequent.[22] The meeting concluded however, that the benefits outweighed the disadvantages, and that the standing arrangements should continue.

Victoria Train

The Southern Railway, on behalf of REC but at the behest of Q(Movements) in the War Office,[23] was responsible for providing rail lift from Dover Marine to London Victoria, and Southampton to Waterloo,[24] to support the movement of individual military personnel between the UK and France.[25] Whilst most of this traffic was leave orientated, there were soldiers returning from sickness, courses, attachments and arriving as individual reinforcements, who also used the services. Inbound from France, when there were no air-raid warnings impeding movement, the

20 TNA WO 167/11: GHQ AG, GHQ (A) A2971/4/65 (PS) dated 18 February 1940, 'Minutes of Leave Meeting held in AG's Office on 16 February 1940', paragraph 5a. French soldiers authorised to take leave in the UK also used the Dover-Calais route at French taxpayers' expense.

21 Memory of John Yeomans; JYIC 241099. Whilst the crossing was short, his morale cannot have been improved by the fact that he was returning to France on his 21st birthday (22 March 1940). Perhaps he would have felt much better had he known that his movements were giving the Finance staff peptic ulcers.

22 The QAIMNS sisters were though made of sterner stuff, and their courage, fortitude and devotion in caring for their patients under fire, during operations in May and June 1940 is a subject that deserves much more academic attention than it has been given hitherto.

23 See, WOOH, *Movements*, Chp 2, Appx A.

24 Victoria was the key rail hub in London for BEF personnel arriving from and departing to France. PSS arranged, with the assistance of the War Office, for the National Provincial Bank to open a branch at the station for transiting soldiers to use. TNA WO 167/11; GHQ, AG PSS, WD, 4 January 1940.

25 Details were published in Administrative Instruction (Leave) No 5, 'Rail Arrangements in the UK and Accommodation of Philanthropic Bodies in London' in TNA WO 167/11: GHQ AG.

P9.2 Victoria Station. The BEF may have long gone but the building retains its 'Southern Railway' title. (Author)

Southern Railway operated three trains per day for the BEF, with special Q paths, X, Y and Z, routed to London Victoria, and a standard path allocated to the Southampton to London-Waterloo route. To mitigate disruption at Waterloo, either through enemy action or serious accident, plans were produced to disperse troops from Clapham Junction and Wimbledon.[26]

The railway emergency planners had great concerns about the enemy's capability to interrupt the operational efficiency of the system through offensive air action and produced various solutions to ensure the effectiveness of attacks would be limited. If enemy air operations had interfered with rail movement, paths X and Y were routed to Victoria, whilst a Q path, ZP, ran from Dover-Marine through to Redhill and then Guildford-Reading-Oxford-Banbury-Leicester-Loughborough-Nottingham-Chesterfield-Sheffield-York. Outbound from UK, there were three paths daily from Victoria to Dover Marine, XR, YR and ZR respectively, with a special available to conduct ZP in reverse if necessary. Personnel living in East Kent, travelled to and from Dover-Marine on local services, whilst those in the South Central and Western parts of England moved directly to and from Southampton on scheduled commercial trains. As it transpired, a much more challenging enemy was the weather, especially in late January and early February 1940, which caused widespread travel disruption throughout the country through a combination of heavy snow, severe frost, freezing rain and dense fog,[27] with 1,500 miles across

26 Whilst there was no damage to London's railway network by enemy air action during the period of the BEF's deployment in France, significant damage was inflicted from August 1940 onwards. See, B W L Brooksbank, *London Main Line War Damage* (London: Capital Transport, 2007).

27 December 1939-February 1940 was the coldest since 1895 and in terms of the persistence of snow upon the ground, the worst since 1879. The temperature fell to -23°C at Rhayader in mid-Wales on 21

P9.3 Blessed Moments. Lance-Corporal Lionel Woodhead of the Corps of Military Police and his wife Hilda on leave. (Courtesy Mary Maginniss)

the rail network closed to traffic despite the operation of 300 snowploughs.[28] Conditions were so bad that many Southern Railway electric services had to be hauled by steam locomotives because of thick ice on the conductor rails,[29] whilst surface sections of the Underground were also severely affected.[30]

The Underground was an essential component of the leave movement system because troops arriving at Victoria and Waterloo used it for dispersal to other London railheads for onward movement. Many soldiers lived in the Midlands, Northern England, and Scotland and needed to travel from Euston or Saint Pancras on London Midland & Scottish Railway (LMS) services, for East Coast destinations, on LNER trains from King's Cross, and for East Anglia, LNER from Liverpool Street, so the Northern Line was essential in enabling a rapid transit across Central London. Personnel taking leave in Wales or the South West required Great Western Railway (GWR) services from Paddington travelling on the District or Circle Lines. Travel to Central Southern England was via Waterloo. For the most part, the process operated effectively but air-raid alerts always caused disruption because the floodgates, protecting the Bakerloo and Northern Line tunnels under the River Thames,

January 1940 and there were long periods when the temperature remained below zero during the day as well as at night. See, Phillip Eden, *Great British Weather Disasters* (London: Continuum, 2008), pp.252-253.

28 O S Nock, *Britain's Railways at War 1939-1945* (London: Ian Allan, 1971), p.57.

29 Ibid.

30 As an example, a Piccadilly Line train left Hounslow West at 1613 but did not arrive at Northfields until 1145, a journey scheduled to take 10 minutes. Ibid, p.58.

were closed.[31] This action was deemed essential in order to prevent ingress of river water into the Tube system, from a tunnel breach caused by a bomb or a mine.[32]

The passage of large numbers of soldiers, usually carrying a plethora of equipment, was an interesting problem for the London Passenger Transport Board (LPTB). Most of the soldiers were not from London, and few had travelled on the Tube before. There were inevitably frustrations as soldiers carrying their shouldered kitbags[33] gathered to read the directional maps, blocked passenger tunnels, crammed escalators and stairs and sometimes lost their way in the subterranean maze. Equally irritating to other passengers and the LBTB was the penchant of some military travellers for removing the rubber hand-grips which were fitted, in lieu of leather straps, to the 1935–1938 built Tube stock. Whatever their capability in assisting the travelling public maintaining a vertical stance, some soldiers decided that they would also make excellent coshes and appropriated them.[34] Some soldiers also opted to break their journey in London and the Left Luggage offices at railway termini were overwhelmed with various items of military equipment and it is an interesting comment upon the culture of the time that they would accept firearms but not great-coats.[35]

The Home Run

Despite the planners' best efforts, travel on the war-time railway network was never particularly relaxing nor timely. Reductions in speeds and train frequency, combined with black-out precautions, enemy action, poor weather and increasing military traffic, created overcrowding on trains, and constant interruptions to services. In late August 1939, as war became imminent, REC began to examine the requirement to implement the War Emergency Schedule for each railway company, in order to allow for more military traffic, whilst minimizing the maintenance burden on locomotives, rolling stock and the Permanent Way. The GWR and LMS commenced their WES on Monday 25 September, the GWR, the LNER on Monday 2 October, and the SR on Monday 16 October 1939. The effects of the reduction in the passenger train services from 1938 level to the 1939, created by the schedules were dramatic. Not only were there fewer trains, with services decreasing between 25 and 64 percent but also scheduled journey times

31 As it transpired, Northern Line under the River Thames from Waterloo to Charing Cross was closed from 1 September 1939 to enable flood protection works to be completed. It reopened, remarkably, and in a most timely manner, on the same day that the BEF's leave programme commenced, 17 December, except for the Kennington - Moorgate section, which was not reopened until 19 May 1940. See, Desmond F Croome & Alan Jackson, *Rails Through the Clay: A History of London's Tube Railways* (London: Capital Transport, 2nd Edn, 1993), p.518.

32 Water ingress of this nature occurred only once during the war, when the disused Hampstead Loop tunnel at Charing Cross was penetrated in September 1940. The flooding was fortunately contained in a 200 yard section by the previous installation of concrete tunnel plugs. Ibid.

33 The 'kitbag' became synonymous with wartime service travel. Not only did it contain the physical components of a soldier's personal life, but it also became a valuable soft seat, ready for immediate deployment whilst hours were spent waiting for trains.

34 Croome & Jackson, *Rails Through the Clay*, p.278.

35 Alan Earnshaw, *Britain's Railways at War* (Penryn: Atlantic Publishing, 1995), p.110.

increased in the range 12 to 34 percent. For personnel proceeding on leave the reduced services and longer times often made their trip home a slow and difficult task.[36]

There were improvements as the schedules bedded-in but the severe winter weather in January and February 1940 was a significant problem, which generated a consequential and extensive backlog of traffic. As an illustration of the chaos, which resulted from the heavy snowfall during the weekend of 27-29 January 1940, there was widespread disruption of services across the country, involving in some areas, a complete stoppage of passenger and goods traffic. Overcrowding was another major and constant issue, with an extreme event occurring at Kettering in Northamptonshire when a lady in a carriage was taken ill, and then died. 95 people had to be ordered, by the stationmaster, to leave the coach, so her body could be removed.[37] At nearly every station BEF personnel would see a large poster of a soldier asking passengers, 'Is Your Journey Really Necessary?'[38] Obviously, every serviceman or woman on leave would have answered unequivocally, 'Yes'.

For some soldiers living on Off-Islands around the Kingdom, such as Skye, the Shetlands and the Isles of Scilly, the end of the rail journey meant the start of another adventure.[39] From the station there would be a short trip to the quay, followed by a sea crossing, which was often longer than the one they had experienced across the English Channel, with of course the possibility of torpedo attack from U-Boats, or being mined. On arrival on the island, they might have to endure another sea journey to reach another Isle, and then walk from the jetty to their home. Those travelling to the North of Scotland were faced with similar difficulties, not only because of

36 For the reduction in rail services, see the table below, compiled from information in Nock, *Britain's Railways at War 1939-1945*.

Table 9.2
UK Main Line Railways
War Emergency Schedule Service Reduction

Railway	From	To	Miles	Trains per day			Average Time		
				1938	WES	% -	1938	WES	% +
LMS	Euston	Birmingham	112.90	20	15	25	2:05	3:10	34
LMS	Euston	Liverpool	193.70	30	16	46	3:39	5:02	27
LMS	Euston	Inverness	568.40	4	2	50	14:30	16:26	12
LNER	King's Cross	Aberdeen	523.20	12	5	58	11:53	14:52	20
LNER	King's Cross	Hull	196.90	14	5	64	4:06	5:32	26
LNER	King's Cross	Norwich	115.00	18	12	33	2:50	3:26	17
GWR	Paddington	Birmingham	110.60	14	8	43	2:05	2:49	26
GWR	Paddington	Bristol	118.30	20	14	30	2:15	2:58	24
SR	Waterloo	Bournemouth	107.90	26	17	32	2:33	3:04	17
SR	Waterloo	Exeter	171.80	13	9	31	3:42	4:15	13

37 Earnshaw, *Britain's Railways at War*, p.93.
38 This poster, drawn by Bert Thomas was by published by the REC in 1940.
39 Dispensations for additional leave to these locations were authorized in Administrative Instruction (Leave) No 3, 'Distant Islands of Great Britain' in TNA WO 167/11: GHQ AG.

the distance, but also because on Sundays there were no trains running North from Inverness[40] and initially soldiers effectively lost a day of leave, although GHQ resolved this dilemma by issuing an instruction to units not to dispatch, on Saturday, leave personnel travelling North of Inverness.[41] At the other extreme, a soldier serving on the MC staff at Calais or Boulogne and living near Dover, could be home in less than three hours. It must though, have been immensely frustrating to see the White Cliffs of Dover from France but not be able to go home. The movement of soldiers to Eire was another problem, the solution requiring required close co-ordination between A Branch and Q (Movements). Personnel on leave in Eire could not travel in uniform, nor carry weapons, so an Eire Leave Reception Centre was established at the Duke of York's HQ[42] in London to support their movement and administration. Firearms and military equipment were placed in storage, the opportunity to wash and eat offered, and if necessary, a set of civilian clothes issued. Upon their return from leave, the process was reversed.[43]

Conclusion

Given Hore-Belisha's intent to 'humanize' the Army, the efficiency and equity of the BEF's leave system was as much a potential political issue as a live practical problem.[44] Leave was a key factor in sustaining morale and failure of the arrangements were sure to damage it, whilst importing an almost assured level of censure from individuals, the media and Whitehall alike. Commercial transportation assets were critical to the success of the task, and GHQ had to compromise with railway and shipping companies in pursuit of its preferred solutions. These movements also required funding, under-written by the financiers, so whilst there were certainly creative tensions between the military and civil servants in this arena, developing the relationship was essential to output.

The staffs of Q Movements, AG PSS and the Finance Branch were in the forefront of not only the planning of the leave programme but also its delivery and there is little doubt that despite the inherent frictions, the officers from these Branches and the MC personnel managing the movements assets achieved a very positive result, whilst unmistakably demonstrating the importance of integrated planning within GHQ. AG PSS was adept in managing the personnel aspects of the BEF's leave process, ensuring that where possible, soldiers should not be disadvantaged by their domiciled locations in UK even if an extension of leave buffered against the G Staffs concerns about the numbers of personnel who were deemed to be Out of Theatre.

The decision of Q Movements and AG PSS to allow senior officers to flex leave with their military duty in the UK and permit medical personnel to travel on hospital ships for leave generated increased travel flexibility, whilst the grafting of movement for visits, courses,

40 This affected those travelling on routes to Wick, Lybster, Thurso and Kyle of Lochalsh and the supporting ferry connections to the Western Isles, the Orkneys and the Shetlands.
41 TNA WO 167/11: GHQ AG PSS, WD, 4 January 1940.
42 The HQ building, designed by John Sanders, the architect of Old College at the Royal Military Academy Sandhurst, is now part of the Duke of York Square development.
43 BEF Administrative Instructions (Leave) in TNA 167/11: GHQ, AG PSS
44 Minney, *The Private Papers of Hore-Belisha*, p.179.

attachments and meetings reduced costs and enhanced effectiveness. Whilst not a condition of the initial plan, the growing numbers of travellers started to build a wealth of experience amongst the MC teams in managing daily flows in excess of 5,000 passengers, which was to bear fruit under very demanding conditions in the coming months.

Diagram 1A
Symbology - Formations, Units and Logistic Functions

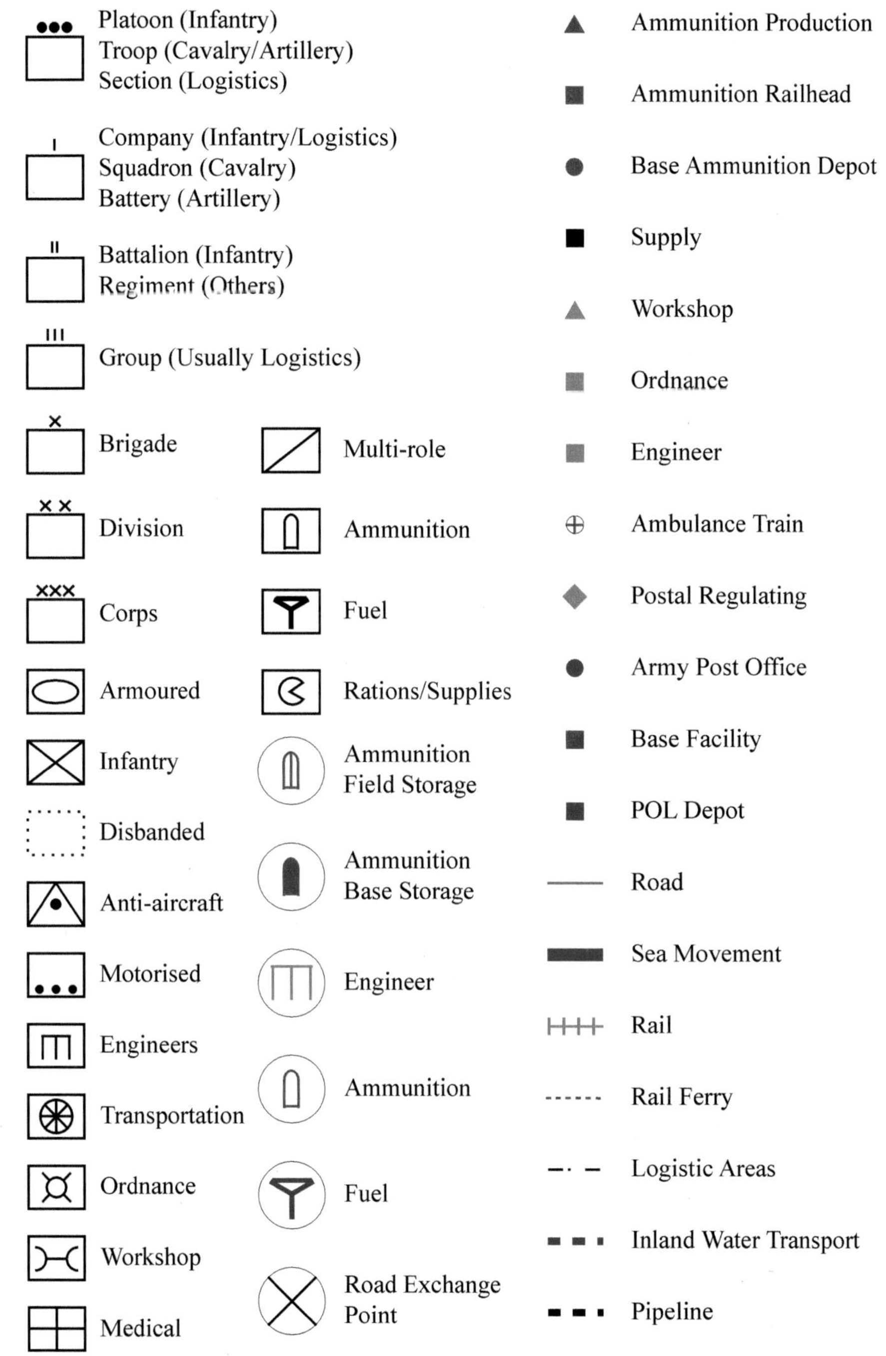

Platoon (Infantry)
Troop (Cavalry/Artillery)
Section (Logistics)

Company (Infantry/Logistics)
Squadron (Cavalry)
Battery (Artillery)

Battalion (Infantry)
Regiment (Others)

Group (Usually Logistics)

Brigade

Division

Corps

Armoured

Infantry

Disbanded

Anti-aircraft

Motorised

Engineers

Transportation

Ordnance

Workshop

Medical

Multi-role

Ammunition

Fuel

Rations/Supplies

Ammunition Field Storage

Ammunition Base Storage

Engineer

Ammunition

Fuel

Road Exchange Point

Ammunition Production

Ammunition Railhead

Base Ammunition Depot

Supply

Workshop

Ordnance

Engineer

Ambulance Train

Postal Regulating

Army Post Office

Base Facility

POL Depot

Road

Sea Movement

Rail

Rail Ferry

Logistic Areas

Inland Water Transport

Pipeline

Diagram 1B
Abbreviations

AA	Anti-Aircraft
AASF	Advanced Air Striking Force
ABD	Advanced Base Depot
AD	Ammunition Depot
Adv	Advanced
AFPU	Air Formation Postal Unit
AFW	Army Field Workshop
AIF	Australian Imperial Force
AP	Ammunition Point
APO	Army Post Office
ARH	Ammunition Railhead
ARP	Ammunition Refilling Point
ASE	Ammunition Section En-Cas Mobile
ATR	Ambulance Train
ATMS	Ambulance Train Maintenance Section
BAD	Base Ammunition Depot
BAPO	Base Army Post Office
BEF	British Expeditionary Force
BMY	Base Marshalling Yard
Bn	Battalion
BOD	Base Ordnance Depot
BOW	Base Ordnance Workshop
BPFC	Base Petroleum Filling Centre
BRT	Bulk Road Tanker
BSD	Base Supply Depot
CAD	Central Ammunition Depot
Can	Canadian
CAP	Corps Ammunition Park
CPP	Corps Petrol Park
CTAC	Corps Troops Ammunition Company
CTSC	Corps Troops Supply Column
DAC	Divisional Ammunition Company
DID	Detail Issue Depot
DPC	Divisional Petrol Company
DSC	Divisional Supply Column
EFI	Expeditionary Forces Institute
ESBD	Engineer Stores Base Depot
Fd	Field
GHQ	General Headquarters
GLOC	Ground Line of Communication
GW	Gas Warfare
HN	Host Nation
HPD	Home Postal Depot
HQ	Headquarters
HRS	Heavy Repair Shop
IWT	Inland Water Transport
LOC	Line of Communication
Log	Logistics
Lon	London
MRW	Mobile Railway Workshop
MT	Motor Transport
MTSD	Mechanical Transport Stores Depot
NZEF	New Zealand Expeditionary Force
OFP	Ordnance Field Park
ORBAT	Order of Battle
PCO	Postal Censorship Office
POE	Point of Entry
POL	Petroleum Oil and Lubricants
POLD	Petroleum Oil and Lubricants Depot
PPRC	Port Postal Regulating Centre
PRC	Postal Regulating Centre
PRH	Petrol Railhead
PWD	Port Workshop Detachment
RAF	Royal Air Force
RAOC	Royal Army Ordnance Corps
RASC	Royal Army Service Corps
RCC	Railway Construction Company
RCO	Railway Construction & Operating Company
RFF	Royal Filling Factory
RGPF	Royal Gunpowder Factory
RHD	Railhead
RN	Royal Navy
ROC	Railway Operating Company
ROF	Royal Ordnance Factory
RRS	Rail Regulating Station
RTC	Rail Tank Car
RTD	Reinforcement Training Depot
RWS	Ramp Wagon System
SA	Sub-Area
SGR	Standard Gauge Railway
SPOD	Sea Port of Disembarkation
SPOE	Sea Port of Embarkation
SRH	Supply Railhead
Svy	Survey
TCC	Troop Carrying Company
TSC	Transportation Stores Company
TSD	Transportation Stores Depot
VRD	Vehicle Reserve Depot
WMT	Wheeled Motor Transport

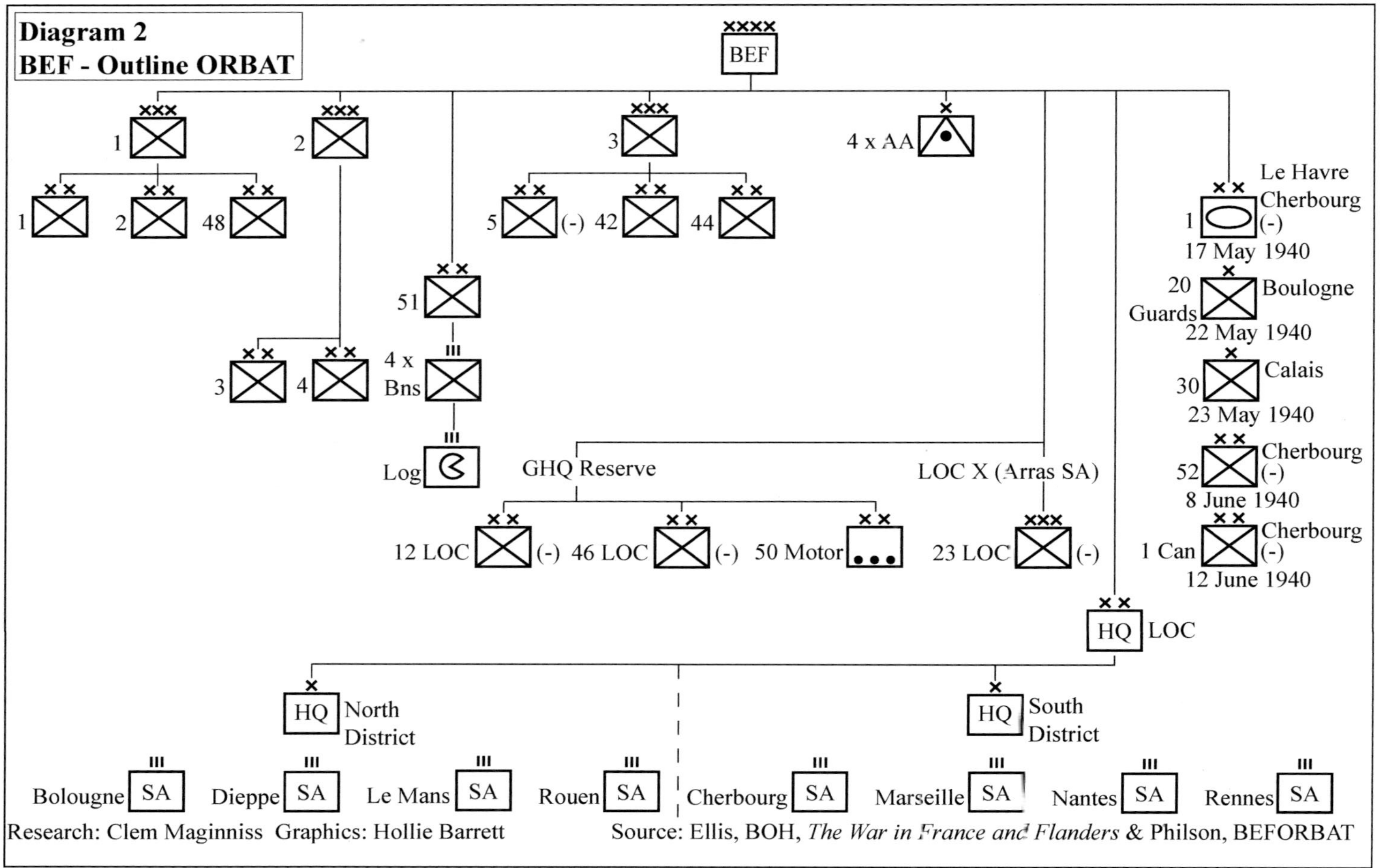
Diagram 2
BEF - Outline ORBAT
BEF
1
2
3
1
2
48
5
(-)
42
44
4 x AA
51
3
4
4 x
Bns
Log
GHQ Reserve
LOC X (Arras SA)
12 LOC
(-)
46 LOC
(-)
50 Motor
23 LOC
(-)
Le Havre
Cherbourg
(-)
1
17 May 1940
20
Guards
Boulogne
22 May 1940
30
Calais
23 May 1940
52
Cherbourg
(-)
8 June 1940
1 Can
Cherbourg
(-)
12 June 1940
HQ
LOC
HQ
North
District
HQ
South
District
Bolougne
SA
Dieppe
SA
Le Mans
SA
Rouen
SA
Cherbourg
SA
Marseille
SA
Nantes
SA
Rennes
SA
Research: Clem Maginniss Graphics: Hollie Barrett
Source: Ellis, BOH, The War in France and Flanders & Philson, BEFORBAT

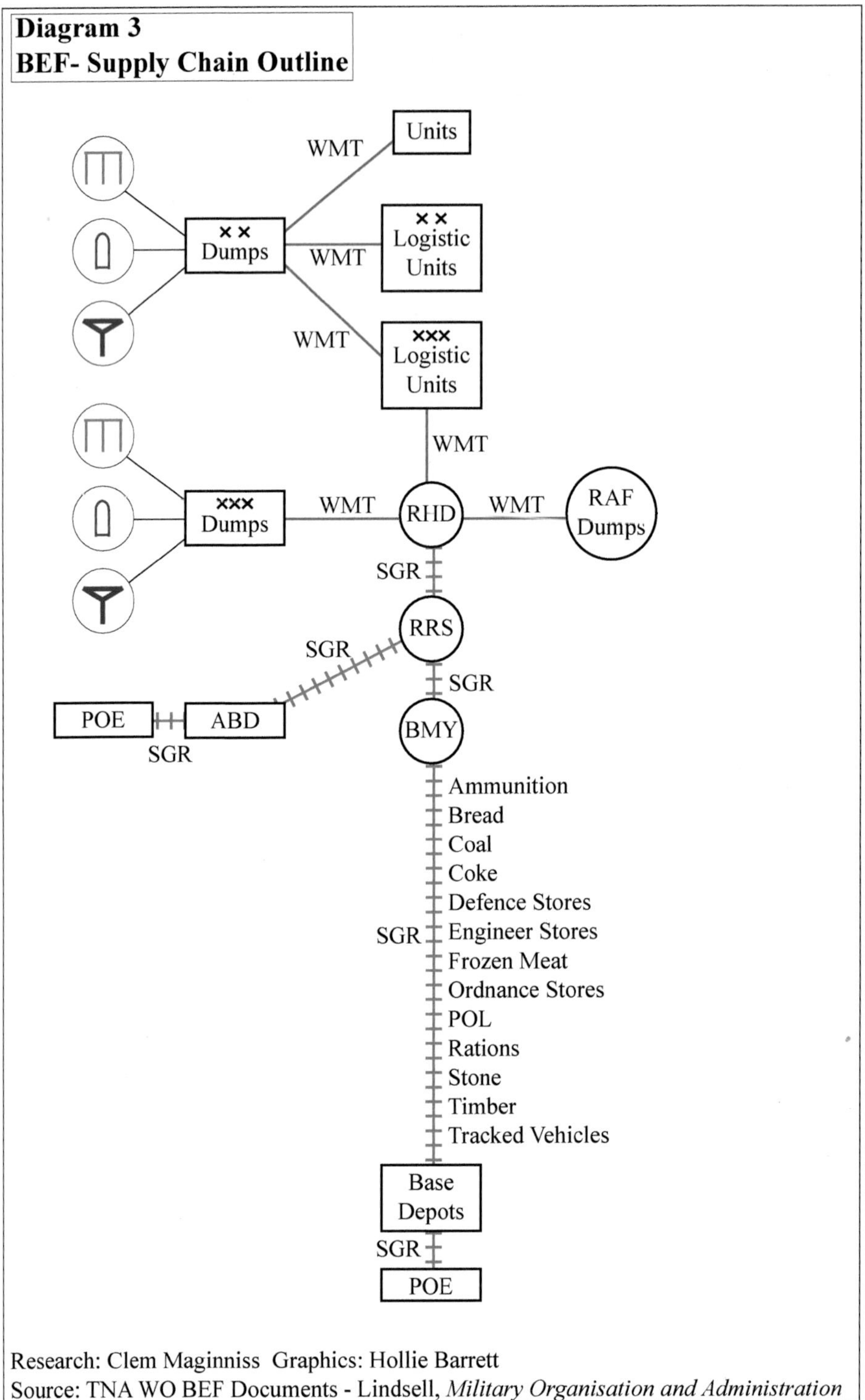
Diagram 3
BEF- Supply Chain Outline
Units
WMT
××
Dumps
WMT
××
Logistic
Units
WMT
×××
Logistic
Units
WMT
×××
Dumps
WMT
RHD
WMT
RAF
Dumps
SGR
RRS
SGR
SGR
POE
ABD
SGR
BMY
Ammunition
Bread
Coal
Coke
Defence Stores
SGR
Engineer Stores
Frozen Meat
Ordnance Stores
POL
Rations
Stone
Timber
Tracked Vehicles
Base
Depots
SGR
POE
Research: Clem Maginniss Graphics: Hollie Barrett
Source: TNA WO BEF Documents - Lindsell, Military Organisation and Administration

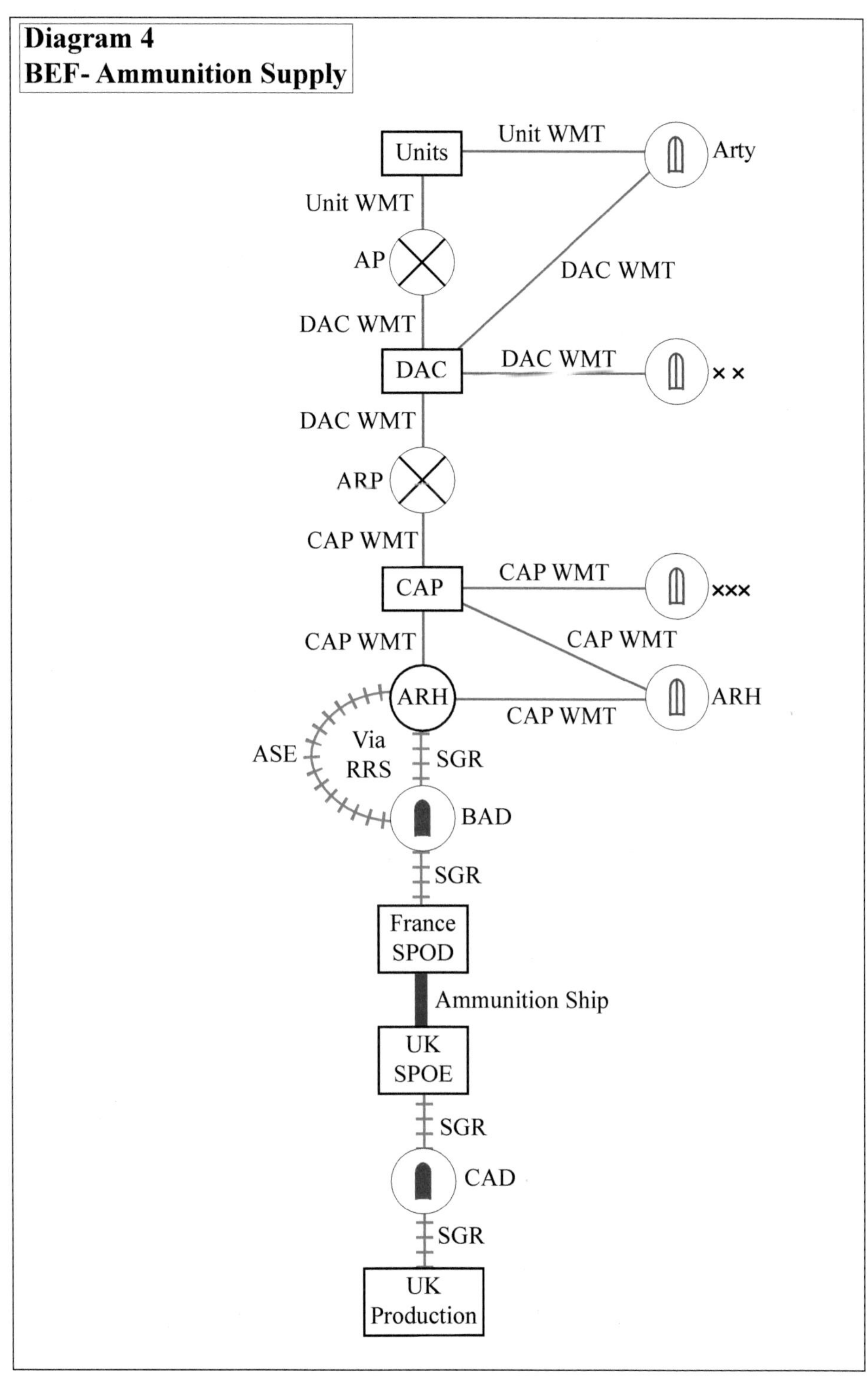
Diagram 4
BEF- Ammunition Supply
Units
Unit WMT
Arty
Unit WMT
AP
DAC WMT
DAC WMT
DAC
DAC WMT
× ×
DAC WMT
ARP
CAP WMT
CAP
CAP WMT
×××
CAP WMT
CAP WMT
ARH
ARH
CAP WMT
ASE
Via
RRS
SGR
BAD
SGR
France
SPOD
Ammunition Ship
UK
SPOE
SGR
CAD
SGR
UK
Production

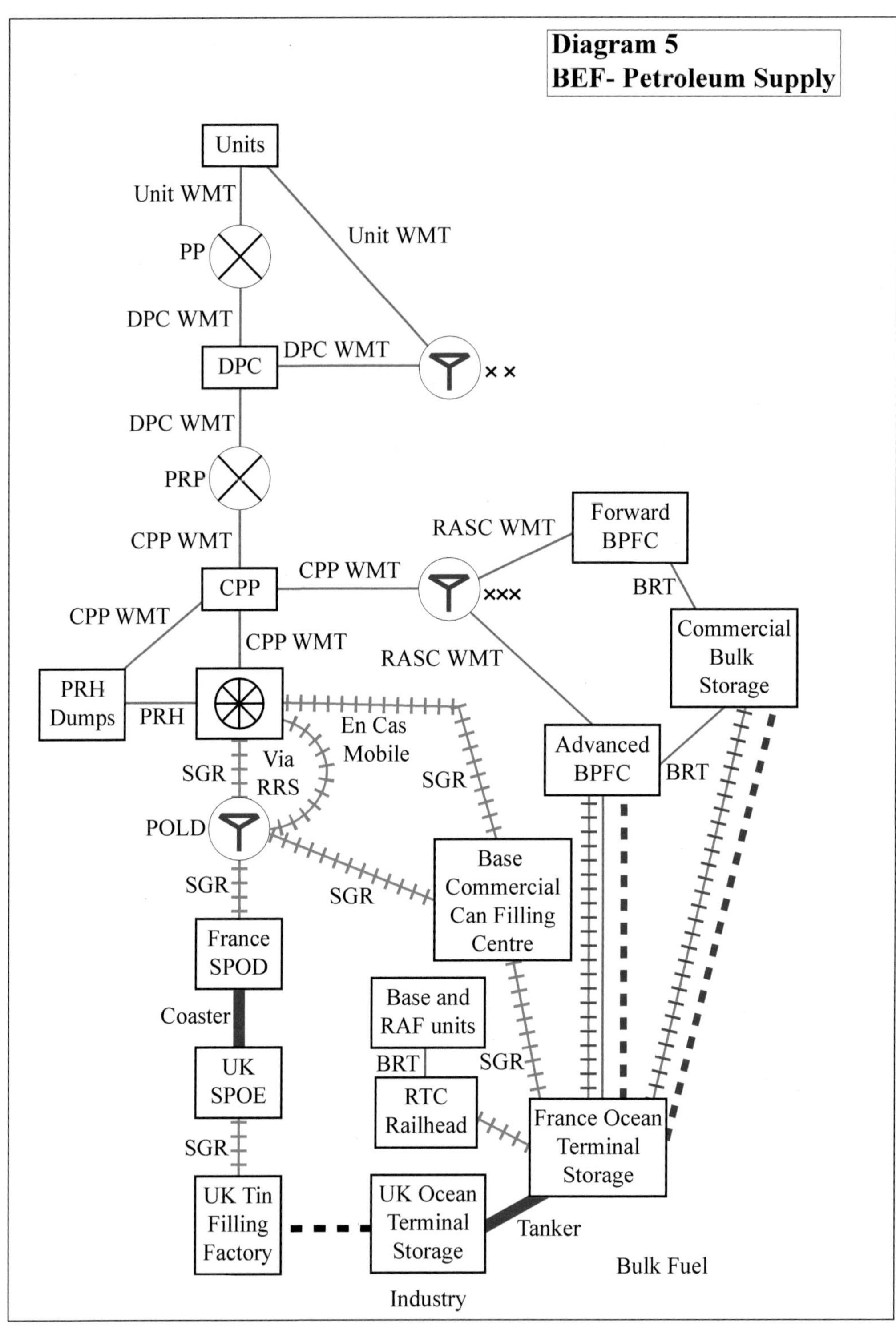
Diagram 5
BEF- Petroleum Supply
Units
Unit WMT
Unit WMT
PP
DPC WMT
DPC
DPC WMT
× ×
DPC WMT
PRP
CPP WMT
RASC WMT
Forward BPFC
CPP
CPP WMT
×××
BRT
CPP WMT
CPP WMT
RASC WMT
Commercial Bulk Storage
PRH Dumps
PRH
En Cas Mobile
Via RRS
SGR
SGR
Advanced BPFC
BRT
POLD
SGR
SGR
Base Commercial Can Filling Centre
France SPOD
Coaster
Base and RAF units
UK SPOE
BRT
SGR
RTC Railhead
France Ocean Terminal Storage
SGR
UK Tin Filling Factory
UK Ocean Terminal Storage
Tanker
Bulk Fuel
Industry

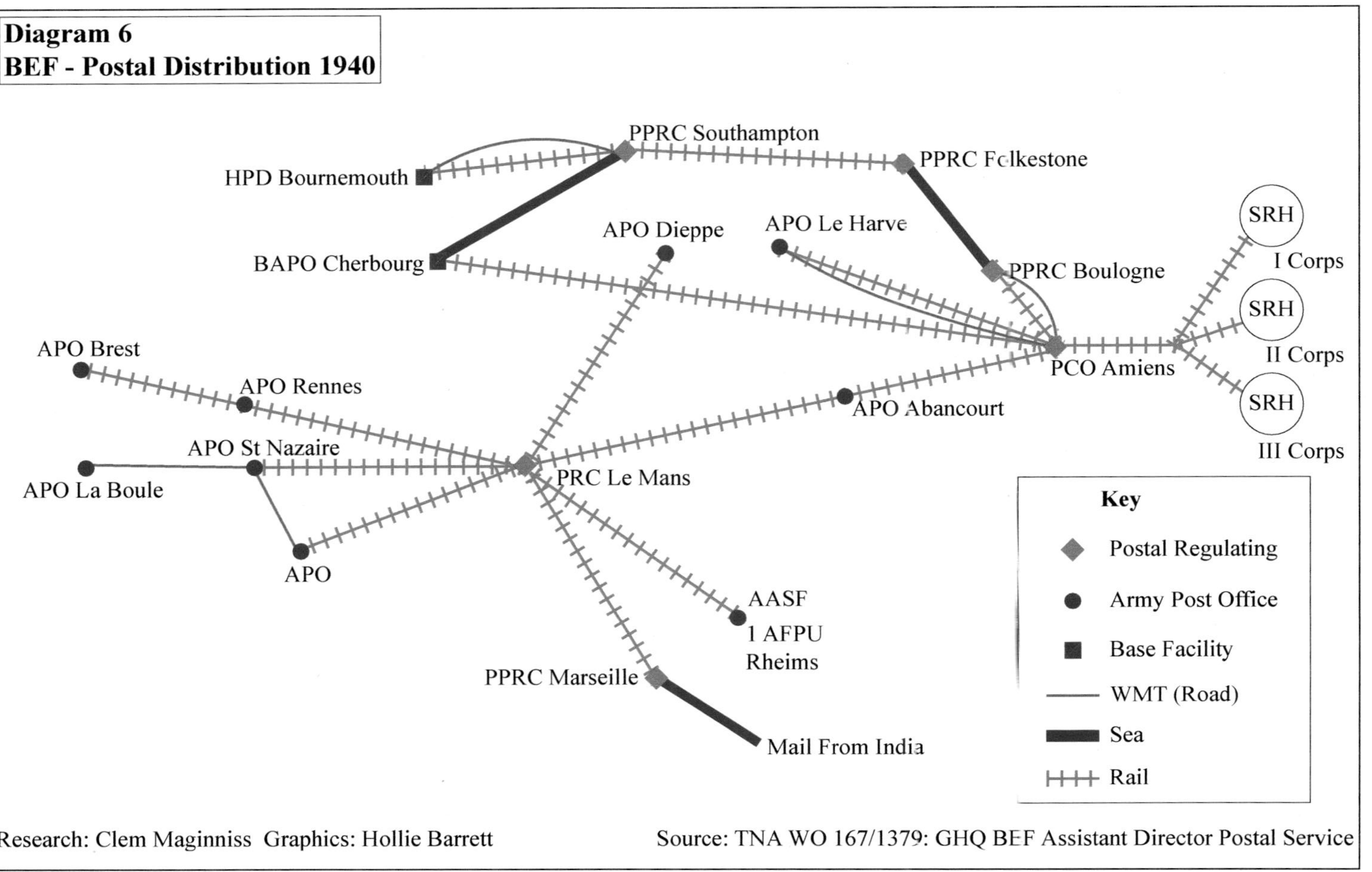

Research: Clem Maginniss Graphics: Hollie Barrett

Source: TNA WO 167/1379: GHQ BEF Assistant Director Postal Service

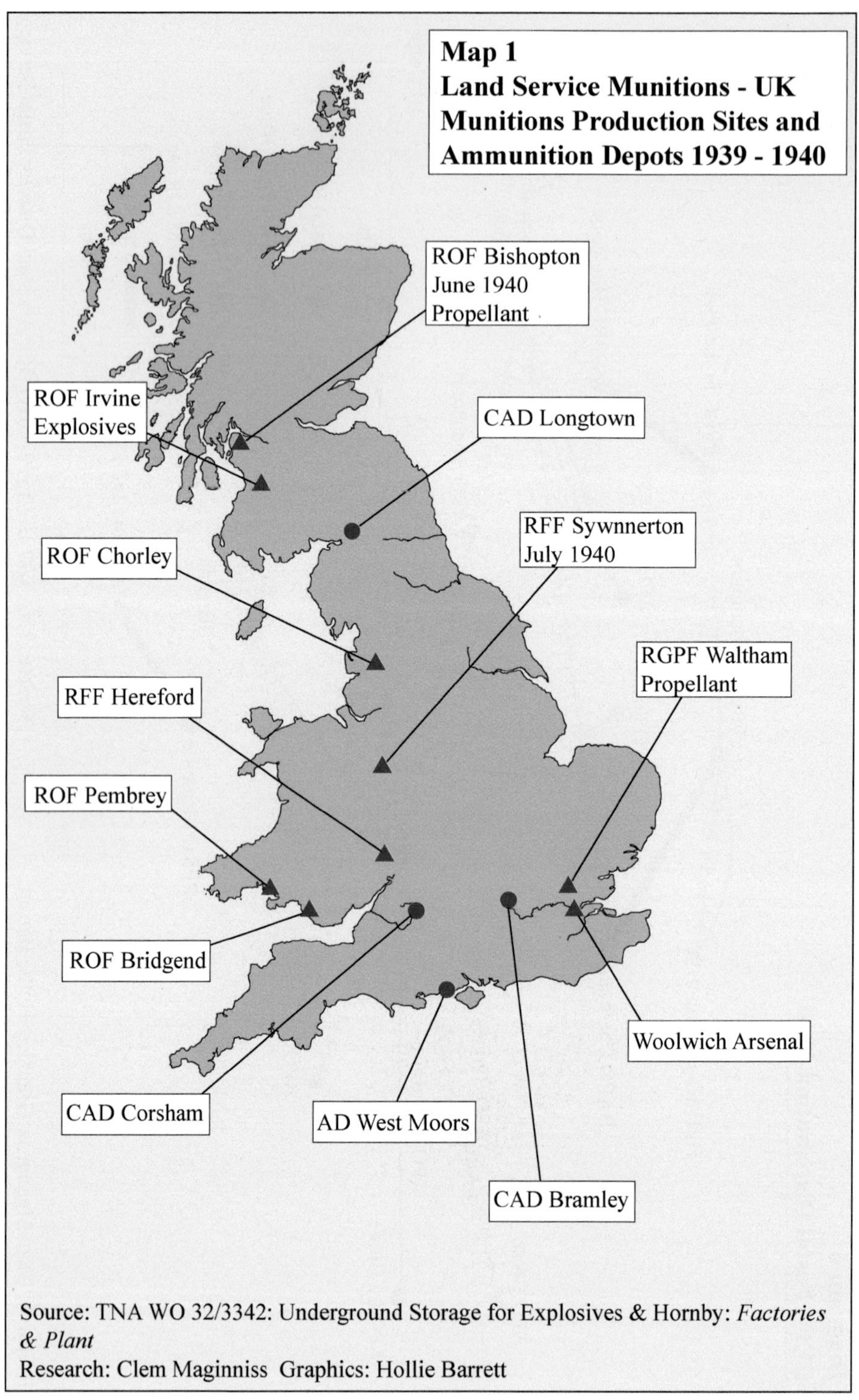

Source: TNA WO 32/3342: Underground Storage for Explosives & Hornby: *Factories & Plant*
Research: Clem Maginniss Graphics: Hollie Barrett

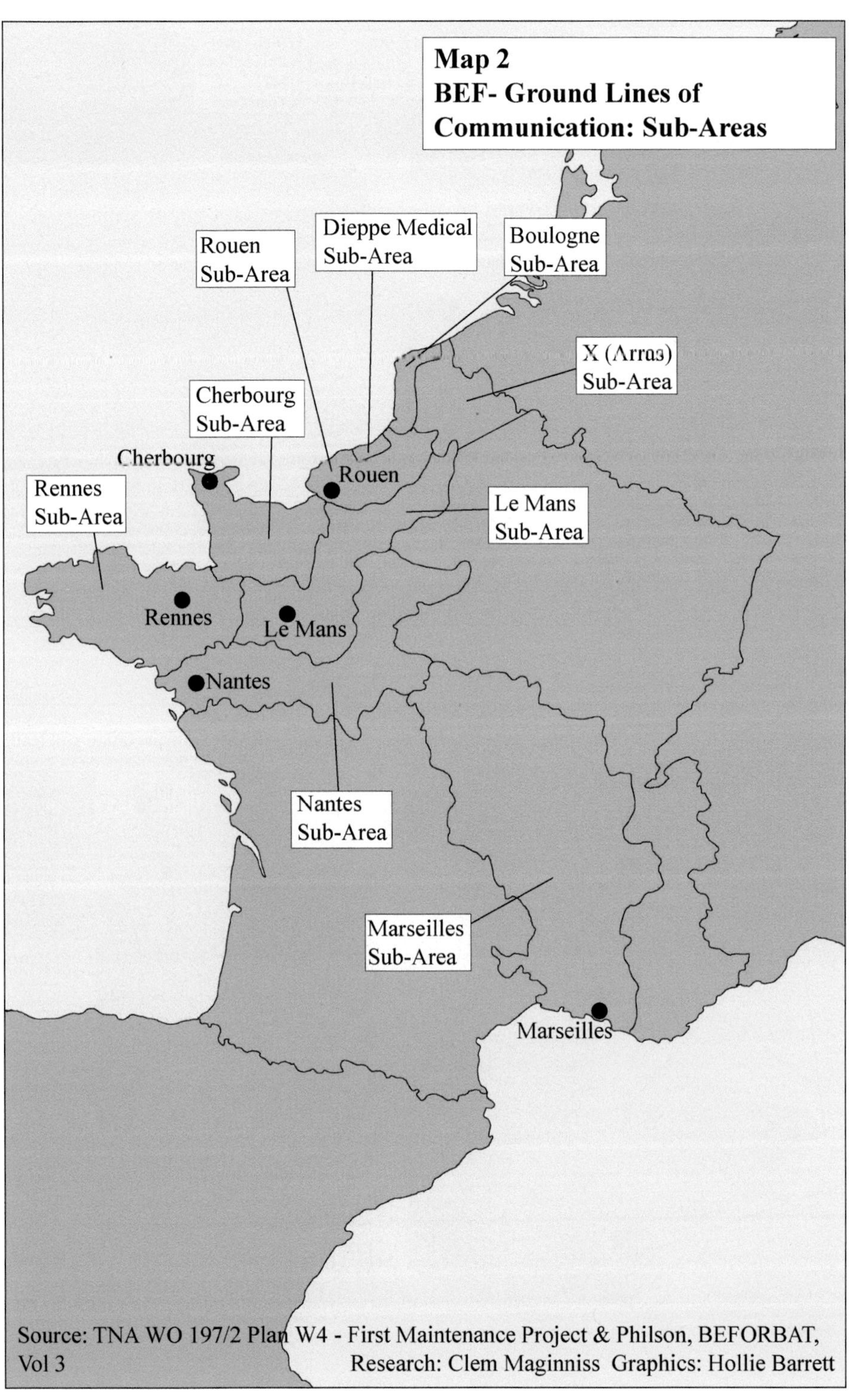
Map 2
BEF- Ground Lines of
Communication: Sub-Areas
Rouen
Sub-Area
Dieppe Medical
Sub-Area
Boulogne
Sub-Area
X (Arras)
Sub-Area
Cherbourg
Sub-Area
Cherbourg
Rouen
Rennes
Sub-Area
Le Mans
Sub-Area
Rennes
Le Mans
Nantes
Nantes
Sub-Area
Marseilles
Sub-Area
Marseilles
Source: TNA WO 197/2 Plan W4 - First Maintenance Project & Philson, BEFORBAT,
Vol 3
Research: Clem Maginniss Graphics: Hollie Barrett

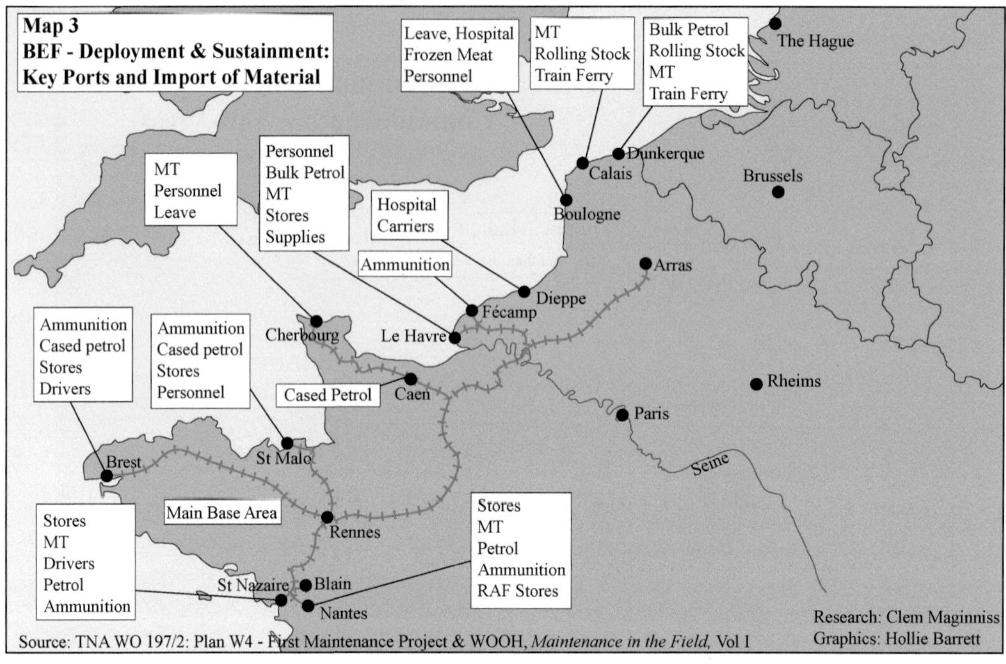
Map 3
BEF - Deployment & Sustainment:
Key Ports and Import of Material
Leave, Hospital
Frozen Meat
Personnel
MT
Rolling Stock
Train Ferry
Bulk Petrol
Rolling Stock
MT
Train Ferry
The Hague
Dunkerque
Calais
Brussels
Boulogne
MT
Personnel
Leave
Personnel
Bulk Petrol
MT
Stores
Supplies
Hospital
Carriers
Ammunition
Arras
Dieppe
Fécamp
Ammunition
Cased petrol
Stores
Drivers
Ammunition
Cased petrol
Stores
Personnel
Cherbourg
Le Havre
Cased Petrol
Caen
Rheims
Paris
Brest
St Malo
Seine
Main Base Area
Rennes
Stores
MT
Drivers
Petrol
Ammunition
Stores
MT
Petrol
Ammunition
RAF Stores
St Nazaire
Blain
Nantes
Research: Clem Maginniss
Graphics: Hollie Barrett
Source: TNA WO 197/2: Plan W4 - First Maintenance Project & WOOH, Maintenance in the Field, Vol I

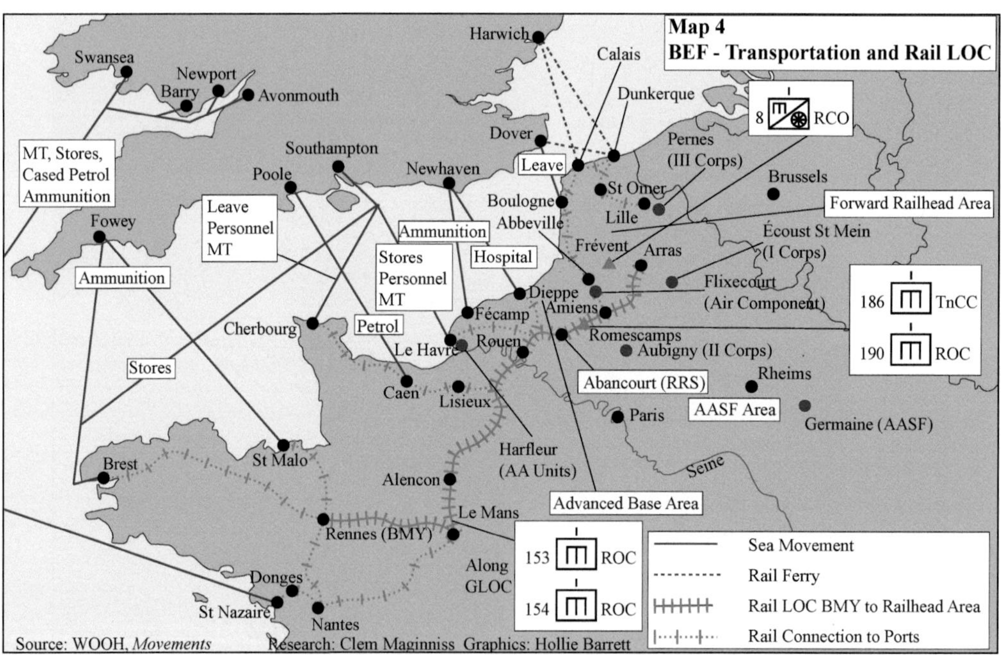
Map 4
BEF - Transportation and Rail LOC
Harwich
Calais
Swansea
Newport
Barry
Avonmouth
Dunkerque
8 RCO
Dover
Pernes
(III Corps)
MT, Stores,
Cased Petrol
Ammunition
Southampton
Poole
Newhaven
Leave
St Omer
Brussels
Boulogne
Lille
Forward Railhead Area
Leave
Personnel
MT
Fowey
Ammunition
Abbeville
Écoust St Mein
(I Corps)
Hospital
Frévent
Arras
Ammunition
Stores
Personnel
MT
Flixecourt
(Air Component)
186 TnCC
190 ROC
Dieppe
Amiens
Fécamp
Cherbourg
Petrol
Romescamps
Le Havre
Rouen
Aubigny (II Corps)
Stores
Abancourt (RRS)
Rheims
Caen
Lisieux
AASF Area
Germaine (AASF)
Paris
Harfleur
(AA Units)
Brest
St Malo
Seine
Alencon
Advanced Base Area
Le Mans
Rennes (BMY)
153 ROC
154 ROC
Along
GLOC
Donges
St Nazaire
Nantes
Sea Movement
Rail Ferry
Rail LOC BMY to Railhead Area
Rail Connection to Ports
Source: WOOH, Movements
Research: Clem Maginniss Graphics: Hollie Barrett

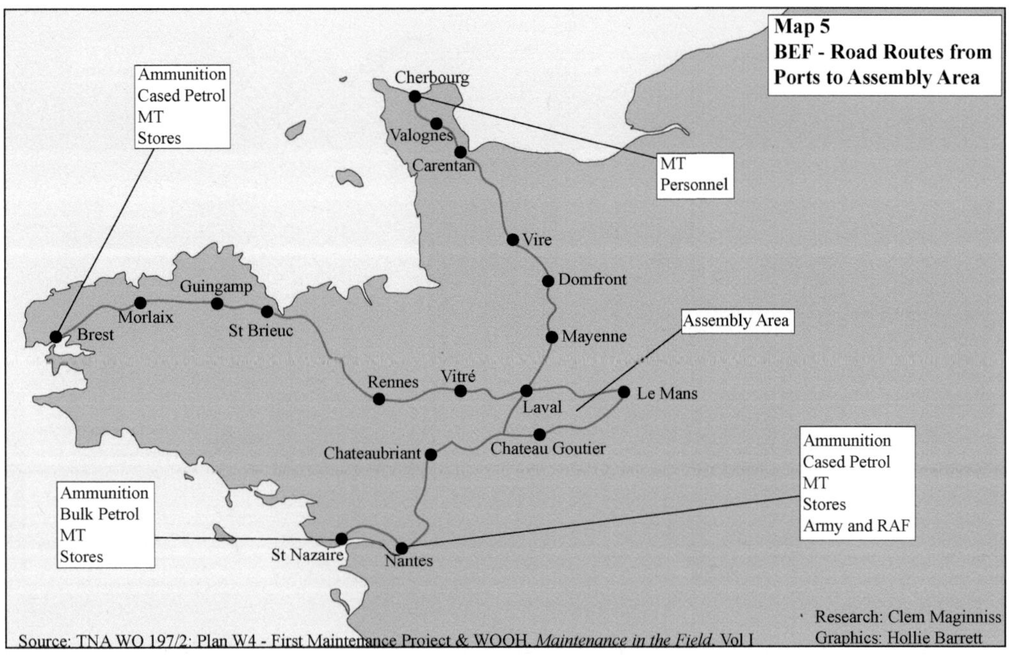
Map 5
BEF - Road Routes from Ports to Assembly Area
Ammunition
Cased Petrol
MT
Stores
Cherbourg
Valognes
Carentan
MT
Personnel
Vire
Domfront
Guingamp
Morlaix
Brest
St Brieuc
Mayenne
Assembly Area
Rennes
Vitré
Laval
Le Mans
Chateaubriant
Chateau Goutier
Ammunition
Cased Petrol
MT
Stores
Army and RAF
Ammunition
Bulk Petrol
MT
Stores
St Nazaire
Nantes
Research: Clem Maginniss
Graphics: Hollie Barrett
Source: TNA WO 197/2: Plan W4 - First Maintenance Project & WOOH, Maintenance in the Field, Vol I

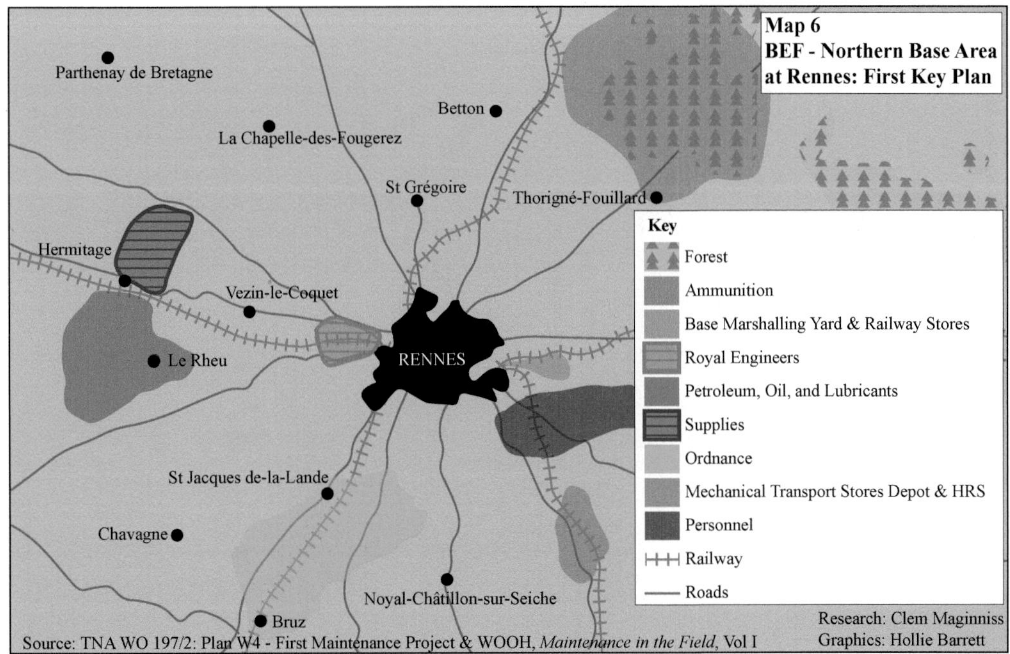
Map 6
BEF - Northern Base Area at Rennes: First Key Plan
Parthenay de Bretagne
Betton
La Chapelle-des-Fougerez
St Grégoire
Thorigné-Fouillard
Hermitage
Vezin-le-Coquet
RENNES
Le Rheu
St Jacques de-la-Lande
Chavagne
Noyal-Châtillon-sur-Seiche
Bruz
Key
Forest
Ammunition
Base Marshalling Yard & Railway Stores
Royal Engineers
Petroleum, Oil, and Lubricants
Supplies
Ordnance
Mechanical Transport Stores Depot & HRS
Personnel
Railway
Roads
Research: Clem Maginniss
Graphics: Hollie Barrett
Source: TNA WO 197/2: Plan W4 - First Maintenance Project & WOOH, Maintenance in the Field, Vol I

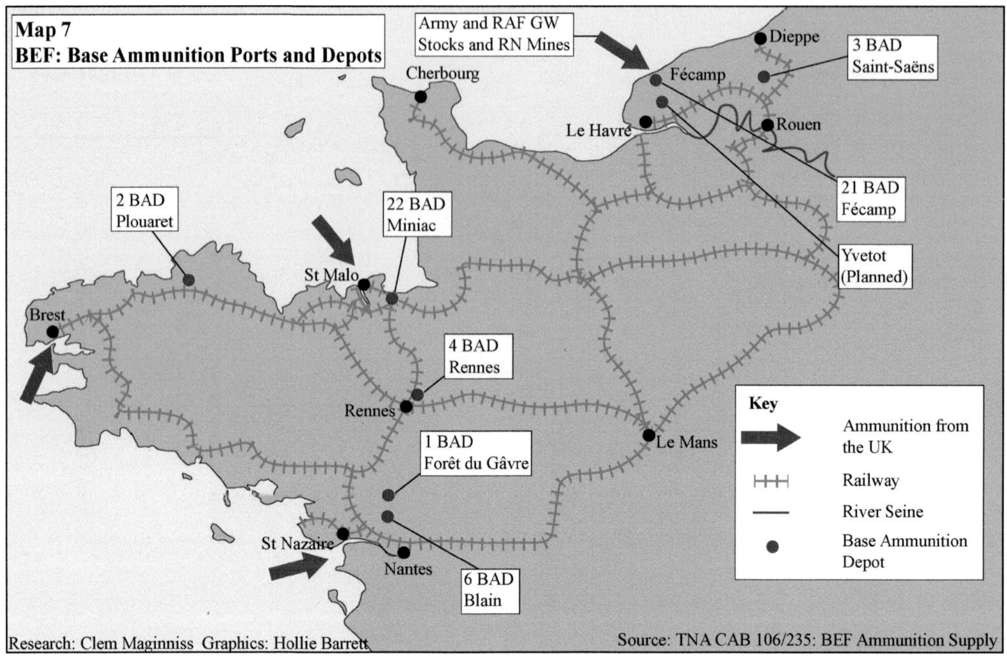
Map 7
BEF: Base Ammunition Ports and Depots
Army and RAF GW Stocks and RN Mines
Dieppe
3 BAD Saint-Saëns
Cherbourg
Fécamp
Le Havre
Rouen
21 BAD Fécamp
Yvetot (Planned)
2 BAD Plouaret
22 BAD Miniac
St Malo
Brest
4 BAD Rennes
Rennes
1 BAD Forêt du Gâvre
Le Mans
St Nazaire
Nantes
6 BAD Blain
Key
Ammunition from the UK
Railway
River Seine
Base Ammunition Depot
Research: Clem Maginniss Graphics: Hollie Barrett
Source: TNA CAB 106/235: BEF Ammunition Supply

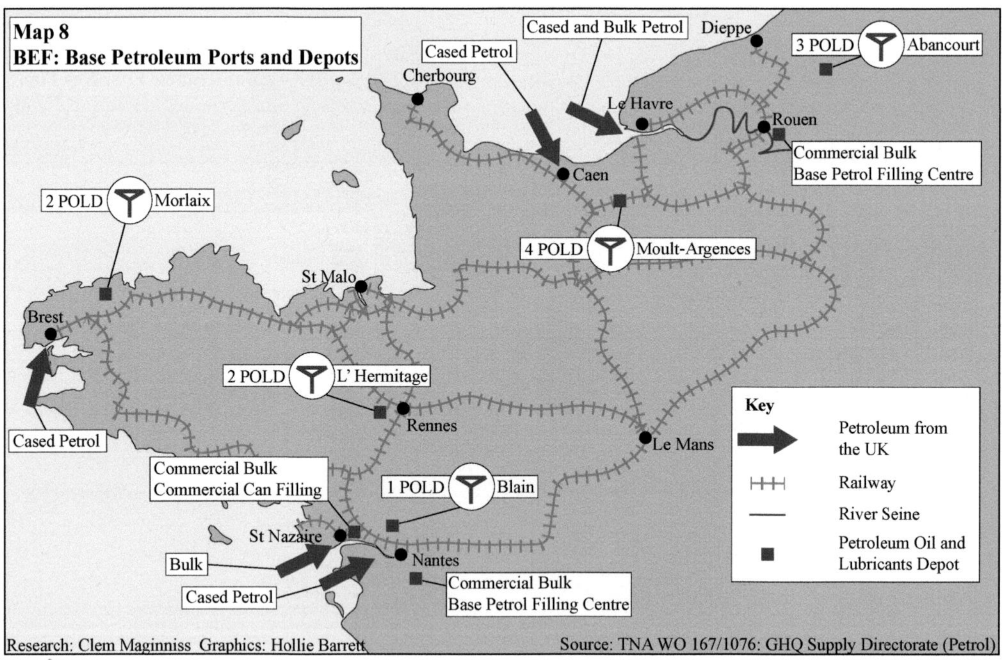
Map 8
BEF: Base Petroleum Ports and Depots
Cased and Bulk Petrol
Dieppe
3 POLD Abancourt
Cased Petrol
Cherbourg
Le Havre
Rouen
Commercial Bulk Base Petrol Filling Centre
Caen
2 POLD Morlaix
4 POLD Moult-Argences
St Malo
Brest
2 POLD L' Hermitage
Rennes
Cased Petrol
Le Mans
Commercial Bulk Commercial Can Filling
1 POLD Blain
St Nazaire
Bulk
Nantes
Cased Petrol
Commercial Bulk Base Petrol Filling Centre
Key
Petroleum from the UK
Railway
River Seine
Petroleum Oil and Lubricants Depot
Research: Clem Maginniss Graphics: Hollie Barrett
Source: TNA WO 167/1076: GHQ Supply Directorate (Petrol)

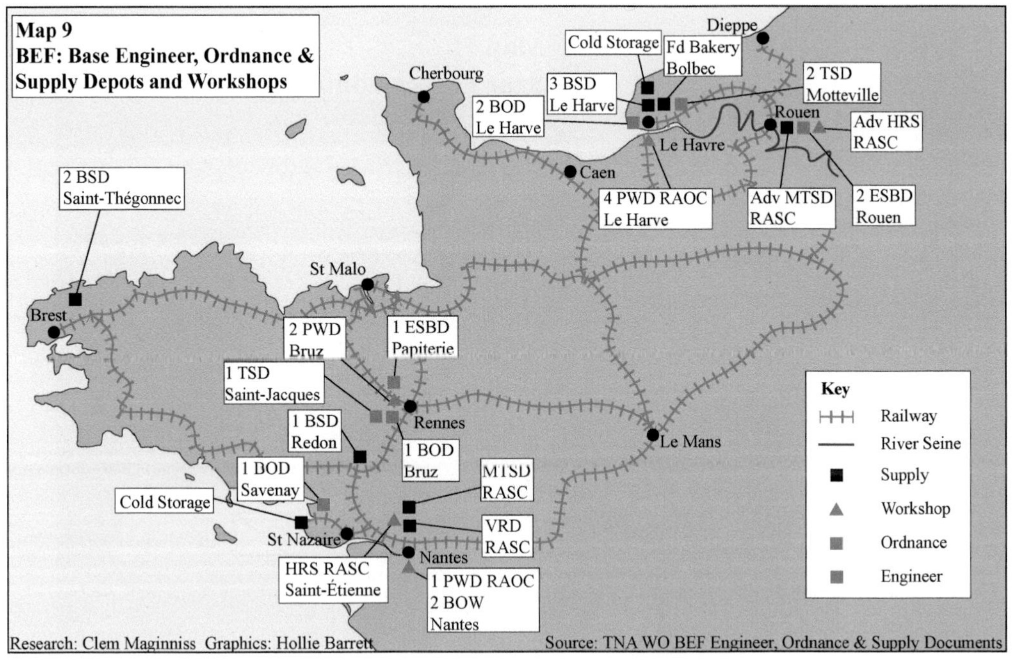
Map 9
BEF: Base Engineer, Ordnance & Supply Depots and Workshops
Dieppe
Cold Storage
Fd Bakery Bolbec
Cherbourg
3 BSD Le Harve
2 TSD Motteville
2 BOD Le Harve
Rouen
Adv HRS RASC
Le Havre
Caen
2 BSD Saint-Thégonnec
4 PWD RAOC Le Harve
Adv MTSD RASC
2 ESBD Rouen
St Malo
Brest
2 PWD Bruz
1 ESBD Papiterie
1 TSD Saint-Jacques
Rennes
1 BSD Redon
1 BOD Bruz
Le Mans
1 BOD Savenay
MTSD RASC
Cold Storage
St Nazaire
VRD RASC
Nantes
HRS RASC Saint-Étienne
1 PWD RAOC
2 BOW
Nantes
Key
Railway
River Seine
Supply
Workshop
Ordnance
Engineer
Research: Clem Maginniss Graphics: Hollie Barrett
Source: TNA WO BEF Engineer, Ordnance & Supply Documents

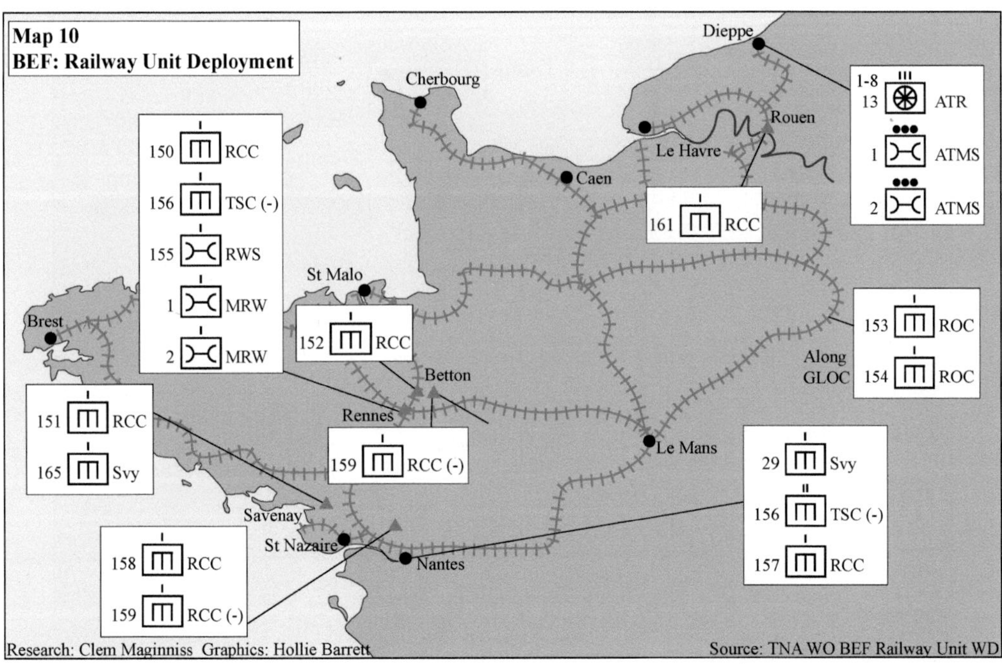
Map 10
BEF: Railway Unit Deployment
Dieppe
Cherbourg
150 RCC
156 TSC (-)
155 RWS
1 MRW
2 MRW
Rouen
Le Havre
Caen
1-8
13 ATR
1 ATMS
2 ATMS
161 RCC
St Malo
Brest
152 RCC
Betton
153 ROC
Along GLOC
154 ROC
151 RCC
165 Svy
Rennes
159 RCC (-)
Le Mans
29 Svy
156 TSC (-)
157 RCC
Savenay
St Nazaire
Nantes
158 RCC
159 RCC (-)
Research: Clem Maginniss Graphics: Hollie Barrett
Source: TNA WO BEF Railway Unit WD

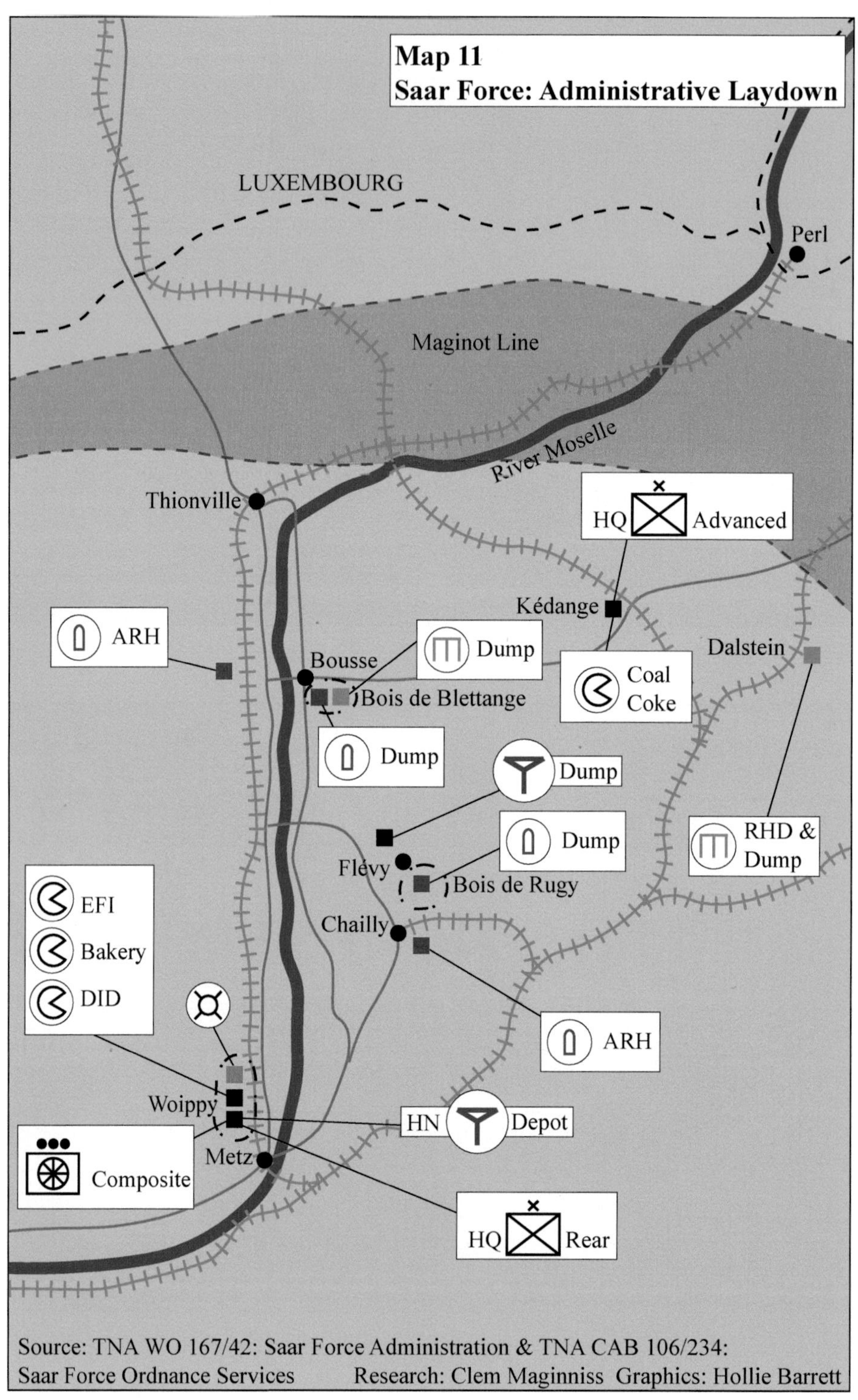

Source: TNA WO 167/42: Saar Force Administration & TNA CAB 106/234: Saar Force Ordnance Services Research: Clem Maginniss Graphics: Hollie Barrett

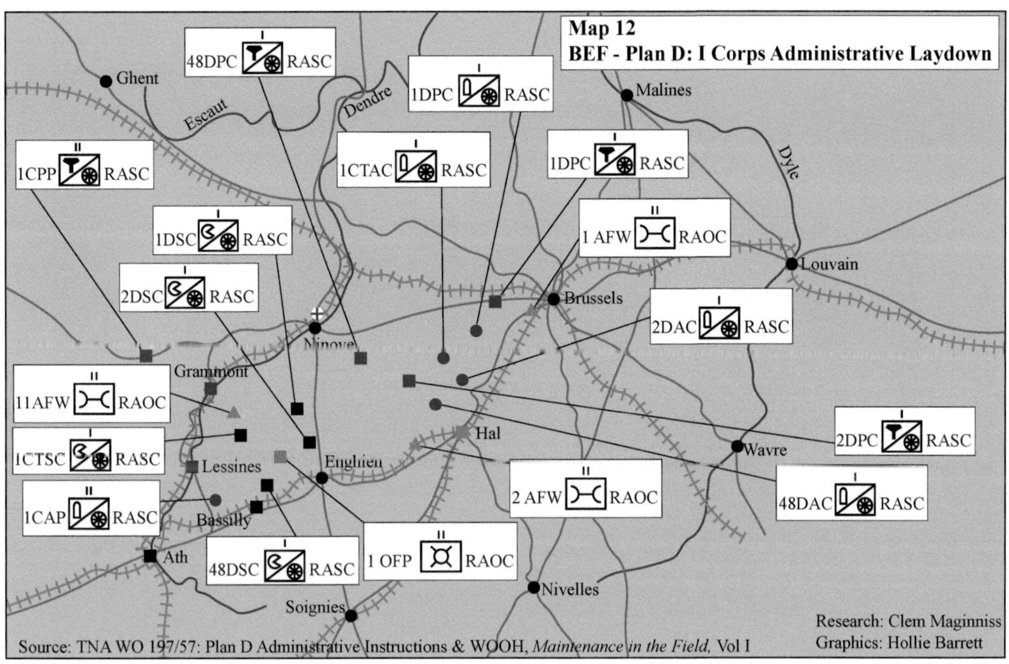
Map 12
BEF - Plan D: I Corps Administrative Laydown
Ghent
Escaut
Dendre
Malines
Dyle
Louvain
Brussels
Ninove
Grammont
Lessines
Bassilly
Enghien
Hal
Wavre
Ath
Soignies
Nivelles
48DPC RASC
1DPC RASC
1CPP RASC
1CTAC RASC
1DPC RASC
1DSC RASC
1 AFW RAOC
2DSC RASC
2DAC RASC
11AFW RAOC
1CTSC RASC
2DPC RASC
2 AFW RAOC
48DAC RASC
1CAP RASC
48DSC RASC
1 OFP RAOC
Research: Clem Maginniss
Graphics: Hollie Barrett
Source: TNA WO 197/57: Plan D Administrative Instructions & WOOH, Maintenance in the Field, Vol I

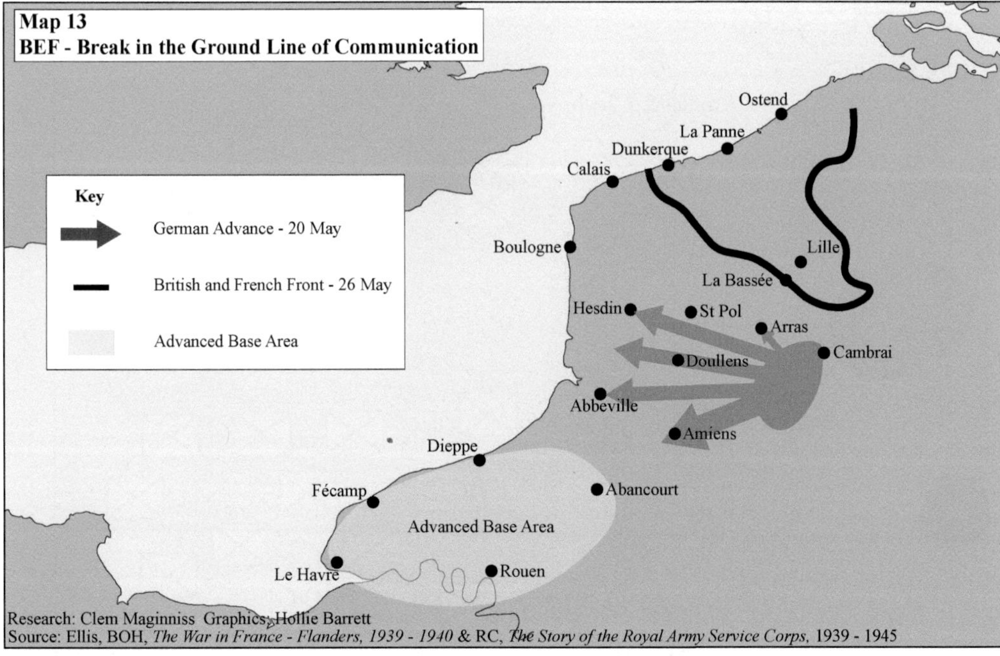
Map 13
BEF - Break in the Ground Line of Communication
Key
German Advance - 20 May
British and French Front - 26 May
Advanced Base Area
Ostend
La Panne
Dunkerque
Calais
Boulogne
Lille
La Bassée
Hesdin
St Pol
Arras
Cambrai
Doullens
Abbeville
Amiens
Dieppe
Abancourt
Fécamp
Advanced Base Area
Le Havre
Rouen
Research: Clem Maginniss Graphics: Hollie Barrett
Source: Ellis, BOH, The War in France - Flanders, 1939 - 1940 & RC, The Story of the Royal Army Service Corps, 1939 - 1945

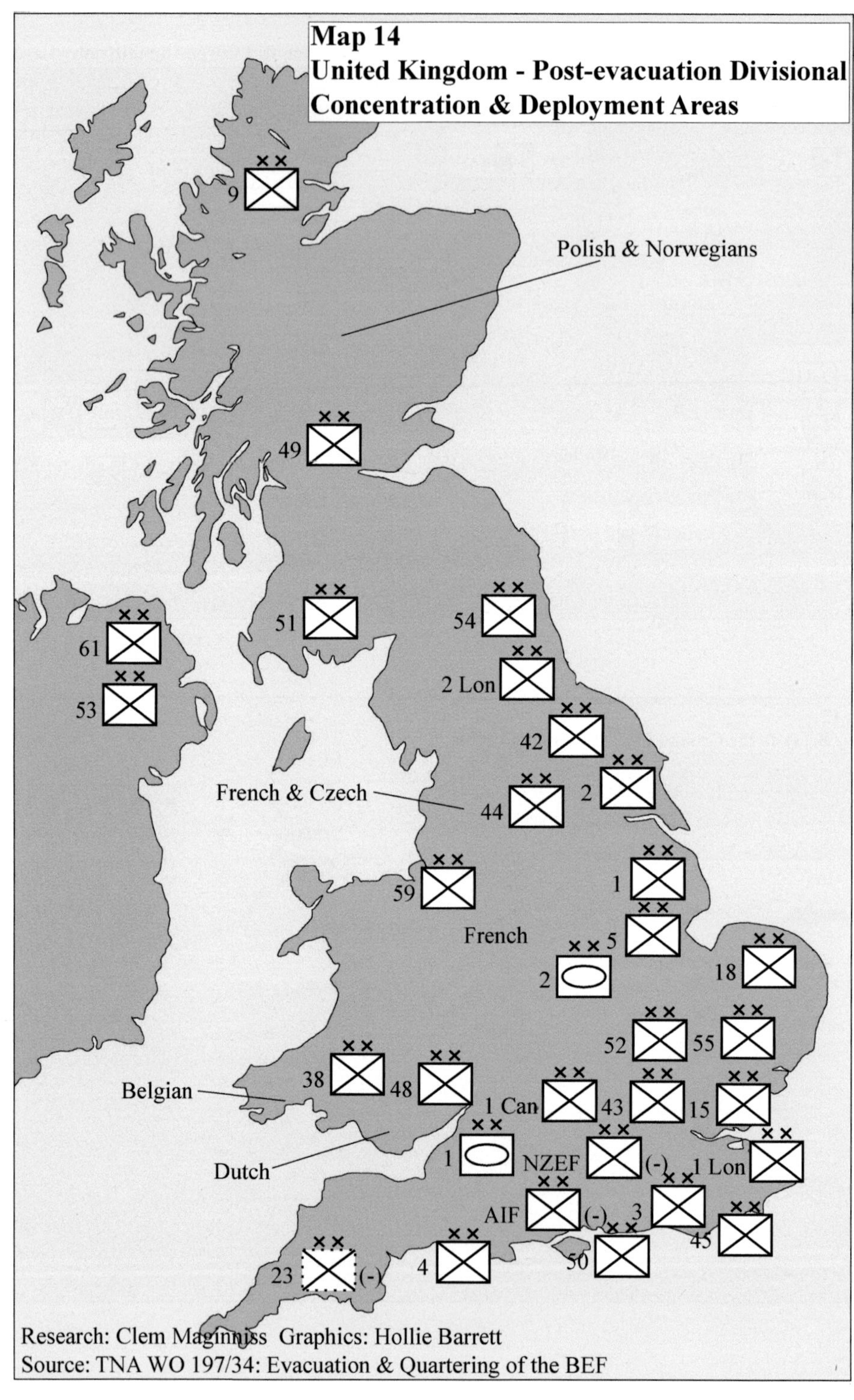
Map 14
United Kingdom - Post-evacuation Divisional Concentration & Deployment Areas
9
Polish & Norwegians
49
61
53
51
54
2 Lon
42
2
French & Czech
44
59
1
5
French
2
18
52
55
38
48
Belgian
1 Can
43
15
1
NZEF
(-)
1 Lon
Dutch
AIF
(-)
3
45
50
23
(-)
4
Research: Clem Maginniss Graphics: Hollie Barrett
Source: TNA WO 197/34: Evacuation & Quartering of the BEF

10

Taken for Granted
The Forgotten Logisticians of the BEF

Ration Trucks

As it expanded, the BEF increasingly relied on a plethora of logisticians whose skills and industry have mostly disappeared into the mists of time and even in 1940, were for the most part, taken for granted by the Staff planners and the soldiers. It is, therefore, the intention of this chapter to shed some light of the operations and contributions of these 'forgotten' logisticians. The establishment of in-Theatre training facilities to improve technical logistic skills and thus enhance effective and efficient outputs, included cookery schools located in the Base at Le Mans, Nantes and Rennes, and the creation of corps MT maintenance schools, the latter a recognition of the fragile standards in the BEF, which was creating a reduction of operational capability in the vehicle fleets. Failure to conduct checks and errors in drill caused damage to power-plants and transmissions, whilst varying standards of driving contributed to the RTA rate, killing and injuring personnel and writing-off vehicles.[1] These training facilities, whilst not viewed by most senior commanders as important in the wider scheme of military operations, were crucial to two areas of technical logistic activity which, affected nearly every soldier in the BEF and most of its daily functionality as a motorized Army.

Food Services in the BEF were, despite the skills of butchers and bakers within the RASC, in need of development, although at battalion level an interested CO could make a significant difference to the Soldiers' lot. Elsewhere, the fare tended to be of variable quality[2] and often rather monotonous,[3] which tempted many to dine outside the military envelope when they

1 Commander II Corps, Lieutenant-General Alan Brooke took a particular interest in his Corps MT school visiting the recently established facility at Sainghin on 18 December 1939. Danchev & Todman, *War Diaries, 1939-1945,* p.26.

2 Whilst individual soldiers complained about the standard of the food, unit war diaries were often as equally as vocal. TNA WO 167/1391: 2 MBU RAOC, WD 26 January 1940, described the food available to officers and soldiers as 'bad'.

3 Private Fred Gilbert of the Royal Warwickshire Regiment would have agreed. Whilst stationed in 2 Infantry Base Depot at Evreux in the Rouen Sub-Base Area, he wrote home on 15 March 1940 stating he was being fed on "bully beef and square biscuits" and on 20 March observed, "we had so much corned beef". Letters in the possession of Elaine Schafer & Rosemary Duxbury.

could.[4] Private Fred Gilbert, a Militiaman of the Royal Warwickshire Regiment, whose Mother ran a butcher's shop in Coventry, obviously enjoyed finer fare at home than the Army offered in France and always sought to dine away from the cookhouse, writing in letter that in a local café he eaten a meal of beef steak, two eggs, bread, *café au lait* and stewed apples for 12 francs.[5] The unknown author of the history of the 46th Division observed that many soldiers choose not to rely entirely upon Army catering to sustain them:[6]

> France, in May 1940, was not an uncomfortable country. Living was cheap, and the people friendly. If their light beer hardly rivalled Burton Special or Tetley's Dynamite, it was nevertheless only four pence a litre.[7] Egg and chips in the local *estaminets* made up for any failure of the Army cooks, who were still unversed in the many variations that can be performed with a tin of stew or bullybeef.[8]

Fortunately for the soldiers and the BEF's medical services, eating in the *estaminets* does not appear to have initiated any appreciable food health concerns in GHQ BEF. Admission to hospital for diarrhoea was 0.32 per 1,000 in October 1939 decreasing to 0.11 in January 1940 and rising slightly to 0.15 in March before dropping to 0.10 in April.[9] There were, however, potential longer term negative health aspects of the access to good living in France, an issue exposed by Second-Lieutenant FitzGerald: 'It was just as well the phoney war ended when it did, otherwise we might have died of obesity and cirrhosis of the liver. All that high living was not good for us'.[10] GHQ BEF was thus keen to improve military food in order to augment health, boost morale, reduce the reliance of the Soldier upon the local economy and to demonstrate that the chain of command took the matter seriously, although arguably it took the formation of the Army Catering Corps in 1941[11] to tackle the structural and cultural issues inherent in the broader context of an expanding Army.[12] Remarkably, senior logistic officers had also

4 Fred Gilbert wrote to his girl-friend Kay Hind on 17 March 1940 that eggs can be purchased from peasants and cafes for six francs a dozen and the troops eat them "at all hours."

5 In 1939, the exchange rate was approximately FF 173.22 to the £, so FF 12 equates to 17d or in decimal currency, 10p. In 2018, this equates to £4.32 using RPI. See *Measuring Worth* <www.paper-dragon.com and www.measuringworth.com>

6 Gilbert letter dated 17 March 1940.

7 In 2018 values, using the Measuring Worth UK conversions, this equates to £0.60 a pint. Private Fred Gilbert also recorded that some of his comrades had slightly more expensive tastes and purchased champagne at 25 francs (£8.77 at 2018 values using RPI), a bottle. Gilbert letter dated 15 March 1940.

8 na, *The Story of 46 Division, 1939-1945* (Graz: Styria University Book Press, nd but c1946).

9 See, Mellor, *Casualties and Medical Statistics*, p.176.

10 Desmond FitzGerald, *Many Parts: The Life and Travels of a Soldier, Engineer and Arbitrator in Africa and Beyond* (London: Radcliffe Press, 2007), p.90. As a Temporary Major, Desmond FitzGerald, later commanded 4 Field Squadron RE being admitted to the DSO for operations in NW Europe 1944-45. TNA WO 373/53/543: Recommendation for Award for FitzGerald.

11 The Army Catering Corps (ACC) was formed on 22 March 1941 under Army Order No 35, although it remained under the control of the RASC until 1 January 1965 when it became an independent Corps under the direction of the QMG.

12 This was not a new issue but the rapid expansion of the Army and the deployment of the BEF to France created additional challenges. In 1937 the Beck Study, initiated by the Secretary of State for War, Leslie Hore-Belisha, had proposed a series of enhancements covering the training and career progression of cooks but which fell at the first financial hurdle. Isidore Salmon was then appointed

P10.1 Water Distribution. A Bedford 4x2 OYC 500 gallon water bowser. The distribution of water is a lacuna in the logistic historiography of the BEF. (RLCM: A1e/MT/5765)

identified, as early as late November 1939, that the wastage of foodstuffs was a growing issue, with the DA & QMG I Corps reminding All Ranks that: 'Don't forget that your families at home are rationed, or about to be, and extravagance in the Field is a disgrace when families at home are short of everything'.[13]

Horrocks and Dowsers

Oddly, the provision of water, a critical resource, is rarely mentioned,[14] except in technical Royal Engineer documents and appears to have been taken for granted,[15] except where access for specific tasks was required such as chemical decontamination operations and major construction

as the Honorary Catering Advisor to the Army and in June 1938 offered a new report resulting in the selection of R A Byford as Chief Inspector of Army Catering in the rank of Colonel, the provision of catering advisors in Home Commands and the construction of a catering school at Saint Omer Barracks in Aldershot. One of the cultural issues, espoused by senior civil servants, including the Permanent Secretary of State at the War Office, was that catering was a civilian function and those that were employed within it should not hold military rank.

13 Open Circular entitled 'Economy' to All Ranks signed by Brigadier J G Halsted OBE MC. TNA WO 167/144: I Corps ADOS, I Corps CRO 30 dated 5 December 1939.

14 One exception is an entry in the 4 Division CRASC war diary, relating to the provision of an agreement for the supply of water to British Troops, with a note from Q Branch that this should be directed to DDST II Corps. As the RE were responsible for water supply, this request must relate to bottled mineral water. TNA WO 167/235: 4 Div CRASC, WD, 27 October 1939.

15 The RE regimental history of the period, Pakenham-Walsh, *The History of the Corps of The Royal Engineers*, Vol VIII, 1938-1948, does not mention water supply in the BEF.

projects, for example the aerodromes, which were usually sited in locations isolated from piped supply. The RE had though, an important remit because it was responsible for finding, raising, collecting, and where necessary, purifying, water before distribution to the user, water being required for drinking, cooking, hygiene, medical, laundry, heating, locomotives, construction, power generation, chemical decontamination, vehicle radiators, equipment wash-downs and animal care.[16] The BEF daily requirement for water was substantial with a Base general hospital needing 250,000 gallons and an infantry base depot 130,000. Logistic facilities were equally demanding as Table 10.1 illustrates, with the figures increasing as sites expanded and activity levels rose. Construction projects could consume significant quantities because 18-24 gallons[17] of water[18] were required for each cubic yard of a cement, sand and aggregate mix to produce concrete,[19] enormous quantities of which, were required to build pill-boxes on the Gort Line[20] and for aerodrome runways.

Table 10.1
BEF – Logistic Facility Daily Water Requirement Planning[21]

Facility	Gallons	Facility	Gallons
Base Ammunition Depot	10,000	Field Bakery	10,000
Base Ordnance Depot	60,000	Field Butchery	10,000
Base Supply Depot	2,500	Heavy Repair Shop	10,000
Engineer Stores Depot	20,000	Static Laundry	150,000
Transportation Stores Depot	80,000	MT Stores Depot	4,000[22]

Given the experience of the Great War on the Western Front, from which the RE published a comprehensive volume on water supply,[23] access to the French public system and the advice from a Professor of Hydrology who had served in a similar role in the Great War and was commissioned to serve on the staff of the Engineer-in-Chief at GHQ, the omission appears comprehensible. This officer had excellent connections with the Host Nation authorities and

16 See *WOOH*, *Military Engineering (Field)*, pp.321-322. For the outline planning aspects, see, Army Council, *Military Engineering*, Vol VII, *Accommodation and Installations*, pp.239-243, Water Supply Installations.
17 The quantity of water required depended upon the size of the coarse aggregate and its grading, the shape and nature of the solids, the power of their absorption and solubility, the aeration of the cement, the temperature of the mixing water and the amount of mechanical mixing. Army Council, *Military Engineering*, Vol VII, p.184.
18 Although clear water was required, purity was not a significant issue unless it contained impurities such as sodium chloride or sulphate in excess of 1.5%, a level above which, adversely affected the strength of the concrete. Ibid, p.185.
19 Ibid. Thus, a 100 cubic yard pill-box might require up to 2,400 gallons of water to construct it.
20 For details, see, Thurlow, *Building the Gort Line*, pp.274-285.
21 Table compiled from information in Army Council, *Military Engineering*, Vol VII, Plate 120.
22 A Vehicle Reserve Depot also required 4,000 gallons *per diem*. Ibid.
23 Army Council, *Military Engineering*, Vol VI, *Water Supply* (London: HMSO, 1922), which runs to 259 pages plus 181 plates and diagrams.

P10.2 Catering Challenge. To enhance BEF food services, emergency catering schools were established in France. (RLCM: ACC/1939/VR/NOR)

experts, which enabled the RE to generate agile planning and delivery work, activities that were supported by an officer on the GHQ Engineer Staff who had considerable experience of 'dowsing'. The hydrologist and dowser worked closely, despite their professional differences, in order to find suitable bore sites. Surprisingly they rarely disagreed, although the dowser was generally more precise in identifying a drill position.[24] There were however, three key logistic issues related to the distribution of potable water that were not resolved until April 1940.

Many units deployed to France deficient to the establishment of water carriage vehicles, a problem compounded by the dispersion of small units that relied on larger ones to treat and distribute their water. Initially, there was no water sterilizing powder available and it was early November 1939 before units began to receive supplies.[25] In the meantime, either Chlorosene, an anti-gas decontamination chemical or *Eau de Javel*, a French preparation of sodium hypochlorite, were used in conjunction with boiling, to create potable water.[26] The failure to ensure the

24 WOOH, *Military Engineering (Field)*, p.322.

25 BOH, *The Army Medical Services, Campaigns*, Vol 1, pp.19-20.

26 For details of the trials relating to pre-war water purification in the Army, see, Major E F W Mackenzie OBE MC RAMC, 'Report on a Series of Tests performed to ascertain the efficiency of the Ammonia

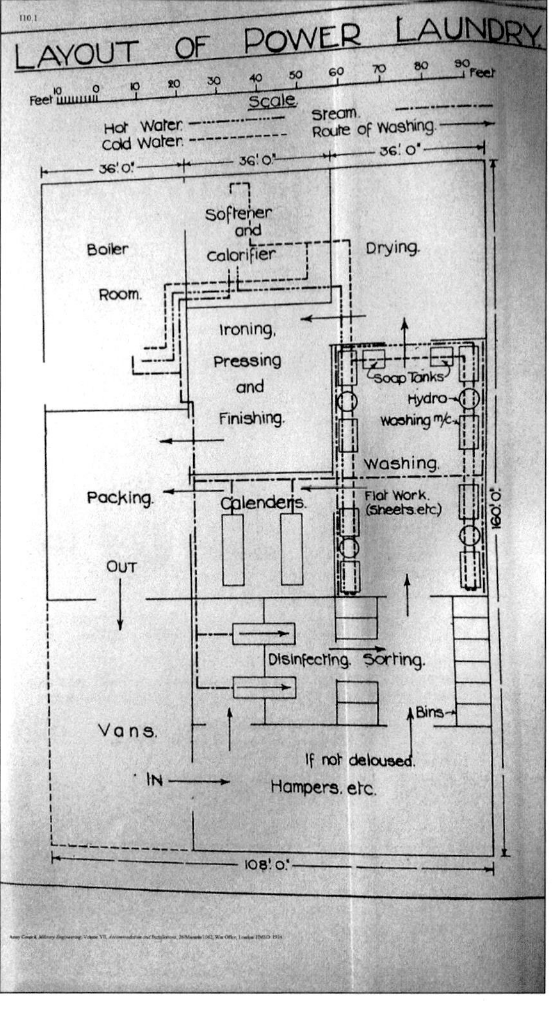

I10.1 Sketch Plan of a Power Laundry. The provision of laundry capability was essential for hospital care, chemical decontamination, and soldiers' health, hygiene and morale. (Army Council, *Military Engineering*, Vol VII, *Accommodation and Installations*, 26/Manuals/1062, War Office, London: HMSO: 1934)

provision of sufficient water treatment apparatus, known as the 'Horrocks Box', which was part of the Complete Equipment Schedule of the water carriage system, meant the correct dosage could not be guaranteed, so inevitably excessive amounts were used making the water distinctly unpalatable,[27] which no doubt, persuaded the troops that consuming the cheap French beer was a much better refreshment option.

Labouring Men

Crucial to all the successful completion of nearly every logistic task in the BEF was the provision of labour, for which the BEF had a voracious appetite. In the combat formations, units provided most of the manpower, although for specific tasks, including the construction of fortifications on the Gort Line and RAF aerodromes, units of the RE general works, road construction and artisan works companies supported by the AMPC were imported to conduct the tasks. Whilst much of the requirement focused upon the provision of unskilled manual labour, construction needed RE skilled manpower such as steel fixers, carpenters, concreters and plant operators,[28] these personnel being recruited from the road construction and building trade industries. Many had no military experience and the pressure to deploy the units to France meant tactical and weapon

Chlorine Treatment of Water applied by a Standardized Method', *Journal of the Royal Army Medical Corps*, Vol LXVI, No 4, April 1936, pp.217-227.

27 Crew, BOH, *The Army Medical Services*, *Campaigns*, Vol 1, pp.19-20.

28 As an example, see Thurlow, *Building the Gort Line*, p.283, Table 8.1, Typical schedule of operations, labour and time for a 100 cubic yard pill-box built in good weather.

training was minimal.[29] In the Base, the AMPC and locally employed civilians were crucial to logistic output, conducting in some locations, such as the Ordnance and Workshop facilities, technical, clerical and manual tasks.

Whether labour was skilled or unskilled, the efficient application of it to create effective outputs was a specialized craft and one that few commanders of any rank outside the RE and AMPC clearly understood, with the chain of command usually focusing upon acquiring numbers. In December 1939, there were 18,600 AMPC personnel in France but GHQ estimated that to support the planned expansion of the BEF, in June 1940, the requirement would be 60,000, with 5,000 a month thereafter until June 1941, a total figure of 120,000. Of the initial 60,000, the War Office identified that to meet current planned projects, 22,000 would need to be skilled RE trades with 582 qualified RE officers to command, lead, manage and administrate.[30] Such a demand could not be fully met from British sources and the War Office examined importing labour from Overseas Territories, especially Cyprus and Malta but the conditions imposed by the governments resulted in other solutions being sought. Local French labour, although restricted by French mobilization, was an option but the complicated identification, payment and accounting systems imposed by the Host Nation made this approach unsuitable in the corps areas, although in the Base, with static units and a more resilient administrative structure, it provided approximately 4,500 personnel per day in the period January – May 1940 to undertake a wide range of tasks.[31] For mobile labour, the most attractive was the formation of *Prestataire* companies[32] comprised of aliens, mainly from Austria, Germany and Spain who had sought asylum in France and who were subject to French military law, thus being liable for call-up.[33] The recruitment of Italians was also pursued, although the Host Nation authorities were uneasy on this matter, having decided not to apply *Prestataire* status because the French Government did not wish to be accused of using Italians to fight Germans.[34] Men of the interned Spanish International Brigade were another option, but because they were effectively deemed to be POWs, guards were required.[35] The total numbers from these sources was not expected to exceed 23,000 by June 1940 and 30,000 by June 1941. As a temporary measure, elements of three TA divisions, 12th (Eastern), 23rd (Northumbrian)[36] and 46th (North Midland)[37]

29 Ibid, p.159, notes that in one company that only three ORs had any military experience, the Company Sergeant Major, the Company Quartermaster Sergeant and a soldier who had last seen active service in the South African War of 1899-1902.

30 TNA WO 106/1777: The British Front, RE (Works) Organization in the BEF: 'Record of Meeting held in the War Office on 5th December 1939'.

31 WOOH, *Miscellaneous 'Q' Services*, p.5.

32 A *Prestataire* Labour Company was established under WE VI/1931/82/1 for 307 personnel, with 276 being labourers organised in four sections. Transport to sites required the provision of RASC or unit WMT and non-British personnel were paid at French Army rates. See, Philson, BEFORBAT, Vol 3 p.126.

33 TNA WO 167/56: HQ L of C, Q Branch, 892/Q dated 15 April 1940, 'Prestataire Memorandum of Agreement'.

34 Rhodes-Wood, *A War History of the Royal Pioneer Corps, 1939-1945*, pp.20-21.

35 Ibid.

36 For the 1940 ORBATs and short historical summaries of 12th (Eastern) and 23rd (Northumbrian) Divisions, see, Philson, BEFORBAT, Vol 4, pp.122-132.

37 For the 1940 ORBAT and short historical summary of 46th (North Midland) Division, see, Philson, BEFORBAT, Vol 5, pp.1-7.

P10.3 Master Butcher at Work. Warrant Officer II Gow RASC at Aldershot in 1935. (RLCM: B2/Depot & Supply/RLCA/21103)

were sent to France in April 1940 to conduct labouring duties, a decision which resulted in controversial decisions to commit them to combat operations.[38]

In the longer term, voluntary recruitment to the AMPC was opened to men in the 18-20 year group, which enabled these soldiers to be deployed to France because the National Service (Armed Forces) Act 1939 had committed not to send those serving under it to operational Theatres until they had reached the age of 20 years. This source was expected to provide 27,000 men to the AMPC by August 1940 and 5,000 per month thereafter. The numbers of older men that had been recruited in the UK also drove the need for additional sources of younger labour because it quickly because clear that many of the older members of the AMPC were not fit to undertake hard manual labour in austere field conditions,[39] an issue aggravated by the tough living arrangements compounded by the severe winter weather. Unsurprisingly, this resulted

38 For an operational review of the Labour Divisions, see, Tim Lynch, *Dunkirk 1940, Whereabouts Unknown, How Untrained Troops of the Labour Divisions were Sacrificed to Save an Army* (Stroud: Spellmount, 2010).

39 Apart from the resilience associated with age, the RPC history observed that many of these men were suffering from malnutrition partly generated by long periods of unemployment in the 1930s. Rhodes-Wood, *A War History of the Royal Pioneer Corps, 1939-1945*, p.19.

P10.4 Age Shall Not Weary Them? AMPC soldiers preparing for deployment to France in October 1939 at the former Butlins Holiday Camp at Clacton-on-Sea, which was opened in 1938. The age group is of note, with many soldiers wearing Great War medals, thus indicating men in their forties plus, the corporal on the left of the picture being an exception. The maturity of mant AMPC soldiers became increasing logistic and health issues during the harsh winter conditions in France. (RLCM: 2016/0067/130)

in AMPC companies having very high levels of sickness in relation to infantry battalions,[40] a situation exacerbated by the failure to resource the AMPC with even basic personal items. Initially, despite protests to the contrary, AMPC soldiers were only issued one set of uniform, which combined with undertaking dirty tasks with scarce opportunities for laundering and bathing, did little for morale, hygiene or presentation. During a gas warfare lecture to men of 44 and 45 AMPC Companies, it was discovered that the dreadful smell was not that of the live agent but the odour of unwashed bodies. The uniform issue was not resolved until an AMPC Group Commander forcefully responded, against the advice of the chain of command, directly to Viscount Gort after the C-in-C expressed his strong disapproval of the ragged and un-military state of AMPC soldiers.[41]

40 For example, 63 AMPC Company had 86 men admitted to hospital in December 1939, whilst constant minor accidents further eroded capability. Ibid.

41 Ibid, pp.27-28.

Reverse Logistics

Reverse Logistics,[42] which has a much longer history than its promotion in 2020 would suggest, had been highly developed on the Western Front in the Great War, initially by the Royal Flying Corps and then generally by the BEF. Whilst nearly all of the ground force material in late 1939 was initially uni-directional and consumable, the experience of the Great War[43] drove the need to quickly develop the processes of salvage,[44] reclamation,[45] reconditioning and re-issue of a variety of *materiel*[46] that was deemed vital to logistic sustainability, a task lucidly articulated in *Field Service Regulations*.[47] As the BEF expanded, Reverse Logistics was expected to create an increasingly important output that would reduce the cross-Channel shipping demand, whilst battlefield clearance supported the re-use and recycling of *materiel*,[48] activities that Great War experience suggested would rely upon French civilian female labour.[49] The Reverse Logistics culture was under-written by constant reminders to economise on the use of everything unless there was an operational imperative not to and the importance of the 'War on Waste' is brilliantly exposed in an open circular entitled 'Economy' to All Ranks signed by DA & QMG I Corps.[50] He ended the circular, with an exhortation: 'While we are not fighting the enemy let us fight

42 Operations related to the reuse of products and materials, by moving them from their typical final destination of use for the purpose of capturing value or proper disposal. Casualty and medical evacuation are in a conceptual sense, a component of Reverse Logistics.

43 Salvage also had a direct financial contribution. In the first six months of 1917, the estimated savings from the Paris Ordnance Depot totalled £961,716, which is £445,800,000 in 2016 values based on the *Measuring Worth UK* Economic Cost measuring the comparison of its relative share in terms of the total output of the economy. TNA WO 95/59: Director of Ordnance Services, WD, 11 November 1917.

44 Salvage had two components. Battlefield Salvage involved weapons, ammunition, shell cases, clothing, equipment, vehicles and trench materials, whilst Normal Salvage consisted of logistic items such as packing cases, wood baulks, dunnage, fuel tins, blankets and accommodation stores. Returnable fuel cans were not 'salvage' unless an item was classified as Beyond Economic Repair (BER).

45 As an example of the wide-ranging reclamation activities, in the month of September 1918, Fourth Army reclaimed 1,057 pounds of solder from bully-beef tins and the like. TNA WO 95/445/5: HQ Fourth Army, 'Solder, September 1918'.

46 Inclusive of clothing, boots, personal carriage equipment, webbing and haversacks, weapons, vehicles spares and brass shell cases.

47 Army Council, FSR, Vol I, *Organization and Administration*, pp.215-223, Sects 136-140, Evacuation of Material.

48 Battlefield clearance is the removal of all military *materiel*, including enemy, from the field of battle, inclusive of human remains, munitions, fuel, vehicles, equipment and supplies. In April 1940, OC III Corps Salvage Unit undertook a Great War Battlefield Tour of the La Bassee area and found derelict ammunition from the previous conflict. TNA WO 167 187: III Corps Salvage Unit, WD, entry 21 Apr 1940.

49 In 1918, the Paris Ordnance Salvage Depot employed nearly 4,000 French women and was focused on clothing salvage. Marcosson, *The Business of War*, offers an active contemporary description of its work.

50 Brigadier J G Halsted OBE MC (1890-1980) was commissioned into the Loyal (North Lancashire) Regiment in 1910, serving in France during the Great War. Twice wounded he received two MIDs and was awarded the MC. Having attended the Army Staff College (1923-1924) he commanded the 1st Loyals in Palestine (1936-1937) receiving a MID and being awarded the OBE. He was AQMG Aldershot Command (1938-1939). Awarded the CB for services in France he was promoted to Major-General in 1941 to assume the post of Chief Administration Southern Command and before retirement in 1946 he was Vice QMG at the War Office in 1945. See, Smart, *Biographical Dictionary of the British Generals of the Second World War*, pp.136-137.

P10.5 Saving Space. With transportation resources at a premium, innovative solutions were sought to reduce the volume of items for recycling. (RLCM: B6/Salvage/248/U/656)

waste'.[51] No doubt his crusade was well supported by the C-in-C who was well known for his antipathy to extravagance,[52] but this particular battle was obviously a hard fought one because in April 1940 a section appeared in *Army Training Memorandum* No 31, entitled, 'Waste is Criminal'[53] and another in July 1940, which stated, 'throughout the Army wastage of material, stores and equipment is still excessive'.[54]

By December 1939, the BEF's Controller of Salvage,[55] had completed a tour of inspection of the GLOC to identify the key development requirements for the Force.[56] Each corps was

51 TNA WO 167/144: I Corps ADOS, I Corps CRO 30 dated 5 December 1939.
52 Colville, *Man of Valour*, p.157.
53 Army Council, *Army Training Memorandum* No 31, April 1940 (War Office, 1940), para 9, p.14. A key sentence reads, 'All officers must realize and impress upon the troops under their command that, in a war of national endurance, waste in any form is criminal …'
54 Army Council, *Army Training Memorandum* No 34, para 8, p.7.
55 Lieutenant-Colonel W T C Huffham OBE MC (1880-1955) an officer of the West Yorkshire Regiment who had been the DAQMG of XIV Corps in 1916.
56 TNA WO 167/38: GHQ Controller of Salvage, 'Report on Tour of Inspection of Lines of Communication carried out from 15-22 December 1939' by Lt Col W T C Huffham OBE MC, SC/13/51/5 nd but late December 1939.

P10.6 War on Waste. Damaged packaging inevitably created product loss. (RLCM: B3/SRB/NOR)

assigned a controller to coordinate the work of the Salvage Units[57] the task being reflected by the continual round of educational and information gathering visits recorded in the war diaries.[58] Military equipment, including weapons, vehicles, webbing, wireless sets, tentage, ammunition brass and accommodation stores were usually returned through the Ordnance system for repair, reissue, return to UK, destruction or local sale, with RE and RASC specialist equipment following a similar process through the relevant chain, although there were occasions when limited access to, or disruption of, transportation interrupted the process.[59] Scrap metal, tyres and waste oil were all items that required careful management with the collection and disposal of this material dependent to an extent upon the effort required to collate and move it, small

57 III Corps was allocated, 7, 9, 10 and 13 SUs. TNA WO 167/187: III Corps Salvage, WD, entries April 1940, with 10 SU assigned to 51st (Highland) Division and 13 SU initially to 50th (Northumbrian) Division.

58 The war diary for I Corps Salvage is not held in the TNA.

59 On 5 February 1940, 4 Division CRASC reported that RTO Arras could not accept any RASC vehicle recoveries to the Base for 14 days. Whilst the reason is not explained in the war diary, the poor weather conditions were probably responsible. TNA WO 167/235: 4 Division CRASC, WD, 5 February 1939.

quantities in isolated locations usually being disposed of through local commercial arrangements with the Host Nation.[60]

Some *materiel* circulating within the BEF's Reverse Logistics system was vital to the distribution system. Divisional HQs and Supply Columns were constantly reminding units to return sacks for vegetables, potatoes and bread, the reuse of which, were essential to effective operation of the distribution system,[61] whilst the RE were keen to recover and reuse cement sacks[62] and unused sandbags.[63] Units were also directed to return empty packing canvas and cases, cardboard cartons, cotton wool, paper and cardboard sheets to the Salvage Units. To save space and thus transport, units were requested to move such items inside returning packing cases.[64] The reintroduction of re-useable cans to the fuel distribution system created another item in the Reverse Logistics loop that became increasingly critical to combat capability, a fragility that was initially under-pinned by the reliance on the disposable 'flimsy', which the soldiers of the BEF were culturally attuned to throw away, a problem that required prompt attention to resolve.

Indeed, the handling of the empty fuel 'flimsies' of which, there was soon a mounting number became a significant task. Scattered units were authorised to sell them locally, which of course created the need for financial audits, but most were returned to salvage dumps or Corps Petrol Railheads from where they were returned the Base POL depots. These 'tin dumps' became a tactical issue because the shiny containers were easily spotted from the air and prompted various attempts to reduce the signature. Flattening the tins was one solution, which also reduced the volume required for transportation but was usually labour intensive, although HQ 1 POLD acquired the services of a diesel road roller to undertake the task.[65] Other uses were also found for the tins, with 4th Division instructing units to deliver them to Petrol Points for onward dispatch to the Royal Engineers for the revetting of defence works,[66] whilst other logisticians utilized them as dunnage for box and case stacks at field sites.[67]

Clean and Tidy

Two key logistic functions, which in the regimental histories receive no attention, were clothing and laundry. In many respects, the deployment in September 1939 created an appreciable challenge in the storage and issue of clothing because the small initial stocks of summer uniforms to meet the First Contingent in the autumn did not meet the demands in

60 TNA WO 167/38: GHQ Controller of Salvage, 'Report on Tour of Inspection of Lines of Communication carried out from 15-22 December 1939'.
61 TNA WO 167/305: 50 Division CRASC, Instruction, 'Supply Arrangements during Thaw Precautions' dated 21 February 1940.
62 TNA WO 167/205: HQ 2nd Division, A&Q, 2 Div Admin Order No 66, dated 4 January 1940, para 1, Salvage.
63 DA & QMG I Corps noted that each hessian sandbag cost 5d, which in 2108 money using the RPI, is £1.28. TNA WO 167/144: I Corps ADOS, I Corps CRO 30 dated 5 December 1939.
64 TNA WO 167/205: HQ 2nd Division, A&Q, 2 Div Admin Order No 66, dated 4 January 1940, para 1, Salvage.
65 TNA WO 167/1148: 1 POLD RASC, WD, entry 12 April 1940.
66 TNA WO 167/235: 4 Division CRASC, WD, 24 October 1939.
67 TNA WO 167/1095: 1 LOC Railhead Company RASC, WD, entries March 1940.

early October for winter items and although stocks were dispatched from UK, a perfect storm started to brew with withdrawals of summer clothing which needed to laundered and stored, clashing with receipts and issues of winter clothing. These initial shortages were so acute that some soldiers, even in regular divisions, deployed wearing the 1922 Pattern Service Dress.[68] The effective prosecution of these tasks was complicated by insufficient suitable storage and no time to generate a sustainable issue plan,[69] a scenario exacerbated by the failure to provision a BEF military laundry capability when it deployed to France, the necessary equipment being awaited from production. Hastily arranged local contracts were therefore, the only solution,[70] although the Royal Engineers were capable of constructing a suitable facility and installing the equipment and supporting utilities.[71]

From an organizational perspective, the most prolific users of the service were the Dieppe Medical Base Sub-Area (MBSA) and the general hospitals, although the Returned Stores Depot, which handled considerable quantities of clothing, also required support. With little available commercial capability accessible in the Main Base Areas and the transport arrangements adding to turn-round times, a laundry in Rouen was contracted to support the MBSA, washing 200,000 pieces weekly. Another laundry in Le Harve delivered a similar output, whilst smaller laundries were either contracted or staffed with RAOC personnel.[72] In early January 1940, the GHQ Ordnance Directorate began planning for the seasonal withdrawal of approximately 1.6 million items of winter clothing including woollen underwear, leather jerkins, greatcoats, sheepskin-coats, third blankets and Boots, Rubber (Knee & Thigh), all of which required cleaning and maintenance in preparation for storage and future reissue.[73] Selected to undertake this task was the largest of the dry cleaning companies in Paris, *Blanchisseries et Teintureries de France* located at Boulogne – Billancourt, a suburb of Western Paris and equipped with modern plant.[74] Clothing arrived by rail at a siding adjacent to the works, and although the commercial company undertook all the dis-infection, cleaning and repair operations, which was extended to web equipment, a RAOC Laundry Detachment of 26 was responsible for conducting checks on standards and controlling all receipts and issues at the railhead. When the enemy occupation of Paris became imminent, all the stocks of clothing and equipment were rendered unusable by the application of caustic soda.[75]

68 TNA WO 167/364: HQ 9th Infantry Brigade, WD, entry 15 October 1939. 9th Brigade was in 3rd Division, II Corps, Ellis, BOH, *The War in France and Flanders*, p.362.
69 Some items, notably woollen gloves, were not available for general Christmas issue. WOOH, *Ordnance Services*, p.145.
70 Local laundry facilities in Nantes had been recorded in No 2 Key Plan from information obtained during the reconnaissance in September 1938 but as it transpired, the capability was small and focused upon French requirements. Ibid, p.147.
71 Army Council, *Military Engineering*, Vol VII, *Accommodation and Installations*, pp.204-208, Laundries and Plate 117, Power Laundry Layout.
72 WOOH, *Ordnance Services*, p.147.
73 TNA WO 197/42: Saar Force Administration, Force W Area Routine Order RO No 8 dated 18 April 1940, Ser 3, Winter Clothing. Oil heating stoves were also withdrawn.
74 To create resilience in case of the works being disabled or destroyed, a dormant contract was let with another company, *Blanchisserie de Frenelle*, which was able to deliver all the cleaning requirements except for leather jerkins. Ibid, p.154.
75 Ibid.

Another key improvement to morale as well as being essential to health and hygiene and thus operational capability, was access to effective bathing facilities. In this respect, the provision or sometimes otherwise of this amenity, is a microcosm of the differentials between the logistic capabilities in the corps areas and those in the Base and the role of support in sustaining the Soldier. Whilst even at corps level it had taken until March 1940 for I Corps to receive and establish its Corps Troops Mobile Bath Unit (MBU)[76] in four locations,[77] at No 2 Base Infantry Depot,[78] Private Fred Gilbert of the Royal Warwickshire Regiment wrote in the same month, that, "Baths are few and far between......we have to wash in water from a pond instead of a well."[79] The RAOC was responsible for the provision of the divisional MBU, although the establishment table indicates that it was effectively an All Arms unit.[80] Capable, in theory, of bathing 120-140 men per hour, the MBU was transported in 2 x 3 ton lorries and consisted of 20 personnel commanded by a subaltern, and included a barber and a plumber. 2 MBU had been operational since 1 December 1939 working closely with 8 Field Hygiene Section RAMC[81] to ensure effective bathing and dis-infection facilities.[82] The OIC 2 MBU, Captain Rowe, had by early January 1940, arranged the establishment of a number of fixed civilian and temporary military bathing venues in the Doullens area, although one of the latter erected by a contractor was found to be unsuitable because the sullage water flowed through a private garage into the street.[83] By mid-month, 2 MBU held 1,000 sets of underwear, winter stockings, shirts and battle-dress, to ensure every soldier had a clean set of clothes to wear once they had bathed.[84] The shortage of spare clothing, including boots, was exacerbated by the cold wet conditions and the often, thick mud in which, some defensive positions were constructed, the problem appearing as early as late October 1939, with some units purchasing Frenchmen's blue canvas trousers, an acquisition considered to be 'invaluable'.[85]

Whilst the weather disrupted some of the construction activities, interrupted troop movement and froze the water, by late January unit bathing periods were 'very numerous',[86] with the facilities at Bavincourt 'working at full capacity' and across the 2 MBU sites, 8,787 men took a bath or shower in the first week of March 1940.[87] Despite this output, the delousing rate was running at seven men per 1,000,[88] which provided an imperative to complete the dis-infestation facility at Bavincourt, which was planned to handle 21,000 soldiers per week and issue them with clean

76 TNA WO 167/1395: 7 MBU RAOC.
77 TNA WO 167/205: HQ 2nd Division A&Q, 1 Corps Admin Order 113 dated 10 March 1940, Sect 11, Baths. This document was SECRET because it gave the grid references of the MBU sections and the unit bath timings. It is unlikely however, that most soldiers considered their bathing activities a military secret.
78 TNA WO 167/122: 2 Base Infantry Depot WD, December - June 1940. 2 IBD was located at Evreux.
79 Letter dated 20 March 1940 from Private Fred Gilbert to his girlfriend Kay Hind in Coventry.
80 For the WET (II/1931/26/1) of a MBU see, Philson, BEFORBAT, Vol 1, p.170.
81 TNA WO 167/1462: 8 Field Hygiene Section RAMC, WD, December 1939 - April 1940.
82 TNA WO 167/1391: 2 MBU RAOC, WD, December 1939.
83 TNA WO 167/1391: 2 MBU RAOC, WD, 4 March 1940.
84 The dirty items were taken to a commercial steam laundry in Amiens and then returned to 2 MBU. TNA WO 167/1391: 2 MBU RAOC, WD, 11 January 1940.
85 TNA WO 167/702: 3rd Grenadier Guards, WD, 27 October 1939.
86 TNA WO 167/1391: 2 MBU RAOC, WD, 23 January 1940.
87 TNA WO 167/1391: 2 MBU RAOC, WD, 23 March 1940.
88 TNA WO 167/1391: 2 MBU RAOC, WD, 30 March 1940.

clothes, blankets and when necessary, web equipment.[89] These outputs did not however, come without significant industry from the men of 2 MBU because the unit operated seven days a week from 0700 to 2200[90] but the 2 MBU appears to have been a motivated organization with plenty of innovative minds.[91] With bathing in full swing, the OIC was then able to consolidate the *ad hoc* commercial arrangements to a centralized facility based upon contracting the facilities of the Doullens Municipal Baths for a year, thus reducing the annual costs from 234,000 French Francs to 30,000,[92] which must have been mood music to the GHQ Finance Office.

Anti-Gas Logistics

A critical logistic task was the maintenance and distribution of Anti-Gas Equipment (AGE), which consisted of items of Individual Protective Equipment (IPE) for example respirators and the supporting ancillaries and those forming stocks of Collective Protective Equipment (CPE) such as bags for contaminated clothing and anti-gas pathways.[93] Specialists within the RAOC BODs were responsible for repairs to AGE, although some items, such as oilskin suits for decontamination squads, were often returned to the manufacturer for refurbishment.[94] The scalings of reserve AGE were complex, and the tables run to eight parts in Appendix XXII of *Gas Warfare*.[95] The calculations were probably never fully understood by most soldiers but the specialist personnel were most industrious in compiling the necessary detail, and acquiring the equipment, although in October 1939, 4 Division CRASC reported that the unit had not received authorized scales to be held by 4 DPC for the division and the temporary mobilization issue received at Colchester required an additional 9 x 3 ton lorries allocated to C Section to enable the stocks to be held on wheels in accordance with RASC doctrine.[96] Logistic unit war diaries include descriptions of Anti-Gas Measures (AGM) training but there are relatively few references to AGE, with, for example, the vehicle loading trial for stocks in 2 DPC not being conducted until 29 February 1940.[97] Table 10.1 lists examples of the IPE and CPE in the AGE inventory and issues to the Army in November and December 1939.

89 TNA WO 167/1391: 2 MBU RAOC, WD, 31 March 1940.
90 TNA WO 167/1391: 2 MBU RAOC, WD, 31 March 1940.
91 One useful idea was to cut the ends off oil barrels, clean them and use them as foot stands so the soldiers could bathe their feet in hot water whilst they were showering. TNA WO 167/1391: 2 MBU RAOC, WD, 29 March 1940.
92 TNA WO 167/1391: 2 MBU RAOC, WD, 28 March 1940. On an exchange rate of FF 173.22 to the £, this is £1,351, which equates to £72,460 in 2018 based upon RPI. Reducing the cost to FF30,000, £173.20, and at 2018 prices £9,293, created a saving of £63,167; no wonder the war diary reported that the plan generated a 'great saving of public money'.
93 WOOH, *Special Weapons and Types of Warfare*, Vol 1 – *Gas Warfare*, is the authoritative document on the subject. Classified SECRET upon publication, it was downgraded to UNCLASSFIED in 1984; MOD D/OR13 (NBC) 22/1 dated 28 September 1984.
94 Ibid, p.96.
95 Ibid, pp.296-308.
96 TNA WO 167/235: 4 Division CRASC, WD, 27 October 1939.
97 The original date was 26 February 1940, but this was cancelled because of the visit of DDST I Corps and 2 Division CRASC, who conducted an inspection of the AGE. TNA WO 167/212: 2 DPC, WD, entries 26 & 29 February 1940.

Table 10.2
Anti-Gas Stores – Individual and Collective Protection[98]
Issues to the Army and Defence deliveries from Industry
November – December 1939

Item	Issues to the Army	Deliveries from Industry
Bleach (Tons)	841	Not shown
Canister, Type E Mk V	229,091	378,049
Detector Paint No 1 (Tin)	24,893	6,221?[99] lbs
Eyeshields, Mk I & II	1,587,783	6,233,189
Facepiece, Respirator	264,250	493,510
Haversacks, Respirator	221,937	306,962
Ointment, No 1 (2 oz tins)	273,278	554,075
Ointment, No 2 (2 oz porcelain jar)	969,176	4,009,614
Outfits, Anti-Dim	269,040	969,744
Pathway, Anti-Gas (Yards)	71,250	120,634

Reserves of AGE, although not every line item, were held at each level of Command: 1st Line stocks by units, 2nd Line with DPCs, 3rd Line with CPPs and the LOC Railhead Company, and 4th Line by the BODs and the quantities required, firmly reinforces the criticality of industry to military capability.[100] The stock levels varied depending upon the item and were based on 12-150 percent holdings, depending upon the item, for three months reserve, across the Theatre. In 1939, it was calculated that it would take a minimum of 14 days for contaminated clothing to be recycled, and this led to 200 percent reserves of clothing being held in France for the First Contingent of the BEF, amounting to around 600,000 sets. As plans for the size of the BEF began to mature, the Staff realized that on this basis, the proposed force of 2,250,000 would, by late 1941, require a stock holding of 9,000,000 sets. As an interim measure, a sliding scale was introduced, which maintained a reserve of 200 percent for 200,000 personnel, and then decreased for each 100,000. The GHQ Chemical Warfare Staff assessment of April 1940 that only 25 percent of the Force might be subject to attack by gas weapons on any one day[101] and only 2 percent contaminated, generated another change to reserve stock holdings.[102]

98 Compiled from information in held in TNA WO 106/1625: Provision of Gas and Anti-Gas Equipment, WO GS MO4 58/27 dated 14 January 1940, Appx A, 'Receipts and Issues of Anti-Gas Stores from 1 November - 31 December 1939'.
99 TNA WO 106/1625: Provision of Gas and Anti-Gas Equipment, WO GS MO4 58/27 dated 14 January 1940, Appx B, Forecast of Production. The table only shows deliveries in lbs and the figure has a question mark.
100 TNA WO 106/1625: Provision of Gas and Anti-Gas Equipment, WO GS MO4 58/27 dated 14 January 1940.
101 TNA WO 193/717: Scale of Gas Attack to which the British Expeditionary Force may be subjected.
102 In May 1940, to provide a 14-day reserve to cater for the recycling process, against a 2% daily contamination rate of 400,000 soldiers, totalling 8,000, required a holding of 112,000 sets.

Decontamination was not a difficult technical challenge, but it was certainly a logistic one. Items of clothing and equipment exposed to Mustard vapour could be decontaminated through weathering by hanging it outside for 24 hours or until the smell had disappeared. Items contaminated with liquid Mustard required boiling, using 1½ gallons of water for every pound of clothing, the time depending on the *materiel*, with respirators and face-tubes requiring three hours. Web equipment, canvas, cotton and linen were decontaminated by the addition of 2 oz of washing soda for every 10 gallons of water, whilst leather items were usually soaked in cold water for an hour and then hot water for four, although Service boots needed six.[103] The task was however, complicated by the acquisition of clothing, known as Anti-Verm,[104] which was temporarily resistant to Mustard gas vapour,[105] although it offered only a small additional protection against liquid splash.[106] By 1938, after three years of research at Porton Down, co-operation with the textile and dry cleaning trades had produced an impregnation process, using 2.4 Dichlorphenyl benzoyl chloroimide, which was capable of being conducted in a standard dry cleaning facility.[107] In 1939, soldiers were not issued with AV Battle-Dress (BD) but a reserve was held for the First Contingent of the BEF consisting of four divisions plus Corps Troops, and this stockpile was increased as production increased. Serge AVBD was stable in storage in temperate conditions and in field conditions Impregnate E was effective for approximately three months. In 1940 however, laundering dirty AVBD posed a problem. Standard laundering, or cleaning with solvents, destroyed the impregnate, whilst the use of a steam disinfector set up a reaction with it, which so damaged the stitching that the garment usually fell apart and had to be scrapped as salvage. Hot air dis-infestation was the solution, but this was a specialist task, and contracts had to be established, through GHQ Ordnance Services, with French companies.[108]

The logistic task in managing the AGE stock was complicated by British intelligence deductions, which were, as it transpired incorrect, concerning the German weaponization of Arsine (SA)[109] an agent coded 'Arthur' by the British GW Staff.[110] Driven by a report from

103 Army Council, FSPB, Pamphlet No 8, 1939, *Protection Against Gas*, p.20, Sect 7, Decontamination.

104 The impregnation process was known as AV as a security precaution and battle-dress so treated was called AVBD. This subterfuge, which suggested anti-louse or insecticide properties, was successful in preventing unwanted interest in the subject but the Germans discovered the process after capturing stocks of AVBD in France. On first issue, AVBD was stiff, a little tacky and had a slight odour of chlorine but these unpleasant properties disappeared after several days of wear.

105 The neutralization of the vapour though, was important because in heavy concentrations it could permeate the BD within 30 minutes.

106 Only rubber or oilskin suits provided protection against liquid Mustard.

107 TNA WO 189/4856: Porton Report, The laboratory preparation of Impregnate E (2.4 Dichlorophenyl benzoyl chloroimide).

108 WOOH, *Special Weapons and Types of Warfare*, Vol 1 – *Gas Warfare*, p.206.

109 Chemically, Arsenic Trihydride is a lethal, non-persistent agent, with a possible smell of garlic, which acts systemically by destroying red blood cells. Even in small amounts it can cause anaemia but unlike other blood agents such as Hydrogen Cyanide (AC) or Cyanogen Chloride (CK) it acts very slowly, taking hours to days to achieve its full effect; it also causes damage to the liver and the kidneys.

110 This was supported by constant reports that the Germans were experimenting with a new gas, which was true: the nerve agent Tabun. The deduction was reinforced when economic intelligence revealed that the Germans had bought large quantities of arsenic on the World metal market. The reality was that some of the arsenic was for general industrial use, whilst that allocated to the chemical weapons programme was intended to make Arsenol, which the Germans used as a diluent in Mustard. In the

the French Army that the German FE 37 respirator filter[111] offered 10 times the protection of the British EA Mark V,[112] the British GW political and military fraternity went into overdrive,[113] despite the fact that both British and French GW experts were clear that its field limitations made it an unsuitable war gas.[114] The possibility that the Germans might have overcome these challenges however, overrode a less cautious approach. The British thus went to an enormous effort to modify the filters in 400,000 service respirators and an even bigger one for the 70,000,000 civilian types,[115] whilst also producing a special detector paper, Type A.[116] As an emergency measure, the connecting tube between the Service Respirator and the Type E Mk V container was cut in half, and an additional container, the Type EA, filled with lime permanganate granules, inserted. Production of the replacement Type E Mark VI filter, which had specially treated charcoal to filter arsine, was rapidly commenced, and remained the standard canister, with some additional refinements to the charcoal, for the rest of the war.

Despite the impact on industrial production and the additional burden upon logistic capacity, commanders were concerned about soldiers' confidence in the respirator, and thus morale. The issue of the emergency canister was welcomed but in the intervening period, those who had only the single buff coloured Type E Mk V felt vulnerable. The new Mark VI was red in colour, which made operational and logistic identification easy, but those soldiers not issued with it, considered themselves to be inadequately equipped. No doubt the morale of the men of 4th Division would have taken a serious dent had they been aware that in late April 1940, the AGE reserve respirators and canisters held by 4 DPC were standard Mark V, which provided little protection against SA. How this situation developed is not clear but when it was discovered immediate logistic action was taken to resolve it, with Mark V EA filters being acquired and fitted to the respirators.[117]

light of this information, the War Office made a deduction that in the event turned out to be too obvious. WOOH, *Special Weapons and Types of Warfare*, Vol 1 - *Gas Warfare*, p.140.

111 F H Hinsley et al, BOH, *British Intelligence in the Second World War: Its Influence on Strategy and Operations*, Vol 2 (London: HMSO, 1981), p.674.

112 The Germans never deployed SA and the high level of protection afforded by the FE 37 against it, was a product of their concerns about Soviet AC. WOOH, *Special Weapons and Types of Warfare*, Vol 1 - *Gas Warfare*, pp.140-141.

113 Arsine is a volatile substance, which can explode on contact with air and disperses in the field very rapidly.

114 WOOH, *Special Weapons and Types of Warfare*, Vol 1 – *Gas Warfare*, p.140.

115 T H O'Brien, BOH, *Civil Defence* (London: HMSO, 1955), p.332.

116 The British action in issuing new respirator canisters and detector paper had though, an influence on the Germans, who deduced that the UK was preparing to deploy SA. Consequently, the Germans increased their previously low level of interest in the agent. WOOH, *Special Weapons and Types of Warfare*, Vol 1 – *Gas Warfare*, pp.140-141.

117 TNA WO 167/235: 4 Division CRASC, WD, 20 April 1940.

Force K6

In a rerun, albeit at a much smaller scale, of the deployment to France of four divisions of the Indian Army Expeditionary Force A in 1914, Force K6[118] arrived at the port of Marseilles on 26 December 1939,[119] having sailed from Bombay in four ships[120] on 10 December.[121] The Force planning figures[122] included 1,723 personnel, inclusive of 411 'Followers', 68 horses, 1,996 mules[123] and 528 carts.[124] The Force arrived with 60 days of 'Working Stocks' and 90 days of War Reserves of those supply items peculiar to the Indian Army except perishables, grain,

118 For a detailed history of Force K6, see the comprehensive Chris Kempton, *Force K6 The Indian Contingent: The RIASC Mule Companies in France & UK, 1939-1944* (Gillingham: Chris Kempton, 2019).

119 See, Maginniss, *An Unappreciated Field of Endeavour*, Chp 6, 'Meerut to Marseilles'.

120 Force K6 sea movement. Table compiled from information in TNA WO 167/1433: HQ Force K6, HQ 5 Base Sub-Area, MCO 21, 'Disembarkation from Mule Ships' dated 26 December 1939 (SECRET), Copy No 30.

Table 10.3
Force K6 – Sea Movement

Ship	Load	Pax	Mules	Cargo (Tons)	Remarks
Rajula	25 & 29 AT Companies	432	501	64	Less 3 x Troops
Rohna	22 AT Company & Section IGH	459	537	444	Plus 1 x Detachment 25 AT Company
Tairea	Force HQ & 32 AT Company	397	493	290	Plus 1 x Detachment 32 AT Company
Talamba	47 SDS, Reinforcement Unit & ARD*	442	500	250	* 300 mules from ARD
Total		1,730*	2,031*	1,048	* Including 368 'Followers' & 22 horses

ARD: Advanced Remount Depot. AT: Animal Transport. IGH: Indian General Hospital. SDS: Supply Depot Section.

121 For details of the arrangements in the Indian Army for sea movement and port discharge, see *Indian Army Service Corps (IASC) Manual (War)*, (Simla: Government of India Press, 1932), pp.87-89.

122 There are small differences between the planning figures and total shipping allocation shown in Table 10.2, created by the planned deployment against the actual movement. See, TNA WO 167/1433: HQ Force K6, table 'Arrival of Force K6 at Marseilles from India', nd but probably 26 December 1939.

123 During the voyage from India Force K6 one riding pony and three mules died of sickness. Personnel casualties included an Indian Other Rank who lost an eye from a mule kicking him in the face and the 2IC 32 AT Company, Captain John Ashdown, the father of Baron Ashdown of Norton-sub-Hamdon, a future leader of the Liberal Democratic Party, who arrived at Marseilles in the sick quarters of the Hired Military Transport (HMT) *Tairea* and was transferred to the Indian General Hospital at Marseilles. TNA WO 167/1433: HQ Force K6, WD, 28 December 1939.

124 The AT carts were two wheeled single axle vehicles with a maximum load of 800 lb hauled by two mules, which were dual-roled pack animals. All carts had been dismantled in India to save shipping space and were loaded thus to rail wagons, except those for 22 AT Company, which were moved by WMT to Camp Roi d'Espagne.

fodder and fuel.[125] The personnel and mules of each unit disembarked in 2½ hour periods during 27 and 28 December in heavy rain with a cold mistral wind blowing, interspersed with snow.[126] The discharge of vehicles and baggage was however, rather slower because of a shortage of dock labour and the availability of WMT, the last of the stores not being cleared from the port until 3 January 1940,[127] whilst the unloading of SS *Rajula*[128] was complicated by the handling of 100 tons of commercial cargo. Some of the forage was directed to be left aboard the ships for the return voyage, although there is no explanation as to why it was required, whilst other stores were held on Mole G for dispatch by rail to unit locations in the Base and corps areas, with all ordnance stores being sent to 2 BOD at Le Harve.[129]

Men and mules,[130] marched the 11 miles[131] to the two transit camps at Chateau Roi d'Espagne and Chateau Reynarde, where ground conditions and administrative arrangements were described as 'poor',[132] the unexpected late arrival of the Commander K6,[133] Lieutenant-Colonel R W W Hills MC RIASC,[134] resulting in the failure to co-ordinate key requirements in the transit camps.[135] In the two corps, the logisticians were rather better prepared, 2 Division CRASC noting in the unit war diary on 19 December 1939 that the I Corps Requisitioning Officer had arranged for sheep to be kept 'on the hoof' for the arrival of Indian troops at Orchies

125 TNA WO 167/1433: HQ Force K6, table 'Arrival of Force K6 at Marseilles from India', nd but probably 26 December 1939.

126 The Force K6 war diary is a comprehensive document, the articulate contents of which are greatly influenced by the hand of its commander, Lieutenant-Colonel Hills, whilst his reports are a lesson in clarity and coherency.

127 TNA WO 167/1433: HQ Force K6, WD, entries 26 December 1939-3 January 1940.

128 The SS *Rajula* of 8,704 GRT was constructed in 1926 for the British India Steam Navigation Company for the Madras to Singapore service. The *Rajula* survived into post-war service until she was scrapped in 1974. Roger Jordan, *The World's Merchant Fleets 1939, The Particulars and Fates of 6,000 Ships* (Annapolis: Naval Institute Press, 1999), p.100 & p.522.

129 TNA WO 167/1433: HQ Force K6, HQ 5 Base Sub-Area, MCO 21, 'Disembarkation from Mule Ships' dated 26 December 1939 (SECRET), Copy No 30, para 6.

130 For details of AT march discipline, see, *IASC Manual (War)*, pp.134-138.

131 Two Watering Points for mules and horses were constructed on route. TNA WO 167/1433: HQ Force K6, HQ 5 Base Sub-Area, MCO 21, 'Disembarkation from Mule Ships' dated 26 December 1939 (SECRET), Copy No 30. Short halts required all girths to be loosened and riding saddles eased, whilst during long halts all saddles were removed, and the animals' backs rubbed by hand. *IASC Manual (War)*, pp.136.

132 TNA WO 167/1433: HQ Force K6, WD, 28 December 1939.

133 The use of the title 'Commander', rather than Commanding Officer, reflected the organization of K6, which consisted of Base and Corps components and was described as a 'Force'.

134 Lieutenant-Colonel Reginald William Welfare Hills (1894-1962) served in the ranks before commissioning as a Second-Lieutenant in the 5th Royal Fusiliers in February 1915. He transferred to the ASC in July 1917 and was awarded the MC and a MID in 1918. He transferred to the RIASC in 1928 serving for most of the 1930s on the North-West Frontier, including the Deputy Assistant Director Supplies July 1937 - August 1939, for which, he received another MID. He was awarded the OBE in 1941, presumably for his service as Commander Force K6, before promotion to Colonel. Dix Noonan Webb of Mayfair auctioned his group of 11 medals in May 2019.

135 Lieutenant-Colonel Hills left Bombay on an Imperial Airways flight to UK on 2 December 1939, but poor weather prevented flying on nine days during the journey. After discussions at the War Office in London, he did not arrive at GHQ Arras until 22 December and Marseilles on 26 December. TNA WO 167/1433: HQ Force K6, WD, December 1939.

in the first week of January 1940 and that the first consignment of 17 animals had arrived at the Corps SRH on the same day.[136] Regrettably the documents do not shed light on the arrangements for managing the animals in the intervening period, although it is probable that a local French farmer was engaged to undertake the task. Plans to deploy K6 were quickly enacted, 29 Animal Transport (AT) Company embarked on two trains at Marseilles Prado Station for Le Mans on 29 December,[137] the Force deployment being shown in the table below.[138]

Table 10.4
Force K6 – Initial Deployment[139]

Sub-Unit[140]	Assigned To	Location	Remarks
K6 HQ	BEF GHQ	Rouvroy	I Corps area
ARD*	5 Base Sub-Area Marseilles	Camp Rcynarde	*Advanced Remount Depot
Reinforcement Unit			
FAO*			*Force Accounts Office[141]
22 AT* Company	5 Base Sub-Area	Camp Roi d'Espagne	*Animal Transport
25 AT Company	II Corps	Wambrechies	Detachment to 5th Division
29 AT Company	2 LOC Sub-Area	Le Mans	
32 AT Company	I Corps	Orchies	Section at Cysoing (2nd Division)
47 SDS*	5 Base Sub-Area	Camp Roi d'Espagne	*Supply Depot Section

136 TNA WO 167/210: 2 Division CRASC, WD entry 19 December 1939.
137 TNA WO 167/1433: HQ Force K6, HQ 5 Base Sub-Area, MCO 22, 'Entrainment of 29 AT Company' dated 27 December 1939 (SECRET), Copy No 45.
138 A section of the Indian General Hospital was also located with 2 British General Hospital at MBSA Dieppe. TNA WO 167/1433: HQ Force K6, WD, December 1939.
139 Table compiled from information in TNA WO 167/1433: HQ Force K6.
140 Officers Commanding of the sub-units were: Majors L W Hitchcock (22 Company), J G Wainwright (25 Company), E C B Shannon (29 Company), J Finlay (47 SDS), H F Gillmore (Reinforcement Unit), S T Apcar (ARD) and Captain H N N Fawcett (Adjutant). TNA WO 167/1433: HQ Force K6, 'Force Nominal Roll of Officers', Appx II to WD, December 1939.
141 For an explanation of Field Service Accounts in the Indian Army, see, *IASC Manual (War)*, pp.110-117.

47 Supply Depot Section (SDS)[142] was responsible for the provision of supplies and equipment for personnel and animals arriving at Marseilles from India,[143] and was supported by 22 AT Company,[144] which remained in Marseilles to assist in the discharge of ships and the transport of cargo to the railhead, although both these units were redeployed to Northern France by rail at the end of April 1940, 47 SDS, less a detachment to Le Harve, and 22 AT Company arriving on 5 May to support 51st (Highland) Division in the Saar.[145] The three AT companies supporting the corps provided sterling service in delivering *materiel* and supplies to units located in positions where WMT was difficult to operate, although it appears from the war diaries that the AT was sometimes under-employed, particularly on the GLOC,[146] although this was not the case with 32 AT Company, which was supporting 1st Division, being described in February 1940 as 'employed to capacity'.[147] One issue was interaction with units, which initially had no experience of working with Pack Transport and thus had to learn the skills and drills for loading parties to prepare the loads for movement and as baggage guards to make readjustments on the march, the muleteers being responsible for supervising the loading and caring for their animals but not conducting the physical tasks of 'humping and dumping'. In favourable conditions, four men could load 60 mules[148] in 60 minutes provided the loads were roped before the task commenced and laid in balanced pairs so the mules could walk between them.[149]

25 AT Company supported RE construction work, which had been curtailed by thaw precautions preventing the movement of WMT,[150] with the ground conditions at some sites so poor that AT was the only transport solution. AT did however, have some limitations.[151] AT companies had to be allocated 2nd Line WMT to deliver combat supplies and forage to

142 OC 47 SDS was Major John Finlay MBE who retired to Bexhill-on-Sea Sussex in April 1939 after a full-service career in the Indian Army, mostly on the NW Frontier. Mobilized in September 1939, he travelled to the Sub-Continent to command 47 SDS but soon returned to Europe and after the evacuation from France, to the UK. In May 1943 he was appointed 2IC of the Indian Contingent as Force K6 had been re-designated and in April 1944 was posted to the India Office in London, retiring as a Lieutenant-Colonel in 1949, 10 years after he thought his military career was complete. See, Hamish Johnston, 'A Corner of Pakistan in Scotland', *Highland Family History Society*, 2012.

143 All the Indian soldiers in Force K6 were Mohammedans. Key imported rations were, curry, *atta* flour and *ghi*. See, TNA WO 167/1433: HQ Force K6, table 'Arrival of Force K6 at Marseilles from India', nd but probably 26 December 1939.

144 22 AT Company had considerable recent operational service having participated in the Loe Agra and Mohmand operations on the NW Frontier in 1936 and a series of actions in Waziristan 1936-1937 when 25 and 32 AT Companies were also in the ORBAT. See, IGS, *Official History of Operations on the NW Frontier of India 1936-37*.

145 TNA WO 167/56: Q Branch L of C, WD, 27 April 1940. The HQ Force K6 Post Operational Report states 7 May. It is probable that the planned date was 5 May and the actual 7 May. TNA WO 167/1433: HQ Force K6, 'Report on Operations in France' dated 19 July 1940. It was ironic that 22 AT Company having served in the Base for most of its deployment in France was the only component of K6 that was captured.

146 The Force K6 war diary suggests that Staff officers were reluctant to intensively employ AT for fear that some WMT might be redeployed. TNA WO 167/1433: HQ Force K6, WD, 19 February 1940.

147 TNA WO 167/1433: HQ Force K6, WD, 27 February 1940.

148 The troops referred to the mules as 'katchas'.

149 *IASC Manual* (War), p.139.

150 TNA WO 167/1433: HQ Force K6, WD, 2 February 1940.

151 One amusing note in the war diary records the requirement for casting a mule and a riding pony in 32 AT Company. The former for being 'old and worn out' and the latter for 'vice'. TNA WO 167/1433:

P10.7Logistic Lesson Learnt. Another post campaign 'logistic lesson learnt', was the provision of integrated mobile laundries. This example was photographed at the Mobile Laundry Training School Hilsea on 17 August 1940. (RLCM: Trades/NOR)

enable AT to function effectively in the BEF environment, although by February 1940 this issue had not been fully resolved.[152] One of the key tasks was caring for the animals in the wet and the cold of the French winter, whilst ice on the pave roads usually prevented AT from operating on them. Camp conditions were generally hard on men and mules because Force K6 infrastructure was not a Works priority,[153] a problem exacerbated by the winter weather and restricted daylight, which reduced the progress of projects. 25 AT Company, whilst waiting for the additional Nissen huts to be constructed authorized by Q II Corps, was able to improve the drainage for the stables and the camp, although overhead cover for the animals was not resolved until the spring by which time the weather was improving.[154] On a positive note, 29 AT Company was accommodated in good billets and had a sub-unit Navy Army & Air Force Institutes (NAAFI) canteen which was recorded as 'doing a good trade',[155] whilst Captain Ashdown, a Detachment Commander in 32 AT Company was commended for organizing 'first-class training'.[156] Ongoing issues in February 1940 were the future command arrangements for Force K7 consisting of two companies of Cypriot Pack animals, the potential utilization of AT to support aerodrome construction, the outstanding decision on the assignment of 22 AT Company to III Corps, a request to GHQ BEF for AT to be deployed to support operations in the Saar and the tireless efforts of the Force Commander to obtain public recognition for the

HQ Force K6, WD, 27 February 1940. Regrettably the war diary does not describe what the 'vice' was but may have been biting, weaving or cribbing.

152 Lieutenant-Colonel Hills visited AQ & QMG II Corps on 7 February 1940 to seek the issue of a van for 25 AT Company to enable the sub-unit to transport supplies purchased locally. TNA WO 167/1433: HQ Force K6, WD, February 1940.

153 Key to the efficient and effective operations of K6 and the morale of its soldiers was the leadership of the Risaldar Major, Mohd Ashraf IDSM. TNA WO 167/1433: HQ Force K6, WD, entries.

154 TNA WO 167/1433: HQ Force K6, WD, 7 February 1940.

155 TNA WO 167/1433: HQ Force K6, WD, 19 February 1940.

156 TNA WO 167/1433: HQ Force K6, WD, 2 February 1940.

work of his 'Men and their Mules'.[157] Viscount Gort offered his appreciation in his despatches, noting that the mules 'proved their usefulness on many occasions'.[158]

EFI

The Expeditionary Forces Institute (EFI), previously titled 'Canteen Service'[159] was recruited,[160] organized and controlled under the RASC cap-badge as an adjunct to the supply service,[161] in order to provide, upon payment, food, equipment, personal requisites, tobacco products and recreational items, which were not issued free through Service channels.[162] In addition, the NAAFI underwrote free services, including newspapers, cinema shows and the provision of sports goods. The first detachments were deployed as part of the component consisting of 500 EFI personnel of the First Contingent, arriving at Brest and Nantes on 12 and 13 September 1939 respectively.[163] By 10 May 1940, EFI strength in France supporting the BEF and the AASF was 2,940[164] operating 225 canteens[165] with a monthly turnover of £288,000,[166] supported by a supply chain of warehouses, bulk issue stores on the basis of one per division,

157 TNA WO 167/1433: HQ Force K6, WD, various entries, February 1940.

158 Lord Gort, *Dispatches on Operations of the British Expeditionary Force, France and Belgium, September 1939 – May 1940*, Supplement to the London Gazette, 17 October 1941.

159 According to the late Lieutenant-Colonel Howard Cole (1911-1983), the Expeditionary Force Canteen (EFC) service was renamed Field Force Institute (FFI) in 1934 and deployed in December of that year with the Saar Force. In late October 1939, the nomenclature was changed after the abbreviation FFI was confused in 2 Base Sub-Area at Nantes, with the FFI used by the Army Medical Services in relation to venereal disease to denote 'Free From Infection' when an order for a FFI medical parade was believed to refer to a formal gathering of all Institute personnel. The BEF Medical Branch understandably, persuaded the General Staff to retain the medical abbreviation, and Expeditionary Forces Institute was introduced. Lieutenant-Colonel Howard N Cole OBE TD DL, *Naafi in Uniform* (Aldershot: The Forces Press (NAAFI), 1982), p.9. Given that the FFI title had been in use for five years it is surprising that it had not been changed before; no doubt, in a TNA War Office file, there is a mountain of correspondence on the matter.

160 Upon mobilization, suitable volunteers from the NAAFI were engaged, solely for service in EFI, as members of the Army Council, TA. Managers were granted temporary commissions whilst other employees were enlisted. FSR, Vol I, *Organization and Administration*, pp.136-137.

161 Ibid, p.135.

162 Ibid.

163 This was the first occasion in British military history when an organized and equipped canteen service had been available to the Army upon mobilization for war. See, Cole, *Naafi in Uniform*, p.10. Howard Cole was a pre-war TA Gunner, commissioning from the Ranks in July 1935. Serving in the Second World War, he commanded 667 Heavy Anti-Aircraft Regiment (1947-1951) whilst employed by the publisher Gale & Polden in Aldershot as military sales manager. A seasoned historian and author, nine of his 13 books covered military subjects, including *Heraldry in War: Formation Badges, 1939-1945* (Aldershot: Gale & Polden, 1946). For his services to Aldershot and Hampshire, including his time as a Deputy Lieutenant (1965-1983), 'Howard Cole Way' in Aldershot was named in his honour in 1979.

164 82 officers and 2,58 Other Ranks. WOOH, *Miscellaneous 'Q' Services*, p.163.

165 Initially units operated regimental canteens but once the EFI was established in France, GHQ requested EFI to open Institutes in the corps areas and at principal personnel railheads for troops departing or returning from leave and courses. Ibid, p.162.

166 Based on the Retail Price Index (RPI) this equated in 2018, to a very handsome £15.45 million, although profits were not so healthy. The Relative Income Value of this turnover, measuring the amount against per Capita GDP, is a staggering £62.950 million. See, Measuring Worth UK.

and railhead storage facilities all organized into four EFI Areas. HQ EFI[167] and HQ Forward, supporting the three corps, was at Arras,[168] with North at Le Harve in the Advanced Base Area, whilst South based at Nantes managed the Main Base Area, GLOC and the AASF around Rheims.[169] Another HQ was formed on 10 May 1940 to support X (Arras) Sub-Area, and across the Theatre, the lay-down of the BEF across France led to some adjustment of the doctrinal approach in *Field Service Regulations* with EFI stocks in the corps areas not following the RASC supply chain.[170]

Conclusion

Whilst the 'sharp-end' of logistics focusing upon ammunition and fuel may have attracted the most attention from commanders, the wealth of supporting activity played a key role in sustaining not only the operational capability of the BEF also the morale and thus effectiveness of its soldiers. Improving the MT skills of the BEF was arguably an under-rated technical task but one that was crucial not only to its logistic support but also to its combat edge. That corps MT schools were established is clear testimony that commanders were alive to the problem and intended to prosecute a solution. The deployment of AT appears at face value to be at best anachronistic, and at worst, a failure to comprehend the changing nature of logistics in the military environment, yet the picture is more complex. Unlike the other Armies that fought in the 1940 campaign, which placed great reliance on the horse, Force K6 was niche, deployed as a precaution to meet a specialist need. Whilst the utilization of K6 was not as envisaged and it was obviously over-faced in manoeuvre warfare, it played a useful role in engineer support work during severe weather conditions that precluded the effective use of WMT and in this respect met its remit of delivering transport capability in places where WMT could not.

Reverse Logistics, the management of AGM equipment and the supply of water have been air-brushed from the published record to the point where these important tasks do not feature in the many histories of the BEF and yet for those involved in delivering them, they were as important as any other activity undertaken by the supporting logistic Corps. Equally significant was the provision of labour, which seemed to expand exponentially not only to support the daily activities of the BEF but also to enable the completion of the growing number of construction projects. Procuring additional skilled trades was always a challenge, whilst access to the French labour market relied greatly on female personnel. Clear improvements to catering appear to have been less successful across the Theatre than GHQ had hoped, the rapid expansion of the

167 The Commandant EFI BEF was Lieutenant-Colonel (later Brigadier) Norman Victor Peters MC, a pre-Great War manager of Gordon Hotels, who joined Navy and Army Canteen Board in 1919, transferring to NAAFI upon its formation on 1 January 1921. Brigadier Peters deployed with the first EFI contingent supporting 21st Army Group in June 1944.

168 Upon arrival in France HQ EFI deployed to HQ LOC at Le Mans but transferred to Arras in November 1939 as the Centre of Gravity of the EFI operation moved North. WOOH, *Miscellaneous 'Q' Services*, p.163.

169 Major R A D Alltoft, who was also the Assistant Commandant, commanded Area North, Major S B Martin Area South and Major J W Martin MBE X Sub-Area and Major N F Hart controlling canteens assigned to the AASF.

170 WOOH, *Miscellaneous 'Q' Services*, pp.162-163.

Force and the spread of responsibility in delivering enhancements proving to be major hurdles in generating effective solutions in the timeframe.

The importance of MBUs and laundries to health and hygiene, morale and thus operational capability, soon became clear and the commitment and industry of the personnel of these specialist organizations has certainly been forgotten. For the most part, operating with improvised equipment or through contracts with French commercial companies, the experience in France generated the knowledge and will to create much more agile and productive military units capable of supporting deployments 'at scale'. Whilst such facilities were often the butt of much soldier humour, the reality was that they were as important to the individual as they were to the Army. That the war diary of 2 MBU exudes a level of professionalism, pride and commitment to their task as high any infantry battalion, speaks volumes for the dedication, industry and morale of the 'forgotten' logisticians.

Part IV

Preparing for Battle

11

Sharpening the Sword
The development of logistic plans and operations in the BEF: November 1939 – April 1940

Sleighs and Drag-Lines

In nearly all histories of the BEF, the period from the completion of the deployment of the First Contingent of four divisions to the commencement of major combat operations offers the impression of relative logistic inactivity, with the main effort to dig in along the Franco-Belgian frontier enlivened by some patrolling from the *Maginot* Line into Germany.[1] This in no way reflected the growing tasks across the whole spectrum within the Theatre from refining matters of accounting detail for the provision of local purchases to crafting plans to support four corps by mid-1940, whilst sustaining expanding complex Land and Air forces, with water, rations, munitions, fuel, supplies, stores, equipment and the material to enable a vast array of infrastructure construction.[2]

Of one of many essential logistic demands in the period was the rapidly increasing demand for timber to support the construction of fortifications, railways, infrastructure and furniture,

1 4031789 Corporal Thomas William Pridy of 1st King's Shropshire Light Infantry was killed in a Blue-on-Blue incident near Grindorff on 9 December 1939. TNA WO 167/124: HQ 1 Corps, GS, WD, entry 11 December 1939. On the night of 3-4 January 1940, 71104 Second-Lieutenant Patrick Everitt of 2nd Norfolks led a three man team on the first British patrol to cross the German frontier since the BEF had deployed to France but he was mortally wounded by machine gun fire in an action on 7 January, 200 yards WSW of Waldwisse railway station during which, the battalion war diary states that he 'exceeded his instructions in moving forward over the hill in this manner as his patrol was a protective mission only'. Everitt was captured and died of his wounds, thereby becoming the first member of the BEF to die through enemy action. On 10 January, Captain F P Barclay and Lance-Corporal M H Davis both of 2nd Norfolks were awarded a MC and MM respectively for a night action during 3-4 January, in which the patrol engaged German positions. In addition to the MC and MM awards, all members of the patrol received a MID. TNA WO 167/794: 2nd Norfolks, WD, entries January 1940.

2 In 1934, the War Office issued a very comprehensive document focusing upon accommodation and installation to support a deployed expeditionary force. Army Council, *Military Engineering*, Vol VII, *Accommodation and Installations*, ran to 401 pages, inclusive of 27 Tables and 18 Appendices, plus an additional 145 plates containing photographs and diagrams.

which prompted the deployment in January 1940 of 129 Forestry Company RE,[3] the members of which were, by 1 February, hard at work logging in the snow-drifts around Crecy, using horses and sleighs to remove the products of their industry from the forests.[4] This activity, conducted in tough winter conditions was perhaps more reminiscent of a scene from British operations in North Russia during 1919[5] rather the BEF in France in 1940 but lucidly illustrates the array of logistic units employed. It was also an excellent example of the vital need to make the necessary arrangements with the Host Nation authorities, without which, the logistic process generally deteriorated into frictional administrative attrition.[6]

Reducing the visual signature of the BEF's military infrastructure, including Base depots, logistic dumps, defence works, gun sites, vehicles, field headquarters, accommodation and aggregate heaps was a critical component of operational security, which relied upon the logisticians.[7] Initially all the nets were made by units from canvas strips which were issued in rolls of 100 yards length. The strips cut from the rolls, were two or three inches in width and garnished nets of 14' x 14' and larger respectively, and were stocked in four shades: dark and light green, brown and loam.[8] Given the developments in infra-red photography, instructions were published to ensure that natural foliage was used in conjunction with the artificial strips to achieve best effect.[9] To increase the availability of the nets a camouflage factory was established in a disused mill at Le Houlme on the main Rouen to Dieppe road equipped with plant from the UK. Production commenced on 11 December 1939 utilizing local French female labour, 44 of whom were employed by Christmas rising to 125 by the end of March 1940 and out-turning, per week, 125 nets, with the supporting frames. In April because of a shortage of twine and an increase in net requirements, a decision was made to use wire netting, which was more difficult to work, necessitating an additional floor space and labour. The factory also produced a prototype dummy tank, five of which could be carried on a 3 ton lorry, and after off-loading, be assembled by three men.[10]

The development of the Advanced Base behind the corps areas consumed a considerable amount of Staff time and effort, whilst the engineering and transportation resources required

3 In June 1940, 129 Forestry Company was employed in the light infantry defence role and was evacuated through Saint Malo on 17 June 1940, except for Second-Lieutenant Condor who was searching for Second-Lieutenant Pollard. The war diary offers no information as to their fate. TNA WO 167/943: 129 Forestry Company RE, WD, June 1940.

4 For details on forest exploitation and timber production, see, Army Council, *Military Engineering*, Vol VII, *Accommodation and Installations*, pp.154-164, Timber Production.

5 TNA WO 32/5705: North Russia Expeditionary Force, October 1918 – October 1919, Report on Field Work and Administrative Services.

6 The OC of 22 BAD, a rail-served site at Chateauneuf-d'Ille-et-Vilaine, eight miles SE of Saint Malo, was taken to task at the end of May 1940 about the damage to young trees on private land adjoining the depot. TNA WO 167/1181: 22 BAD, Part I Orders, No 27 dated 31 May 1940, Serial 113.

7 WOOH, *Works Services and Engineer Stores*, p.106.

8 Strips were cut to lengths of 18 to 36 inches. A 14 x 14 feet net required two 2 inch rolls; a 24' x 24' net, four 3 inch rolls; a 29' x 29' net, six and a 35' x 35' net, eight. Army Council, Pamphlet No 4, 1939, *Field Engineering*, p.64, Sect 12, Concealment and Camouflage.

9 Ibid, pp.63-65, Sect 12, Concealment and Camouflage.

10 Thurlow, *Building the Gort Line*, pp.184-185.

to construct and improve GLOC capacity,[11] Base facilities[12] and camps competed with the very significant tasks to build fortifications on the Gort Line and construct, improve and maintain the aerodromes for the Air Component of the BEF and the AASF.[13] CRE I Corps calculated in October 1939 that the corps defence works and road improvements[14] would need *per diem*, 1,200 tons of sand, 1,000 tons of cement, 1,000 tons of aggregate, 20 cubic metres of planks and 3,000 sandbags, supported by 37,000 railway sleepers, expanded metal mesh, rolled steel joists, timber shuttering, steel reinforcing rods, road metal, hessian rolls, wire-netting, pickets, brushwood and hoop-iron.[15] To construct a Standard Base Supply Depot required 1,094 tons of cement, 2,647 cubic yards of sand, 5,294 cubic yards of aggregate, 264 windows, substantial quantities of timber and galvanized sheets, plus timber and 553 lbs of four different types of nails.[16] The construction or modification of workshops was equally challenging, depending upon their function, which might be, ordnance, engineer, locomotive, carriage & wagon, transportation, heavy MT repair or ammunition.[17] As GHQ looked to the future, the provision of the special facilities at the Royal Armoured Corps (RAC) Training Centre at Pacy-sur-Eure, 50 miles West-North-West of Paris, to support and train the embryonic armoured divisions became an emerging theme,[18] which involved a considerable logistic component. Plans were agreed in April 1940 with the Host Nation to construct in the Armoured Fighting Vehicle (AFV) Base Area, integrated Base Ordnance Depot (BOD) and Base Ordnance Workshop (BOW) facilities of sufficient capacity to support ten armoured divisions, potentially expanding to twelve.[19]

The initiation of this work had commenced in November 1939 when Director Ordnance Services had been informed that the planning date for the arrival of the first armoured division in France was 1 May 1940, which led to a review of future requirements for specialist officers, provisioners, suppliers, artificers and craftsmen, to ensure that the Equipment Support in the form of spares and repairs for the increasing numbers of AFVs was effectively delivered, and to progress this work, an Ordnance officer was attached to the GHQ AFV Branch from February

11 The RE had a comprehensive planning document for infrastructure, which covered personnel accommodation, storage depots, productive installations including timber and concrete, workshops, medical and veterinary facilities, power production, water supply and aerodromes. See, Army Council, *Military Engineering*, Vol VII, *Accommodation and Installations*.

12 TNA WO 106/1777: The British Front, RE (Works) Organization in the BEF: 'Record of Meeting held in the War Office on 5th December 1939'. At this meeting, the provision of engineer units to develop the GLOC and Base was directed to be the priority, with assets for the Gort Line to be a high secondary.

13 For a brief summary of the RE contribution to aerodrome construction, improvement and maintenance, see, Pakenham-Walsh, *The History of the Corps of The Royal Engineers*, Vol VIII, 1938-1948, pp.15-18. For details of the technical tasks, see, Army Council, *Military Engineering*, Vol VII, *Accommodation and Installations*, pp.301-315, Work for the Royal Air Force.

14 For technical details, see, Army Council, *Military Engineering*, Vol V, *Roads*.

15 TNA WO 167/129: I Corps, CRE, CE S/1 dated 14 October 1939, 'Supply of Engineer Stores'.

16 Army Council, *Military Engineering*, Vol VII, *Accommodation and Installations*, Appx IX, List of Materials Required for Construction of Various Base Depots.

17 Ibid, pp.209-234, Workshops and Appx X, List of Materials Required for Construction of Various Base Workshops.

18 The RAC Training Centre, complete with training areas, ranges, staff, accommodation, ordnance depot and armoured workshops, was expected to number 2,000 personnel by mid-August 1940. TNA WO 167/56: Q Branch L of C, WD, entries March 1940.

19 WOOH, *Ordnance Services*, p.155.

1940 to advise on the supply of specialist stores.[20] None of the proposed facilities were built, the German offensive ending the development of the site, although there was an interim plan to use existing accommodation at Bonnieres-sur-Seine to house a small ordnance depot for AFV spares and stores.[21] More transient logistic planning and execution involved the movement of 1st Cavalry Division in late December 1939 and January 1940 from the UK to Palestine via Dover by sea and rail to Marseilles,[22] and the withdrawal in April 1940 of 5th Division from its corps area to the Advanced Base at Le Harve in preparation for recovery to the UK as War Office Reserve and the dispatch via UK, of its 15th Infantry Brigade for operations in Scandinavia.[23] Other smaller but nonetheless necessary moves, included the 1st Welsh Guards from Gibraltar via Marseilles to La Hutte[24] and in April 1940, 5th Scots Guards from UK via Le Harve to Chamonix for 'special training with the French'.[25]

The logistic tasks continued to expand throughout the period, creating a concomitant need for military and civilian labour not all of which could be resourced. The Royal Engineers in particular began, increasingly, to utilize plant to improve productivity, although sometimes the ground conditions were not conducive to their employment, CRE 2nd Division noting that on one major project, 'There are 20 men and 20 colossal machines,[26] most of which get stuck in the mud'.[27] The RE formed a specialist unit, 135 Excavator Company[28] to utilize much of the heavy plant such as bulldozers, scrapers, draglines and drag-shovels, with new equipment arriving ex-factory, from UK and the USA, in France via the Harwich - Calais Train Ferry.[29] Interestingly, the company was recruited from All Arms because technical skills and experience were more important than cap-badge and the first OC, Major S A Westrop,[30] was a TA infantry officer, whose professional civil engineering knowledge was fundamental to the effective use of the equipment. Many engineer resources were also allocated to the building and expansion of

20 Ibid, p.149.
21 Ibid, p.155.
22 Denis C Bateman, 'Goodbye to Boots and Saddles, The Twilight of the British Cavalry', *British Army Review*, No 114, pp.75-89.
23 TNA WO 167/245: HQ 5th Division, AQ, WD, April 1940.
24 TNA WO 167/56: Q Branch L of C, MCO R6 dated 6 November 1939, 'Move of Welsh Guards Marseilles - La Hutte'.
25 This was winter warfare training in preparation for operations in Scandinavia. See, TNA WO 167/56: Q Branch L of C, WD, entries March 1940. The activities included improving skiing skills in a tactical environment and operating in a cold climate, although the soldiers, some of whom were civilian volunteers, were billeted in 'great comfort' in hotels. For the bizarre but fascinating story of the battalion's recruitment, formation, training and deployment, see, David Erskine (Comp.), *The Scots Guards, 1919-1945* (London: William Clowes and Sons, 1955), pp.21-26.
26 For a review of the types of machinery in use with the RE, see, Army Council, *Military Engineering*, Vol VII, *Accommodation and Installations*, pp.288-300, Constructional Plant.
27 TNA WO 167/207: HQ 2nd Division CRE, WD, 15 October 1939.
28 For a brief summary of 135 Company operations, see, Pakenham-Walsh, *The History of the Corps of The Royal Engineers*, Vol VIII, pp.202-203 and Thurlow, *Building the Gort Line*, pp.156-158, and for details of its work, the unit war diary in TNA WO 167/944.
29 The first shipment details are shown in WO/Q14A/17/3 dated 17 October 1939 (MOST SECRET) held in TNA WO 167/56: Q Branch L of C, although the document is over classified.
30 Later Brigadier CBE DSO.

Base depots, ammunition and fuel sites, railway infrastructure,[31] transit and training camps[32] and the improvement of RAF airfields,[33] which sometimes led to rather intriguing logistic arrangements to deliver the output. On one occasion, to unload two barges of sand, HQ 2nd Division hired a commercial crane, which was operated by a French soldier. Personnel from a field ambulance loaded the grab-bucket, which tipped the sand into lorries provided by 2 Division Ammunition Company (DAC).[34]

Stuck in the Mud

The immense burden that the adverse weather, especially in late December 1939 and January and February 1940, placed upon the soldiers and civilians attempting to deliver logistic capability must be placed into context[35] and it would be true to state that 'Mother Nature' was a more challenging enemy than the German Army and the *Luftwaffe*. Heavy snow and hard frosts were often followed by thaws and rain before the cycle recommenced, with on occasions extreme conditions creating chaos to transport and communications.[36] The war diary scribe of 21 Base Ammunition Depot (BAD)[37] near Fecamp recorded, 'The outside temperature did not rise above freezing point … trees, poles and pylons were hurled to the ground by the weight of ice. Telephone communications were cut off'.[38]

Whilst the worst of this weather was in the corps areas, the whole of the BEF from port quay to front trench was affected at some point and the conditions adversely affected all military activities including key logistic outputs such as road and rail communications and depot and construction operations, although the soldiers of 2 Division Petrol Company (DPC) were not prevented from participating in the 2nd Division football competition at Orchies[39] nor holding swimming parades at Douai, which presumably had a heated indoor pool.[40] The distribution of supplies was however, disrupted at a time when there was a concomitant and sharp increase in demand for coal and anti-freeze, whilst the numbers of vehicles damaged or written-off in RTA and through the failure of frost precautions, not only reduced transport lift but also generated

31 TNA WO 167/879: 1 Railway Construction and Maintenance Group RE; WO 167/880: 2 Railway Construction and Maintenance Group RE and WO 167/881: 3 Railway Construction and Maintenance Group RE.
32 TNA WO 167/56: Q Branch L of C, GHQ Q (Maint) Loose Minute Q/35 dated 4 February 1940, lists the progress and plans for most of the Infantry Base Depot sites and the Convalescent Depot.
33 TNA WO 1671422: AASF CRE, WO 167/1423: AASF CRE (East), WO 167/1424: AASF (North) and WO 167/1425 (South).
34 Thurlow, *Building the Gort Line*, p.275.
35 The cold conditions persisted into late March 1940. According to Signalman Yeomans serving in GHQ Arras, there was lying snow when he returned from UK leave on Good Friday 22 March 1940. JYIC 241099.
36 For a unit perspective, see, Gun Buster, *Return via Dunkirk*, pp.78-81.
37 21 BAD was constructed specifically to store GW munitions, although some conventional ammunition was also stored temporarily.
38 TNA WO 167/1179/1: 21 BAD RAOC, WD, 29 January 1940.
39 TNA WO 167/212: 2 DPC RASC, WD, 26 February 1940.
40 TNA WO 167/212: 2 DPC RASC, WD, 26 February 1940.

the requirement for distributing new equipment and spares.[41] The records of 1st Royal Welch Fusiliers noted, 'When the winter set in with heavy rain, the whole area became a morass of thick mud, making all road movement difficult'.[42] Snow blocked roads requiring labour and improvised four snow-ploughs to clear them,[43] whilst ice reduced road movement transit times, resulted in more RTAs or caused the chain of command to cease or curtail traffic operations.

The 'Freeze-Thaw' cycle was particularly aggressive to *pave* laid on earth, with many of these routes closed until repairs could be affected, whilst on another roads transit was restricted to light WMT of 15 cwt or less with a 12 mph speed limit. This level of damage came as little surprise to the Royal Engineers, Commander RE I Corps identifying the need to ensure improvements to the road network in the I Corps area in mid-October 1939,[44] whilst the relevant technical RE document reminded users that high speed and axle loads were the 'greatest enemy of the road'. *Military Engineering*, Volume V, *Roads*, [45] suggested from an engineering perspective, the following speed limits for long-term use: Tanks, 3 ton lorries and tractors, 15 mph; 30 cwt load-carriers, 25 mph and cars: 35-40 mph, which was in stark contrast to the advice given in other official military publications.[46] These suggested the cruising speed of the Car, Light Armoured Reconnaissance was 50 mph, and Cruiser tanks and 3 ton lorries, 25 mph. Professional intervention and experience adjusted this guidance to 30 mph for the armoured car and 20 mph for the Cruisers, in addition to a number of other amendments.[47]

Inland Water Transport (IWT), which the BEF increasingly utilized to transport sand and aggregate for construction was also affected, with barge traffic on rising river levels caused by heavy rain and snow melt, unable to make headway upstream because of the current, whilst there was insufficient headroom, especially for vessels in ballast, under bridges because of the height of the water. Railways were also affected, with snow and ice blocking tracks and clogging switches, whilst cargo such as sand became so frozen that air hammers had to be used to break it out of the wagons,[48] which not only caused disruption to the flow of material but also congestion in the rail yards. These demanding conditions, particularly during 'thaw' periods generated a raft of new arrangements to ensure units were supplied, whilst constraining the movement of heavy WMT and thus the consumption of petrol and diesel. When the weather improved, the

41 Entries by OC 4 DSC RASC in 4 Division CRASC WD, January - February 1940. TNA WO 167/235. The OC was Major E D G Galley RASC, an officer awarded the MC and the AFC for his service in the RFC and the RAF. Before the war, he was serving at the Supply Reserve Depot Deptford.

42 Lieutenant General Jonathon Riley CB DSO, Lieutenant Colonel Peter Crocker & the late Lieutenant Colonel Richard Sinnett, *Regimental Records of the Royal Welch Fusiliers*, Vol IV, *1918-1945*, Part One, *November 1918 - May 1940* (Warwick: Helion, 2019), p.442.

43 TNA WO 167/916: 23 Field Company RE, WD, entries, February 1940.

44 TNA WO 167/129: CRE 1 Corps, CE F2 dated 15 October 1939, 'Road Improvements - I Corps Area'.

45 Army Council, *Military Engineering*, Vol V, *Roads*, p.27. With the improvements in tyres and suspensions before 1940, the speeds of modern 3 ton lorries became less restrictive.

46 Including Army Council, FSPB, Pamphlet 6, 1939, *Mechanized Movement by Road*, Appx 1.

47 Army Council, *Army Training Memorandum* No 28, January 1940 (War Office, 1940), p.27, Appx D, General Staff Publications, Revision of Cruising Speeds.

48 Thurlow, *Building the Gort Line*, p.276.

Corps Petrol Parks (CPP) and DPCs were heavily tasked to deliver sufficient fuel to enable units to build a 'Thaw Reserve.'[49]

The poor weather also coincided with the arrival of the first elements of the Territorial divisions of the Second Contingent,[50] thereby placing additional stress on logistic planning and personnel. Nonetheless, the BEF pressed on with training, individual and collective, culminating in live-firing shoots[51] and divisional tactical and movement exercises, supported by the preparation of unit defensive positions and the construction of fortifications along the Gort Line. The logistic practice and experience obtained during these exercises varied considerably. 3rd Division held four divisional tactical exercises, each of which lasted for several days, whilst 2nd Division only conducted two short movement schemes.[52] The four day 5th Division exercise 24-28 March 1940 along the River Authie, included a night move, occupying a defensive position, a night attack and infantry-tank assault co-operation. This exercise was certainly worthwhile because it identified a number of deficiencies, especially in relation to junior leadership, which in the divisional logistic combat environment in May 1940, proved crucial.[53] Supporting these operations was a wealth of developing logistic activity, most of which, has never received any exposure or analysis and yet it was a crucial period in the expansion of the BEF's capability. The coordination and integration of the many facets of the logistic diamond was vital to the effective and efficient utilization of the allocated resources but the dispersion of the assets across 500 miles of the GLOC created a consequential challenge in delivering the output, a problem compounded, initially at least, by unreliable communications, a frustration exacerbated by the extreme winter weather.

A Quiet Day in the Office

In early January 1940, GHQ RASC recorded: 'Great difficulty experienced in inter-communication between this HQ and RASC units as telephones are scarce, lines always engaged and DRs[54] unable to operate'.[55] The over-load on the cable infrastructure was such that GHQ introduced 'phone-less' days, which whilst an interesting solution did little to assist the BEF in delivering capability. Whilst a 'quiet day in the office' may have suited some Staff officers, dynamic logistic specialists imported from industry were much less impressed. Used to quickly

49 TNA WO 167/212: 2 DPC RASC, WD, 22 December 1939.

50 42nd (East Lancashire), 44th (Home Counties), 48th (South Midland), 50th (Northumbrian) and 51st (Highland).

51 Whilst infantry battalions, and to a lesser extent medium artillery regiments equipped with field guns, could utilize inland French ranges, logistic to support live firing for the heavy guns was more complex. 5th Heavy Regiment for example, withdrew one 8-inch gun from the line at a time in order to fire on full charge from a site near Calais into the English Channel. Thurlow, *Building the Gort Line*, p.240.

52 See, David French, *Raising Churchill's Army, The British Army and the War against Germany, 1919-1945* (New York: Oxford University Press, 2000), p.179.

53 TNA WO 167/21: GHQ, SD & Trg, 'Report on talk by Commander 5 Div on the Divisional exercises carried out from 24-28 March 40'.

54 Motor-cycle Despatch Riders (DR) were a key Command, Control & Communications (C^3) asset in all logistic units but particularly at corps and division. The winter weather sometimes made it extremely dangerous to ride motor-cycles and COs often withdrew them from the roads, despite the disruption to logistic C^3. TNA WO 167/235: 4 Division CRASC, WD, 17 February 1940.

55 TNA WO 167/24: GHQ RASC, WD, January 1940.

accessing telephonic and telegraphic services to conduct commercial business, the concept of not being able to rapidly communicate with the 'movers and shakers' was completely alien to them; these officers and those in GHQ Petrol from the oil industry were a particular example, brought the paucity and fragility of the BEF's communication systems into sharp relief.[56] In the Base, communications relied mainly upon the Host Nation civil telephone and telegraph networks, supported by local military field systems at depots and docks, which were often supplemented by the bicycle to enable inter-personal action. DRs were an essential component of the logistic communication matrix, ensuring the relatively rapid distribution of detailed written orders and information, supported by the Army Postal Service, which was rather slower. At the tactical level, the issues were worse, with, for example, RASC Troop Carrying Companies (TCC)[57] not being routinely issued with wireless equipment, which given the critical role of the TCC in mobile operations, was a failure that significantly eroded operational flexibility.[58]

Developing the relationship with the Host Nation at every appropriate level was critical to the logistic capability of the BEF. Strategically, given the logistic lay-down and the BEF's limited WMT and fuel resources, the deployed corps relied almost completely upon SNCF to provide the rail transportation at 3rd Line that was vital to sustaining the Force on the Franco-German border, although as the Advanced Base developed, the rail resources required to support the BEF reduced. Co-ordination with the Host Nation was essential to secure the additional infrastructure needed to expand capacity,[59] and to move to new sites offering improved access to railheads or enhanced productivity.[60] There was also the question of resolving real estate legacy issues, relating to access to port and storage facilities, which had emerged during the deployment phase.[61] Relations between the BEF's logisticians and their Host Nation counterparts were generally professional, usually cordial and, when time permitted, especially social, although inevitably, the competition for resources sometimes generated creative tension. Language was sometimes the greatest barrier, especially at unit or sub-unit level, unless liaison officers with the appropriate linguistic skills had been appointed. Some units were fortunate to have officers and soldiers whose knowledge of French enabled technical logistic business to be discussed, with OC 2 DPC being particularly fortunate in employing a Driver Ferrari[62] of the RASC as interpreter.[63]

November and December 1939 were months of consolidation for the logisticians. The priority was to ensure the wheel kept turning in delivering the Maintenance Project Plan (MPP),[64]

56 TNA WO 167/1076: GHQ Supply (Petrol), WD, entries, September 1939 - May 1940.

57 Each GHQ Troops TCC was capable of lifting 225 tons of cargo or the marching personnel of an infantry brigade with each section carrying one infantry battalion, the TCC could be allocated to divisions for specific operations. See Philson, BEFORBAT, Vol 1, p.154, WEIII/1931/44A/1.

58 For an engaging analysis of the BEF's communications systems, or rather lack of them, see, Smalley, *The British Expeditionary Force, 1939-40*, pp.84-111. The impact of fragile communications upon logistic operations both in the Base, and at corps level, is certainly worthy of exploration.

59 TNA WO 167/1168: 1 BOD/2 dated 22 September 1939.

60 TNA WO 167/1076: GHQ, Supply Directorate (Petrol), WD, 12 November 1939.

61 TNA WO 167/1115: 1 BSD RASC, WD, September 1939.

62 The son of Ranieri and Pia, T252233 Daniele Ferrari hailed from Leyton in Essex. He was killed on 28 May 1945 as a result of an accident Italy.

63 TNA WO 167/212: 2 DPC RASC, WD, entry 26 October 1939.

64 TNA WO 197/2: First Maintenance Project: Reception of Forces in France and system of maintenance in the initial stages.

P11.1 Fortification Construction. Whilst not on the Gort Line in France but on the GHQ Stop B Line at Moor Park Farnham Surrey (SU 866463), this FW 3/28 pillbox for a 2 pounder anti-tank gun illustrates the quantity of material and labour required for construction, often in locations with poor transportation access. Photographed in 2002. (Author)

which was focused upon importing sufficient stocks to sustain the BEF, whilst building the vital in-Theatre War Reserves of ammunition, fuel, supplies, equipment, stores, vehicles and spares in preparation for major combat operations. The provision of rations was the most stable of these items because the scales per person were fixed. With no combat consumption, ammunition stocks, with some type exceptions, continued to rise, with only training issues, banned batches or damaged munitions drawing on the inventory. Deteriorating munitions however, plagued the BEF, particularly during the winter because much of the ammunition was stored in field sites and dumps, where a mixture of poor management, climatic conditions and non-waterproof containers created a constant trickle of ammunition flowing through the reverse supply chain for remedial attention or disposal, a post-campaign report observing that, 'Much had to be returned to the base on account of damage caused by carelessness or ignorance'.[65]

65 TNA CAB 106/235: BEF Ammunition Supply (Gibson Report), p.10.

Fuel was the critical commodity because issues with tin-filling in UK and heavier than planned consumption within the BEF adversely affected the build of War Reserve stocks. By 31 December 1939 however, 44 days of reserves of cased MT spirit based upon a consumption rate for the Force of 500 tons per day had, despite the winter weather, been accumulated, although in December 1939, issues exceeded imports by 984 tons and in January 1940 by a much more significant 4,351 tons, recovering to surplus in February by 700 tons, despite an increase in daily consumption.[66] III Corps logisticians finding their feet upon the formation of the Corps in late March 1940, struggled throughout April 1940 to bring order to the delivery and management of ammunition, liquid fuel, coal, and potatoes and sought support from II Corps,[67] which was not always forthcoming.[68] The inexperience of the logistic Staff, units and individuals all contributed to a series of failures and frictional issues in III Corps, which in the circumstances was perhaps to be expected. Indeed, before the Corps left the UK a chronic shortage of WMT in many units prevented them from practicing key aspects of motorised movement or march discipline.[69] Ammunition lorries from the CAP and DAC were often incorrectly loaded and the munitions not recovered when they were dumped,[70] whilst DAC vehicles were, without orders, filling from the Corps ARH, instead of the CAP.[71] In a specific incident, poor drills by 44th Division logistic units drawing from a railhead, offered a superb target for the *Luftwaffe*, the miscreants being instructed by HQ III Corps to ensure it 'never happened again'.[72] On the same day, an officer filling his cigarette lighter from a 4-gallon can of aviation spirit started a fire at the Benguin petrol dump, which must have brought the DDST to the point of exasperation.[73]

At a Furious Pace

WMT was always in demand from everyone but constantly under siege from the weather and a shortage of spares yet despite this pressure it was not solely assigned to BEF military tasks. In April 1940, 1 LOC Railhead Company RASC was allocating WMT daily to move agricultural produce for the Host Nation. Loads included grain, wheat, straw, potatoes and cattle fodder, with some of the loops being a distance of 50 miles, and one, involving the movement of farm machinery, being 125 miles along rural roads.[74] 2 LOC Railhead Company, whilst focused upon supporting the BEF rather than Host Nation civilian requirements, handled a variety of transport tasks including the attachment in mid-February 1940 'for an indefinite period on coal duties' of 25 x 3 ton vehicles to 3 GHQ Company, although the distribution of the stocks was

66 Figures collated from information in TNA WO 167/1076: GHQ, Supply Directorate (Petrol), 'Cased MT Petrol Position - November 1939 to February 1940'.
67 TNA WO 167/180: III Corps, DDST, WD, entries April 1940.
68 On 11 April, 5th Division was unable to drawn petrol from II Corps. It took the intervention of III Corps DDST with his counterpart for II Corps to 'reluctantly agree' to supply 1500 gallons. TNA WO 167/180: III Corps, DDST, WD, 11 April 1940.
69 TNA WO 163/49: OS11 'Memorandum by the CIGS on the Training of III Corps: Appendix A - Report by GOC 3 Corps,' 21 January 1940.
70 TNA WO 167/180: III Corps, DDST, WD, 30 April 1940.
71 TNA WO 167/180: III Corps, DDST, WD, 23 April 1940.
72 TNA WO 167/180: III Corps, DDST, WD, 22 April 1940.
73 TNA WO 167/180: III Corps, DDST, WD, 22 April 1940.
74 TNA WO 167/1095: 1 LOC Railhead Company RASC, loose Table 'Civilian Details, April 1940'.

P11.2 Pressed for Space. As vehicle production increased, The increasing flow of military specification 4x2 WMT equipment from the factories enabled the logisticians to commence reducing establishment deficiencies from the VRDs in the Spring of 1940, a process, which continued post campaign to replace the substantial WMT losses in France. Covered storage, however, was at a premium and equipment often had to be stored in the open creating problems with security and reliability. Lorries stored at VRD Feltham seen in 1941. (RLCM: A1/MT/RLCA/20581)

immediately disrupted by the imposition of 'thaw precautions' banning all movement of routine WMT in excess of 15 cwt to reduce damage to the roads.[75] In early March, the main effort for 2 LOC Railhead Company was moving the components of Nissen huts for RAF aerodromes before all RE allocated WMT was withdrawn on 23 March to move 78,000 gallons of fuel on a loop of 90 miles from Vignacourt to the dump at Rebreuve – Ranchincourt.[76]

The high level of WMT activity, accidents and failures kept the corps Ordnance Field Parks (OFP) occupied. The shortage of WMT spares was a critical issue, which was an inevitable consequence of the pre-war decisions relating to procurement and sustainability.[77] Repair improvisations, cannibalisation of damaged vehicles for spares, and local purchase of parts,

75 TNA WO 167/1096: 2 LOC Railhead Company RASC, WD, entries 18-28 February 1940.
76 TNA WO 167/1096: 2 LOC Railhead Company RASC, WD, 23 March 1940.
77 In October 1940, 4 Division CRASC recorded that the demands submitted for RASC vehicle spares from the Motor Transport Stores Depot had been returned with a covering letter requesting that a re-submission be made in 14 days. TNA WO 167/235: 4 Division CRASC, WD, 27 October 1939.

whilst not the preferred GHQ solutions, were, in the circumstances, the only options, although utilizing additional labour and time to achieve the result. Local purchase of spares to support corps units and the OFPs was undertaken by the Advanced Ordnance Depot at Arras but was not without considerable frustrations. As many items had no part numbers, acquisition by ordnance and workshop personnel was undertaken by eye, whilst the complex inventory of impressed vehicles created yet more challenges.[78] On a positive note, by the spring of 1940, military vehicle production in the UK, especially in the 1-3 ton range, saw a step change in holdings and activity, which enabled some of the unit deficiencies to be filled. In April, 1 OFP received 439 WMT variants and motorcycles, mainly by road from 2 BOD,[79] before issuing them 'at a furious pace day and night'.[80] By early May, there was a brief respite, the soldiers having sufficient time to attend a concert-party and enjoy daily bathing in the Chateau lake, which the unit had cleared of weeds, recreational activity that the German invasion brought to an abrupt end.[81] The OFPs were also responsible for the provision of artillery and signals equipment, which were deemed to be priority *materiel* and the OFPs dedicated considerable time to ensuring that the correct quantities of these key items, each marked with a red code, could be loaded to specified vehicles in the event of an emergency order to move location.[82]

Technical and Tactical

In addition to 'keeping the wheel turning' logistic Staffs and units had internal business to resolve. In the Base there was an urgent necessity to enhance productivity by revising procedures, enhancing trade training and procuring additional equipment, whilst at the corps level there was an imperative to generate greater tactical and technical synergy. In this respect, there was always an underlying creative tension both in the Base and in the corps to developing skills whether trade, tactical, logistic or military. Skill at Arms was a particular issue in many logistic units, with HQ 5th Division upon its formation in December 1939, identifying that 690 personnel had never fired their personal weapon.[83] These problems were never entirely resolved whilst the BEF was in France, with much of the focus being 'On-The-Job' training, the standard and intensity of which, varied depending upon commanders, tasks and resources, although increasing numbers of personnel from units in UK were attached to the BEF to enhance their knowledge and experience of operational and technical tasks.[84] The regular pre-war divisional units of the RASC were the most resilient, whilst the Base units, formed upon mobilization,

78 TNA WO 167/1194: 2 OFP RAOC, WD, entries February 1940.

79 Given the distances, the wear on the equipment and the manpower involved, it is surprising that most of the WMT moved by road. It is approximately 350 miles from Nantes to Arras and 145 from Le Harve to Arras.

80 TNA WO 167/1192: 1 OFP RAOC, WD entries April 1940. Some of the convoys were of appreciable size. On 1 April 1940, 100 WMT vehicles and motorcycles arrived at 1 OFP and on 25 April, 87 WMT vehicles and 30 motorcycles.

81 TNA WO 167/1192: 1 OFP RAOC, WD entries 1-10 May 1940. 1 OFP also erected diving boards.

82 TNA WO 167/1194: 2 OFP RAOC, WD, entries February 1940. 2 OFP was however, six months after deploying to France, short of cookhouse tables. 2 OFP, WD, 25 March 1940.

83 576 soldiers had not fired the rifle and 114 the revolver. See, Thurlow, *Building the Gort Line*, p.235.

84 For example, Captain Bridges of 43rd (Wessex) Division RASC was attached to 2 DPC for 'learning petrol duties'. TNA WO 167/212: 2 DPC RASC, WD entry 18 February 1930.

with a varying mix of personnel, had the greatest challenge in 'sharpening the sword'. The capability of the Corps Ammunition and Petrol Parks matured once the combat formations were located on the Franco-Belgian frontier, COs making the best of the opportunities to conduct some individual and technical training, whilst practising collective operating procedures.

DPCs were kept busy in their daily logistic role and had less time to allocate to military and tactical training but equally became well practised in their technical work, a process, which applied to the TA divisional RASC units once the formations were operating in France. Whilst much of the fuel distribution was routine, there were numerous special tasks to engage CPPs and DPCs. In early March 1940, the Host Nation demanded that vehicles carrying petrol tins and cans[85] should not be located in villages, which meant that either woodland locations for WMT had to be found or the stocks had to be ground loaded and camouflaged in field sites.[86] On 12 March 1940, II CPP[87] opened a petrol replenishment park for 4th Division, which included 3,000 gallons of dieselite and 2,000 gallons of M160 lubricating oil, which was to be transported by 4 DPC to support a special force formed to counter enemy parachutists.[88] In mid-April 1940, II CPP assisted the newly formed III Corps with managing the Petrol Railhead (PRH) at Houdais and the nearby field fuel site at Beugin in preparation for III Corps taking over these facilities. There were loose ends that required tying because the change of responsibility occurred around the period that the first 4-gallon returnable cans were flowing into III Corps, which required close supervision of the reverse supply chain and the imperative to solve the outstanding failure to camouflage the petrol-tin salvage dump at Beugin.[89]

With no major combat activity to support, the DACs had the least practice in their operational role, which in theory should have enabled these sub-units to allocate more time to training and equipment maintenance but the shortage of WMT to meet numerous tasks in the corps areas and the need to control and guard ammunition on the ground, which the DACs were not resourced to undertake, eroded the slack. 5 DAC,[90] for example, received a constant stream of tasks including the movement of RE stores, 'on-call' coal duties, the collection of scrap iron for the French civil authorities and the transport of troops.[91] Whilst these tasks offered the opportunity to practise road movement drills and clearly demonstrated the flexibility of appropriately controlled WMT, it meant that ammunition had to be ground-loaded by manual labour to generate the lift and then be correctly stacked ready for inspection and movement. This requirement created several issues, including site selection, camouflage, security and

85 This directive only applied to cargo and not to the reserve 1st Line vehicle fuel carried in the reusable cans.

86 TNA WO 167/1095: 1 LOC Railhead Company RASC, WD, entries March 1940.

87 The OC was Major H T Gilchrist MBE RASC.

88 TNA WO 167/161: II CPP RASC, WD. This entry is interesting from a military perspective because it firmly authenticates that the BEF was more tactically and logistically innovative than some authors have suggested and the deployment of airborne forces by the Germans was not an operational surprise. See also, Army Council, *Army Training Memorandum* No 32, May 1940 (War Office, 1940), pp.12-13, para 7, Parachute Troops.

89 TNA WO 167/161: II CPP RASC, WD, entries, 15-23 April 1940.

90 TNA WO 167/250: 5 DAC RASC is most unusual in having RASC Section (ie platoon) war diaries, which contain much interesting information on 5 DAC operations, tasks, administration and soldiers, with detail in some cases down to individual vehicles and drivers.

91 TNA WO 167/250: 5 DAC RASC, WD, entries, February-April 1940.

resources. Wood dunnage was needed to prevent ammunition boxes being in direct contact with the ground and tarpaulins were required for weather protection and camouflage; both these stores were usually in short supply.[92]

Occasionally Exciting

Life in logistic units varied from the mundane and routine, through to demanding and occasionally exciting. On 13 January 1940, as a result of intelligence assessments, CAP vehicles were ordered to be loaded with War Scales of ammunition from local dumps and ARHs,[93] all leave was cancelled and units placed on four hours Notice To Move.[94] As part of the plan for I CAP, lorries from 1 & 2 Ammunition Sub-Parks loaded with demolition explosives were attached to 1 DAC and 2 DAC respectively.[95] Moderate snowfall all day on 16 January, disrupted the completion of these tasks but much to the relief of the soldiers, the alert was cancelled the next day.[96] It was, to use the terminology of the time, a 'flap', a military drama that was delightfully described by the war diary scribe of CRE 2nd Division: 'There is no other single word that implies crises, troop movement, orders, counter orders, packing, unpacking, packing again, destroying files, looking for letters destroyed … The word, in fact, implies the whole gamut of military activity when everybody wants to gets something done but nobody is quite sure what'.[97]

The following days were an anti-climax, involving an outbreak of scarlet fever and measles, CAP personnel assisting RAOC ammunition technicians with work on 40 mm charges, transport lifts for infantry battalions and the induction of reinforcements from 1 General Base Depot.[98] Not until 20 March 1940 was the focus returned to operational ammunition tasks, when a dumping programme commenced, with the Q Staff directing that, 'as far as possible sites were to be located outside villages',[99] an instruction that was no doubt a great relief to the local rural villagers. HQ 4th Division however, was unable to adhere to the directive and had to initiate a 'Q' examination of the DAC arrangements, which included some munitions storage around La Madeleine, a small town to the North-East of Lille, although the assessment concluded that, 'There is no danger to local inhabitants by the storage of this Ammunition and this has been represented to 2 Corps'.[100] Clearly, an internal British Army evaluation cut relatively little ice with the local French authorities or the population, and there was an on-site meeting between 4 Division CRASC and the Mayor, resulting in the ammunition remaining in its original location.[101]

92 TNA WO 167/250: 5 DAC RASC, WD, entries, January 1940.
93 Ammunition was not usually collected from a rake of rail wagons but from dumps either at the ARH or sites nearby.
94 TNA WO 167/137: 1 CAP RASC, WD, 14 January 1940.
95 TNA WO 167/137: 1 CAP RASC, WD, 15 January 1940.
96 TNA WO 167/137: 1 CAP RASC, WD, entries 13-17 January 1940.
97 TNA WO 167/207: 2nd Division CRE, WD, 25 April 1940.
98 TNA WO 167/250: 5 DAC RASC, WD, entries, January - March 1940.
99 TNA WO 167/250: 5 DAC RASC, WD, 20 March 1940. Underlining in original document.
100 TNA WO 167/235: 4 Division CRASC, HQ 4th Division Q letter 1/Q dated 5 February 1940.
101 TNA WO 167/235: 4 Division CRASC, WD, 21 February 1940.

The Divisional Supply Columns (DSC) were constantly engaged in ensuring the supported formations were supplied with rations, medical consumables, soldier comforts and mail. The key routine activity was unloading the daily section of the 'Pack Train' allocated to the division and distributing the contents. During the extremes of weather in January and February, delayed trains and impassable roads often disrupted the programme, resulting in alternative arrangements having to be planned and briefed. For example, during a 'thaw' period, 50 Division CRASC directed that units only use light WMT to draw directly from the Divisional Supply Railhead (SRH) at Famechon, with a request that neighbouring units co-ordinate the lift to reduce the number of vehicles on the road. Each drawing unit was allocated a time-slot at the SRH, which, if it was missed, was deferred until the daily programme was complete.[102] Even when the weather did not disrupt operations, there was usually a myriad of supply issues to be resolved.

Rations arriving on pack trains were sometimes found not to be to scale. Whether this was the result of the non-availability of items, pilfering or mal-administration needed to be investigated, whilst the deficient rations had to be supplemented with local purchase of the same or other items.[103] The DSC was also responsible for delivering EFI stores, although units keen to ensure an early and complete arrival of their stocks often dispatched WMT to the SRH, which caused congestion, delayed train unloading and wasted precious fuel.[104] On a more positive note, the logisticians were pleased to advise upon the forthcoming issues of extra 'luxuries'. 4 Division CRASC recorded in the war diary, with considerable pleasure, the arrival of the first tobacco ration on a pack train[105] and that 'Golden Syrup would be issued once a week when available'.[106] OC 1 LOC Railhead Company, keen to ensure the security of the precious unit rum and chocolate rations, ordered that the stocks of these two items be 'stored in a lock-up under guard'.[107]

Plan D and J Day

During the period from the deployment of the BEF to France until the commencement of the German offensive, GHQ operational and logistic planners developed the orders and instructions to support the advance from the Franco-Belgian frontier to the Rivers Escaut and Dyle, with the latter the priority.[108] Despite the planning and the resources, Viscount Gort was pessimistic about the success of the initial deployment, commenting, 'even the movement to the Dyle would impose such a severe test unless carried out under peace conditions',[109] a fragility compounded by the indecision by the War Office to form III Corps in France caused by the plan to deploy

102 See, TNA WO 167/305: 50 Division CRASC, 'Supply Arrangements during Thaw Precautions' dated 21 February 1940.
103 TNA WO 167/235: 4 Division CRASC, WD, 23 October 1939.
104 TNA WO 167/235: 4 Division CRASC, WD, 23 October 1939.
105 TNA WO 167/235: 4 Division CRASC, WD, 26 October 1939.
106 TNA WO 167/235: 4 Division CRASC, WD, 26 February 1940.
107 TNA WO 167/1095: 1 LOC Railhead Company RASC, WD, 9 November 1939.
108 For the wider political and military issues relating to planning for the move of the BEF into Belgium, see, Brian Bond, *France and Belgium, 1939-1940, The Politics and Strategy of the Second World War* (London: Harper Collins, 1975.)
109 TNA WO 167/21: GHQ SD & Trg, Lord Gort to Under Secretary of State for War, February 1940.

some of the assets to Scandinavia and withdraw 5th Division from the BEF to the UK as a War Office reserve. In addition, ammunition, equipment, supplies and vehicles, which were due to arrive in France, were held at readiness in the UK for possible deployment to Norway. The one positive outcome GHQ obtained from this development was the retention in France of 5th Division, albeit under War Office control, although the formation had to be transferred from its corps area to the ABA near Le Harve, which created additional logistic complexity to Plan D.

Unsurprisingly, with changing scenarios and dynamic ORBATs, several versions of Plan D, often described in documents and war diaries using the codeword DAVID, were produced, and a constant stream of amendments issued. The last version, GHQ Operational Instruction No 37, was dated 6 May 1940 and the logistic support plan, GHQ Administrative Instruction No 12, was dated 7 May 1940.[110] I Corps was to be on the right, II Corps on the left and III Corps to secure the advance before occupying the line of the River Escaut. The I and II Corps forward deployments to the River Dyle were to be supported by eight RASC Troop Carrying Companies (TCC) with one TCC in GHQ Reserve,[111] lifting I and II Corps Troops plus 2nd, 3rd and 4th Divisions between Zero Hour on J Day[112] and J+90 hours. 44th Division was to be lifted between J+5 – J+7, 50th Division J+5 – J+9, 5th Division J+8 – J+10[113] and 1st Division was to follow when the other movements were complete.[114] The only lacuna in the plan was that whilst it relied on speed to reach the River Dyle as quickly as possible, the lead TCC commanders did not have the opportunity to conduct as reconnaissance of the routes. GHQ sought however, to create additional flexibility by maintaining a WMT reserve consisting of the two LOC Railhead Companies and two General WMT companies.[115]

One key task was the forward positioning of RE mines & explosives to prepare the river defence lines of the Dendre, Dyle, Escaut and Senne. Large quantities of explosives were stored at ARHs in order to conduct bridge demolitions and crater roads within the defence zones in accordance with the counter-mobility plans, whilst stocks of anti-tank mines were also positioned forward with some the balance held in readiness at BADs for loading to the first ammunition trains. To save the transport of engineer stores during the initial advance, secret arrangements were made with the Belgian Army, through the British Military Attaché in Brussels, to create two dumps of defence stores, including wire, pickets, revetting, timber

110 Copy No 9 is held in TNA WO 167/57: HQ L of C, Q Movements, whilst the operational documents are mainly located in WO 167/58: Plan D - Operational Instructions. The codeword in use on 10 May 1940 to place units at a Notice To Move state was DONALD, which perhaps, as it transpired, unfortunate. TNA WO 167/57: HQ L of C, Q Movements, Forward Move of the BEF (Plan D) – Administrative instructions and correspondence, GHQ Administrative Instruction (AI) No 12 dated 7 May 1940, para 1, Information.

111 Nos 1, 2, 3, 4, 9, 11, 12 and 14, with 13 as GHQ Reserve. TNA WO 167/57: HQ L of C, Q Movements, GHQ AI No 12, para 3, Road Movements.

112 J Day was the day upon which Zero Hour occurred when the first BEF troops crossed into Belgium. TNA WO 167/57: HQ L of C, QMG Movements, GHQ AI 12, para 1, Information.

113 Although 5th Division was held in War Office reserve, it appears in Plan D. TNA WO 167/57: HQ L of C, Q Movements, GHQ AI No 12, para 3, Road Movements.

114 TNA WO 167/57: HQ L of C, Q Movements, GHQ AI 12, para 3, Road Movements.

115 No 1 & 2 Railhead Companies and 8 & 9 (less one section) Reserve MT Companies. TNA WO 167/57: HQ L of C, Q Movements, GHQ AI 12, para 5, Transport.

and tools, to the West of the River Dyle, each supporting one British corps; these stocks were mainly complete when Plan D was initiated.[116]

The criticality of controlling the corps road routes is lucidly illustrated by the formation of the Corps Road Control Centres, whilst the importance of military railway capability to the operation was underpinned by the early forward deployment of 151 Railway Construction Company (RCC) and 153 Railway Operating Company (ROC),[117] which were to be concentrated at Lille and Ath respectively by J+2.[118] The BEF rail route allocation was Lille-Baisieux-Tournai-Ath-Grammont[119] based upon a flow rate of 36 trains per 24 hours controlled by the French Rail Zone HQ at Baisieux, which was the last station on the line in France. Given that that most of this route was in Belgium, there may have been some carefully controlled secret co-ordination planning, not shown in the documents, with the Belgian railway authorities. The plan to locate 153 ROC at Ath lucidly suggests however, that GHQ BEF was concerned that the Belgian railways would need at the least, military reinforcement, which given that rail movement was crucial to the successful execution of Plan D, was a vital backstop.

Several units, including two Casualty Clearing Stations (CCS), two pioneer battalions, four artillery regiments and a tank regiment,[120] were planned to move forward by rail and there was also a comprehensive plan to deliver additional ammunition and fuel to established railheads in France for I Corps and to allocated ones in Belgium for II and III Corps, with alternatives if enemy action precluded the priority locations.[121] The railheads in Belgium may have been subject to covert reconnaissance, although there is no supporting evidence in contemporary logistic documents[122] but it is unlikely that officers tasked with operating them would have been involved because this work was the responsibility of the Q Staff at corps level.[123] Each corps was assigned an ARH, a PRH and SRH, an Ambulance Railhead (ATR) and one for RE Stores, each of which had individual two letter codes.[124] Four Standard Ammunition Trains (SAT)[125] were to be held to the East of the River Somme and two located to the West by J+1, delivering to forward ARHs two trains per corps by J+4, with four trains per day arriving at

116 WOOH, *Military Engineering (Field)*, p.8.
117 TNA WO 167/57: HQ L of C, Q Movements, GHQ AI 12, para 2, Rail Movements.
118 TNA WO 167/57: HQ L of C, Q Movements, GHQ AI 12, para 1, Information.
119 Now Geraardsbergen Belgium.
120 1 CSS for I Corps and 6 CCS for II Corps; 51st Heavy Artillery Regiment and 4th, 58th & 59th Medium Artillery Regiments for II Corps, plus 4th Royal Tank Regiment. TNA WO 167/57: HQ L of C, Q Movements, GHQ AI 12, Appx A, Movement Table - Troop Trains.
121 TNA WO 167/57: HQ L of C, Q Movements, GHQ AI 12, Appx D, Railheads.
122 Such activity was highly sensitive in the political arena and the reports, if they were produced, probably classified as MOST SECRET and in any retreat, a priority for destruction.
123 Gregory Blaxland, *Destination Dunkirk: The Story of Gort's Army* (London: William Kimber, 1973), pp.60-61, explains that in March 1940, Commander I Corps Artillery, Brigadier Davidson, accompanied by the British Military Attaché, Colonel Blake, was granted tacit permission from King Leopold to conduct a covert reconnaissance of the Dyle Line. To retain anonymity, they wore civilian clothes dispatched specially from the UK, remained in the car and used maps and binoculars with care. The team identified a new trunk road that was not on British maps, plotted gun positions and identified the limitations of the Belgian defence scheme and fortifications.
124 TNA WO 167/57: HQ L of C, Q Movements, GHQ AI 12, Appx D, Railheads.
125 Each SAT was loaded with 50% of the planned Daily Ammunition Expenditure Rate (DAER) based upon a corps of three divisions plus Corps Troops. TNA WO 167/57: HQ L of C, Q Movements, GHQ AI 12, para 8, Ammunition.

P11.3 Calm before the Storm. Logisticians from 4 Company RASC in April 1940 (RLCM: RASC/ATB/1088)

ARHs from the Base from J+5 onwards.[126] Labour was key to the clearance of these railheads and GHQ allocated four sections of AMPC to ARH Aubigny and two to ARH Ecoust, whilst to support the forward dumping programme, two sections of AMPC were to be deployed at the Pernes ammunition dump, with all these resources to be operational from J+3. SRH Avion was assigned two AMPC sections on J+3 and PRH Beaumont two sections on J+5.[127] RE Stores were to be loaded on J+1 to two trains at Farbus and the next pair on J+4.[128] The Expeditionary Forces Institute (EFI) was to be prepared to open bulk canteens at the forward SRHs from J+4 upon receipt of orders from GHQ.[129] The key Ordnance Services task in Plan D was for the OFPs to complete, as far as stocks allowed, the issue of vehicles, equipment and stores to cover deficiencies in units under the priorities issued by corps HQs.[130]

126 These trains were planned to be loaded in the BADs from J+2 onwards. TNA WO 167/57: HQ L of C, Q Movements, GHQ AI 12, para 8, Ammunition.
127 TNA WO 167/57: HQ L of C, Q Movements, GHQ AI 12, para 12, Labour.
128 TNA WO 167/57: HQ L of C, Q Movements, GHQ AI 12, para 16, RE Stores.
129 TNA WO 167/57: HQ L of C, Q Movements, GHQ AI 12, para 14, Canteens.
130 TNA WO 167/57: HQ L of C, Q Movements, GHQ AI 12, para 9, Ordnance.

Force W

The creation of Force W[131] based upon an infantry brigade group[132] to serve in the Saar area as part of the French forces[133] manning the *Maginot* Line required the generation of specific 2nd Line logistic and medical components,[134] with the logistic ORBAT comprising RE, RASC and RAOC assets.[135] The RASC provided a Composite Transport Company (CTC) RASC,[136] consisting of one section each for ammunition, petrol and supply, plus a Detail Issues Depot (DID), a field bakery section and an EFI. The RAOC contribution comprised a Light Aid Detachment (LAD) and specialist personnel to operate two small depots, for ammunition and one for ordnance,[137] whilst the RE provided the Force postal detachment. There was also much discussion on the deployment of animal transport from the Royal Indian Army Service Corps (RIASC) to support the Force W brigade group. By mid-February 1940, HQ Force K6 was pressing GHQ to make a positive decision to integrate an Animal Transport (AT) company but this was rejected[138] and the matter lay effectively dormant until Force W was expanded with the deployment of 51st (Highland) Division in late April 1940 when 22 AT Company was assigned to the ORBAT. The Force W logistic capability was split, with Forward and Reserve components as follows:

131 From 1 December 1939 to 21 April 1940, nine different brigades served on rotation in Force W, after which the 51st (Highland) Division was deployed.

132 Three infantry battalions, an anti-tank company, a MMG company and a field company RE.

133 The deployment of the brigades offered 'the experience of the front Line and a smell - not much more, in view of the short periods allotted - of cordite' and to demonstrate the coherency of the Anglo-French alliance, whilst showing that the BEF was not fighting 'to the last Frenchman'. TNA WO 197/42: Saar Force Administration, 'Brief for Incoming Saar Area Commandant', Major Lee DSO RA by Area Commandant, Major Gardiner RA, nd but February 1940.

134 The medical ORBAT consisted of a field ambulance forward with the brigade, a CCS section in the Legouest military hospital in Metz, and an ambulance train on call. The Legouest is now an Army Training Hospital. TNA WO 197/42: Saar Force Administration, 'Location of Units in Reserve Area', nd but February 1940.

135 For the logistic laydown, see Map 11: Saar Force - Administrative Laydown.

136 TNA WO 167/210: 2 Division CRASC, WD, 23 January1940. The 2nd Division RASC Composite Company left for Metz by train on 23 January 1940.

137 The documents record the ammunition depot as a dump but because specialist technical personnel operated the site, it was doctrinally a depot. The ordnance store was a Force not a unit asset and thus also a depot. TNA WO 197/42: Saar Force Administration, 'Location of Units in Reserve Area', nd but February 1940.

138 TNA WO 167/433: HQ Force K6, WD, 19 February 1940 and GHQ (O) GR/567/O (S) dated 17 March 1940 in WO 197/42: Saar Force Administration, refers.

Table 11.1
BEF Force W – Logistic ORBAT[139]
February 1940

Unit	Component	Location	Remarks
Composite Company RASC (-)*	Forward	Brigade area	*Ammo & Petrol sections
Light Aid Detachment RAOC		Veckring	
Ammunition Depot RAOC	Reserve	Bois de Rugy	Chailly-les-Ennery
Composite Company RASC (-)		co-located DID	* Supply Column section
Detailed Issues Depot RASC		Saint Agathe NE Woippy	Including coal & coke
EFI RASC		Woippy	
Fuel Depot		Haute Guenange	Host Nation
Field Bakery Section RASC		co-located DID	
Ordnance Stores Depot RAOC		co-located DID	
Postal Detachment RE		co-located DID	

Appointed by and reporting to GHQ[140] in order to co-ordinate the operations of the Reserve Area logistic component with the Force W Brigade and HQ Third French Army, was an Area Commandant whose duties were laid down in *Field Service Regulations*[141] but from practical experience these were locally amended by the incumbent to deliver the relevant outputs.[142] Effectively the Area Commandant was the Deputy Assistant QMG (DAQMG) to Force W, although the post also involved ensuring RE material was appropriately supplied, which was usually the responsibility of a CRE, and acting as Assistant Provost Marshal. This was an appointment that whilst only graded at the rank of major, required an officer, whose inter-personal and professional skills, in dealing with a combination of brigadiers and above, Host Nation HQs and the technical logistic experts in the Force, needed to be of the highest quality. The Area Commandant's key internal task was monitoring logistic stock levels to ensure the appropriate combat capability was maintained. This was of especial importance during the winter months because of the adverse influence of the weather upon the flow of *materiel* from the Base as demands usually took six to nine days to arrive and on one occasion a railway

139 Table compiled from information in TNA WO 197/42: Saar Force Administration, 'Location of Units in Reserve Area', nd but February 1940. This document contains eight figure grid references for each site.
140 The first incumbent in the post of Area Commandant is wholesome in his praise of all the GHQ Branch members with whom he dealt. TNA WO 197/42: Saar Force Administration, 'Brief for Incoming Saar Area Commandant'.
141 Army Council, FSR, Vol I, *Organization and Administration*, Chp XVI, Sect 143, pp.230-232.
142 TNA WO 197/42: Saar Force Administration, 'Brief for Incoming Saar Area Commandant'.

wagon was in transit for 17 days.[143] Externally, the key task was liaison with HQ Third French Army. The most significant concern was developing a close relationship to ensure that French logistic support was effective and that the rotating brigades remained inside the French military and civilian social envelope. Matters such as obtaining large quantities of food from the local economy by units, which generated area shortages and price inflation, the protection of farm animals and the care of billets, were all contentious issues that required constant attention from the Area HQ and two specific concerns, which HQ Third Army raised, involved units burning unprotected candles in barns[144] and discarding razor blades into farm straw.[145]

A particular issue was the effective operation of the reverse logistic chain for the refilling of the French 10 litre fuel cans and 50 litre drums, the return of which, was critical to the French fuel distribution system. This problem was partly cultural because the BEF relied for the most part on the disposable 4-gallon 'flimsy' and units were not attuned to return them but equally the French drums were often mis-appropriated for 'various purposes,'[146] an action that was such an irritation to the French logisticians in Third Army that a serious complaint over the loss of 'a very large number' was made in February 1940 by French *Grand Quartier General*, which required the personal intervention of the commander of the British 1st Guards Brigade.[147] Units were ordered to search for and collect all empty drums and deliver them to the RASC CTC Petrol section for return to the Host Nation but the problem was still an on-going issue in April.[148] Regulatory issues relating to rail and road movement were a constant theme, with WMT and tracked A vehicle speed limits and 'thaw precautions' being of especial concern to HQ Third French Army because a substantial component of French military transport was horse-drawn.[149] On a more mundane level, but likely to cause irritation to the Host Nation if it was not resolved, was the requirement, covering both Q and APM responsibilities, to ensure all military bicycles conformed to French traffic regulations, especially in relation to lighting.[150]

Conclusion

For logisticians, the period between the completion of the First Contingent deployment and the execution of Plan D was one of constant industry and activity. Whilst the media suggested that the BEF was a static operation, the development of its logistics was a constant dynamic as planners and soldiers sought to enhance the resilience and scope of its support. The greatest

143 TNA WO 197/42: Saar Force Administration, 'Brief for Incoming Saar Area Commandant'.
144 The hazard of fires in farm barns is well described by Gun Buster, *Return via Dunkirk,* pp.68-72.
145 TNA WO 197/42: Saar Force Administration, 'Notes by Area Commandant Saar Force on Administrative Matters' dated 2 April 1940, para 8, Billets.
146 TNA WO 197/42: Saar Force Administration, Loose Minute to Commander 1st Guards Brigade from Saar Force Area Commandant ACW 251 dated 14 February 1940.
147 TNA WO 197/42: Saar Force Administration, Loose Minute to Commander 1st Guards Brigade from Saar Force Area Commandant ACW 251 dated 14 February 1940.
148 TNA WO 197/42: Saar Force Administration, Force W Area Routine Order RO No 8 dated 18 April 1940, Ser 9, Petrol Drums.
149 TNA WO 197/42: Saar Force Administration, Loose Minute to Commander 4th Infantry Brigade from Saar Force Area Commandant ACW 86 dated 2 January 1940, 'Restrictions on Traffic after a Thaw'.
150 TNA WO 197/42: Saar Force Administration, Force W Area Routine Order RO No 13 dated 1 May 1940, Ser 3, Bicycles, directing units to indent for rear lights and supporting brackets.

challenge in the winter months was undoubtedly the weather, which disrupted construction, movement and training, whilst creating additional rigours for soldiers living in the field and the arrival of the spring was greeted with much relief. Whilst the logisticians did their best to keep the wheel turning during these three months, there is little doubt that the harsh conditions bent the logistic development programme out of shape.

The logisticians, however, made, for the most part, good use of the time, particularly in maturing relations with the Host Nation at every level, although there were inevitable frictions, especially with local civil authorities and agencies. These were usually resolved with positive intervention from logistic commanders through the French liaison officers, but it was a task that required careful management and positive inter-personal skills. Interaction with technical military and civil logistic organizations and Commands were usually professional and cordial but required shaping to ensure the most effective use of resources, with the influence of national military logistic culture often being a challenging issue, the fuel can subject in Force W being an example. The demands upon WMT were relentless. This resulted in not only sometimes ruthless measures to create efficiency but also an adverse influence upon tactical, technical and military training in logistic units, an issue compounded by the provision of WMT support to the Host Nation civil authorities.

The supply, fuel and ordnance components of the BEF's logistic system were well practised by April 1940, albeit in a non-operational static environment, whilst the ammunition element was the most fragile. The key logistic planning work was devoted to maturing the administrative plan and supporting instruction to enable the movement of the BEF's corps to the defensive line on the River Dyle. The documents were constantly being revised to take account of changes in the operational plan, new logistic information and the arrival of reinforcing combat and logistic units but the key challenge was the apparent paucity of current information from Belgium. There were presumably some unofficial contacts with the Belgian railway authorities and other material may have arrived from War Office intelligence sources and the British Military Attaché, but all this is opaque in the logistic documents and requires a study to examine the extent to which logistic planning was degraded by this situation.

12

Tracks Across France
Railway operations during the preparatory phase September 1939 – May 1940

Setting the Scene

The lay-down and ORBAT of the BEF and the AASF had a strong influence upon the requirement for railway units and their structure, training and employment. The Royal Engineers, the Corps responsible for conducting British military railway operations, had significant experience of supporting global deployments, especially during the Great War. In June 1918, on the Western Front, the Railway Operating Division (ROD),[1] was employing, 18,235 operating and workshop personnel, with another 14,080 involved in Standard Gauge Railway (SGR) construction and maintenance, supporting the operation of 1,247 SGR locomotives, increasing to 1,421 by December.[2] This key pool of capability, whilst greatly reduced, had not entirely evaporated, with Great War soldiers serving in the Regular Army, Regular Reserve, Territorial Army and Supplementary Reserve (SR).[3] The War Office and RE planners were also cognizant of the failure to deploy sufficient railway operating and construction units to France in August 1914 as a result of the agreement between the British and the French that the Host Nation would be responsible for all railway operating for the BEF.

This was a mistake that the Staff were not intending to repeat, so in addition to the three Regular railway companies, the War Office had created seven SR companies, each of which was sponsored and 'manned' by one of the 'Big Four' commercial railways.[4] Indeed, one of

1 For ROD operations particulars, see, *Transportation on the Western Front*. For railway operations in the operational context see, Major-General H L Pritchard (ed.) *The History of the Corps of Royal Engineers*, Vol V, *The Home Front, France, Flanders and Italy in the First World War* (Chatham: The Institution of the Royal Engineers, 1952) and the classic illustrated work, William A T Aves, *ROD, The Railway Operating Division on the Western Front, The Royal Engineers in France and Belgium, 1915-1919* (Donington: Shaun Tyas, 2009).

2 War Office, *Statistics of the Military Effort of the British Empire, during the Great War, 1914-1920* (HMSO, 1922), p.600 (i), Table (iii) - Establishment and Strength of the Railway Personnel Employed in the various Theatres of War.

3 The role of the railways in supporting the BEF and RAF leave movement is examined in Chp 9, 'White Cliffs'.

4 Great Western, London Midland & Scottish, London & North Eastern and Southern.

the key features of the BEF's railway component was the reliance on the early mobilization of the SR units, which until January 1940, provided 86 percent of the operating and construction capacity and 100 percent of the railway stores and workshop output. Brigadier D J McMullen, Director-General Transportation (DGT) in GHQ BEF, assisted by two deputies and their supporting Staffs was responsible for directing and managing British military railway resources in France. The efficiency of the British contribution was enhanced because the BEF's railway component was controlled through one Corps, the Royal Engineers, which was responsible for infrastructure construction and repair, railway operating and signalling, and locomotive and rolling stock maintenance. This level of integration, which was reinforced by the experience of the Great War on the Western Front,[5] replicated commercial practice, although with generally greater corporate interactions across the departments but also created synergies across the logistic chain, which would have been impossible to generate through other arrangements.

During the deployment, the focus was solely upon the enhancement and utilization of the SGR[6] system, although there were suggestions, based upon the experience of the Great War, that within depots, Narrow Gauge Railways (NGR)[7] using 60 cm gauge *Decauville* rail system should be constructed to move material. The lead Deputy-Director Transportation, Colonel Woodhouse, wrote a cogent response to these proposals,[8] explaining that the introduction of NGR would increase double-handling of stocks,[9] divert labour from SGR projects, create more competition for shipping space, introduce yet more motive power equipment types to the Theatre with a concomitant requirement for spares and repairs and generate the need to skilled operatives to operate the systems.[10] On balance he was, 'Generally speaking,.......averse to the proposal....' but was gracious enough to comment that the views of his fellow Deputy Director, Colonel Waghorn might 'perhaps point to a different conclusion.'[11] A large amount' of NGR equipment is recorded as having arrived on aboard the SS *Melrose Abbey* on 20 January 1940 but none of the Railway Construction Company (RCC) war diaries make reference to its disposal,[12] although some of the assets were used to support the construction of fortifications and aerodromes,[13] reinforced by assets from French contractors, many of which acquired the materiel from BEF disposal sales after the Great War.

5 For an analysis within a wider strategic logistic perspective, see, Ian Malcolm Brown, *British Logistics on the Western Front, 1914-1919* (Westport Connecticut & London: Praeger, 1998).
6 A railway that has a track gauge of 4 feet 8½ inches (1435 mm). In 2020, Standard Gauge is rated between 1432 mm and 1435 mm to account for those SGRs, which have been reduced in gauge by 3 mm, to improve the ride of high-speed trains. In some documents and publications, SGR is described as Broad Gauge, which is technically incorrect but was a term used by some personnel in the BEF, and their forebears in the Great War, and appears in contemporary documents.
7 A railway with a track gauge of less than 4 feet 8½ inches (1432-1435 mm).
8 TNA WO 167/51: GHQ, Transportation, DG Tn R/46 dated 8 November 1939.
9 He noted that, 'Labour is short and this proposal will entail double handling, which is, I believe, most important to avoid'. TNA WO 167/51: GHQ, Service, Transportation, DG Tn R/46 dated 8 November 1939.
10 The *Decauville* track panels were a particular issue.
11 TNA WO 167/51: GHQ, Transportation, DG Tn R/46 dated 8 November 1939.
12 TNA WO 167/876: 2 Docks Group RE, WD.
13 See comment and diagram in Thurlow, *Building the Gort Line*, pp.281-282.

The RE initially deployed two Regular units, 8 Railway Construction & Operating Company (RCO)[14] and 29 Railway Survey Company,[15] and from the SR, three RCCs: 150 (London & North Eastern Railway (LNER))[16] and 151 (Great Western Railway (GWR))[17] arriving in mid-September 1939 and 152 (GWR)[18] in mid-October. 156 (Southern Railway) Transportation Stores Company (TSC), a key rail logistic unit, also from the SR,[19] arrived in September,[20] followed, in November 1939, by 186 Transportation Construction Company,[21] which was equipped with heavy plant,[22] although this unit was also assigned to tasks involving field defence and fortification works. Initially, the Director of Railways was responsible for the rail construction projects but in February 1940, a Directorate of Transportation Construction was formed in order to bring greater coherency to civil engineering for the Transportation Service, encompassing railway works and port improvements. This action was timely, in that 165 Survey Company[23] arrived in Theatre in January with one RCC arriving each month from January to April 1940.[24] Of the operating units, only one was Regular, two were SR and one Militia, whilst of the construction companies, three were SR and five mainly conscripted Militia.[25]

With the emphasis on rail construction, the deployment of Railway Operating Companies (ROC) was held in abeyance until December 1939 when 154 (GWR) ROC arrived,[26] after which there was a pause until early March 1940 when 153 (LNER) ROC[27] deployed followed by 190 ROC[28] in April. A ROC was large sub-unit with an establishment of 360 personnel of

14 8 RCO remained in France until April 1940 when it was withdrawn to UK in preparation for a potential deployment to Norway. TNA WO 167/906: 8 RCO RE, WD, April 1940.

15 TNA WO 167/918: 29 Railway Survey Company RE, WD, entries September 1939.

16 TNA WO 167/945: 150 RCC RE, WD, entries September 1939.

17 TNA WO 167/946: 151 RCC RE, WD, entries September 1939.

18 TNA WO 167/947: 152 RCC RE, WD, entries October 1939.

19 These SR units were well established organizations recruiting suitable personnel from the commercial railway companies and conducting structured annual training at the RE Railway Training Centre at Longmoor. See, 'The Woolmer Instructional Military Railway', *The Railway Gazette*, 25 November 1932 and for details of training, the comprehensive David Ronald & Mike Christensen OBE, *The Longmoor Military Railway: A New History*, Vol One: *1903-1939* (Lydney: Lightmoor Press, 2012).

20 TNA WO 167/951: 156 TSC RE, WD, entries September 1939.

21 Company HQ and one section arrived in November and the other two sections in December.

22 The WE (IV/1931/17A/1) included 6 angle dozers, 2 heavy-duty rooters, 20 scrapers, 36 excavators and 36 dumpers. Personnel totalled 371. See, Philson, Vol 3, pp.64-65.

23 TNA WO 167/956: 165 Railway Survey Company RE, WD, entries December 1939.

24 157 RCC on 21 January 1940; TNA WO 167/952, WD. 158 RCC on 6 February; TNA WO 167/953. 159 RCC on 31 March; TNA WO 167/954. 161 RCC in mid-April; TNA WO 167/955.

25 The youth of the soldiers in the Militia units is highlighted by the ages of those lost from 159 RCC who were aboard HMT *Lancastria*. Judging from the ages of those killed in the Rennes train bombing, the SR ROCs were comprised of older men, with most casualties being in their mid-thirties.

26 TNA WO 167/949: 154 ROC RE, WD, December 1939. Regrettably, the war diary has few details relating to operations in France.

27 TNA WO 167/948: 153 ROC RE, WD, March 1940. Regrettably, the war diary has few details relating to operations in France.

28 TNA WO 167/960: 190 ROC RE, WD, April 1940. 190 ROC was a Militia unit and after post evacuation service in the UK, deployed to the Middle East to operate, in conjunction with 153 ROC, railways in Persia December 1941 - January 1943. See, R M Robbins, *190 in Persia* (London: Published Privately, 1951). His private papers from his military railway service in Iran and Greece are

P12.1 Railway Construction Training. 152 (GWR) RCC RE, a Supplementary Reserve unit at Hopkins Bridge LMR in July 1935. Although not Regular units, the RE railway SR companies were embedded as a core logistic deployment capability in the BEF and were generally well trained in comparison to other SR units. (WDLMRC: DRMC/V1/141)

mixed trades including 54 Drivers, Railway Engine,[29] 54 Locomotive Firemen, 74 Brakesmen and Shunters, 14 Traffic Operators, and 26 Railway Checkers and Clerks.[30] As the BEF expanded, the War Office sought to ensure that railway capability kept pace with the task, an aspiration that sometimes created friction with the Government's Railway Executive Committee (REC), which controlled the UK's civil railways. The key challenge always remained the shortage of trained manpower, a problem compounded by the recognition that the commercial railways in the UK were critical not only to the economy but also the prosecution of the war and that mobilizing railway staff from the civilian sector for military service required careful management.[31] Conscripting the right people however, made a significant difference.

held in IWM/Documents.21752. Michael Robbins (1915-2003) had a distinguished post-war career in London Transport, as a transportation historian and a societal contributor, including originating the London Transport Museum. Obituary, *The Times*, 3 January 2003.

29 The Army was specific about the term 'Driver' because there were several trades including MT, Horse Transport and Locomotive.

30 WE IV/1931/18/2, in Philson, BEFORBAT, Vol 3, pp.67.

31 At the beginning of the Great War, thousands of men had left the railways to join the Army, mainly infantry units, which were outside their trade, creating shortfalls in key areas, whilst failing to generate military capability related to their skill-set. By 15 August 1914, 27,600 railway staff had been mobilized (Territorial Force and Reserves) or volunteered for military service. In mid-September, the War Office

Sapper Thomas Brownbill was a Militiaman and a Passed Cleaner on the LMS, but after three months training at the RE No 1 Railway Training Centre (RTC) at Longmoor in Hampshire, he quickly found his feet serving in 190 ROC, adapting to 'living on the locomotive' during operations in France.[32]

Concepts and Doctrine

The significance of railways to British Army operations has declined since the Second World War but in 1939, railways were the transportation method of choice for intra-Theatre strategic movement. Whilst the term C4IRM (Command, Control, Communications, Coordination Intelligence & Resource Management) was not in use at that time, the effective utilization of railway assets relied explicitly on these processes. In particular, the co-ordination of the British Army's requirements with the Host Nation railway, the nationalized SNCF,[33] was key in balancing the needs of the BEF with those of the French defence effort and the civil need. Doctrinally, rail operations[34] were focused upon delivering the key component of surface transportation[35] from the 4th Line Base[36] to 2nd Line road units and operated mostly as a 3rd Line system.[37] Although often 'grouped' for technical command, railway capability was based upon specific to role sub-units: Construction, Operating, Stores, Workshops and Signal & Telegraph.[38] Railway units allocated to the Base were 4th Line assets, whilst those operating forward of it, were 3rd Line. The rear element at 4th Line consisted of a rail grouping located within the Base Sub-Areas (BSA) encompassing dock railways at the Sea Ports of Debarkation (SPOD) with its associated sorting and exchange sidings, through to rail-served base depots and one or more Base Marshalling Yards (BMY).

The BMY had four key tasks: first, the sorting and marshalling of traffic from the depots, in order to create trainloads for formations; secondly, the re-circulation of empty wagons from the corps railheads to the docks and depots; thirdly, local regulation of passenger and ambulance trains and fourthly, control of ex-port traffic, which could be sent directly to depots. Entraining and detraining at stations assigned for unit personnel, reinforcements and vehicles were not a Transportation task and not therefore, a component of the BMY. A mixture of British Army units and the Host Nation railway organization usually conducted railway operating

directed recruiting offices not to accept railwaymen unless they had a certificate of release from their company. See, Edwin Pratt, *British Railways and the Great War: Organization, Efforts, Difficulties and Achievements*, Vol I (London: Selwyn & Blount, 1921), pp.348-378.

32 Memory of Sapper Thomas Brownbill of 190 ROC RE, quoted in Aves, *Supporting the British Expeditionary Force*, pp.43-44.

33 Until 1937, the SNCF had consisted of five commercial companies. It was a modern Western European system operating 15,000 locomotives and 450,000 wagons and although organized in five regions had a Central Movement Service (CMS) coordinating inter-regional and international traffic.

34 See, Army Council, *Military Engineering*, Vol VIII, *Railways*.

35 Surface Transportation included rail, road and IWT.

36 In 1939, British logistic doctrine directed that 4th Line assets be deployed to theatres as a forward component of the UK Base.

37 For a comprehensive explanation, see, Quartermaster-General, *Notes on Military Railway Engineering*, Part IV, *Operating* (War Office 1942), pp.9-22.

38 Known to railwaymen as S&T. For an outline of the military arrangements, see, WOOH, *Signal Communications*, Colonel T B Gravely OBE (Comp.) (War Office, 1950), pp.377-381.

and maintenance in BSAs. The intermediate element was a Main Line component, which might consist of several allocated routes usually operated by SNCF. The third element was the Railhead Sub-Area (RSA) usually consisting of a Regulating Station to control the flow of traffic and several railheads[39] in the Corps Rear Area, often allocated to task: pack supplies, petroleum products, ammunition, engineer stores and ambulance trains. Operations forward of these corps' railheads were usually the responsibility of the Host Nation during the deployment phase but were assigned to a BEF RCO[40] or ROC once active operations had commenced.[41] This enabled railheads to be pushed forward to the divisional rear areas if the logistic situation demanded it and the tactical scenario allowed it.

Civil Railway Engineering

In a re-run of the deployment of the BEF to France in 1914, the SNCF initially handled all British Army traffic and was responsible for maintaining and upgrading the private and SNCF sidings used by the BEF, either using SNCF staff or through contract.[42] The BEF focus was therefore, on constructing rail access to depots with most of these works being conducted by the RE or civilian contractors supervised by them, with the exception of the switches and signalling for connections to the French network, which was a SNCF responsibility.[43] Railway infrastructure design and assessment was vested in two railway survey companies,[44] whilst construction was the responsibility of the RCC supported by AMPC labour and occasionally supplemented by RE general construction companies. Whilst RCCs could deliver construction and repair capability in the combat environment, AMPC and Host Nation civilian labour was critical to the progression of major projects and effective in increasing output in smaller ones. The construction of railway facilities[45] to support British military and air operations was a very significant task that continued to expand throughout the period of the BEF's deployment, with SNCF and French Army engineering assets supplementing British resources.

39 A railhead is a transhipment point between rail and another type of transport. In 1940, a railhead was defined as a point on the railway along the line of advance or withdrawal that was deemed to be the terminus for rail operations and at which transhipment to another mode of transportation was enacted; this was usually by WMT. By doctrinal definition therefore, points along the railway at which units drew personnel, material, supplies and ammunition were not railheads. See, Army Council, *Military Engineering*, Vol VIII, *Railways*, p.97.

40 The RCO Company was established to conduct railway operating and Permanent Way (PW) repair in a tactical environment. In 1939, there was only one RCO, 8 Company RE.

41 In May 1940, the task was given to 153 ROC SR because the Regular unit, 8 RCO was, in late April 1940, withdrawn from France to the UK, in anticipation of a deployment to Norway, which then matured. TNA WO 167/906: 8 RCO, WD.

42 Memorandum of the Agreements concluded with the Delegation of the *Commission Centrale de SNCF* headed by M Besnerais, *Directeur Générale de la SNCF* dated 21 September 1939. TNA WO 167/51: GHQ Transportation Service.

43 TNA WO 167/51: GHQ Transportation Service.

44 The 29th, a Regular company and 165th, a Reserve unit.

45 For a contemporary resume of the technical aspects, see Army Council, *Military Engineering*, Vol VIII, *Railways* and QMG, *Notes on Military Engineering*, Part I, *Survey* and Part II, *Engineering* (War Office, 1940).

P12.2 Railway Drama. Training did not always mature as planned. A toppled self-propelled steam excavator at Whitehill on the LMR. Repair and re-railing skills learned in the inter-war period were invaluable during operations in France. (RLCM: A2/MT/RLCAB/0001918/1)

The order of priority for works was establishing the Transportation Stores Depots (TSD), building the BMY at Rennes,[46] constructing rail spurs and sidings to serve the expanding Base depots, creating hospital sidings for ambulance trains and lastly, installing feeder lines to the sites of new airfields in Northern France to enable the delivery of the thousands of tons of sand, aggregate and cement needed to complete these RAF infrastructure projects for which the Army, through the RE, was responsible.[47] These tasks required such prodigious quantities of material that rail movement was the only meaningful solution and had the additional benefit that once the construction task was complete the railway could be used to deliver munitions, stores, fuel and supplies.[48] Last but certainly not least, was the repair of BEF and SNCF railway facilities, damaged by accident or enemy action.[49]

The RE with all the professional zeal for which, the Corps is renown, started work in short order, supported by eight railway labour companies of the AMPC.[50] 150 RCC commenced

46 This was agreed at a meeting between DGT, the French Army and SNCF at the *Ministre de la Guerre* in Paris on 27 October 1939. TNA WO 167/51: GHQ Services, Transportation.

47 Army Council, FSR, Vol I, *Organization and Administration*, p.149.

48 BEF and RAF - Construction of Rail Served Depots at Appx to Chp 12 summarizes the key projects.

49 One of the 'Lessons Identified' from the enactment of this task was the need to have sufficient WMT within the construction units to create the relevant mobility.

50 TNA WO 167/51: GHQ Services, Transportation, Railway Labour, A/139 dated 23 October 1939. The document from DGT, Brigadier D J McMullen, requested the Director of Railways, Colonel E

constructing a siding at Braye, a SNCF marshalling yard to the South-East of Rennes for No 1 TSD RE using materials and tools from SNCF, on 15 September 1939, two days after the unit arrived in France. The siding was completed on 26 September with work commencing on constructing the rail works in the depot, supported by labour from 17 Company AMPC, on 2 October,[51] a detachment of 186 Transportation Construction Company arriving on 3 December equipped with excavators and dumpers to speed the construction activity.[52] On 20 November, work started at Bruz to build the rail facilities for 1 Base Ordnance Depot (BOD), SNCF installing the connection to the main line on 18 December, whilst construction of the railway sidings for 4 Petroleum Oils & Lubricants Depot (POLD) at Moult Argences was initiated on 20 December.[53]

Essential to these outputs was the work of 156 TSC, which arrived in mid-September[54] and was responsible for supplying rail, switches, fishplates and supporting railway infrastructure accessories. 156 TSC controlled No 1 TSD at Braye and managed the development of No 2 TSD at Carquefou to the North of Nantes, which was in-loaded during October with 5,371 tons of stores on 19 trains.[55] Holdings on 31 October 1939 were sufficient to construct nine miles of single track and by the end of November this had increased to 31.34 miles.[56] During October 1939, it handled receipts and issues of 8,500 tons in 602 wagons, increasing to 11,455 tons in 679 wagons by December 1939. Also essential to railway construction was ballast, 1,000 cubic yards of which, was required to each mile of single track.[57]

One RCC required 1,000 unskilled labourers to operate at maximum efficiency. In the summer, a RCC could lay about four miles of track per week, and in the winter, 2.5 miles.[58] The reduced output was not only a product of the more challenging winter meteorological conditions but also less daylight, which in Northern France is only eight hours in mid-December, or possibly less depending upon the weather conditions but in excess of 16 hours in mid-June. The 156 TSC war diary summarized the problem: 'No work has been done at night. It is very difficult and somewhat dangerous to off-load rails and sleepers by hand at night, unless very good floodlighting can be arranged'.[59] The winter of 1939-40 in Northern France and the United Kingdom was the coldest since 1895,[60] compounded by the most persistent lying snow since 1879, so there was severe disruption to the progression of some of the works, many of which were not completed before the evacuation in June 1940.[61]

A Johnston, thus: 'Will you please ensure that they are allocated to Railway Construction as early as possible if they are not already so employed'.

51 TNA WO 167/945: 150 RCC RE, WD.
52 TNA WO 167/956: 186 Transportation Construction Company RE, WD.
53 TNA WO 167/945: 150 RCC RE, WD.
54 196 TSC deployed in April 1940 to reinforce 156 TSC. TNA WO 167/961.
55 Initially SNCF shunted the trains into the depot but with the pace of activity increasing SNCF assigned a diesel-shunter to the site. TNA WO 167/951: 156 TSC RE, WD, entry 24 October 1939.
56 TNA WO 167/951: 156 TSC RE, WD, entry 31 October 1939.
57 TNA WO 167/51: GHQ Transportation, DGT 39/31 dated 11 October 1939, 'Assessment of the Requirement for Railway Ballast, November 1939 - April 1940'. The total amount was 200,000 tons.
58 See, *The Nautical Almanac* published annually by HMSO.
59 TNA WO 167/951: 156 TSC, WD, entry 24 October 1939.
60 Eden, *Great British Weather Disasters*, p.252.
61 By mid-May 1940, the following had been achieved: 17 miles of track laid with 90 Pound Per Yard (PPY) rail with 210 turnouts (points) and 124 miles of track laid with 75 PPY rail with 455 turnouts.

The daily stone requirement for aerodrome construction and BEF defence works required 14 trains *per diem* but the output from the quarries usually only delivered eight, so inevitably these projects fell behind schedule.[62] The severe cold of February and March 1940 did however, create a railway civil engineering opportunity. At the airfields, the aggregate for the concrete usually arrived at a railway spur or siding and was then transferred to the site by road, a considerable task as an average of 10,000 tons was required for each site.[63] With the ground frozen hard, the SGR spurs were often extended onto the runway work sites on un-ballasted track thereby removing double handling using WMT, which thus increased the distribution flow rate, whilst reducing the labour demand. Once the thaw came in late March, these temporary tracks became unusable and were removed but they were a most useful temporary expedient.[64]

Mechanical Railway Engineering

Military mechanical engineering capability was delivered by three discrete components: two Railway Workshop Companies (RWC),[65] two Mobile Railway Workshops (MRW)[66] and an ambulance train maintenance company comprising two sections. The Railway Workshops Group, the CO of which was also assigned as the Chief Mechanical Engineer, controlled all these assets. Initially because there were no British locomotives or rolling stock in-Theatre, there was no requirement for railway mechanical repair units in France, but once British motive power was assigned to the BEF it was decided to provide appropriate military support. 155 (LMS) RWC arrived in late January 1940, its tradesmen then suffering from an influenza epidemic in the unit, although during February engineering machinery was installed in a disused locomotive shed at Saint Nazaire.[67] In early March, soldiers from 155 RWC were assisting 156 TSC with the manual handling of rail stores, which was perhaps not the most effective use of their skills, but by the middle of the month technical work had commenced to modify the incoming 0-6-0 Dean Goods freight locomotives from the GWR for operating on the French rail network, to undertake running repairs and manufacture items for the TSC and Docks Groups.[68]

To increase capability, negotiations were in hand to utilize part of the SNCF Batignolles locomotive workshops in Paris as a heavy repair shop and to provide light assets at Savenay and Abancourt, with a third proposed for Saint Malo. The MRWs were located at Saint Nazaire and Rennes being tasked with conducting minor repairs to locomotives and rolling

70% of this work was completed by the RE and supporting units, with the balance undertaken by the French Army and the SNCF.

62 WOOH, *Military Engineering (Field)*, p.7.

63 Ibid, p.284.

64 Ibid.

65 For the RE layout of a Railway Workshop, see, Army Council, *Military Engineering*, Vol VII, *Accommodation and Installations*, Plate 112, Railway Workshops Layout.

66 An officer in No 1 MRW was a Second-Lieutenant William Stanier, son of the famous Chief Mechanical Engineer of the LMS.

67 TNA WO 167/950: 155 RWC RE, WD, entries February 1940.

68 The modifications included a Westinghouse air-braking system, the installation of brake pipes on the tenders and the fitting of Flaman speed indicators and recording equipment. TNA WO 167/950: 155 RWC RE, WD, entries March 1940. For a detailed description of the technical work undertaken in the UK and in France on the Dean Goods locomotives, see, Aves, *Supporting the British Expeditionary Force*, pp.25-30.

stock but more importantly, to execute a programme, in conjunction with 155 RWC, to fit ex-GWR locomotives with Westinghouse brakes for operating in France and spark arrestors for operations in ammunition and POL depots and port areas.[69] 199 RWC[70] arriving in May 1940, was established in a disused shed at Martainville near Rouen. No 1 Ambulance Train Maintenance Section arrived in January 1940. Based at Dieppe, its work was essential to the delivery of medical evacuation capability. No 2 Section deployed from the UK in May 1940 to Etaples, but the German advance prompted its evacuation to UK before it was fully operational.

Taking The Strain

The railways in France were critical in delivering and sustaining the BEF's deployment including logistic support, engineering projects, defence works, airfield construction, unit, personnel and equipment reinforcement, leave, course, training and rotation programmes and medical evacuation. Without the railways, the BEF, like the French Army, could not have functioned, which is why they were central to defence planning in Western Europe in 1939 and 1940. The table below, showing the BEF's military imports, less flying aircraft, to France, concisely exposes the size and scope of the railway transportation task:

Table 12.1
BEF and AASF – Military Imports[71]
September 1939 – June 1940

Commodity	Quantity
Ammunition	109,000 tons
Petroleum Products	166,000 tons
General Stores	449,000 tons
Tanks	704
MT Vehicles	68,618
Motor Cycles	21,161
Personnel	732,531

As the logistic requirements and operational imperatives of the BEF continued to grow, it became obvious to the planners that the manpower, motive power and rolling stock available to the SNCF would be insufficient to support the British and French defence efforts and the French civilian economy. The British therefore, agreed in late October 1939, to import additional military and civil resources in order to assume responsibility for railway traffic from the ports to the Base depots and from December 1939 onwards, British railway capability was

69 Aves, *Supporting the British Expeditionary Force*, p.72.
70 There is no war diary for 199 RWC in the TNA for the campaign in France but it is assessed that the untitled RWC mentioned in WOOH, *Transportation*, p.42, is this unit.
71 Table compiled from information in WOOH, *Movements*, Appendices to Chp 10.

P12.3 Rail Wagons. The BEF sought to import wagons from British railway companies until sufficient stock designed for BEF use in the UK and France could be manufactured. (Author)

reinforced with a steady stream of units. All railway units were under the operational command of the DGT GHQ except for the ambulance trains. Within this matrix, HQ No 1 Railway Operating Group had control of all railway operating units, whilst the HQs No 1, 2 and 3 Construction & Maintenance Groups were responsible for directing new builds, repair and maintenance activities through control of allocated assets, although units were often detailed to provide detachments to support operating outside their geographic boundaries. The key point to highlight is that whilst the BEF was the only army in the French campaign that was fully motorized,[72] the deployed formations relied almost entirely upon the railway for its logistic support from the Main Base areas.

To meet this rapidly expanding demand, the War Office was obliged to increase the outputs from the training system, initially relying upon No 1 RTC, the Army's oldest railway training facility opened in 1903 based at the Longmoor Military Railway (LMR),[73] which also supported

72 With the exception of the specialist animal transport component.

73 See, Ronald & Christensen, *The Longmoor Military Railway: A New History,* Vol One: *1903-1939*, pp.113-197 and Vol Two: *World War Two and the Cold War Era* (Lydney: Lightmoor Press, 2013),

the Bordon-Longmoor-Liss military complex and the associated TSDs, with connections to the Southern Railway at Bordon and Liss.[74] To reinforce this capability, the War Office opened No 2 RTC on the Melbourne Military Railway,[75] a requisitioned section of the LMS line between Ashby-de-la-Zouch and Melbourne Junction.[76] The centre also provided engineer rail construction training and serviced the King's Newton (No 2 UK) TSD , whilst also serving several commercial facilities including a soap works, a colliery, a lime factory and a quarry, the latter important for stone in the Air Ministry's airfield construction programme.[77]

To generate more lift capacity, an order was placed in December 1939 in the UK for the manufacture of 10,000 x 12 ton tare weight box vans for use in the French wagon pool.[78] Based upon a French design with centre sliding doors to accommodate 40 men & 8 horses, these wagons had some detachable parts to enable them to run on the UK system and were constructed for ease of repair in the field; none reached France before the evacuation of the BEF. In the interim, 500 British freight wagons were shipped to France, although because they were

pp.355-359. The LMR was also the setting for the remarkable train chase in the film, *The Great St Trinian's Train Robbery* (1965).

74 The connection diagrams are shown in Richard Harman and Gerry Nichols, Gerry, *Atlas of the Southern Railway* (Addlestone: Ian Allan, 2016), Map 55.

75 See, Alan Cooper, Peter Leggott & Cyril Sprenger, *The Melbourne Military Railway, A History of the Railway Training Centre at Melbourne and King's Newton: 1939-1945* (Headington: Oakwood Press, 1990).

76 Chellaston East Junction to a point one mile North of Ashby-de-la-Zouch Station.

77 Cooper, Leggott & Sprenger, *The Melbourne Military Railway.*

78 As a planning yardstick, the BEF used the load tables below when calculating the material and equipment movement based on a 10 ton rail freight wagon. Army Council, FSPB, Pamphlet No 7, 1939, *Movement by Sea, Rail and Air*, p.16.

Table 12.2
Rail Movement Planning – Wagon Loads in Tons

Commodity	Load (tons)	Remarks	Commodity	Load (tons)	Remarks
Ammunition	10		Mail	5	
Ballast	10	For rail construction	MFO Parcels	5	
Canteen Stores	5		Medical Stores	5	
Cement	10		Metal	10	Brass, copper, iron, scrap
Clothing	5		Ordnance Stores	5	
Coal	10		Petrol	8	In tins and cased
Coke	6		Railway material	9	Excluding PW ballast
Engineer Stores	7		Supplies	7	Including rations
Forage	5		Timber	6	Scantlings & hut sections

not fitted with air-brakes, the French placed strict operating conditions upon their use; these wagons were left in France.[79]

A key objective to improve the efficiency of military rail movement was undertaken by the 4th Department of the French General Staff to classify every tracked and wheeled vehicle in the BEF inventory to match it to one or more of five classes in the SNCF wagon fleet. The driver for this project was to assess the SNCF fleet capability for the French Army and the BEF, which would provide the information required, to take a decision on whether additional wagons for vehicle movement were required.[80] To execute this work, the 4th Department required the vehicle dimensions and axle weights of every vehicle type[81] and DGT BEF initiated, on behalf of the War Office, the collation of this information in October 1939 but it was made more onerous and time-consuming by the vast array of impressed WMT.[82] The DGT Staff also exposed to the French Army and SNCF rail representatives that regardless of the output from the study, the construction of specialist flats to transport future tanks that were heavier and larger, was under consideration.[83] In particular, the War Office was desirous of engaging with the French Railway Central Committee to design a wagon capable of moving on both British and French rail networks and be incorporated to French consists.[84] Another specialized wagon the BEF required, was an Insulated Ice Cooled Van for the movement of frozen meat, a foodstuff the BEF handled considerable quantities of. DGT requested 140 be provided either from production or from the UK railways but as a temporary measure hired 200 vans in the 6-15 ton range through the *Société Francais de Transport et Entrepots Frigerifiques*. As plans matured, the UK ordered an additional 60 cool vans and hired a further 70.[85]

Appropriate wagon lift remained therefore, a constant issue for the BEF and was a problem compounded by three factors. The first was the failure to tightly control wagon loading and unloading at Base depots, which greatly increased turn-round times. Generated by a mixture of hurriedly planned depot layouts, infrastructure constraints and a shortage of engineer construction resources and labour, it was sometime before these matters started to be resolved.

79 The importance of this stock in resolving the shortage of lift is lucidly illustrated by BEF contracts to use French commercial IWT to move petrol, sand and aggregates. TNA WO 167/51: GHQ Services, Transportation, DGT IW/1 dated 14 October 1939, Directorate of IWT.

80 GHQ DGT Loose Minute dated 10 November 1939, Memorandum of the Meeting held in the General Manager's Office of the SNCF, 88 Rue Saint Lazare on 27 October 1939. TNA WO 167/51: GHQ Services, Transportation.

81 GHQ DGT Loose Minute dated 10 November 1939, Memorandum of the Meeting held in the General Manager's Office of the SNCF, 88 Rue Saint Lazare on 27 October 1939. TNA WO 167/51: GHQ Services, Transportation.

82 TNA WO 167/51: GHQ Services, Transportation, DGT R/105 dated 25 October 1939. The SNCF vehicle carrying wagons had a classification number from 1-4 with number 5 being denoted by a plain grenade.

83 The A12 (Matilda II) had a combat weight of 26.50 tons, whilst the A22 (Churchill Mk III) weighed in at 39.0 tons. Chamberlain, Peter and Ellis, Chris, *British and American Tanks of World War Two* (London: Arms & Armour, 2000).

84 GHQ DGT Loose Minute dated 10 November 1939, Memorandum of the Meeting held in the General Manager's Office of the SNCF, 88 Rue Saint Lazare on 27 October 1939; TNA WO 167/51: GHQ Services, Transportation.

85 GHQ DGT Loose Minute dated 10 November 1939, Memorandum of the Meeting held in the General Manager's Office of the SNCF, 88 Rue Saint Lazare on 27 October 1939; TNA WO 167/51: GHQ Services, Transportation.

Secondly, for operational reasons, there was a growing desire to place stocks on railway wheels in order to generate a flexible and response reserve of combat supplies. Whilst entirely logical from the military logistical and operational perspectives, in uncontrolled environments it could easily immobilize precious lift and the issue was one of the commercial imperatives for the railways to charge wagon demurrage to persuade customers not to use railway assets as free storage facilities. Thirdly, several trains dispatched to Ammunition Railheads (ARH) had munitions insecurely loaded in open wagons without sheets, resulting in boxes being damaged and ammunition exposed to the rain.[86] These trains had therefore, to be returned to the depot, unloaded and reconstituted with box vans and new loads; hardly the model of logistic efficiency or indeed of operational capability.[87]

The BEF also required additional motive power, which was provided, as in the Great War, by the acquisition of locomotives from the UK commercial railways, although these required several modifications[88] to operate on the SNCF system. The preparation and deployment of these assets was conducted under the code-name Operation DERWENT. The original plan was to dispatch 100 x 0-6-0 Tender locomotives for heavy shunting duties[89] to arrive by the end of January 1940 followed by 300 x 2-8-0 main line freight locomotives,[90] with a phased deployment commencing in February 1940 at 40 per month. In the event, the 0-6-0 delivery schedule was delayed, with only 79 arriving by May and a decision was taken not to commence the deployment of 2-8-0 locomotives until June 1940, so fortunately none of the latter arrived. In addition, 16 shunting locomotives from the LMS were also dispatched to the BEF: 8 x 350 hp 0-6-0 Diesel-Electric[91] and 8 x steam 3F 0-6-0T Jinty.[92] The three rail ferries operating on

86 In 1940, many ammunition boxes were made of wood.

87 According to a post-war report on ammunition supply in the BEF, 1 BAD RAOC was responsible for these failures. See, TNA CAB 106/235: BEF 1939-40, Ammunition Supply, Brigadier C Gibson, 1945.

88 For the shunting and main line locomotives, these included the removal of the vacuum braking system, Automatic Train Control (ATC) equipment and water scoops and the fitting of Westinghouse air brakes and Flaman speed recorders. Some of these modifications were made in the UK, others by railway units in France. Spark arrestors were also fitted to locomotives operating in fuel and ammunition depots.

89 The locomotives selected were from the GWR 2301 Class (Dean Goods) and all of them required varying degrees of overhaul or repair. Despite their age (those selected had been built between 1890 and 1899) these tender 0-6-0 locomotives were generally reliable and had a relatively low axle and total weight. In addition, the class had been widely deployed with the ROD on the Western Front during the Great War. William A T Aves has investigated the fate of these 79 Dean Goods in *Supporting the British Expeditionary Force*, pp.44-76 and pp.83-87.

90 Pending the delivery from production of War Department 2-8-0 locomotives from the LMS it was planned to dispatch 300 ex-Great Central Railway (GCR) locomotives serving with the LNER. Many of these engines were veterans of the ROD.

91 No 7069 is the sole survivor of the 95 steam and DE locomotives dispatched to France. Captured by the Germans in 1940, it is in private ownership in UK.

92 Five of these locomotives were recovered from France, returning via the Dunkerque-Dover rail ferry between August 1948 and July 1949, and were returned to service with British Railways after overhaul at Derby. Aves, *Supporting the British Expeditionary Force*, p.70. The Jintys remained in British Railways service until 1967 and nine of the type are in preservation, although the none of the BEF survivors are amongst them.

the Harwich-Calais LNER service[93] and the one on the Dover-Dunkerque (Southern Railway) route were essential to the swift delivery of these assets. The early agreement with the Host Nation to import locomotives from the UK to support BEF rail operations[94] led to an urgent need to assess the provision of coal from the UK, the French being unable to provide suitable stocks. By 3 October 1939, the War Office had advised the Mines Department of the monthly requirement in the period October 1939 to September 1939. Commencing with 2,000 tons per month in October including a 1,000 tons initial reserve, the demand rose to 4,000 tons in January 1940, 14,500 in May and 30,500 tons by September.[95] Whilst the details of future rail operations had yet to be decided, it is clear that from his experience in the Great War, DGT BEF envisaged rail activity 'at scale' and directed his Staff to plan accordingly.

Planning and Manning

In addition to the specific railway units allocated to task, there were numerous supporting players on the BEF's railway stage. RE general construction and AMPC companies were essential to the building and repair of the Permanent Way (PW) and a wide range of supporting infrastructure. AMPC companies were also deployed to supply labour at railheads and in the depots. Close liaison was maintained between the BEF and the SNCF at every level. Movement Control elements were vital to the effective management of the BEF's railway system, ensuring effective and efficient use of the assets. A central timing office was established in Paris to co-ordinate rail operations with SNCF HQ and was the rail clearing house for all BEF train schedules, although all initial movement requests were passed through the French Army movements organization. BEF RTOs were deployed at each railway HQ: central, regional and district. Contracts with Host Nation civilian companies and agencies were an indispensable element of the BEF railway matrix and involved many activities including the purchase of stone and sleepers, the hire of accommodation, the negotiation of workshop services, the leasing of sidings, the provision of labour and the delivery of rail services. Finance was also a key task controlled by Director Transportation, the DGT Finance and Accounts Office being located at Rennes with a staff of 27.[96] Originally established to negotiate financial arrangements with the SNCF,[97] it expanded into other transportation arenas, although rail was always the focus. Its

93 These ferries were those built in 1917 and imaginatively named Train Ferry Nos 1-3. These ships operated on the Richborough – Calais and Southampton – Dieppe routes from February 1918. See, Robert Butler, *Richborough Port*, (Ramsgate: Ramsgate Maritime Museum & East Kent Maritime Trust, 1999), pp.15-22 and A J Mullay, *For The King's Service, Railway Ships at War* (Easingwold: Pendragon, 2008), p.64.

94 Memorandum of the Agreements concluded with the Delegation of the *Commission Centrale de SNCF* headed by M Besnerais, Directeur Générale de la SNCF dated 21 September 1939. TNA WO 167/51: GHQ Transportation Service.

95 TNA 167/51: GHQ Services, Transportation, War Office BM/DTn/18 dated 3 October 1939 letter to L G Lowry, Mines Department. The letter noted; 'The coal should be good quality Welsh steam coal and should be shipped from a South Wales port'.

96 Established in September 1939, it consisted of one officer and three Other Ranks, expanding to five officers, 20 Other Ranks and two French civilians. The Finance Office operated until 16 June 1940, being evacuated to the UK the next day.

97 The BEF paid the same rates as the French Army. Most of the financial arrangements were staffed on a rolling basis. A finance convention between GHQ BEF and the SNCF was drafted but was not signed

remit included managing contracts for the hire of private sidings, the leasing of coaching stock for billeting, financial arrangements for traffic on private railways, the charges for BEF motive power and rolling stock running on French tracks and the rates for British locomotives hauling French military and civilian trains.

The RAF also generated what might have been the greatest challenge to the military railways in France. In April 1940, plans were maturing to expand and enhance the RAF infrastructure in France to improve the operational and logistic capability of existing units and to enable heavy bomber squadrons from the United Kingdom to be temporarily based in France. These plans involved constructing 48 new aerodromes, upgrading the maintenance at 36 existing ones, enhancing damage repair outputs and specifically for heavy bombers, delivering appropriate refuelling and arming capabilities.[98] The plan required the positioning of at least 500,000 tons of stone, the erection of 2,000 temporary buildings[99] and the distribution and storage of thousands of tons of bombs, Small Arms Ammunition (SAA), aeroplane spares and aviation spirit. The manpower requirements for this mammoth project were estimated to be 50,000 personnel, whilst the runways, circuits and roads on each aerodrome equated to the construction to ten miles of arterial route in the United Kingdom. The Engineer Staff assessed that an average of 55 x 3 ton lorries, preferably tippers, would need to be allocated for each project to lift the stone from the nearest railhead to the work site,[100] so to reduce the WMT demands during the building phase and to sustain future re-supply operations, HQ BAFF sought to select sites near the railway so spurs could be built into the airfields. Although there was an initial capital and engineer investment in constructing the PW, creating additional tensions in the allocation of resources, the plan lucidly demonstrates the railway's capability, in the appropriate environment, as a logistic force multiplier. Apart from the very substantial resources required from so many different agencies, the German attack on 10 May 1940 prevented progression of the airfield project but it is clear that the railways would have been crucial to its success.

The SNCF also delivered rail services to niche British military activity, including the Mediterranean Line of Communication (MEDLOC). This LOC, running from Marseilles to Cherbourg was established in October 1939 to support Force K6 and to return small parties of service personnel and unaccompanied families from the Middle East, India and the Far East.[101] Two trains were usually required for each vessel that docked and an early move that tested the arrangements was the deployment of 1st Welsh Guards from Gibraltar via Marseilles to France for employment as the GHQ Defence Battalion.[102] Train A carried 620 officers and soldiers of 1st Welsh Guards plus 42 Other Ranks, four women and three children travelling to the UK via Le Mans and Cherbourg. Train B, consisting of 25 flats, two stores wagons and a

before the evacuation in June 1940. It would be interesting to know whether there are any outstanding payments due.

98 TNA AIR 35/66: Aerodrome Construction in France - Requirements and Policy, HQ BAFF S.4202/AD Plans dated 27 April 1940.

99 HQ BAFF to Air Ministry (AMSO) S/4201/Admin Plans dated 24 April 1940 in TNA AIR 35/66. To highlight the significance of the issues, the letter was signed by the AOC.

100 HQ BAFF to Air Ministry (AMSO) S/4201/Admin Plans dated 24 April 1940 in TNA AIR 35/66.

101 This arrangement saved shipping space and naval escorts, especially in the Eastern Atlantic, whilst also reducing travel time and the risk of attack.

102 Major L F Ellis, CVO CBE DSO MC, *Welsh Guards at War* (Aldershot: Gale & Polden, 1946), p.8.

P12.4 Railway Movement Training. Morris CDSW 6x4 Field Artillery Tractors towing 25 pounders are loaded at Louisburg Ramp on the LMR in 1938. Note the 'Capes, Anti-gas' providing protection against the rain. Such training was vital to ensuring strategic mobility in France. (WDLMRC: DRMC/V1/175a)

passenger coach, carried the battalion WMT, baggage, stores and a guard party.[103] Departing on 10 November, the journey from Marseilles to La Hutte-Coulombiers, a country station approximately 23 miles North of Le Mans was pathed to take 29 hours 45 minutes,[104] reinforcing the importance of logistic planning to ensure units were appropriately sustained in transit.

Traffic also began to flow South, in particular, personnel, bombs and equipment for the RAF Experimental Bombing Station near Perpignan, which led to an expansion of the staff and the facilities in No 5 Base-Sub Area at Marseilles.[105] The largest operational move over the MEDLOC was the deployment of the 1st Cavalry Division[106] from the UK to Palestine commencing in December 1939. Animal parties travelled from Dover to Dunkerque by ferry and thence by rail to Marseilles; personnel moved on the route Southampton – Cherbourg for onward rail movement.[107] The total transported strength was 11,976 personnel and 8,758 animals.[108] A much smaller move but one that was highly sensitive, was the transit of a small

103 TNA WO 167/157: L of C HQ 'Q' (M) Movements, HQ L of C Admin Instr Q/240/1/2 dated 6 November 1939 (SECRET), Move of Welsh Guards to La Hutte.
104 TNA WO 167/157: L of C HQ 'Q' (M) Movements, HQ L of C Admin Instr Q/240/1/2 dated 6 November 1939 (SECRET), Move of Welsh Guards to La Hutte, para 4.
105 TNA WO 167/112: 5 Base Sub Area (Marseilles) Headquarters.
106 Consisting of the 4th, 5th and 6th Cavalry Brigades. For a short history of the division in this period, see, Dennis C Bateman, 'Goodbye to Boots and Saddles, The Twilight of the British Cavalry', *British Army Review* 114, pp.75-89.
107 TNA WO 167/157: L of C HQ 'Q' (M) Movements WD, February 1940, Move of Cavalry.
108 WOOH, *Movements*, pp.184-285.

team of Gas Warfare (GW) specialists, tasked with conducting secret trials in the Algerian Desert, using aerially delivered chemical sprays, in order to enhance the UK's offensive and defensive GW capability.[109] A rather different rail movement was the tour of the BEF, in December 1939, of 80 students from the War Staff Officers Course at Camberley.[110]

Medical Evacuation

Prior to the advent of medical evacuation by air,[111] ambulance trains[112] delivered the strategic and some operational movement capability in the Land environment and comprehensive arrangements were enacted to provide this support to the BEF. Pre-war Anglo-French staff conversations generated two outputs. First, an offer to provide the BEF an initial capability using converted French stock[113] and secondly, the decision by the War Office to import British ambulance trains from the UK, although because the Army held no deployable stock, the trains were provided through a contract with the 'Big Four' railway companies, the LMS being the lead company and thus providing all the rolling stock and producing the relevant conversion drawings. The other companies, GWR, LNER and Southern, in conjunction with the LMS, allocated, to their workshops, specific projects within the programme, each company delivering a particular type of vehicle. All coaches were LMS 57 foot stock and converted for ambulance train operation in France. Conversions included couplings, draw-gear and air-brakes for Continental running, steam heating connections for French locomotives and bottom step-boards for ground level access. Each carriage was painted khaki, with a red cross on a white

109 The documents in this file are mostly classified as VERY SECRET, the forerunner of TOP SECRET. TNA AVIA 15/254: Report on Trials in Algeria.

110 The locomotive that hauled the train, War Department 106, a GWR 0-6-0 Dean Goods (No 2419) was captured by the Germans and scrapped in Poland after the war. Aves, *Supporting the British Expeditionary Force*, pp.74 & 77.

111 The AASF operated an improvised aero-medical evacuation service for some RAF personnel. This initiative was generated by evacuation timelines by road to the nearest British General Hospital, which meant it was quicker to evacuate casualties by air to the UK from the AASF area. See, TNA AIR 35/336: Use of Air Transportation Service for the evacuation of casualties and Rexford-Welch, *The Royal Air Force Medical Services*, Vol 1, *Administration*, pp 481-489.

112 There is surprisingly little published on ambulance trains. The classic volume for a history of ambulance train operations in the British Armed Forces is John H Plumridge, *Hospital Ships and Ambulance Trains* (London: Seeley Service, 1975) but it only contains four pages on BEF operations.

113 The plan is summarized in the table below. Information collated from Plan W4 First Maintenance Project, p.17, para 19d, in TNA WO 197/2: First Maintenance Project: Reception of Forces in France and system of maintenance in the initial stages.

Table 12.3
French Ambulance Train Plan – BEF Deployment (Z) Day

Train Type	Available	Capability	Quantity
Couche	Z+7	300 x stretcher	1
Mixte	Z+7	120 x stretcher & 240 x sitting	1
Couche	Z+16	300 x stretcher	1
Mixte	Z+20	120 x stretcher & 240 x sitting	1

background on both sides, whilst the roof was also painted white with a large red cross.[114] Each train consisted of 16 coaches, with a total length of 970 feet excluding the locomotive and a loaded weight of 460 tons. Lift capability was 320 stretcher cases and 40 sitting. The composition and marshalling of BEF ambulance trains, [115] each with a total of 51 personnel,[116] is shown in the table below:

Table 12.4
BEF Ambulance Train Consist[117]

Order	Coach	Quantity	Remarks
1	Brake	1	Including ward for infectious cases
2	Staff Car	1	Medical Officers and Nurses
3	Kitchen Car	1	Area for sitting officer patients
4-7	Ward Car	4	Sitting & Stretcher (36 beds per car)
8	Pharmacy	1	Including controlled drugs
9-12	Ward Car	4	Sitting & Stretcher (36 beds per car)
13	Ward Car	1	Sitting and psychiatric
14	Kitchen	1	ORs Mess
15	OR staff accommodation	1	
16	Brake	1	Medical and G1098 stores

Ambulance trains were scaled on the provision of one train per deployed division, although only nine trains were operational in May 1940,[118] with control being vested in Deputy Director Medical Services HQ LOC. On arrival in France, the trains were railed to the Medical Sub-Base Area (MBSA) at Dieppe to be staffed with personnel, issued with the medical inventory and ordnance equipment before preparation for deployment in-Theatre. Ambulance trains operated in two medical zones: the Evacuating Zone running between Casualty Clearing Stations (CCS) and Base General Hospitals (BGH) and the Distributing Zone between BGH and the maritime hospital carriers.[119] Until the German attack in May 1940, ambulance train personnel led a relatively leisurely existence running an alternate daily service from Dieppe to the Ambulance Train Railheads (ATR) at Drocourt and Beuvry for I and II Corps respectively

114 Nock, *Britain's Railways at War, 1939-1945*, pp.48-49.
115 TNA WO 222/2137: BEF Ambulance Trains.
116 WE IV/1931/46/2. Philson, BEFORBAT, Vol 3, p.109.
117 Table compiled from information in Army Council, *Notes on Military Railway Engineering*, Part IV, *Operating*, pp.170-173.
118 Ambulance Trains 1-8 & 13. British personnel were also briefly allocated to two French Ambulance Trains, 336 & 368, during May and June 1940.
119 Plumridge, *Hospital Ships and Ambulance Trains*, p.34, describes a 'hospital carrier' as an inferior type of hospital ship, although titled His Majesty's Hospital Ship (HMHS). Registered under the Geneva Convention and marked as hospital ships, they were suited to the cross-Channel routes, which did not require the comprehensive clinical facilities of a hospital ship.

and later, III Corps, whilst the GLOC was supported by a 3½ day schedule. No 3 Ambulance Train for example, undertook ten runs over ten weeks in the period December 1939 – February 1940 to both corps and GLOC ATRs, transporting a total of 1,951 patients to Dieppe for evacuation to the UK. The ambulance train departed Dieppe collecting patients *en route* and then dividing at Rennes, one part travelling to Brest and the other to Nantes to evacuate soldiers from Base areas before the halves were reunited at Rennes for movement to Cherbourg where patients were transferred to a hospital carrier.[120]

Practical experience identified numerous operating, logistic and technical issues, which reinforced the importance of attention to detail. The ambulance train length restricted the choice of stabling locations, which was important because the units needed to be separate from military operations such as munitions trains, with the best sites being sidings at small village stations.[121] From the medical and practical perspective, smooth braking was important because of the importance of avoiding distress to patients, whilst as a precaution, it was necessary to secure equipment to prevent damage to it and personnel. The heating systems, which used steam from the locomotive, were discovered to be ineffective in the cold winter of 1940 with the rear coaches remaining cold, a problem unresolved by the few Valor paraffin stoves held on the ambulance train Ordnance Equipment Table (OET). In addition, without a locomotive, there was no heating on the train because no auxiliary arrangement had been provided.

Watering was another difficulty because although there were plenty of water-points available, a hose with suitable connections had been omitted from the OET, which meant that the tanks had to be filled by bucket; a most inefficient arrangement. The Equipment Support component of the capability was also fragile because initially there was no ambulance train maintenance unit, with repairs and servicing being conducted on an *ad hoc* basis by one Sapper in 8 RCO who was not fully conversant with the equipment.[122] The blackout and lighting arrangements also posed a challenge.[123] The windows had been painted to permit the use of interior light at night but this meant using artificial light during the day thus draining the batteries, or opening the windows, which during inclement weather conditions was not conducive to either patient care or staff efficiency; both these matters were partially resolved by engineering action.[124]

120 Crew, BOH, *The Army Medical Services, Campaigns*, Vol 1, p.24. Russell Plummer, *The Ships That Saved an Army: A comprehensive record of the 1,300 'Little Ships' of Dunkirk* (Wellingborough: Patrick Stephens Limited, 1990), pp.55-66, lists nine ferries that were converted to the hospital carrier role. During the period September 1939 to early May 1940, most of the carriers were relatively inactive.

121 Given the outcome of the Rennes incident of 17 June 1940, this proved to be a wise policy. TNA WO 361/114: Rennes Train Bombing, although there were instances during operations when ambulance trains were stabled, if only briefly with ammunition and troop trains.

122 DGT BEF proposed that a RE Carriage & Wagon technician conversant with the electrical and heating systems should be assigned to each train, a solution fully enacted with the arrival of the Ambulance Train Maintenance Sections. TNA 167/51: GHQ Services, Transportation, letter DGT R/48 dated 11 October 1939 to War Office Director Transportation.

123 Repairs to the lighting systems were complicated because although they were all 24 volts, there was not commonality across the fleet. TNA 167/51: GHQ Services, Transportation, letter DGT R/48 dated 11 October 1939 to War Office Director Transportation.

124 Battery charging systems were purchased, and blackout boards were procured from the LMS Workshops at Derby. TNA 167/51: GHQ Services, Transportation, letter DGT R/48 dated 11 October 1939 to War Office Director Transportation.

Conclusion

The BEF's increasing rail capability was just getting into its stride when the German attack commenced, with some units still deficient in personnel and equipment, whilst others were working up to meet their operational commitments, so the BEF's rail capability was not fully matured. Out-with 8 RCO, training was initially a serious concern, especially in the Militia units, the Rank & File of which consisted mainly of conscripts. Whilst many were rail tradesmen mobilized from commercial railway companies in the UK, and thus brought some excellent technical skills, they had little experience of operating as a component of a cohesive team in a challenging military environment, especially in a foreign land and much had to be learned, as indeed was the case in many of the Base logistic operations, 'On The Job'.

Given the massive investment in the Base depots and the inherent reliance upon rail to transport material to and from them, it was inevitable that the initial emphasis would be on rail infrastructure development, a process reflected by the deployment of RCCs over ROCs. Despite a challenging start, the ambulance train capability improved consistently throughout the deployment period, building regular loop cycles and enhancing medical and technical team skills, which were to prove invaluable during operations in May 1940. The proposed airfield expansion project would certainly have posed an interesting challenge to the British railway capability in France, which would probably have required reorganization to ensure efficient utilization of the resources and personnel reinforcement to ensure the BEF components continued to be effectively supported. From the equipment perspective, the plans to introduce substantial numbers of additional locomotives and wagons to the Continent unambiguously reinforced the firm British commitment to expanding its military forces in France and ensuring they were properly sustained. The most critical task however, was yet to come.

Appendix to Chapter 12

Table 12A.1
BEF Railway Units
Deployment Table – May 1940[125]

Unit	Deployment	Remarks
HQ 1 Railway Operating Group	Rennes	Rail operating in Brittany
HQ 1 Railway Construction & Maintenance Group	Rennes	
HQ 2 Railway Construction & Maintenance Group	Nantes	Arras from January 1940
HQ 3 Railway Construction & Maintenance Group	Rouen BSA	Rouen from mid-May 1940
29 Railway Survey Company (Regular)*	Nantes	
8 Railway Construction & Operating Company (Regular)	Various	Redeployed to Norway April 1940
150 (London & North Eastern) Railway Construction Company (SR)	Rennes	Elbuef Rouen May - June 1940
151 (Great Western) Railway Construction Company (SR)	Savenay	Lille & Belgium May 1940
152 (Great Western) Railway Construction Company (SR)	Betton	Boulogne & Calais May 1940
153 (London & North Eastern) Railway Operating Company (SR)*[126]	Various	Lille & Belgium May 1940
154 (Great Western) Railway Operating Company (SR)*[127]	Rennes	Detachment at Bruz
155 (London Midland & Scottish) Railway Workshops Company (SR)	Rennes	Controlled 1 MRW

125 This table has been compiled from several sources including war diaries, Aves, *Supporting the British Expeditionary Force* and Philson, BEFORBAT, Vol 3.
126 Some sources describe this unit as RCC. The WD held in TNA Kew, states ROC. TNA WO 167/948.
127 Some sources describe this unit as RCC. The WD held in TNA Kew, states ROC. 154 Company had a detachment operating in the Cherbourg BSA. TNA WO 167/949.

156 (Southern) Transportation Stores Company (SR)*	Nantes (Carquefou)	Rennes (Braye)
157 Railway Construction Company	Nantes	Saint Malo June 1940
158 Railway Construction Company	Blain	
159 Railway Construction Company *	Foret du Gavre	Detachment at Blain
161 Railway Construction Company	Rouen	May - June 1940
165 Railway Survey Company	Savenay	Located with 151 RCC
186 Transportation Construction Company [128]	Betton	Romescamps & Motteville
190 Railway Operating Company*[129]	Various	Abancourt then Saint Malo
196 Transportation Stores Company[130]	Various	
HQ Railway Workshops Group	Rennes	
199 Railway Workshops Company	Martainville	
1 Railway Mobile Workshop	Rennes	Redeployed to Saint Nazaire
2 Railway Mobile Workshop	Rennes	
1 Ambulance Train Maintenance Section (Dieppe)	Dieppe	
2 Ambulance Train Maintenance Section (Etaples)	Dieppe	
1-8 & 13 Ambulance Trains	Dieppe MSBA	
HQ Railway Telegraph Company	Rennes	
71 (Railway) Telegraph Operating Section	Rennes	
72 (Railway) Telegraph Operating Section	Rennes	
21 (Railway) Line Maintenance Section	Rennes	

* Elements aboard HMT *Lancastria*

128 186 Transportation Construction Company was equipped with heavy earth moving machinery. The Company HQ and one section (troop) arrived in France in November 1939 and the other two sections in December. The Company was used to assist in railway construction projects.

129 Some sources describe this unit as RCC. The WD, held in TNA Kew, states ROC. TNA WO 167/960.

130 Support to railway construction projects as required.

Table 12A.2
BEF and RAF – Construction of Rail Served Depots[131]

Location	Role	Base Sub Area	Remarks
Abancourt	3 Base Supply Depot	No 3 (Rouen)	Not completed
Abancourt	3 Petrol Oil & Lubricants Depot	No 3 (Rouen)	Not completed
Abancourt	Machine Bakery	No 3 (Rouen)	Not completed
Beauvoir-Wavrans	Airfield	Corps Area	
Blain	1 Petrol Oil & Lubricants Depot	No 2 (Nantes)	Not completed. Plus one Sub-Depot
Bougennais	Base Aircraft Depot	No 2 (Nantes)	
Braye	1 Transportation Stores Depot	No 1 (Rennes)	Plus one Sub-Depot
Bruz	1 Base Ordnance Depot	No 1 (Rennes)	Not completed
Dieval	Airfield	Corps Area	
Elbeuf	2 Heavy Repair Shop RASC	No 3 (Rouen)	Not completed
Farbus	Forward Engineer Park	Corps Area	Work not started
Foret de Gavre	6 Base Ammunition Depot	No 2 (Nantes)	Not completed
Foret de Rennes	4 Base Ammunition Depot	No 1 (Rennes)	
Foret de Tanouarn	2 Petrol Oil & Lubricants Depot	No 1 (Rennes)	Not completed
Grevilliers	Airfield	Corps Area	
Guichen	Siding for railway ballast	No 1 (Rennes)	
Le Manoir	2 Engineer Stores Base Depot	No 3 (Rouen)	Not completed
L'Hermitage	2 Base Supply Depot	No 1 (Rennes)	Not completed
Miniac	22 Base Ammunition Depot	No 1 (Rennes)	
Monchy-Breton	Airfield	Corps Area	
Motteville	2 Transportation Stores Depot	No 3 (Rouen)	Not completed
Moult Argences	4 Petrol Oil & Lubricants Depot	No 1 (Rennes)	
Nuncq-Hautecote	Airfield	Corps Area	

131 This table has been compiled from several sources including war diaries, volumes of the WOOH, Aves, *Supporting the British Expeditionary Force* and Philson, BEFORBAT, Vol 3.

Rennes (Papeterie)	1 Engineer Stores Base Depot	No 1 (Rennes)	
Romescamps	Regulating Station	No 3 (Rouen)	HQ 2 Railway Operating Group
Savernay	1 Base Ordnance Depot	No 2 (Nantes)	Two Sub-Depots
Staple	Airfield	Corps Area	Work not started
St Etienne	1 Heavy Repair Shop RASC	No 2 (Nantes)	
St Gildas de Bois	2 Base Stores Depot	No 2 (Nantes)	
St Jacques	1 Transportation Stores Depot	No 1 (Rennes)	Not completed. Two Sub-Depots.
St Joseph	Tank Loading Ramps	No 2 (Nantes)	
Vertou	Base Petrol Filling Centre	No 2 (Nantes)	

13

Chasing the Rhino
An analysis of logistic support for the 1st Armoured Division during 1939-1940

The Challenge

The aim of this chapter is to analyse the concepts, organization and equipment of the units providing logistic support[1] to the 1st Armoured Division[2] during 1939 – 1940.[3] The divisional unit allocation table, illustrating the changing ORBAT during the period is in the Appendix to the chapter.[4] The chapter will not examine the limitations of the armoured doctrine, organizational structure,[5] the ORBAT[6] or the weapon systems, except where this is relevant to logistic issues.[7] A key challenge in developing a coherent and capable logistic system was the shortage of trained manpower because the logistic Corps, in line with all parts of the Army,

1 The logistic issues of the period in supporting mobile warfare are encapsulated and challenged in Shaw, *Supply in Modern War*.
2 1st Armoured Division is abbreviated in the fn to 1 AD, except where documents are referenced, or a quote uses the title in full.
3 One of the challenges of researching this subject has been recovering primary information relating to 1 AD. Records relating to the ORBAT and operations exist in The National Archives (TNA) at Kew and the Tank Museum at Bovington but there is little information regarding the logistic components. The Royal Logistic Corps Museum at Deepcut and the Imperial War Museum have no relevant documents. In this respect, some of the crafting of this article relies on deductions by examining available supporting primary and secondary information; the conclusions are therefore, inevitably not all based on the former.
4 The allocation of units to 1 AD from its formation to its return from France is shown in Table 13A.1. The information contained in it has been compiled from various sources, including Philson, BEFORBAT, Vol 4 , Part 1 and for the ORBAT, Vol 5, p.35 and HQ 1st Armoured Division S/520/A dated 25 April 1940, Mobilization (SECRET) held in WO 166/798: HQ 1 AD, AQ. Allocation does not mean that units were at War Establishment in personnel or equipment, or that units were available for operations.
5 For an analysis of the mechanization of the cavalry regiments, which formed 2nd Armoured Brigade, see, Salmon, *Everything Worked Like Clockwork.*
6 For the establishment by unit, see, Philson, BEFORBAT, Vol 4, Part 1 and Vol 5, p.35.
7 For an assessment of British inter-war armoured doctrine, see, Harold R Winton, *To Change an Army: General Sir John Burnett-Stuart and British Armoured Doctrine, 1927-1938* (Kansas: University of

expanded quickly between September 1939 and May 1940. In common with most of the BEF, the personnel in logistic units were conscripts, Territorials and Supplementary Reservists (SR), few of whom had much experience of the Army and even less supporting a mechanized force in an era of manoeuvre warfare,[8] an especial problem for 1st Armoured Division.[9]

To compound these issues, the significance of delivering effective collective logistic training as a component of formation activity whilst perhaps understood, was for several reasons not effectively executed, which created a de-gradation in combat capability.[10] That the requirement for and significance of, logistic integration within this new formation had been cogently articulated by the QMG in late 1935 makes the failure all the more frustrating. Responding to a paper on the future organization of the Army by the QMG wrote: 'It is equally important that the detailed composition of the Mobile Division is settled. Administratively it is a completely new "technique" and we must get the maintenance of this formation settled and put into practice in peace',[11] an assessment which firmly contradicts the perceived wisdom that senior officers were oblivious to the criticality of logistics in armoured operations. Should these problems have been insufficient, the War Office was constantly raiding the division for logistic units, which were then dispatched to the BEF in France. This constant erosion of any capability that was created was not only a personal irritation to the GOC, Major-General Roger Evans[12] but had in his opinion, the making of a serious future military failure, which was another prescient observation. He had no hesitation in making his professional views clear: 'Owing to the present policy of withdrawing personnel, units and equipment from my formation, I cannot have the formation fit for war by Z-9 months if that policy is continued.'[13] As it transpired, the 1st

Kansas Press, 1988) and J P Harris, *Men, Ideas and Tanks, British Military Thought and Armoured Forces, 1903-1939* (Manchester: Manchester University Press, 1995).

8 Manoeuvre Warfare: 'A style of warfare that seeks to destroy an enemy's cohesion and his will to win through a series of rapid, violent and unexpected actions that create a turbulent and rapidly deteriorating situation with which he cannot cope. Essentially, it aims to defeat the enemy'. *British Defence Doctrine*, Joint Warfare Publication (JWP) 0-01 (UK MOD, 1996), p.G8.

9 1 AD was not the only armoured formation in the British Army. There was the Armoured Division in Egypt, which became 7th Armoured Division, and staff work was progressing in June 1940, to form the 2nd and 3rd Armoured Divisions and four tank brigades in addition to 1st Army Tank Brigade, which was deployed with the BEF.

10 The 1 AD Troop Training Directive of October 1939 does not mention logistic support, although the Administrative Services are on the distribution. Document held in the Tank Museum Library (TML) MH5 Box 1 (355.486.4).

11 TNA WO 32/4612: Future Army Organization – 1935, QMG Response dated 16 December 1936 to CIGS SECRET Paper, 'Future Reorganization of the British Army' dated 9 September 1935.

12 Major General Roger Evans CB MC (1886-1968) was commissioned into the 7th Hussars in 1907, serving in India before the Great War and in Mesopotamia (1917-1918). He was a student at the Army Staff College (1920-1921) and on the Directing Staff (1924-1927) with contemporaries including: Alan Brooke, Jack Churchill, Lindsell, Montgomery, Paget, Pownall and A F A N Thorne. He commanded 5th Inniskilling Dragoon Guards, (1929-1933) and attended the Imperial Defence College in 1934. He was appointed GOC 1 AD in 1938 after a tour in the War Office as Deputy Director Military Operations (DDMO). His eldest son died on Active Service in 1942. For further details, see, Smart, *Biographical Dictionary of the British Generals of the Second World War*, pp.97-98.

13 1st Armoured Division 79/Mob/3244 dated 6 October 1939. Letter summaries held in TML MH5 Box 2 (355.486.4). Underlining in the original.

P13.1 Logistic Challenges. The rapid deployment of 1st Armoured Division to France created a whole series of logistic fragilities, from which, the formation never recovered during operations in France. This photograph at Cherbourg Quay on 23 May 1940 is of a Spring peace-time scene, with the threat of aerial attack seemingly absent but is replete with fascinating logistic detail. In the background, a sign proclaims 'Movement Control' by a line of Bedford OYD trucks. In the foreground, there are two A13 Mk I Cruisers of 2 RTR plus cased petrol and a cone funnel. Supporting crated stores and equipment, together with the tanks, await rail transportation, via the ramp to the left, whilst to the right rear, a Matilda II awaits a 2 pdr barrel. (Tank Museum: 2447/A2)

Armoured Division[14] was the penultimate British formation to deploy to the Continent[15] and it did so into a military scenario that was, from the Allied rapidly disintegrating. Its operational

14 In 1939, the formation badge of the 1 AD was a static rhino. In September 1942, a Sapper from No 3 Troop Cheshire Field Squadron RE was tasked to repaint the sign outside the Divisional HQ and crafted a much more spirited animal at the charge, which gained the vibrant approval of the GOC. See, Lieutenant-Colonel Howard N Cole OBE TD, *Formation Badges of World War Two, Britain, Commonwealth and Empire* (London: Arms & Armour Press, 1993), pp.32-33.

15 52nd (Lowland) Division deployed in early June 1940 supported by leading elements of a Canadian brigade group from 1st Canadian Division, which were both components of the 2nd BEF but they were withdrawn within days of landing. Ellis, BOH, *The War in France and Flanders,* p.296.

performance was deemed by the War Office to be a dismal failure and there has been little written of its campaign.[16]

Logistic ORBAT and Organization

Within the armoured division, the 2nd Line assets were two RASC Armoured Brigade Companies (ABC) and one RASC Support Group Company, each of which was organized into a headquarters, a workshop section and three 'commodity' sections:[17] ammunition, petrol and supply, thus creating the more flexible 'composite' companies required for armoured operations. The RASC Armoured Divisional Troops Company had four 'commodity' sections: ammunition, petrol and two supply.[18] To enhance its logistic capability, the division also had under command, allocated 3rd Line assets. These were, the RASC Petrol[19] and Ammunition Sub-Parks (ASP),[20] and the divisional slices of a Reserve Supply Park (RSP)[21] and a RAOC Armoured Corps Ordnance Field Park (OFP) and Workshops,[22] all usually corps level organizations. The allocation of 3rd Line resources as divisional assets, which thus differed to that of an infantry division, meant that 21 percent of the divisional manpower served in logistic units. The table below summarizes logistic assets:

16 1 AD has no published history and there are few works on its operations and performance, having arrived in France deficient in units, weapons, munitions, stores, equipment, training and cohesion. A summary of its deployment and combat is in Captain B H Liddell Hart, *The Tanks: The History of the Royal Tank Regiment and its Predecessors*, Vol II, *1939-1945* (London: Cassell, 1959), pp.18-35. Jean Paul Pallud, *Blitzkrieg in the West, Then and Now*, (Plaistow: After The Battle, 1991), pp.398-403, has some interesting illustrations relating to its deployment. The best two short summaries of its operations are to be found in Philson, BEFORBAT, Vol 5, pp.35-40 and David Fletcher, 'The White Rhino's Baptism of Fire, 1st Armoured Division in France, 1940', *Military Illustrated 86*, July 1995, pp.36-38. The Post Operational Report (POR) by the GOC, Major-General Evans is held in TNA WO 32/9392: Operations of 1st Armoured Division in France.

17 A RASC 1940 Section equates to an infantry platoon and a Sub-Section, a Section.

18 For details of the War Establishments and strengths, see, Philson, BEFORBAT, Vol 3, p.35.

19 TNA WO 167/343: 1 AD Petrol Sub-Park RASC, WD, May - June 1940.

20 TNA WO 166/804: 1 AD ASP RASC, WD, 1939-1941.

21 The RSP established under WE I/1931/10G/1 was organized, structure and equipped to carry three days of rations for an armoured division. See, Philson, BEFORBAT, Vol 4, p.64.

22 TNA WO 167/345: 1 AD Workshop RAOC, WD, April - July 1940.

Table 13.1
1st Armoured Division – Logistic Assets[23]

Unit	Corps	Personnel	Task Vehicles
Commander RASC Staff	RASC	38	11
2 Armoured Brigade Company	RASC	360	87
3 Armoured Brigade Company	RASC	360	87
1 Support Group Company	RASC	303	72
1 Armoured Division Troops Company	RASC	344	65
1 Armoured Division Ammunition Sub-Park	RASC	383	99
1 Armoured Division Petrol Sub-Park	RASC	205	51
1 Armoured Reserve Supply Park	RASC	183	33
Armoured Ordnance Field Park (Element)	RAOC	215	21
25 Mobile Bath Unit	RAOC	20	2
1 Armoured Division Postal Section	RE	25	3
Total		2,436	531

All RASC units were commanded by CRASC,[24] from divisional headquarters, there being no Regimental Headquarters (RHQ). The operational command of the non-RASC units within the logistic support envelope is difficult to ascertain. Some documents indicate that CRASC directed their operations, others, that the divisional HQ staff branches controlled their tasks. It was probably a combination of the two depending upon the scenario and timing. Corps logistic capability was designed to act as a buffer during operations, and, where possible, stocks were delivered daily from the Base for direct onward movement to the divisional area. The rationale for this was to maintain momentum by keeping, in the divisional area, stocks on wheels, whilst the corps logistic units provided *materiel* in reserve, either in dumps or on rail. With no British corps upon which to base a logistic buffer, 1st Armoured Division had to utilize its allocated divisional 3rd Line slice to effect the output. In some respects, having direct control over it generated greater divisional agility, but poor communications and the structure and resources within divisional HQ to control it, offset this advantage.

There were two key logistic concerns about the structure and organization of 1st Armoured Division: supporting battle-winning equipment and the integration of the logistic component into divisional capability. These issues were overlain by two fundamental problems; evolving armoured doctrine and the constant re-organization and removal of units. The significant differences between the armoured and infantry division ORBATs, particularly in relation to

23 The table has been compiled from information extracted from Philson, BEFORBAT, Vol 4, pp.33-66.
24 The 1 AD CRASC in France was Major (Temporary Lieutenant-Colonel) J R Allen. One of the HQ officers, Major T E Bartleet, was from the Royal Indian Army Service Corps (RIASC). The war diary is held in TNA WO 167/337 but like many of the Division's records, it is a tad thin.

P13.2 Armoured Operations Enabler 1. 1st Armoured Division relied greatly upon rail movement to create its strategic and operational mobility. On 21 June 1938, Light and Medium Armour is loaded to 'Rectank' wagons in Woolmer Yard on the LMR as part of a logistic component of the Army Staff College (ASC) demonstration, which also included railway operating and construction. Whilst the ASC DS and students watch the rail action, the gentleman with the hat in civilian clothes in the left foreground appears to be 'lubricating' the wagon springs. (WDLMRC: DRMC/V1/178b)

logistic hungry armoured mobile fighting platforms, was a king-pin within the experiential process. Each of the two brigades had three armoured regiments, totalling a divisional War Establishment of 342 tanks. 1st Armoured Division had therefore, a different logistic support ORBAT to the infantry divisions, which, because of the greater mobility of its manoeuvre units, placed more emphasis on support at brigade rather than divisional level. Secondly, the structures, organization and ORBAT of the division were constantly changing. From the logistic perspective, this meant reshaping where necessary, logistic units, the training of which, was concomitantly disrupted, inevitably resulting in further de-gradation of capability.

Unsurprisingly, there was little training by logistic units at formation level between September 1939 and March 1940, partly because the division seems to have had only one regular assigned RASC Company, No 10. The files of HQ 1st Armoured Division AQ[25] also have little comment on integrated logistic support tasks until spring 1940, which is reinforced by other unit war diaries although entries relating to these activities become more numerous from April 1940, reflecting a new focus upon preparing the division for overseas service. There were however, three key logistic tests for the division. The first was the move in late October/early November 1939 from the Salisbury Plain area to southern East Anglia to conduct home defence tasks. The

25 TNA WO 166/798: HQ 1 AD, AQ, WD.

second was the re-deployment in January 1940, to Dorset and the third was the move from War Stations to Southampton Docks, for the deployment to France.[26]

Between its formation in 1938 and its deployment to France, the 1st Armoured Division was, for various reasons, unable to conduct meaningful formation training.[27] In particular, the available logistic components were not to establishment, others were missing from the ORBAT and there was almost no integration beyond unit tasks and training.[28] The failure to mature a clearly defined armoured doctrine prevented the refinement, through intellectual rigour and sound planning, of an integrated logistic capability able to support high tempo operations, a problem compounded by the shortage, rotation and training of logistic units.[29] The deficiency of logistic units within the division is illustrated by the experiences of 10 Company RASC. Assigned as the Support Group Company, it was for a period in 1939, the Heavy Armoured Brigade Company before being re-roled and re-organized in November, as a composite Armoured Divisional Company.[30] The recently retired QMG, Lieutenant-General May, must have been greatly dismayed by the outcome.

Tank Logistics

The key logistic driver within the armoured division was the tank but because the doctrinal issues under-pinning divisional operations were not mature, a lacuna in the development of the supporting logistic concepts quickly appeared. The table below summarizes the complexities:

26 TNA WO 166/798: HQ 1 AD AQ, WD.

27 One of the interruptions was an outbreak of Foot & Mouth disease in October 1939. See, TNA WO 166/799: 1 AD Support Group, WD.

28 A common entry in RASC war diaries is: 'Work and training progressing normally'.

29 The unit war diary also highlights issues relating to personnel stability. 911 Anti-Aircraft (AA) Company RASC was a TA unit that was re-designated 1 AD ASP on 2 April 1940. On 22 April, the OC received an order to post 63 Supply personnel to No 6 Base Supply Depot at Barry; such decisions did not bode well for divisional capability. TNA WO 166/804: 911 Anti-Aircraft (AA) Company RASC, WD.

30 The reorganized 10 Company ORBAT is shown in the table below. For details, see 1st Armoured Division Administrative Order No 2 dated 20 November 1939 in TNA WO 166/798.

Table 13.2

10 Company RASC – Composite ORBAT

Task	Sections	Remarks
Ammunition	2 Sub-Sections	
Petrol	2 Sub-Sections	
Supplies	1 Sub-Section	
Manoeuvre	3 Sub-Sections	1 each for Heavy & Light Brigades. 1 for Support Group

Table 13.3
1st Armoured Division – Tank Logistic Factors[31]

Tank[32]	Weight[33] (Tons)	Main Armament	Rounds	MG	Rounds	Fuel[34] (gallons)	Range (miles)	mpg[35]	Crew
Lt Mk VI A/B	5.24	0.5-inch (12.7 mm)	500	1 x 0.303-inch	2500	35.0	130	3.71	3
Lt Mk VIC	5.24	15 mm	175	1 x 7.92 mm	2700	35.0	130	3.71	3
A9	12.75	2 pdr (40 mm)	100	3 x 0.303-inch	3000	72.0	150	2.08	6
A9 CS	12.75	3.7-inch (94 mm)	40	3 x 0.303-inch	3000	72.0	150	2.08	6
A10	14.15	2 pdr (40 mm)	100	2 x 7.92 mm	4050	98.0	100	1.02	5
A10 CS	14.15	3.7-inch (94 mm)	40	2 x 7.92 mm	4050	98.0	100	1.02	5
A11	11.00	0.303+ or 0.5-inch	+4000	None	NA	42.0	80	1.90	2
A12	25.00	2 pdr (40 mm)	93	1 x 0.303/7.92	2925	46.5	70	1.50	4
A13 Mk 1	14.00	2 pdr (40 mm)	87	1 x 0.303-inch	3750	110.0	90	0.82	4
A13 Mk 11	14.75	2 pdr (40 mm)	87	1 x 0.303/7.92	3750	110.0	90	0.82	4

From an analysis of the table, a series of instructive logistic issues arise. First, is the requirement for fuel, particularly for the A10 and A13s, which had a consumption on the road of approximately one mile per gallon and much less cross-country. With no bulk refuelling capability at 1st or 2nd Line, the delivery of sufficient fuel in the manoeuvre environment would definitely be a challenge. For example, a full fill for an A13 required 27 x 4-gallon tins, each of which required manual handling. The positive news from the logistic perspective was that

31 The details in the table have been compiled from the platform Technical Handbooks in the TML and *Army Operations Research Group Manual*, Vol I, British Tanks (86/Research/324 (ScI)) dated October 1955. Copy No 40 is held by the TML.
32 For archive film footage of the tanks employed within 1 AD, see, DVD, *British Tanks of the Second World War, 1939-1945* (Strike Force Entertainment, 2010).
33 Cruiser tank weights were limited to a maximum of 14 tons to meet bridge weight restrictions, but it became clear that the necessary protection could not be delivered within this limitation and later models were much heavier.
34 One Imperial gallon converts to 4.546 litres.
35 Fuel consumption is based on best rate travelling by road. Cross-country, mpg could be twice this figure.

all the division's tanks were fuelled with a single fuel type, petrol.[36] Secondly, there were the disparate types and quantities of ammunition; four natures for the main armament and two for the secondary armament. The difficulty was not bulk or weight but the complexities of detail, a problem compounded when armoured regiments were issued with a mix of tanks, which made distribution within squadrons more challenging. Bulk storage and transport had some flexibility because all of the 2 pounder ammunition was solid shot, the 3.7-inch projectiles being smoke and High Explosive (HE). The Close Support (CS) A9 and 10 tanks, equipped with a 3.7-inch howitzer, were established in HQ squadrons[37] to provide smoke cover because the 2 pounders mounted on the Cruiser tanks only had a solid-shot armour piercing round. The 3.7 could also fire High Explosive (HE) rounds against soft targets but the stowage plan, 36 rounds smoke and four HE, plainly illustrates its primary role. The concept of procuring a tank for the purposes of firing smoke seems bizarre now but was believed necessary when the design was progressed.[38] Indeed, in France, with all the other divisional tactical limitations, the provision of an effective smoke-screen, especially to cover withdrawal, was often vital.

Practically, dedication and diligence created carefully crafted establishment tables with a theoretical balance of suitable logistic equipment but the efficiency and effectiveness so vital to manoeuvre operations never had the opportunity to develop within a doctrinally robust environment. Nonetheless the logistic thinking and application driven by the RASC was certainly sound. Each echelon of the Divisional Supply Column (DSC) had one section dedicated to Divisional Troops, whilst the other three were allocated to brigade support. The RASC divisional logistic concept was designed to have a clear focus on delivering stocks to units thus offering greater mobility by holding stocks on wheels. Generating this capability was a key task in the 1930s and is neatly summarized by Lieutenant-Colonel Shaw RAOC in his book, *Supply in Modern War*: 'From the foregoing it is clear that the salient features of mechanized operations will be the dispersion of forces and their speed. Dispersion implies decentralization, and this – from a supply angle – connotes some measure of self-containment in both unit and formation'.[39]

Transportation and Recovery of Armour

Two critical logistic shortfalls in the 1st Armoured Division were the transport and recovery of tanks. The BEF had a considerable number of vehicles, both military and civilian,[40] many

36 The A11 (Matilda I) and A12 (Matilda II) were designated as Infantry Tanks and were therefore, not on the establishment of 1 AD units. The A11 had a Ford 70 hp petrol engine and the A12, unusually for the time, was powered by diesel - two AEC 87 hp bus engines, totalling 174 hp. In France, an Independent Infantry Tank Squadron (-) was formed and assigned to 3rd Armoured Brigade. The squadron probably consisted of 4 x A12 and 2 x A11. See, R K Huggins, 'The Crisis Formation of the Infantry Tank Squadron Placed Under Command of 1st Armoured Division, BEF, France, May-June 1940', Unpublished, TML, 1 AD, Box 1.

37 See, WET, WE I/1931/5E/1, Philson, BEFORBAT, Vol 4, p.12.

38 Some publications suggest that the CS tanks were fitted with a 3 inch howitzer; the A10 CS example in the Tank Museum at Bovington has a 3.7; David Fletcher and the author measured it.

39 Shaw, *Supply in Modern War*, p.188.

40 The BEF lost 95 military and 336 civilian 10 ton variants in France and some of these assets were taken into German service. See, WOOH, *Fighting, Support and Transport Vehicles*, Part II, *Unarmoured*

P13.3 Armoured Operations Enabler 2. Scammell Pioneer 20 ton Tank Transporter 'Snow White' with a Cruiser IV negotiates the refugee traffic in the market square in Le Neubourg on 9 June 1940. The significant shortage of these vehicles critically restricted the operational manoeuvre capability of 1st Armoured Division. (Tank Museum: 4256/B4).

of which, had drawbar trailers, that were capable for transporting armour with a Gross Vehicle Weight, which was not in excess of 10 tons. Most of these equipments were allocated to regimental Light Aid Detachments (LAD) for the movement and recovery of the Light Mark VI tank,[41] which was the only one in the BEF's inventory weighing 10 tons or less.[42] The BEF

Vehicles, p.61, Appx B (I) Approximate Losses of B Vehicles by Types in the Evacuation of France. Whilst few of these vehicles were designed to move tracked vehicles, most proved to be capable of doing so.

41 WOOH, *Fighting, Support and Transport Vehicles*, Part I, *Common Problems*.

42 A summary of British tank characteristics may be found in Blaxland, *Destination Dunkirk, The Story of Gort's Army*, p.406. For more details on the limitations, capabilities, development and industrial production of British armoured vehicles, see, David Fletcher, *Mechanized Force, British Tanks between the wars* (London: HMSO, 1991) Chp 9 and Fletcher, *The Great Tank Scandal, British Armour in the Second World War*, Part 1, Chps 1 & 2. See also, Peter Chamberlain & Chris Ellis, *British and American Tanks of World War Two, The Complete Illustrated History of British, American and Commonwealth Tanks, 1933-1945* (London: Arms and Armour, 1969). *The Tank Museum* website <www.tankmuseum.org> has an excellent electronic archive of tank characteristics.

also had around 25 Heavy Equipment Transporters (HET),[43] each capable of lifting 20-40 tons, all but two being impressed from the civil sector, the exception being the military Scammell 6x4 Pioneer Transporters.[44] The operational movement and recovery of Cruiser and Infantry tanks in the BEF and 1st Armoured Division thus relied on 25 HETs and the railway.[45]

The experience in France however, lucidly indicated that whilst strategic rail movement was an excellent force multiplier and a critical asset, tactically it could be a fragile option and the HET offered the most effect operational link between the strategic and the tactical for deployment and recovery of the key combat platforms; it was therefore, unfortunate that there were so few of them. The GOC's Post Operational Report (POR)[46] specifically identified the hazardous nature of loading damaged vehicles to rail-flats at forward railheads[47] during the withdrawal in an environment in which, the *Luftwaffe* maintained air superiority but this lesson, and the fragility in having the entrainments so far forward during dynamic ground manoeuvre operations, appear to have be missed by the War Office. The Staff of HQ 1st Armoured Division though, clearly understood the tactical risks because the operations at the railheads[48] were conducted during the hours of the short June darkness and were protected by the guns of 44th Light Anti-Aircraft (LAA) Battery.

It is difficult, given the paucity of documentation, to define the key reason why the General Staff failed to fully comprehend the importance of procuring suitable HETs to deliver the deployment and recovery capabilities, especially given the experience of moving tanks in the Mobile Brigade experiments during the 1930s.[49] There are several possibilities, although probably it was a combination of them. The failure to craft a coherent doctrine certainly set

43 22 were left in France but at least one civilian vehicle and the two Pioneer Scammell 20 ton transporters were recovered, the latter by 1 AD. Figures calculated from the table, Approximate Losses of B Vehicles by Types in the Evacuation of France in WOOH, *Fighting, Support and Transport Vehicles*, Part II, *Unarmoured Vehicles*, p.61, Appx B (I).

44 The Scammell 6x4 HET was purchased to move the Vickers Medium Mark II Tank of which 120 were built. One key asset was a powered winch to recover tanks and vehicles with no mobility, a capability essential to all military HETs. For technical details, see, Tank Museum, *Data Book of Wheeled Vehicles, Army Transport,* pp.210-212 and for a short history, see, Georgano, *World War Two Military Vehicles*, p.49.

45 An influencing factor upon British tank design until 1945 was the constraint of the UK rail structure gauges. The last British in-service tank able to travel with little restriction on the UK National Rail Network was the Cruiser, A34, Comet. The French rail structure gauge was more generous.

46 The POR is entitled 'Report of Operations of 1st Armoured Division in France', S/158/G dated 22 August 1940 and is held in TNA WO 32/9392 and by the Tank Museum Library (TML). This document is known as the 'Evans Report' although only Part 1 exists in these archives and the covering note of Part 2. A mix of chronology and assessment, it is a product of work from divisional Staff officers and the GOC's recollections and perspectives, and his personal frustrations with the War Office unmistakably and constantly, permeate the document. It has though, little relating to logistics. When he signed the document on 22 August 1940, Roger Evans had been told on 19 August that his removal from command would be effective on 24 August.

47 Whatever the technical capability of the emerging armoured divisions, their tactical deployment was always a cause for concern because the railhead had to be well forward to reduce the tracking distance to the battle. This solution was fraught with risk in manoeuvre warfare, and there was more than one occasion when German tanks destroyed French armoured units, whilst the latter were detraining.

48 The entrainment railheads were at Blangy, Gamaches and Vieux Rouen and detrainment at Louvries. TNA WO 32/9392: Evans Report, p.2.

49 See, Winton, 'The Quest for a Mobile Division', *To Change an Army*, pp.174-219.

the scene, compounded by a shortage of tanks in the division during 1939 upon which, to create practical exercises that might have exposed the crucial nature of their role. No doubt the expense and complexity of such specialist vehicles was another factor and one that certainly attracted the attention of the Staff, who were grappling with Armoured Fighting and General Service B vehicle design and the costs, and levels of production. In this respect, the planners responsible for progressing the procurement of future HETs were not entirely wrong in having reservations about potential problems in design and production. The two military Scammell Pioneer military transporters, whilst having that precious military capability of effective off-road mobility, had, as a result, a high load-bed on the trailer,[50] which restricted the freedom of movement on some routes because of overhead obstructions such as bridges[51] thus resulting in the need to off-load the tank to negotiate the obstacle.[52] From an engineering perspective, the challenges of producing, in the UK, a sufficiently powerful and reliable engine to power the HET with a weight of 15-20 tons and the tank of 25 tons and growing, were problematic and never overcome during the war,[53] the War Office eventually obtaining the prime-movers from US industry, although trailers manufactured by British companies delivered sterling service.

Grasping The Nettle

Despite clear comprehension of the need for logistic integration, if not delivery, at formation level, there were only two opportunities to practise some of the skills in the field before 1st Armoured Division deployed to France. In October 1939, the division moved to Hertfordshire and southern East Anglia to execute home defence duties.[54] Once the move was complete, logistic activity returned to routine tasks supporting widely dispersed units and assisting in the move of squadrons to firing camps, all during the bitter winter in December 1939 – January 1940.[55] Whilst the weather conditions provided some much needed practical experience in operating in a harsh environment, it did little to enhance logistic capabilities within the formation. In January 1940, the division redeployed from southern East Anglia and Hertfordshire to Dorset in the Wimborne, Wareham and Ringwood Triangle. This move involved 19 trains, with the balance of the division moving by road using two Main Supply Routes (MSR), which were protected by two troops of 60th Light Anti-Aircraft and Anti-Tank Regiment. From the logistic perspective, it was an excellent opportunity to practise a divisional

50 Tank Museum, *Data Book of Wheeled Vehicles, Army Transport*, p.211.

51 WOOH, *Fighting, Support and Transport Vehicles*, Part II, *Unarmoured Vehicles*, p.97.

52 This is still a procedure in the 21st Century, although it is more usually because the axle weight of the loaded HET exceeds the bridge classification.

53 Albion produced, in 1942, a 20 ton transporter to a General Staff specification but despite using the most powerful truck engine in UK it was beset by reliability and braking issues, resulting in the load capacity eventually being reduced to 15 tons, although this did not prevent its introduction to service in a fleet of 750 equipments. For details, see, WOOH, *Fighting, Support and Transport Vehicles*, Part II, *Unarmoured Vehicles*, p.98.

54 The division had three tasks: defence of the divisional area within boundaries against airborne assault, support to 18th Division against a seaborne invasion and ditto for 54th Division. Documents held in TNA WO 166/796: HQ 1 AD GS.

55 For details, see, TNA WO 166/796: HQ 1 AD GS, WD. Conditions were such that no tanks from 2 RTR were allowed to leave barracks from 25 December 1939 to 7 January 1940. TNA WO 166/1403: 2 RTR, WD.

move and within the constraints of personnel and equipment availability, full advantage was taken. The deployment involved Divisional Rear HQ, logistic units and all B Echelons moving to a forward concentration area supported by three railheads: supply at Luton, petroleum at Harpenden and ammunition at Dunstable, whilst road refilling points were established for petroleum at Great Missenden and ammunition at Stokenchurch; 21 tanks moved by rail.[56]

Once these deployments were complete, it appears that interaction between divisional HQ, brigades and logistic units returned to a routine arrangement but in early April 1940, the war diaries lucidly expose an increase in tempo, with training being reinvigorated and supported by series of visits by the GOC to logistic units.[57] 1 Armoured Division Ammunition Sub-Park (ASP) participated in a Tactical Exercise Without Troops on 10 April 1940, focusing upon the logistic contribution to 'Harbour Schemes' for armour,[58] whilst the Reserve Supply Park was involved in a divisional harbour exercise South-West of Blandford on 10 April[59] before detaching officers and NCOs to view a gas spray demonstration at Home Crossing in the New Forest on Thursday 11.[60] The ASP participated in another divisional harbour scheme on 18-19 April,[61] whilst the Divisional Troops Company (–) participated in a similar exercise 18-19 April[62] and the RSP operated a divisional Supply Railhead (SRH) at Sturminster Marshall[63] on 23 April. On 22 April, the War Office issued the order for 1st Armoured Division to mobilize, re-organize and prepare to move overseas by 1 June 1940.

Bon Voyage

The 1939 War Establishment (WE) contained a heavy armoured brigade and a light one; the 1940 WE converted these to two armoured brigades, each planned to have the same mix of equipment. The third manoeuvre formation was the Support Group, composed of two infantry

56 The March Table, AD AO S/467/7/Q dated 23 January 1940, is held in the HQ 1 AD AQ file in TNA WO 166/798. It is possible that some tanks partially tracked, were carried portee or were moved by commercial assets.

57 1 AD RSP RASC, which moved from Ramsgate to Poole on 31 March 1940, received a visit on Wednesday 3 April between 1045-1130 hours. The company also had an issue of vehicles from the MT Depot at Slough. TNA WO 166/809: 1 AD RSP RASC, WD. The Divisional Troops Company based at Poole was also visited by the GOC and, according to the entry in the unit war diary, 'he expressed great satisfaction at what he found'. TNA WO 166/806: 1 AD Divisional Troops Company, WD, April 1940 - June 1941.

58 On 2 April 1940, 911 AA Company RASC was re-designated 1 AD Ammunition Sub-Park. Given its change of role, a key component of capability was re-orientating training. TNA WO 166/804: 1 AD ASP RASC

59 TNA WO 166/809: 1 AD RSP RASC, WD.

60 TNA WO 166/809: The Ordnance Survey GRID SU 319061 shown in the war diary indicates that Home Crossing is approximately two miles to the SE of Lyndhurst in the area of Park Hill. Presumably, given the proximity of Lyndhurst to the site, live agents were not used in the demonstration.

61 TNA WO 166/804: 1 AD ASP RASC, WD.

62 TNA WO 166/809: 1 AD RSP RASC, WD.

63 The station at Sturminster Marshall, on the Somerset & Dorset Joint Railway was known as Bailey Gate to prevent confusion with the station at Sturminster Newton. The railway closed in 1969 and the goods yard where the railhead was operated is now the Bailie Gate industrial estate. For period photographs, see, Mac Hawkins, *The Somerset & Dorset, Then and Now* (Wellingborough: Patrick Stephens Ltd, 1986), pp.182-183.

battalions and one dual-roled artillery regiment comprising LAA and anti-tank capabilities. Engineer Support consisted of one field and one field park companies. The WE was 11,327 personnel and 342 tanks.[64] On Saturday 20 April, the War Office directed that the 2nd Battalion The King's Royal Rifle Corps (KRRC), 1st Battalion The Rifle Brigade (RB), 1 Field Ambulance and the Wireless Troop of 2 Squadron Royal Signals plus various individuals, to assemble at Aliwal Barracks at Tidworth to provide the basis for the emergency formation of 30th Infantry Brigade, in preparation for a potential deployment to Norway, which was another serious blow to the combat capability of the division.[65] Not content with effectively further degrading the formation's strength and capability, the War Office ordered that the organization and WE of 1st Armoured Division be amended with effect from 1 May 1940, which caused much confusion as the division prepared to deploy to France, a situation compounded by the rapid redeployment of 3 Royal Tank Regiment (RTR) from 3rd Armoured Brigade for convoy escort duties at Calais.[66]

The initial deployment ORBAT therefore consisted of two armoured brigades,[67] one with three mechanized cavalry regiments, and the other with two battalions from the RTR.[68] 4th Border, a TA battalion, was assigned to replace the division's two motor infantry battalions, 2 KRRC and 1 RB, from the 1st Support Group.[69] There was no organic artillery, reserve tanks or bridging capability. Other changes included the deletion of the 3rd Line RSP, a function assumed by the Petrol Sub-Park. The 1940 manpower WE totalled 11,112 personnel,[70] whilst the 1939 WE was 8,965. The deployed division however, reflected neither the 1939 or 1940 WE; strength on 16 May 1940 was 9,542. Considering the order, counter-order and dis-order that ensued, it is surprising that any logistic structure remained within the division but remarkably it did, if only just. The dysfunctional deployment is concisely described, although with the important omission of logistics, by the 9th Queen's Royal Lancers regimental history: 'It cannot be too strongly stressed that the 1st Armoured Division was not a division at all. Armoured troops cannot fight effectively by themselves. Artillery, infantry and engineers are a vital adjunct and the co-operation of all arms is essential for success in battle'.[71]

64 These figures are drawn from Ellis, BOH, *The War in France and Flanders*, p.54. Liddell Hart, *The Tanks*, Vol II, p.23, states 134 Light and 150 Cruiser. For details of the WEs, strengths, units and ORBATs, see, Philson, BEFORBAT, Vol 4.

65 In the event, 30th Guards Brigade deployed to Calais.

66 3 RTR located near Fordingbridge in the New Forest, was in the process of preparing for a move to the BEF Tank Training Area at Pacy-sur-Eure. See, Liddell Hart, *The Tanks*, Vol II, p.19.

67 The ORBAT of the deployed brigades was: 2nd Armoured Brigade: Bays, 9th Lancers and 10th Hussars. 3rd Armoured Brigade: 2 RTR and 5 RTR.

68 Tank units formed from the cavalry were titled regiments, those from the RTR, battalions.

69 For a short summary of the units in the ORBAT and the types of equipment, see, Ellis, BOH, *The War in France and Flanders*, Appx 1, pp.367-371. For more detail, including the establishment of every unit, see, Philson, BEFORBAT, Vol 4.

70 This figure did not include the 3rd Line Ordnance Field Park. See, Philson, BEFORBAT, Vol 4, p.70.

71 Joan Bright OBE (ed.) *The Ninth Queen's Royal Lancers, 1936-1945: The Story of an Armoured Regiment in Battle* (Aldershot: Gale & Polden, 1951), p.24. This regimental history, apart from providing a fascinating insight into operations in France during 1940, is unusual in being edited by the most capable Joan Bright (1910-2008) who held several demanding and interesting posts during the Second World War, including employment by Military Intelligence (Research), the forerunner of the Special Operations Executive, and service with the Joint Planning Committee. She also dated Ian Fleming

The 1st Armoured Division thus deployed to France with 103 Light Tanks and 128 Cruisers[72] but with deficiencies in radios, sighting telescopes and armour piercing ammunition. Based upon an undated handwritten summary in the Tank Museum Library, the distribution by type and units was:

Table 13.4
1st Armoured Division – Distribution of Tanks by Type and Unit

Brigade	Unit	Mark VI*	A9	A10	A13	Total	Remarks
2	Queen's Bays	21	4	3	22	50	
	9th Lancers	20	3	2	18	43	
	10th Hussars	20	3	0	15	38	
3	2 RTR	21	8	1	18	48	
	3 RTR	21	6	2	23	52	Detached to Calais
	5 RTR	21	4	3	24	52	
	Total	**124**	**28**	**11**	**120**	**283**	

*Cavalry regiments held the VIC and the RTR battalions, VIB

The following logistic units[73] were mobilized for service in France: [74]

and is considered to be one of three or four women whose persona created the basis for the character Miss Moneypenny

72 Confirming the number of tanks 1 AD deployed is an interesting challenge. The table below summarizes the difference of the key sources:

Table 13.5
1st Armoured Division – Source List of Tank Numbers on Deployment to France

Source	Light Mark VI		Cruiser		Total	
	Total	-3 RTR	Total	-3 RTR	Total	-3 RTR
Bulk Operational Holdings of Light and Cruiser Tanks (TML)	143	122	172	141	315	263
TML Hand-written Summary (TML)+	124	103	159	128	283	231
Blagden Memorandum (TML)*	135	114	193	162	328	276
Liddell Hart, The Tanks, Vol II, p.23	134	113	150	119	284	232

+ This document lists the tanks by unit, type and quantity. 3 RTR is listed as having a strength 21 x Mark VIB and 31 x Cruisers.

* Memorandum on the position regarding tanks in the BEF as known to the AFV Branch of GHQ, Cherwell Papers, G364/30 held in the TML.

73 The RAOC also provided the Armoured Workshop based at Alderholt 2.5 miles SW of Fordingbridge and the Divisional Section Armoured Corps Workshop located at Winton in Bournemouth. Both these units delivered Equipment Support capability.

74 Authority was HQ 1st Armoured Division S/520/A dated 25 April 1940, Mobilization (SECRET) held in WO 166/798: HQ 1 AD AQ.

Table 13.6
1st Armoured Division – Logistic Units Mobilized for Deployment to France

Unit	UK Location	Remarks
HQ RASC[75]	Kinson Bournemouth	
2 Armoured Brigade Company	Poole	RASC
3 Armoured Brigade Company	Blandford	
1 Support Group Company	Poole	
Divisional Troops Company	Poole	
Ammunition Sub-Park	Poole	
Petrol Sub-Park	Poole	
Armoured Corps Ordnance Field Park[76]	Alperton Middlesex*	Divisional element from No 3 Ordnance Field Park* RAOC
Divisional Post Unit[77]	Fordingbridge	RE

Bizarrely, given the GOC's persistent attempts to ensure the division was correctly manned and equipped, there was a mad rush to allocate vehicles and personnel to units, with all the dramas that might be expected of such arrangements. This was complicated by the amendments to the AFG 1098 mobilization equipment and stores schedules as a result of the change to the WE, so there were no approved scales within the armoured regiments, whilst attempts to preserve peacetime accountancy processes generated yet more frustrations.[78] The experience of the 9th Lancers was typical:

> We eventually received all our "B" vehicles but the tanks - a good proportion of them transfers from other units and in very bad condition - continued to arrive in driblets up to the last moment. A certain number of A9 and A10 Cruisers and some close-support tanks were also received but no one in the Regiment had driven or maintained this type before; we hoped we should have a chance to train with them in France.[79]

Given the frenetic activity and the dynamic developments in France, the move to Southampton from UK War Stations and the sailings to France appear to have been relatively efficient. The few movement orders remaining in the files are logically structured and there is no adverse comment on the execution elements in the regimental histories, although inevitably given the speed of the mobilization there must have been minor frustrations, misinterpretations and

75 S/520/A dated 25 April 1940 has HQ CRASC located at Kinson and not with Divisional HQ at Fordingbridge. TNA WO 166/798: HQ 1 AD AQ.
76 The divisional slice was a component of the Armoured Corps OFP, which was deployed forward to support manoeuvre operations. 1 AD OFP consisted of three sections: Reserve, Corps and Division with one sub-section per brigade and one for the Support Group.
77 The DPU is shown in the organigram held in the TML but not on the mobilization order in TNA WO 166/798: HQ 1 AD AQ.
78 Bright, *The Ninth Queen's Royal Lancers*, p.2.
79 Ibid, p.3.

delays which were not recorded in the war diaries. One significant amendment however, was the decision to change the SPOD from Le Harve to Cherbourg because of German bombing and aerial mining of the port, and an escalating perception of the threat posed by German ground forces.[80] The Ammunition Sub-Park's war diary[81] certainly gives a vivid impression of the fast pace, whilst lucidly describing the competing priorities in a logistic unit in delivering real-time support to the division at the same time as preparing for deployment. In particular, the war diary is replete with entries relating to the collection of 1st and 2nd Line ammunition from depots in Southern England,[82] issues and inspection of equipment and the return of stores and billets. 9th Lancers were pressed to complete the departure tasks because of late arriving equipment and had to transport some of the tank ancillaries by rail to Southampton with the personnel party, whilst the C Squadron Leader used his private car to carry machine guns, belt boxes and sighting telescopes.[83]

Table 13.7
1st Armoured Division
Logistic Support Units - Movement to France

Unit	Mov No	SPOD	Date
HQ RASC	BS 6	Le Harve	17 May 40
2 Armoured Brigade Company	BS 6	Le Harve	17 May 40
3 Armoured Brigade Company	BS 7	Le Harve	20 May 40
1 Support Group Company	AS 9	Cherbourg	24 May 40
Divisional Troops Company	BS 6	Le Harve	17 May 40
Ammunition Sub-Park	AS 8	Le Harve	23 May 40
Petrol Sub Park	BS 7	Le Harve	20 May 40
Armoured Corps Ordnance Field Park	AS 7	Cherbourg	21 May 40
Divisional Post Unit	BS 7	Le Harve	20 May 40

Logistic Issues in France

The person responsible for directing the Staff of the AQ Branch in HQ 1st Armoured Division, and thus bringing coherency to the output of the logistic units was the Assistant Adjutant & Quartermaster-General (AA & QMG), a General Staff Officer 1. The incumbent, recently

80 TNA CAB 44/67: The BEF in Belgium and Artois, 10 May - 3 June 1940, entry 19 May. The decision made by the War Office on the advice of the GOC. 1 AD were at sea for Le Harve on SS *Amsterdam* and SS *Vienna* when the ships were ordered to divert to Cherbourg. Regimental Committee, *The 10th Royal Hussars in the Second World War* (Aldershot: Gale & Polden, 1948), p.6.
81 TNA WO 167/342: 1 AD ASP RASC, WD, May 1940.
82 Bramley in Hampshire, Corsham in Wiltshire and Woolwich.
83 Bright, *The Ninth Queen's Royal Lancers*, p.3.

arrived in early May 1940, fresh from the Directing Staff at the Army Staff College Camberley, was a most able cavalry officer, Lieutenant-Colonel Charles Keightley,[84] and he had certainly had plenty to occupy his attention as the division deployed to France. One of his key tasks was to grip the supply chain from the Main Base Areas. This was much easier said than done, not only because of the fragility of signal, telegraph and telephone communications but also the dynamic and often conflicting priorities. In addition to the structural and organizational issues within the Division, which were creating logistic dilemmas that the AA & QMG could do little to immediately resolve, there were a mounting number of problems that required the attention of the Q Staff in the AQ Branch.

In 1940, as now, armoured operational capability relied greatly upon the ability to deliver, Equipment Support and thereby 'prepare, repair, recover and recondition', to restore armoured combat capability as quickly as possible and maximize equipment availability. A key shortage of spares for the tanks, compounded by the different types and variants, placed the delivery of this key output, immediately in doubt. Keightley grasped this particular nettle hard, arranging for urgent demands to be sent by teleprinter from Assistant Director Ordnance Services (ADOS) 1st Armoured Division to Ordnance Services 5 at the War Office, which then arranged for the items to be delivered by air. Priority stocks arriving by sea were collected from the dockside by RAOC vehicles and taken to the Armoured Fighting Vehicle (AFV) Sub-Depot and field park sections for immediate issue to the relevant workshop.[85]

One of many issues was a manufacturing fault in some of the track plates, causing cracks in the metal, thus requiring the plates to be replaced. This was a general problem because of the shortage of track plates and an especial one with the A10 Mark II tanks because the cotter pins were made from high tensile steel and could not be removed with the standard tool kit, one of many apparently small but nonetheless important issues that so easily eroded combat capability. On a more positive note, the 1st Armoured Division's logistic load carrying vehicle fleet, unlike most of the BEF, had few impressed civilian platforms and consisted mostly of 4x2 military variants, with the 3 ton Bedford OY prominent. Creating a relatively standardized logistic vehicle fleet equipped with more robust platforms built to military specifications reduced the holdings of spares lines that were required, as well as decreasing the repair and driving training burden, thereby generating improved efficiencies and operational outputs. Whilst obviously a great improvement on other formations in the BEF, the 4x2 platforms in the armoured divisions, imported mobility limitations, a lesson re-learned in the Western Desert, which resulted in

84 Charles Keightley (1901-1974) was commissioned into the 5th Dragoon Guards in 1921. He held several key Staff appointments in the interwar period, including Brigade Major of the Cairo Cavalry Brigade, which was a component of the Mobile Division. Having returned from France, he had, unlike his GOC, a meteoric rise, commanding 30th Armoured Brigade, 6th Armoured Division and 78th Infantry Division before being appointed, aged 43, to command V Corps in Italy. Knighted in 1945, he held a succession of post-war senior command appointments, including C-in-C BAOR, Far East Land Forces, Middle East Land Forces and Governor and C-in-C Gibraltar. For additional details, see, Smart, *Biographical Dictionary of the British Generals of the Second World War*, pp.175-176.

85 The Mobile Workshop and field park sections were scaled to hold AFV spares at 2% of the armoured division vehicle establishment. The scaling included: engines, gearboxes, track, sprockets, bogie wheels, springs and dynamos. The Mobile Workshop was supported by a static facility at Nantes and the AFV Sub-Depot at Nantes.

tactical re-supply constraints, a problem later partially mitigated by the introduction of 4x4 logistic load-carriers.

The one logistic component that was absolutely critical to an armoured division was fuel supply, a subject, which appears to have received little attention and even less comment. British armoured formations never properly exercised fuel distribution before their deployment to France, and despite the emphasis which had been placed on the speed and mobility of the Cruisers, petroleum support at 3rd, 2nd and 1st Line relied on the 4-gallon disposable tin and reusable can. 1st Armoured Division operations during late May and early June 1940 reinforced the importance of robust and flexible fuel distribution in manoeuvre warfare, although it appears that few tanks were abandoned because of a failure in the system, which may explain the dearth of analysis. The secondary sources indicate that many tanks ran out of fuel and had to be abandoned but their crews were often captured, and the loss was attributed to enemy action, rather than ineffective logistic capability. Examination of the unit war diaries in the TNA, offer a more complex picture, with tanks having technical fuel problems, including blocked filters and lines, which suggests an issue with fuel quality or maintenance standards.

A handwritten report[86] from Commander 3rd Armoured Brigade, Brigadier Crocker,[87] offers some illuminating points upon logistics within the Division. Of particular note, was the allocation of RASC assets in the form of the Armoured Brigade Companies (ABC), whilst the Ordnance capability was retained as a divisional resource, Crocker being clear that brigades should have allocated repair, recovery and OFP sections. He also highlighted the disruption caused by the excessive separation between Division Forward and Rear. This was of especial importance because the ABCs became divorced from the OFP and the ammunition and petroleum sub-parks, an issue compounded by the dynamic operational environment interrupting co-ordination with the assets available on the GLOC. The outcome was almost a reversion to pre-Napoleonic operations, with RASC units, including the ABCs scouring empty barracks, abandoned dumps, chaotic docks and sundry railheads in the search for supplies. Another key observation was that transport units, especially the ABCs operated from woods or forests and never urban locations, including villages.[88] An obvious deduction from this scenario was the requirement for 4x4 load-carriers with a cross-country capability, which could reach

86 Brigadier J Crocker, Comments on 3rd Armd Bde Narrative dated 29 July 1940; handwritten document held in TML - 1 AD boxes.

87 Born in 1896, John Crocker enlisted as a Private in the Artists' Rifles in 1915 before commissioning into the Machine Gun Corps (MGC), being awarded the DSO and MC. In 1919, Crocker left the Army to train as a solicitor but re-commissioned into the Middlesex Regiment in 1920 before transferring to the Royal Tank Corps in 1923 and attending the Quetta Staff College in 1929. In April 1940, he was appointed to command 3rd Armoured Brigade and upon his return to UK from France was promoted to major-general as GOC 6th Armoured Division. He commanded I Corps for Operation OVERLORD and the subsequent North-West Europe campaign. He retired in 1953 as Adjutant-General to work as the Vice-Chairman of the Imperial War Graves Commission and serve as the Lord Lieutenant of Middlesex. He died in 1963. His only son, Wilfrid, an officer in the 5th Royal Inniskilling Dragoon Guards, was killed in Holland in October 1944. For details, see, Smart, *Biographical Dictionary of the British Generals of the Second World War*, pp.72-73.

88 The observation was emphasised thus: 'NEVER used a village'. Lecture, un-referenced and handwritten, on the 'Movement of 1 AD from Eng [land] to Somme, May 1940 and Lessons Learnt', held in TML. Why this was the case is not explained in the notes. but it may have been driven by the concerns about the threat from Fifth Columnists.

the AFV hides, although there is no suggestion in any report that armoured units should be supported by a tracked logistic platform.

The evacuation of failed AFVs was another subject that received Crocker's attention. The role of the HET was one point, whilst the procedures for re-deploying the crews, was another. Armoured units were well practised in recovering failed or damaged tanks by using the key capability to hand, which was another tank but there was relatively little capability to execute recovery to railheads, so immobile tanks were repaired *in situ*, abandoned or occasionally destroyed. It was however, obvious that using gun tanks as the primary recovery vehicles reduced combat power often when it was most needed, but given that a handful of Armoured Repair & Recovery Vehicles (ARRV) based on the Mark V tank had been deployed on the Western Front during the Great War this most certainly a pre-war omission and one that remarkably required the experience of the Western Desert to reinforce.[89]

Armoured Logistics in Action

That there was any logistic support to 1st Armoured Division in France was very much the result of the dedication and commitment of the practitioners and the efforts of the Staff officers rather than the War Office planners. The BEF GHQ Operational Instruction AFV 1 dated 23 May 1940 directed to GOC 1st Armoured Division, was, in relation to logistics, brief and to the point; paragraph 5 reads: 'L of C, North District are arranging supplies for your advance'.[90] Remarkably, given the *Luftwaffe's* assault on the French rail network, train movement, at least during the initial deployment, was robust if quirky, a point highlighted in the 3rd Armoured Brigade war diary.[91] A regimental perspective from the 10th Hussars concerning the move from Cherbourg around 22 May summarizes the rather surreal conditions:

> Between Cherbourg and Caen there is a very long gradient and on this the train stopped just as darkness was falling. Having heard of the wide ramifications of the fifth column, many thought that this halt was engineered by enemy agents. The suspicion was strengthened when it was explained by a railway official, who had overtaken the train on a bicycle, that the engine had broken down. The Commanding Officer now examined the more intimate parts of the engine … he formed the opinion that, in view of the class of locomotive and its state of dilapidation, which allowed far more steam to escape into the atmosphere than reach the working parts, it was not capable of pulling a train-load of tanks up the rest of the gradient. The opinion had already been formed by the railway official, who sent for another engine, which arrived in due course and the rest of the journey was completed without incident.[92]

89 57/Vehs A880, Report on a visit to armoured formations in the Middle East, Feb-Mar 1941, cited in WOOH, *Fighting, Support and Transport Vehicles*, Part I - *Common Problems*, p.225.

90 Copy No 9 is held by the TML. According to the stamp, it is still classified as SECRET.

91 TNA WO 167/421: HQ 3rd Armoured Brigade, WD, May 1940. See also, Edward Wilson, *Press On Regardless, The Story of the Fifth Royal Tank Regiment in World War Two* (Staplehurst: Spellmount, 2003), pp.10-14.

92 Regimental Committee, *The 10th Royal Hussars in the Second World War*, p.7. The CO was Lieutenant-Colonel John Derrick Hignett, who features regularly in the unit war diary, TNA WO 167/466. His

With a dearth of HETs, the movement of tanks by rail continued throughout the campaign, a capability that depended greatly upon the availability of Railway Construction Companies (RCC) of the Royal Engineers to build the ramps that enabled loading and off-loading if the selected railhead no side or end loading ramp.[93] 150 and 161 RCCs constructed a ramp at Neufchatel-en-Bray[94] in mid-May for the arrival of 1st Armoured Division and 161 RCC moved to Louviers between Rouen and Evreux to construct one for the RAOC Armoured Workshop.[95] On 2 June, 82 tanks and scout cars arrived at the workshop for repair followed by an additional 70 on 3 June.[96] The workshop out-loaded, during the withdrawal, a train of damaged and un-repaired tanks from 2nd Armoured Brigade that included an A12, which arrived at Brest Docks on 17 June. A second train loaded by 9th Lancers for Cherbourg never arrived, and the tanks fell into German hands.[97]

Tank main armament ammunition was another issue. No HE rounds were initially available in France for the 3.7-inch howitzers of the A9 Close Support tanks and a limited number of smoke rounds, which meant than none of the tank force could deliver HE nor was there sufficient smoke to cover advances and withdrawals. The regimental history of the 9th Lancers summarized the situation: 'There was not one round of ammunition for this useful weapon'.[98] The failure to ensure the integration of motorized artillery to the deployed ORBAT compounded this issue but at least this resolved the task of delivering artillery ammunition. The logistic main effort seems therefore, to have been the supply of fuel to widely dispersed units, which with disintegrating communications was a major challenge. The most successful coherent logistic operation during operations in France supported the withdrawal, from Le Neubourg to Cherbourg, of the 3rd Armoured Brigade. To enable this operation, a RASC Supply Company was task organized with fuel, rations, water and ammunition and dispatched to Vire to await the arrival of the brigade, although there was minor disruption to the replenishment plan because of the requirement to re-route the formation around the town. Remarkably, only two light tanks and one cruiser failed to reach Cherbourg Docks, a tribute to the foresight, dedication and competence of commanders, planners, crews, logisticians and mechanics. That this operation had many logistic similarities to the three major divisional moves in the UK must have contributed to its success.

knowledge of steam locomotives was gained through working in a ship-yard and in deep-sea fishing. For a biography, see, Derek Lewin, *Parson, Politician and Gentleman* (Leicester: Troubador, 2009).

93 The provision of the Ramp Wagon System (RWS) introduced to the British Army in 1918 would, in many instances, have resolved the requirement for deploying RCC for this type of task, thereby creating more engineer resources for rail projects and generating greater tactical flexibility for the armoured units. The RWS was a sound concept and an effective design, which remained in service, with new equipments, until the end of the 20th Century. For details of the design and operation of the RWS, see, *Royal Corps of Transport Training*, Vol IV, *Transport Operations - Rail Transport* (UK MOD, 1975), Annex K, Appx 1, pp.264-265 and for the construction of a sleeper ramp, QMG, Notes on Military Railway Engineering, Part II, Engineering (War Office, 1940), Plate 56, Improvised Tank Ramp Constructed from Railway PW Materials..

94 TNA 167/945/2: 150 RCC RE, WD, May 1940.

95 TNA 167/955: 161 RCC RE, WD, May 1940.

96 TNA WO 167/345: 1 AD Workshop RAOC, WD, June 1940.

97 Bright, *The Ninth Queen's Royal Lancers*, p.22.

98 Ibid, p.22.

P13.4 Logistic Agility. The provision of military specification 4x2 WMT to logistic units in 1st Armoured Division reduced demands upon Equipment Support facilities and spares, whilst enhancing operational capability. Motorcycles, whilst not the safest form of transport, were vital to control logistic road movement. (RLCM: A1/MT/RLCA 20780)

The Ammunition Sub-Park moved location eight times in the period 1-14 June but except for the odd minor traffic accident, survived the campaign with no serious casualties, although it struggled to obtain rounds for the 0.38-inch Revolver, 0.5-inch Vickers Machine Gun, 15 mm BESA, 40 mm Beaufort and 0.303-inch tracer ammunition. This situation was not the result of insufficient effort because as the unit war diary[99] noted, nearly every dump and ARH along the GLOC was visited with almost no success. The OC had however, a better outcome with his entertainment planning; 500 soldiers from the Park and surrounding units, attended, on 14 June, a concert organized by one of the officers, at a French chateau.[100] One of the key lessons noted in the war diary was the importance of passive and active air defence procedures through

99 TNA WO 167/342: 1 AD ASP RASC, WD, June 1940.

100 Lieutenant Cowell was the appointee. The event was hosted on a stage complete with theatre lights; the improvisation of British soldiers is amazing. The Park also held, presumably the next day, Sunday 15 June, a communion service, attended by the rather smaller congregation of 80 personnel.

concealment, camouflage, sentries and AA weapons. The Petrol Sub-Park has less luck; four soldiers were seriously injured in motor-cycle accidents[101] and two taken ill requiring them to be admitted to hospital. One interesting event on 5 June 1940 was the capture, near Roncherolles, to the East of Rouen, of four *Luftwaffe* personnel from a crashed Heinkel 111,[102] by four RASC officers from the Sub-Park attired in dressing gowns, pyjamas and steel helmets; sadly, the unit war diary is silent on the names of these nocturnally tailored logistic adventurers.[103] The unit was though, to engage in plenty of tasking until 16 June, when, five miles from Brest, it received the order to withdraw via the port.[104] The unit denial party destroyed or neutralized its 80 vehicles[105] and drained, through puncturing the tins, 16,000 gallons of cased petrol. On 17 June, the 205 personnel marched five miles to Brest docks with personal kit, rifles, Bren LMGs, Boys anti-tank rifles and the company records in tin boxes.[106]

101 Motor-cycles were essential to logistic C^3, reconnaissance and convoy control. Then, as now, they were not the safest method of wheeled transport. Trooper Ernest Ronald Whitworth, a Despatch Rider in 10th Hussars, was a fatal casualty of a motor-cycle accident when at around 0230 on 15 June, he collided in the dark near Le Mans with a 10th Hussars tank travelling in the opposite direction. He lies At Rest in Guipavas Communal Cemetery 5 miles NE of Brest, the sole British serviceman to so do. Regimental Committee, *10th Royal Hussars*, p.26.

102 The *Luftwaffe* mounted a raid on Rouen at 0615 and lost three aircraft near the target. This aircraft is either He 111P 1G+AH from I/KG27 shot down by French Blochs of GC II/10 or a HE 111H of 3/KG27, shot down by Hurricanes of 1 Squadron RAF. See, Cornwell, *The Battle of France,* pp.428-429, which also lists the names of the German air crews.

103 TNA WO 167/343: 1 AD Petrol Sub-Park RASC, WD, June 1940.

104 TNA WO 167/343: 1 AD Petrol Sub-Park RASC, WD, June 1940.

105 The table below is based upon WE 1/1931/10F/1 in Philson, BEFORBAT, Vol 4, p.63 and the unit war diary in TNA WO 167/343: 1 AD Petrol Sub-Park RASC. The Sub-Park must have been one of the few units in the BEF to have a task vehicle strength in excess of the WET.

Table 13.8

1st Armoured Division Petrol Sub-Park - Vehicle Establishment & Strength

Type	Estab	Strength	Remarks
3-ton, Bedford OY	36	46	Battle Winning Equipment (BWE)
3-cwt, Thornycroft	5	5	
1-ton, Fordson, LMG	4	1	Mobile AA capability
Lorry, Technical	4	1	
Car, 4 Seats	2	1	
Car, 2 Seats	3	3	
Motor-Cycle	16	16	4 damaged in RTAs
Trailer, Water	3	2	
Total	73	80	

106 The unit war diary, which is neatly typed, gives an excellent insight into matters of company detail but unfortunately little on its contribution to operations in support of the Division. TNA WO 167/343. The reconstitution of 1 AD, and in particular its logistic units, is another fascinating story. The RASC was especially well served in delivering this capability because the Corps Mobilization Centres, which no other Arm or Service had. They were, to quote the Director of Staff Duties at the War Office 'as valuable to the Country as gold mines'. Needless to say, the War Office had tried to dis-establish them as an economy measure. See, WOOH, *Supplies and Transport*, Vol I, Colonel D W Boileau late RASC (War Office, 1954), p.127.

In addition, there was a myriad of logistic failures and irritations, many of which were created by the friction of war and remind logistic planners that '*Le Diable dans les Detail*'.[107] The 1st Line HE and smoke rounds were initially left on the docks at Southampton, some tanks were deficient wireless sets, sighting telescopes and gunners' shoulder pieces. There was insufficient tank track in the GLOC supply chain, track pins were prone to failure and tanks sailed with their cannons still boxed and packed with grease. Had the division not deployed into battle, these issues would have been grist to the Staff mill but the enemy ensured such matters became a logistic crisis. It was of course, not planned to be like this. The original concept was for 1st Armoured Division to deploy to France, and conduct regimental and brigade training, including firing camps and logistic integration within the AFV Advanced Base Area (ABA) around Pacy, approximately 35 miles South-South-East of Rouen. Two key logistic components of the ABA were the Base Ordnance Depot (BOD) and Base Ordnance Workshops (BOW) specifically created to support the initial three armoured divisions, with an expansion capability to ten and then twelve.[108] Whilst these vast facilities were being constructed, No 1 BOD and No 2 BOW, located at Nantes were designated to operate as the AFV Base with a small advanced depot at Bonnieries-sur-Seine in the ABA.[109] The German attack unbalanced this plan by divorcing this important logistic capability from the sole deployed armoured division. The GOC[110] summarized his frustrations of the outcome in his POR, noting that the 'severe shortage of mechanical spare parts for the repair of the fighting vehicles and the absence of any reserve of fighting vehicles with which to replace casualties' were key logistic failings that contributed to the disastrous outcome in France.[111]

Conclusion

1st Armoured Division's logistic units, although not always to establishment in manpower and equipment and often suffering from an initial lack of individual technical and tactical skills upon which to build, handled the rapidly evolving scenarios sufficiently competently to sustain the operation and acquit themselves well in battle. The Petroleum Sub-Park and 10 Company were the most practised at their art because their services were required daily, whilst the Ammunition Sub-Park delivered an impressive performance given the change of role two months before. The shape, size, composition and role of the logistic divisional units were not always in accordance with the Staff plan and there was much frustration relating to training and tasking but in the round, most units were able to deliver sufficient capability to support operations. The GOC indisputably recognized the significance of formation logistic training in 1940 but without the

107 The Devil is in the Detail! I am indebted to Colonel Dan Duffau of the *Service des Essences des Armees* (French Military Fuel Service) for this most pertinent logistic quote.

108 For details, see, WOOH, *Ordnance Services*, p.155.

109 In preparation for the deployment of the armoured divisions, the RAOC sent selected officers and SNCOs on AFV stores courses and posted a specialist officer to advise GHQ on the receipt, storage, maintenance and issue of AFVs and spares.

110 Relieved on 24 August 1940, Major-General Evans was posted to command Aldershot Garrison. Alanbrooke, whilst C-in-C Home Forces, wrote: '19 August 1940. In the afternoon Roger Evans came to see me to ask why he had been removed from the Armoured Division. This resulted in an unpleasant interview'. Danchev & Todman, *War Diaries*, p.101.

111 TNA WO 32/9392: Evans Report, pp.18-19.

resources, it was impossible to deliver it,[112] whilst the crucial importance of individual technical logistic competence was clearly highlighted.

The campaign in France rejuvenated many old logistic chestnuts, although it is unfortunate that the formation war diaries shed such little light upon the challenges at brigade and divisional levels.[113] That there is so little comment probably indicates that logistics was perceived to have operated remarkably well in the circumstances, but from the historical perspective it may be deduced that fundamentally, its effective delivery was undermined by the manner of the operational deployment, compounded by the failure to hone the relevant formation logistic skills, although the vital issue relating to the shortage of tank spares and reserves did little to support a positive outcome. Interestingly, the Bartholomew and Evans Reports are also mostly silent on these issues.[114] Brigadier Crocker highlighted a series of pertinent points, not least of which, was the importance of ensuring that the appropriate 1st and 2nd Line logistic slices were allocated to armoured brigades, regiments and squadrons that were detached to other formations and units.[115]

The War Office failed to grasp the importance of generating a robust solution for the forward recovery of armour, only belatedly initiating work on an armoured recovery vehicle based on the Churchill I tank chassis as a result of operational experience in the Western Desert.[116] The failure to procure a HET for tank deployment and recovery is more understandable given the experience of the Great War and the expectation that tank railheads in France would be well forward,[117] but incredibly the dramatic experience in France in 1940 failed to prompt any

112 See, summary note of 79/Mob/3244 held in TML MH 5 Box 2 (355.486.4).

113 None of the files researched shed light on the combat supplies scales in France. The TML has one document relating to the 1 AD in UK during September 1940, which is brief but of interest, especially as the division is allocated to VII Corps with 1st (Canadian) Division. Rations: 3 days preserved in all AFVs and vehicles in 'A' Echelon and one 24 hour Iron Ration per man. Petrol: RASC 3rd Line to refill from Corps dumps. 1st Line to refill from dumps, using 4-gallon tins, only in an emergency. Ammunition: 2nd or 3rd Line RASC to refill from Corps dumps. Ordnance: 2nd Line through the Petrol Sub-Park and 3rd Line through Command Ordnance Depots (COD). Anti-Gas IPE - one set per man. TNA WO 166/798: HQ 1 AD AQ, 1st Armoured Division Administrative Instruction No 2 (SECRET) S/10 Home Forces dated 8 September 1940.

114 The Bartholomew Report and its supporting evidence is held in TNA WO 106/1741 and 1775; it was also published in the *British Army Review* No 129 (UK MOD, Spring 2002), pp.87-104 and was the War Office's immediate post operational assessment of the BEF's performance. The Bartholomew Committee consisted of five officers, which took evidence from 36 officers from lieutenant-general to major. The report was a considered examination of the lessons identified and the proposed remedial measures. The committee did not examine the 1 AD campaign, the only relevant sections appertaining to the utilization of armour being the operations of armoured car regiments and divisional cavalry allocated to infantry and motor divisions. The Evans Report was planned to be an integral component of the Bartholomew Report but was not crafted in the same style or structure.

115 Brigadier J Crocker, 'Comments on 3rd Armd Bde Narrative' dated 29 July 1940; handwritten document held in TML - 1 AD boxes.

116 The initial vehicles had no winch fitted, relying on tractive effort to effect the recovery, which user experience had firmly identified as an issue and future production equipments had winches. Minutes: 13th Meeting, AFV Recovery and Committee, 3 March 1942, 57/Tanks/2866 cited in WOOH, *Fighting, Support & Transport Vehicles*, Part I – *Common Problems*, p.226.

117 For an analysis of the Great War experience, see, 'Without Trucks to Move Them: The role of logistics in delivering armoured capability in the BEF', Maginniss, *An Unappreciated Field of Endeavour*, pp.294-312.

change and it took the fighting in North Africa compounded by the paucity of rail capacity in the Theatre to ram home the lesson that the acquisition of HETs was essential to military success.[118]

By definition, the demands of the situation created extemporization, and the RASC for example, provided lorries to lift the equipment and ammunition of the four dismounted troops formed in the 10th Hussars after they had insufficient tanks to crew.[119] Such logistic flexibility received positive assent, reinforcing the need to ensure agility in the manoeuvre environment but re-heating the debate in the RASC about whether companies should be commodity or task based. The most important lesson however, was importance of divisional logistic units having robust, well-trained soldiers, who were capable of fighting when necessary and implicit in this process was that they should be equipped with suitable weapons, be able to use them, and be led by determined and able officers and NCOs who were prepared to seize the initiative.

118 The US Army, despite the British experience North Africa, failed to recognize its importance and had to learn the hard way of the critical edge that HETs offered to armoured combat capability. As a consequence of this inertia, US industry did not start production of 40 ton HETs until April 1943. To facilitate the HETs operating forward, later US models had armoured cabs for the crews, a feature which has re-appeared on 21st Century equipments. See, WOOH, *Fighting, Support and Transport Vehicles*, Part I – *Common Problems*, pp.227-228.

119 Regimental Committee, *The 10th Royal Hussars in the Second World War*, p.20.

Appendix to Chapter 13

Table 13A.1
1st Armoured Division – Unit Allocation

Arm or Service	Unit	Remarks
Divisional HQ	22 Employment Platoon	Detached to 2nd Armoured Division
	1 Armoured Division Intelligence Section	
	37 Field Security Police Section	
2nd Armoured Brigade	Queens Bays	
	9th Queen's Royal Lancers	
	10th Royal Hussars	
3rd Armoured Brigade	2nd Royal Tank Regiment	
	3rd Royal Tank Regiment	Detached to 30th Brigade in April 1940
	5th Royal Tank Regiment	
1st Support Group	1st Battalion The Rifle Brigade	Deployed to 30th Brigade before deployment to France and replaced by 4th Border
	2nd Battalion King's Royal Rifle Corps	
Artillery	1st Royal Horse Artillery	Detached to BEF in October 1939
	2nd Royal Horse Artillery	Detached to BEF in October 1939
	101st Light Anti-Aircraft & Anti-Tank Regiment	
Engineers	HQ Royal Engineers	
	Field Squadron	
	Field Park Troop	
Signals	1st Armoured Division Signals Company	

Supply & Transport	HQ 1 Armoured Division RASC	
	2 Armoured Brigade Company	
	3 Armoured Brigade Company	
	1 Support Group Company	
	1 Armoured Division Troops Company	
	1 Armoured Division Ammunition Sub-Park	Ex 911 AA Company RASC
	1 Armoured Division Petrol Sub-Park	
	Reserve Supply Park	Task subsumed by Petrol Sub-Park
Medical	1 Light Field Ambulance	
	2 Light Field Ambulance	
	1 Armoured Division Field Hygiene Section	
Ordnance	1 Armoured Division Workshop	
	2 Armoured Brigade Light Repair Section	
	3 Armoured Brigade Light Repair Section	
	20 Armoured Brigade Light Repair Section	
	Mobile Bath Unit	Not shown on the deployment table
Provost	1 Armoured Division Provost Company	
Postal	1 Armoured Division Postal Unit RE	

14

Operation FLANNELFOOT
Supporting the Gas Warfare capability of the BEF

A Hidden Inventory

Amongst the thousands of soldiers and airmen that formed the BEF and the British Air Forces France (BAFF) was a group of specialists, supported by other Arms and Services, whose task was to conduct, in support of the BEF, offensive and defensive operations using chemical weapons or 'Gas Warfare' (GW) in the parlance of the day. Training and deployment were conducted in great secrecy and perhaps not surprisingly, little has been written on the BEF's GW capability in 1939-1940,[1] the Official History of the campaign, *The War in France and Flanders 1939–1940*, not mentioning it.[2] The specialist history of British GW preparations during the Second World War, *Special Weapons and Types of Warfare,* Volume I, *Gas Warfare*[3] was, until 1984, graded SECRET, when it was downgraded to UNCLASSIFIED.[4] A rare but fascinating document, discussion on the logistic aspects of preparations for BEF GW is, perforce of coverage, zero and it is the aim of this chapter to fill this lacuna in this important but nonetheless little known, historical dimension of the BEF.

In 1939, Chemical Warfare (CW) was defined as those aspects concerned with the offensive and defensive use of gas, incendiary and smoke munitions, and those defence measures required to protect British Forces. GW related specifically to the employment, in military operations, by any nation of any chemical substance, solid, liquid or gas,[5] designed to have a poisonous or

1 Sometimes this secrecy pervades the logistic war diaries with veiled terms being used to describe the handling, movement and storage of Gas weapons, which in research terms is frustrating in that it is not always possible to clarify from the documents the specific weapon systems.
2 Ellis, *The War in France and Flanders.*
3 WOOH *Special Weapons and Types of Warfare*, Vol I, *Gas Warfare*, Lieutenant-Colonel D J C Wiseman (Comp.), (War Office, 1951). Hereafter, WOOH, *Gas Warfare.*
4 This document was downgraded to UNCLASSIFIED by MOD D/OR13 (NBC) 22/1 dated 28 September 1984.
5 46 chemical agents are listed in Lieutenant-Colonel Augustin M Prentiss PhD and Major George J B Fisher, *Chemicals In War: A Treatise on Chemical Warfare* (New York: McGraw-Hill Book Company, 1937), pp.6-7.

irritant affect, upon the human body,[6] and this included tear gases. Consequently, gas was deemed to be a 'Special Weapon' (SW) and one that required different controls to incendiary and smoke munitions.[7] Strategically, the use of gas in retaliation was considered to be a defensive act,[8] whilst at the operational and tactical levels, the BEF General Staff planned to use GW[9] to support offensive and defensive ground operations with land based and air delivered gas munitions. The Army had, or planned to have, SW for offence and defence, whilst the RAF inventory was entirely offensive; some Army systems could be utilized for both, whilst others were designed for a specific type of operation.

The British Army had several Arms and Services involved in storing, securing, moving, deploying and employing its offensive and defensive SW. The Army was also responsible for assisting the RAF in deploying its SW to and from the Continent, and in an early successful period of 'Jointery', the two Services worked closely to achieve these tasks. The RAOC was responsible for storing SW in Base Ammunition Depots (BAD), controlling a designated field site, 21 BAD, near Fecamp[10] in Northern France, specifically for storing SW, which it was perceived, ensured not only greater secrecy, although there was debate on this point but also the capability to swiftly evacuate the stocks to UK, which as it transpired proved to be the case.[11] The Corps of Royal Engineers (RE) was responsible for constructing the depot, and the Corps controlled SW movement by rail and ship, although most of the assets were civilian. The AMPC provided labour for building and handling tasks in the depot, and at the ports. The RASC took the lead role in deploying SW by road at the corps and divisional level, also providing vehicles and personnel for internal depot tasks, the loop between 21 BAD and the port, and the depot and railheads. The Royal Artillery (RA) handled SW 'Grey Shell' as conventional rounds, although there were special controls over issue and employment, whilst the RE No 1 Chemical

6 Home Office, *Air Raid Precautions*, Handbook No 1, *Personal Protection Against Gas* (London: HMSO, 1938), p.2.

7 In RAF documents relating to the period held in the TNA, gas weapons are almost invariably described as chemical weapons, which is not incorrect, but this descriptor also included smoke and incendiary munitions.

8 Whilst the War Office and GHQ BEF were developing GW plans, the paper proposing the arrangements for the delegated authority to C-in-C BEF to retaliate with GW if British Forces were attacked with gas weapons had not been presented to the War Cabinet for approval. WOOH, *Gas Warfare*, p.7.

9 Anti-Gas Measures (AGM) now termed Chemical Defence, were an integral part of the planning process for GW operations, and the Staff carefully studied the impact of the enemy's capability on British Forces. See, TNA WO 193/717: Scale of Gas Attack to which British Expeditionary Forces may be subjected. For a summary of British AGM inter-war trials and development, see, G B Carter, *Chemical and Biological Defence at Porton Down, 1916-2000* (London: The Stationary Office, 2000), pp.29-43 and for military AGM systems, see, WOOH, *Gas Warfare*, pp.192-233.

10 The depot was sited at Tourville-les-Ifs, four miles South of the SPOD at Fecamp, although in almost all documents that refer to it, use the nomenclature, Fecamp.

11 The Air Ministry plans Staff had mixed views on the establishment of Fecamp, preferring to store RAF SW at railheads for an agile response. After due consideration, an Air Ministry letter S.2187/WO2 dated 21 November 1939 noted the 'risk' of forward railhead deployment and thus decided to 'accept the slight delay which will ensue in getting stocks up to the forward area if it becomes necessary to use gas', by storing some weapons at 21 BAD. TNA AIR 35/130: British Air Forces in France - Gas Policy.

Warfare (CW) Group[12] composed of three CW Companies,[13] was responsible for the Livens Projectors, chemical mines and the Bulk Contamination Vehicles (BCV).[14] The RAF provided specialists at the ports and 21 BAD for the handling, movement and storage of RAF SW, and also had facilities constructed to support the AASF.[15]

Ground Delivered Offensive Special Weapons

The main land force GW offensive capability was to be delivered by artillery. Initially, the BEF's punch was restricted to 6 and 4.5-inch howitzer shells designed to contaminate ground, and to a lesser extent personnel and equipment. These munitions had a bursting charge, activated by a percussion fuse, which broke the casing, thereby releasing the agent. In September 1939, the shells were held as empty cases from ammunition produced during the Great War but filling of both types with a blister agent, HS Mustard,[16] commenced in October 1939. 28,000 rounds of 6-inch were ready by the end of November and 18,000 rounds of 4.5-inch by the end of December. GHQ BEF had a plan to fill 50 percent of the 4.5-inch ammunition with the lachrymatory agent Bromobenzyl Cyanide (BBC)[17] but this was never enacted.

The GHQ Operations and GW Staffs eagerly awaited the arrival of Base Ejection (BE) air-burst chemical ammunition for the 25 pounder. The Mark I (Y) shell weighed 20 lb, contained 2 lb of Mustard, and was designed as an anti-personnel weapon to support defensive operations. For offensive operations, the shell had a 'B' fill of BBC, which although relatively persistent created, in comparison to Mustard, a very small contact hazard.[18] Design and production difficulties, however, interrupted the planned issue programme and GHQ calculated that there would be no deliveries of any 25 pounder gas ammunition until mid-September 1940. In the event, the prediction was accurate; on 1 October 1940 there were 200 rounds of HS Mustard charged shells and 2,000 awaiting filling.[19] Gas rounds for this system were planned to be 10 percent

12 For the War Establishment (WE) of the HQ CW Group (WE III/1931/14B/1) and the CW Company (WE/1931/15/3), see, Philson, BEFORBAT, Vol 1, pp.131-133.

13 58, 61 & 62 Companies RE. WOOH, *Gas Warfare*, p.273, Appx XIII, Order of Battle – Chemical Warfare Troops. A fourth company, No 63, remained at Bulford on Salisbury Plain.

14 Perforce of operational circumstances, with no chemical mines or BCVs to deploy, the campaign lucidly demonstrating the tactical limitations of the Livens Projectors, and that GW seemed increasingly unlikely to be used in France, No 1 CW Group was tasked to general engineer and defence tasks. See, *The History of the Corps of The Royal Engineers*, Vol VIII, 1938-1948, p.31.

15 RAF SWs were stored in the brickworks next to the AASF's ARH at Germaine, located 12 miles South of Rheims and at a Forward Air Ammunition Park at Nogent l'Abbesse, 5 miles East of Reims.

16 Coded a 'Y' fill.

17 BBC, first produced in 1881, was introduced into French Army service in July 1918 and was part of the British inventory in 1940. Artillery shells filled with BBC had to have a minimal bursting charge to prevent the decomposition of the chemical, a constraint that reduced its dispersal area. WOOH, *Gas Warfare*, p.131.

18 An agent with an odour of soured fruit, BBC had several advantages and disadvantages. It was in 1940, the only tear gas, which required decontamination with strong alkali, for example, slaked lime, or organic solvents, so it had much merit for defensive operations but in the offence, careful judgement was required, as it had considerable persistency. In the open, it can last three days, in woods seven, and in soil between 15-30. Ibid.

19 Ibid, pp.247-248, Appx II, Stocks of Air and Army Gas Weapons and War Gases (3 September 1939 - 31 December 1941).

of total holdings, with 50 percent being charged with Mustard and 50 percent BBC. GHQ also looked into the future by planning GW operations for the 5.5-inch gun, proposing that all gas ammunition for this weapon system should contain blister agent. The RASC Divisional Ammunition Companies (DAC) distributed GW artillery rounds, 'Grey Shell' in the colloquial of the day, in the same manner as conventional munitions, though subject to special control and handling measures; specific training for the task appears to have been very limited.

In 1940, the other offensive gas weapon held by the BEF was the Livens Projector operated by RE CW Companies. Developed during the Great War, it consisted of a cast iron tube 3 feet in length and 8 inches in diameter, which fired a large cylindrical drum[20] by means of a charge box placed in the bottom of the projector,[21] giving a maximum range of 1,800 yards with the No 9 Projector[22] using a No 30 charge.[23] By design, a weapon of static warfare, with the projector and drum weighing in at 220 pounds, some of the tubes were mounted on dedicated WMT[24] vehicles to make them more tactically responsive, but they still had to be dug in for firing.[25] The Livens drums in April 1940 were filled with HS Mustard in order to contaminate ground and personnel, although GHQ also planned to fill some Livens drums with a 'G' fill of Phosgene,[26] a potent lethal agent for its day, and one that could have given the Livens Projector a more offensive edge.[27] By 19 April 1940, stocks stood at 4,700 drums, which was sufficient for seventeen company shoots. This level of capability would have had little adverse effect on the Germans at the operational level, although given the right scenario, the tactical impact could have been considerably greater but until stocks were increased, the BEF was restricted to small shoots, or very local contamination operations. Nearly all of the Livens Projectors were lost during the evacuation from France but emergency production in the summer and

20 The common term for a Livens cylinder was a 'drum', although it was cylindrical in shape.

21 The Tri-Service Defence CBRN Centre at Winterbourne Gunner has an example of the projector and the drum.

22 There were five different projectors: Nos 3, 4, 7, 9 and 10; General Staff, *The Tactical and Technical Employment of Chemical Weapons*, Military Training Pamphlet (MTP) No 32, Part II – *The Projector*, 26/GS Pubns/363 (War Office, July 1940), p.5.

23 The short range, which was a maximum of 1,800 yards, was a problem. Not only did it give friendly forces little stand-off protection from the vapour hazard if the wind changed direction but also the chances of securing surprise was greatly reduced unless meticulous security precautions were taken. Range was adjusted by altering the quantity of the charge. See, General Staff, MTP No 32, Part II – *The Projector*.

24 None were 4x4, thereby restricting tactical deployment.

25 To bring a CW company into action with this weapon was a ponderous activity and the sections were particularly vulnerable to enemy artillery whilst recovering the projectors. A full salvo of 270 drums from the one shot tubes could though, produce a 'crash concentration' of gas, so as an area weapon it packed a short but powerful punch, which was the key capability of the system, with the potential to produce large numbers of casualties before enemy personnel had time to adopt protective equipment. See, General Staff, MTP No 32, Part II – *The Projector*.

26 As it transpired, charging in the UK did not commence until August 1940. 9,000 filled drums were in stock by 1 October. WOOH, *Gas Warfare*, pp.247-248.

27 In the round though, its short range and immobility, made it unsuitable for offensive operations, so despite its high weight to gas ratio, it was a defensive rather than an offensive system, and it is surprising that it was classed as the latter. Given its interesting variation of shot, both in range, and deflection it was probably best suited to the one task it was never given by GHQ BEF: area contamination of ground during an out of contact withdrawal.

autumn of 1940, of this simple weapon soon replaced the losses.[28] Ammunition and projectors were supplied to the CW companies through the GHQ Company RASC. The two echelons of the RASC company carried one refill of 270 drums and 20 spare projectors for each CW company. When a CW company was detached from GHQ Troops, an element of the GHQ RASC Company was attached to the relevant formation RASC company, which at divisional level was the DAC.

Ground Delivered Defensive Special Weapons

In addition to the offensive capability provided by the Livens Projector, the CW companies also had the task of deploying SW in defence. All three of the systems, the BCV, the chemical mine and the ground contamination bomb, were, because of production problems, not brought into service until after the BEF was evacuated from France but plans were developed to store and maintain them in France.[29] The BCV[30] was based on a Morris CS 8 truck chassis of 15 cwt, upon which was mounted a de-mountable 140 gallon water cart, capable of containing 126 gallons of liquid HT Mustard.[31] Un-armoured, it was vulnerable to small arms fire and artillery, which limited its deployment during a withdrawal in contact. There was also a plan to issue the carts on trailers, to be drawn by a tank or Universal Carrier, and thereby offer a small measure of protection to the laying crew. BCVs were not a permanent CW company asset and were held centrally, being issued as required, on a scale of 50 per company. 240 were allocated for deployment to France and GHQ intended that 120 would be held in BADs and 120 at Ammunition Railheads (ARH). CW companies were tasked with collecting BCVs from the ARH but given their many tasks it is probable that the DACs would have been responsible for positioning these vehicles in the operational area, although the providing the additional drivers would no doubt have been a challenge. The refilling procedures for the BCVs, whilst clearly a requirement, does not appear in the documents but it is likely that the GHQ Staff planned to return the empty equipment to the UK, although refilling by the French could have been an option.

28 Stocks of drums rose rapidly. There were 16,000 drums charged with mustard by 1 October 1940, and 9,000 filled with phosgene; 5,000 were stored empty. WOOH, *Gas Warfare*, pp.247-248, Appx II.
29 By 1 October 1940, there were ready for issue, 65 equipments charged, and another 109 empty. Ibid.
30 For details of the system, see: General Staff, MTP No 32, Part IV – *The Bulk Contamination Vehicle*, 26/GS Pubns/348 (War Office, June 1940).
31 The agent was discharged by pressurizing the container with compressed air at 20 psi, from a medium pressure cylinder with a maximum operating pressure of 250 psi, which forced the agent through a discharge valve, and thence to a horizontal spreader pipe. Designed to heavily contaminate ground, and particularly roads and tracks, in defence or withdrawal, one vehicle, moving at 5-6 miles per hour, was capable of laying one gallon of blister agent every 25 yd^2, over a continuous belt 14 yards wide and 200 yards long. General Staff, MTP No 32, Part IV – *The Bulk Contamination Vehicle*.

The chemical mine was a commercial pattern cylindrical steel drum with a burster in the neck, two handles to carry it, and a filled weight of 65 lb.[32] Charged with four gallons of HS Mustard, it was designed for use on terrain that could not be reached using the BCV and for the contamination of demolitions.[33] Chemical mines were never issued to the BEF because production started after the evacuation but by 1 October 1940, 4,500 charged mines were available, with another 525 empty. Designed as an All Arms weapon, the Bomb, Ground, 6-lb[34] was charged with 2 pints of HS Mustard and used for small-scale contamination operations, particularly of trenches and small buildings.[35] The ground bomb was too late into production to see service with the BEF, but by 1 October 1940, stocks stood at 73,300 charged and 92,000 empty. The CW companies did not carry mines or ground bombs permanently, but by ground loading the Livens Projectors, there was sufficient transport to lift 864 mines and 7,920 ground bombs.[36] The only gap in the doctrine was the supply of chemical mines and contamination bombs, for which Military Training Pamphlet No 32, Part I, stated: 'Special provision, must therefore be made'[37]. To date, no documentary evidence has emerged from the BEF's files, which would indicate how these munitions were to be distributed but it is probable that the RASC DACs would have been tasked.

Air Delivered Special Weapons

The RAF was responsible for the offensive GW main effort and the key weapon in the operational and tactical armoury was the Smoke Curtain Installation (SCI)[38] filled with HT or HTV Mustard, designed to discharge high and low level spray. There were two types of SCI in service by April 1940.[39] 250 lb SCI charging had commenced in September 1939, and by 19 April 1940, stocks had risen to 361 charged, 261 of which were in France,[40] with 39 held empty in UK as a reserve. Stocks of the 500 lb SCI were higher. Of the 815 charged systems, 809 were held in France on 19 April and there were 85 in the UK awaiting a fill.[41] The 1000 lb SCI went into production in April 1940 and would have been deployed to France for use by those

32 For the technical details and tactical employment, see, General Staff, MTP No 32, Part V - *The Chemical Mine*, 26/GS Pubns/263 (War Office, February 1940).

33 It could heavily contaminate, with accuracy (50 gm/m^2) 70 yd^2 of ground, and lightly contaminate (10 gm/m^2) 1,000 yd^2, and thereby impose delay on enemy movement or the use of ground. WOOH, *Gas Warfare*, p.165.

34 For the technical details and tactical employment, see, General Staff, MTP No 32, Part VI - *Bombs, Ground, 6 lb*, 26/GS Pubns/289 (War Office, March 1940).

35 The Bomb, 6-lb could heavily contaminate 10 yd^2 and lightly contaminate up to 100 yd^2. WOOH, *Gas Warfare*, p.165.

36 Ibid.

37 General Staff, MTP No 32, Part I - *Chemical Warfare Units*, p.3.

38 In all published training sources, the term Smoke Curtain Installation is used, with explicit explanations that SCI was to be referred to in this manner as a security precaution. Most Air Ministry (AIR) and Ministry of Aviation (AVIA) and some War Office (WO) documents in the TNA use the nomenclature, Spray Container Installation, thereby describing, with brevity, its GW task.

39 WOOH, *Gas Warfare*, pp.247-248, Appx II.

40 The balance of 100 had been dispatched to Egypt. Ibid.

41 Ibid.

forward-based elements of the Heavy Bomber Force equipped with the Wellington had the evacuation from the Continent not intervened.[42]

To compliment the spray systems, the RAF also fielded iron bombs filled with HS Mustard. Bombs, Aircraft, Low Capacity (LC) 250 lb and Mk I LC 30 lb, were fuzed weapons of conventional appearance. They functioned on impact using the tail ejection principle in which a small internal burster blew off a lightly welded tail plate, the liquid fill being dispensed around the point of impact with the minimum loss into the crater.[43] Individual Mk I 30 lb bombs contaminated a much smaller area but dropped in sticks, accuracy was not only less important than with the 250 lb LC weapon but also several areas of contamination were created across the target.[44] There were 42,000 Mk Is charged with HS Mustard, held in the UK, although because of a fuze production failure, only 10,000 were ready for issue and another 18,900 awaited filling.[45] The Bomb, Aircraft, LC, 30 lb, Mk II, was a fuze-less weapon, loaded to an eight-bomb cluster container.[46] The key logistic issue with the Mk II was the short shelf life after the fill, which precluded ready use stocks in France. 4,000 empty bombs were therefore, held in the UK ready for charging, which of course created a transportation issue in moving quickly them to the AASF. Plans were also discussed, which aimed to enhance SW capability by filling petrol tins and 45 gallon oil drums with HS Mustard to make up shortfalls in 30 lb and 250 lb bomb production; this proposal was, to the relief of those who were tasked with handling them, abandoned.

Inter-Theatre Movement Operations

The movement of SW to France was a highly sensitive activity, which was run under the codename Operation FLANNELFOOT.[47] The planning and delivery of the operation was the subject of considerable debate within the War Office, the Air Ministry and the Ministry of Transport. The planning and movements Staffs had the experience in handling and storing SW from the Great War to guide them, and more recently, the shipment, in August 1939, of

42 The reason why there were SCIs of different sizes was to ensure that the systems offered flexibility across the spectrum of the offensive aircraft capability. The Lysander could carry 2 x 250 lb SCIs, the Battle and Blenheim, 2 x 500 lb SCIs, and the Wellington, 1 x 1000 lb SCI.

43 The 250 lb bomb could heavily contaminate 70 yd^2, lightly contaminate 550 yd^2, and given a wind speed of 10 mph, force personnel to don respirators with an area of 2,300 yd^2. The 250 lb bomb was the weapon of choice if internal contamination of buildings was required. WOOH, *Gas Warfare*, p.176 and p.289, Appx XX.

44 One Mk I 30 LC bomb could heavily contaminate 10 yd^2 against a hard target, lightly contaminate 75 yd^2 and create an anti-personnel effect over an area of 400 yd^2. Ibid, p.176 and p.290, Appx XX.

45 Ibid, pp.247-248, Appx II.

46 The bomb casing disintegrated on impact dispersing the contents, and thereby heavily contaminating 40 yd^2, lightly contaminating 100 yd^2 and creating an anti-personnel effect over an area of 250 yd^2. Ibid, p.177 and p.290, Appx XX.

47 The term was based upon the Metropolitan Police nick-name of a cat-burglar, Harry Edward Vickers (1888-1942) who eluded conviction from 1921 to 1937. His trademark was to bind his shoes in socks, cloth or flannel to reduce noise, which thus earned him the tag. His story also spawned a 1953 film entitled *Flannelfoot* directed by Maclean Rogers and produced by F J Fancey at Walton Studios. Vickers served in 9th Rifle Brigade, 1916-1918.

filled SCIs and 250 lb LC bombs to Egypt.[48] This was undoubtedly useful in focusing minds on some of the complexities relating the management of SW but many had to be resolved as they appeared. In 1939, SW, regardless of whether they contained propellants or High Explosives, were classified as Group XIII explosives, the storage, transport, maintenance and disposal of which, were subject to civil[49] and military regulations.[50] 'Heavy case' weapons, as shells and Livens drums[51] were described, had been moved during the Great War, and this knowledge was put to good use in 1939. Leakage did occasionally occur but for the most part, the robust nature of the containers reduced the chance of failure. The carriage of 'light case' weapons, such as the SCIs, BCVs and chemical mines, created a different problem. The container skins were designed to be thin to permit a high liquid to weight ratio, but this made them vulnerable to damage in transit. Much effort was therefore, expended to ensure that the appropriate safety procedures were applied: 126 gallons of liquid Mustard spilling from a ruptured BCV onto a busy dockside was not a matter to be taken lightly. The chemical mine, although only containing four gallons of Mustard but fitted with a gunpowder burster charge required equal respect.[52] The instruction manual noted: 'The Mine, Chemical, No 1, Mk I, BV, is a substantial steel drum, and will withstand fair wear and tear. It must not however, be handled roughly, and when transported care should be taken to see that there is no chance of the drum being punctured or dented by bolts or other projections in the floor or side of the vehicle'.[53]

The deployment of GW capability, both weapons and specialists, was subject to political assent, which was granted in principle during October 1939. There were however, practical issues to be resolved and clearance for the dispatch of SW was not initiated until the War Cabinet's 79th Meeting, held on 11 November 1939, during which, at Item 5 – Poison Gas, it was decided: 'To authorize the Secretary of State for War to make the necessary arrangements for the dispatch of supplies of gas and equipment to France, on the understanding that every possible precaution should be taken to prevent observation'.[54] The emphasis on security sparked a raft of interesting loose minutes between Director Staff Duties (Weapons) (DSD) (W)), Director Military Intelligence (DMI) and Director Movements, all of whom disagreed on everything except the fact they that believed it was highly unlikely that security could be maintained. DSD (W), well ahead of his time in risking taking, took the view that SW should be handled in the same manner as conventional munitions, stating that: 'Stevedores must work under conditions similar to those, which prevail when they are loading ammunition. This

48 Note in MO4 B/M 1/182 dated 14 November 1939 in TNA WO 193/716: Despatch of Gas and Equipment to the BEF.

49 *Instructions as to the Conveyance of Explosive, Inflammable Liquid, Corrosive and Poisonous Chemical, Compressed or Liquefied Gases and other Dangerous Goods by Rail, Road or Water* (London: Railway Executive Committee, 1939).

50 TNA WO 287/161: General Staff, *Regulations for the Storage, Transport, Maintenance and Disposal of Chemical Weapons* (RSTMD), CONFIDENTIAL (War Office, 1941).

51 If Livens drums contained a Phosgene charge, they had to be handled as a light case munition. TNA WO 287/161: RSTMD, p.28, Appx VII.

52 SW fitted with gunpowder burster charges were a challenge to store because of the requirement to handle them in accordance with the chemical munitions and Magazine regulations.

53 General Staff, MTP No 32, Part II - *The Projector*, p.2, Sect 3.

54 TNA WO 193/716: Despatch of Gas and Equipment to the BEF, Note in MO4 B/M 1/182 dated 14 November 1939.

P14.1 A Significant Logistic Risk? Newhaven Harbour was utilized for the dispatch of GW weapons and the receipt of the BEF's hospital carriers. Photograph taken in 2002. (Author)

involves the risk of casualties, but this must be accepted. Stevedores must however, be warned that they are handling dangerous material'.[55] In addition, he believed that all markings must be obliterated during transit but that the captain of the ship must be informed of the cargo. Director Movements took a different view. He believed that SW must be marked, every ship and train should have a decontamination squad, special ships should be used for transit to France, soldiers should replace stevedores, and that all those involved in SW storage and movement should carry their respirators in the 'Alert Position'. DMI argued that this would give the game away, so he suggested that the decontamination squads and their equipment should remain out of sight unless they were required to clear a spill.

Director Movements replied, noting that in his opinion, the French decision to allow only Fecamp to be used to in-load SW stocks would arouse German interest.[56] DSD (W) then trod on Director Movements' turf by proposing that other *materiel* be brought in, to indicate that

55 TNA WO 193/716: Despatch of Gas and Equipment to the BEF, Note in MO4 B/M 1/182 dated 14 November 1939.

56 TNA WO 193/716: Despatch of Gas and Equipment to the BEF, Note in MO4 B/M 1/182 dated 14 November 1939.

Fecamp had become another Channel supply port.[57] Frustrated by the continuing debate, DSD (W) wrote a stinging note, in which he expressed his view that there were no major difficulties in moving 'this stuff" and that shipment should commence at the earliest opportunity, a point reinforced by the Deputy Director Military Operations.[58] In this, he was supported by the Secretary of State,[59] who was becoming increasingly concerned about the slow rate at which SW would arrive in France and abandoning a little of the previous caution, stated that: 'The risk must be taken owing to the vital importance of our army being equipped for defensive [ie retaliatory] purposes'.[60] The result of this lengthy discussion was that full identification and hazard markings were removed from all crates and boxes, although the shells, bombs and SCIs retained their grey paint.[61] Asset tracking however, remained a key issue and at Air Ministry insistence, the SCIs had a blue band painted around the case with a stencilled shipping code, which was tagged to a SCI serial number denoting the SCI type, the agent, and the factory and date of charging. In the covering letter of a SECRET annex, the Ministry reinforced the importance of matching the serial numbers to the ships codes: 'It is essential that these weapons should not lose their identity and normal markings should be restored at the earliest opportunity consistent with the maintenance of security'.[62] The arguments under-pinning this long running debate were though, lucidly exposed four years later In Italy on 2 December 1943.[63] The normal identification and hazard markings for a SCI crate are shown below. The colour of the crate was, in keeping with the convention, grey. HMF/R was the abbreviation for the charging factory,

57 There must have been some compromise on this point because according to a post-war War Office monograph, ammunition, to the sum of 18,000 tons was received into the port at Fecamp, much of which came through Newhaven. WOOH, *Movements*, p.201, Annex D to Chp 10 - Approximate Tonnage of Stores Shipped to France for the BEF, September 1939 - June 1940. That Newhaven was also used as the main medical evacuation reception port in the UK for the BEF did not prevent its use for the trans-shipment of conventional and gas munitions.

58 TNA WO 193/716: DDMO Loose Minute (MOST SECRET) dated 15 November 1939.

59 Leslie Hore-Belisha.

60 TNA WO 193/721: Chemical Warfare, Strategy XIII: Gas Policy and Despatch of Supplies, Note from DMO & P BM of 13 November 1939.

61 WOOH, *Movements*, p.140, notes: 'In December 1939, it was at Newhaven that the first shipment of gas bombs was loaded, the security arrangements in connection with the cargo being so successful that they did not know the nature of the stores they were handling'.

62 TNA AIR 35/131: Holding of Gas Weapons (Policy), Air Ministry S.2187/DDWO dated 13 April 1940.

63 On this date, a German air attack on the Italian port of Bari illustrated the hazards of failing to ensure the correct authorities knew of, and were prepared for, a major chemical spill from a ship or train. Amongst the many vessels involved, was the American Liberty Ship *John Harvey*, with a cargo of 100 tons of 2,000 American M47A1 Mustard bombs. Those who were aware of the cargo were killed during the raid, and as the contents of the bombs were released, no alarm was given, and the appropriate defensive measures thus not taken. During the action, over 1,000 Allied military personnel and an unknown number of civilians died, the casualty figures being undoubtedly increased by the presence of Mustard. For details, see, Glenn B Infield, *Disaster at Bari* (New York: Macmillan, 1971) and Karel Margry, 'Mustard Disaster at Bari', *After The Battle Magazine No 79* (Plaistow: Battle of Britain Prints International Ltd, 1993), pp.34-46. TNA WO 193/712: Chemical Warfare - Offensive Policy, contains a document, 'Toxic Gas Burns Sustained in Bari Harbour Disaster'.

RAF Spray Container Installation – Crate Marking & Dimensions. The level of identification of gas weapons generated much debate within the War Office and Air Ministry. (Author)

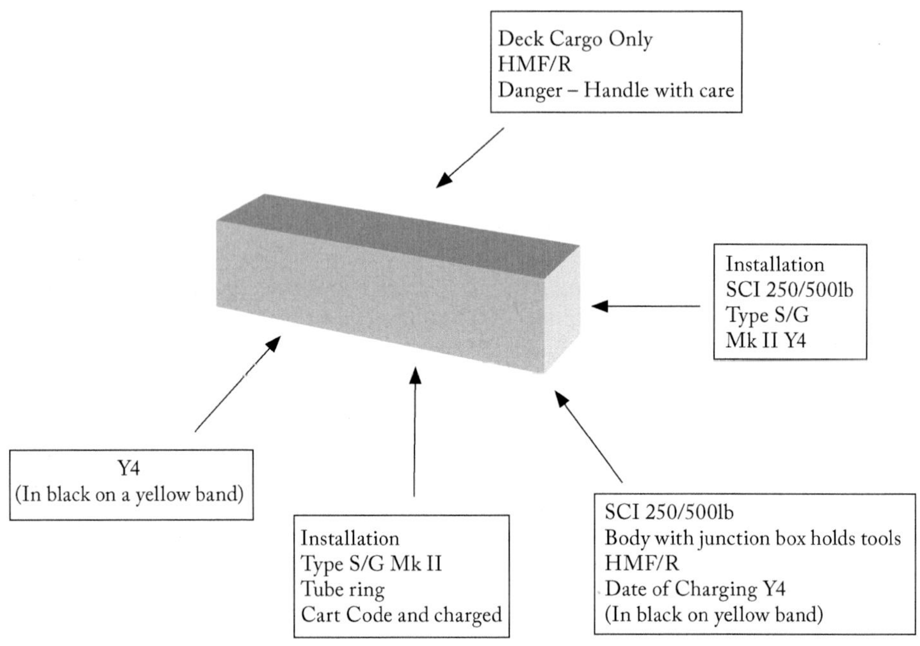

in this case, His Majesty's Factory/Randle.[64] A 500 lb crate with a charged weapon had the following dimensions: Width: 2' 6", Height: 2', Length: 6', Weight: 7 cwt.

Storing Gas in France

The deployment and storage of SW did not generally follow the GLOC procedures, which had been established to support the BEF. Storage in the Main Base Areas and movement by rail to the corps areas created unease in the War Office, which perceived difficulties in rapidly extracting the weapons from Theatre. It was therefore, decided to store most of them in the Advanced Base Area using a short sea crossing and from the few records that remain, it would appear that all the BEF's SW were shipped from Newhaven in Sussex to Fecamp in France and the SS *Clewbay*, a steam collier of 645 tons GRT, undertook most of the voyages.[65]

64 HMF Randle was established on Wigg Island to the SE of Widnes in 1937. For a history of its operations, see, Major T I J Toler, 'Poison Gas Manufacture in the UK', *After The Battle Magazine No 79*, London: Battle of Britain Prints International Ltd, 1993, pp.16-18.

65 Built 1914 as the *G Player* at Troon by the Ailsa Shipbuilding Company, she was renamed *Clewbay* in 1914 and survived the war, to be broken up in Belgium in 1959, having been renamed *Ballygilbert* in 1952. See, Plummer, *The Ships That Saved an Army*, p.69. The SS *Clewbay* was later involved in Operation AERIAL. See, Winser, *BEF Ships*, p.74 & p.145.

The first SW arrived at Fecamp on 12 December 1939, for onward movement to 21 BAD. It was not rail-served location, depot stocks being in-loaded and out-loaded by road or via a local Host Nation rail siding. There were no details of the shipment, but it almost certainly contained SCIs for the RAF. The few references in published accounts state that all the SW were stored at 21 BAD but research indicates that this was not the case. The table below, compiled from GHQ Q Maint Q/1193 (b1) dated 15 February 1940,[66] and the BAD war diaries, summarizes the outline deployment of Army controlled SW in the BADs until June 1940. Apart from 6 BAD, which was only used for SW during the evacuation, all the depots storing SW were road-served, with stocks being moved from Host Nation railheads.

Table 14.1
BADs in France Storing Army SW– February 1940

BAD	Name	Town	Access	SW	Remarks
1	Foret du Gavre	Nantes	Road	Yes	
2	Plouaret	Brest	Road		
3	Saint Saens	Rouen	Road	Yes	Forward BAD
4	Rennes	Rennes	Rail		
5	Le Gavre	Nantes	Rail		
6	Blain	Nantes	Rail	Yes	During evacuation - May 1940
21	Fecamp	Le Harve	Road	Yes	Main SW Depot
22	Miniac	St Malo	Rail		Formerly 8 BAD

The pressure the BADs were under, to accept gas munitions, is clearly illustrated by the experience of 3 BAD.[67] It mobilized at Bramley on 10 November 1939 and deployed to France, still short of key personnel, before Christmas and began to establish a road-served BAD near Rouen, with three 21,000 ton sub-depots, and the Depot railhead at Buchy. A team carried out a reconnaissance for a Grey Shell area on 25 December, and SW stocks arrived on the SS *Clewbay*, which docked at Fecamp during 2 January 1940. Whilst the war diary[68] does not indicate what the shipment contained, a note on 3 February 1940 gives greater detail, stating that 3,258 rounds of 6-inch Grey Shell had been receipted into No 1 Sub-Depot and there were more receipts on 6 February.[69] 1 BAD also receipted SW, although whether its existence was discussed in April with the Army Staff College reconnaissance team, visiting in preparation for the student group tour in June, is not recorded.[70] An interesting but mysterious activity in 21 BAD was the arrival on 19 April 1940, from UK, of 150 tons of unspecified naval

66 TNA WO 167/10: GHQ, QMG Maintenance (Q).
67 3 BAD comprised an HQ plus 8, 9 and 10 Ordnance Ammunition Companies.
68 TNA WO 167/1177: 3 BAD RAOC, WD.
69 TNA WO 167/1177: 3 BAD RAOC, WD.
70 TNA WO 167/1175: 1 BAD RAOC, WD.

ammunition.[71] On 12 May, Movement Control at Le Harve issued instructions for 120 tons of Naval Expeditionary Force stores to be out-loaded by road[72] to Mommenheim, a small town North-North-West of Strasbourg, with the balance of 30 tons being despatched by rail under naval guard on 16 May.[73] The war diary does not elaborate on either manifest but highlights a visit by Rear-Admiral Fitzgerald[74] to inspect the road out-load so whatever the cargo was it must have been of some significance and sensitivity.[75]

As plans developed, some Army weapons were deployed to other BADs whilst HQ BAFF arranged the out-load of some of the air delivered SW to locations near to the operational airfields to create a rapid response to any German gas attack. The stocking of offensive gas air-delivered munitions for operations in Europe, although originally the logistic SW main effort, had suffered a delay in August 1939, when stocks had been dispatched to Egypt, but by March 1940, despite the many challenges, the BAFF stock inventory started to rise. In particular, 250 lb LC Bomb reserves were complete, and the SCIs stock position positive. Only in 30 lb LC Bomb reserves did the Air Staff have cause for concern. The table below illustrates the gains made in the planned stock positions for munitions held in France.

Table 14.2
Air Gas Weapons – Stock in France
January-April 1940[76]

Munition	25 January	1 March	15 March	19 April	Planned	% Complete
30 lb LC Bomb Mk I	Nil	Nil	1,000	7,500	24,500	30.61
250 lb LC Bomb	1,300	1,300	3,350	3,350	3,350	100.00
250 lb SCI	70	70	225	261	340	76.76
500 lb SCI	540	540	770	809	1,070	75.60

71 TNA WO 167/1179: 21 BAD RAOC, WD.
72 This task was executed by 4 MT Reserve Company RASC. TNA WO 167/1179: 21 BAD RAOC, WD, 13 May 1940.
73 TNA WO 167/1179: 21 BAD RAOC, WD.
74 The war diary states the rank as Admiral. Rear-Admiral John Uniacke Penrose Fitzgerald commanded Operation ROYAL MARINE, for which, he was awarded the CB. Aged 52, he was lost at sea on 11 December 1940, whilst serving as the Commodore of Convoy HX 92 on the SS *Rotorua*, sunk by a torpedo from U-96, 110 nautical miles West of Saint Kilda. He is commemorated on the Liverpool Naval Memorial.
75 The circumstantial evidence suggests that 21 BAD had been storing fluvial mines, which were deployed during Operation ROYAL MARINE, which was designed to disrupt barge traffic and damage bridge piers on the River Rhine. Mines were placed in French rivers, which were tributaries of the Rhine, thus explaining why Mommenheim was the destination. See, TNA CAB 121/308: Operation ROYAL MARINE - Proposals for laying mines in the River Rhine and TNA ADM 1/10494: Minelaying on the Rhine - Awards to Naval Expeditionary Force personnel.
76 These figures have been derived from two main sources. First, WOOH, *Gas Warfare*, pp.247-248, Appx II and secondly from documents in TNA AIR 35/130: British Air Forces in France, Gas Policy. There are differences in some of the figures, and accounting or otherwise, for weapons in transit, probably causes this. The author believes that the figures in the tables are accurate to within plus or minus 5%.

A plan was produced to store SCIs forward in the brickworks next to the AASF ARH at Germaine.[77] Phase 1 of the redeployment involved moving 270 x 500 lb SCIs and although this was completed by 20 March 1940, a number of practical difficulties soon emerged, which resulted in the new depot only being able to out-load 50 SCIs per day to the surrounding airfields. This caused considerable concern at HQ BAFF, and after much discussion, it was decided to re-allocate the Phase 2 move of 234 x 500 lb SCIs to the Forward Air Ammunition Park at Nogent L'Abbesse, through a railhead at Witry.[78] A little of the flavour of the SW out-load operations can be obtained from the 21 BAD war diary.[79] On 17 April, orders were received to dispatch 90 x 500 lb SCIs to ARH OZ at Germaine. Loading at the depot railhead commenced at 0645 and the eight wagons were released to SNCF at 2225. There was another issue of 90 x 500lb SCI on 27 April. Positioning of SW to support combat operations continued until the enemy threat generated a rapid review of the requirement to hold them in France. One result of this was a rail move of 23 wagons of RAF SCIs from 21 BAD at Fecamp to 6 BAD at Blain. After brief storage, the SCIs were then out-loaded by road to Pont Pietan, a village five miles from the depot, where they were transferred to three canal barges for onward movement to Saint Nazaire and recovery to the United Kingdom.[80] The war diary is silent on why it was necessary to engage in this rather complex and time-consuming transportation solution but it was presumably initiated either by a desire to deceive the enemy as to the location of these weapons or by a shortage of WMT. The practicalities of managing the arrangements soon however, exceeded the demands of security and all future receipts of RAF SW to 6 BAD were retained on the trains for dispatch direct to the port.[81]

SCI Recharging Plans

One logistic task that was not conducted in France was SCI field refilling although considerable effort was devoted to generating a solution. The initial concept was that the SCIs would be one-shot systems, the containers being jettisoned over enemy territory when the gas spray had been completed but security issues and a shortage of containers prompted a review, the outcome of which, generated a host of issues related to stock replenishment which were to tax the Air Staff, air operations planners, armament experts, movements personnel and suppliers. To solve the lacuna in their plans for supporting offensive gas operations, the War Office and Air Ministry Staff proposed to return, by sea and rail, SCIs to HMF Randle for refilling but a logistic check quickly revealed two problems. First and foremost, was the turn-round timescale, estimated to be three weeks. One solution to reduce the time-lines was to fly the 'empties' back to the UK in Armstrong Whitworth AW 27 Ensigns, a civilian airliner, six of which were requisitioned for RAF service.[82] Careful scrutiny soon exposed the practical limitations of this proposal. The

77 TNA AIR 35/131: Holding of Gas Weapons (Policy), HQ BAFF 4430/Org 3 dated 12 March 1940.
78 TNA AIR 35/131: Holding of Gas Weapons (Policy), HQ AASF S.3563/Org dated 20 March 1940.
79 TNA WO 167/1179/1: 5 BAD RAOC, WD.
80 The road out-load and transfer to the barges took 60 hours and the canal journey to Saint Nazaire another 72. TNA WO 167/1180: 6 BAD RAOC, WD, 'Report on the Work, Moves, Activities etc, of No 6 Base Ammunition Depot from 1 May 1940 in 12 July 1940' dated 6 August 1940.
81 TNA WO 167/1180: 6 BAD RAOC, WD, 'Report on the Work of 6 BAD'.
82 The payload of the Ensign Mk I was 9,500 lb. For a history of the AW 27, see, Oliver Tapper, *Armstrong-Whitworth Aircraft since 1913* (London: Putnam, 1973), p.235-254.

average daily availability was only two aircraft, whilst loading the SCIs into the aircraft by hand was by no means an easy task.[83] Indeed, one of the first problems was to ensure the SCIs had been correctly decontaminated, which was a particular difficulty because there was no suitable field equipment in service, trained teams or any field drills, to support the operation,[84] whilst the Royal Engineers threw in another problem: shortage of water at most of the airfields, with only Berry–au-Bac having sufficient.[85] The planners thus turned to another solution: refilling in the field. Porton Down, the RAF Suppliers and the Armaments Staff were aghast at the idea, but it appeared to be the only workable concept. At first, the Armaments Staff demurred, stating it was impossible to fill in the field; their argument though, was demolished after someone had read the Algerian Technical Field Trials Report, which clearly indicated that the trials team had conducted field filling.[86] An important task was equipping and training the ground crews but such was the pressure of the moment, the view from HQ BAFF, was that not only must risks be taken but also that these risks were manageable; Porton Down, in the belief of the planners, had overstated the risks involved. HQ BAFF estimated that they would require 200 SCIs refilled per day, although how they calculated this figure is now difficult to confirm, but the Air Ministry issued instructions for the training of the first 20 of over 200 personnel who were to form the initial SCI refilling team in France;[87] the selected candidates must have been delighted when they found out what their task was to be. Production orders were also issued, for the thousands of 5-gallon cans, which would be needed for the field filling; each 500 lb SCI required six, and a 250 lb SCI, three.

The logistic challenges however, remained, the key issue becoming whether it was worth the effort to train and equip teams for decontamination[88] and field filling, when by July or early August, SCI stocks would have risen to the point that the argument became academic. The subject inevitably generated an appreciable raft of correspondence but before a decision could be taken, the German assault began. The policy of jettison thus continued as the most likely

83 There was no Material Handling Equipment (MHE) to lift the crates to the doors, and even had there been some, handling inside the aircraft had to be done manually.

84 The first Air Ministry instructions relating to field decontamination do not appear to have been issued until 4 June 1940. S.49832/03 dated 4 June 1940 in TNA AIR 14/419: Smoke Curtain Installation, Technical Trials. The instruction had a diagram of a decontamination area and stated that the team should consist of an officer or NCO plus five airmen.

85 Most of the airfields could have been provided with water from artesian wells because the RE had several well-drilling companies. They were though, deployed on other important tasks such as supporting hospitals and the priorities would have required amendment.

86 TNA AVIA 15/254: Chemical Warfare: Research and Development, Reports on Gas Spraying Trials, 'Report on Trials in Algeria' (VERY SECRET).

87 TNA AIR 2/5117: Chemical Warfare, Air Staff Policy, Air Ministry Loose Minute of 13 May 1940, which expressed clear urgency in its tone, 'There is no time for further discussion'.

88 Live trials were conducted at RAF West Raynham and RAF Horsham St Faith in Norfolk during the period 29-31 October 1940, a Blenheim dispensing HTV from an SCI and although the location is not noted in the file was probably over the North Sea. The trials concluded that SCI decontamination was not a difficult task, but it did require properly equipped trained teams conducting slick drills. In a sustained effort, experiments revealed that a team of 5 could decontaminate 5-6 x 500 lb SCIs per hour. Anti-Gas IPE if correctly utilized offered 100% protection to personnel, but the trial highlighted the care required to prevent cross-contamination and the importance of changing the location of the decontamination area if the wind changed. TNA AIR 2/5200: Air Ministry Bacteriological and Chemical Warfare.

operational solution, but this created two complications. If the SCI equipment was to be kept secret, the security Staff argued that the SCIs should not be dropped on territory controlled by the enemy and defacto, this meant releasing them on territory controlled by the Allies, which would inevitably mean contaminating parts of it as the weapon struck the ground. One option proposed by HQ BAFF was to establish a dirty airfield, where SCIs could be removed and dumped. Before this proposal could be progressed, the war had moved on, but it was an idea, which was revived in UK during the anti-invasion preparations. The plan to decontaminate and refill the SCIs was, in the circumstances, a sound one but no thought had been given to the resource implications. Militarily, it was far more effective to jettison the SCIs than to establish a substantial field organization to decontaminate and refill them, although imperatives in the summer of 1940 generated this solution for operations flown from the UK.[89] Essentially though, by adopting this process, the SCI programme, instead of creating a force multiplier, became a logistic burden involving more personnel, equipment and training.[90]

The Trials of 21 BAD

Whilst the War Office files are replete with policy, the war diary of 21 BAD,[91] the unit holding most of the SW stocks, highlights the constant round of inspections, concerns over security and the daily grind of operating with a shortage of experienced trained personnel. This aspect is of particular relevance because it is remarkable, given the military significance, political sensitivity and technical challenge of the tasks, that the War Office and GHQ BEF, failed to grasp the importance of ensuring 21 BAD was properly resourced to execute its work. Despite much staffing and prodding from the unit, through the chain of command, the War Office insisted that 21 BAD was an ARH and refused to recognize neither its SW status or its Port Ordnance responsibilities; consequently, it was never granted a Special Establishment.[92]

Despite its operational and logistic importance, 21 BAD was never issued with the correct stores and the Quartermaster found it difficult to acquire them, the war diary noting a shortage of labour, WMT and stationery, and the requirement for a mobile crane to handle the SCIs and 250 lb LC bombs.[93] The fact that the unit diarist had to write on blank paper because the relevant form, the AFC 2118, was not available until mid-February 1940, is perhaps a clear example of the many frustrations the personnel of 21 BAD faced. Whether the War Office position was part of a security cloak, or an impressive piece of incompetence, is impossible to

89 TNA AIR 2/5200: Air Ministry Bacteriological and Chemical Warfare, Air Ministry, Director of Plans letter dated 12 July 1940.

90 The draft drill for SCI decontamination was issued as SD 129 Leaflet B11. See TNA AIR 14/2735: Chemical Warfare Decontamination of SCIs. The equipment requirement involved 30 different items, including SCI crates, trestles, drip trays, pails, bleaching powder, rope, canvas screens, cotton waste, spanners (various), screwdrivers, pliers, tommy bars, tongs, pins, knives, bituminized bags, petrol, earth, sand, and full Anti-Gas IPE for all personnel.

91 TNA WO 167/1179/1: 21 BAD RAOC, WD.

92 On 11 May 1940, with the German attack in full swing, the war diary noted that ADOS (Ammunition) had advised that the establishment would be that of an ARH, whilst also reporting the possible presence of enemy parachute troops between Le Harve and Fecamp. Needless to say, the urgency of combat operations interrupted further discussion on the subject.

93 TNA WO 167/1179/1: 21 BAD RAOC, WD, entry 14 December 1939.

determine from the documents, but the depot commander's frustrations are lucidly expressed in the war diary. It was indeed unfortunate, that the visit of the BEF's Quartermaster General, Lieutenant-General Lindsell on 19 March 1940, was cancelled; there was much he needed to see.[94] Apart from that, the OC,[95] had made special arrangements for him to have a hot bath.

A summary of the BAD personnel deployment for 29 March 1940, manifestly exposes the problems inherent in failing to create a meaningful ORBAT for a specialist task;[96] only 18.5 percent of the personnel in the BAD were cap-badged RAOC, although the RAF personnel were employed as specialists and members of the RASC were also deployed. At the end of March 1940, there were five soldiers from No 3 LOC and 4th Reserve MT Companies and another 58 from the 50 Divisional Ammunition Sub-Park RASC, nearly all of whom were employed to in-load, by road, SW, from the port at Fecamp. There were though, more problems in the structure and command of the organization, which merit further examination because on 7 May 1940 key personnel were being employed on fatigues as well as ammunition work.[97] No doubt their specializations held no weight with the Sergeant Major's clerk but one detects within the war diary, pressure upon the OC from all the detachment commanders, to ensure that every soldier, regardless of his trade, did his fair share of duties. As they struggled to complete their tasks, the officers and soldiers of 21 BAD had to operate in the coldest winter since 1895, the war diary provides ample testimony to the terrible conditions of January 1940 and the fragility of some of the AMPC manpower, an issue which was the subject of a letter from GHQ to the War Office.[98]

At 2100 hours on 21 May, with German armoured forces on the Channel Coast, HQ 21 BAD received information from the Chief of Staff at 2 Base Area[99] that all SW were to be returned to the UK or moved to other locations in France. Whilst the planning was being executed for this task, two officers were involved in a fight, which resulted in one of them being placed in

94 It is also of note that C-in-C BEF never visit 21 BAD, or indeed any other logistic element of the GLOC, which given the sensitivity of the site and its stocks is certainly an omission on his part.

95 Captain J A Tandy MC RAOC.

96 The strength and consist of 21 BAD is shown in the table:

Table 14.3

21 BAD – Personnel on 29 March 1940

Unit	Personnel
21 BAD RAOC	30
4 Reserve MT Company RASC	4
No 3 Line of Communication Company RASC	1
50 Divisional Ammunition Sub Park RASC	58
Highland Light Infantry	31
106 Company AMPC	24
Royal Air Force	14
Total	162

97 TNA WO 167/1179: 21 BAD RAOC, WD.

98 TNA WO 197/72: Appreciation of British retaliatory position in the event of Chemical Warfare - GHQ (A) A/3221 (O) dated 31 January 1940.

99 A RAF Group Captain held this appointment.

arrest; the pressures of operations had begun to take their toll.[100] With D Company 2/6th East Surreys as the security guard, out-loading began almost immediately but it took the depot staff, 4 MT Reserve Company RASC and 106 Company AMPC until the evening of 24 May[101] to move the 2,000 tons from the depot.[102] 1,400 tons of SW were transported by road to the small port of Fecamp where the munitions were loaded to the SS *Malrix*[103] for a voyage to Fowey[104] in Cornwall, with the balance being railed to Saint Nazaire via 6 BAD.[105] Most published sources indicate that all the BEF's SW were eventually recovered to UK or the 'leakers' dumped at sea. The War Office monograph however, states that: 'the major part of our stocks of gas weapons were evacuated from France'[106] and tucked away in a file at the TNA, there is an intelligence report that supports the suggestion that not every SW was recovered. Paragraph 65 of CSDIC (UK)/SIR 14 dated 3 July 1943 states that: 'some of our war chemicals fell into the hands of the enemy after Dunkirk and were extensively studied'.[107]

Unfortunately, the report does not state which types or quantities, which were involved but given the effort to clear 21 BAD it is improbable that the weapons came from this site.[108] More likely, the Germans acquired these SW from other BADs,[109] or perhaps an ARH.[110] The CW companies abandoned all the Livens Projector tubes but a special effort was made to evacuate the SCIs because it was believed that the system and the capability, was unknown to the Germans. Only two were left in France, both of which had been given to the French for experimental purposes, so it is possible the Germans acquired a SCI from this source. On 27 May, 15-20 parachute troops were recorded as having been sighted four miles West of what had been 21

100 TNA 167/1179: 21 BAD RAOC, WD, entry 22 May 1940.
101 OC 21 BAD declared the depot clear of stocks at 2015, with the train departing from the SNCF railhead at 2230. TNA 167/1179: 21 BAD RAOC, WD, entry 24 May 1940.
102 WOOH, *Movements*, p.194, states a total of 2,000 tons, whilst the 21 BAD war diary lists 1,800 tons but does not specify the tonnage split, only noting that most of the SW were shipped to UK with the balance dispatched to another depot in France; TNA WO 167/1179.
103 The 21 BAD war diary does not state the name of the ship, but *Winser*, *BEF Ships*, p.77, lists the *Malrix* arriving at Fecamp on 23 May 1940, then sailing from Fowey on 31 May. The *Malrix* was a coaster, similar in size at 703 GRT to the *Clewbay*'s 645. The SS *Malrix*, from Hull to London with coal, was sunk by a mine explosion in the Thames Estuary between Southend and Whitstable on 17 December 1940 with the loss of seven sailors who are commemorated on the Tower Hill Memorial London. Admiralty, *British Merchant Vessels Lost or Damaged by Enemy Action*, p.15.
104 WOOH, *Movements*, p.194, records that one shell fell into the dock during discharge at Fowey.
105 The 21 BAD war diary states that the OC was at Saint Nazaire on 31 May 1940 to confirm that all the SW dispatched by rail from Fecamp had been accounted for. TNA 167/1179: 21 BAD RAOC, WD, entry 31 May 1940.
106 WOOH, *Gas Warfare*, p.8.
107 TNA WO 193/723: Chemical Warfare - Intelligence.
108 TNA WO 167/1179: 21 BAD RAOC, WD. The entry of 26 May 1940 is explicit in stating, 'dump cleared'.
109 Brigadier Gibson noted that at one BAD, the Chief Ordnance Officer made a final inspection of the depot to ensure all the SW stocks had been cleared and discovered one grey shell, which he arranged to have taken to the Base port and dumped in the sea. Unfortunately, Gibson does not record the BAD, but it was either 1 or 6. It is therefore, possible that a SW shell or bomb was left at a BAD site. TNA CAB 106/235: BEF Ammunition Supply (Gibson Report), p.11.
110 When the Germans occupied the French Army Chemical Warfare Laboratory at Le Bouchet they discovered British reports and experimental items that had been given to the French. See, Carter, *Chemical and Biological Defence at Porton Down*, p.51.

P14.2 Impact of Gas Warfare. A section conducting a demonstration of vehicle decontamination drills to remove liquid GW agents. Although this is a military event, the soldiers are wearing the civilian pattern respirator, so may be members of the Home Guard. (RLCM: Trades/NOR)

BAD; the clearance had been completed with little time to spare.[111] The decision to remove the BEF's SW capability from Theatre was driven by the political and military consequences arising from their capture. Such considerations far outweighed the possibility that it might be necessary to reply in kind and the recovery became a priority activity.

Recovery and Reconstitution

The RAF's SW were shipped to Fowey in Cornwall from where they were transferred by rail to Harpur Hill, two miles South of Buxton in Derbyshire, one of the RAF's main reserve ammunition depots controlled by 28 Maintenance Unit (MU),[112] which was part of 42 Armament Group. RAF Harpur Hill was a rail-served underground storage facility, which

111 TNA WO 167/1179: 21 BAD RAOC, WD.
112 The activities of 28 MU are detailed on RAF Form 540, the Operational Record Book (ORB), which is the RAF equivalent of the Army War Diary (AFC 2118).

had been constructed from an open cast limestone mine,[113] with a technical site on the surface to support the facility.[114] Whilst it offered protection for SW, Harpur Hill was not best placed to store them. The depot had only opened in March 1940, construction work was ongoing, and there were a raft of problems relating to procedures and security, few of which had been resolved. In addition, the storage of gas weapons in an underground facility required especial care, particularly with regard to ventilation and checks for 'leakers'.[115] These matters were the subject of much discussion by the depot staff because Harpur Hill was not designed or equipped to handle SW; indeed, it was not until May 1941 that the E Group, which was established to control the storage of such weapons, was fully functioning.

A consignment of 72 rail wagons arrived from the port of Fowey courtesy of the GWR and LMS Railway, on 26 May 1940, causing considerable consternation because there was no movement documentation or packing lists.[116] Members of the depot staff were thus unable to produce a storage plan until they had examined each wagon to confirm its load, a task, which took 24 hours to complete. The tally was: 1,081 x 30 lb Mk I bombs, 469 x 500 lb SCI and 461 x 250 lb SCI.[117] There was problem handling the 500 lb SCIs because the filled weapon in its crate weighed 7 cwt.[118] To provide a solution, hand lift trucks were borrowed from HMF Randle where the SCIs were filled, whilst 42 Group authorized the purchase of trucks from the manufacturer, so the HMF equipment could be returned. The RAF's SW were though, fundamental to the United Kingdom's anti-invasion plans and as these matured, SW were deployed to other sites including Air Ammunition Parks and airfields. The 4.5 and 6-inch shells from Fecamp were despatched to CAD Longtown, a facility still under construction, whilst the Livens drums, and 6 lb Ground Bombs when they were received ex-factory, were stored at Bedale, Longtown, Savernake and Shefford, whilst as the BCVs came into service, they were initially stored at Savernake. The stock position on 1 October 1940 is shown in the table below.[119]

113 Harpur Hill consisted of seven concrete arch chambers in a limestone quarry, which, were then covered with 45 feet of spoil, limestone and concrete to provide protection and camouflage. For a brief description and illustrations of its construction, see, AMOH, Air Publication 3236, *Works*, pp.263-267.

114 The Health & Safety Executive occupy the technical site and the underground storage is in commercial use.

115 TNA AIR 29/990: Air Ministry S49833/1 dated 25 May 1940 confirms that SW ex-21 BAD were being stored underground at RAF Harpur Hill before the Fecamp site was evacuated and noted the requirement for chemical decontamination and additional guards to patrol the exchange railway sidings.

116 TNA AIR 29/990: 28 MU RAF, ORB, entry 26 May 1940.

117 TNA AIR 29/990: 28 MU RAF, ORB, entry 27 May 1940.

118 784 lb.

119 These figures have been derived from WOOH, *Gas Warfare*, Appx II, Stocks of Air and Army Gas Weapons and War Gases, 3 September 1939 - 31 December 1941.

Table 14.4
Ground Delivered Gas Munitions – Stock in the United Kingdom
1 October 1940

Munition	Filling	Charged	Empty	Remarks
4.5-inch Howitzer	Mustard	17,436	Nil	
6-inch Howitzer	Mustard	25,070	Nil	
25 pdr Base Ejection	Mustard	200	2,000	
Livens Drums (Y)	Mustard	16,000	5,000	
Livens Drums (G)	Phosgene	9,000		
Bombs, Ground, 6 lb	Mustard	73,000	92,000	
Mines, Chemical	Mustard	4,500	525	Production reduced by bombing
Bulk Contamination Vehicle	Mustard	65	109	

Conclusion

Preparations for gas warfare by the Army and the RAF is a little-known aspect of the 1939-1940 campaign in France. There has been a perception over the last 80 years that the British GW capability was purely designed for deterrence and if necessary, retaliation and whilst there is no suggestion in the files to request use in a 'first strike' scenario,[120] the documents do clearly indicate that there was a concerted effort to increase the British assets as quickly as possible, and to employ them to military effect if they were required. The logistic Corps were, despite limitations in training and resources, fundamental to the GW capability and they enacted their hazardous duties in rigorous and demanding conditions with industry and dedication. The RAOC had the greatest exposure to SW through the storage at 21 BAD and to a lesser extent, at other depots. Reference to 'Grey Shell' in RASC documents at corps and divisional level is very rare and the deduction must be that except for ammunition movement by 50 Divisional Ammunition Sub-Park between depots and ports, practice in handling and distributing SW within the RASC in the BEF was probably zero, with the existence of SW being opaque to the units.

Of especial significance though was the logistic Corps' performance, in conjunction with the Merchant Marine, in recovering nearly all the SW to the UK. That they arrived in, and departed from, France in non-descript small coasters that belied the sensitivity and importance of their cargoes, certainly reinforced decision to adopt a low-key security approach during transportation, whilst the commercial railways contribution to swiftly moving the SW in UK must be highlighted. The success in evacuating a substantial component of Britain's GW munitions not only prevented the stocks being captured by the Germans but it also ensured

120 Indeed, the reverse is true, with most documents being specific that it would only be used in response to a German gas attack. TNA AIR 35/131: Holding of Gas Weapons (Policy), Air Ministry S.4392/S6 dated 29 April 1940 is an example.

that the UK retained its GW capability during the period that the Germans were preparing to execute Operation SEALION. Indeed, it is clear that Winston Churchill was prepared, as the Prime-minister, and against great opposition from various departments, to sanction its use as a 'first strike' weapon, if there was a chance of changing the military balance during an invasion.[121] In this respect, the logisticians played a fundamental part in ensuring that the United Kingdom maintained, what was perceived at the time, a significant military and political asset.

121 'In my view there would be no need to wait for the enemy to adopt such methods. He will certainly adopt them if he thinks it will pay ... Everything must be brought to the highest pitch of readiness, but the question of actual employment must be settled by the Cabinet'. MOST SECRET Memorandum from the Prime-minister to General Ismay in TNA WO 193/732: Policy - Use of Gas in Home Defence.

Part V

Combat Operations

15

Riding the Rails
The role of the railway in supporting BEF combat operations

On and Off the Rails

In a 'Lessons Identified' paper of 11 October 1939, the Director-General Transportation (DGT) BEF, Brigadier McMullen wrote:

> In general the SNCF have done extraordinarily well under very difficult circumstances. They were very heavily taxed with the French concentration during the first 3 to 4 weeks and the moves of British Units from Port 46[1] to the Northern and Southern Bases and to the assembly area cut right across the French concentration moves. They have an extensive system of telephonic control and their traffic working has been excellent. What would happen if the telephonic circuits were cut is difficult to visualize.[2]

The SNCF initially conducted all railway operating on behalf of the BEF, although as the deployment proceeded, British military railway units took over some tasks, including the operation of specified SNCF sections, the lines being mostly in the areas of the Main Base Areas (MBA). By the end of April 1940, RE units were working main lines for traffic between Saint Malo and Rennes, in addition to manning all British rail-served depots and marshalling yards in the Nantes and Rennes Bases. Railway Operating Companies (ROC) were also deployed at Abancourt Regulating Station later transferring locally to Romescamps and operating the airfield spurs in the rear of the BEF corps areas.[3]

Plans were well developed with SNCF, using a J-Day as the planning initiator for the rail movement of units, ammunition, fuel and *materiel* into the Corps Rear Areas to support the forward deployment of the BEF into Belgium under Plan D,[4] although SNCF did not allow the

1 Cherbourg. TNA WO 167/1379: GHQ BEF Assistant Director Postal Services (ADAPS). Diagram dated 26 September 1939, Appx 30.
2 TNA WO 167/51: GHQ Services, Transportation, DG Tn, 'Lessons' dated 11 October 1939.
3 Map 4: BEF - Transportation and Rail Line of Communication and Map 10: BEF - Railway Unit Deployment.
4 Q (MC) SD/S/87/22 dated 22 April 1940 (SECRET), Movement Table, Troop Trains. One notable feature is the number of bicycles assigned for rail movement, with an infantry brigade assigned cargo

ROCs to drive trains on the French network in the BEF's corps areas until after the German attack, which prevented the requisite training to enhance operational capability. The most significant tasks therefore, were focused upon the delivery of railway transportation outputs in the growing number of docks, depots and sidings that the BEF acquired or constructed, although some depots were served solely by road, with WMT operating from private or SNCF sidings to the site; the BEF used 69 such facilities. Others had a rail link into the depot making it 'rail-served' but internally, WMT moved material to the storage areas. Others were 'rail-operated', with stocks being delivered direct to the sheds or dumps, by rail.

The railway was an integral constituent of several elements forming the BEF's forward and mobile supply systems.[5] To ensure ammunition stocks were available to combat forces at the commencement of operations, dumping commenced around nominated Corps Ammunition Railheads (ARH),[6] whilst six days of RAF munitions and POL were held at Air Component Railheads.[7] ARH sites were the responsibility of the RAOC ARH Detachments found from the establishment of Base Ammunition Depots (BAD).[8] Five Days of Supply (DOS) for ammunition were held for I Corps and seven DOS for II Corps; the execution of plans for III Corps was disrupted by the German invasion[9] but there was approximately 1,000 tons at the III Corps ARH equating to three DOS. Initially, no combat supplies were held at railheads for the AASF, but this approach changed in early 1940 when stocks were deployed at the established Germaine ARH and 82 Advanced Railhead Detachment RAOC was improvised to operate AASF railheads.[10]

The BEF GHQ logistic planners were though, much concerned that there would be insufficient lift at the commencement of operations to replenish what they expected to be

space for 110. TNA WO 167/56: Q Branch L of C.

5 For the general principles, see, Army Council, *Military Engineering*, Vol VIII, *Railways*, pp.18-42.

6 Corps ARHs were initially as follows:

Table 15.1
Corps Ammunition Railheads - Initial

Formation	Initial Deployment		Pre-Plan D		Remarks
	Name	Location	Name	Location	
I Corps	Evron	30 miles WNW Le Mans	Ecoust	10 miles SE Arras	Code OX
II Corps	Noyen*	16 miles SW Le Mans	Aubigny	8 miles NW Arras	Code OY
AASF	Germaine	10 miles South of Rheims	Germaine	10 miles South of Rheims	Code OZ

*Meslay-du-Maine replaced Noyen as the deployment commenced. TNA CAB 106/235: BEF Ammunition Supply (Gibson Report), p.4.

7 Appx A to HQ BAFF 4864/Org 3 dated 17 April 1940, 'Memorandum on the Scale of Reserve Stocks of Fuel, Bombs and Ammunition to be held in France' (SECRET) lists the stocks, planned and actual, of all key Air Service munitions. TNA AIR 35/123: Reserve stocks of aviation fuel, bombs and small arms ammunition, 1940.

8 An ARH Detachment had a WE of two officers and 27 Other Ranks.

9 An additional four DOS for each corps that had been delivered by rail through the ARH were dumped under corps arrangements forward of the ARH.

10 TNA WO 167/1428: 82 Advanced Railhead Detachment RAOC, WD. The last entry on 31 May 1940 reports: 'All remaining stores salvaged successfully except 2 bicycles in QM Stores. The latter had been broken into by French troops and the bicycles misappropriated'.

high expenditure rates in the opening engagements of a major defensive battle and sought to create a robust solution. When GHQ adjusted the BEF posture to an advance to a defence line, the fundamental concept underpinning this approach became irrelevant because leaving stocks further forward than they would otherwise have been, caused some difficultly during the withdrawal of the BEF as they were perceived to be inappropriately sited. Some were lost to the enemy but as it transpired, these dumps proved to be the salvation of the BEF when the German advance cut the GLOC. Given the doctrinal British focus upon creating mobility, it may appear surprising that the forward storage solution was adopted but it was the product of the long GLOC and a shortage of WMT that prompted its adoption.

The French, however, were uneasy about the static stocking of so much *materiel* forward believing it to be vulnerable to enemy action[11] and much preferred the *En-Cas-Mobile* (ECM)[12] arrangement, which the French Army had developed, with the British, during the Great War, although interestingly the pre-war *Field Service Regulations* clearly identified the concept and its application.[13] This was a system based on a group of railway wagons, barges or WMT kept under load for immediate despatch, although for practical purposes this was mostly ammunition held on rail.[14] By 1940 the BEF had developed this concept to include a range of combat supplies, vehicles and material held on wheels, both road and rail. The BEF system consisted of these two components. The rail element consisted of three parts: POL, rations and ammunition, of which the latter was the most important. Interestingly, one of the reasons the British adopted the ammunition ECM was because the French objected to the deployment of advanced ammunition depots, so ECM was expanded as a compromise.

The rail ECM plan had two DOS on wagons located within 36 hours of the respective Corps ARH plus an additional two DOS for I Corps within 12 hours. Ammunition ECM trains were loaded with an agreed pack of ammunition natures authorised by the G Staff at GHQ and were originally designated Standard Ammunition Trains (SAT) but were re-titled Ammunition Section En-Cas-Mobile (ASE). The SAT concept in 1940 had though, two limitations. First, not all the corps had the same weapon populations, which in addition, were constantly changing, and secondly, the ammunition expenditure rates were not sufficiently scientific. The GHQ Administrative Instruction for Plan D (Dyle)[15] also listed three ration and three petrol trains[16]

11 British logistic doctrine directed that *materiel* with predicted usage rates, such as rations and clothing, should be held to the rear, being delivered forward by daily trains. Items that had more volatile daily expenditure or consumption rates, such as ammunition and liquid fuels, should have an allocated component held forward.

12 Literally, 'movable if necessary'. Henniker, BOH *Transportation on the Western Front*, p.xxxi.

13 The pre-Great war FSR articulates the conditions for forming the equivalent of ECM in the rail environment: 'This rule does not apply to such train loads of supplies or ammunition as the IGC may direct to be kept ready at certain stations for immediate despatch to the troops in case of necessity. The amount so retained will be strictly limited and should not exceed one day's supplies for the force served'. Army Council, FSR, Part II, *Organization and Administration*, Chp VIII, Transport, Sect 63, para 6, p.95.

14 Henniker, BOH, *Transportation on the Western Front*, p.xxxi.

15 TNA WO 197/57: Forward move of BEF (Plan D) Administrative Instructions.

16 These assets were planned to come under command of X (Arras) Base Sub-Area with 23rd (Northumbrian) Infantry Division as the formation responsible for rear area defence.

as part of the ECM plan and a summary of BEF Land Service ammunition stocks held on rail[17] in May 1940, is summarized in the table below:

Table 15.2
BEF – Rail Held Land Service Ammunition Stocks[18]

Facility	DOS	Response Time	Remarks
I Corps ARH	5	Immediate	Dumped at ARH
II Corps ARH	7	Immediate	Dumped at ARH
III Corps ARH	3	Immediate	Dumped at ARH
I Corps ASE	2	Within 12 hours	Held on rail - 3 x ASE
I Corps ASE	2	Within 36 hours	Held on rail - 3 x ASE
II Corps ASE	2	Within 36 hours	Held on rail - 3 x ASE
III Corps	Unknown	Unknown	Estimated to be 1,000 tons

The RAF also decided to hold stocks of Air Service ammunition for the AASF on rail, pending the completion of the AASF Advanced Base; an ECM ammunition reserve was therefore, held on wheels at Barbonne,[19] consisting of the stocks shown in the table below:

Table 15.3
AASF Rail Held Air Service Ammunition – ASE Barbonne[20]

Aerially Delivered Munitions	Quantity	Small Arms Ammunition	Quantity
Bomb, 250 lb, General Purpose	1,546	0.303-inch, Ball	494,000
Bomb, 40 lb, General Purpose	3,608	0.303-inch, Armour Piercing	176,000
Bomb, 20 lb, Fragmentation	1,920	0.303-inch, Incendiary	59,000

The road element of the ECM system was the LOC Railhead company of the RASC, the role of which, was to carry on WMT, one DOS of POL, rations, clothing and Anti-Gas Equipment (AGE) for a deployed force to provide a reserve in case of rail delivery being interrupted. The BEF had two LOC Railhead companies, one each for I and II Corps; the planned deployment of two additional companies to support III Corps and the never

17 In addition, each corps held four DOS, delivered via the respective Corps ARH, in dumps in the corps and divisional areas.
18 Table compiled from information in WOOH, *Ordnance Services*, and WOOH, *Maintenance in the Field*, Vol I.
19 HQ BAFF 4864/Org 3 dated 15 April 1940, 'Memorandum on the Scale of Reserve Stocks of Fuel, Bombs and Ammunition to be held in France' (SECRET) in TNA AIR 35/123.
20 Table compiled from information in Appx B to HQ BAFF 4864/Org 3 dated 15 April 1940, 'Memorandum on the Scale of Reserve Stocks of Fuel, Bombs and Ammunition to be held in France' (SECRET) in TNA AIR 35/123.

formed IV Corps, was prevented by the evacuation.[21] 4 Company RASC was fully engaged in the I Corps areas, whilst 108 Company, which arrived in early February 1940[22] had A Section allocated to the Dieppe Medical BSA, three sections in the II Corps area and E Section supporting the Rouen BSA. Upon a GHQ Notice to Move order being issued, A and E Sections were to rejoin 108 Company on J+1 and both companies were to load the allocated 120,000 rations and 400 tons of POL that had been ground loaded in preparation for operations, with any spare lift to be assigned to AGE.[23] A LOC Railhead company was, with an establishment of 150 task 10 ton lorries[24] and 411 personnel organized in five sections[25] plus a HQ and a workshop,[26] a major logistic sub-unit, although the establishments did not however, reflect the strengths, with, for example, on 10 May 1940, the strength of 4 Company being 422 and that of 108 Company, 352.[27] The 10 ton vehicles[28] were also a mixed bag as many were impressed commercial lorries bringing with them the usual issues of more complex maintenance and a shortage of spares.[29]

Without Liability to Congestion

The BEF's Land and Air Components, and the AASF, required thousands of gallons of fuel per day to operate. When mobile, the combat formations of the Land Component consumed over 330,000 gallons[30] per day,[31] the Air Component approximately 27,276 gallons on high activity levels[32] and the AASF on a maximum effort strike mission, 38,000 gallons,[33] although fuel consumption figures for the two RAF elements never exceeded 27,000 gallons per day before the ground campaign started in May 1940. Much of this fuel was delivered to the corps areas and the airfields by rail, mostly in cans, although road tanker bulk capability did exist at 3rd Line and Rail Tank Cars (RTC) could be used to supply some airfields from a rail spur or

21 4 Company RASC supported I Corps and 108 Company, II Corps, although with detachments supporting other formations. WOOH, *Supplies and Transport*, Vol II, Appx VA, p.365.
22 8 February 1940. Ibid, Appx VB, p.366.
23 BEF GHQ QMG, Q1081/2 dated 21 April 1940, 'L of C Railhead Companies' in TNA WO 167/1095: 1 LOC Railhead Company RASC.
24 The established allocation was: 115 for Supplies, 15 for AGE and 10 as reserves. For details, see, Philson, BEFORBAT, Vol 1, p.153.
25 In 1940, the RASC used the term 'section' to describe what was a platoon sized organization and 'sub-section' for the smallest RASC grouping.
26 The establishment authority was WE IV/1931/34B/1. Philson, BEFORBAT, Vol 1, p.153.
27 TNA WO 167/1095: 1 LOC Railhead Company RASC and WO 167/1096: 2 LOC Railhead Company RASC, Field Returns.
28 The Bartholomew POR noted that the 10 ton lorries on the establishment of the LOC Railhead companies were considered to be too heavy for ECM operations. TNA WO 106/1775: Bartholomew Committee - Report on lessons to be learnt from operations in Flanders; evidence, report and action arising, Transport, para 29a.
29 The 4 Company RASC transport details sheet for April 1940 records six different makes: AEC, Albion, Armstrong-Saurer, Atkinson, ERF and Leyland. TNA 167/1095: 1 LOC Railhead Company RASC, 'Civilian Details, April 1940'.
30 Based upon 26,670 gallons per day for an infantry division.
31 This equates to nearly 82,500 x 4 gallon cans.
32 Based upon 12 aircraft per squadron on the ORBAT.
33 Based upon 12 x Battles per Light Bomber squadron and 12 x Hurricanes per Fighter squadron.

nearby siding. The pre-war doctrine directed that all reserves of POL in the corps areas should be held on wheels in 3rd or 2nd Line transport in the Corps Petrol Park (CPP) and Divisional Petrol Companies (DPC) respectively and that there should be no dumped stocks forward of the Petrol Railhead (PRH) but in the winter of 1939-1940 practicalities overcame the doctrine and surplus stocks, amounting to several hundred tons of different fuels began to accumulate at the PRHs. With disruptions to rail deliveries caused by severe winter weather in February 1940, a decision was made to retain these stocks as a reserve, which required the use of resources from Supply and Pioneer companies to control the static PRH stocks. These assets proved inadequate and elements of the CPP, which despite the nomenclature were transport units, had to be imported to support the task, thereby reducing the capability of the mobile reserve, whilst still not ensuring that dumped POL stocks were effectively stored and accounted for, resulting in fuel loss and quality issues.

Another key component of the BEF that was integral to railway output was the Divisional Supply Column (DSC) of the RASC. The function of the DSC was to lift rations and stores from the Corps Supply Railhead (SRH) to divisional units, over a planning operating distance of 40 miles. Pack trains for supply items usually consisted of 38 wagons and were dispatched daily from the MBA on a scale of one pack train per day per two divisions. Rail was also vital to the strategic movement of the BEF's armour and tracked vehicles, being used extensively during the BEF's deployment from the ports to the Assembly Area at Le Mans in September and October 1939 and then subsequently to the Concentration Area. Rail was also critical to the deployment of 1st Armoured Division in May 1940. Whilst most of these moves were strategic in nature, rail was also used at the operational level because of the shortage of wheeled Heavy Equipment Transporters (HET)s. The railheads, which were essential logistic facilities, serviced the 'End to End' delivery capability of the railway and commanders and Staff recognized how important it was to choose them with care. The two key imperatives for selection were succinctly summarized in a contemporary publication: 'A railhead should, as far as possible, be protected from bombardment by guns or aeroplanes. The roads in the vicinity of a railhead should be suitable for the carriage of considerable traffic without liability to congestion'.[34] The BEF was soon to learn how true this statement was.

Combat and Courant

Whilst railway units are not usually perceived to be at the forefront of operations during May and June 1940 many were to see a remarkable amount of combat. As part of the German assault, the *Luftwaffe* strafed trains and attacked a large number of railway junctions in the Eastern and Northern Railway Regions, which initially caused considerable disruption to operations in the BEF corps areas, whilst several trains were captured or destroyed by the enemy. Of 26 ammunition trains[35] dispatched from BADs in the period 10-17 May, only six were unloaded at constituted ARHs with others off-loaded in *ad hoc* locations. In the wider round however, enemy disruption to the BEF's *courant*[36] was clearly less than expected, as the Bartholomew

34 Lindsell, *Military Organization and Administration*, p.92.

35 WOOH, *Ordnance Services*, p.156.

36 A *courant* (literally a stream) is a continuous flow of empty trains to entraining stations, of loaded trains from them to detraining stations and of returning empty trains. Henniker, BOH, *Transportation on the*

Committee's Final Report on the campaign in France noted: 'The delays caused by air attack on railway junctions, marshalling yards and other centres were often of a temporary nature only, as a diversion could soon be arranged. Damage to running lines at awkward spots, and at a distance from the repair facilities of railway centres, caused more lasting delays'.[37]

151 Railway Construction Company (RCC) RE moved from Frevent to the SNCF depot at Lille, with elements deployed forward with the company suffering three fatal casualties on 10 May in an incident involving a crashed Heinkel 111P from KG27.[38] A detachment of 153 ROC[39] moved forward from Romescamps to Ath in the corps areas as part of Plan D but because the Belgian Railways initially continued to function, it had little work to conduct, although by 16 May, it had lost five soldiers missing in action whilst tasked to retrieve trains from forward locations.[40] 151 RCC and 153 ROC deployed with locomotives, additional tenders for water and supporting wagons, with 153 ROC forming an *ad hoc* breakdown train, searching for flat-wagons to move heavy artillery and hauling troop and ambulance trains using UK and Belgian motive power.[41]

Operating in Belgium was a particular challenge because the RE railway units had conducted no reconnaissance, liaison or training with the Belgian Railways, a product of the country's neutrality. In addition, the operationally dynamic scenario disrupted the flow of information from the chain of command and 153 ROC often received their primary information warning of German advances from SNCF. Once the withdrawal began on 18 May 1940, 153 ROC train crews were increasingly employed in keeping traffic moving, sometimes under aerial attack. The operating conditions were challenging, with the whole line from Ath to Lille blocked with trains head to tail moving in occasional spasms, a problem resolved by using both tracks under 'wrong-way' working procedures.[42] 153 ROC however, did sterling work, rescuing a stranded ambulance train, delivering wagons of 6-inch howitzer ammunition and entraining the 2/5th Foresters.[43] Cut off by the German seizure of the Channel coast at Abbeville, elements of 153 ROC were evacuated from Boulogne on Wednesday 22 May 1940 and others from Calais the next day,[44] the latter group having been part of an anti-tank road block eight kilometres to the South of the port.[45]

Western Front, p.xxxi.

37 TNA WO 106/1741: Bartholomew Committee 1940 - Final Report, para 10b.

38 Heinkel 111P (1G+CL) crashed near Ferme Jourdain at Borre, East of Hazebrouck at approximately 0500 LOCAL. It exploded 45 minutes later, killing two of the crew and three members of 151 RCC: 71422 Lieutenant John Ross Rhedyneg Price, aged 28, and two NCOs, Lance-Sergeants, 394136 Frederick Martin and 18442255 Reginald Paul; they rest in the Merville Communal Cemetery Extension. Other bystanders were injured. For the aircraft details, see, Cornwell, *The Battle of France*, p.210.

39 8 Construction & Operating Company (RCO) was assigned to this task but redeployed to the UK in late April 1940. TNA WO 167/906: 8 RCO RE, WD.

40 TNA 167/948: 153 ROC RE, WD, entries May 1940.

41 TNA 167/948: 153 ROC RE, WD, entries May 1940.

42 WOOH, *Transportation*, p.42.

43 153 ROC operated the Melbourne Military Railway (MMR) in Derbyshire November 1939 - February 1940, deploying to France on 9 March 1940. TNA WO 167/948: 153 ROC RE, WD.

44 For a description of the actions of the various ROC and RCC during the Battle for France, see, Aves, *Supporting the British Expeditionary Force*, pp.48-52.

45 TNA WO 167/948: 153 ROC RE, WD.

There was little interdiction along the GLOC with no marshalling yards or motive power depots suffering appreciable damage, although in the corps areas aerial strafing of trains occurred and there were bombing attacks on the Permanent Way. The only significant assault against the wider French railway system was on 3 June 1940, when 200 bombers raided Paris in Operation PAULA,[46] attacking railways, factories and aerodromes; 22 stations and various parts of the rail infrastructure of the Paris *Ceinture* lines received damage.[47] Ironically, it was French Army engineers, executing bridge demolitions, which caused the major harm, particularly across the River Marne.[48] A significant disruption though, to rail traffic, was not physical injury to the network but the attempts to withdraw the maximum number of wagons and locomotives to the South of the River Somme; the Allies were, much to German satisfaction, inflicting logistic chaos on themselves. The post-war War Office monograph observed: 'Although the Germans bombed stations, junctions and marshalling yards, the obstruction by evacuated rolling stock was by far the most potent cause of delay to traffic'.[49] Decisions as to the destruction or evacuation of stocks were almost always hampered by the dislocation of communications preventing the receipt of clear orders, or by the inability of junior officers on the ground to make balanced judgements from often fragmentary and dated information. With timely situational awareness a constant challenge, rumour abounded, which was usually not good for morale and certainly not for coherent decision-making.

Ambulance Train Actions

The ambulance trains unfortunately, probably saw more action than nearly any other railway unit and the story is one of grit, determination and incredible heroism, under the most trying conditions.[50] One particular problem that became an increasingly difficult to surmount as the campaign progressed was preventing unauthorised persons boarding the ambulance trains, including civilian refugees and military stragglers, although wounded women and children were often treated if there was capacity.[51] Ambulance trains were, despite displaying the Red Cross, often subjected to aerial attack by bombing and strafing, although not necessarily deliberately, whilst the ambulance train staffs had to adapt to dynamic medical evacuation operations, including the care of German POWs. No 3 Ambulance Train (ATN) for example, took casualties direct from field ambulance units because 6 Casualty Clearing Station (CCS) was closing and unable to accept new patients. Arriving at Verneuil it was initially stabled with an ammunition train and a troop train, the former fortunately departing before an air attack commenced, a bomb killing a medical orderly and wounding nine others wounded, whilst the train was badly damaged, with No 5 Coach crumpled like a crushed matchbox, thus leaving 3

46 Operational intelligence and signals intercepts provided the Allies with nearly all the details of this raid except the date. 250 fighters were dispatched to intercept it. Cornwell, *The Battle of France*, p.415.
47 WOOH, *Movements*, p.182.
48 Ibid.
49 WOOH, *Transportation*, p.42.
50 For details of the medical arrangements for the BEF, see, Crew, BOH, *The Army Medical Services, Campaigns*, Vol 1, pp.1-113.
51 TNA WO 222/2137: BEF Ambulance Trains.

ATN with only three operational coaches.[52] No 4 ATN became stranded in Belgium whilst recovering patients from Ninove West of Brussels because of railway infrastructure issues, only being recovered to Dieppe with the patients because of the determined actions of three RE locomotive drivers from 153 ROC,[53] none of whom had any experience of operating on the railways in the area. Their actions were in the highest traditions of the railway service because in addition to the depredations of aerial attack they also had to operate points and signals in locations where the Belgian operatives had left their posts. Through their courage, supported by some good luck, 4 ATN was able to keep just ahead of the German advance, passing through a burning Tournai as I Corps units were preparing defensive positions on the River Escaut.

Having reached Dieppe Harbour on 21 May 1940, the patients were prepared for disembarkation to enable the train to depart on another tour to evacuate patients from 3 and 11 Base General Hospitals (BGH)[54] but whilst it was on the quay at 1700 with over 600 patients aboard,[55] the train was set on fire by flames from the receiving hospital carrier HMHS[56] *Maid of Kent*,[57] which had been hit by aerial bombs.[58] The train was evacuated but some patients were subsequently killed in the continuing attack and 118 patients were dispatched to 3 and 10 BGH for treatment. Six coaches and two baggage vans with a large amount of equipment were lost but the remainder of the stock was uncoupled by a courageous and sadly unrecorded French railway shunter and manually relocated 200 yards from the incident. With the addition of some French vans, 4 ATN moved its remaining patients to Rouen where it received further damage from air attack before travelling to Rennes to discharge some of them to 8 BGH. It then moved to La Baule to transfer the balance of the casualties to 4 BGH before returning to Rennes for repair and reconstitution with French ATN stock.[59]

52 Nursing Sister Pike (QAIMNSR) summarized of her shock of the action explaining that "Our beautiful ambulance train was cut in two". She also highlighted the bravery of one of the orderlies and her sadness at having to leave the body of Orderly F W Jones in the wreckage. Information extracted from a letter by Sister Pike in TNA WO 222/2137: BEF Ambulance Trains. Research has not confirmed the identity of this soldier, but it is probably 7256004 Private John William Jones, aged 38, of the RAMC who is remembered on the Dunkirk Memorial, Column 143.

53 See, 153/39/459 dated 29 July 1940 in TNA WO 167/948: 153 ROC RE.

54 BOH, *The Army Medical Services, Campaigns*, Vol 1, p.43.

55 Other sources suggest the much lower figure of 252 but this may refer to stretcher cases. Ibid, states 600.

56 Apart from a lesser clinical capability, hospital carriers were in all other respects marked, lit and registered under the Geneva Convention as hospital ships, and were titled His Majesty's Hospital Ship (HMHS).

57 The *Maid of Kent* of 2,693 GRT was a Southern Railway cross-Channel ferry that had been operating as a hospital carrier on the Newhaven-Dieppe loop since 10 September 1939. See, Winser, *BEF Ships*, p.60.

58 HMHS *Maid of Kent* was burned out and came to rest the on the harbour bottom next to the dock wall, with the loss of 43 lives, 17 crew, 11 members of the RAMC and 15 soldiers. TNA WO 361/13: Evacuation of Dunkirk: losses on hospital carrier Maid of Kent, 21 May 1940. Of the nine hospital carriers listed in Plummer, *The Ships That Saved an Army*, pp.55-66, there were two losses: the *Maid of Kent* and HMHS *Paris*, which sank under tow on 3 June 1940 after being disabled by air attack. Two of the ship's crew were lost; both are buried in Sussex.

59 Crew, BOH, *The Army Medical Services, Campaigns*, Vol 1, p.43.

5 ATN recovered the personnel and equipment of 5 CCS by attaching the 22 wagons in which it was loaded, to the ambulance train, uncoupling them at Hazebrouck, whilst 7 ATN entrained 1 CCS and 1 Advanced Medical Stores Depot at Ninove. 6 ATN was trapped at Albert by bomb damage to the track, the OC[60] persuading the three nursing sisters[61] to make their escape to prevent them becoming POWs. They had a harrowing time moving 19 miles on foot, farm-carts and bicycles to Doullens from where they were evacuated to Cherbourg;[62] the remaining ambulance train staff and all the patients were captured. The Principal Matron at HQ LOC must have been relieved to learn on 28 May 1940 that the QAIMNS staff from ATNs 5, 6, 8, 9 & 13 had been evacuated to the UK but very concerned the next day to receive a signal stating that nothing was known of ATNs 1, 3 and 7.[63] The ATN movement programme was thoroughly disrupted by the German drive to the Channel coast and access to the six BGH in 1 MBSA at Dieppe, the six in 2 MBSA around Boulogne and the six in the Main Base Area in North-West France, was denied. An improvised service was directed to Dunkerque with the aim of direct evacuation from the rear of the CCSs to the UK. All the nine ambulance trains remained in France to be captured by the Germans, although some of the stock was recovered in 1944; fortunately, most of the staff were evacuated. All these exploits were in the highest traditions of the Army Medical Services and exposed the immense courage and skills of the military railwaymen.[64]

Ramassage[65]

Rail played a significant role in evacuating personnel and material, especially along the GLOC and there was furious activity in the Base depots to support three different tasks: the evacuation of material and personnel to the UK, preparations for the arrival of the 2nd BEF and maintaining British forces South of the River Somme. By the third week of May 1940, 150 RCC was tasked, assisted by 161 RCC, to urgently construct tank-loading ramps[66] to support the deployment of 1st Armoured Division.[67] By the first week of June, the 150 RCC main effort was damage repair, with a particular focus on enabling the recovery of SNCF locomotives and rolling stock.

60 Captain (Temporary Major) H Clain RAMC. TNA WO 222/1517: Medical Staff Units, BEF Order of Battle.
61 J H Dabbs, E Alty and L Williams QAIMNS. TNA WO 222/2137: BEF Ambulance Trains.
62 TNA WO 177/14: WD, 1939-1945, Medical Services, QAIMNS, September 1939-June 1940.
63 M/135/4 dated 28 May 1940 (Folio 254) and 2/GEN/1416/664/LMS dated 29 May 1940 (Folio 225) in TNA WO 177/14.
64 The remarkable exploits of the BEF's ambulance train staff deserve much greater recognition.
65 A French railway term for sweepings, applied to trains made up of odd vehicles of miscellaneous traffic as distinct from supply, reinforcement, remount and other trains of definite kinds of traffic. Henniker, BOH, *Transportation on the Western Front*, p.xxxii.
66 The provision of the Ramp Wagon System (RWS) introduced to the British Army in 1918 would, in many instances, have resolved the requirement for deploying RCC for this type of task, thereby creating more engineer resources for rail projects and generating greater tactical flexibility for the armoured units. For a constructional diagram of a temporary ramp, see, QMG, *Notes on Military Railway Engineering*, Part II, *Engineering*, Plate 56, Improvised Tank Ramp Constructed from Railway PW Materials.
67 TNA 167/945: 150 RCC RE, WD. Construction commenced by 18 May at Neufchatel-en-Bray before redeployment to Louviers between Rouen and Evreux.

On 7 June, six bomb cuts between Dieppe and Longueville were repaired, the 150 RCC train being attacked by air the next day, but fortunately without casualties or damage.[68] On 12 June, 150 RCC conducted an impressive operation at Serquigny[69] to recover the stranded 161 RCC train. The military railwaymen salvaged tools from it, repaired the damage to the track and then manually pushed the stock to the North of the station to enable SNCF to recover its locomotives from the engine shed.[70]

SNCF continued to the last to make a positive, although not always successful, contribution to sustaining and then evacuating the BEF. A long forgotten operation commenced at 0200 on 14 June, the day after the last elements of 51st (Highland) Division from Force W[71] had been evacuated from France, when the remaining logisticians manning the Force W Rear Area installations at Woippy[72] three miles North-North West of Metz departed by rail.[73] This recovery appears to have been another example of confusion and failure because the stocks had been evacuated by 8 June and the units, with the exception of the field bakery ovens,[74] were expecting to leave the same day.[75] With 64 trains on the same track in front of it, the BEF train did well to reach Chavelot, 78 miles to the South, after 25 hours. The frustrating delays were mostly caused by disruption to locomotive water supplies, which was blamed upon sabotage[76] and the railway crews resorted to filling the tender from wells, ponds and ditches using village manual fire pumps and bucket chains manned by the passengers,[77] although not every soldier or civilian was willing to lend a hand.[78] At Belrupt, subjected to bombing and strafing by the *Luftwaffe*, the train stopped and the passengers disembarked to disperse into the adjoining woods and fields. The attack over, the passengers re-embarked, the train then chuffed slowly on, leaving Vesoul on 16 June at 1000, 60 minutes before German tanks arrived, which then engaged a French armoured train whilst causing appreciable damage to other trains, with resulting personnel casualties. Swirling around the military rail evacuation were thousands of refugees some of whom had been driven over the edge of insanity by their traumatic experience.[79]

68 TNA WO 167/945: 150 RCC RE, WD.
69 Approximately 30 miles SW of Rouen.
70 TNA WO 167/945: 150 RCC RE, WD.
71 The Force W also known as the Saar Force.
72 These included RASC soldiers manning the DID, 4 Field Bakery and the EFI and RAOC personnel operating the Ordnance Depot.
73 TNA CAB 106/234: Saar Force – Ordnance Services.
74 These weighed 35 cwt and required a suitable crane to load them to a lorry or railway wagon. When the order was given to move on 13 June, no crane capable of the task was available. TNA WO 217/16: Private Diary of Lieutenant K R Gough RASC, entry 13 June 1940.
75 Lieutenant Gough ascribes the delay to supporting the *Entente Cordiale*. See TNA WO 217/16: Private Diary of Lieutenant K R Gough RASC, entry 13 June 1940.
76 TNA CAB 106/234: Saar Force - Ordnance Services, notes that, 'somebody, probably fifth columnists had cut off water supplies'.
77 TNA WO 217/16: Private Diary of Lieutenant K R Gough RASC, entry 16 June 1940.
78 This report is second hand. TNA CAB 106/234: Saar Force – Ordnance Services.
79 TNA WO 217/16: Private Diary of Lieutenant K R Gough RASC, entry 17 June 1940.

P15.1 Ramping It Up. During the deployment and the campaign, the RCCs were often tasked with constructing improvised rail loading ramps, which were critical to effective and efficient rail transportation operations, and thus military capability. A Vickers Mark I Medium tank confirms a successful build at Longmoor in 1937. (WDLMRC: DRMC/V1/004)

At Vellerois-Le-Bois, the RAOC officer in charge of the party[80] resorted to using an armed escort commanded by Conductor Hawley to unpick the traffic chaos at the station, enforcing order at the point of a bayonet and rifle in order to enable trains to continue their journeys.[81] At a location approximately 14 miles North-North-East of Besancon, this intrepid rail expedition ended. A *Luftwaffe* aircraft dropped a bomb on a 300 mm rail mounted artillery piece killing two French soldiers and blocking the line, and whilst the BEF train was stationary, it was rammed in the rear by the locomotive of the following train, although fortunately the speed was low and there were no casualties from the collision.[82] The logisticians dismounted and a plan was discussed, which involved marching South to Marseilles but close to Swiss frontier, thus enabling internment in Switzerland as a last resort. The stores wagons on the train were fired to destroy equipment and burn the Imprest account funds but the flames were extinguished after

80 Major Milnes. TNA CAB 106/234: Saar Force - Ordnance Services.
81 TNA WO 217/16: Private Diary of Lieutenant K R Gough RASC, entry 16 June 1940.
82 TNA CAB 106/234: Saar Force - Ordnance Services.

the parties left the site. The contingent moved off in three groups each of 70 men,[83] each of whom were issued some rations,[84] led by a reconnaissance team commanded by Lieutenant Burghope RAOC.[85] Near L'Ecouvotte, contact with the RASC group led by Lieutenant Gough RASC was lost[86] and it was increasingly clear that groups of 70 were too large to move undetected, so parties of 5-6 or less were formed. The OIC's party covered 125 of the 450 plus miles of the march to Bordeaux before a German WMT convoy captured its members[87] near Chalon-Sur-Saone on 26 June. Lieutenant Kenneth Gough had better fortune having eventually made the decision in the light of increasing German military activity to strike for Switzerland, which his group of 54 out of the original 68,[88] reached on 23 June after a remarkable and long-forgotten exploit of evasion by an eclectic mix of logisticians.[89]

156 Transportation Stores Company (TSC)[90] was instrumental in supporting the arrival of 1st Armoured Division out-loading 28 tank ramps to 151 RCC in the period 16-19 May, of which eight were returned to depot on 24 May, the remainder being used to support the movement of tanks by rail.[91] In June, 156 TSC focused upon the evacuation of key railway stores by rail for transhipment by sea to the UK, including bridges, mobile rail cranes and 8,700 sleepers.[92] The soldiers of 2 Transportation Stores Depot (TSD) at Carquefou,[93] having out-loaded most of its stocks, were witness in the first two weeks of June to the chaos of the withdrawal of Allied

83 These groups consisted of a RAOC, RAMC and Area Commandant's party commanded by Major Milnes RAOC; the 10 Salvage Unit and 4 Field Bakery party under Captain Wright and a RASC party led by Lieutenant Kenneth Gough RASC. TNA WO 217/16: Private Diary of Lieutenant K R Gough RASC, entry 17 June 1940.

84 The 7 lb tins of meat on the train were mostly left behind because they were difficult to carry. Each man was issued with a 12 oz tin of corned beef, two or three packets of biscuits, an emergency ration pack plus a tin of beans or salmon. TNA WO 217/16: Private Diary of Lieutenant K R Gough RASC, entry 17 June 1940.

85 The Ordnance Services report in TNA CAB 106/234 does not mention how the soldiers were fed during the extraction, although the RASC group solutions are described in TNA WO 217/16: Private Diary of Lieutenant K R Gough RASC.

86 Although Major Milnes was unaware of the reason, it was an intentional act by the OIC RASC party to reduce the risk of being identified by the enemy. TNA WO 217/16: Private Diary of Lieutenant K R Gough RASC, entry 17 June 1940.

87 Several W Force soldiers who were captured later escaped and reached neutral territory. These included Sergeant Edward Patrick RASC of 4 Field Bakery and from the RAOC, Privates Larning and Cope. TNA WO 208/3298: Escape and Evasion Reports.

88 Second-Lieutenant Kerr and 12 soldiers were captured, whilst Corporal Burnham, despite a hip injury, waited near Morteau for Captain Wright but reached Switzerland later. TNA WO 217/16: Private Diary of Lieutenant K R Gough RASC.

89 TNA WO 217/16: Private Diary of Lieutenant K R Gough RASC. Three of the fortunate soldiers were Sergeant N Blakeley and Private H Unwin from 3 Supply Company RASC and Private J Seymour RASC. TNA WO 208/3298: Escape and Evasion Reports.

90 156 TSC had suffered a fatal casualty the day before the German attack. 1983712 Sapper Richard Tilbrooke, aged 32, of 1 TSD at Braye failed to parade at Tattoo on 9 May 1940 and his body was found in the River La Vilaine at 2035 on 11 May 1940. His death was recorded as due to accidental drowning and he was buried at the Cimitiere de l'este Rennes on 14 May, where he rests. TNA WO 167/951: 156 TSC RE, WD.

91 TNA WO 167/951: 156 TSC RE, WD.

92 TNA WO 167/951: 156 TSC RE, WD.

93 Located immediately to the North of Nantes.

Forces.[94] A succession of evacuated Belgian locomotives and stock steamed through the station heading to Nantes and Saint Nazaire, whilst a stream of military units, including British, Dutch and French and units, passed through the village.[95] On 13 June, 1 TSD at Braye dispatched an urgent consignment of railway material to Saint Malo port for the construction of an improvised bridge to enable a train ferry to dock.[96] On 14 June 157 RCC was dispatched from Nantes to Saint Malo port to conduct the work and whilst the unit war diary[97] does not mention why this was necessary, one assumption must be that there was a plan to evacuate locomotives, freight wagons and ambulance trains from France using rail ferries. The withdrawal certainly overtook whatever was being considered with all British railway equipment in varying states of repair and operability, being captured by the Germans. Prepared demolition planning and execution was rare, although, war diaries indicate that some 'wrecking',[98] was undertaken in order to prevent immediate use.[99] Stories of locomotives being run over dock walls into harbours are almost certainly a myth[100] but the shunting locomotive at 1 Heavy Repair Shop (HRS) based at Saint Etienne de Montluc was steamed into a set of buffers.[101]

Amongst other adventures, 190 ROC had an interesting evacuation commencing on 16 June 1940, when a locomotive hauling 75 Ferry Vans, many loaded with ordnance stores and four containing the messes, cookhouse and fitter's workshop left the Bruz depot for Nantes hauled by six Great Western Dean Goods 0-6-0 freight locomotives and a LMS 0-6-0 Jinty, which must have been an amazing sight to behold. The local French signalman would not however, grant access to the mainline, so the British railway-men dismantled the de-railer,[102] pulled the ground levers and steamed into Bruz Station, halting for long enough to appropriate a piano on the platform before departing for their destination.[103] Operating on the procedure of *Marche a Vue*, 'go as you see', the train trundled towards Nantes collecting refugees, including a French priest who gave piano recitals during the journey. The unpleasant task of cleaning ash-pans and

94 Concern about the activities of the Fifth Column and German collaborators are an underlying feature of the entries in the war dairy, which is replete with the vehicle registration marks and descriptions of stolen Belgian and French cars and lorries. TNA WO 167/951: 156 TSC RE, WD, June 1940.

95 The British units included the ground crew of a RAF squadron and No 2 War Graves Unit, the latter billeted in Chateau de l'Epinay. TNA WO 167/951: 156 TSC RE, WD, June 1940.

96 TNA WO 167/951: 156 TSC RE, WD, June 1940.

97 TNA WO 167/952: 157 RCC RE, WD.

98 A common procedure was to leave the fire burning, which resulted in the fusible plugs in the fire-box melting.

99 For details of basic rail demolition procedures, see, QMG, *Notes on Military Railway Engineering,* Part II, *Engineering,* Chp IX. Demolition.

100 The various fates of the 95 locomotives are described in Aves, *Supporting the British Expeditionary Force.* Some of them were destroyed in the war, a few were in German service on the Eastern Front in the USSR, others remained on the Continent after 1945, mainly with the SNCF, but a few steamed on behind the Iron Curtain, whilst many were returned to the UK for scrapping or refurbishment. A few went to China as part of a United Nations Aid programme and one, GWR 0-6-0 War Department 188 became the subject of a long-running ownership dispute between the UK and the USSR, but was scrapped in Austria in 1951.

101 The war diary states that the locomotive was 'destroyed' although the cited action seems unlikely to have led to this result. TNA 167/1155: 1 HRS RASC, WD, entry 16 June 1940.

102 A metal block placed on the track mechanically or manually to prevent runaway locomotives or rolling stock from a siding or depot from entering the main line.

103 Another case it would appear, of uncontrolled looting by the BEF.

smoke boxes was conducted at halts on the main line, with the locomotives watering at Savenay. In their quest to follow their orders, the men of 190 ROC must have broken nearly, if not all, of the rules in the military railway rule book, and most those of SNCF.[104]

A Tragic Finish

On Saturday 15 June 1940, 4 BAD near Rennes, was tasked by ADOS Ammunition at HQ LOC with out-loading 9,150 tons of ammunition to the UK.[105] By 2200 on 16 June, 2,100 tons had been dispatched in three trains to Saint Malo via the Rennes Base Marshalling Yard (BMY) but further work was halted because empty rail wagons were unavailable[106] although the industry of the 4 BAD staff was to have unforeseen consequences only 12 hours later. Bizarrely, the railway at 4 BAD was also busy in-loading ammunition from 6 BAD at Blain, which on 14 June had, after three weeks of deliveries, 2,200 tons on hand;[107] all these munitions were abandoned to the enemy. The order to evacuate to the UK was certainly a surprise to many railway units and their soldiers, a scenario, which, says as much about the speed of the German advance, as it does about the British communication of situational awareness. The war diary of 159 RCC, a unit located at 6 BAD,[108] summarizes the feeling:

> The news of evacuation came as a shock and the order to move at 1830 hrs can only be alluded to as a bombshell ... the general order was to destroy nothing and this was acted upon though many times since we have all wished that we had disobeyed orders and burnt the train.[109]

BEF railway unit casualties had been light during the pre-combat period with exception of various accidents one would expect operating railways in a foreign land under challenging circumstances. After combat operations commenced on 10 May 1940 there were relatively few casualties caused by attacks or accidents to BEF trains, with the first significant incident occurring at the Gare de Saint-Roch in Amiens when the train carrying the 7th Sussex was bombed, badly damaging the tender of the locomotive and the first coach; eight officers were killed and another 72 members of the battalion were wounded.[110] As it transpired, the BEF was only to suffer serious loss during railway movement during evacuation operations on the penultimate effective day of the British ground campaign. On 17 June 1940 at Rennes, 60 miles North-East of Saint Nazaire, a BEF troop train, bound for that port with four wagons of ammunition attached, was delayed with another four trains awaiting paths in the yard or the station at the *Quai Militaire*. Awaiting despatch were a refugee train from Paris and Liseaux, two

104 Memory of Sapper Thomas Brownbill of 190 ROC RE, quoted in Aves, *Supporting the British Expeditionary Force*, pp.45-46.
105 250 tons were destined for Cherbourg, 4,400 tons for Saint Malo and 4,500 tons for Saint Nazaire. TNA WO 167/1178: 4 BAD RAOC, WD.
106 TNA WO 167/1178: 4 BAD RAOC, WD.
107 Mainly RAF bombs, 3 and 3.7-inch AA rounds and SAA. TNA WO 167/1180: 6 BAD RAOC, WD.
108 159 RCC deployed to France on 29 March 1940 taking over from 151 RCC at Rennes.
109 TNA WO 167/954: 159 RCC RE, WD, entry 15 June 1940.
110 TNA WO 361/165: BEF - Bombing of Train at Amiens, 18 May 1940.

French troop trains[111] and an ammunition train,[112] when, at approximately 0950,[113] a Dornier Do 17Z aircraft from III/KG 76 attacked the station and marshalling yard.[114] The aerial bombs, the ensuing fire and the subsequent explosions of munitions, severely damaged or destroyed at least five trains, demolished buildings and inflicted heavy troop and civilian casualties;[115] the initial crater from detonation of the ammunition train was estimated to be 240 feet long, 60 feet wide and 15 feet deep. Rescue and recovery efforts were hampered for the next 24 hours by exploding munitions and the intense fire; some of the victims were never recovered.

Many sources suggest that it was an exploding French ammunition train that caused most of the damage. Research in the TNA offers a nuance to this interpretation because the 4 BAD WD[116] is specific in stating that between late 15 June and 2200 on 16 June 1940, three ammunition trains had been dispatched to the Rennes BMY, for consignment to Saint Malo, so it remains a strong possibility, given the interruption to train paths that British munitions were at least partly responsible for the post-attack explosions.[117] Whatever the catalyst, the result was approximately 805 military and civilian fatalities and a 1,000 wounded.[118] 177 British troops[119] are believed to have died[120] with 78 of those soldiers un-identified.[121] BEF railway units lost at least 26 men[122] but six hours later, an even greater catastrophe was to befall the

111 One contained the personnel of 203rd and 212th Artillery Regiments and the other, 222nd Artillery Regiment.
112 *BBC Peoples War Stories* <www.bbc.co.uk/history/ww2peopleswar/stories/24a7501024.shtml> contains the 2005 research of David Grundy.
113 Most sources indicate around 1000 hours; the 4 BAD WD states 0950. TNA WO 167/1178.
114 Some publications suggest that the Fifth Column informed the Germans about the location of the ammunition trains.
115 Photographs of the incident are available at *Lancastria Archive* <www.lancastria.org.uk/>
116 TNA WO 167/1178: 4 BAD RAOC, WD.
117 Interestingly, the 4 BAD evacuation report in the war diary does not mention any British munitions contribution, stating that the incident involved a British and French troop train and a French munitions train. See, 4 BAD/BW/1 dated 23 June 1940, Report on Evacuation of 4 BAD by Commanding Officer, Lieutenant-Colonel G Caruana Dingli, in TNA WO 167/1178.
118 The figures are believed to be: French military 591, British military (Army and RAF), 177 and French civilians 37. An extract from the war diary of 8 BGH RAMC records that approximately 200 wounded British and French soldiers and civilians were admitted for treatment. TNA WO 361/114: Rennes Train Bombing, R Cas (Liverpool) typed note. The war diary of 8 BGH is not shown in the TNA catalogue.
119 The Roll of Honour is available at *Lancastria Archive* <www.lancastria.org.uk/Victim_List/Rennes_bombing_17th_June_1940>
120 The dead were initially buried communal graves in fields nearby at St Helier and Cesson. The local French authorities transferred the remains to Rennes East Cemetery in September 1940.
121 Until the early 21st Century, these 78 men were assumed, by the CWGC, to have been killed aboard the *Lancastria*. Through extensive research by Brian Crabb and others, we know this is not the case. Whilst the names of these men do appear, mistakenly, in some lists of *Lancastria* dead, including the first edition of Brian Crabb's book, *The Forgotten Tragedy*, it appears their remains, although unidentifiable, were buried in the communal plot of Rennes Eastern Cemetery. See, Brian James Crabb, *The Forgotten Tragedy: The Story of the Sinking of HMT Lancastria* (Donington: Shaun Tyas, 2002). It is a reasonable assumption that given the inability to identify these men, it is likely they were closest to the initial and most serious blast when the French munitions train exploded. At least two of the victims, buried in the cemetery, died of their wounds in the days following the attack.
122 The author has compiled a Rennes railway unit casualty summary based on the CWGC casualty register and the Lancastria Association Roll of Honour, which is summarized in the table below:

railwaymen when the largest number of casualties suffered by railway units in any one action in the campaign occurred at sea during the sinking of the Hired Military Transport (HMT) *Lancastria*[123] on Monday 17 June 1940. How many railway troops were lost on the *Lancastria*[124] is the subject of continuing debate[125] but was probably 87, with 159 RCC suffering 83 percent of the casualties.[126]

Table 15.4
Rennes Rail Bombing
Railway Unit Casualties

Unit	Casualties
152 Railway Operating Company	1
154 Railway Operating Company	13*
156 Railway Stores Company	1
190 Railway Operating Company	5
Total	20

*1983641 Lance Sergeant Reginald Robert Tucker, (29) is sometimes shown as a member of 115 RCC but this unit did not exist; the CWGC entry states his unit as 154 ROC. 115 was the number of an AMPC Company.

123 See Chp 18, 'Run Rabbit Run'.

124 Over 30 harrowing first hand accounts are contained in John L West (Comp.) *The Loss of Lancastria* (Rossendale: Millgate, 1988). There are three accounts by railway construction unit soldiers: 1891823 Sapper Norman Driver of 159 RCC (pp.24-25) Sergeant Miller, 159 Company (pp.65-66) and Sapper (?) Potts, 190 Railway Operating Company (p.80). The heroism of Major Armitage (OC 159 RCC) is articulated in the memories of Sapper G Hillyard (p.49). John West, then serving with the Royal Army Pay Corps (RAPC), was a survivor of the disaster.

125 The table below has been compiled from several sources, including CWGC casualty rolls and the *Lancastria* Association Roll of Honour.

Table 15.5
HMT Lancastria
Railway Unit Casualties

Unit	Casualties
29 Railway Survey Company	4
154 Railway Operating Company	3
156 Transportation Stores Company	5
159 Railway Construction Company	72
176 Transportation Stores Company	1
190 Railway Operating Company	2
Total	87

126 159 RCC suffered the greatest number of casualties to a railway unit of the campaign, losing 72 of its members during the sinking of HMT *Lancastria.* Only 66 men, some badly burned, returned to the UK. The war diary entry for 21 June 1940 is melancholy: 'Nothing much done except compile Nominal Roll.' TNA WO 167/954: 159 RCC RE.

Conclusion

That the SNCF was capable of continuing to function in such chaotic conditions is testament to the courage of its people, resilience of its infrastructure and the flexibility of its systems. The SNCF organization retained its cohesion long after the French military in the North-East of France had disintegrated and only collapsed when the German Army overran its central HQ.[127] Railway controls were adept at efficiently diverting traffic and the civil engineering staff generally conducted critical repairs with commendable speed. Railways operations continued even in the shrinking pocket in North-East France, but capability was slowly eroded by the German advance and aerial attacks. Whilst there was confusion on occasions and much frustration, the railway system stood the test of war remarkably well, with sufficient tempo being maintained to support military operations.

The BEF's increasing rail capability was just getting into its stride when the German attack commenced, with some units still deficient in personnel and equipment, whilst others were working up to meet their operational commitments, so the BEF's rail capability was not fully effective. Of the operating units, two were Regular, two Supplementary Reserve and one Militia, whilst of the construction companies, three were Supplementary Reserve and five mainly manned by Militia.[128] Whilst many were rail tradesmen mobilized from commercial railway companies in the UK, they had little initial experience of operating as a component of cohesive team in a challenging military environment, especially in a foreign land, so coherency was sometimes a constraint, especially in the Militia units but taking 190 ROC's evacuation experience as an example, there was certainly no shortage of initiative or confidence and it is remarkable that they achieved what they did in very trying circumstances.

The railwaymen operating in the corps areas did well to keep the wheels rolling and there is no doubt that the railway units of the BEF gave of their absolute best in delivering military capability; their story, especially the staff of the ambulance trains, deserves much greater recognition. The BEF planners recognized the significance of a forward military rail deployment but were unable to practise the relevant skills in the locale because of French reluctance to allow British soldiers to practise on site, whilst Belgian neutrality prevented reconnaissance, liaison and training to support Plan D. The BEF could not however, have functioned without the wide range of military railway capability in France nor could it have operated without the French railways whose staff proved to be more than equal to the task until the Nation began to collapse. The courage of the soldiers in BEF railway units involved in combat action during this period has mostly been forgotten but the dedication, diligence and courage of this small band of people with all their niche skills deserves to be remembered.

127 Around 20 May 1940, Second-Lieutenant R L Charlesworth RE, reported SNCF morale in the Boulogne and Calais sector to be good. TNA WO 167/948: 153 ROC RE, WD.

128 The youth of the soldiers in the Militia units is highlighted by the ages of those lost from 159 RCC who were aboard HMT *Lancastria*. Judging from the ages of those killed in the Rennes train bombing, the SR ROCs were comprised of older men, with most casualties being in their mid-thirties.

Dedication

This chapter is dedicated to the memory of all those British and French railway men and women, military and civilian, who gave their lives in the cause of freedom during the Battle for France 1940.

16

Still Obscure
Maintaining an operational Ground Line of Communication

A Fire in the Garage

The first BEF logistic loss on 10 May 1940 was not caused by enemy action. 2 Ordnance Field Park (OFP) supporting II Corps was based in the Sallaumines district of Lens when a fire broke out in a garage the unit occupied, the resulting conflagration destroying five motorcycles, a battery carrier and several charging lorries with a 6-inch howitzer badly damaged, which was hardly an auspicious start to the campaign.[1] A rather sadder event in II Corps on the same day was the death of the AQMG and two RASC soldiers from the HQ in an air raid[2] whilst conducting a railhead reconnaissance in the Belgian town of Alost[3] 15 miles North-West of Brussels, the corps commander, Lieutenant-General Brooke learning of the incident when he visited the Corps Road Control Centre on 11 May.[4] That Brooke should visit this HQ was an important reminder of the vital role of efficient traffic control,[5] particularly during the advance or a withdrawal, to the operational capability of an army, a lesson that would be firmly reinforced during the campaign in France.[6]

The forward deployment of I and II Corps to the defence line on the River Dyle was conducted using rail and road. Trains conveyed supplies, stores, ammunition, petrol, some troops and

1 TNA WO 167/1194: 2 OFP RAOC, WD entry 10 May 1940. The May war diary was typed on blank paper after the evacuation with a date of 1 July 1940 and is therefore, a summary of events. The diary records an air raid on Lens the same day.

2 Colonel Aeneas Francis Quinton Perkins MC, late RE, and a well-known figure in pre-war RE cricket matches and golf tournaments was 47 and the son of Brigadier-General A E J Perkins CB. His previous appointment was CRE 4th Division. He lies At Rest in the Aalst Communal Cemetery, Belgium with S/97042 Corporal Thomas Baird Andrews, aged 21 and T/73640 Driver Ernest Wilson, aged 31, both RASC, who were killed on the same day and were part of the railhead reconnaissance team. Colonel Perkins was the first officer from the BEF to be killed on operations in Belgium.

3 Alost is the French name of the town of Aalst. Why AQMG II Corps was conducting a reconnaissance of the Supply Railhead assigned to III Corps is not explained in the documents. TNA WO 167/57: HQ L of C, Q Movements, GHQ AI 12, Appx D, Railheads.

4 Danchev & Todman, *War Diaries*, p.60.

5 Army Council, FSPB, Pamphlet No 6, 1939, *Mechanized Movement by Road.*

6 This point was clearly articulated in Army Council, *Military Engineering*, Vol V, *Roads*, p.27.

various tracked vehicles, to nominated railheads, whilst the rest of the Force travelled by road,[7] with the armoured cars of 12th Royal Lancers in the van.[8] The move of the three corps was a very significant operation because by 1940, an infantry division was established for 1,812 wheeled cargo vehicles, artillery tractors and ambulances, 216 tracked armoured vehicles, 715 motor-cycles, 172 trailers and 138 cars, totalling 3,053 equipments.[9] The re-deployment of 5th Division, located to the area around Le Harve, in preparation for a potential return to the UK, added additional complexity to the execution of Plan D.[10]

Rail movement, transporting tracked armour, played a significant role in the deployment of 1st Army Tank Brigade, consisting of two tank battalions, 4 RTR and 7 RTR, supported by a RAOC workshop[11] and a RASC composite Armoured Brigade Company (ABC),[12] the planning complicated by the recent arrival of the brigade in France.[13] 4 RTR was at Pacy conducting RAC training, whilst the tanks of 7 RTR were *en-route* by rail from the docks, which were then un-loaded on 13 May to be re-loaded the next day.[14] On 15 May, two trains for 4 RTR were unloaded at Hal and three for 7 RTR at Sint-Agatha-Berchem, tracking at night to the Foret de Soignes, a distance of 12 miles.[15] The withdrawal from the Dyle began on 16 May, although the rail moves from Hal were initially transferred to the railhead at Enghein because of bomb damage, a location also rendered immediately inoperable through air attack, resulting in the tanks tracking to reach Tournai.[16] This decision was not however, taken lightly. Despite the damage assessment estimating that the railway yard at Enghien had been struck by approximately 300 bombs, attempts were made with SNCF to procure trains for the move, but further air attack suggested a road move was the best option,[17] although as it transpired, the

7 TNA WO 197/57: HQ L of C, Q Movements, Forward Move of the BEF (Plan D) - Administrative instructions and correspondence: GHQ Administrative Instruction No 12 dated 7 May 1940.

8 12th Royal Lancers were equipped with 39 Lanchester armoured cars; all were lost in France. See, TNA CAB 106/272: Equipment Losses, Extract from RAC Progress Report No 2 (1-31 May 1940) and note to the BOH Historian, Major Ellis from DRAC dated November 1950.

9 Philson, BEFORBAT, Vol 4, p.126. An infantry division was also established for 327 bicycles, an equipment that added little combat capability but was a useful administrative item.

10 Map 12: BEF - Plan D: I Corps Administrative Laydown.

11 1 Army Tank Brigade Workshop RAOC WET authorized a workshop of 202 personnel and three LADs each of 18, thus totalling 256 officers and soldiers; WE III/1931/52A/1 refers. Philson, BEFORBAT, Vol 1, p.44. Personnel strength on deployment was below establishment at 198 All Ranks, Ibid, p.4.

12 1 ABC WET comprised four sections: ammunition, petrol, supplies and workshop, established for 349 personnel in 12 trades operating 63 task load-carriers at 2nd and 3rd Line transport, with the supplies section working to the double-echelon system; WE III/1931/39A/2 refers. Ibid, pp.39-41. Personnel strength on deployment was slightly above establishment at 354 All Ranks, although there was one officer deficient, p.4.

13 1st Army Tank Brigade also had a field ambulance; see WET WE III/1931/46/2, Philson, BEFORBAT, Vol 1, p.43.

14 The records suggest that 112 tanks were moved by rail. 4 RTR had 5 x Light VIB and 50 x Infantry Mk I, whilst 7 RTR had 7 x Light VIB, 27 x Infantry Mk I (A11 - Matilda) and 23 Infantry Mk II (A12 - Matilda II). See the Blagden Memorandum 'on the position regarding tanks in the BEF as known to the AFV Branch of GHQ', Cherwell Papers, G364/30 held in the TML.

15 TNA WO 167/414: HQ 1st Army Tank Brigade, WD, May 1940.

16 TNA WO 167/414: HQ 1st Army Tank Brigade, WD, May 1940.

17 Account of 1st Armoured Brigade Commander, Brigadier Douglas Pratt, late RTR, Liddell Hart, *The Tanks:* Vol II, p.11.

challenges of tank recovery,[18] tactical spacing, the flood of refugees and rubble in the streets, all reminded the planners of the advantages of rail movement. Road movement initiated a continual decline in capability as mechanical failure took its toll, especially affecting the A12 Matilda II tanks, causing, in conjunction with battle damage, availability to drop from 100 A11 and A12 tanks[19] on 13 May to 74[20] on 21 May and after the action at Arras[21] to 35 on 22 May[22]. Such a massive reduction in battle-worthy equipment was a timely reminder of the failure to ensure the allocation of appropriate logistic support to sustain armoured formations, especially the provision of spares, recovery assets and Heavy Equipment Transporters. Reserve ammunition lift for the brigade, split equally between 2nd and 3rd Line components of the ABC, included 9,600 rounds of 2 pounder AP, 2,052 smoke dischargers, 10,500 HMG 0.50-inch rounds and 542,000 rounds of 0.303-inch SAA.[23] Fuel consumption was a concern, the road move eating into the 75 mile reserve carried by the ABC petrol section at 2nd and 3rd Line, an issue complicated by the introduction to the brigade of the A12 Matilda II, which was powered by a compression ignition engine, thus requiring the distribution of diesel to 7 RTR, which initially held all these tanks but later also to 4 RTR when the ORBAT was adjusted by Brigadier Pratt[24] to meet the tactical dynamics of the operations. This example exposes the increasing complexity of logistic support to dispersed armoured formations using a mix of vehicles, equipment and weapons,[25] but the challenges of effectively executing the tasks was sometimes obfuscated by HQ I Corps, to which the brigade was attached, obviating the brigade HQ and issuing orders directly to the tank battalions.[26]

The role of WMT and particularly the RASC Troop Carrying Companies (TCC) in generating increased infantry mobility and combat capability was central to the deployment of the BEF to the River Dyle, the concept being the subject of a detailed analysis by Major Lockhart RA in an *Army Quarterly* article of 1937,[27] based upon the completion of a divisional move of 42 miles in 16 hours, although whether this focused piece of work influenced the development

18 At one point, the three Scammell Tractor 6x4 wheeled recovery vehicles of the brigade workshop were tasked with moving 30 failed tanks. Ibid.

19 77 x A11 and 23 x A12. Blagden Memorandum.

20 58 x A11 and 16 x A12. Liddell Hart, *The Tanks*, p.11.

21 For summaries of this action on 21 May 1940, see, Ellis, BOH, *The War in France and Flanders,* pp.87-96 and Hugh Sebag-Montefiore, *Dunkirk, Fight To the Last Man* (London: Viking, 2006), pp.142-145. For a focus on the operations of 1st Armoured Brigade, see, Philson, BEFORBAT, Vol 5, pp.44-45.

22 TNA WO 167/414: HQ 1st Army Tank Brigade, WD, May 1940.

23 Philson, BEFORBAT, Vol 1, p.42.

24 Douglas Henry Pratt (1892-1958) CB DSO MC was commissioned into the Royal Irish Regiment in 1911, serving initially in India and then in France. Transferring to the Tank Corps in 1916, he was awarded the DSO, MC and received three 3 MIDs before the end of the Great War. An Army Staff College student (1923-1924) he was an exchange officer at the Australian RMC Duntroon (1931-1933), commanding 2 RTR (1936-1937) before his appointment as Assistant Director of Mechanization in 1938. Promoted to the rank as Major-General AFVs in Washington, he became Deputy Director British Supply Mission in the USA, retiring from the Army in 1946.

25 The role of the logisticians in supporting 1st Armoured Brigade operations during the campaign in France deserve further study.

26 Account of 1st Armoured Brigade Commander in Liddell Hart, *The Tanks,* p.11.

27 Major L K Lockhart MBE MC RA, 'Movement of a Division by Mechanical Transport', *The Army Quarterly*, Vol XXXIV, April-July 1937, pp.98-106.

P16.1 Thornycroft Workshop lorry interior. Repair of combat platforms, logistic vehicles, weapons and a wide range of equipment was critical to BEF operational capability. (RLCM: A1/MT/RLCA/20526)

of Plan D is unknown.[28] There were two key concerns identified by the author.[29] First, the impact of an adverse air scenario and thus a concomitant potential reversion to a night move that reduced speeds to 9 miles in the hour (mih) resulting in the division being unable to complete the operation even during December with 16 hours of darkness, without using two main deployment routes and two TCCs.[30] Given that Plan D involved distances, which were more than twice the 42 miles assessed by Lockhart and the move was conducted in May, then the significant challenges become clear. Secondly, Lockhart exposed the crucial role traffic control played in managing the move of the 2,166 prime movers in an infantry division, which even based on the maximum density of 50 vehicles to the mile (vtm),[31] and no tactical unit spacing, occupied over 43 miles of 'road space',[32] although for planning purposes 'road time' was the dominant factor,[33] an issue

28 Lockhart focused upon the creation of the most effective combat output from the move.

29 Leslie Keith Lockhart (1897-1966) served on the Western Front in the Great War being awarded the MC. He attended the Army Staff College (1932-1934), serving in the War Office (1939-1940) as a GSO 2 and GSO 1 before promotion to Colonel on the British Army Staff Washington (1940-1942). He returned to the War Office (1942-1943) as Deputy Director RA, then commanded AA Brigades in NW Europe (1944-1945), receiving a CBE in 1946. Promoted to Major-General in 1947, he commanded 5 AA Group, being awarded a CB in 1949, then held the post of GOC East Anglian District (1951-1952) before retiring in 1952.

30 Lockhart MBE MC RA, 'Movement of a Division by Mechanical Transport', *The Army Quarterly*, Vol XXXIV, April - July 1937, p.105.

31 The 50 vtm was the normal planning maximum in order to accommodate the passage of long bridges. 20 vtm was assessed to reduce the effecting of strafing and bombing from aerial attack, whilst 5 vtm was expected to have a high chance of avoiding attention from the enemy; although movement at a density of 5 vtm would result in a division occupying over 433 miles of road space. See, Army Council, FSPB, Pamphlet No 6, 1939, *Mechanized Movement by Road*.

32 The key vehicles occupying the road-space were the 1,812 trucks, lorries, tractors and ambulances, 216 tracked vehicles and 138 cars.

33 Road-time was the length of time a unit occupied a section of road to complete a specified distance. Lockhart, 'Movement of a Division by Mechanical Transport', *The Army Quarterly*, Vol XXXIV, April

complicated by the sustainable speed dissonance between tracked and wheeled vehicles. These assessments led Lockhart to firmly state that the allocated traffic control resource, the Divisional Provost Company, was 'totally inadequate' to conduct the operation in war.[34]

Vulnerable to Enemy Bombing

Most of the BEF's RASC TCCs were committed to supporting the transport of I and II Corps infantry units to the River Dyle, leaving 5th Infantry Division mostly reliant upon unit WMT and the marching power of the infantryman's legs, which, whilst part of the soldiers' lot inevitably reduced the speed of deployment and combat power in battle and clearly reinforced the significance of this vital logistic asset. The move of 143rd Infantry Brigade, tasked to conduct route protection duties for I Corps, reinforced this point when on 10 May, 9 TCC was several hours late in reaching unit lines, resulting in the three battalions[35] not reaching the operational positions until almost midnight.[36] 2 TCC RASC assisted in the deployment of 5th Division from Le Harve to the concentration area at Estaires and 8 Reserve MT Company RASC[37] from Estaires to Hal on the River Senne but some of the infantry battalions, had a very tiring march in the May heat against an almost overwhelming flood of Belgian refugees. 2nd Northamptons[38] of 17th Infantry Brigade marched 25 miles from Camps-en-Ameinnois to Bernaville on 11 May, then 12 miles to Ligny-sur-Cache on the next day followed by 13 miles on 15 May arriving at Hernicourt on the afternoon of the 16th and Mekinghem on the morning of 17 May.[39]

On 18 May, 17th Brigade was ordered to withdraw, with the battalions planned to be lifted by 60 RASC lorries from 5 Division Ammunition Company (DAC)[40] and 5 Division Petrol Company (DPC).[41] Unfortunately, despite an additional 10 x 3 tonners from 9 Reserve MT Company being attached to 5 DAC[42], only 24 vehicles were available, so battalions were ordered to march.[43] At approximately 0130 on 19 May, with battalions *en-route* both on foot and using unit WMT, the arriving RASC vehicles arrived in the dark from the opposite direction, causing a traffic jam of monumental proportions, which took over two hours to resolve, the imperative being to clear it before first-light and the potential arrival of the *Luftwaffe*.[44] In the Base however, apart from an increase in the defence alert state and the tempo of out-loading, military life had more than a peace-time feel to it. On 12 May, 2 Base Supply Depot (BSD)

- July 1937, p.102.
34 Ibid, pp.105-106.
35 1st Ox & Bucks, 1/7th Warwicks and 8th Warwicks.
36 TNA CAB 44/67: The BEF in Belgium and Artois, 10 May - 3 June 1940, entry 10 May 1940.
37 TNA WO 167/1092: 8 Reserve MT Company RASC, WD, May 1940.
38 Jervois, *The History of the Northamptonshire Regiment, 1934-1948*, p.55.
39 George Aris, *The Fifth British Division, Being an account of the Journey and Battles of a Reserve Division in Europe, Africa and Asia* (London: The Fifth Division Benevolent Fund, 1959), p.28.
40 TNA WO 167/250: 5 DAC RASC, WD.
41 TNA WO 167/250: 5 DAC RASC, WD.
42 80 Company RASC.
43 Jervois, *The History of the Northamptonshire Regiment, 1934-1948*, p.56.
44 The Northamptons' regimental history recorded that; 'the congested road would have been very vulnerable to enemy bombing'. Ibid, p.56.

lost 3-13 at Rugby football to 4th Borders but regained their spurs on 15 May with a 2-1 win in an Association game after a 'hard struggle' against a 'clever team' from the same battalion.[45] There can be little doubt that their weary infantry and logistic comrades engaged in combat would have much preferred to have been participating in similar competitions but from the perspective of BEF morale, it was fortunate they remained unaware of the sporting prowess and entertainment facilities on-going in the Base.[46] It was not however, all play at 2 BSD because the commencement of German offensive operations quickly fired the Base tempo, with for example, 2 BSD dispatching on 24 May, 44 rail wagons of supplies, consisting mainly of potatoes, a cargo which must have required much manual labour to load, in addition to 320,000 preserved rations,[47] although with the cut in the GLOC many of these loaded wagons were returned to the depot.[48]

As part of the logistic lay-down to support Plan D, reserves of ammunition, fuel and supplies were in-loaded to advanced railheads and areas to the East of Tournai but sites in this location proved to be vulnerable to aerial attack and were drawn down. Some of the explosives and ammunition were out-loaded to 2nd Division to support the defence of the Dyle Line, the former enabling the demolition of bridges across the river and the latter ensuring D Company 2nd Durham Light Infantry had sufficient ammunition and grenades for Second-Lieutenant Dickie Annand[49] and his platoon to delay the Germans crossing the demolished bridge at Gastouche on 15-16 May, an action for which he was awarded the Victoria Cross.[50] This operation also lucidly demonstrated the level of logistics that were required to support intense combat because in two hours the company expended 20,000 rounds of 0.303-inch SAA and 100 grenades.[51] As the alternative solution, combat supplies were held on rail wagons North of the Somme as *En-Cas Mobile* (ECM), and 1 BAD continued to out-load these trains until 22 May.[52] This arrangement was not entirely satisfactory because not all the trains arrived at the nominated railheads as a result of *Luftwaffe* air interdiction. This focused upon major railway stations and junctions,[53] although the later selection of railheads at minor countryside stations,

45 TNA WO 167/1116: 2 BSD RASC, WD, May 1940. Driver Johnson scored the sole 2 BSD try in the rugby match.

46 On 18 May 1940 the members of 2 BSD were entertained at a concert party by the 'Strolling Players'. TNA WO 167/1116: 2 BSD RASC, WD, May 1940.

47 Of this total, 120,000 were dispatched to the I Corps SRH, 120,000 to the II Corps SRH and 80,000 to GHQ Troops. TNA WO 167/1116: 2 BSD RASC, WD, May 1940.

48 TNA WO 167/1116: 2 BSD RASC, WD, May 1940.

49 Dickie Annand's Armed Services career began in 1933 when he joined the Royal Navy Volunteer Reserve, with the intention of entering the Royal Navy but was rejected through age in 1937 and he was commissioned into the DLI as a Supplementary Reservist in 1938.

50 David Rissik, *The DLI at War, The History of the Durham Light Infantry, 1939-1945* (Durham: The Depot, nd but 1952), pp.14-15 and TNA WO 98/8/717: Victoria Cross details for Annand. Although wounded, he returned to the UK but suffered hearing loss to the point where further operational service was impossible and he served in training and staff appointments. Invalided from the Army in 1948, he devoted much of his time to assisting the disabled, but his courage came to the fore again in February 1979, when, aged 64 he saved his wife, Shirley, from drowning in the River Tyne. Dickie Annand died aged 90 on Christmas Eve 2004.

51 Rissik, *The DLI at War*, p.14.

52 TNA WO 167/1175/2, 1 BAD RAOC, WD, 22 May 1940. These trains were named Ammunition Section ECM (ASE).

53 TNA WO 197/112: Movement & Maintenance in the BEF, p.3.

P16.2 Logistic Success. Site of the successful delaying action by 2nd DLI on the River Dyle at Gastuche Belgium, which was enabled by sufficient ammunition and explosives. Photograph taken in May 2019. (Author)

whilst not doctrinally pure, attracted much less enemy interest,[54] lucidly demonstrating that the BEF's logisticians were quick to learn and adapt. The key BEF rail route through Tournai was not cut but damage to the network elsewhere led to diverted French military traffic delaying BEF trains and using routes GHQ expected would be allocated solely to the BEF.[55] The dumps at the advanced railheads however, proved most useful during the withdrawal from the River Dyle to the River Escaut and the three corps were adequately sustained.[56]

Divisional RASC units commenced ammunition and POL dumping programmes in brigade rear areas on 13 May[57] and the next day, 2 DAC began in-loading anti-tank mines to enable 2nd Division RE to reinforce the River Dyle defence line,[58] whilst 2 Division Supply Column (DSC) issued units one day of preserved rations as a reserve,[59] although tasks were interrupted for a period whilst logistic units adjusted their Anti-Gas Measures posture upon receipt of a message that indicated that a German gas attack on the Western Front was believed to be imminent'.[60] More disruption was caused by the failure to ensure the issued maps of Belgium reflected the

54 TNA WO 197/112: Movement & Maintenance in the BEF, p.3.
55 TNA WO 197/112: Movement & Maintenance in the BEF, p.3.
56 TNA WO 197/112: Movement & Maintenance in the BEF, p.4.
57 TNA WO 197/210: 2 Division CRASC, WD, 13 May 1940.
58 TNA WO 197/210: 2 Division CRASC, WD, 14 May 1940.
59 TNA WO 197/210: 2 Division CRASC, WD, 14 May 1940.
60 TNA WO 197/210: 2 Division CRASC, WD, 14 May 1940.

existing routes, 2 Division CRASC war diary[61] recording that they were 'out of date and most inaccurate',[62] an issue that affected nearly all corps and divisional logistic units, which reinforced the importance of motor-cycles for reconnaissance.[63] On 18 May, the CRASC[64] attended a conference at HQ 2nd Division, reporting to his sub-unit commanders that the operational situation was 'still obscure',[65] whilst on 20 May CRASC was advised by the HQ 2nd Division Q Staff that no more ammunition, petrol or supply trains would arrive for 'at least four days', which initiated a series of operations by the sub-units to secure ammunition, petrol and rations from dumps and local sources,[66] at which point, commanders may have begun to remember a most pertinent quote in a British Army logistic handbook: 'Men without weapons and food, guns without ammunition, tanks without petrol, are useless encumbrances to an army in the field'.[67] Whilst the RASC engaged in an urgent search for combat supplies 18 Field Park Company RE in a rather different logistic operation, took over a barbed wire factory at Sweyeghem order to supply 100 tons a day to the BEF.[68]

Final Cut

When 2nd Panzer Division reached the Channel Coast, having seized Abbeville on 20 May 1940,[69] a catastrophic disaster befell the BEF in France.[70] Not only was it separated from the

61 The 2 Division CRASC war diary is a lucid and informative document, which touches upon relevant unit detail, whilst ensuring the actions of the divisional RASC are embedded to the wider operational and logistic picture. Between 1-21 May the war diary is written in light blue ink but has water damage to the top half of each page, which in a few places renders the script impossible to read. From 22 May, the scribe writes in pencil; presumably, the Adjutant could not obtain further supplies of ink. TNA WO 197/210: 2 Division CRASC, WD, 1-21 May 1940.

62 TNA WO 197210: 2 Division CRASC, WD, 16 May 1940. The WD continued: 'Some rds bear no relation to those printed on the maps and this is in spite of the fact that maps produced by OS at Southampton in 1938.'

63 Army Council, *Army Training Memorandum* No 34, July 1940, Appx G, Lessons from Experience for the RASC, p.24.

64 Lieutenant-Colonel Cecil Montague Clavell Luff was born in 1898 and attend the Royal Military College Sandhurst before commissioning into the Army Service Corps, deploying to France in August 1916, being attached to the Dorset Regiment for a period in 1917. He commanded the divisional RASC throughout the campaign in France and was still CRASC when 2nd Division deployed to India in April 1942, promoting to Temporary Colonel as DDST XXXIII Corps in Burma and being gazetted as an Acting Brigadier in 1946. *Supplement to London Gazette*, 28 November 1946, p.5833. He was awarded the OBE for his services in Burma. TNA WO 373/80/183: Recommendation for Award for Luff. His seven medal group was sold at auction by Dix Noonan Webb of Mayfair on 19 September 2013.

65 TNA WO 197/210: 2 Division CRASC, WD, 18 May 1940.

66 TNA WO 197/210: 2 Division CRASC, WD, 20 May 1940.

67 Lindsell, *A&Q, or Administration in the Field*, p.7.

68 TNA CAB 44/67: The BEF in Belgium and Artois, 10 May - 3 June 1940, entry 19 May 1940.

69 Ellis, BOH, *The War in France and Flanders,* p.85 and Situation Map facing p.86.

70 In 1938 Brevet Lieutenant-Colonel Donald Portway, Senior Tutor in engineering of Saint Catharine's College and CO Cambridge University Officers' Training Corps, wrote a most prescient statement, relating to the British Army's operational organization: 'Even in the handy and more mobile form that is the product of recent changes, infantry divisions are liable to be pinned to the ground by a mechanised enemy with the ever present dangers inherent in belts of persistent gas, raids on communications by air

main group of French Armies to the South of the River Somme but also more significantly for its survival, the Germans cut the GLOC.[71] In 10 days, the German Army had not only conquered a large area of Northern France, but they had rendered the Continental Army of France's main ally, incapable of effectively supporting its fighting forces. Whether the layout of the GLOC affected the German plan for their ground offensive is difficult to quantify but given their plan to drive to the coast and split the Allied Armies in two, *Oberkommando des Heeres* (OKH) must have appreciated the effect it would have on the logistic sustainability of those forces. The German attack in March 1918 was also designed to drive a wedge to the coast but because the British GLOC was run from the French Channel Ports there was never much of a possibility that they could have cut it; the BEF of the day intended to fall back along its GLOC. 1940 however, was very different and by 19 May, it was clear to General Gort that the BEF was in a perilous situation: '.......the administrative situation made it unlikely that sustained operations could be undertaken. Communication with the bases was on the point of being interrupted. The mobile echelons of gun and small arms ammunition were full, but once they were exhausted I could not safely reckon on being able to replenish them'.[72] The BOH summary of the position is more succinct: 'The British Expeditionary Force was outflanked and the sensitive lines of communication on which its life depended stretched out, practically undefended, across the path of the German armour."[73]

Gort was now in the unenviable position of having his ORBAT determined by the enemy, for the BEF now consisted of two armies; one to the North of the Somme and one to the South. The former, with the bulk of the fighting formations, had little coherent logistic support beyond 2nd and 3rd Line assets, whilst the latter consisted mainly of 4th Line Base and GLOC units. The GLOC combat formations, with vary levels of capability, included the deploying 1st Armoured Division,[74] less two infantry battalions and 3rd Royal Tank Regiment, sent to defend Calais,[75] and 51st (Highland) Division re-deploying on a 400 mile journey by rail and road from the Saar,[76] having undertaken fortress duties in the *Maginot* Line, with 52nd (Lowland) Division[77] and a brigade group of the 1st Canadian Division arriving from the UK in early June. In addition, there were the poorly equipped and trained 12th (Eastern)[78] and 46th (North Midland)[79] Divisions, plus three un-brigaded infantry battalions and manpower from reinforcement depots providing assets to create the *ad hoc* Beauman Division.[80]

The reorganization of these forces is a remarkable story. When the GLOC was cut there were approximately 229,300 troops in the Northern element and 113,000 in the area South of

action and tank formations ...' David Portway, *Science and Mechanisation in Land Warfare* (Cambridge: W Heffer & Sons Ltd, 1938), p.51.

71 Map 13: BEF: Break in the Ground Line of Communication.
72 *WOOH, Maintenance in the Field*, Vol, I, p.53.
73 Ellis, BOH, *The War in France and Flanders*, p.74.
74 TNA WO 32/9392: Operations of 1st Armoured Division in France.
75 Fletcher, 'The White Rhino's Baptism of Fire, 1st Armoured Division in France', 1940, *Military Illustrated 86*, (July 1995), pp.36-38.
76 TNA WO 167/315: 51st Division AQ, WD, May 1940.
77 TNA WO 167/327: 52nd Division AQ, WD, June 1940.
78 TNA WO 167/259: 12 (Eastern) Division, CRASC, WD, May - June 1940.
79 TNA WO 167/286: 46th (North Midland & West Riding) Division, GS, WD, May - June 1940.
80 TNA WO 167/1413: Beauman Division, Q, WD, June 1940.

the Somme,[81] although this increased to 180,000 by 30 May as other formations were taken on strength for support but not necessarily under command for operations, reducing to 125,000 as the withdrawal commenced. Once it became clear that the GLOC had been irretrievably cut, commanders and Staff at the highest level reacted quickly to the situation. The War Office took over responsibility for supporting the BEF in North-East France and Belgium, whilst the forces deployed to the South of the Somme were initially placed under Commander L of C Area until 23 May, when a newly appointed GOC, Lieutenant-General Karslake,[82] arrived in theatre,[83] GHQ BEF then ceased to control the GLOC, although for various reasons Karslake's command status was never ratified and most of the formations were under French command at some time.

A New Line of Communication?

Although on 19 May, road and rail communications to Abbeville were intact, Gort's appreciation was that German forces would cut the GLOC within 24 hours leaving one of three options: restore the GLOC, create a new GLOC or evacuate the force. The experience of 1914-1918 remained a powerful influence upon British military thinking, the first instinct of the Chief of the Imperial General Staff, General Ironside, being to direct Gort to immediately withdraw South-West through the Arras-Bethune area in order to restore the GLOC and thus continue operations in conformity with the French.[84] This intent was, remarkably, clearly expressed to the logisticians on the GLOC, the war diary of LOC DDST, noting that all RASC transport not employed on essential services was to be collected in the vicinity of Rouen to be available 'at short notice to carry ammunition, supplies and petrol to Corps as soon as breakthrough is obtained'.[85] By 25 May the size of the transport requirement had matured to 800 x 3 ton lorries to deliver one day's maintenance to the three corps of the BEF,[86] a figure highlighting the key role of the railway to military logistics. The operational realities however, dictated an alternative course and the QMG to the BEF, Lieutenant-General Lindsell was effectively faced with making the same decision as the QMG to the BEF in 1914, Wully Robertson, in creating a new GLOC.[87]

On 19 May, he therefore requested the War Office to open an emergency base served by the French Northern Channel Ports (NCP) of Boulogne, Calais and Dunkerque, the decision

81 Regimental Committee, p.67.
82 Lieutenant-General Sir Henry Karslake (1879-1942) KCB KCSI CB CMG DSO was commissioned into the Royal Artillery in 1898 serving in South Africa during the Second Boer War and being awarded the DSO. He served on the Staff in France during the Great War before spending most of his post-war career in India, retiring from the Army in 1938.
83 TNA CAB 44/67: The BEF in Belgium and Artois, 10 May - 3 June 1940, entry 22 May 1940.
84 Ellis, BOH, *The War in France and Flanders*, p.84.
85 TNA WO 167/1077: LOC DDST, WD, 24 May 1940.
86 TNA WO 167/1077: LOC DDST, WD, 25 May 1940.
87 The criticality of ensuring the BEF retained the ability to fall back along its GLOC had been tested in 1914 when the BEF's QMG Wully Robertson faced with the force being divorced from it whilst conforming with French strategic direction had solved this conundrum by directing that the Base be relocated. See, Maginniss, *An Unappreciated Field of Endeavour*, pp.159-163.

being taken on 21 May,[88] although on 20 May, the BEF's AQMG, Lieutenant-Colonel Hewer travelled by air to the UK for a meeting at the War Office to discuss arrangements for a possible evacuation, a proposal initially rejected.[89] Whether these two GHQ approaches were the result of assessed contingency planning or a conceptual dissonance within the HQ is difficult to define from the documents. Either way, the NCP option was the only effective solution to maintain or evacuate the BEF in the North and the logisticians applied their industry and talent to creating a GLOC from the facilities and units that were *in-situ*.[90] A Base Sub-Area HQ was established in Dunkerque, located with a GHQ QMG Staff Section, both of which were closely integrated to the British and French naval authorities,[91] whilst the Army logisticians, Royal Navy and Merchant Marine demonstrated the ability to not only 'hot' plan but also deliver and support *ad hoc* forces to France.

Upon the direction of the War Office, 3 BSD at Le Harve had loaded 2,500 tons of general supplies to the SS *Belgravian*,[92] the ship sailing for Boulogne on 21 May.[93] 20th Guards Brigade deployed as a protection force to the port on 22 May, the disembarkation being delayed by military evacuees crowding the quays, whilst discharge had mostly to be undertaken by hand because power to the dock cranes had failed.[94] To protect logistic operations in Calais elements of 30th Brigade also began landing the same day.[95] The work to create this new GLOC has, understandably, been completely overshadowed by the later evacuation from Dunkerque but it is clear that given different operational conditions there are strong reasons to suggest that it was a sustainable solution, although there were several key enablers identified by the BEF QMG Staff planners, without which, failure was considered inevitable. These included: effective active air defence measures by the RAF and Army AA units;[96] each port being able to handle 1,000 tons *per diem* and be supported by rail and road out-load capacity; sufficient supplies being delivered to sustain Belgian and French forces and feed the civilian population.[97] These were certainly tall orders and from the logistic perspective, operations were assessed to be achievable provided

88 TNA CAB 120/247: British Expeditionary Force: Lord Gort's Despatches, p.5919.

89 TNA WO 197/115: Notes on the Operations in France between 10-31 May 1940 from a Movement Point of View, nd.

90 TNA WO 197/74: A Brief Summary of the Administrative Situation of the BEF - 22 May 1940.

91 TNA CAB 44/67: The BEF in Belgium and Artois, 10 May - 3 June 1940, entry 22 May 1940.

92 The SS *Belgravian* was an Ellerman Lines cargo ship of 3,136 GRT launched in 1937. The *Belgravian* was taken up from trade in October 1939 to support the BEF and participated in Operations CYCLE and AERIAL. She was sunk by a torpedo from U-372 on 5 August 1941 when voyaging from Port Harcourt and Freetown for Hull with a cargo of 3,534 tons of kernels and groundnuts, and 412 tons of tin ore. Admiralty, *British Merchant Vessels Lost or Damaged by Enemy Action*, p.25.

93 TNA WO 167/1077: LOC DDST, WD, 24 May 1940.

94 For a summary of operations, see, Philson, BEFORBAT, Vol 5, pp.93-95. 20th Guards Brigade comprised, 2nd Welsh Guards, 2nd Irish Guards and 5th Loyals.

95 For a summary of operations, see Ibid, pp.96-98. 30th Infantry Brigade comprised two motor battalions, 1st Rifle Brigade and 2nd King's Royal Rifle Corps plus 1st Queen Victoria's Rifles and the divisional motor-cycle battalion of 1st (London) Division.

96 TNA CAB 44/67: The BEF in Belgium and Artois, 10 May - 3 June 1940, entry 23 May 1940.

97 TNA WO 197/74: Administrative Situation of the BEF and TNA CAB 44/67: The BEF in Belgium and Artois, 10 May - 3 June 1940, entry 22 May 1940.

P16.3 Known unto God. An unusual part of the BEF story. This unknown Royal Naval sailor lies At Rest in Wavre Communal Cemetery and is believed to be a casualty of Operation ROYAL MARINE which involved the rail movement of floating mines from Fecamp to place into the River Rhine. Photograph taken in May 2019. (Author)

that German artillery was kept out of range of the ports and installations and the offensive elements of the *Luftwaffe* kept at bay.[98]

The viability of the railways was critical to NCP out-loading, and although traffic had been significantly disrupted by the evacuation of stock, SNCF was confident that sufficient capacity to work BEF and French military trains would be restored by 24 May.[99] That the SNCF was capable of continuing to function in such chaotic conditions is testament to the courage of its people, resilience of its infrastructure and the flexibility of its systems. The BEF QMG Staff calculated that the Force would require *per diem*, 400 tons of supplies, 1,000 tons of ammunition and 600 tons of petrol, a level of imports that would leave flexibility for disruption and a reserve to assist in sustaining French and Belgian forces and support civilian feeding.[100] On 22 May, GHQ QMG sent a telegram to the QMG at the War Office pressing for swift action: 'No railway line for supply of BEF or 1st French Army now remains open.[101] About one day's supplies and 100 rpg ammn in hand. Essential to push ammn supplies and petrol through BOULOGNE CALAIS DUNKIRK. To make this possible adequate air protection of ports must be provided'.[102] At 2010 on 23 May, Gort reinforced the rapidly deteriorating logistic situation in a personal telegram to the Secretary of State for War, offering a gloomy summary of the maintenance situation, exposing not only the absolute need for effective air defence of the ports, but also a request from the Belgians for logistic support:

98 TNA WO 197/74: Administrative Situation of the BEF.
99 TNA WO 197/74: Administrative Situation of the BEF.
100 TNA WO 197/74: Administrative Situation of the BEF. Ammunition requirements were based on 35 rpgpd for artillery and for petrol on 60 tons *per diem* per division.
101 This point refers to rail communications from the Base areas and not within the Northern Allied perimeter.
102 TNA CAB 44/67: The BEF in Belgium and Artois, 10 May - 3 June 1940, entry 22 May 1940.

P16.4 Bray Beach 2019. A poignant moment in time. Almost impossible to believe that this is the site of such dramatic logistic action in 1940. (Author)

> Ammunition very little now available in excess of echelons. Railways and docks seriously damaged by bombing and capacity to receive stores much reduced. Belgian army also in very bad state for supplies and asks us to supply 400,000 rations daily, which I am unable to do. No equipment replacements now available. Consider adequate maintenance impossible unless sufficient air protection can be provided for ports.[103]

On 24 May 1940, CIGS replied:

> First essential, you retain in Dunkirk all personnel who may possibly be of value in working the port and getting stores forward as labour or in any other capacity. Secondly, equally essential, you retain all fighting personnel. If you have personnel other than the above, you are at liberty to evacuate to UK under strict control by such ships as may be available. The AA defences were reinforced by 85 HAA Regt, less 220

103 TNA CAB 44/67: The BEF in Belgium and Artois, 10 May - 3 June 1940, entry 23 May 1940.

Bty, (16 x 3.7 inch guns), 60 HAA Regt (12 x 3 inch guns) and 51 LAA Regt, less 1/2 tp to 151 Bty (15 Bofors).[104]

What was missing from these communications was the importance of creating a coherent air defence capability, including UK and French GBAD and aerial fighter capability from the British and French air forces.

Down at the Beach

The War Office was in effect one step ahead of GHQ because in the period 23-24 May, 4,200 tons of supplies, 2,900 tons of ammunition and 1,100 tons of cased petrol were directed to arrive at the NCP and although the petrol shipments were temporarily suspended, this plan still exceeded the capacity of the ports.[105] On the evening of 18 May the War Office QMG Branch ordered Supplies & Transport (ST) 6 to prepare rations to be loaded to three ships to act as an ECM reserve to be deployed as required. Recognizing that delivery of the BEF Field Service Ration Scale was unsustainable, ST 6 initiated Special Scale E,[106] the items of which were loaded to the first ship in bulk. ST 6 however, immediately decided that a 'pack' solution was tactically and logistically more resilient and effective, thus greatly increasing the chances of ensuring a balanced ration being issued to the Soldier.[107] Stocks were embarked to ships at 1 Supply Reserve Depot (SRD) Deptford wharf, whilst trains were loaded at 2 SRD at Barry in South Wales ready for dispatch to Dover, Littlehampton, Newhaven and Southampton. Soldiers from a Supply Personnel Section were sent to these ports to form RASC Port Detachments, whilst the Embarkation Supply Depot at Southampton came in 'for more than its usual customary hard labour'.[108] The net tonnage of supplies delivered to the BEF from the SRDs via this scheme was 6,500.

At sea, lighters brought to evacuate troops, arrived on the beaches loaded with ammunition, rations and water, so the RASC could establish dumps above the High Water mark.[109] POL was much less of a problem because there were considerable stocks of packed and bulk spirit in storage areas and filling centres, whilst supply requests diminished as the BEF withdrew, and then destroyed many of its vehicles. As a precaution however, ST 6 earmarked cased POL supplies for continental deployment, loading some to ECM ships commencing 19 May,

104 Telegram No 7 1905, CIGS to Commander Dunkirk dated 24 May 1940 in TNA CAB 44/67: The BEF in Belgium and Artois, 10 May - 3 June 1940.

105 TNA WO 197/74: Administrative Situation of the BEF and TNA CAB 44/67: The BEF in Belgium and Artois, 10 May - 3 June 1940, entry 22 May 1940.

106 The daily ration per man comprised: 12 oz preserved meat, 12 oz biscuit, and in tins, 2 oz sugar, 2 oz condensed milk, 2 oz cheese, 2 oz jam, 2 oz eating chocolate with supplements and alternatives including cigarettes, matches, rum, salmon and meat loaf. WOOH, *Supplies and Transport*, Vol II, Appx IX/4, p.436.

107 TNA WO 197/134: Evacuation from France and Quartering of the BEF - Activities of DST in the Evacuation from France.

108 TNA WO 197/134: Evacuation from France and Quartering of the BEF - Activities of DST in the Evacuation from France.

109 One such sailing barge was the *Barbara Jean* from Ipswich, which was towed across the Channel on 31 May by the tug *Fairplay One* and positioned on the beach at Bray Dunes, where she was unloaded and then abandoned. Winser, *BEF Ships*, p.33, p.103 & p.109.

and in anticipation of further short notice orders, in-loaded stocks to Blandford for immediate dispatch to Poole and Southampton.[110] One of these ECM small coasters, the MV *Spinel*, was dispatched to Dunkerque loaded with cased petrol[111] but was abandoned in the harbour when fires in the docks precluded discharge from the vessel.[112] Of greater import was the supply of water, a problem exacerbated when the civil purification plant in Dunkerque was rendered inoperative by aerial bombing.[113] Whilst there was access to canned supplies held in units, DSCs and a few supply trains scattered around the area held by the BEF and in small quantities from village sources, it was clear to the logisticians that water might become a defining factor in the outcome of operations and considerable effort was devoted to delivering this precious liquid in returnable 4 and 2-gallon petrol tins.[114] 80,000 x 4-gallon cans were issued and 40,000 x 2-gallon, of which 24,000 and 37,500 respectively were written off from account through enemy action or operating loss.[115]

The planners estimated that the Force would initially require 2,000 tonnes of stocks per day and given the availability of the ports, this would have been easily sustainable but as their capacities rapidly declined through enemy action, support became more difficult and soon impossible.[116] The imminent fall of Boulogne and Calais prompted, on 24 May, a GHQ AQMG reconnaissance of two Belgian ports, but operating issues and the aerial and ground tactical situations prevented development of these options,[117] leaving Dunkerque as the sole port to sustain the BEF and to evacuate units and personnel no longer essential to the operation. An ammunition ship arrived on 24 May and the providential arrival of the ARH Detachments from the corps railheads at Ecoust-sur-Mein and Aubigny provided the technical personnel to identify the natures in the holds. Unfortunately, the vessel had not been tactically loaded and the ammunition components needed to be matched before the munitions could be distributed to Corps Ammunition Parks, a task impossible on the quayside. Inevitably, during the transfer of the cargo to a less vulnerable location, some items went astray, thus rendering some of the ammunition unserviceable.[118]

Trains continued to be loaded at and dispatched from the port of Dunkerque until 25 May and although most of them did not reach the intended destinations, un-loading at alternative

110 TNA WO 197/112: Movement and Maintenance in the BEF.

111 Winser, *BEF Ships*, p.13.

112 MV *Spinel* was later sunk by an aerial bomb but was salvaged by the Germans. Admiralty, *British Merchant Vessels Lost or Damaged by Enemy Action*, p.5.

113 TNA WO 197/112: Movement and Maintenance in the BEF.

114 The assumption is that they were new cans. There appear to be no references in the files consulted, to contamination of water by petrol from water issued from UK, nor any observations relating to decontamination of cans for use as water carriers.

115 TNA WO 197/134: Evacuation from France and Quartering of the BEF - Activities of DST in the Evacuation from France.

116 TNA CAB 44/67: The BEF in Belgium and Artois, 10 May - 3 June 1940, entry 22 May 1940.

117 At Ostend there was only one small ship carrying food for Belgian refugees, but discharge had ceased after a bombing raid, whilst at Nieuport the nature of the harbour restricted operations to small ships entering and departing at High Water only. In addition, the reconnaissance team discovered the harbour congested with barges. At neither location was any Belgian GBAD in place. TNA WO 197/115: Notes on the Operations in France between 10-31 May 1940 from a Movement Point of View, nd.

118 Fernyhough & Harris, *History of the RAOC, 1939-1945*, p.95.

P16.5 Exposed. Looking WSW towards Dunkerque on the beach horizon, showing how exposed any logistic operations were between the water's edge to the Dunes and the buildings, both from the enemy and the weather. (Author)

railheads enabled combat formations to draw ammunition, fuel and rations,[119] an achievement which clearly exposed the amazing courage and commitment of some of the SNCF train crews. The rail out-load was supported by road using 2 LOC Railhead Company RASC,[120] although movement was greatly impeded by refugees,[121] a feature of the campaign that not only introduced immense friction to movement but whose plight not only touched the hearts of British soldiers

119 TNA WO 197/112: Movement and Maintenance in the BEF.

120 TNA WO 197/112: Movement and Maintenance in the BEF. The war diary for 2 LOC Railhead MT Company for May 1940 was lost during the evacuation; TNA WO 167/1096.

121 The influence of refugees, especially upon military movement and soldiers is a regular feature of many unit war diaries and PORs. The After Action Report (AAR) produced by the Bartholomew Committee, highlighted the importance of ensuring the effective execution of a 'Refugee Plan' preferably in conjunction with the Host Nation and was deemed of such significance that the AAR contained a separate annex on the subject. Para 7 of the annex noted that: 'In the final withdrawal to the coast refugee traffic had largely stopped, the inhabitants realising there was nowhere safe for them to go'. The caveat is 'largely stopped' as RASC war diaries in particular, noted civilian movement impeding military activity. See TNA WO 106/1775: Bartholomew Committee – Report on lessons to be learnt from operations in Flanders; evidence, report and action arising, paragraph, 27 and Annex A, Refugees. See also, Gun Buster, *Return via Dunkirk*, p.135 highlighting the paucity of a coherent Host Nation civil support services.

and also sometimes caused immense emotional distress.[122] This situation probably accounts for the 2 Division CRASC observation that 'The system of road loads as visualised never functioned properly in fact practically no sups came through DUNKIRK'.[123] By 26 May, the damage caused to the dock, road and rail infrastructure by air attack[124] was such that all British military logistic operations in the port ceased,[125] supplies, including ammunition, rations and water, were thereafter landed on the beaches using barges and lighters.[126] On the same day, orders were issued for the BEF to withdraw to the coast to ports East of Gravelines, in order to evacuate to the UK.[127] The level of destruction wrought to the transportation and storage infrastructure in the port and surrounds of Dunkerque was precisely what the logistic planners had sought to avoid by locating the original SPODs in the West of France, although the outcome in the NCP absolutely reinforced the vital importance of effective air defence systems.

Conclusion

The advance to the Dyle, whilst not without its challenges, especially in relation to traffic control, was a success for the BEF's logisticians. Once contact was made with German ground forces, the BEF's logistic system for the most part, kept the combat formations supplied and had the GLOC been maintained through the campaign would have continued to do so. When the GLOC was cut, the logistic planners in the War Office, GHQ and HQ LOC all reacted with commendable speed to create contingency plans, which sought to ensure that the BEF stayed in the fight during what was initially thought to be a temporary scenario. From an historical perspective, the cutting of the GLOC was the defining moment in the campaign for the BEF, although at the time this was not perceived as such by the logistic planners, who recognizing the serious of the situation also sought to create solutions to overcome the problem.

HQ LOC prepared WMT convoys loaded with combat supplies, ready for rapid dispatch to the corps areas if the GLOC was restored, whilst the War Office and GHQ BEF began preparations to create a new GLOC using the NCP in case the restoration was not achieved. Once it became clear that the German advance precluded this outcome, HQ LOC disbanded the

122 Post-war, an officer of the Grenadier Guards told the regimental historian that the sight of refugees 'cut to pieces' in a field by a strafing attack by the *Luftwaffe* was 'the most terrible sight he had witnessed throughout the war'. Captain Nigel Nicolson MBE and Patrick Forbes, *The Grenadier Guards in the War of 1939-1945*, Vol I, *The Campaigns in North-West Europe* (Aldershot: Gale & Polden, 1949), p.22 See also, Gun Buster, *Return via Dunkirk*, pp.135-136.

123 TNA WO 197/210: 2 Division CRASC, General Notes - Supplies.

124 The issue of air defence had been raised by the Admiralty on 22 May, highlighting that the 'French AA guns at DUNKERQUE inadequate. Continued use of port likely to become impractical unless AA guns reinforced'. TNA CAB 44/67: The BEF in Belgium and Artois, 10 May - 3 June 1940, entry 22 May 1940.

125 According to Brigadier N W Routledge OBE TD, *History of the Royal Regiment of Artillery, Anti-Aircraft Artillery 1914-1955* (London & New York: Brasseys (UK) 1994), p.118, an ammunition ship with AA rounds arrived at Dunkerque on 26 May and was unloaded by personnel from 2nd AA Brigade.

126 TNA WO 197/115: Notes on the Operations in France between 10-31 May 1940 from a Movement Point of View, nd.

127 The codename for this evacuation was Operation DYNAMO. TNA WO 106/1618: Evacuation of BEF from France.

WMT convoys and requested SNCF to return trains to the Base depots, whilst the deteriorating operational scenario increasingly suggested to GHQ BEF that the proposed new GLOC would need to be re-orientated to deliver evacuation rather than support. Given a different operational scenario, the plan to support the BEF through the NCP was a practical solution and one, which because of the evacuation of the BEF has disappeared in the historical mist.

17

Worst Job of the Lot
BEF combat logistics from Abbeville to Dunkerque and Beyond

Very Badly Hit

When the GLOC was cut, the three corps held on WMT, 2,000 tons of ammunition, 700 tons of petrol but no supplies,[1] although materiel was held in dumps, and on trains the movements of which, had been disrupted by the German attack. RASC units sent reconnaissance teams out to establish the location and contents of the trains, which were estimated to be 300 tons of ammunition, 1,350 tons of petrol and 450 tons of supplies[2] and from this point, the ingenuity, zeal and improvisation of the BEF's logisticians flourished. To sustain dynamic brigade operations DSCs created supply report centres to control the flow of supplies through Supply Points to units, whilst one formation RASC created mobile supply refilling points using 3 ton lorries with canvas shelters.[3] At divisional level, the logistic RASC ORBAT, a company for ammunition and one for petroleum, plus the Divisional Supply Column (DSC), initially restricted flexibility because if any one of these sub-units became separated from the formation, divisions encountered severe logistic support problems,[4] and the structure created difficulties in support dispersed deployments of independent brigades or changing tactical organization within the division.[5]

1 TNA CAB 44/67: The BEF in Belgium and Artois, 10 May-3 June 1940, entry 22 May 1940. The entry notes that 'On 21 May Corps had only three days RASC supplies in the forward area'.
2 TNA CAB 44/67: The BEF in Belgium and Artois, 10 May-3 June 1940, entry 22 May 1940.
3 Army Council, *Army Training Memorandum* No 34, July 1940, Appx G, Lessons from Experience for the RASC, p.24.
4 The commodity based ORBAT was the subject of much discussion in the inter-war period. Whilst the commodity solution was applied to the infantry divisions, a composite company structure was created for 1st Armoured Division. The RASC re-organization of August 1941, whilst not eliminating commodity companies created greater integration by the introduction of composites. WOOH, *Supplies and Transport*, Vol II, pp.313-319, Appx IIC. Composite sections were created in January 1940 by 2 Division CRASC to support the brigade group Saar deployments. TNA WO 167/210: 2 Division CRASC, WD, entry 23 January 1940.
5 Royal Logistic Corps Museum, 'The Operation of an Armoured and Infantry Divisional RASC', nd, but c1946, para 2b (c).

In recognition of the more demanding operational logistic environment, 48 Division RASC dispensed with the doctrinally pure 'commodity' companies and created 'composite' sections within the Divisional Ammunition Company (DAC), Divisional Petroleum Company (DPC) and the DSC.[6] This lucidly demonstrated the learning agility of the RASC logisticians and is the more remarkable for the 48 Division RASC being a TA unit, although there is evidence that in many ways this promoted innovation because the Volunteer military culture was less constrained by precedent and regulation. Given the severity of the situation, GHQ issued instructions on 20 May to ensure the conservation of the stock of preserved rations, the 'utmost care in the use of SAA' and restricted the consumption of artillery ammunition to five rounds per gun *per diem*, a II Corps Operation Order instructing that 'except in case of emergency, expenditure will be strictly limited to 5 r.p.g per diem which will be used for minor tactical necessities'.[7] Whilst all three directives were logistically sound, they were certainly not tactically welcome,[8] and firmly reinforced the influence of logistics upon tactical scenarios and operational planning.

The logisticians were in the fight from the beginning of the campaign with the most unlikely of units engaging German combat units, and thus the prescient concern in 1935 by the QMG to the Forces about the vulnerability of the Administrative Services to enemy ground attack during mobile operations matured.[9] In this respect, an early loss to BEF logistic capability was the capture of the greater part of 1 LOC Railhead Company RASC,[10] one of only two such units in the BEF,[11] although not before it had engaged German tanks,[12] an action for which, the OC, Major C B Langdon,[13] received one of the ten DSOs[14] awarded to RASC officers during the war,[15] whilst 70735 Driver A N Sanson, a Despatch Rider in the Company was awarded the MM for his courage in maintaining communications to the chain of command.[16]

6 TNA WO 167/294: 48 Division CRASC, WD, 25 May 1940.

7 Underlined in the original. II Corps Operation Order 232005 May 1940, para 6, Ammunition. TNA CAB 44/67: The BEF in Belgium and Artois, 10 May-3 June 1940, entry 23 May 1940.

8 TNA CAB 44/67: The BEF in Belgium and Artois, 10 May-3 June 1940, entry 20 May 1940.

9 Writing to the CIGS, he observed: 'At the moment it appears that insufficient attention is given to this question of protection ... I feel that more consideration should be given to the question of the defence of the administrative services'. TNA WO 32/4612: Future Army Organization – 1935, QMG Response dated 16 December 1936 to CIGS SECRET Paper, 'Future Reorganization of the British Army' dated 9 September 1935.

10 4 Company RASC, which pre-war, was based in Bulford, Wiltshire.

11 LOC Railhead companies were established on the authority of WE/IV/1931/34B/1 for 15 x Boys 0.55-inch Anti-Tank rifles which suggests that the Army, and its logisticians, were very much alive to the threat of enemy mobile armoured operations in the Corps Rear Areas. Philson, BEFORBAT, Vol 1, p.153. LOC Railhead companies were organized into five sections of 10 ton lorries, with one section per railhead. A company also carried 3rd Line reserves of AGE. See, WOOH, *Supplies and Transport*, Vol II, p.308.

12 The war diary for May 1940 was lost during the engagement. See, TNA WO 167/1095.

13 Major Cyril Bailey Langdon was a logistician of courage, resourcefulness, determination and talent, also being awarded the OBE for services to operations in Burma. TNA WO 373/81/26: Recommendation for Award for Langdon.

14 *Supplement to the London Gazette*, 29 April 1941, p.2425.

15 Regimental Committee, *The Story of the Royal Army Service Corps, 1939-1945*, p.xix.

16 TNA WO 373/15/47: Recommendation for Award for Sanson.

Whilst ground action became an increasing feature of forward logistic units, air attack was a constant threat throughout the area of operations. Five RASC soldiers and several civilians were killed in the bombing of Moulle on 21 May.[17] Personnel from 2 OFP located in the neighbouring village of Houlle[18] were deployed to clear the crossroads in the centre of the village, the unit war diary recording that: 'This area had been very badly hit, and the road was blocked with burning vehicles and dead and wounded refugees'.[19] Such scenes must have weighed heavily upon the minds of the technical RAOC logisticians tasked with dealing with the aftermath but the pressures of war directed that 2 OFP complete its immediate task in order to deploy to Wylder.[20] Morale in both units would certainly not have been improved by the knowledge that the disruption to the GLOC and AA actions against constant *Luftwaffe* attacks[21] had created a particular shortage of AA ammunition,[22] with 1 AA Brigade Company RASC[23] struggling to find supplies to replenish the regiments protecting the three corps of the BEF.[24]

Dead at the Wheel

Whilst the search for AA rounds continued, the RASC was even more engaged in provision of artillery ammunition, the expenditure of which, reached prodigious proportions on some occasions and is a very clear indication of the ferocious combat in which the BEF was engaged,[25] with on one day, consumption being 12,852 tonnes, the equivalent of 33 ammunition trains.[26] As an example, the artillery fire-plan to support the withdrawal of the three brigades of 2nd Division to the River Lasne on the evening of 15 May 1940 consumed in 4½ hours, 10,250

17 TNA WO 167/1194: 2 OFP, WD entry 21 May 1940. The war diary does not identify the unit to which these five soldiers belonged, whilst the contemporary record may not accurately reflect the casualties. The CWGC records no burial in local cemeteries and the soldiers must presumably be remembered at the Dunkirk Memorial.

18 The 2 OFP war diary spells these villages Houle and Moule; no such villages or towns with this spelling exist in France. The villages are ½ mile apart with Houlle to the North and Moulle approximately 6 miles NW of Saint Omer.

19 TNA WO 167/1194: 2 OFP, WD, 21 May 1940.

20 TNA WO 167/1194: 2 OFP, WD entries 21-22 May 1940.

21 For an account of the AA and ground defence operations of the BEF's six AA brigades in Belgium and France, see, Brigadier N W Routledge OBE TD, *History of the Royal Regiment of Artillery, Anti-Aircraft Artillery 1914-1955* (London & New York: Brasseys (UK) 1994), pp.113-126.

22 The RA history of AAA, Ibid, makes only one mention of a shortage of AA ammunition, p.118, which relates to operations at Dunkerque but the war diaries of RASC AA companies offer a different picture.

23 The lift capability of the company was degraded by a deficiency of 3 x 30 cwt trucks, 9 x 3 ton 4x2 lorries and no water trailers from a total establishment of respectively, 24, 76 and 5. TNA WO 167/425: 1 AA Brigade Company RASC.

24 TNA WO 167/425: 1 AA Brigade Company RASC, WD, entries 21-22 May 1940. On 24 May, 190 x boxes of 3-inch ammunition were obtained from Mont Noir.

25 For an account of the BEF's artillery operations in Belgium and France, see France, see, Farndale, *History of the Royal Regiment of Artillery: The Years of Defeat 1939-41*, pp.30-94.

26 Lindsell, *Military Organization and Administration*, p 116.

rounds of five different natures.[27] It was therefore, fortuitous that considerable stocks had been dumped in preparation for the forward deployment to the River Dyle and the Corps Ammunition Parks (CAP) were kept busy in the initial stages of the movement out-loading ammunition from the ARHs to designated ammunition refilling points for transfer to the DACs or conducting dumping programmes, especially for 6-inch stocks, although occasionally confused orders or misinterpretation of instructions disrupted the flow.

On 22 May, I CAP dumped 'a very large quantity' of 25 pounder ammunition at the incorrect location, thereby creating a shortage of stocks for collection by 48 DAC.[28] Issues at corps and unit level also degraded the efficient distribution of ammunition, the former often caused by Staff inexperience in controlling logistic assets and the latter by tactical dynamics and poor communications. On 22 May, 48 Division CRASC noted the problems caused by I CAP being located too far from the DACs to effectively complete the ammunition delivery loop, whilst the failure of unit guides to RV at the agreed meeting points, is an issue frequently mentioned in the CRASC and DAC war diaries.[29] Flexibility was proving to be a key asset. On 17 May, 6 Ammunition Sub-Park of II CAP dumped 6-inch howitzer rounds at Tiegehem before delivering 40 tons of explosives[30] and 3,200 anti-tank mines to II Corps RE, then on 19 May, lifting an infantry brigade and recovering a number of guns on behalf of II Corps artillery.[31] The Sub-Park was then tasked to support the *ad hoc* Pol Force based upon elements of 46th Division, a key initial activity being to dump explosives at La Bassee[32] for demolitions.[33]

27 Table collated from information in TNA CAB 44/67: The BEF in Belgium and Artois, 10 May-3 June 1940, entry 15 May 1940.

Table 17.1
Artillery Rounds - Consumption
2nd Division withdrawal to the River Lasne

Ammunition	Quantity
25 pdr	7,200
4.5-inch Gun	700
6-inch Gun	150
6-inch Howitzer	2,000
8-inch Howitzer	200

28 TNA WO 167/294: 48 Division CRASC, WD, 22 May 1940.

29 TNA WO 167/294: 48 Division CRASC, WD, 20 May 1940.

30 The post campaign operation After Action Report (AAR) produced by the Bartholomew Committee, highlighted the acute shortage of weather-proof, ie plastic, explosive. TNA WO 106/1775: Bartholomew Committee - Report on lessons to be learnt from operations in Flanders; evidence, report and action arising, paragraph, 42

31 TNA WO 167/159: II CAP, WD entries of 17 and 19 May 1940.

32 TNA WO 167/159: II CAP, WD entry 23 May 1940.

33 The quantity of explosives required for demolitions was not inconsiderable. For planned operations on the River Dendre, the RE requirement was: Gun Cotton – 11 tons, Ammonal in tins - 6.5 tons, Ammonal in cartridges - 6.5 tons and Gelignite - 3.5 tons. See, TNA WO 197/84: Preparations for demolition in Belgium and supply of explosives - GHQ E-in-C No 568 dated 13 May 1940, 'Explosives for River Dendre demolitions'. For details of the types and quantities of explosives used by 208 Company RE in bridge demolitions, see, list in Morling, *Sussex Sappers*, Appx F, G, H & J.

Based upon Daily Ammunition Expenditure Rates (DAER) for the Force there were approximately four days in corps and divisional dumps forward of the Corps Railheads, with 5 x DAER on the ground at the I Corps ARH at Ecoust-sur-Mein, 7 x DAER at the II Corps ARH at Aubigny and about 1,000 tons at the recently formed III Corps ARH at Pernes,[34] stocks upon which the corps drew as the Germans were engaged. The enemy advance however, threatened both I and II Corps ARHs and the ARH detachments were ordered to destroy the remaining stocks. Destruction of munitions by demolition carried significant risks to troops and civilians, so generally fuzes were removed and propellant burnt. Some success was achieved at Ecoust-sur-Mein but at Aubigny the dump was alongside a main road crowded with military traffic and refugees, resulting in the stocks being abandoned, although the two ARH detachments were evacuated to UK after a perilous journey via Hazebrouck, Boulogne and Dunkerque.[35] Once the GLOC was cut however, ammunition was the most challenging combat *materiel* to acquire and some RASC officers went to extreme lengths to recover stocks. Lieutenant R S Wicks[36] discovered an ammunition train, a section of which was on fire. With the assistance of a SNCF crew, the burning wagons were detached and the train, despite being subject to air attack, reached a railhead at Hazebrouck.[37] By 19 May however, the SNCF had effectively ceased to function in the III Corps apart from a few local crews.[38]

By 21 May, DACs were no longer able to draw stocks from the CAPs because ammunition trains were no longer arriving at the Corps ARHs and the DACs thus sought out dumps, some of which had been stocked as early as January 1940.[39] 2 DAC was busy collecting SAA and 25 pounder artillery ammunition from 2nd Division dumps around Saint Amand and Beuvry, whilst on 22 May, authority was granted for 25 pounder ammunition to be drawn from a 1st Division dump at La Vacque and 4.5-inch howitzer rounds from Huguinville.[40] Artillery units sometimes accessed these dumps directly using unit 1st Line transport to ground-load the ammunition near gun-lines or create regimental dumps. Whilst effective if the rounds were fired, this arrangement generated additional work for the DACs because if the artillery had to move before the ammunition was consumed there was usually insufficient 1st Line transport to lift the balance, which drew in vehicles from the DAC to ensure stocks were not lost to the enemy.[41] On 21 May, Second-Lieutenant J K Mansfield and his section soldiers from 50 DAC[42] displayed enormous courage and professionalism in maintaining an ammunition point in Rochlincourt under air attack and shellfire,[43] before mounting, despite the presence of German

34 TNA CAB 106/235: BEF Ammunition Supply – Gibson Report.
35 Fernyhough & Harris, *History of the Royal Army Ordnance Corps, 1939-1945*, pp.94-95.
36 Regimental Committee, *The Story of the Royal Army Service Corps 1939-1945*, p.74 notes his rank as Captain but the recommendation in the TNA states his substantive rank as Lieutenant, suggesting he was holding acting rank.
37 Lieutenant Wicks was awarded the MC for this action. TNA WO 373/16/410: Recommendation for Award for Wicks. Regrettably, the names of the equally courageous SNCF crew have not been recorded or honoured in the same manner.
38 TNA CAB 44/67: The BEF in Belgium and Artois, 10 May - 3 June 1940, entry 19 May 1940.
39 TNA WO 197/210: 2 Division CRASC, General Notes – Ammunition.
40 TNA WO 197/210: 2 Division CRASC, WD, entries 21-22 May 1940.
41 TNA WO 197/210: 2 Division CRASC, General Notes - Ammunition.
42 522 (Ammunition) Company RASC (TA).
43 Sometimes the courageous actions of the logisticians did not result in the desired combat effectiveness. On one occasion, Lieutenant E W S Ford, 3rd Grenadier Guards, delivering ammunition to forward

P17.1 The Road to Dunkerque. View NNW from the 577 feet height of Mont Cassel of the D916 road towards Wormhoudt and then Dunkerque. The British possession, through the heroic and stubborn resistance of 145th Infantry Brigade of 48th (South Midland) Division, until the night of 29-30 May 1940, of this important tactical feature, prevented the Germans having over-watch of British logistic movements. (Author)

patrols,[44] a night operation to replenish the section with 25 pounder ammunition from a dump at Violaines near La Bassee.

The search for petroleum products was equally challenging, although the quest was aided by detachments of bulk petrol companies and access to some civil and dumped BEF stocks. A key asset though, was the Advanced Base Petrol Filling Centre at Lomme near Lille, which despite interruptions through air raids and a temporary evacuation of the commercial site it occupied,[45]

companies discovered that the incorrect boxes had been selected from the battalion dump and instead of SAA were mostly Very cartridges. As it transpired, firing these cartridges confused the Germans, who taking them for a check-fire, ceased to mortar the Grenadier's positions. Ford received a MID for his campaign service. Nicolson & Forbes, *The Grenadier Guards in the War of 1939-1945*, Vol I, *The Campaigns in North-West Europe*, pp.35-36.

44 TNA WO 167/305: 50 DAC WD, 11 June 1940. These were impressive military logistic feats for such an inexperienced junior officer from a TA unit and for these two actions Mansfield was awarded the MC. TNA WO 373/15/186: Recommendation for Award for Mansfield.

45 The site is now a Distribution Park but the large rail complex, a key feature of which is the landmark U loop, is extant in 2020.

continued to fill cans until 26 May when the unit suspended operations and withdrew.[46] Once the GLOC was cut the Corps Petrol Parks could no longer draw fuel from the PRHs but sought supplies in dumps or ran the loop from the BPFC at Lomme.[47] DPCs were almost completely dependent upon dumps,[48] and although civil stocks were an option, 2 DPC[49] avoided their use to obviate the possibility of using fuel that had been sabotaged with sugar by the Fifth Column.[50] Short-term urgency often overtook longer-term importance in distribution and after being tasked to provide fuel for units from other divisions, 2 DPC issued the last stocks on 27 May.[51] Distributing fuel was not without risk. Low-level strafing by the *Luftwaffe* was a constant threat and during daylight RASC units usually moved in small groups of vehicles to mitigate the effects of an attack. Indeed, experience quickly suggested that 10 vehicles to the mile was the maximum density that could be operated safely in an adverse air environment,[52] but despite these precautions, dive-bombers attacked 50 DPC[53] at Estaires on the evening of 22 May resulting in one soldier killed and eight wounded, with several vehicles destroyed and damaged.[54] 2 DPC also suffered a fatal casualty on 25 May 1940 when approximately eight fighters attacked three lorries near La Bassee, the section commander factually reporting that Driver Booth,[55] driving the middle vehicle, 'was dead at the wheel shot through the head, he was killed while the vehicle was in motion, because his lorry had crashed into the back of the leading lorry.'[56] Death, wounds and injuries inflicted upon vehicle drivers mounted as the BEF retreated to the coast to the point that the War Office dispatched 200 reinforcements to Calais but the ship was unable to dock and returned to England.[57]

Never Better Fed

Supplies arriving by rail from the Base were soon affected by the cut in the GLOC, with no pack train arriving at the III Corps SRH on 17 May and the last the next day,[58] the RASC

46 Regimental Committee, *The Story of the Royal Army Service Corps 1939-1945*, p.74. 3 BPFC arrived in France on 23 April 1940 to reinforce the can filling operation. Unfortunately, the war diary for May 1940 is not in the TNA; WO 167/1144: 3 Base Petrol Filling Centre RASC.
47 The full work of the CPPs is difficult to establish because the II CPP war diary for May 1940 was lost during the evacuation. TNA WO 167/161, HQ II Corps, DDST, 2ST/170/P dated 13 March 1941 to War Office Records C7.
48 TNA WO 197/210: 2 Division CRASC, General Notes - Petrol.
49 24 Company RASC.
50 TNA WO 197/210: 2 Division CRASC, General Notes - Petrol.
51 TNA WO 197/210: 2 Division CRASC, General Notes - Petrol.
52 Army Council, *Army Training Memorandum* No 34, July 1940, Appx G, Lessons from Experience for the RASC, p.25.
53 523 (Petrol) Company RASC.
54 TNA WO 167/305: 50 Division CRASC, WD, 22 May 1940. Losses were: 3 x 3 ton, 1 x AA truck and 1 x 2 seat Austin staff car, plus 7 x 3 ton damaged.
55 The body of T/1024189 Frank Robert Booth aged 40 and husband to Mary, was not recovered and he is remembered on the Dunkirk Memorial Column 135.
56 TNA WO 167/212: 2 DPC RASC, hand-written report by T/3596737 Lance-Corporal G J Owen of A Section dated 29 June 1940.
57 TNA WO 197/134: Evacuation from France and Quartering of the BEF – Activities of DST in the Evacuation from France.
58 TNA CAB 44/67: The BEF in Belgium and Artois, 10 May-3 June 1940, entry 18 May 1940.

thus reverting to foraging for foodstuffs, thereby engaging in the one activity its existence was supposed to prevent, although there were however, missed opportunities. A pack train had arrived at Hazebrouck for I Corps in the early hours of 21 May but there was no DSC to unload it and was subsequently damaged in an air raid at 1200, thus demonstrating the importance of timely logistic action. Attempts were made to salvage some of the stocks but further *Luftwaffe* raids prevented much work and an alternative SRH was opened at Blaringhem the next day.[59] This SRH never received a train, the town being captured by the Germans on 23 May with the SRH detachment being engaged in its defence[60] before withdrawing, fortunately with no casualties, to Lynde.[61] In the 2nd Division, the DSC operated autonomously, the CRASC noting that they: 'had to function as an independent unit and find sups themselves'.[62] The officers and soldiers of the column set to work with a will, accessing the abandoned NAAFI[63] in Lille,[64] and collecting from the countryside around it, abandoned cattle for milk and meat,[65] and 50,000 eggs in a store.[66]

The French Army *Intendance* Service also sustained the BEF, holding large stocks of rations in Lille and the senior supply officer in HQ 2nd Division was fortunate in acquiring the equivalent of 38,000 rations on 20 May but noted that bread and potatoes had become unobtainable. Acquisition of supplies however, was not in itself a solution because 2 DSC had equal difficulty in distributing them as many unit locations were unknown.[67] 5 DSC[68] was grateful to discover an abandoned supply train on 22 May with 180,000 rations aboard,[69] whilst 42 DSC[70] was fortunate to access well-stocked warehouses in Lille including one operated by the eponymous mass-distribution retail business of *Felix Pontin*, the stocks from which, enabled units to be issued with tinned asparagus and lobster in lieu of the standard fare, 42 DSC calling

59 TNA WO 167/144: ADOS I Corps – SRH RAOC, WD, 21 May 40.
60 The SRH Detachment war diary recorded the actions of a RE officer Major Gwynne who was the *de facto* acting OC at Blaringhem on 23 May: 'At great personal risk and exposed to enemy fire, Major Gywnne succeeded in smashing 3 containers holding large quantities of alcohol, thereby liberating the liquid which flowed into the canal. He then ignited same. But for the fact of the run of the tide, his action would have severely hampered the enemy advance……'. TNA WO 167/144: ADOS I Corps - SRH RAOC WD, 23 May 40.
61 TNA WO 167/144: ADOS I Corps - SRH RAOC, WD, 23 May 40.
62 TNA WO 197/210: 2 Division CRASC, General Notes - Supplies.
63 Navy, Army & Air Force Institute. The RASC was responsible for the Expeditionary Forces of NAAFI and whilst not a combatant component of the Corps, members of EFI were KIA, wounded and taken prisoner, although some made remarkable escapes, worthy of any thriller. The EFI suffered its greatest number of casualties during the sinking of the HMT *Lancastria* on 17 June 1940, when the majority of the 109 killed and seven missing in the campaign were lost. For an informal record of its operations in May - June 1940, see, Cole, *NAAFI in Uniform*, pp.13-22.
64 In addition to 2 DSC drawing on the NAAFI for distribution to brigades and Divisional Troops, it appears that units, including 2nd Coldstream Guards were also doing so, presumably as 'direct collect' from 2 DSC operating the site. See, Michael Howard and John Sparrow, *The Coldstream Guards, 1920-1946* (London, New York & Toronto: Oxford University Press, 1951), p.48.
65 Regimental Committee, *The Story of the Royal Army Service Corps 1939-1945*, p.73.
66 TNA WO 197/210: 2 Division CRASC, General Notes - Supplies.
67 TNA WO 197/210: 2 Division CRASC, WD, 21 May 1940.
68 2 Company RASC.
69 TNA WO 167/249: 5th Division CRASC, WD, 22 May 1940.
70 503 Company RASC.

the improvised scale the 'Felix' ration.[71] The DSC also discovered a pack train destined for Comines at a railhead in Choques and duly cleared it, concurrently persuading local bakers to produce some bread,[72] whilst RASC butchers in 48 DSC[73] slaughtered cattle to provide the division's meat ration.[74] The DSC also started bread production in an improvised bakery an enemy air attack in the vicinity of it prompted a withdrawal and put an end to baking.[75] A 3 DSC officer was equally enterprising but more fortunate than his counterpart in 48 DSC. Having discovered a stock of flour in an empty bakery,[76] he obtained from 7th Guards Brigade a master baker and 20 soldiers who had been in the trade pre-war.[77]

In some places, the activities of the DSCs became irrelevant as soldiers in units also applied their innovative logistic skills to the problem. Near Bray Dunes, 3rd Medium Artillery Regiment was fortunate to find several abandoned loaded French ration lorries, the contents of which were, 'purloined'.[78] In Halluin, after the provision of fresh meat and bread through the military supply chain failed, 2nd Royal Fusiliers was placed upon half-rations, although this had little practical effect because the battalion requisitioned cattle from surrounding farms and other food was procured by local purchase.[79] The CO 1st Coldstream Guards[80] recorded:

> We were told that the BEF was now cut off from its normal supplies, and we were to collect all the local produce we could and to live off the country. By the time we had left, our cooks' lorries were groaning with beef and pork, chickens and ducks, not to mention fresh eggs and milk. It is safe to say that from this day[81] onwards the Battalion was never better fed'.[82]

71 Regimental Committee, *The Story of the Royal Army Service Corps 1939-1945*, pp.42-43.
72 Ibid, p.73.
73 518 Company RASC. The OC, Major W H Summers had a baptism of fire, having returned from leave in the Channel Islands on 14 May 1940. TNA WO 167/297: 48 DSC RASC, WD.
74 TNA WO 167/297: 48 DSC RASC, WD, 22 May 1940.
75 TNA WO 167/297: 48 DSC RASC, WD, 24 May 1940.
76 Although utilizing existing bakeries to supplement field bakeries was a simple solution, some RE units were capable of improvising or constructing power bakery facilities. See, Army Council, *Military Engineering*, Vol VII, *Accommodation and Installations*, pp.202-203, Bakeries.
77 Regimental Committee, *The Story of the Royal Army Service Corps 1939-1945*, p.72.
78 na, *The History of the 3rd Medium Artillery Regiment Royal Artillery, 1939-1945*, p.63.
79 na, *A Short History of the 2nd Battalion Royal Fusiliers (City of London Regiment) during the First Year of the War*, p.16.
80 Lieutenant-Colonel Arnold de Lerisson Cazenove DSO MVO. Cazenove was promoted to Brigadier in August 1940 and subsequently commanded 7th Guards Brigade, 73rd Infantry Brigade Group and 140th Infantry Brigade. Howard & Sparrow, *The Coldstream Guards, 1920-1946*, p.474.
81 Wednesday 22 May 1940.
82 Howard & Sparrow, *The Coldstream Guards, 1920-1946*, p.35. Michael Howard (1922-2019) was an officer in the 3rd Coldstream Guards being awarded the MC for gallant service in Italy. Post-war he founded the Department of War Studies at King's College London and subsequently enjoyed a most distinguished academic career receiving several official honours including the CBE in 1977, Knight Bachelor in 1986 and the Order of Merit in 2005. John Sparrow (1906-1992), a pre-war academic and barrister, was also commissioned into the Coldstreams, serving in a series of Military Assistant posts including MA to the Adjutant-General. He was also the author of WOOH, Morale (War Office, 1949).

P17.2 Half-Rations? Whilst the BEF was placed on half-rations many units were more than well-fed, although improper acquisitions from the French local population caused considerable friction. (RLCM: RAOC/WTB1/RAO/373/2)

This reversion to 'living off the country', an action that the DSC was designed to prevent,[83] was not greeted with much enthusiasm by the civil populace because sometimes it was based more on official looting[84] than authorized acquisition,[85] although in some instances, such as at Camphin-en-Pevele, the fleeing inhabitants requested the BEF to destroy or remove property

83 In addition to its military supply responsibilities, the Divisional RASC was established for a Requisitioning Officer who was authorized to arrange for acquisitions in accordance with FSR. On 27 October 1939, the RO of 4 Division CRASC reported that 4,000 French Francs (£1,402 at 2018 values) had been stolen from a suitcase. Whilst the matter was reported to the Military Police, the culprit escaped retribution. TNA WO 167/235: 4 Division CRASC, WD. There remains of course, the possibility, no doubt considered by the investigating officer, that the RO was responsible for the theft.

84 Some of this looting was personal rather than official, with elements of it committed by officers as Lieutenant Jimmy Langley of 2nd Coldstream Guards discovered when he occasioned upon a captain shooting the locks off the desk belonging to the owner of a large brewery, presumably in the search for cash and valuables, his actions having no military justification. Lieutenant Colonel J M Langley MBE MC, *Fight Another Day* (London: Collins, 1974), pp.33-34.

85 Army Council, FSR, Vol I, *Organization and Administration*, pp.278-290, Chp XIX, Regulations for the Utilization of the Local Resources of a Country.

to prevent the Germans seizing it.[86] This was unfortunate because the chain of command was acutely aware of the need to support the local economy and not to engage in rapacious activity upon it but it is clear that occasionally during the withdrawal to the coast, BEF units treated the resources and inhabitants of France as if the country was a conquered enemy[87] rather than an Allied nation.[88] The officers at the War Office in Supply & Transport 6 however, could little have imagined that in the midst of the chaos of war, soldiers would dine in bizarre ways, occasionally giving physical and mental sustenance to those fortunate enough to participate in them. At Dunkerque, with the evacuation in full flow, the scribe of an *ad hoc* Squadron of 4th/7th Royal Dragoon Guards recorded of Sunday 2 June, 'All took our lunch down to the beach for the day ... Found the only tin of Ration Biscuits on the beach. Unfortunately, they didn't last long, as the Officer on Guard over them slept at his post. Riley produced a bottle of Red Wine – not quite the right temperature but very welcome'.[89] 1st Berkshire were evacuated from Dunkerque on the MV *Royal Daffodil*,[90] the regimental history recording that once the ship was out of range of German artillery, 'immaculate stewards served lunch; and after it, unbelievably, presented the bill!'.[91]

No Opportunity for Sleep

The pressure on the logisticians was beginning to mount. III Corps A&Q recorded, 'G plans have little relation to the administrative situation and it was necessary for QMG to intervene…….the very limited reserves of petrol are rapidly being exhausted.[92] Medical stores are running short…..Orders are changed more rapidly than units can keep pace with, and this in turn is exhausting troops and reserves'.[93] In this respect, the Q Staff officers at HQ III Corps at least understood what units were grappling with. Those tasked with combat operations immediately upon arrival in Theatre certainly found it particularly difficult to adjust to the rigours of a dynamic fight during mobile operations. OC 13 TCC summarized the challenge

86 TNA CAB 106/204: BEF Unit Narratives, 2 DPC.

87 Equally, officers and soldiers believed that it was better they had the rations rather than the Germans. See, Gun Buster, *Return via Dunkirk*, p.103.

88 The regulations appertaining to the acquisition of resources were clearly articulated in FSR and were subject to additional controls in friendly countries. FSR, Vol I noted 'In the utilization of local resources direct contact between troops and inhabitants will be avoided as far as possible'. Ibid, p.279, para 5.

89 This squadron was attached to the 5th Dragoon Guards. See na, *Actions of the 4/7th Dragoon Guards, May - June 1940* (Uckfield: Naval & Military Press, nd), p.35.

90 MV *Royal Daffodil* was a diesel vessel of 2,060 GRT, a passenger capacity of 2,073 and a maximum speed of 21 knots, launched in January 1939. During Operation DYNAMO, *the Royal Daffodil* evacuated 7,461 personnel in seven lifts before being damaged by a bomb on 2 June 1940 but was repaired in time to recover British soldiers and civilians from Guernsey during Operation AERIAL. The *Royal Daffodil* has the distinction of evacuating more personnel than any other ship during Operation DYNAMO. Winser, *BEF Ships*, p.61. She was scrapped in 1967, her last voyage, to Ghent for breaking, being shown on BBC TV.

91 Blight, *The History of the Berkshire Regiment, 1920-1947*, p.208.

92 This comment refers to the III Corps situation as GHQ recorded that: 'The petrol situation, fortunately, gave no cause for concern ... there still remained a large army bulk filling station near Lille.' TNA CAB 44/67: The BEF in Belgium and Artois, 10 May-3 June 1940, entry 22 May 1940.

93 TNA CAB 44/67: The BEF in Belgium and Artois, 10 May - 3 June 1940, entry 23 May 1940.

P17.3 Bray Dunes 2019. Carrying water, rations and ammunition from the barges at the water's edge was a dangerous and manpower intensive task. (Author)

in a report to GHQ after one week of deployment and it dispels any notion that the logisticians in the BEF had it 'easy' and how quickly logistic capability could be eroded.[94]

> Since its arrival in FRANCE on the 14th May, it has been continuously employed day and night on Troop Carrying duties. Many miles have been covered and the drivers have had practically no opportunity for sleep. The unit has frequently been bombed and machine-gunned and it has moved at such speed and over such a wide area that it has not been possible to maintain adequate touch with the supplies and petrol … I am very short of equipment … My officers and dispatch riders have no pistols … There are only four maps in the unit … and some 50 drivers are unaccounted for. Briefly this Unit needs rest, the vehicles are urgently in need of maintenance and replacement vehicles are required.[95]

94 A soldier from 13 TCC, Driver Stanley Patrick, aged 19, was one of only two survivors from the 640 Army personnel aboard HMS *Wakeful* when a torpedo sank her on 29 May 1940.
95 TNA 167/1111: 13 TCC, WD, 'Report by OC to GHQ' dated 22 May 1940.

Fear of German collaborators in civilian clothes or British Army uniforms conducting sabotage and subversion was rife during the campaign,[96] an environment succinctly captured by the CO[97] of the TA unit tasked with denial and demolition, the Kent Fortress Royal Engineers:[98] 'It must be appreciated that the area was flooded with fifth columnists, spies and other enemy agents. Parachutists were captured and shot, and rumour was rife sedulously fostered no doubt by the Boche.[99] Hence it was not really surprising that everyone was suspicious of the rest of humanity'.[100] Quite whether every instance of sabotage and Fifth Column activity reported was accurate is open to conjecture but the war diaries in some cases are specific about the incidents.[101] 1 OFP for example, detained 'many' suspected espionage agents in Marcq a town to the North-East of Lille and, in accordance with instructions, handed them over to the French Gendarmerie,[102] whilst I Corps SRH Detachment RAOC recorded SAA fire through the windows of the unit billets[103]. The detachment also handled a suspected spy in British Army uniform at Templeuve who claimed to be a RE officer who had been given orders to report to the War Office with all speed and needed transport to reach a Channel port without delay, the investigation discovering that his case was genuine.[104]

In the circumstances therefore, it is not surprising that there are references in BEF unit war diaries of soldiers witnessing the lynching, in French towns and villages, of civilians in suspected of being spies, saboteurs or members of the Fifth Column. Inevitably the logisticians were involved in some of the darker aspects relating to these activities. 5 Group AMPC, in addition to its labouring tasks in unloading ammunition and 100 tons of explosives from a ship in Boulogne Harbour,[105] deployed its soldiers in a combatant role during which a detachment assaulted a house inside the perimeter from which the Pioneers were receiving SAA fire. Several

96 Concern about the activities of the Fifth Column and German collaborators are an underlying feature of the entries in unit war diaries. That of 156 Transportation Stores Company for example, is replete with vehicle registration marks and descriptions of stolen Belgian and French cars and lorries, which the chain of command assessed might be used by Germans in civilian clothes or members of the Fifth Column. TNA WO 167/951: 156 TSC, WD, June 1940.

97 Lieutenant-Colonel C C H Brazier RE, later Brigadier OBE.

98 The KFRE was responsible for the provision of the XD parties. For a history of its operations in France, see, Brigadier C C H Brazier, *XD Operations: Secret British Missions Denying Oil to the Nazis* (Barnsley: Pen & Sword, 2004), pp.40-92.

99 Lieutenant-Colonel Brazier relates a story of a bogus British RE major who had stolen a British staff car from a lieutenant in Rouen, Ibid, p.54.

100 Ibid, p.49.

101 For example, on 18 May 1940, 76th Field Regiment RA 'dealt with several civilians found cutting wire or signal cable in their area'. TNA CAB 44/67: The BEF in Belgium and Artois, 10 May-3 June 1940, entry 18 May 1940.

102 TNA WO 167/1192: 1 OFP RAOC, WD, 14 May 1940.

103 This incident occurred at Anvaing in Belgium 11 miles NE of Tournai in the early hours of 18 May 1940. TNA WO 167/144: ADOS I Corps – SRH RAOC WD, 18 May 40.

104 TNA WO 167/144: ADOS I Corps – SRH RAOC WD, 19 May 40. It transpired that this person was Major Gywnne RE, who is almost certainly L E A Gwynne, later Colonel CBE TD.

105 Pakenham-Walsh, *The History of the Corps of The Royal Engineers*, Vol VIII, 1938-1948, p.32. The 100 tons of explosives were transported by volunteer drivers under the direction of Major H H C Withers RE of the Engineer-in-Chief's Staff; the cold courage of these men driving vehicles loaded with sensitive explosives deserves to be remembered, as does the bravery of Major Withers and his driver who engaged German tanks with rifle fire, having dismounted from a car loaded with detonators.

armed men in civilian clothing were detained, one with a sub-machine gun, the regimental history recording that, 'These were disposed of'.[106] Another incident resulted in the execution of four 'spies' in Cysoing on 21 May by 2 Division Provost Company,[107] whilst Sergeant Arthur Chapple, alias Lang, a member of the EFI was taken prisoner and achieved notoriety by becoming a renegade and broadcasting for the Nazi regime on Radio National.[108]

Individuals and Innovation

As the BEF withdrew towards Dunkerque, the delivery of logistic capability was increasingly sustained by good fortune and personal initiative. On 27 May, 5 DSC[109] deployed to draw rations from a dump at the Steenwercke railhead but discovered that most of the supplies at the site consisted of full rum jars, a substance, which if not properly controlled, was not conducive to operational capability or military discipline. Given there were no RASC personnel manning the dump it is surprising that there had not been a drama before 5 DSC accessed it. 5 DSC was also fortunate in chancing upon several abandoned lorries loaded with Belgian supplies, enabling it to establish a supply point until the unit received orders to move for embarkation, [110] whilst 48 DSC arriving on 29 May at Bray Dunes, carried a welcome two days of rations.[111] During this period, 50 Division RASC was still collecting ammunition and supplies, including NAAFI stores, from abandoned dumps,[112] whilst also taking receipt of the remaining ammunition stocks from 5 Division RASC at Adinkerke.[113]

Unlike many battalion actions in which, senior leadership directly influenced combat engagements, RASC Junior NCOs often directed logistic operations, with results that might affect outcomes at divisional level or beyond. A small and long forgotten action on 25 May 1940 not only lucidly demonstrated this dynamic but also clearly illustrated the capability and flexibility of RASC WMT when 2 DPC was ordered to detach a sub-section of five lorries to 5th Infantry Brigade at Estaires.[114] Commanded by Corporal Shortland, the sub-section was tasked by brigade HQ at 1230 to lift troops and equipment of 1st Queen's Own Cameron Highlanders to La Bassee to reinforce the Eastern flank of 2nd Division.[115] The sub-section made five return trips, each of 20 miles, being shelled on the approach to La Bassee, although fortunately all the rounds fell short of the road. Whilst unloading the last detail, the sub-section suffered air attack.[116] After an exhausting day under fire, Corporal Shortland, his men and the

106 Rhodes-Wood, *A War History of the Royal Pioneer Corps, 1939-1945*, p.37.
107 TNA WO 167/215: 2nd Division Provost Company, WD.
108 TNA KV 2/443: Security Service: World War II, Renegades and Suspected Renegades, Chapple. He was sentenced to 15 years imprisonment in 1946, later reduced to 10.
109 2 Company RASC.
110 Regimental Committee, *The Story of the Royal Army Service Corps 1939-1945*, p.77.
111 TNA WO 167/297: 48 DSC RASC, WD, 29 May 1940.
112 TNA WO 167/305: 50 Division CRASC, WD, entries May 1940.
113 TNA WO 167/249: 5 Division CRASC, WD, entries May 1940.
114 TNA WO 167/212: 2 DPC RASC, WD, 25 May 1940.
115 Ellis, BOH, *The War in France and Flanders*, Situation Map op p.182.
116 Aircraft recognition, a neglected subject in many units, received increasing attention as the campaign developed. 2 DPC was certainly one unit that mis-identified an action on 11 May 1940, when the war diary recorded that a Spitfire shot down a Heinkel 111. This was presumably a Hurricane or a French fighter because apart from the unarmed Photographic Reconnaissance Unit (PRU) aircraft no Spitfires

lorries returned in his words, 'all safe & sound', to the DPC at 1900.[117] This, and many other operations, conclusively confirmed the effectiveness and importance of small well led logistic teams, without which, the combat formations of the BEF could not have fought as they did.

There was certainly no lack of ingenuity from logistic Staff and units. Between 22 and 24 May several rakes of rail wagons loaded with ammunition, fuel and rations were extracted from sidings almost in the front line and hauled to sites where they could be unloaded in the dark.[118] 5 DAC unloaded ammunition trains at La Bassee but discovered that there were no explosives or SAA tracer,[119] whilst 5 DPC[120] alighted upon 76,000 gallons of cased aviation and MT spirit at an abandoned RAF aerodrome.[121] Air supply was utilized to deliver rations, water and SAA using air landed and air-drop, techniques.[122] On 22 and 23 May, 50 tons of preserved meat and biscuit were delivered in 30 sorties[123] flying from Croydon Airport to Merville,[124] using civil transports from the British Overseas Airways Corporation (BOAC)[125] and the Belgian airline Sabena.[126] This operation was not without risk, despite the RAF Hurricane fighter escort.[127] On 23 May, Me 109 fighters strafed the airfield whilst the BOAC AW 27 aircraft were unloading, resulting in *Elysian* being burnt out, whilst on the return flight to Croydon, *Euryalus* was struck in two engines by SAA fire from an enemy aircraft and upon landing at Lympne in Kent was seriously damaged when the under-carriage collapsed.[128] Further flights to

were deployed in operations over France on this date. Assuming the identification is correct, the most likely candidate is the Heinkel 111P 1/LG1 from shot down by Hurricanes from 79 Squadron RAF, which crashed at Masnuy-Saint-Jean. See, Cornwell, *The Battle of France,* p.241, which also lists the names of the German air crew.

117 TNA WO 167/212: 2 DPC RASC, Hand-written report by T/45367 Corporal J Shortland, nd but late May 1940.

118 TNA WO 197/115: Notes on the Operations in France between 10-31 May 1940 from a Movement Point of View, nd.

119 69 Company RASC.

120 TNA WO 167/249: 5 Division CRASC, WD, 22 May 1940.

121 TNA WO 167/249: 5 Division CRASC, WD, 21 May 1940. It is not clear why this fuel was not denied to the enemy but probably the RAF either urgently evacuated the airfield or that the POL was left with the expectation that the site would be re-occupied.

122 For an explanation of the procedures, see, Army Council, FSPB, Pamphlet No 7, 1939, *Movement by Sea, Rail and Air*, Sect 8-10, Movement by Air – Carriage of Supplies, pp.21-22 and Air Council, *Royal Air Force Pocket Book*, Air Publication 1081, Air Ministry (London: HMSO, 1937), Chp IX, Sect 42, Movement.

123 The first flight of three aircraft departed at 1730 on 22 May 1940 transporting 21,680 lbs gross of preserved meat and biscuit followed at 1915 by seven aircraft loaded with 27,544 lbs of rations. TNA WO 197/134: Evacuation from France and Quartering of the BEF - Activities of DST in the Evacuation from France.

124 TNA WO 197/134: Evacuation from France and Quartering of the BEF - Activities of DST in the Evacuation from France.

125 BOAC provided five Armstrong-Whitworth 27 Ensign Class, with an individual payload of 9,500 lb. Tapper, *Armstrong-Whitworth Aircraft since 1913*, p.247.

126 Sabena provided a Douglas DC-3 and two Savoia Marchetti airliners. Ibid.

127 The execution of this operation was conducted under the caveat that the supplies would be dispatched by air only if they were 'really urgent owing to the large escort required'. TNA CAB 44/67: The BEF in Belgium and Artois, 10 May - 3 June 1940, entry 22 May 1940.

128 *Euryalus* was dismantled and taken to Hamble with the intention of repair but was used for spares. Echo landed at Heston with damage to the tail-plane. Ibid.

lift the remaining 320 tons that had arrived at Croydon Airport were cancelled when Merville Airfield was captured, with some of the stocks that had been delivered.[129]

On the evening of 26 May, the RAF received a request to drop combat supplies to forces holding the Citadel in Calais. At first light on 27 May, 12 Lysanders dropped water, whilst at 1000, 17 Lysanders delivered ammunition.[130] Given the air situation, it was a courageous action and it is surprising that only three Lysanders were lost. Sadly the effort was in vain because the Germans had captured the Citadel on the evening of 26 May.[131] There were additional drops elsewhere because 2 DSC, whilst foraging in a supplies dump in the Foret de Nieppe, discovered bully beef and biscuit tins, which, 'appeared to have been dropped by aeroplane',[132] whilst 48 DSC drew on air-dropped supplies in the Bois de Flines.[133] Although a classic example of improvisation, and lucidly demonstrating the co-ordination of the many different components required to deliver logistic output, the airlift was unsustainable. The unfavourable air situation demanded a fighter escort, yet still involved the loss of transport aircraft, whilst poor communications also played a part because the RASC WMT could not be briefed if the destination airfield changed.[134]

For Their Departed Mates

Whilst these aerial logistic operations were in full swing, an entirely different technological transportation capability was slowly moving to the coast. 25 and 32 Animal Transport (AT) Companies of Force K6 had many trials and tribulations during operational swirl of the withdrawal, the pace of their movement often resulting in marches along small country lanes to leave the roads free for WMT and AFVs. 25 AT Company abandoned its animals and equipment near Teteghem and embarked for passage to England from the Dunkerque Mole on 29 May. Remarkably, 'in spite of violent enemy action', the unit suffered not one casualty during the withdrawal and evacuation, which the Commandant put down to good fortune, excellent training and the leadership of the OC, Major J G Wainwright.[135] 32 AT Company, allocated to I Corps, eventually withdrew to the village of Socx, nine miles South of Dunkerque and gifted the animals to local farmers before embarking for England on 25 May having only suffered two casualties.[136] Remaining on an animal theme, logisticians performed many tasks inside the Dunkerque perimeter, some of them logistic, others tactical but, a sad one undertaken by Major Vaux, OC 2 DPC, should be recorded. Moved by the pathetic howling of the dogs on the Mole calling 'for their departed mates', he commenced shooting them before dropping them over the

129 Regimental Committee, *The Story of the Royal Army Service Corps 1939-1945*, p.74.
130 For the procedures, see, Air Council, *Royal Air Force Pocket Book*, Chp IX, Sect 43, Supply Dropping, pp.141-142.
131 Ellis, BOH, *The War in France and Flanders*, p.170.
132 TNA WO 197210: 2 Division CRASC, General Notes – Supplies.
133 TNA WO 167/297: 48 DSC RASC, WD, 24 May 1940. The Bois de Flines was an area probably quite well known to the soldiers of 48 DSC because the unit was located, before the German invasion, at Dechy, 7 miles to the SSW.
134 TNA WO 197/134: Evacuation from France and Quartering of the BEF – Activities of DST in the Evacuation from France.
135 TNA WO 167/1433: HQ Force K6, 'Report on Operations in France' dated 19 July 1940, para 12.
136 TNA WO 167/1433: HQ Force K6, 'Report on Operations in France' dated 19 July 1940, para 15.

side into the water, until, having had to borrow more ammunition, there none were left alive. Despite the human death and destruction around the unit, the author of the war diary, who witnessed the event, described it as, 'The worst job of the lot'.[137] Meanwhile on the beaches, members of 50 Division RASC Band were engaged in burying their instruments in the sand in the hope that at some point they might be recovered.[138]

There were many cases of quiet heroism amongst the logisticians, especially those driving ambulances and unloading the lighters on the beaches, some of whom did not survive and lie At Rest in the surrounding cemeteries or are remembered on the Dunkirk Memorial, their names carved in perpetuity in stone. One was Staff Sergeant Lloyd RAOC who was the armourer of 2nd Coldstream Guards,[139] a battalion forming part of the BEF's rear-guard. Ordered as a logistic technical specialist to seek embarkation from the beaches, he chose to remain in the fighting line and was KIA.[140] Second-Lieutenant John Carpenter,[141] commanding a section in 522 Ammunition Company (TA)[142] in 50 DAC, having been ordered to reach Dunkerque, marched his soldiers to the sands at Bray Dunes. Seizing the moment, he waded into the sea and brought in an abandoned lifeboat, which his men rowed from the beach. Subjected to a *Luftwaffe* machine gun attack, the section was rescued by a Dutch coaster and reached England. Many other logisticians were also fortunate to return to the UK, although with mixed experiences, the men of 2 DPC being representative of many of them because the unit was split into several groups, which although they all returned to the UK, did so in various ways.[143] Those men directed to serve as ambulance drivers near the beach areas did not leave until 1 June, and for the most part had to wade and swim out to small boats, thus crossing the English Channel in various ships and arriving at Hereford and Halifax in 'dribbles' by many routes.[144] The party aboard the SS *Prague* departing from Dunkerque with some of the 95 German POWs the unit had transported from Steenwerke[145] had a safe and uneventful crossing, with the ship's

137 TNA WO 167/212: 2 DPC RASC, WD, 29 May 1940.
138 The precious pieces were never recovered by the Band post-war and may still lie under the beach. The story passed into regimental folklore and remains alive and well in its successor, 150 Transport Regiment RLC.
139 Howard & Sparrow, *The Coldstream Guards, 1920-1946*, p.52, record his name as Loyd but the correct spelling is Lloyd.
140 7876211 Staff Sergeant Oliver Charles Lloyd RAOC, aged 31, and husband to Amy Joyce of Elson Gosport, lies At Rest in Warem Communal Cemetery, France.
141 I am indebted to the late Major-General V H J Carpenter CB MBE (1921-2009) for kindly sharing with me, some of his traumatic experiences of his service in the BEF. He subsequently served in Palestine, Iraq, North Africa, Sicily, Normandy and NW Europe. He remained in the Army post-war, attending the Army Staff College and serving in Palestine, Korea, the Arabian Peninsula and BAOR. Promoted to Major-General in 1971, he was appointed Transport Officer-in-Chief (Army) retiring in 1975 as Director of Movements (Army). He was National Chairman of the Dunkirk Veterans Association (1974-1991) and then its President until its disbandment in 2000. His obituary appeared in the Daily Telegraph on Wednesday 12 August 2009.
142 Although a Regular officer, John Carpenter was posted to a TA unit and received a baptism of fire because he arrived in the unit on 9 May 1940.
143 The 2 DPC war diary is clearly a compilation of the experiences of several groups, written at Halifax, although the manuscript suggests the author is one person, who given his grasp of the many activities within the unit may have been the OC, Major J F Vaux RASC.
144 TNA WO 167/212: 2 DPC RASC, WD, 1 June 1940.
145 TNA WO 167/212: 2 DPC RASC, WD, 27 May 1940.

P17.4 Dunkerque Mole and Outer Harbour May 2019. Unbelievably calm and peaceful. (Author)

company doing 'everything possible' for the soldiers before docking at Folkestone to find food and refreshments as well as a 'surprisingly enthusiastic welcome'.[146]

The 2 DPC party commanded by Captain Westwood RASC sailing on the MV *Hird*[147] however, had a very different experience and, for military evacuees from Dunkerque a rather unusual one. The ship was 'packed with French and British troops,' German POWs, some under the control of the 2 DPC party, and a number of refugees, all estimated to total 3,500 souls.[148] During the crossing, despite the threat of air, surface and submarine attack, the *Hird* stopped to

146 TNA WO 167/212: 2 DPC RASC, WD, 29 May 1940.

147 The MV *Hird* was a diesel-powered cargo ship of 4,950 GRT, owned by the Norwegian company Vard. The *Hird* was sunk on 15 September 1940 by a torpedo fired from U-65 whilst on passage from Bermuda to Manchester in convoy HX 72 with a general cargo of 8,101 tons. The Icelandic trawler *Poroflur* rescued the crew.

148 BR 1736 (32), *Second World War,* Battle Summary No 41, *The Evacuation from Dunkirk, Operation Dynamo, 26 May - 4 June 1940,* TSD 64/48, Tactical and Staff Duties Division (Admiralty, 1949), p.37. Given the numbers aboard, it was most fortunate that the *Hird* was not sunk otherwise a disaster on the scale of the *Lancastria* could have occurred.

P17.5 *Compagnons d'armes.* Memorial at Bray Dunes to the soldiers of the French 12th Motorized Infantry Division. The logistic interfaces between the BEF and the French Army are opaque aspects of operations in France and worthy of study. (Author)

lower a boat at 0515 to rescue Commander R L Fisher RN,[149] the Captain of HMS *Wakeful*.[150] Having had no water, rations or sleep for two days, and little of any of those luxuries on the MV *Hird*, the party were aghast to discover that standing off Dover,[151] the ship was ordered to sail to Cherbourg with the evacuated soldiers included the wounded, still aboard.[152] The war diary records that having almost reached England, 'Men broke down with disappointment',[153]

149 Commander Ralph Lindsay Fisher (1903-1988) had a series of remarkable adventures after the sinking of HMS *Wakeful* and was certainly lucky to survive his ordeal. He was awarded a DSO for his actions at Dunkerque and retired as a Rear Admiral CB DSO OBE DSC in 1957.

150 BR 1736 (32), *Second World War*, Battle Summary No 41, p.37. HMS *Wakeful* was a W Class destroyer sunk at 0045 by a torpedo from an E-Boat S-30 with heavy loss of life, with only 25 of the crew and two of the 640 soldiers aboard surviving, one being a RASC soldier Stanley Patrick, aged 19, who was serving with 13 Troop Carrying Company and the other, Jim Kane of the Royal Tank Regiment.

151 According to Winser, *BEF Ships*, p.17, Commander Fisher disembarked from the *Hird* off Dover.

152 Oddly, the *Hird* is not mentioned in Russell Plummer, *The Ships That Saved an Army*, perhaps because it did not dock at Dover and upon its return from Cherbourg was never recorded as having completed an Operation DYNAMO voyage.

153 TNA WO 167/212: 2 DPC RASC, WD, 29 May 1940.

manifestly suggesting that by then, morale was fragile, reinforced by a presumption that they were being returned to France to conduct further operations.[154] Interestingly, the war diary does not make comment upon this nor the reason for the diversion to Cherbourg, but the most likely reason was to repatriate the French troops, whom presumably the Admiralty believed to be in the majority.[155] The *Hird* reached Cherbourg on 30 May, morale being uplifted by the capable seamanship of the Master and by the strong leadership of OC Troops, Major Hunt RASC, who, upon the docking of the ship, swiftly arranged the transfer of the POWs to the French[156] and for the British troops the provision of water, rations and some rest at a transit camp.[157] Suitably refreshed, the 2 DPC soldiers arrived at Southampton aboard two ships on 1 June, the unit war diary describing the administrative arrangements for their reception as 'bad' with no food or refreshments and they only received hot tea and sandwiches from the industrious lady volunteers at Salisbury railway station at 0200 on 2 June.[158]

South of the Somme

Operations South of the Somme, although initially less pressured, were more complex. Immediate efforts were made to restore control of the supply situation, which had deteriorated to a parlous state by 22 May. The War Office stopped further shipments of anything but priority stores to ports South of the Somme and plans were drafted for the return of specified *materiel* to the United Kingdom. Ships *en-route* were recalled, whilst others in port were often re-loaded with the same stocks they had recently discharged.[159] The Staff of HQ LOC Area had a challenging time over the next month coping with the many conflicting tasks placed upon them, which were an intriguing mix of withdrawal, re-organization, re-deployment, evacuation and reinforcement, and their efforts were all the more impressive given that they were not structured or tasked to support divisional formations. Nonetheless, a semblance of order was created, and the logisticians adapted to the rapidly changing scenario, although orchestrating support to the *ad hoc* formations of Macforce,[160] Petreforce,[161] Polforce,[162] Usherforce[163] and smaller fluctuating

154 It is possible that the 2 DPC experience of sailing from Dunkerque to a UK port, diverting to Cherbourg and docking in France is unique.
155 TNA WO 167/212: 2 DPC RASC, WD, 29 May 1940. It can only be presumed that despite the priority in evacuating troops from Dunkerque, the Admiralty had sufficient shipping lift to divert the *Hird* to Cherbourg.
156 The German POWs were indeed fortunate because they were released under the terms of the 1940 Armistice. Their wartime fates are unknown.
157 TNA WO 167/212: 2 DPC RASC, WD, 30 May 1940.
158 TNA WO 167/212: 2 DPC RASC, WD, 1 June 1940.
159 WOOH, *Maintenance in the Field*, Vol, I, p.53.
160 TNA WO 197/86: Macforce – Operational Message and Notes. For a resume of operations, see, Philson, BEFORBAT, Vol 5 (Milton Keynes: Military Press, 2007), pp.99-100.
161 Petreforce was based 12th (Eastern) Division. A light tank squadron was formed with 12 tanks from an Ordnance depot. Ibid, pp.102-103.
162 Polforce was based upon 46th (North Midland & West Riding) Division. Ibid, pp.1-7.
163 Ibid, pp.104-105.

units, some based on enlarged platoons, such as Don Details, Cobbet's Force, Cook's Light Tanks and Woodforce,[164] was a demanding, if not occasionally hopeless, activity.

War Stocks had to be issued to improvised formations including Beauman Division[165] but *materiel* shortages led to many of the units being improperly equipped. For example, 'A' Field Regiment Royal Artillery consisting of four batteries, was planned to be equipped with 48 x 25 pounders but the ordnance depot could only issue 24 x 25 pounders, 4 x 18/25 pounders and 2 x 4.5-inch howitzers, which created logistic challenges in supply of the ammunition and the provision of spares.[166] Reserve stocks for the BEF continued to be ring-fenced held in case the GLOC was reopened and the order to release this *materiel* for other purposes was not issued until 29 May, three days after the declaration of evacuation through Dunkerque was promulgated. The Base depots also had to maintain support to the recently deployed 1st Armoured Division and the withdrawing 51st (Highland) Division, as well as receiving *materiel* from the UK to enhance the operational capability of these formations, with the distribution of AFV spares being an especially important aspect. The transport of POL was a problem although supplies were ample; on 4 June stocks amounted to 100,000 tons with a daily consumption of only 650,[167] sufficient to last 153 days.

Events moved quickly for the logistic Staffs at every level of command. Evacuation of stocks to the UK increased after 24 May, when the War Office ordered an urgent return of 50,000 rifles,[168] 50,000 respirators and 12,500 tonnes of ammunition.[169] The inference that all British forces were to leave France was however, soon changed by the War Office. Once it was clear that the BEF in the North would have to withdraw to the UK, plans were drafted for the establishment of a 2nd BEF to the South of the Somme, comprising sufficient forces for the creation of initially one, expanding to two corps, based on the following divisions: 1st Armoured, 51st (Highland), 52nd (Lowland), Beauman and 1st (Canadian); additionally there was also a proposal to re-constitute 3rd Division recently returned from Dunkerque. Churchill, who wished to continue Britain's Continental commitment in order to keep the French in the fight and Britain in Europe, drove this military concept hard. On the face of it, based on the assumption that French forces could still offer cohesive resistance, the proposal made sound political and military sense because whilst France was in the war, the Germans were unlikely to attack Britain. The tempo of operations however, rendered the plan impractical, since by the second week in June, the 1st Armoured Division was no longer combat effective, whilst 51st

164 Woodforce was formed to defend GHQ at Hazebrouck and consisted of 3 x 25 pdrs, 1 x 25 mm anti-tank gun, 300 men from GHQ and a Welsh Guards platoon armed with 11 x anti-tank rifles, 3 x Vickers MMG, 13 x LMG and 300 rifles, plus a Belgian detachment manning 12 x MG and from France, 200 Engineers and 18 x FT 17 tanks. See, Philson, BEFORBAT, Vol 3, p.41.

165 For an operational resume, see, Ibid, pp.38-41.

166 Ibid, p.41 and TNA CAB 44/67: The BEF in Belgium and Artois, 10 May-3 June 1940, entry 18 May 1940.

167 WOOH, *Supplies and Transport*, Vol I, p 127.

168 The recovery of these rifles came to the attention of the Prime-Minister, Winston Churchill, who was advised, incorrectly, by the Ministry of Supply that there had been significant losses from Base depots. It would appear that the 50,000 were received in the UK from the BEF BODs in the period 15-24 June 1940, with further consignments totalling 45,848, being received later. Initially, losses were assessed to be 24,557, revised downwards to 6,152. See, TNA PREM 3/183: Material lost in and evacuated from France, Letter Secretary of State for War (Anthony Eden) to Prime-Minister of July 1940 but nd.

169 WOOH, *Ordnance Services* (War Office, 1950), p 158.

(Highland) Division, less 154th Brigade, had in less than two days between 8-10 June been cut off from its withdrawal route to Le Harve or Rouen and could no longer be supplied through the GLOC, even by road.[170] So quickly did the British operational scenario deteriorate that in the same period the option of supporting 51st Division by sea through Dieppe or Fecamp had also evaporated,[171] leaving evacuation through the small port of Saint Valery-en-Caux and the adjoining beaches as the only alternative. From the logistic perspective, the last hours of the Highland Division's battle on 12 June were summarized by the experience of 1st Black Watch: 'For some hours there had been no food or water; by noon there was no ammunition'.[172]

An Appalling Traffic Jam

The re-deployment continued apace, despite the German advance and crumbling French resistance, creating many difficulties for the logisticians. On the one hand, they were attempting to recover stocks to the UK under Operation AERIAL but on the other, generate support for incoming forces including 52nd (Lowland) Division[173] and the first brigade group of 1st (Canadian) Division; it was a confusing situation, which created conflicts of priority and left subordinate commanders to decide the main effort. The military element of the plan would have been much more meaningful had the mission been to recover the enormous stocks from the Base areas, although this would have created serious political repercussions. One forgotten aspect was the late withdrawal of the logistic elements of Force W from the Saar. Whilst 51st (Highland) Division was withdrawing to the coast, most of the logisticians supporting Force W were tasked with recovering the stocks located in the Woippy area near Metz. 22 AT Company RIASC, which joined Force W on 5 May 1940,[174] remained to assist in the movement of ammunition to a railhead after which, it was planned to rail the unit to Saint Nazaire to undertake similar work with ordnance stores but by the time the relevant orders were given this was no longer achievable nor was a secondary plan to evacuate it by WMT and the company was captured, the only Force K6 component to suffer this fate.[175] The RASC and RAOC components were only able to evacuate once the Third French Army had made arrangements with SNCF for trains to move them but by then, although valiant efforts were made, the operational situation resulted in the logisticians leaving the trains to march on foot but they were eventually either mostly captured or sought internment in Switzerland.[176]

170 Ellis, BOH, *The War in France and Flanders*, Situation Map opp p.282.
171 Ibid, Situation Map opp p.294.
172 Bernard Ferguson, *The Black Watch and the King's Enemies* (London: Collins, 1950), p.45.
173 TNA WO 167/327: 52nd Division A&Q, WD, June 1940. The RASC also provided 10 TCC to act as a 3rd Line Ammunition Sub Park. TNA WO 167/1077: LOC DDST, WD, 13 June 1940.
174 TNA WO 167/56: Q Branch L of C, WD, 27 April 1940. The HQ Force K6 Post Operational Report states 7 May. It is probable that the planned date was 5 May and the actual 7 May. TNA WO 167/1433: HQ Force K6, 'Report on Operations in France' dated 19 July 1940.
175 It was ironic that 22 AT Company having served in the Base for most of its deployment in France should be the only component of K6 that was captured. The Commander, Lieutenant-Colonel R W W Hills RIASC was not informed of the presumption of capture, learning of it from a public announcement, an arrangement that much distressed him. TNA WO 167/1433: HQ Force K6, 'Report on Operations in France' dated 19 July 1940, para 5.
176 See Chp 15, 'Riding the Rails'.

The air situation remained in the Germans favour, but this had rather less effect on the Base areas than the planners had envisaged because incendiaries delivered by air could have caused considerable destruction in the Base depots. For most of the time however, the *Luftwaffe* focused its activity on providing Offensive Air Support (OAS)[177] and although logistic activity was constantly interrupted, there was never a concerted effort to execute integrated Air Interdiction (AI)[178] on a widespread basis, thereby enabling key logistic activities to continue despite German air superiority over much of France. This good fortune enabled the RASC to participate in two particularly successful operations during the withdrawal of 52nd (Lowland) Division. On 17 June, after an urgent request from 157th Infantry Brigade to deliver combat supplies, a composite convoy of 20 lorries from LOC Area delivered rations, ammunition and petrol from dumps at Rennes.[179] How this logistic crisis developed is not clear but it was either the result of HQ 52nd (Lowland) Division failing to allocate logistic resources to 157th Brigade after the withdrawal of the balance of the Division[180] or that 'G' at HQ LOC agreed to arrange support but did not consult 'Q'. The LOC DDST war diary is clear that 'Q' was not informed that the brigade had not been evacuated but sheds no light on the logistic planning processes with HQ 52nd Division,[181] although the failure to deploy, in a timely manner, the RASC assets to meet the initial mission in France suggests fragility in this arena. That on 15 June 1940, CRASC was tasked with providing two sections of 30 x 3 ton lorries, with both 155th and 156th Brigades each receiving one to lift an infantry battalion per formation, seems to suggest that the focus was on evacuation rather than support and the 157th Brigade requirement was forgotten.[182] In another logistic success, 18 TCC RASC[183] withdrew all the non-motorized elements of 157th Brigade, 226 miles from Saint Anne Loir-et-Cher[184] to Cherbourg in 24 hours during 16-17

177 OAS consisted of Battlefield Air Interdiction and Close Air Support. See, *Air Publication* (AP) *3000, British Air Power Doctrine*, 2nd Edn, pp.62-63.

178 See Glossary.

179 TNA WO 167/1077: LOC DDST, WD, 16 June 1940. The arrival of these stocks is not mentioned in the TNA WO 167/413: HQ 157th Brigade WD, which given that the HQ was focused on evacuating the brigade is an understandable omission, although a strange one not only because of the criticality of the delivery but also the otherwise detailed entries. See also, WOOH, *Supplies and Transport*, Vol I, p 128.

180 The three sub-units forming 52 Division RASC embarked on the SS *Rohistan* at Cherbourg on 17 June 1940. TNA WO 167/330: 52 Division CRASC, WD, 17 June 1940. 10, 15 and 18 TCC were assigned to the division for operations but were not organic to it.

181 TNA WO 167/1077: LOC DDST, WD, 16 June 1940.

182 TNA WO 167/330: 52 Division CRASC, WD.

183 Regimental Committee, *The Story of the Royal Army Service Corps 1939-1945*, p.87 states 226 Company but there is no war diary for 226 Company RASC for the period in the TNA, the earliest reference being Home Forces in July 1940: WO 166/4942. Two TCCs, 15 and 18 were attached to 52nd Division, deploying on 8 June 1940. HQ 157th Brigade war diary is specific that 18 TCC conducted the move, TNA WO 167/413, entries 16-17 June 1940 and WO 167/1110: 18 TCC RASC, WD. The distance between Saint Anne Loir-et-Cher is shown as 226 miles on the AA Route-planner; a co-incidence or a transposition in *The Story of the Royal Army Service Corps*?

184 Saint Anne Loir-et-Cher lies approximately 50 miles SSE of Le Mans. The non-motorized elements of 157th Brigade had travelled from Conches to Saint Anne in French buses. George Blake, *Mountain and Flood: The History of the 52nd (Lowland) Division, 1939-1946* (Glasgow: Jackson, Son & Co, 1950), p.28.

June.[185] The move was particularly challenging in that not only were the roads[186] crowded with refugees and uncontrolled military traffic but also it crossed three lateral routes mainly occupied by the French Cavalry Corps withdrawing West to Brest.[187] There was a significant delay in the Foret de Domfront during which, a single *Luftwaffe* aircraft strafed the brigade column that was part of an 'appalling traffic jam'[188] but there were no casualties.[189] In this respect, the Germans missed another golden opportunity to severely dislocate the withdrawal South of the Somme and British forces escaped with fewer losses than might have been expected.[190] One of the key factors in the success of the move apart from providence was the strong co-ordinating grip of the Brigade Major.

Conclusion

The logisticians' critical role in supporting the BEF's combat operations in the Battle for France has effectively been ignored for the past 80 years but hopefully this chapter has exposed their contribution and commitment. With the GLOC cut, the corps and divisional logisticians were quick to seize the moment, securing combat supplies from BEF dumps and civilian sources, sometimes under direct fire from German forces. Ironically, it was the doctrinally impure pre-attack dumping of substantial quantities ammunition and the subsequent ability to distribute it, which enabled the BEF to take the fight all the way back to the North Channel Ports; had these stocks not been available, most of the BEF would almost certainly have been captured. In this respect, the logisticians played a fundamental role in the BEF's survival that to date has never been fully recognized.

Throughout the campaign, the paucity of communications was a constant constraint on logistic planning and delivery, so the achievement of the Staff and units is even more remarkable. Equally impressive are the maturing 'Learning Steps' developed during combat operations. The move to minor railheads to reduce logistic signature, the developing tactical agility of distribution and the growing initiative, courage and confidence of junior officers and NCOs were three unmistakable indicators of an organization ready to rapidly adopt new 'skills and drills' to obviate emerging threats and there is little doubt that had the campaign resulted in a different outcome, the combat logisticians would have been a honed professional component of the BEF but the evacuation blunted the blade of the logistic axe.

185 TNA WO 167/413: HQ 157th Brigade WD, entries 16-17 June 1940.

186 One particular, and presumably irritating feature of many of the moves during the deployment of 52nd (Lowland) Division, was closed gates on railway level crossings but no keepers to open them. Blake, *Mountain and Flood*, p.25. The Brigade Major 157th Brigade however, also found level crossings a useful RV for WMT. TNA WO 167/413: 157th Brigade WD, entries 16-17 June 1940.

187 TNA WO 167/413: HQ 157th Brigade WD, 17 June 1940.

188 TNA WO 167/413: HQ 157th Brigade WD, 17 June 1940.

189 TNA WO 167/413: HQ 157th Brigade WD, 17 June 1940. The war diary observed that: 'it was a miracle that more attacks were not delivered as the French colns were blocking the roads for miles in many places and tpt was nose to tail - in fact, in many places a one well directed bomb would have held up the coln for hours. However, the enemy missed their opportunity'. The divisional history observed of situation of the stationary convoys: 'if the German bombers had come upon it, the carnage must have been frightful'. Blake, *Mountain and Flood*, p.29.

190 TNA WO 167/413: HQ 157th Brigade WD, entries 16-17 June 1940.

18

Run Rabbit Run
Denial and Departure

Cycling Stragglers

There were five separate evacuation operations from France. The process commenced with what originally was a re-deployment. In order to adjust the logistic and operational posture of the BEF, in the period 19- 26 May, before Operation DYNAMO[1] commenced, 21,410 Army[2] and RAF personnel, 4,992 casualties[3] and 1,534 Allied soldiers and refugees totalling 27,936 people had been landed at Dover, Folkestone, Newhaven and Southampton.[4] This activity was a most valuable prelude to DYNAMO, the most famous of the evacuation operations, which recovered the BEF and later Allied Forces from the port of Dunkerque and the neighbouring beaches to the East-North-East. Operation CYCLE was successful in evacuating the majority of troops from the base around Le Harve, including 154th Brigade[5] but the attempt to lift the main body of 51st (Highland) Division and additional units, from Saint Valery-en-Caux, was, with the exception of the fortuitous extraction from the beach at Veules-les-Rose,[6] for the most part

1 For the official naval history of Operation DYNAMO, see, BR 1736 (32), *Second World War*, Battle Summary No 41, *The Evacuation from Dunkirk, Operation Dynamo, 26 May-4 June 1940*, TSD 64/48, Tactical and Staff Duties Division, Admiralty, 1949. See also, ADM 234/360: Operation Dynamo.

2 Many of these soldiers were specialists from GHQ Troops. Initially a process of re-deployment, the withdrawal included railway operators and construction troops, military survey staff and bakers. Other groups, such as offensive chemical personnel and intelligence staff were also withdrawn to prevent them from being captured.

3 The casualties accumulating in the Casualty Clearing Stations (CCS) around Bailleul had, once the Germans had cut the GLOC, only the road and railway to Dunkerque to provide a perilous route to the coast.

4 TNA WO 197/134: Evacuation and Quartering of the BEF, para 7 and Peter Tatlow, *Return from Dunkirk: Railways to the Rescue, Operation Dynamo (1940)* (Usk: Oakwood Press, 2010), p.51.

5 11,000 troops, including those from Ark Force were evacuated from Le Harve in the two days of 12-13 June 1940. TNA WO 106/1739: Operation CYCLE - Evacuation Reports.

6 900 French soldiers and 1,300 members of the BEF were rescued from the beach at the base of the cliffs, including 500 men from the 2/7th Duke of Wellington's Regiment and another 161 from 385 Battery 1RHA, some of whom had used improvised ropes made from blankets and rifle slings to descend the 300 feet of vertical rock, with several falling to their deaths. In addition, approximately 800 troops were lifted from small fishing ports along the coast. For a detailed account of this operation, see,

thwarted by the German advance and thick fog,[7] although a total of 3,335 British and French military and civilian personnel[8] were landed in the UK, which given the circumstances was a remarkable and courageous action by the Royal Navy and Merchant Marine.[9] Some of these soldiers were rescued from small boats in which they had set sail with the intention of crossing the English Channel and the courage of those taking passage in such vessels, sometimes with little or no experience of the sea is truly remarkable.[10] The total numbers landed in the UK from 51st (Highland) Division was 4,499, from an initial strength of 13,582. The Divisional RASC was fortunate to recover 54 percent of its personnel; 589 officers and soldiers from a total of 1,087 although none of the 26 members of the Divisional Postal Unit or the 16 soldiers of 8 Mobile Bath Unit escaped.[11] One of the logisticians fortunate to return to the UK was Driver Bisset of 527 Supply Company RASC, who was evacuated with a French contingent.[12]

Operation AERIAL, despite the challenges, was a remarkably successful operation, recovering stores and personnel mainly through the ports of Brest, Cherbourg, La Pallice, Saint Malo, and Saint Nazaire, although the Inter-Departmental Howard Committee established to report on the 'Evacuation of the BEF from French Ports, South of the Somme', believed that more equipment could have been evacuated.[13] Operation AERIAL also included the brief reinforcement[14] and then evacuation[15] of the Channel Islands, to which, nine ships were allocated, supported by four local vessels for inter-island transfers.[16] To illustrate the logistic dynamics of

Saul David, *Churchill's Sacrifice of the Highland Division, France 1940* (London & Washington: Brasseys 1994), pp.214-225.

7 Ibid.

8 2,137 British, 1,184 French and 34 seamen and civilians. WOOH, *Movements*, p.202, Appx E to Chp 10 and TNA WO 106/1739: Operation CYCLE - Evacuation Reports.

9 For details of the critical naval and mercantile contribution to Operation CYCLE, see, TNA ADM 179/158: Operation CYCLE and ADM 276/126: Operation CYCLE Reports.

10 The most spectacular escape was from Saint Valery harbour under the observation of the enemy, by Second-Lieutenant Jim Walker and 18 men of Company 7th Norfolks. Using shovels as paddles they escaped to sea to be rescued by the destroyer HMS *Harvester*. Lieutenant-Commander P K Kemp RN, *The History of the Norfolk Regiment*, Vol III, *1919-1945* (Norwich: Regimental Association of The Royal Norfolk Regiment, 1953), p.121.

11 Philson, BEFORBAT, Vol 5, 51st Division state upon returning to the UK, p.26.

12 David, *Churchill's Sacrifice of the Highland Division*, p.218.

13 TNA WO 33/2384: 'Report on the Committee on the Evacuation of the British Expeditionary Force from French Ports', hereafter, Howard Committee Report.

14 This involved two infantry battalions from the UK and RAF ground staff from France to support Hurricane fighters from 17 and 501 Squadrons, flying from the Islands to cover the evacuations from Cherbourg. The LAA battery in the ORBAT was not deployed and the proposal to use the Islands as a staging point for the evacuation from Saint Malo was also cancelled. Winser, *BEF Ships*, p.49.

15 TNA WO 106/1615: Evacuation of BEF France - Plan AERIAL, Admiralty Immediate (MOST SECRET) Message 0252/15 dated 15 June 1940. The British Government declared that the Channel Islands would be demilitarized but the evacuation included 25,000 civilians, most of whom left by sea, although 319 people departed by civilian De Havilland Express DH-86 aircraft, between 16-19 June, landing at Exeter. Despite the demilitarization, there were losses. Several ships including the Southern Railway SS *Isle of Sark*, a cross-Channel ferry, were docked in Saint Peter Port harbour on 28 June when six Heinkel He 111 bombers attacked. The bomb damage was mainly to the harbour where 49 lorries loaded with tomatoes for export were parked. 34 people died and 33 injured, and in a similar attack in Jersey, nine people were killed.

16 Winser, *BEF Ships*, p.49.

this operation, RAF ground units consisting of 188 personnel, WMT and equipment, arrived in Jersey from Saint Malo early on 18 June 1940, disembarked from the small coaster SS *Farfield*,[17] supported Hurricane fighters from 17 and 501 Squadrons flying patrols to cover the evacuation from Cherbourg before embarking on *Train Ferry No 1* for Southampton on 19 June.[18] By mid-August 1940, despite the short notice to effect, Operation AERIAL had recovered 139,812 British service personnel including 2,626 casualties, 315 artillery pieces and AA guns, 2,282 vehicles, 3,414 tons of ammunition and 1,783 tons of stores,[19] which added to the material that had been previously salved. A little-known sub-evacuation, which although conducted under AERIAL was effectively a separate task, was the on-going recovery of BEF stragglers,[20] the many foreign contingents, some civilians and the staff of the Marseilles Sub-Area from the South and South-West of France,[21] an operation, which continued until mid-August 1940. 46,515 Allied service personnel arrived in the UK by way of Operation AERIAL, including 163 Belgians, 4,938 Czechs 17,062 French and 24,352 Poles.[22]

Operation DYNAMO has been covered in detail by many authors and Operations AERIAL and CYCLE also, although to a lesser extent, with the focus being the evacuation of personnel rather than material.[23] This chapter will therefore, examine the evacuation and denial of logistic assets to the South of the Somme,[24] tasks which, were beset by a complex Allied chain of

17 The *Farfield* of 468 GRT then embarked civilian evacuees, departing Jersey on 20 June and arriving at Weymouth the next day. Ibid, p.138. On 15 (some publications state 13 or 14) July 1941, the SS *Farfield* was bombed and strafed, sinking 5 nm West of South Stack Anglesey with the loss of all the eight crew, with only the RN gunner being rescued. Admiralty, *British Merchant Vessels Lost or Damaged by Enemy Action*, p.25.

18 TNA AIR 27/1949: 501 Squadron RAF, ORB, June 1940.

19 TNA WO 106/1615: Evacuation of BEF France - Plan AERIAL, War Office QMG note Q (M) 2 dated 15 August 1940, 'Personnel Returned from the BEF (Aerial Plan)'.

20 Three British soldiers had escaped from France and arrived at Bilbao in Northern Spain before obtaining passage on a ship to Glasgow. TNA WO 106/1615: Evacuation of BEF France - Plan AERIAL, War Office QMG note Q (M) 2 dated 15 August 1940, 'Personnel Returned from the BEF (Aerial Plan)'.

21 This included extraction from minor ports including Bordeaux-Verdon in the West, Bayonne to the NE of Biarritz and Saint Jean de Luz to the SW. From this latter port approximately 17,000 Polish personnel were evacuated in addition to British military and civilian personnel. Winser, *BEF Ships*, p.50.

22 These figures are 'as at' 14 August 1940. TNA WO 106/1615: Evacuation of BEF France - Plan AERIAL, War Office QMG Q (M) 2 dated 15 August 1940, 'Personnel Returned from the BEF (Aerial Plan)'

23 Two books of note have been published on the evacuation operations to the South of the River Somme. Basil Karslake, *1940: The Last Act: The Story of the British Forces in France after Dunkirk* (London: Leo Cooper, 1979), was written by the eldest son of Lieutenant-General Karslake, the author having personal involvement with a senior officer who commanded key parts of the operations. In the author's note, he wrote, 'It is hoped that the following account will, at long last, fill a gap in the history of the Second World War, thereby completing the history of the BEF in France', which perhaps applied to the operational aspects but not the logistic ones. Michael Glover, *The Fight for the Channel Ports: A Study in Confusion* (London: Leo Cooper, 1985), adds more to the operational perspective, particularly in relation to the relationship with the French and a little to the British logistic one. Both books are invaluable in explaining the operational context in which the logisticians were working.

24 There are though, occasional references to denial operations undertaken by units to the North of the River Seine.

command and the complications of execution exacerbated by the introduction on 23 May of a senior officer as the GOC LOC, Lieutenant-General Karslake, who had been retired from the Army for two years and had spent the previous 10 serving in India. He was not therefore, currently conversant with either the structure of the LOC or the Base nor the fast moving events in France.[25] As GOC LOC, he commanded Beauman Division and the disparate units under Commander Depots, Ports and Supplies, Major-General de Fonblanque but attempted to execute his responsibilities with an inadequate and unpractised Staff, whilst most of the other British formations South of the River Somme were under various French commands.

It is clear that Lieutenant-General Alan Brooke, sent to France to command the 2nd BEF, believed Karslake was adding no value to the operation, informing him the day after Brooke arrived in France that 'he could go home'. He recorded in his diary, 'After greeting Karslake I informed him that he need not wait any longer than he wanted. He told me he had a plane standing by and was off at once!'[26] One has to conclude in 2020, as Brooke did in 1940, that Karslake was not a commander capable of bringing any order to the crisis that was engulfing the logisticians on the GLOC, though regardless of the personalities, the challenges remained as the constant. That Major-General de Fonblanque was effectively with the departure of Karslake re-instated as GOC LOC, unknown to his superiors and subordinates, terminally ill,[27] compounded the problems generated by sometimes obscure missions and collapsing communications but at least with the arrival of Brooke on 13 June he received clear orders.[28]

Writing on the Wall

Evacuation of stocks to the United Kingdom increased after 24 May, when the War Office ordered an urgent return of: 50,000 rifles, 50,000 respirators and 12,500 tonnes of ammunition;[29] someone had seen the writing on the wall. As planning for withdrawal gathered pace, the Staff focused their minds on five important logistic tasks: sustaining the 2nd BEF, ensuring the safe recovery of the Army and RAF Gas Warfare weapons,[30] returning as much conventional ammunition as possible and preventing the enemy from capturing the very sizeable stocks of British petroleum products, the latter issue having been examined in late 1939 to gather

25 According to Karslake, *1940: The Last Act*, p.53-54, the general had identified that by bringing the fighting lines parallel to the LOC, the Allies had created a recipe for disaster, which was indeed the case.

26 Danchev & Todman, *War Diaries, 1939-1945, Field Marshal Lord Alanbrooke* (London: Weidenfeld & Nicolson, 2001), p.79, diary entry 13 June 1940.

27 His service in France adversely affected his ailing health and he died on 2 July 1940 two weeks after his return to UK. He is buried in the Commonwealth War Grave Commission's General Service section of the Cambridge City Cemetery.

28 Brooke remarked in his diary, 'To my consternation I found that there were still some 100,000 men from the BEF - L of C troops! In addition, masses of dumps of clothes, equipment, vehicles, stores, petrol etc etc. I instructed him to keep on evacuating home as many of these unarmed personnel as he could, only retaining personnel essential for the maintenance of four Divisions'. Ibid, p.79, diary entry 13 June 1940.

29 TWOOH, *Ordnance Services*, p.158.

30 The recovery of GW munitions is described in Chp 14, 'Operation FLANNELFOOT'.

P18.1 A Forgotten Logistician. The resting place of Major-General Philip de Fonblanque DSO in the Cambridge City Cemetery Grave 9586. His fate was not to be KIA in France commanding his soldiers but to die of a terminal illness a fortnight after returning to England having served his Country to the end. He receives but one passing period factual mention in the *History of the Corps of Royal Engineers*, Volume VII, p.13 but Churchill remarks positively upon his service in France in *The Second World War* Volume II, p.172. His brother Edward (1895-1981, CB CBE DSO ADC) served with distinction in the Royal Artillery, competing in the 1924 Olympics in equitation and also achieving the rank of major-general. Photograph taken in March 2020. (Author)

information upon which, to construct outline denial plans.[31] The War Office solution for retaining a force in France, an idea that had as much political imperative as military inspiration, was to create a 2nd BEF[32] initially consisting of a re-constituted 1st Armoured Division, 51st (Highland) and 52nd (Lowland) Divisions and 1st (Canadian) Division,[33] with the Force to be supported initially through Cherbourg and Saint Malo. This directive, which included the need to continue to support the AASF, gave the logistic planning Staff clear guidance for the retention and location of stocks but also a series of challenges. In particular, the timescale for

31 The definition of denial is: 'to prevent enemy use of military equipment and supplies by means of destruction, removal or pollution, although the deliberate contamination of water and food is unlawful'. *Army Field Manual*, Vol 1, *The Fundamentals*, Part 6, *Combat Service Support*, Appx 1 to Annex B to Chp 4 refers.

32 TNA WO 197/89: Evacuation of the Line of Communication, War Office MO4 Telegram 72409 of 28 May 1940.

33 A second tranche was to have included a reconstituted 3rd Division, recently returned from France but it soon became clear that a complete withdrawal from the Continent was inevitable.

meaningful staffing was woefully inadequate and although the logisticians did their best to adjust the logistic posture in a dynamic operational scenario, the constant changes in emphasis from the War Office inevitably unbalanced the ability to generate efficiency and effectiveness in any one project. Sustaining these units led to resources being diverted from stock evacuation tasks as well as a cultural confusion as to the main effort, an issue compounded by the requirement to receipt incoming *materiel*, including ammunition, vehicles[34] and technical stores, especially for 1st Armoured Division.

To expedite urgent deliveries by air and sea, special arrangements were made, which of course utilized precious specialist personnel to ensure efficient execution and thus dispersed still further, widely deployed logistic capability.[35] In this respect, DDST at HQ LOC was constantly battling three issues: the dispersal of RASC units, fragile communications and the tendency of the Q Branch to authorize the loan of small packets of WMT for specific tasks, which were then sequestered for other duties, with the assets disappearing from the HQ LOC radar.[36] Such actions wasted Staff officers' time, eroded vehicle reserves, disrupted maintenance and degraded centralized control, all of which reduced the capability to support critical outputs at the operational level.[37] The provision of support to the 2nd BEF was an excellent example of the challenge, a problem exacerbated because there were no authorized reserves of combat supplies, equipment or *materiel* for it. 3 ton lorries in particular were in demand, with only 100 vehicles in the Le Mans Vehicle Reserve Depot (VRD) on 7 June, 25 of which, were ear-marked to replace battle-casualties in 51st (Highland) Division[38] and an instruction was issued to return to the VRD, 50 lorries on loan to Nantes Sub-Area.[39] The growing shortage of BEF WMT available to meet the transport task led to requests to the Host Nation for the provision of hired vehicles to work at Nantes and Rennes, a solution which created much frustration when the assets failed to materialize.[40]

Orders were issued by HQ LOC to out-load stocks from logistics sites in the Le Harve and Rouen areas,[41] the movement of which, partially depended upon the operational capability of SNCF, although most of the *materiel* was shipped from the port of Le Harve. On 30 May 1940, there were 48,000 tons of rations and stores and the intention was to back-load them to Nantes or Saint Nazaire. Given that Operation DYANMO was reaching its peak, the plan was illogical, and the ships used to transfer the stores to the Western French ports would have better utilised in evacuating them to the UK, except for the fixation of creating a 2nd BEF. That the majority of the holdings were evacuated from the Le Harve area between 30 May and 11 June is all the more remarkable because the personnel of 2 Base Ordnance Depot (BOD), 3 Base

34 For example, 50 cars were planned to arrive at Cherbourg on 5 June 1940 and required movement to VRD Le Mans. TNA WO 167/1077: LOC DDST, WD, 3 June 1940.

35 WOOH, *Ordnance Services*, p.159.

36 In one instance, the Staff of DDST HQ LOC spent much time attempting to identify the location of 42 x 3 ton lorries from 3 and 8 Reserve MT Companies RASC that had been dispatched to La Hutte. TNA WO 167/1077: LOC DDST, WD, 8 June 1940.

37 TNA WO 167/1077: LOC DDST, WD, 3 June 1940.

38 TNA WO 167/1077: LOC DDST, WD, 7 June 1940.

39 TNA WO 167/1077: LOC DDST, WD, 7 June 1940.

40 55 were assigned to Nantes and 45 to Rennes; TNA WO 167/1077: LOC DDST, WD, 8 June 1940.

41 TNA WO 197/89: Evacuation of the Line of Communication, HQ L of C OQ/12/1 dated 29 May 1940.

Ammunition Depot (BAD) and 3 Docks Group were all deemed to be non-essential troops and ordered to evacuate South across the River Seine by ferries for onward movement by rail to the Western Ports.[42]

Fortunately, this instruction was rescinded, the troops returning to their tasks but their zeal and industry in evacuating the stocks makes the failure to make the right decision regarding the destination all the more galling because some of these stocks, 1,500 tons of rations and other supplies, 300 tons of fodder and 315,000 empty returnable 4 gallon fuel cans,[43] were later destroyed by enemy air action, although on 8 June, there remained 1,500 tons of rations and supplies in 3 Base Supply Depot (BSD), 300,000 rations in Detail Issue Depot (DID) Harve,[44] 435,000 empty returnable fuel cans at Le Harve and another 300,000 at Rouen.[45] In addition, left *in situ*, were 2,500 tons of NAAFI goods, awaiting WMT to the port and 1,000 tons of frozen meat, which HQ LOC noted was 'desirable' to be moved as soon as possible. On 1 June, the intention was to transfer the meat to Nantes or 'further South'[46] rather than evacuating it to the UK, for which no refrigerated shipping was available, but movement was prevented by the dynamic operational scenario, the non-availability of insulated rail wagons and difficulties in acquiring cold storage in Nantes.[47]

Stocks from 2 BOD at Le Harve were transferred by rail to 1 BOD at Bruz and Savernay, whilst all ordnance stores and tentage from hospitals evacuating the Dieppe Medical Base Sub-Area were to be dispatched to 1 BOD, except for the equipment to build a 2,000 bed Base General Hospital at La Baule-Escoublac.[48] Much of this material reached the Base at Nantes but overwhelmed the resources of dock labour and the shipping programme and thus remained in France to be captured by the Germans.[49] Indeed, despite the best efforts of the officers and soldiers of 1 BOD, at least 20,000 tons of ordnance stores were abandoned to the enemy.[50] Planning commenced on 28 May to out-load to UK, 900 tons of spares holdings from the Advanced MT Stores Depot[51] at Elbeuf and 80 lorries awaiting repair at the Advanced Heavy Repair Shop.[52] Unfortunately another 750 tons were out-loaded by ship to Nantes arriving on 12

42 WOOH, *Movements*, p.193.

43 The sources are at variance over the figures. The LOC DDST WD states that 300 tons of hay were destroyed with 315,000 cans during the night raid on Le Harve 4/5 June. TNA WO 167/1077: LOC DDST, WD, 5 June 1940. WOOH, *Movements*, p.194, notes 100 tons of fodder and 250,000 cans. Both documents agree the loss of rations, 1,500 tons being destroyed by a night raid 7/8 June. TNA WO 167/1077: LOC DDST, WD, 8 June 1940.

44 TNA WO 167/1077: LOC DDST, WD, 8 June 1940.

45 TNA WO 167/1077: LOC DDST, WD, 5 June 1940.

46 TNA WO 167/1077: LOC DDST, WD, 1 June 1940.

47 TNA WO 167/1077: LOC DDST, WD, 1 June 1940.

48 TNA WO 197/89: Evacuation of the Line of Communication, HQ L of C OQ/12/1 dated 29 May 1940. La Baule-Escoublac is 10 miles West of Saint Nazaire.

49 WOOH, *Ordnance Services*, p.160.

50 Ibid, p.161.

51 761 tons of workshop material was loaded to 55 x railway wagons and loaded to the SS *Fair Head*, which sailed on 5 June. The evacuation was timely; on the same day, bombs were dropped 200 yards from the HRS sheds. TNA 167/1156: Advanced Sub-Depot MT Stores Depot. The SS *Fair Head* of 1,719 GRT, was seriously damaged by a parachute mine in Dufferin Dock Belfast, on 5 May 1941. She was towed to Bangor, beached and scrapped. Admiralty, *British Merchant Vessels Lost or Damaged by Enemy Action*, p.22.

52 TNA WO 167/1077: LOC DDST, WD and WOOH, *Supplies and Transport*, Vol I, p.128.

June, thus adding to the stocks that required evacuation to the UK.[53] Serving in the Advanced Base during this period was for logisticians not just a period of intense labour because enemy air action claimed many lives, 6 Reserve MT Company RASC having six killed and 28 wounded on the night of 4/5 June,[54] with other WMT units also suffering casualties in the same period.

Despatch and Denial

In the BSDs, diligent and industrious regimental logisticians, in receipt of sometimes conflicting or confusing orders from the chain of command, were working to dispatch stocks to units, evacuate material to the UK or to transfer holdings to the Host Nation. 1 BSD at Redon had been focused upon the receipt of supplies from Le Harve, in preparation for transport to the UK when the CO was ordered to transfer all the supplies to the Town Mayor and evacuate unit personnel through Saint Nazaire, embarking upon the ill-fated Hired Military Transport (HMT) *Lancastria*.[55] The last task before the unit departed from Redon was to load and dispatch a pack train to Cherbourg with 90,000 rations for 52nd (Lowland) Division.[56] 2 BSD[57] at Saint Thegonnec 30 miles East-North-East of Brest, continued to operate until 16 June, and on that day dispatched 700 tons of supplies by road and rail to Brest for BEF and French units, and civilian refugees arriving in the port. The remaining 3,000 tons were transferred *in-situ* to the Host Nation civil authorities and the personnel departed the site.[58] 3 BSD put in an impressive performance, out-loading 11,000 tons of rations,[59] initially at a rate of 500 tons per day,[60] mostly by rail and ship for evacuation, with the balance by road to local units,[61] although 1,500 tons of supplies were destroyed by air action on the night of 7/8 June.[62]

1 HRS RASC, located at Saint Etienne de Montluc between Saint Nazaire and Nantes had prepared an evacuation scheme, which despite the shortage of time and transport, worked remarkably well. The CO[63] was particularly careful to impress upon his officers and soldiers the need for both urgency and secrecy, with special arrangements being made not to alert the civilian employees.[64] The unit was able to pack 30 cases of valuable equipment such as lathes,

53 TNA WO 167/1077: LOC DDST, WD, 12 June 1940.
54 TNA WO 167/1077: LOC DDST, WD, 5 June 1940.
55 Regimental Committee, *The Story of the Royal Army Service Corps, 1939-1945*, p.85.
56 WOOH, *Supplies and Transport*, Vol I, p.128.
57 The CO was Lieutenant-Colonel E W F Aylwin-Foster DSO RASC. His Great War personal file is held in TNA WO 374/25170.
58 Regimental Committee, *The Story of the Royal Army Service Corps*, 1939-1945, p.85.
59 Orders to close 3 BSD were issued by DDST LOC at 1600 on 3 June 1940, with arrangements for an urgent shipment of frozen meat from Le Harve to Saint Nazaire being put in hand at 1630. TNA WO 167/1077: DDST LOC Area, WD.
60 TNA WO 167/1077: LOC DDST, WD, 5 June 1940.
61 Regimental Committee, *The Story of the Royal Army Service Corps, 1939-1945*, p.85. 150,000 rations were issued to DID Le Harve. TNA WO 167/1077: DDST LOC Area, WD, 2 June 1940.
62 TNA WO 167/1077: LOC DDST, WD, 8 June 1940.
63 Lieutenant-Colonel E Studdy RASC. The military service of this officer is the subject of a project by the Royal Logistic Corps Museum at Worthy Down.
64 TNA WO 167/1155: 1 HRS RASC, WD, 15 June 1940. Civilian employees were directed to work away from the shops and stores, leaving the military element to focus upon the move.

generators and drilling machines[65] but because the derrick lift of the ship allocated to the task, the HMT *Marslew*[66] had a limit of five tons, the generator sets and heavy machine tools had to be dismantled to meet the weight restriction.[67] 1 HRS was however, unable to move some of the electrical equipment packed to cases because the assigned lorry was re-tasked to troop carrying operations. In addition, two workshop and three stores lorries reached the quay where the ship was berthed but later arriving RAF technical vehicles were 'deservedly given priority'[68] so the HRS WMT and equipment had to be left on the dock. Denial was not authorised by the chain of command but on his initiative the CO ordered the HRS plan to commence. Some equipment was buried and vehicles awaiting repair were in some way damaged to prevent immediate use by smashing cylinder blocks, gear-boxes and crank cases and by using oxy-acetylene torches to cut frames and axles. Stores in the Quartermaster's Department were all doused with acid and the 5 ton transportable crane disabled.[69] 1 MT Stores Depot had especially good fortune. When a unit evacuation plan was first drafted it was expected it would take seven days to out-load the site but with the assistance of SNCF, in 36 hours, the soldiers cleared by rail, all the engines, major assemblies and tools,[70] although 300 tons of other stores had to be abandoned, along with 11 railway wagons loaded with vehicle tyres, which were left at La Chapelle Station.[71]

The large stock of winter clothing and blankets at the dry cleaning contractors in Paris, was however, denied to the enemy by the industry of the RAOC Laundry detachment, whose OIC arranged for the removal and then subsequent spoiling of the stocks.[72] Denial by destruction using explosives or petroleum, whilst an option preferred by many officers and soldiers, had its hazards, as some members of 3rd Medium Regiment Royal Artillery discovered, when C Troop destroyed its 6-inch howitzers[73] by placing a shell with a 101 fuze in the muzzle and then fired another with a 106 fuze[74] from the chamber using a 200 yard length of signal cable as a lanyard.[75] The first attempt blew the howitzer into several pieces and the troop commander, Captain Reggie Wiskin was blown off his feet. The second demolition resulted in the death of

65 Regimental Committee, *The Story of the Royal Army Service Corps, 1939-1945*, p.86 states that 12 cases were received in the UK. The HRS war diary entry 30 June 1940 provides a summary of the *materiel* received to the depot at Ashchurch, which indicates that 10-12 cases of miscellaneous stores were returned but a separate document lists another six cases plus a raft of heavy machinery. TNA WO 167/1155: 1 HRS, WD, 30 June 1940.

66 The SS *Marslew* of 4,542 GRT had been supporting the BEF since September 1939 but was another wartime shipping casualty, being sunk by a torpedo from U-69 on 23 February 1941, 300 nm NNW of Rockall. 13 souls were lost and 23 saved. Admiralty, *British Merchant Vessels Lost or Damaged by Enemy Action*, p.17.

67 TNA WO 167/1155: 1 HRS RASC, WD, 15 June 1940.

68 TNA WO 167/1155: 1 HRS RASC, WD, 15 June 1940.

69 TNA WO 167/1155: 1 HRS RASC, WD, 16 June 1940.

70 WOOH, *Supplies and Transport*, Vol I, p.128. The result was even more impressive given that there were so few 3 ton lorries available and much of the WMT consisted of 30 cwt vehicles and vans. TNA 167/1157: 1 MTSD RASC, WD, June 1940.

71 TNA WO 167/1157: 1 MTSD RASC, WD, 16 June 1940.

72 WOOH, *Ordnance Services*, p.160.

73 Gun Buster, *Return via Dunkirk*, pp.237-238, describes the demolition of a battery's guns inside the Dunkerque perimeter.

74 The 101 B & E fuzes were percussion graze and the 106 percussion direct action. See, War Office, *Textbook on Ammunition*, 26/Manuals/1543 (HMSO, 1936).

75 na, *The History of the 3rd Medium Artillery Regiment Royal Artillery, 1939-1945*, p.62.

a cow which had all of its legs amputated by flying metal, whilst the fourth wounded Gunner Short in the head, leading to his medical evacuation and subsequent capture.[76] Paddy Mooney from the Light Aid Detachment was fortunate to survive, when having poured 20 gallons of petrol into the rear of a stores lorry, he threw in a match; the explosion lifted him bodily from the ground and deposited him 30 yards away.[77] It is appropriate given the unit experience with delivering effective denial that the regimental history should record the results appertaining to the destruction of some of the British Army's thousands of vehicles: 'The scene at Houthem was unforgettable……..here the last vehicles of the BEF were burnt or destroyed. Hundreds and hundreds of vehicles were lined up in the fields burning furiously and exploding. The whole area was covered with the usual black smoke of burning petrol, while tongues of flame shot high into the air'.[78]

1 Ordnance Field Park (OFP) drove some vehicles into the canals around Dunkerque,[79] whilst many others were used by the Royal Engineers to form piers on the beaches to assist the evacuation and were thus damaged by salt-water. At Furnes, the MT Platoon of 1st Coldstream Guards undertook the destruction with little enthusiasm, the CO recording, 'It was sad, particularly for the Motor Transport Officer, Lieutenant Graham-Clarke,[80] to see those vehicles which we had so carefully looked after since War began, being thus cast away'.[81] Whilst this denial of material was undoubtedly necessary, the ruthless abandonment and destruction of vehicles and equipment certainly infuriated French officers, who were sometimes almost incandescent when the BEF established road-blocks to ensure the French did the same, to the point when, on occasions, force was threatened between Allies. This tension occurred at Dunkerque and emerged again in later evacuations when the British attempted to destroy French infrastructure and supplies to prevent them being utilized by the enemy.[82] Not all vehicles though, were destroyed or disabled as the immediate choice. On 29 May, 5 Division CRASC,[83] requested the unit French liaison officer to offer the unit vehicles to a French armoured division *in lieu* of destruction but the chaos overwhelmed any chance of a handover.[84] 1st Coldstream Guards kept the battalion combat platforms operational to the end of the fighting[85] whilst I Corps Petrol Park was ordered to leave the unit WMT loaded on the allocated vehicle parks; the CO queried these orders with the Corps DDST, who confirmed them. It was indeed a confusing picture.[86]

76 Ibid.
77 Ibid.
78 Ibid.
79 TNA WO 167/1192: 1 OFP RAOC, WD, 25 May 1940.
80 67095 Lieutenant Lionel John Graham-Clarke aged 24 and husband to Jean, was KIA whilst attacking a German pontoon with a Bren LMG on 30 May 1940, the day after he had been involved in the destruction of most of the battalion's MT. He is At Rest in Veurne Communal Cemetery Extension, Belgium. Howard and Sparrow, *The Coldstream Guards, 1920-1946*, p.38.
81 Ibid, p.37.
82 Brian Bond, 'Dunkirk: Myths and Lessons', *The RUSI Journal*, Vol 127, Issue 3, 1982, p.5, discusses the wider issues.
83 Lieutenant-Colonel L W Walsh RASC.
84 TNA WO 167/249: 5 Division CRASC, WD.
85 Howard & Sparrow, *The Coldstream Guards, 1920-1946*, p.37.
86 TNA WO 167/143: I CPP RASC, WD, 27 May 1940.

Waste and Misuse

Completely forgotten has been the dedicated work of the RAOC GHQ Salvage Unit (GSU) that scoured abandoned camps and dumps for ordnance stores, where evidence was quickly found of 'the most appalling waste and misuse of material', including using blankets to pad trenches and to fill sandbags instead of earth.[87] The commandant of Force K6,[88] was 'appalled' by the quantity of *materiel* that was abandoned to the enemy, describing the failure to issue and execute clear orders for recovery or destruction as 'foolhardy'.[89] 1 General Base Depot at Forges les Eaux was identified as a classic example of failure in this respect, with over 1,000 tons of ordnance stores abandoned with no attempt to recover any items.[90] The depot was planned to have accommodation for up to 15,000 personnel but the GSU estimated that tentage and accommodation stores for 30,000 had been hoarded, along with so much clothing that in some of the stores it was two feet deep, and along with the ration stores, had been thoroughly looted.[91] Such failure reflected very poorly upon the BEF; it was certainly not the action of a professional Army.

Formed at Camp 13 Rouvcrary, the GSU consisted of four companies consisting of a total 12 officers and 324 Other Ranks (ORs) recruited from the Base Ordnance Workshop, Advanced Ordnance Workshop, Advanced Ordnance Depot and 2 BOD.[92] Resourced and organized to operate 24 hours a day, in the first week of June, the unit salvaged 350 tons of stores and equipment dispatching the stocks in 50 railway trucks to 1 BOD at Nantes. The companies worked in two shifts. During the day, stores were collected by 20 x 15 cwt Bedford trucks from the camps to assembly points from which, in the dark hours, 20 x 3 ton RASC lorries transported the equipment to nominated railheads for loading to rail wagons.[93] *Materiel* included accommodation stores, tents, blankets, uniforms, anti-gas clothing, web equipment, bayonets and scabbards, plus RE stores, a 6-inch howitzer and three gun limbers.[94] Also recovered, was the equivalent of 34 railway wagons of similar equipment, which had to be stored in Nissen huts at the assembly points of Forge les Eaux and Rouveray because there was no WMT to transfer the assets to a railhead.[95]

A further 700 tons of stores and 500 tents had to be left at the various sites because it was necessary to withdraw from them but not before the GSU had transferred between 80-100 tons of NAAFI stocks from the supply depot at Formery to the EFI Area Controller at Forge.[96] Such actions assisted the EFI, given the significant losses of military stores, to recover, mainly from the Nantes area, over 7,000 tons of stocks,[97] including sports equipment, tobacco, cigarettes, tea

87 TNA WO 167/144: I Corps ADOS, GHQ Salvage Unit Report, nd, p.6.
88 Lieutenant-Colonel Hills MC RIASC.
89 TNA WO 167/1433: HQ Force K6, 'Report on Operations in France', dated 19 July 1940, p.9.
90 TNA WO 167/144: I Corps ADOS, GHQ Salvage Unit Report, nd, p.11.
91 TNA WO 167/144: I Corps ADOS, GHQ Salvage Unit Report, nd, p.12.
92 TNA WO 167/144: I Corps ADOS, GHQ Salvage Unit Report, nd, p.6.
93 TNA WO 167/144: I Corps ADOS, GHQ Salvage Unit Report, nd, p.4.
94 TNA WO 167/144: I Corps ADOS, GHQ Salvage Unit Report, nd, p.2.
95 TNA WO 167/144: I Corps ADOS, GHQ Salvage Unit Report, nd, pp.2-3.
96 TNA WO 167/144: I Corps ADOS, GHQ Salvage Unit Report, nd, p.3.
97 WOOH, *Miscellaneous 'Q' Services*, p.163.

and boot polish but *materiel* to the estimated value of £1,930,722 had to be written-off,[98] which at 2018 values, is a very hefty £103.60 million.[99] Units and individuals 'salved' some of these goods[100] before the local population and the Germans had their pick.[101] EFI personnel also made appreciable contributions to the recovery of funds. One lieutenant arrived at Saint Nazaire from Nantes for evacuation with £5,000[102] in cash secured in a box but was not allowed to board the ship with it. Undeterred by this set-back, he motored South over 260 miles to Bordeaux and found passage for himself and the EFI's money on the small coaster SS *Rhineland*[103] to Falmouth, accompanied by 36 soldiers and seven nurses.[104] In a more daring escape, a sergeant restaurant manager and three soldiers were captured at Abbeville and imprisoned in the EFI canteen with no uniforms. Under the cover of darkness, wrapped in blankets, they collected the cash and books before escaping.[105]

Worried and Angry

There was a concerted effort to recover conventional munitions stocks from the BADs, although perforce of circumstances, including the arrival of yet more ammunition from the UK and a convoluted ammunition control chain, this work was not as successful as it could have been, with the command issue being a particular problem. The Assistant Director Ordnance Services (ADOS) Ammunition (Ammn) based at HQ_LOC Le Mans was part of the QMG Branch in GHQ_BEF and had little interface with HQ_LOC except for the administration of the ammunition depots but confusingly received orders and instructions directly from Ordnance Services (OS) 2 in the War Office, to which he reported after communications were cut with GHQ on 19 May,[106] although of course OS 2 was not conversant with operations on the GLOC. Despite this lacuna in the command arrangements, ADOS (Ammn) seized the initiative and despite the claim by the post-evacuation Howard Committee Report that only with 'an earlier

98 Ibid.
99 Relative value based upon RPI.
100 Wilson, *Press On Regardless*, p.13.
101 As an example, on 5 June 1940 at Harstad in Norway, the EFI closed its operation and abandoned the base canteen and its stocks valued at £8,000, which at 2018 prices using RPI is £429,100. WOOH, *Miscellaneous 'Q' Services*, p.189. 6 (L of C) Provost Company was tasked with preventing looting by the local population but effectively supervised the 'out-loading' of the site by individual soldiers. Most personnel chose to select tobacco and cigarettes, but one soldier filled two kit-bags with boot polish on the basis he had heard a rumour that it was in short supply in the UK. Memory of 2555235 Lance-Corporal Lionel Woodhead (1903-1984) of 6 (L of C) Provost Company.
102 Based upon RPI, this equates to £268,200 in 2018.
103 The *Rhineland* was completed in December 1922 by AG Weser Bremen as the *Altengamme* for Schlüter & Maack, Hamburg but sold in 1926 and renamed *Rhineland* for James Currie & Co Ltd, Leith. She was sunk by a torpedo from U-201 whilst in convoy OG-74 about 800 nm NNE of the Azores on 21 September 1941. There were no survivors from the crew of 26. Admiralty, *British Merchant Vessels Lost or Damaged by Enemy Action during the Second World War*, p.27.
104 Cole, *Naafi in Uniform*, p.15. The *Rhineland* departed Bordeaux on 17 June arriving at Falmouth on 20 June. Winser, *BEF Ships*, p.50.
105 Winser, *BEF Ships*, p.50.
106 TNA WO 33/2384: Howard Committee Report, Appx B, Ammunition, Petrol, Ordnance Stores, Supplies, para 2. It was not until 5 June 1940 that ADOS (Ammn) commenced attending the HQ_LOC conferences.

decision and more energetic steps' could stocks have been reduced,[107] the first key action was taken on 24 May, when 1 BAD was ordered to out-load 6,000 tons to the ports, although the execution of the task was disrupted by the requirement to receipt ammunition on trains being returned to the depot because of the closure of the GLOC to the corps areas.[108] On 29 May, OS 2 instructed ADOS (Ammn) to evacuate to the UK, 50 percent of all ammunition stocks not required for operations in France,[109] which appeared to be a simple order but the calculations involved to issue detailed instructions to the BADs as to the types and quantities to be exported were based upon a dynamic force structure. ADOS (Ammn) chose, therefore, an initially cautious solution by returning those stocks, which were in obvious surplus, namely 6-inch howitzer and 25 pounder munitions. ADOS (Ammn) also raised the issue of the denial and possible destruction of ammunition in-Theatre, although the three formal requests to GOC LOC for the latter failed to elicit a decision,[110] with the result that whilst the BADs prepared plans for denial and demolition, only the former was enacted.

On 1 June, the CO 1 BAD was directed by ADOS (Ammn) to out-load a further 7,000 tons of ammunition to the UK, close the depot by 25 June[111] and establish an Advanced Ammunition Depot (AAD) at Bretueil between Le Mans and the Seine.[112] A reconnaissance revealed that the site was unsuitable and with events overtaking the logistic planning, the BAD were ordered to move stocks to a site near Niort to the North-East of La Rochelle but this option was also abandoned.[113] At this point the main effort was clearing the depot in the Foret du Gavre and in addition to out-loading stocks to the ports, there were substantial issues of demolition explosives to the Royal Engineers and two convoys of AA ammunition were dispatched to Saint Nazaire.[114] Arrangements were then made to destroy by demolition the remaining ammunition but the CO received specific orders from HQ Nantes Sub-Area that

107 TNA WO 33/2384: Howard Committee Report, Appx B, Ammunition, Petrol, Ordnance Stores, Supplies, para 7b, Observations. It is possible to see this comment in the wider strategic sense of reducing the planned stock holdings across the Theatre and reposition them in the UK Base, although this is not explicit in the report.

108 TNA 167/1179: 21 BAD RAOC, WD, 24 May 1940.

109 TNA WO 33/2384: Howard Committee Report, Appx B, Ammunition, Petrol, Ordnance Stores, Supplies, para 3b.

110 TNA WO 33/2384: Howard Committee Report, Appx B, Ammunition, Petrol, Ordnance Stores, Supplies, para 5c.

111 There is no war diary for June 1940, depot operations being recorded in a typed report by the CO dated 13 July 1940 held in TNA WO 167/1175/2: 1 BAD.

112 Whilst the 1 BAD report does not explain the reasoning for the location of the AAD, the presumption must be that it was sited to support 1st Armoured Division and 51st (Highland) Division, with the expectation these formations would be reinforced by 52nd (Lowland) Division and 1st (Canadian) Division.

113 The 1 BAD war diary does not expose the co-ordination with the Host Nation, the approval of which, was required to use these sites, although presumably ADOS (Ammn) at HQ LOC initiated the staffing.

114 TNA WO 167/1175/2: 1 BAD RAOC, Report by CO 1 BAD dated 13 July 1940.

'nothing whatever was to be blown up'.[115] CO 2 BAD faced a similar problem.[116] A denial and demolition plan had been produced and the CO ordered the denial part to be executed, in expectation that the Brest Garrison Commander would then give the order to 'apply the match' to complete the task, although as it transpired, no such order was received by the CO.[117] Fuzes, tubes and detonators were trucked to the coast and dumped in the sea, whilst the depot staff commenced burning the cartridge propellants and crushing the RAF bomb-tails. On 15 June, demolition parties prepared all the dumps with fuzes and detonators but when they came to conduct checks the fuzes had been removed, the suspicion being that members of the local French military were involved because the Town Mayor had stated that the population was 'very worried and angry' about the possibility of their villages being damaged if the dumps were destroyed.[118]

In addition to the demolition plan, the staff established a dump near Brest for 200 tons of ammunition to support the local defence scheme.[119] The personnel of 3 BAD having been ordered to evacuate the depot, returned to conduct ammunition issues to 1st Armoured Division before clearing the site.[120] Trains were dispatched to Brest, one of which, carrying 9.2 howitzer shells, was late arriving on 7 June but fortunately the precious cargo was loaded to the SS *Zaafaran*[121] and arrived in the UK.[122] On 15 June, ADOS (Ammn) at HQ LOC ordered 4 BAD to out-load its remaining stock of 9,150 tons to the UK, with the priority being RAF bombs, then anti-tank and Bofors ammunition.[123] 4,400 tons were to be dispatched to Saint Malo and 4,500 tons to Saint Nazaire,[124] plus 250 tons of infantry and artillery natures to Cherbourg to support the withdrawal of 52nd (Lowland) Division.

By 2200 on 16 June, 2,100 tons had been dispatched in three trains to Rennes Base Marshalling Yard labelled for Saint Malo, although they remained in the yard and were *in situ* when the Rennes train bombing occurred on 17 June.[125] Further out-loading work was halted because empty rail wagons were unavailable, a problem overtaken by the order to evacuate the depot personnel,[126] with the CO receiving a specific order not to engage in destruction,

115 TNA WO 167/1175/2: 1 BAD RAOC, Report by CO 1 BAD dated 13 July 1940. This quotation is in black ink inserted to the typescript and is clearly a later addition before the CO signed the document. It is possible, if not indeed probable, that the CO had learned of the investigation into the failure to destroy the remaining stocks and wished to be clear that this outcome was not his intent nor order.

116 There is no war diary for June 1940, the depot operations being summarized in a letter 2 BAD/16 dated 27 June 1940 signed by the CO. TNA WO 167/1116: 2 BAD RAOC, WD.

117 TNA WO 167/1116: 2 BAD RAOC, CO letter 2 BAD/16 dated 27 June 1940.

118 TNA WO 167/1116: 2 BAD RAOC, Report, nd but probably mid-July 1940, written by Lieutenant Forsdick, Inspecting Ordnance Officer.

119 TNA WO 167/1116: 2 BAD RAOC, CO Report dated 27 June 1940.

120 WOOH, *Ordnance Services*, p.158.

121 The SS *Zaafaran* of 1,559 GRT survived until 5 July 1942, when acting as rescue ship, she was one of 24 ships sunk from convoy PQ 17 sailing to Archangel. Admiralty, *British Merchant Vessels Lost or Damaged by Enemy Action*, p.38.

122 TNA WO 167/876: 2 Docks Group RE, WD, 7 June 1940.

123 TNA WO 33/2384: Howard Committee Report, Appx B, Ammunition, Petrol, Ordnance Stores, Supplies, para 5a.

124 TNA WO 167/1178: 4 BAD RAOC, WD.

125 See, TNA WO 361/114: Rennes Train Bombing and Chp 15, 'Riding The Rails'.

126 TNA WO 167/1178: 4 BAD RAOC, WD.

denial or demolition,[127] leaving 6,000 tons of operational ammunition on the site.[128] Whilst the other depots were out-loading stocks, 6 BAD, operational since 24 May[129] seems to have been nominated as a repository for unwanted ammunition, with 2,200 tons consisting mainly of RAF bombs, AA ammunition, both 3.7-inch and 3-inch 20 cwt, plus SAA, being accumulated by 14 June.[130] The CO received less than 10 hours' notice to evacuate the depot and the records do not mention any preparations for demolition.[131]

Burning Spirits

For petroleum products, the War Office decided that with the exception of canned or cased 100 octane aviation spirit for the RAF, denial or destruction rather than recovery would be the priority,[132] although by 7 June, the QMG, through ST 6 at the War Office had authorized the issue of cased petrol to the Host Nation[133] and an additional port, Granville,[134] located on the South-West coast of the Cherbourg Peninsula had been ear-marked to import petrol to support 52nd (Lowland) Division.[135] To assist the British Forces in France to conduct the denial and destruction of fuel stocks, the War Office directed that small demolition sections, called XD Parties, be created utilizing soldiers from a TA unit, the Kent Fortress Royal Engineers (KFRE) based in the county.[136] The XD parties were dispatched from the UK in RN destroyers, and in conjunction with in-Theatre RASC personnel, were tasked to destroy packed and bulk fuel stocks.[137] Destroying bulk stocks held in Host Nation facilities was politically sensitive[138] and in some places the French prevented such action, although extensive

127 CO 6 BAD received similar instructions. TNA WO 167/1180: 6 BAD RAOC, WD entries June 1940.
128 TNA WO 167/1178: 4 BAD RAOC, WD. The CO was Lieutenant-Colonel G Caruana Dingli RAOC, late of the Royal Malta Artillery, who was appointed the CO CAD Kineton in July 1942.
129 There is almost nothing of import in the 6 BAD WD, depot operations being covered in the 'Report on the Work, Moves, Activities etc, of No 6 Base Ammunition Depot from 1 May 1940 to 12 July 1940' dated 6 August 1940 in TNA WO 167/1180: 6 BAD RAOC.
130 TNA WO 167/1180: 6 BAD RAOC, 'Report on the Work of 6 BAD', p.3.
131 That the order to evacuate was last minute is reinforced by the war diary of 159 RCC, which recorded that, 'The news of evacuation came as a shock and the order to move at 1830 hrs can only be alluded to as a bombshell..........the general order was to destroy nothing and this was acted upon......'. TNA WO 167/954: 159 RCC RE, WD, 15 June 1940.
132 Some of the destruction was undertaken by private soldiers on their own initiative. See the actions of Trooper Bing Coller in Wilson, *Press On Regardless*, p.13.
133 TNA WO 167/1077: LOC DDST, WD, telecon DDST staff with Major Bond of ST 6.
134 Granville, a small fishing port and home of the Dior family became a health resort in the 1920s, being known as the 'Monaco of the North'. Whilst the documents do not explain why Granville was selected, it was probably because it was not an obvious target for the *Luftwaffe*, whilst the small coasters used for the carriage of packed fuel were able to use the facilities.
135 TNA WO 167/1077: LOC DDST, WD, 11 June 1940.
136 For the operational history, see, Brazier, *XD Operations*, although some elements of detail do not accord with the war diary records.
137 Every effort was made to recover to the UK 100 octane aviation spirit, so vital to RAF fighter performance. TNA AIR 29/781: 5 Air Stores Park, AASF, WD, May - June 1940.
138 Commander McKye RN, the RN liaison officer to the French Atlantic Fleet at Brest stressed the importance of not firing the oil tanks unless the French naval commander gave authority. Brazier, *XD Operations*, pp.82-83.

damage was inflicted upon the storage infrastructure at Le Harve and Rouen,[139] assisted by the *Luftwaffe*, which in a night raid on Le Harve destroyed 315,000 returnable 4 gallon cans,[140] leaving 435,000 in stock, with another 300,000 at Rouen.[141] At other sites, the British chain of command intervened to prevent un-necessary friction with the French authorities, thus saving for example, the storage tanks at French commercial oil farm Donges, which had been prepared for demolition.[142]

1 POL Depot (POLD) in the forest at Blain and Havardais was stocked with aviation fuel in barrels and cased MT spirit totalling 10,000 tons plus another 660 tons of cased diesel.[143] The stocks were however, successfully destroyed, although as with all such operations, it was not without significant risk. Having used all the explosives on other tasks, the only solution was to puncture some of the tins in each stack with pickaxes and bayonets with the possibility of sparks creating a premature fire.[144] Once this was complete, with the smell of petrol vapour wafting through the trees, the XD party commanded by Captain Peter Keeble,[145] used a Very light[146] to ignite the leaking fuel from an upwind position.[147] The forest was tinder dry and the vapour from the fuel aided the conflagration so quickly that two men were seriously burned and a third was never found.[148] 2 POLD was ordered to hand over the 7,000 tons[149] of cased products to the French, although by the time this was enacted the stocks had been reduced to 4,500 tons, consisting of 500 tons of aviation spirit, 3,000 tons of MT spirit and 1,000 tons of lubricating oil.[150] The French civilian authorities were greatly relieved by this decision because

139 TNA WO 167/1077: LOC DDST, WD, 9 June 1940, records that the stocks at Rouen were fired on 8 June. See also, Brazier, *XD Operations*, p.56.

140 TNA WO 167/1077: LOC DDST, WD, 5 June 1940. Also lost by fire, was 300 tons of hay.

141 There had been maturing plans to move these 1,050,000 returnable cans to the UK, to the point where the DDST Staff had calculated the transportation requirements for the 750,000 cans at Le Harve, amounting to 625 rail wagons and the equivalent of 18,750 tons of shipping space. TNA WO 167/1077: LOC DDST, WD, 1 June 1940.

142 Brazier, *XD Operations*, p.63.

143 Regimental Committee, *The Story of the Royal Army service Corps, 1939-1945*, p.75.

144 There is conflicting information on who enacted this task. Brazier, *XD Operations*, p.61, states that the XD party was responsible but the 1 POLD WD records that Lieutenant-Colonel Brazier had instructed OC Troops, Major Simson to direct the depot staff to conduct this work as a pre-requisite for the XD parties to complete the demolitions. TNA WO 167/1148: 1 POLD RAOC, WD, entry 15 June 1940.

145 Keeble was awarded the DSO for his part in these actions. TNA WO 373/16/259: Recommendation for Award for Keeble.

146 This appears to have been a common method of ignition. See, Wilson, *Press On Regardless*, p.13

147 Obituary, Major Peter Keeble DSO MC, *The Daily Telegraph*, Friday 29 October 2004.

148 Ibid and Brazier, *XD Operations*, p.61.

149 There is a slight difference in the presentation of the figures between the 2 POLD WD and the Howard Committee Report, generated by the presence of unloaded stocks on railway wagons, which presumably had not been taken onto account. The 2 POLD war diary in TNA WO 167/1149, states 7,000 tons and the report 7,060. TNA WO 33/2384: Howard Committee Report, Appx B, Ammunition, Petrol, Ordnance Stores, Supplies, para 4b, Petrol Depot Taule.

150 TNA WO 167/1149: 2 POLD RAOC, WD, 17 June 1940. The Howard Report suggests 1,578 tons of aviation sprit, 4,240 tons of MT spirit and 1,000 tons of lubricating oil, totalling 5,760 tons, plus 1,300 tons of cased products on 110 rail wagons. TNA WO 33/2384: Howard Committee Report, Appx B, Ammunition, Petrol, Ordnance Stores, Supplies, para 4b, Petrol Depot Taule.

there were many refugees living in wooden shanties near to the depot.[151] The stocks at 4 POLD at Moult-Argences were being cleared at a rate of 800 tons per day mainly to 2 POLD,[152] although by 15 June only 46 personnel remained at the site with the sole task of supplying petrol to Beauman Division. The French authorities accepted responsibility for the remaining stocks but were unable to provide a unit to take over the inventory and under orders from HQ Beauman Division[153] the 1,000,000 gallons plus of petrol and 60,000 gallons of lubricating oil were fired.[154]

Unwise to Overrule Them

Concurrently, the arrival of 52nd (Lowland) Division, a component of the 2nd BEF, provided the LOC Area DDST staff with an additional problem because the formation's petrol and supply companies had been dispatched to arrive at the tail of the division, an unfortunate outcome because it tasked to move as quickly as possible from the SPOD.[155] WMT from local resources were thus placed under command of 52 Division CRASC and lorries from the VRD were allocated to 157th Brigade, which was in the vanguard.[156] In addition, the War Office directed LOC Area to form the 3rd Line Ammunition Sub-Park from in-Theatre resources.[157] It proved impossible to generate one from a Reserve MT Company and after five days of staff work, 10 TCC RASC was assigned to the task,[158] thereby demonstrating the absolute need for flexibility in the utilization of WMT.

As the operational focus moved to the West of France, with evacuation and denial operations being increasingly driven at pace, plans were maturing for the establishment of a re-located Base at La Rochelle to support the 2nd BEF, the War Office dispatching a reconnaissance team on 12 June.[159] The outline plan included a BOD, BAD and a Base Ordnance Workshops and was sufficiently advanced for 1 BOD to be instructed to commence packing 50 percent of war and MT stores with a completion date of 22 June, the order being confirmed in writing on 13 June from the QMG at the War Office to GOC LOC Area.[160] The DDST Staff exposed the key freedoms and constraints in developing this proposal during a conference with the War Office reconnaissance team led by the DQMG BEF Brigadier Parminter[161] at HQ LOC at Le Mans

151 TNA WO 167/1149: 2 POLD RAOC, WD, 17 June 1940.
152 TNA WO 167/1077: LOC DDST, WD, 13 June 1940.
153 GOC Beauman Division was also given the responsibility for ordering the destruction of the fuel dump at Evreux. TNA WO 167/1077: LOC DDST, WD, 9 June 1940.
154 Regimental Committee, *The Story of the Royal Army service Corps, 1939-1945*, p.85.The Howard Report agrees with the figures appertaining to the lubricating oil but records the petrol as 4,688 tons, though noting that the information was 'as at' 13 June 1940 and that some POL stocks had been dispatched by rail and issued to local units before the destruction occurred. TNA WO 33/2384: Howard Committee Report, Appx B, Ammunition, Petrol, Ordnance Stores, Supplies, para 5, Petrol Depot Moult.
155 TNA WO 167/1077: LOC DDST, WD, 13 June 1940.
156 TNA WO 167/1077: LOC DDST, WD, 14 June 1940.
157 TNA WO 167/1077: LOC DDST, WD, 9 June 1940.
158 TNA WO 167/1077: LOC DDST, WD, 13 June 1940.
159 The orders for the reconnaissance are in IWM/LBY K.49621.
160 WOOH, *Ordnance Services*, p.160.
161 Temporary Brigadier R H R Parminter DSO MC, late Manchester Regiment, was the AA & QMG GHQ BEF September 1939 - March 1940 before being appointed as DQMG. TNA WO 167/1719:

on 14 June; the scenario did not have much to commend it, with few of the former and rather too many of the latter.[162] The only asset immediately available was a field bakery, although its third section required equipment. 30 percent of the GLOC WMT had been lost to enemy action or accidents, with much of the balance requiring maintenance, repair or reorganization. In summary, all the key units needed to be imported from the UK, including a BSD, HRS, VRD, Advanced MTSD, LOC MT Company and a Reserve MT Company.[163]

The proposal to form a new Base undoubtedly disrupted stock evacuation operations but with orders to evacuate the 2nd BEF, the scheme was dropped, and the party focused upon assisting executing the evacuation of the reconnaissance team, advance parties and other personnel through La Pallice, the port of La Rochelle. Apart from withdrawing material for later evacuation to the UK, the concept made absolutely no sense because it was in the opposite direction to the forces deploying into the Cherbourg peninsula, whilst the sea voyage from UK was much longer than to either Brest or Saint Nazaire. 2,500 RAF personnel were embarked on two requisitioned colliers, one of which was only partially discharged, together with a number of military personnel, 10-12 tons of special RAF ammunition,[164] four motor cars plus ancillary artillery equipment,[165] leaving on the docks four 3.7-inch HAA guns, four LAA Bofors and 350 to 400 vehicles, all of which required cranes to load them aboard ships.[166] The pressure to depart in short order was driven by the growing concern that the impending Franco-German Armistice might result in the internment of all British service personnel by the French, a decision supported by the Howard Committee,[167] although officers on the Royal Navy destroyer HMS *Mackay* arrived on 19 June and arranged for the evacuation of 4,000 Poles on 20 June, with some stragglers also being collected on 22 June.[168]

Additional diversions included the issue of weapons and equipment to the various *ad hoc* forces that were formed, including Beauman Division[169] and the recovery of material when

BEF Appointments. He was awarded a CBE for his service in France, including actions at Dunkerque. TNA WO 373/75/460: Recommendation for Award for Parminter. Post-war he was Head of the United Nations Relief and Rehabilitation Administration's Mission to Austria before retiring from the Army in 1948.

162 TNA WO 167/1077: LOC DDST, WD, 14 June 1940.

163 The conference members agreed to propose to the War Office that 3 BSD and the Advanced HRS, both recently evacuated to UK, should be returned to support the 2nd BEF. TNA WO 167/1077: LOC DDST, WD, 14 June 1940.

164 Whilst the documents are silent on what constituted this 'special' ammunition, one conclusion must be that the statement referred to Gas Warfare munitions, which is illuminating because no other sources suggest that these munitions were evacuated to the South of the GLOC.

165 These ships arrived at Newport in South Wales on 20 June 1940. In stark contrast to the deployment of the BEF in September 1939, the War Office was unconcerned about the comfort or victuals of the troops on the voyage.

166 Most of these vehicles were subject to denial action except for the large lorries on loan from the Host Nation, which were left for the French to recover. TNA WO 33/2384: Howard Committee Report, Report on Evacuation of La Pallice, para 5, Embarkation.

167 TNA WO 33/2384: Howard Committee Report, Report on Evacuation of La Pallice, para 4, Decisions.

168 TNA WO 33/2384: Howard Committee Report, Report on Evacuation of La Pallice, para 4, Decisions.

169 HQ Rouen Sub-Area issued instructions for the maintenance of 1st Armoured Division, 51st (Highland) Division and Beauman Division on 3 June 1940. Beauman Division maintenance planning was based upon sustaining it for a minimum period of six weeks. TNA WO 167/1077: LOC DDST Area, WD, entries 2 & 3 June 1940.

they were disbanded,[170] and the order, received by HQ LOC Area on 11 June to be prepared to re-equip 51st (Highland) Division, another task that was swiftly shelved.[171] The War Office then made a concerted effort in the middle of June to recover as many stocks as possible by dispatching MT, stores and ammunition ships,[172] supported by coasters[173] as shown in the table below, with orders that personnel should travel on all MT and stores vessels subject to agreement by the Master.

Table 18.1
Operation AERIAL – Cargo Ships[174]

SPOE France	ex UK	Ammo	MT	Stores	Coasters	Remarks
Brest	Southampton		4			
Brest	Southampton		4	1		
Brest	Fowey	1				
Cherbourg	Southampton		2			
Granville	Newhaven				2*	*Stores or personnel
Nantes	Barry			2		
Nantes	Plymouth		4			
Nantes	Port Talbot			1		
Saint Malo	Fowey	1				
Saint Malo	Newhaven	2*				* Stores alternative cargo
Saint Malo	Southampton				2*	*Stores or personnel
Saint Nazaire	Avonmouth		4			
Saint Nazaire	Newport	2				
Saint Nazaire	Plymouth		4			
Saint Nazaire	Port Talbot	1				
Total		7	22	4	4	

170 TNA WO 197/89: Evacuation of the Line of Communication, War Office MO4 Telegram 72409 of 28 May 1940.
171 WOOH, *Ordnance Services*, p.160.
172 All of these ships sailed from the UK on 14-15 June 1940. TNA WO 197/105: Operation AERIAL, War Office 'DQMG Appx Schedule of Empty Ships ordered to French Ports' dated 15 June 1940.
173 29 coasters were allotted to Operational AERIAL, but the documents suggest that only four sailed to France. TNA WO 197/105: Operation AERIAL, Admiralty SECRET Message 252 of 15 June 1940, lists the vessels by name.
174 Table collated from information in TNA WO 197/105: Operation AERIAL, War Office 'DQMG Appx Schedule of Empty Ships ordered to French Ports' dated 15 June 1940.

Movement Control at Brest had several challenges, including the assembly at the port of 2nd Brigade Group of 1st (Canadian) Division, which was deploying to France when the order to evacuate was received, and the refusal by the French to accept the transhipment of ammunition in the docks. Despite these restrictions, 1st and 2nd (Canadian) Brigade Groups, AASF personnel, some WMT from 1st Armoured Division, elements of the Rennes Sub-Area, 24 x 25 pounder guns and 12 x 40 mm Bofors plus various supporting stores, equipment and vehicles were safely evacuated, although the Howard Committee assessed that given another 48 hours an additional 1,100 vehicles could have been recovered.[175] In Le Harve, the remarkable actions of Second-Lieutenant J S Cumming, Assistant Adjutant of 75th Field Regiment RA, whilst highly praised by the Howard Committee, received no mention in the regimental history of the Royal Artillery.[176] Cumming found guns of 17th Field Regiment abandoned in the streets and determined to salve them. On 12 June, accompanied by a French liaison officer, Pierre Fabre-Luce, he persuaded the French Admiral commanding the port to authorise the use of French shipping on the quays before organizing, with the assistance of British soldiers and French sailors, the recovery and loading of 14 x 25 pounders and 14 vehicles to a ship, unfortunately losing a gun and a truck which fell from the ship's crane slings into the sea.[177] Regrettably, Cumming did not have time to evacuate the 1st Line WMT of the 154th Brigade's infantry battalions, which had been abandoned on the quaysides.[178] Had there been more officers with the tenacity and determination of Second-Lieutenant Cumming there is no doubt that much more equipment could have been returned to the UK.[179]

The arrival of MT and stores ships, however, did not guarantee that vehicles and equipment at the docks would be loaded. In the rush to depart from the ports in the belief that the Germans would suddenly arrive on the dockside, material was either abandoned or loading had ceased because of a shortage of stevedores or operational wharf cranes, although this did not prevent 10th Hussars in the Brest Docks from man-handling two Bofors LAA guns onto the deck of the SS *Manx Maid* and more would have been brought aboard had it not been for a direct order to the unit to abandon further work.[180] At Saint Malo there were mixed results. Although vehicle embarkation was not planned, approximately 100 cars and light vehicles, including ambulances, plus 400 motor-cycles were reported to have been loaded to the decks of personnel ships in a display of initiative that was described as 'refreshing compared with the lack of it shown at some other ports'.[181] The plan to move 600 lorries to another port for

175 TNA WO 33/2384: Howard Committee Report, Report on Evacuation of Brest. Most of the vehicles left at Brest were damaged in some way to prevent immediate use.

176 Farndale, *History of the Royal Regiment of Artillery: The Years of Defeat 1939–41*.

177 This loss was presumably the result of the inexperience of the soldiers and sailors in conducting the loading task.

178 TNA WO 33/2384: Howard Committee Report, Report on Evacuation of Le Harve, para 6. Cumming's efforts also recovered 2 x motor-cycles, 3 x 2-inch mortars, 4 x Bren LMGs and 4 x Boys anti-tank rifles.

179 Whilst commending Second-Lieutenant Cumming, the Howard Committee was rather less complementary about his commander, Brigadier A C L Stanley-Clarke DSO of 154th Infantry Brigade, although he was awarded a CBE later in the war.

180 Regimental Committee, *The 10th Royal Hussars in the Second World War*, p.27.

181 TNA WO 33/2384: Howard Committee Report, Report on Evacuation of Saint Malo, para 4, Evacuation of Vehicles.

evacuation was mainly thwarted when some of the drivers, many from hastily organized *ad hoc* units, deserted their vehicles and took passage on departing ships. The remainder of the WMT was abandoned owing to French objections to destruction and 'it was considered unwise to overrule them', a decision fully supported by the Howard Committee, which noted in its report that 'it would have been unjustifiable at this stage to antagonise the French, whose assistance was of great value'.[182]

The pressure, frustration and confusion were concisely summarized in the war diary of HQ 157th Brigade evacuating through the port of Cherbourg. The Brigade Major exercised immense energy in searching for transport to lift the personnel of the brigade HQ from Transit Camp D to the docks, and 'eventually lorries were promised in an hour', the plan proving useless because by then the general rumour was that ships were all sailing within an hour'.[183] Meanwhile the brigade Staff Captain and the Motor Transport Officer, demonstrating the strength of character and resolute determination that in a crisis is so crucial in delivering effective logistic output, were engaged in leading a team to load the brigade HQ WMT, even persuading the brigade commander[184] to take a break from arranging the provision of tea for the troops to put a 'shoulder to the wheel', although by all accounts he did not require much encouragement. The work commenced in the dark, but their efforts were not in vain because all the WMT was loaded except for the 8 cwt vehicles, the Staff Captain reporting that if there had been more drivers available, additional WMT could have been loaded,[185] which confirms that greater quantities of equipment could have been recovered with more planning and grip. Despite the frenetic activity on the quaysides of the French ports, there were officers and soldiers who brought calm and order to the confusion, much of which was caused by the last-minute orders for the evacuation, poor communications and the inevitable chaotic unit arrival by train, vehicle and boot. A member of 1st Armoured Division remembered:

> I must say that what impressed me about the docks in Brest was the sense of order. There was no alarm or undue agitation; and that must have been due, at least in part, to this same Embarkation Staff Officer. I have no idea who he was, and in the ordinary course of nature he must be dead by now; but I gladly pay my tribute to him here ... He was the sort of man of whom, like Milton's sonnets, there are "alas, too few".[186]

182 TNA WO 33/2384: Howard Committee Report, Report on Evacuation of Saint Malo, para 4, Evacuation of Vehicles.

183 TNA WO 167/413: HQ 157th Brigade WD, 17 June 1940.

184 Brigadier (later Major-General) Sir John Emilius Laurie (1892-1983) DSO, late Seaforth Highlanders. After Great War service on the Western Front, during which he was awarded the DSO in 1916, a Bar in 1918, and Mentioned in Despatched on five occasions, he served in Egypt and India before commanding 2nd Seaforth Highlanders (1934-1938). He was then posted to China as Commander British Troops Tientsin (1939-1940), being recalled to command 157th Brigade. He was appointed CBE for his leadership in France and commanded the 52nd (Lowland) Division March 1941 - September 1942. For further details, see, Smart, *Biographical Dictionary of the British Generals of the Second World War*, p.181. Blake, *Mountain and Flood*, p.23, described him as a 'cool, resolute and skilful commander'.

185 TNA WO 167/413: HQ 157th Brigade WD, entry 18 June 1940.

186 'No Truce With Time', David B Erskine, *Tank Journal*, May 1990, p.22. In this article, Erskine, responsible for the ciphering machines at HQ 1st Armoured Division, provides, from a personal perspective, an erudite resume of the withdrawal and evacuation.

Far removed from the cut and thrust of armoured warfare, 47 Supply Depot Section (SDS) of Force K6 arrived at Le Harve from Marseilles on 10 May, being subject to several heavy raids from 20 May onwards. Evacuated South across the River Seine on the Caudebec Ferry on 21 May, 47 SDS was returned in short order to Le Harve to assist in operating the Advanced Base facilities.[187] 47 SDS entrained for Saint Thegonnec on 7 June arriving safely on 10 June, the *Luftwaffe* fortunately not attacking the railway infrastructure or rolling stock *en-route* and the unit reached Plymouth on 19 June aboard the RMS *Strathaird*,[188] which had embarked, 6,500 military personnel. To the South, the Force K6 Reinforcement Unit, Advanced Remount Unit and 29 Animal Transport (AT) Company departed on the march from Le Mans at 0015 on 10 June, the first two units being ready at one hour's Notice to Move. Despite the crowded roads, they arrived at Heric, the evacuation assembly area, 30 miles from Saint Nazaire on 16 June, where they were ordered to abandon all animals and equipment.[189] Commandant Force K6, Lieutenant-Colonel Hills RIASC directed that the units handover both to the local French populace, with an instruction to distribute the animals to farmers and the equipment to refugees.[190] WMT took the 700 troops to the port, via a waiting area in woods and fields five miles from the docks to reduce the chance of casualties from air attack. The units embarked on the SS *Floristan* on 17 June but due to confusion about the loading of personal kit much was left on the quay, together with some of the Force records, a failure, which greatly exercised the Commandant.[191] Despite damage to hull plates caused by an unfortunate grounding, the ship, with 3,000 troops aboard and only making a maximum speed of eight knots, arrived at Plymouth on 19 June.[192]

Ebb and Flood

The air situation remained in German favour, but this had rather less effect on the Base areas than the planners had estimated; incendiaries delivered by air could have caused considerable destruction, particularly in the BODs. The Germans certainly missed a golden opportunity to severely dislocate the withdrawal in the South, and British forces escaped with fewer casualties than was expected. There were however, some very dramatic and tragic losses, including the attack on Rennes railway station[193] causing 805 military and civilian

187 TNA WO 167/1433: 'Report on Operations in France' dated 19 July 1940, para, 16-19.

188 TNA WO 167/1433: 'Report on Operations in France' dated 19 July 1940, para, 20-22. Of 22,281 GRT, this P&O liner survived the war to be scrapped in Hong Kong in 1961.

189 The move was lubricated by the 'invaluable' industry of the French liaison officer, Sous-Lieutenant le Comte F de Champeaux, who organized billeting and water for both personnel and animals.

190 TNA WO 167/1433: 'Report on Operations in France' dated 19 July 1940, paras, 40-41.

191 TNA WO 167/1433: 'Report on Operations in France' dated 19 July 1940, para, 46.

192 Lieutenant-Colonel Hills noted that although in a small convoy, the *Floristan* had only four lifeboats, almost no lifebelts and 'very little woodwork'. TNA WO 167/1433: 'Report on Operations in France' dated 19 July 1940, paras, 47-51.

193 See, Chp 15, 'Riding the Rails'.

P18.2 Tragedy and Courage. Many logisticians were lost as a result of the aerial bombing attack upon, and the sinking, of HMT *Lancastria*. 2188669 Private Hubert Thomas Hickerton 73 Company AMPC is commemorated on the Dunkirk Memorial, Column 152. This is his private memorial at the National Arboretum. (Author)

fatalities[194] and the sinking of HMT *Lancastria*[195] at Saint Nazaire[196] on 17 June, with the loss of between 3,000 and 5,000 lives.[197] Many of the dead and wounded were from the logistic

194 The figures are believed to be: French military 591, British military (Army and RAF) 177 and French civilians 37. TNA WO 361/114: Rennes Train Bombing.

195 The Cunard /White Star passenger liner Royal Mail Ship (RMS) *Lancastria*, the former *Tyrrhenia* (16,243 tons) was in service as a Hired Military Transport (HMT) and its sinking by aerial bombing led to the largest loss of life at sea suffered by the UK in one incident and depending upon the baseline calculations, between the 6th and the 14th largest maritime disaster of the Second World War. For updates and casualty research, see *Lancastria Association* <www.lancastria-association.org.uk/> and *Lancastria Association of Scotland* www.lancastria.org.uk/.

196 On 16 June 1940, whilst entering Quiberon Bay, the *Lancastria* and the *Fraconia* were attacked by a single *Luftwaffe* aircraft. The *Lancastria* escaped damage but the underwater bomb explosions sprung some hull plates on the *Franconia* and caused internal engine misalignment resulting in the ship returning empty to the UK for repairs. Crabb, *The Forgotten Tragedy*, pp.60-61.

197 Casualty estimates vary considerably because they are calculated as the difference between those on board and the number of survivors; unfortunately, there are discrepancies in the former baseline. The Association of Lancastria Survivors estimate that up to 9,000 people were aboard HMT *Lancastria* when she was sunk; official assessments suggest 5,310 to 5,506. The compiler of the 159 RCC RE war

Corps[198] of the Army and the supply and engineer branches of the RAF and the loss of the *Lancastria* challenged the courage and fibre of everyone involved. At approximately 1548, whilst lying at anchor in the Charpentier Roads,[199] in the River Loire off Saint Nazaire, a Junkers 88A of KG 30 bombed the ship,[200] which capsized and then sank, all in 24 minutes.[201] Squadron Leader Shipp RAF[202] succinctly summarized the trauma of the event:[203] 'We came face to face with those army boys, many suffering from terrible wounds, others showing on their faces mental havoc which had been wrought in so short a time. The cries of suffering from those badly wounded and needing help was the worst problem …'[204] In the middle of this chaos however, logisticians from the RASC engaged the enemy with three members of 1

diary states in the AFC 2118 that he was informed that there were approximately 5,100 people. See, TNA WO 167/954. The figure of 3,750 is often quoted including Army, RAF Merchant Marine and civilians; the RN and Royal Marines appear to have been fortunate in suffering no loss. The *Lancastria Roll of Honour* <www.ipresent.co.uk/rollHonour.htm> and *Lancastria Association* <www.lancastria.org.uk/> websites, compiled by Brian Crabb, lists all those personnel known or believed to have been lost on HMT *Lancastria*, which totals 1,738 names but the author articulates that it is not definitive. See also, Crabb, *The Forgotten Tragedy*. The subject is not well served by poor research. David L Williams, *In Titanic's Shadow, The World's Worst Merchant Ship Disasters*, (Stroud: History Press, 2012), p.26, notes units of the Royal Logistic Corps, which was not formed until 1993, were aboard.

198 A list of the units is in Geoffrey Bond, *Lancastria* (London: Oldbourne, 1959), pp.252-256. Logistic units included: 1 & 2 BOD RAOC, 1 BSD RASC, 1 HRS RASC, 1 & 2 Field Bakery RASC and EFI AASF. There were several railway companies aboard the *Lancastria*, 29 Survey, 154 ROC, 156 Transportation Stores, 159 RCC, 176 Transportation Stores and 190 ROC, but the inclusion of 7 Railway Company RE in publications must be an error because it did not deploy to France. TNA WO 222/1529: Aerial Plan - Reports. Logistic corps losses are believed to be: RASC (268), RAOC (85) and AMPC (435). RE railway units are believed to have suffered 87 fatalities, 72 of which were from 159 RCC.

199 The wreck of HMT *Lancastria* lies in 26 metres and stands 12 metres proud of the seabed in position 47° 09.049N 002° 20.389W.

200 TNA AIR 35/352: 67 Wing Operational Summaries 1940.

201 The most comprehensive publication is Crabb, *The Forgotten Tragedy* but see also, Bond, *Lancastria* and Jonathan Fenby, *The Sinking of the Lancastria, Britain's Greatest Maritime Disaster and Churchill's Cover-Up* (London: Simon & Schuster, 2005).

202 Squadron Leader E M C Shipp MBE RAFVR was the OIC MT Section, HQ BAFF.

203 Churchill deemed the news of her loss so bad, that he forbade publication of the story. He wrote: 'the newspapers have got quite enough disaster for to-day at least … .I forgot to lift the ban, and it was some time before the knowledge of this horror became public'. Winston S Churchill, *History of the Second World War*, Vol II, *Their Finest Hour* (London: Cassell, 1949), p.172. He was correct in his assumption; *The Times* did not carry the story until the late edition of Thursday 25 July 1940, whilst the Daily Mirror ran it as headline news on Friday 26 July. His decision had though, some unintended negative consequences because rumours of the disaster quickly began to circulate in Plymouth and these were repeated as the survivors were re-located across many parts of the United Kingdom. When the newspapers ran the story 38 days later, long after the sinking had been announced on German radio, the public trust in official bulletins was undermined and the delay attracted much adverse criticism from the population adding another frictional dimension to British morale during the Battle of Britain. See, Paul Addison and Jeremy A Crang (eds), *Listening to Britain: Home Intelligence Reports on Britain's Finest Hour, May-September 1940* (London: The Bodley Head, 2010), pp.270-292. The media implications of the *Lancastria* disaster are examined in: C H Maginniss, 'Leadership, Propaganda and Popular Morale during the Battle of Britain', C H Maginniss, Warwick University Thesis (unpublished), 1977.

204 Crabb, *The Forgotten Tragedy*, p.134.

BSD firing their Bren guns until the water reached the decks,[205] whilst 1 HRS claimed that 'all the automatic weapons in action on the Lancastria with one exception, were manned by HRS personnel. The exception was one RAF Lewis gun ... The action of these Guns Teams was exemplary and would have done credit to veteran troops'.[206]

In spite of the sinking of the *Lancastria* and damage to other ships, 42,000 personnel were evacuated from Saint Nazaire in less than 48 hours, a most creditable feat which has mainly been forgotten.[207] The plan during 15-18 June to recover vehicles and equipment was thwarted by the impossibility, within the timeframe, to sail appropriate ships. Hundreds of vehicles including specialist equipment such as workshop lorries had to be abandoned, although often destroyed or rendered unfit for immediate use. Several hundred tons of ordnance tools and miscellaneous stores, 3 x 25 pounder guns and radar equipment were however, brought to UK.[208] The evacuation from St Nazaire in the period 16-18 June was the largest after Dunkerque, with 57,200 personnel being recovered. Most of these soldiers were GLOC troops and AASF personnel. Commandant Force K6, in his After Action Report, credits OIC Movement Control at Saint Nazaire, an infantry officer, Major Richard Ware MC of the Durham Light Infantry,[209] for keeping a close grip on operations, stating, 'Without his careful organization the embarkation might well have developed into a rabble',[210] a short sentence in a war diary thus quietly understating the calm demeanour of another forgotten officer, whose actions enabled the BEF to reach England.

Equally, there were other successes. 31,360 personnel were evacuated from Cherbourg and 21,474 from Saint Malo without loss of life or vessels, by enemy action.[211] Other units were fortunate to escape through the incredible gallantry and sea-faring professionalism of the mainly unsung heroes of the Merchant Marine, bringing with them precious military *materiel.* 10th Royal Hussars were delayed at Brest by aerial mines, which the *Luftwaffe* had deployed into the shipping channel and the French naval authorities had yet to clear them. The skipper of a 'rusty old cargo vessel'[212] had however, taken bearings on the mines as they fell into the water and offered to lead the ship, the SS *Manx Maid*, in which the unit was embarked, to the open sea. After the *Manx Maid* cleared the channel unscathed, the soldiers gave his ship and

205 118836 Second-Lieutenant J C Medlicott-Vereker RASC was awarded the MC. TNA WO 373/146/67: Recommendation for Award for Medlicott-Vereker. Sergeant J Clarke and Corporal J Durrant both received the MM for their actions.

206 Report by Captain D F Abbott RASC in TNA WO 167/1155: 1 HRS RASC, June 1940. The report notes that Lance-Corporal Bolton was missing but he survived the sinking. The names of the 16 gunners are listed in Crabb, *The Forgotten Tragedy*, Appx 3.

207 TNA WO 33/2384: Howard Committee Report, Report on Evacuation of Saint Nazaire, para 2b, Evacuation.

208 TNA WO 33/2384: Howard Committee Report, Report on Evacuation of Saint Nazaire, para 3, Salving of Equipment.

209 After the evacuation Richard Fenwick Ware was promoted to command 11th DLI, which was deployed to Iceland as part of 70th Brigade. Ware also commanded 16th DLI during operations in Tunisia in early 1943 with 46th Division. Rissik, *The DLI at War*. As Movement Control was a Royal Engineer responsibility, he may have been filling a temporary post in the organization. He died in 1987 and is buried in Wolvercote Cemetery Oxfordshire.

210 TNA WO 167/1433: HQ Force K6, 'Report on Operations in France', dated 19 July 1940, p.10.

211 Ellis, BOH, *The War in France and Flanders*, p.302.

212 Regimental Committee, *The 10th Royal Hussars in the Second World War*, p.27.

its brave crew[213] a regimental cheer, to which the vessel's captain replied with his siren. The regimental history recorded. 'We never knew his name or those of his volunteer crew but this gallant action is remembered by the Regiment'.[214] The members of the 10th Hussars were not the only soldiers to be grateful to the Merchant Marine, with the master of the SS *Floristan*[215] receiving wholesome praise from the Commandant Force K6, who noted in his AAR that the 'outstanding work' of Captain E Wilson 'merits a reward'.[216] To these civilian logisticians, such as these crusty Old Sea Dogs, the BEF owned its survival.

As the ships cast off from the quays on 17 June, a meeting was held at Gwydyr House London[217] to examine the wider issues relating to the evacuation from France.[218] Chaired by Lord Hankey and attended by 21 representatives from all the key government departments, including the Armed Services, Cabinet Office, Economic Warfare, Foreign Office, Home Office, Labour, Shipping and the Anglo-French Co-ordinating Committee, the agenda included the repatriation of British refugees, demolition of French ports and oil storage facilities,[219] the evacuation of Polish troops and *Luftwaffe* POWs, recovery of diamonds and 250 skilled die drillers, the acquisition of machine tools, the diversion of French aircraft purchased from the USA arriving in France from Canada[220] and the transport of nine LAA guns from Switzerland by commercial air charter.

Another long forgotten aspect of the evacuation from France was the departure of the personnel and equipment of the Marseilles Sub-Area, which was, despite the best efforts of its commander, Brigadier Hawes,[221] a shambles that could have easily been avoided with clear direction from HQ LOC.[222] In the light of events in Northern France and the increasing possibility that the Italians would join the conflict and invade Southern France, Hawes had reduced the shape, size and scope of the operation, and with the exception of items to run

213 The skeleton crew consisted of the captain, two engine-room staff, the quartermaster and a deck-hand. Ibid.

214 Ibid.

215 The SS *Floristan* was lost on 19 January 1942 loaded with a mixed cargo of locomotive parts, copper wire, military vehicles, tanks, tin and gold specie, when, whilst on a voyage from Manchester to the Persian Gulf, she ran aground in Kilchiaran Bay in Islay Scotland; the crew survived the sinking. The wreck lies in 15 metres of water, the highest part standing 12 metres proud; divers have recovered some gold coins. Richard & Bridget Larn, *Shipwreck Index of the British Isles*, Vol 4, *Scotland* (London: Lloyd's Register of Shipping, 1998), Sect 6.

216 TNA WO 167/1433: HQ Force K6, 'Report on Operations in France', dated 19 July 1940, p.10.

217 Gwydyr House is in Whitehall SW1 and houses the Office of the Secretary of State for Wales. The front exterior was used to represent the building hosting the fictitious Department of Administrative Affairs in the BBC TV political comedy *Yes Minister*.

218 TNA CAB 115/378: Evacuation of Personnel and Material from France, 'Gwydyr House Meeting Minutes' dated 17 June 1940.

219 The Committee took note that the French authorities at Saint Malo were unwilling to agree to such demolitions. TNA CAB 115/378: Evacuation of Personnel and Material from France, 'Gwydyr House Meeting Minutes' dated 17 June 1940, para 2, Material.

220 These included crated aircraft in cargo ships and 73 planes aboard the French aircraft carrier *Bearn* that had sailed from Halifax on 16 June 1940. TNA CAB 115/378: Evacuation of Personnel and Material from France, 'Gwydyr House Meeting Minutes' dated 17 June 1940, para 2, Material.

221 Hawes was a substantive Colonel, holding Local rank.

222 TNA WO 197/131: Evacuation of Marseilles Sub-Area, Personal Letter (SECRET) from Brigadier Hawes to Commander South District, Brigadier F W Bissett DSO MC dated 17 June 1940.

the transit camps, had packed 1,560 tons of equipment and stores ready for entrainment but received no orders until 15 June, which then suggested either destruction or a move by rail and road to evacuate through La Pallice.[223] As it transpired, neither occurred, although the weapons and ammunition were dispatched by rail to 1 BOD. As a result, most of the ordnance stores and RASC supplies were transferred to the Host Nation, with officers from the French Army *Intendance* assuming control of the Ordnance and Supply depots.[224] Brigadier Hawes summarized the challenge in a letter to the chain of command: 'There are 140,000 Italians in Marseilles at this moment and all our revolvers have been withdrawn. Dont [sic] laugh, it might be quite unpleasant'.[225] All BEF personnel were therefore, prepared for evacuation, with the exception of a RASC supply section, supporting 53rd HAA Regiment, which was attached to the RAF to assist in the defence of the French airfields of Le Vallon and Salon-de-Provence in Southern France near Marseilles, which were to host two Wellington bomber squadrons, deployed to attack, if ordered, targets in Northern Italy under Operation HADDOCK.[226] In a finale, which was in keeping with the almost comic affair, the RASC supply section then arrived on the quay to embark having been informed by 53rd HAA Regiment that the RAF elements were also leaving. The parties thus set sail for Gibraltar on four cargo vessels, the SS *Alma Dawson*, the SS *Coultarn*, and the SS *Finland*,[227] with 20 WMT vehicles on a fourth ship, the SS *Toussika*.[228] Unfortunately, in the confusion and rush, compounded by dock labour issues, several 3-inch AA guns were left in Marseilles, a contentious issue that was still 'doing the rounds' in November 1940,[229] although the LAA Bofors were embarked on the *Alma Dawson*.

Endgame

Despite the constantly shifting sands upon which the evacuation plans were based, the logisticians were remarkably adept in reacting to the operational requirements, although they were sometimes unable to provide the support because of the shortage of critical assets. Whilst stock evacuation had commenced in late May, there is little doubt that the orders to mount a scale evacuation of stocks and equipment was left too late, an outcome which, was incontrovertibly

223 TNA WO 197/131: Evacuation of Marseilles Sub-Area, Memorandum by Colonel (Retd) H F Hawes dated 21 November 1940, p.3.
224 TNA WO 197/131: Evacuation of Marseilles Sub-Area, Memorandum by Colonel (Retd) H F Hawes dated 21 November 1940, p.2.
225 TNA WO 197/131: Evacuation of Marseilles Sub-Area, Personal Letter (SECRET) from Brigadier Hawes to Commander South District, Brigadier F W Bissett DSO MC dated 17 June 1940.
226 TNA AIR 35/323: Haddock Force Operations.
227 The SS *Finland* of 1,333 GRT had loaded cargo at Marseilles in early June for a voyage to Italy but had been anchored in the roads. The *Finland*, in contrast to many other BEF ships, had a long life at sea, being lost as the SS *Bulwark* on 1 April 1963 after running aground in fog 0.4 nm West of Danger Point Cape Province in South Africa whilst on a voyage from Cape Town to Durban carrying fishmeal and liquor. Winser, *BEF Ships*, p.44.
228 SS *Alma Dawson* (3,985 GRT), the SS *Coultarn* of GRT 3,759 and the SS *Tousika* (1,828 GRT). All three ships were lost later in the war. The *Dawson* struck a British mine in November 1940, the *Coultarn* was torpedoed by U-69 in March 1941 and *Toussika* seized by the Vichy French at Casablanca on 30 June 1940, being scuttled as a blockship at Port Lyautey in November 1942. Lloyd's Register.
229 TNA WO 197/131: Evacuation of Marseilles Sub-Area, Memorandum by Colonel (Retd) H F Hawes dated 21 November 1940, p.4.

influenced by the vision of an expanding 2nd BEF to assist the French to stay in the fight. Situational awareness, or rather its absence, resulted in flawed decision-making, with rumour rather than fact becoming the driver, adversely influencing logistic commanders' comprehension of the speed of the enemy advance, the various interpretations of impact of the Franco-German armistice upon the status of the BEF and departure times of allocated shipping, all of which compressed the perceived time-space continuum.

Plans to move a smaller Base to the South, whilst an understandable reaction to the German advance not only wasted valuable Staff effort, depot time and logistic resources but also lost touch with the ability of the Sea Line of Communication to support operations or evacuate personnel and *materiel*. The decision to send significant numbers of cargo and MT ships in a 'last throw of the dice' failed to consider the logistic realities in France of the availability of depot labour, rail wagons, train paths, locomotives and declining port capacity, all of which were crucial to enabling stocks to be evacuated. In the final event however, the greatest frustration for the logisticians was to deliver *materiel* to the quay, for ships to leave without a full load because of a rumour that the Panzers were outside the dock gates.

Part VI

Aftermath

19

Back in Blighty
The contribution of National and military logistics to the reception of the BEF in the United Kingdom

---

Defining Images?

The evacuation from Dunkerque continues to hold centre stage in the historical analysis of late May and early June 1940, with perhaps the most iconic images being those of an army of civilian volunteers feeding weary soldiers of the BEF with tea and wads at a host of stations on the Southern Railway and beyond. In this respect, whilst the human aspect is first and foremost in these photographs, they rightly and lucidly illustrate two key components of transportation and rationing, which were part of the immense military and civilian logistic operation, without which, the recovery from the Dunkerque Mole and the neighbouring beaches would have ended with chaos at the South East Ports (SEP). Mostly forgotten, or perhaps ignored, in the historiography, are the two further recoveries from France in mid-June delivered by Operations AERIAL and CYCLE and the series of evacuations of British Forces from Norway in May and June. In the published literature, logistics does not feature greatly and the amazing story of the reception and reorganization of the various components of the BEF, evacuated from France in 1940, remains for the most part, opaque to public view, although one book, the excellent *Return from Dunkirk,*[1] is the exception.

The importance of the UK operations within the annals of military endeavour though, is firmly under-written by the fact that the BEF is the only British Army to be evacuated to the Home Base under attack and within sight of the United Kingdom. This alone should have ensured that significant attention was later paid to the logistic planning and execution that ensured the success of the operation, but this has not been the case, despite the contemporary visibility of the returning troops in a manner that was the complete opposite to those evacuated from Norway. The incredible improvisation has never been given the public credit it deserves, except in the 1971 film Dad's Army, when a senior German general announced, 'Do not under-estimate the

1 Peter Tatlow, *Return from Dunkirk: Railways to the Rescue, Operation Dynamo (1940)*, (Usk: Oakwood Press, 2010), is the classic text on the railway and catering operations supporting these evacuations, which captures not only the detail but also the atmosphere.

British; like us, they are great organizers!'[2] It is therefore, the intention of this chapter to correct this lacuna in the historiography of the BEF and indeed of British military operations.

Planning the Priorities

The War Office was accused of many failures during the Second World War but in planning and executing the evacuation of the BEF from France, the logistic planners showed nothing but industry and foresight and logistics, which although not much in the headlines, was of crucial importance, the tasks at home being different but no less formidable than those in France. The outcomes were even more remarkable given that the War Office was juggling with eight dynamic operations, four of which were not connected with the BEF. Whilst operations in France held centre stage in May and early June, the stunning German advance turned the attention of the War Office to the increasingly pressing matter of Home Defence.[3] Initially none of the intelligence agencies[4] had a firm handle on what the Germans were planning but strategic wisdom indicated that invasion[5] was not improbable and that some form of air campaign was likely to precede it.[6] Overlying the intelligence outputs there was always a suspicion at many levels of command, which was very understandable given the events in France, that the Germans might have an innovative surprise in store. An assault from the sky, whether from air attack, parachutists or air-landed troops, was perceived to be a distinct immediate possibility, and planning for these situations had a concomitant effect upon the logisticians.

Support[7] to the dispersed Anti-Aircraft (AA) divisions,[8] which were an integral component of the Air Defence of Great Britain (ADGB)[9] involved the RAOC furnishing AA personnel

2 The German general was played by Paul Dawkins (1918-1979). See *Dad's Army*, Columbia Pictures, 1971.

3 Basil Collier, BOH, *The Defence of the United Kingdom* (London: HMSO, 1957), pp.119-125.

4 See, F H Hinsley et al, BOH, *British Intelligence in the Second World War*, Vol 1 (London: HMSO, 1979), pp.159-190.

5 For a comprehensive explanation of German invasion plans, capabilities and equipment, see, Peter Schenk, *The Invasion of England 1940* (London: Conway Maritime Press, 1990).

6 Air Intelligence initially overestimated *Luftwaffe* strength and thus its offensive capability. Air operations analysts however, assessed that it would take 3-4 weeks from mid-June 1940 before the *Luftwaffe* was capable of mounting major operations against the UK from captured bases. In late June, low grade SIGINT, the Enigma and Photographic Reconnaissance were able to confirm this judgement. See, Hinsley, BOH, *British Intelligence in the Second World War*, Vol 1, p.174.

7 This was a major task because during a major raid on London, the AA guns would fire 600 tons of ammunition. By comparison, on the night of 14 November 1940, the *Luftwaffe*, during its raid on Coventry dropped 503 tons of High Explosive. For a very brief explanation of the logistic support system to AA Command, see, Regimental Committee, *The Story of the Royal Army Service Corps, 1939-1945*, pp.434-435. This is certainly a subject that would benefit from study.

8 AA Command comprised during this period, seven divisions deployed throughout the UK plus the Orkneys and Shetlands Defence (OSDEF). The allocation of guns to divisions on 11 July 1940 is shown in Collier, BOH, *The Defence of the United Kingdom*, pp.448-449, Appx IX.

9 ADGB consisted of four major organizations: Fighter Command (RAF) Balloon Command (RAF) AA Command (Army) and the Observer Corps. Fighter Command Groups, Balloon Command and the Observer Corps, were under command HQ Fighter Command at Bentley Priory; AA Command was under operational control.

with Small Arms,[10] so detachments could be given a ground defence role against parachutists, whilst the RASC AA divisional companies wrestled with the complexities of operating with impressed lorries[11] and the growing multiplicity of AA ammunition natures.[12] The rapidly expanding Home Guard,[13], driven by the threat of air desant forces,[14] was another growing activity that concerned the logisticians, as the War Office Staff debated who would be responsible for supporting the new organization.[15] With the best of the Army's formations returning from France bereft of equipment,[16] the reorganization of the Home Defence divisions[17] became a priority, whilst a major task was the maintenance of the expanding Army, including quartering, equipment, unit formation and movement, challenges which were complicated by sustaining the recruit and trade training of the 275,000 men who joined the colours between June and August 1940. As if all of these tasks were of insufficient magnitude, there were four additional operations ongoing or developing. The maintenance and then evacuation, reception, dispersion and reorganization of the North Western Expeditionary Force (NWEF) from Norway[18] is a

10 The War Office released 4,000 LMGs and 32,800 rifles from stock for issue to AA units. See, General Sir Frederick Pile, *Ack-Ack: Britain's Defence Against Air Attack during the Second World War* (London: George G Harrap & Co, 1949), p 118.

11 Upon the outbreak of war in September 1939, the AA Command released many of its War Department pattern vehicles for service with the BEF and they were replaced with a variety of impressed or hired equipment. A shortage of spares, the enactment of driver training and some unsatisfactory soldiers, were just three of the problems faced by the RASC in attempting to effectively support AA operations.

12 In June 1940, AA Command was equipped with 4.5-inch (static) 3.7-inch, 3-inch, 40 mm (Bofors) 20 mm (Hispano) and the 0.303-inch LMG Lewis. In addition, General Pile pressed for the introduction of an anti-tank round for the 40 mm Bofors. The frustrations he met in pursuing this matter are summarized in Ack-Ack, p.127. It is surprising though, given the anti-armour performance of the German 88 mm in France, that more attention was not paid to the anti-tank capability of the 3.7-inch.

13 The Home Guard was formed on 17 May 1940 by a Defence Order in Council, as the Local Defence Volunteers, with the abbreviation LDV, said by many to stand for Look, Duck, Vanish. Some small para-military groups in rural areas had been informally active well before Eden's radio announcement on 14 May 1940 and that the Government intended to create an official force was a decision, which was almost certainly hastened by the need to regularize these emerging unofficial armed militias. For a contemporary account of its activities, see, A G Street, *From Dusk Till Dawn* (London: George Harrap & Co 1943). Norman Longmate, *The Real Dad's Army* (*London:* Arrow Books, 1974) is a concise history. For a comprehensive academic review, see, S P Mackenzie, *The Home Guard: A Political and Military History* (Oxford: Oxford University Press, 1995). Interest in the Home Guard continues to be generated by the BBC series, *Dad's Army*.

14 In May 1940, the Germans had the capability to deliver light forces by glider, parachute and aircraft. British ground defence commanders were rightly concerned about their ability to destroy the combat capability of such forces to prevent them securing Drop Zones and airfields.

15 There are many Home Guard histories, which generally give an excellent flavour for organization and operations but almost nothing on logistics, which is another aspect that deserves study. For a brief description of platoon logistics, see, Lieutenant Colonel C H Maginniss, 'Hearts of Oak: The Stoneleigh Home Guard Platoon Group in the Defence of Middle England, 1940-1944', *British Army Review*, No 124 (UK MOD, Spring 2000), p.69.

16 The return of the BEF to the UK, added the manpower strength, but not the combat capability, of 12 divisions to the Home Defence ORBAT. Collier, BOH, *The Defence of the United Kingdom*, pp.119-125.

17 For details of divisional deployments in the UK in May and June 1940, see, Ibid, pp.127-134.

18 See, T K Derry, BOH, *The Campaign in Norway* (London, HMSO, 1952).

P19.1 Port Clearance. Rail was critical to delivering the swift movement of the BEF's soldiers from the UK SPODs. (Author).

mostly forgotten activity but occupied the time and talent of logisticians from April to July.[19] Mostly opaque but important from an Imperial perspective, was the reception, support and integration of Australian and New Zealand Forces to the UK ORBAT, tasking that required logistic planning, resources and delivery. The deployment to Iceland of some units from 49th (West Riding) Division,[20] elements of which had recently returned from Norway[21] was another logistic task overshadowed by the deployment, support to and subsequent evacuation of, the 2nd BEF in Normandy. Perhaps unsurprisingly, given the rapidly developing scope and scale of many of the tasks, the War Office looked to the commercial and voluntary sector to assist in providing the Army with the critical logistic capability it required.[22]

19 WOOH, *Maintenance in the Field*, Vol I, pp. 62-86.
20 WOOH, *Maintenance in the Field*, Vol I, pp.86-91.
21 I am indebted to the then 2555235 Lance-Corporal Lionel Woodhead (1903-1984) of No 6 (L of C) Provost Company, for his personal experiences of the deployment, operations and recovery of the NWEF from his service in Harstad. Lionel Woodhead, a bus driver, had served in the TA in Leeds for 18 years before being mobilized in 1939.
22 TNA WO 197/134: Evacuation and Quartering of the BEF, 'A Short Account', para 3.

Burning the Midnight Oil

The speed and direction of the German advance rapidly rang alarm bells in Whitehall. On 10 May 1940, a Tri-Service body, the Home Defence Executive [23] was formed, with C-in-C Home Forces[24] in the chair, which was tasked with executing a drastic overhaul of home defence organizations in the light of new German dispositions, tactics and weapons. In the War Office, the Military Operations Directorate monitored the land battle in Belgium and France with growing concern. By 18 May, the War Office Staff began to seriously examine the possibility that a withdrawal of the BEF, or at least elements of it, might be necessary, and it was considered wise to prepare contingency plans for that event. A contemporary report summarized the challenge: 'The problem confronting the Quartermaster-General's Department, and in particular the Quartering Directorate, was a formidable one, and on a scale without precedent in the history of war'.[25] With that as the starting point, a conference was convened in the War Office on 19 May 1940,[26] attended by representatives from the QMG's Department, in particular Movements, the Directorate of Army Quartering and the Home Commands, to discuss the arrangements that would have to be enacted to rehabilitate[27] the BEF[28] by receiving, transporting, distributing, accommodating, reorganizing and re-equipping an unknown number of units.[29]

In order to progress the planning process, the Staff made a number of assumptions, which, through a careful appreciation of a dynamic operational situation, generated a number of deductions, most of which proved to be substantially correct,[30] and all of which were underpinned by the application of the 'Principles of Logistics': foresight, efficiency, simplicity, co-operation and flexibility. The planners were able to quantify, within working limits, the logistic requirement, by utilizing the process of what is now called DQUAD: Destination, Demand, Distance and Duration.[31] The importance of their sound and balanced appreciation was to become clear within a very short space of time. As the Staff started to burn the midnight

23 For a Tri-Service perspective on the challenges of Home Defence in the period May to August 1940, see, Collier, BOH, *The Defence of the United Kingdom*, pp.119-146.
24 General Sir Edmund Ironside between May and July 1940.
25 TNA WO 197/134: Evacuation and Quartering of the BEF, para 2.
26 TNA WO 197/134: Evacuation and Quartering of the BEF, para 1.
27 Rehabilitation encompasses two activities in the British Army: Reconstitution and Regeneration. The former restores combat power to a specific level and the latter to the original level. For further explanation, see, *Army Field Manual* Vol 1, *The Fundamentals*, Part 6, *Combat Service Support*, Glossary, p.xv.
28 For the most part, the BEF was reconstituted, that is rehabilitated to a specific level, in this case well below that of the original, commensurate with the available resources, rather than the anticipated mission.
29 The process of rehabilitation is largely logistic in nature, although subsequent training will be of importance in restoring combat power. For details of the present approach, and the fundamentals were very similar in 1940, see *Army Doctrine Publication* Vol 3, *Logistics*, pp 4-8 to 4-10, paras 0420-0422.
30 Fortunately, unlike Doctor Watson in the Blue Carbuncle, they were not too timid in drawing their inferences. See, Arthur Conan Doyle, *The Adventures of Sherlock Holmes: The Blue Carbuncle* (Oxford: Oxford University Press 1993), p.152. "On the contrary, Watson, you can see everything. You fail, however, to reason from what you see. You are too timid in drawing your inferences."
31 For an explanation of the application of DQUAD, see, ADP, Vol 3, *Logistics*, pp 2-3 to 2-5, paras 0207-0211. See also, The Royal Logistic Corps, Vol 1, Pamphlet 1, *Logistic Support Doctrine*, pp.3-4 to 3-5.

oil, events in France had initiated the requirement to move troops and casualties from the SEP and by the time Operation DYNAMO[32] was ordered on 26 May 1940, 21,410 Army and RAF personnel, 4,992 casualties and 1,534 Allied soldiers and refugees totalling 27,936 people had had landed at Dover, Folkestone, Newhaven and Southampton.[33]

First, the planners believed it would probably only be possible to recover soldiers and their personal equipment.[34] In the event, this was the case, and, in the evacuation from the French Northern Channel Ports, almost certainly inevitable.[35] Salvage parties from the RAOC[36] were deployed at the SEP debarkation ports but contemporary observers were unimpressed, if not dismayed, by the scale of the abandonment of arms,[37] ammunition and equipment.[38] There was consequently much less reclamation than expected,[39] with the main items being blankets, rifles, revolvers, grenades and Small Arms Ammunition (SAA), although many of the weapons had been exposed to sand and salt-water and required reconditioning. Units may not however, have been entirely at fault in failing to recover what the chain of command expected. 50th Division, evacuating from Bray Dunes, recorded that its units were ordered to make every effort to return automatic weapons and optical instruments, especially for the artillery, the divisional history noting that, 'When the time came, no unit in the Division failed to salve the machine-guns and instruments'.[40] The regimental history of 3rd Medium Regiment Royal Artillery noted: 'small arms, wireless sets, dial sight, binoculars and compasses were saved, and these were carried with a great deal of trouble onto the ships. The Navy stepped in at this point and threw them all in the sea'.[41] Lance-Corporal Gillian of the regimental Signal Section showed much greater determination in returning a type-writer, saving it from the water when the rowing boat he was in, sank.[42]

32 For the official naval history of Operation DYNAMO, see, BR 1736 (32), *Second World War*, Battle Summary No 41, *The Evacuation from Dunkirk, Operation Dynamo*. See also, ADM 234/360: Operation Dynamo.

33 TNA WO 197/134: Evacuation and Quartering of the BEF, para 7 and Tatlow, *Return from Dunkirk*, p.51.

34 TNA WO 197/134: Evacuation and Quartering of the BEF, 'A Short Account', para 3.

35 Unfortunately, initially at least, this concept was transferred to the planning of the evacuations from South of the Somme, with the consequential loss of otherwise recoverable material, although this outcome was also the result of late decisions, poor intelligence and weak communications.

36 TNA WO 197/134: Evacuation from France and Quartering of the BEF - Activities of the Directorate of Ordnance Services in the Evacuation from France.

37 On occasions, soldiers had an excellent reason for not disembarking in the UK with a firearm. Signalman John Yeomans was questioned on arrival on the quay in UK as to the whereabouts of his rifle, to which he had great pleasure in replying that he had never been issued with one. JYIC 241099.

38 The War Office official history commented: 'Those who can recall the deficiencies of rifles in the British Army during the remainder of 1940 will appreciate this point from the provisioning angle, quite apart from the disciplinary issues involved'. WOOH, *Maintenance in the Field*, Vol 1, p.60.

39 This was entirely understandable for soldiers rescued from the beaches, West to East: Malo-les-Bains, Zuydcoote Sanatorium, Bray Dunes and La Panne (Belgium).

40 Major Ewart Clay MBE, *The Path of the 50th: The Story of the 50th (Northumbrian) Division in the Second World War, 1939-1945* (Aldershot: Gale & Polden, 1950), pp.25-26.

41 na, *The History of the 3rd Medium Artillery Regiment Royal Artillery, 1939-1945*, p.62.

42 Ibid, p.66. Regrettably the author does not offer any visibility upon its operational state after its immersion in sea-water but there is little doubt a RAOC Workshop would have refurbished it.

Perhaps because of the poor results from the salvage parties during Operation DYANMO, they were not widely deployed to the South-West ports to receive the ships from Operations CYCLE and AERIAL. This was a missed opportunity to bring some early order to the equipment issue at Command level because many units withdrawing from the Western and Normandy ports seized the chance to enhance equipment stocks, often from *materiel* abandoned by less disciplined units. Whilst every man in 5th King's Own Scottish Borders returned with a rifle, the Regimental Quartermaster greatly enhanced the battalion's holdings by salvaging abandoned weapons from the quay at Cherbourg, so upon arrival at the Reorganization Station at Ramsay in Huntingdonshire, the main shortage was blankets and personal ablution items, quantities of which were kindly donated by local people.[43]

The 9th Queens' Royal Lancers regimental history identified not only a pertinent command and control issue but also a downstream Quartermaster problem, which whilst initially benefiting the regiment caused wider problems for the Army. When the ship SS *Lady of Man* voyaging from Brest arrived at Plymouth, 'Orders to disembark resulted in an indescribable muddle; much equipment including arms and ammunition, was left on board, an omission which was probably due to the fact that most of the troops were stragglers and not formed bodies'.[44] This opportunity was too good to miss and an inventory check at the regiment's half-completed camp near Warminster discovered that, 'we had brought with us rather more than our establishment of small arms: 'A' Squadron for instance, had thirty-six Bren guns instead of the five to which they were entitled….'.[45] One logistic unit fared rather less well despite their best efforts to retain their equipment as the system began to effectively collate *materiel*, CRASC 2 Division reporting that his soldiers arriving at Halifax in Yorkshire were without caps, rifles and respirators, which he discovered had been removed from them in the Reception Area camps.[46]

Secondly, an assumption was made that the number requiring reception would be around 300,000 British soldiers,[47] whilst it was deemed unlikely that unit coherence would be maintained so the reception process would need to reform units in a later phase. This outfall from this assessment was the creation of a three stage process, involving an initial move from the port to a Reception Area, thence to Divisional Redistribution Areas and finally to Reorganization Areas.[48] The evacuation of French and Allied contingents was also examined.[49] Whilst the planners had no idea how many Allied soldiers might require evacuation, movement, accommodation and rationing, an estimate was generated based on the numbers of foreign personnel thought to be in France, although it was expected that French military and naval personnel would be repatriated to France if shipping permitted. Planning for the

43 Captain Hugh Gunning, *Borderers in Battle: The War Story of the King's Own Scottish Borderers, 1939-1945*, (Berwick-upon-Tweed: The Regiment, 1948).
44 Bright, *The Ninth Queen's Royal Lancers, 1936-1945*, p.24.
45 Ibid, p.25.
46 TNA WO 197/210: 2 Division CRASC, WD, entry 7 June 1940.
47 TNA WO 197/134: Evacuation and Quartering of the BEF, 'A Short Account', para 3 (iv).
48 TNA WO 197/134: Evacuation and Quartering of the BEF, 'A Short Account', para 3 (ii).
49 As it transpired, 147,838 Allied personnel landed in the UK. WOOH, *Movements*, p.202, Appx E to Chp 10.

reception of Allied contingents developed with the operational scenario[50] and the War Office made outline arrangements on the following basis:[51]

Table 19.1
Allied Contingents – Reception Planning

Contingent	Command	Location	Planning Figures
Belgian	Western	Tenby	10,000-15,000
Czech	Western	West Lancashire	15,000-20,000
Dutch	Western	Porthcawl	5,000
French – Foreign Legion	Western	Trentham - Staffordshire	Unknown
French – Free	Western	South Lancashire	Unknown
French – Transit	Southern	South Coast[52]	60,000
Norwegian	Scottish	South Highlands	Unknown
Poles	Scottish	Not confirmed	100,000

Thirdly, the Staff appreciated, that given the *Luftwaffe's* capability to mount, though not necessarily sustain, operations across the English Channel, a rapid dispersal of forces arriving in United Kingdom ports was vital, otherwise heavy losses might result.[53] The decision to dispatch

50 Whilst this was a dynamic process, by November 1941, the numbers of Allied contingents had become relatively static and the location of them mostly reflected the planning of May and June 1940. Table collated from information in WOOH, *Quartering*, p.29.

Table 19.2
Accommodation of Foreign Troops in UK - November 1941

Contingent	Command	Location	Officers	Other Ranks	Total
Belgian	Western	South Wales & Tenby	104	1,775	1,879
Czech	Western	Royal Leamington Spa*	576	2,307	2,883
Dutch	Western	Wolverhampton	100	1,544	1,644
Free French	Aldershot	Old Dean Common Camberley	60	654	714
Norwegian	Scottish	Coatbridge & Dumfries	140	1,716	1,856
Polish	Scottish	Fife Angus	3,599	13,797	17,396
Total			4,579	21,793	26,372

*The HQ of the Free Czechoslovak Army (FCA) was at Harrington House, demolished in 1967, in Newbold Terrace, with the main camp at Moreton Paddox, 8 miles to the South. The FCA in Royal Leamington Spa will always be associated with Operation ANTHROPOID, which led to the assassination of Reinhard Heydrich.

51 Table collated from information in TNA WO 197/134: Evacuation and Quartering of the BEF, para 19.

52 The War Office planned, with the assistance of the civil authorities, to billet French soldiers in private houses in Bournemouth (25,000), Plymouth (15,000) Southampton (15,000) and Weymouth (5,000) until repatriation to France. TNA WO 197/134: Evacuation and Quartering of the BEF, para 12. The P&O liner RMS *Strathaird* was also anchored in Plymouth Sound as floating temporary accommodation for French personnel awaiting repatriation. Winser, *BEF Ships*, p.42.

53 TNA WO 197/134: Evacuation and Quartering of the BEF, 'A Short Account', para 3 (v).

P19.2 Logistic Plan B. Commercial buses and coaches were held in reserve to cover disruptions to rail services. (Author)

all troops arriving at the SEP to Reception Areas without any reorganization greatly aided this plan. The ability of Fighter Command to maintain local air superiority over the port areas in Southern England was therefore, a vital, if little exposed, aspect of the operation. Military and railway planners certainly expected the *Luftwaffe* to intervene, and had plans to sustain the momentum of the operation.[54] Essential Permanent Way repair materials were already located at key points as part of the Strategic Defence Plan, and road transport was allocated to cope with emergencies, whilst the Royal Engineers stationed military railway construction and maintenance troops[55] at selected locations to assist the Southern Railway in their infrastructure

54 Brigadier C N Barclay CBE DSO, *The History of the Cameronians (Scottish Rifles)*, Vol III (London: Sifton Praed, nd but 1947), p.50, notes, 'A remarkable feature of these events was the failure of the German Air Force to bomb the ports of disembarkation'. No doubt the regiment's officers and soldiers took some comfort from the fact that a key player in the arrangements was General Sir Thomas Riddell-Webster, the Colonel of the Regiment.

55 TNA WO 197/134: Evacuation from France and Quartering of the BEF - Activities of DGT in the Evacuation from France.

repair operations.[56] Although intelligence gave no clue as to the possible use of Gas Warfare (GW) agents, and the operational situation in France indicated that such weapons were unlikely to be used, the railways were prepared for such an eventuality, being capable of deploying reconnaissance, survey and decontamination teams,[57] in addition to completing repairs in Individual Protective Equipment.[58]

The Staff identified the need to have a rapid, robust and flexible transport plan, which they based on rail movement, supported by road transport. To deliver effective output, close co-ordination with the railway companies at every level was required, created by liaison with the Railway Executive Committee and the deployment of Railway Traffic Officers to major stations. Military and civilian vehicles were employed to provide lift at the ports to entraining locations if trains could not reach the dockside and to disperse personnel from terminal stations to reception camps. Road transport was also ear-marked to provide alternative lift in the event of rail routes to the ports being interrupted by enemy action or accidents. The Ministry of War Transport provided 200 commercial motor coaches, with their civilian drivers, all on 12 hours' Notice To Move for use in Kent, where the Operation DYNAMO debarkation ports were located.[59] 4 Ambulance Car Company RASC[60] was allocated to Eastern Command, to support ambulance train operations,[61] which were run from Dover Marine Platform 3, Newhaven and Ramsgate, although some patients were transferred by road directly to local military or civilian medical facilities.[62] Fourthly, the challenges in feeding and quartering the returning soldiers required some innovative solutions, requiring assistance from the Voluntary sector. Last, but not least, Staff officers were keenly aware of the importance of the clerical aspects of the reception, especially in relation to the public interest. Field and personnel records would require

56 HQ No 4 Railway & Construction Group RE and 160 and 162 Railway Construction Companies (RCC) were assigned to this task. No 4 Group HQ deployed to the Southern Railway HQ at Deepdene House to the South-East of Dorking, whilst 160 RCC deployed two sections to Ashford and two to Redhill. 162 RCC remained in reserve at No 1 Railway Training Centre Longmoor Hampshire. TNA WO 197/134: Evacuation from France and Quartering of the BEF - Activities of DGT in the Evacuation from France.

57 For further details of GW defence preparations on British railways during the war, see, Earnshaw, *Britain's Railways at War*, pp.88-89 and Tim Bryan, *The Great Western at War, 1939-1945*, Tim Bryan (Sparkford: Patrick Stephens Limited, 1995), pp.31 & 75.

58 For an interesting selection of photographs of railway staff training in IPE, see *British Railways Illustrated*, Vol 6, Number 8, May 1997, pp.376 - 377.

59 TNA WO 197/134: Evacuation from France and Quartering of the BEF - Activities of DST in the Evacuation from France.

60 Five ambulances were allocated to eight SPODs and two at each of the initial *halt-repas*, plus a reserve. Tatlow, *Return from Dunkirk*, p.61.

61 Outside the scope of this chapter but nonetheless very relevant, is the immense mental and physical trauma suffered by many of the soldiers during the evacuation, often within a very short period of time, although they may not have been classified as casualties. The experiences of Signalman John Yeomans, provides an insight into this significant personal perspective. Having worked in GHQ, he waited his turn, under air attack, on the Dunkerque Mole for a place on a ship to England. The Dutch schuyt in which he sailed was attacked and sunk. The casualty list is unknown, but he and others, survived in the water to be rescued by a Royal Navy destroyer. JYIC 241099.

62 For the role of the civilian hospital services in supporting the treatment of casualties, see, C D Dunn, (ed.), *Medical History of the Second World War* (MBOH) *Emergency Medical Services*, Vol I (London: HMSO, 1952), pp.100-103.

re-instatement, partly to inform the next of kin of those who were safe and those who were killed, missing or POW. Additional problems emerged during the recovery, which required the assistance of other agencies. MI5 were involved with Customs & Immigration to screen civilian returnees[63] to seek out spies and Fifth Columnists,[64] whilst the soldiers returned with at least 170 dogs[65] that required quarantine for rabies.[66]

Hopelessly Split Up

War Office planners produced a simple but effective solution, which was conducted in three stages. Stage 1 was the movement by rail from the Sea Port of Disembarkation (SPOD) to a Reception Area, which, with the exception of sites in South and West Wales[67] and the South Midlands,[68] were in the South of England, with the majority in the Aldershot–Bordon and Salisbury Plain military areas.[69] To reduce initial travelling distances, and thus sustain the return of passenger rolling stock, the Northern limit for Northern Command was South of a line from The Wash to Derby. The plan was based on utilizing the facilities of existing garrisons and the soldiers in them to host returning members of the BEF on a one to one basis, which dictated the numbers that each Command would be expected to

63 This is a subject that requires exploration and lucidly illustrates that not everyone evacuated wore a military uniform. Two were Belgian waitresses, Simone Duponselle (19) and Elaine Madden (17) whose remarkable escape, with the BEF, from the Belgian town of Poperinghe to Dunkerque would grace the pages of any regimental history or indeed action story. See, Egbert Kieser, *Hitler On The Doorstep*, (translated by Helmut Bogler), (London: Arms & Armour Press, 1997, pp.59-62. Elaine Madden (1923-2012), Simone's niece, joined the Special Operations Executive and parachuted into Belgium in 1944 before transferring to the Special Allied Airborne Reconnaissance Force. She modestly observed that, 'I.....was willing to do anything except join the ATS! I wasn't a heroine but I can still look in the mirror and feel proud'. Tatlow, *Return from Dunkirk* states one soldier brought his French wife to UK disguised in battle-dress. 157th Brigade war diary records that three British ladies were evacuated from Cherbourg with the brigade HQ. TNA 167/413: HQ 157th Brigade, WD, entry 16 June 1940. There were also many civilians aboard HMT *Lancastria.*

64 The Official History of MI5 recorded that none of the individuals evacuated from Dunkerque proved to be of importance from the espionage perspective. There is no mention of other evacuations. John Curry, *The Security Service, 1908-1945, The Official History* (London: The Public Record Office, 1999), p.228.

65 The regimental history of 3rd Medium Regiment RA records that amongst several dogs, the regiment had found a home for Poppy, a small brown woolly puppy rescued from the rubble of a building in Poperinghe, which was smuggled to England on a RN destroyer and reached Lichfield, where 'an angry infantry colonel found her and had her shot, presumably for being a fifth columnist'. See na, *The History of the 3rd Medium Artillery Regiment*, p.63.

66 Tatlow, *Return from Dunkirk*, p.65, states the dogs had to be put to sleep.

67 Brecon, Cardiff, Llantwit Major, Newport, Pembroke Dock, Porthcawl, Tenby and Usk.

68 Northampton, Stratford-upon-Avon and Warwick.

69 See, Tatlow, *Return from Dunkirk*, pp.168-175.

take.[70] The departure stations and destinations of DYNAMO trains is a clear indication of the traffic flows from the SEP, with Dover Marine[71] being the main SPOD, then Ramsgate and Folkestone Harbour,[72] although Harwich, Newhaven and Sheerness were also used.[73] Banbury was the Rail Regulating Station for Northern Command. Soldiers would arrive at the SEP be entrained, fed at a halt on the journey and then be de-trained at a station near a suitable camp. Soldiers then marched,[74] or if they were fortunate, transported in WMT, to their temporary accommodation. On arrival, each soldier was double-bunked with a garrison man, who offered him some relevant comforts, such as a bed, blanket, eating utensils and a little hospitality, until the BEF soldier could be re-equipped with basic personal equipment, a process which placed a major burden upon the RAOC. The Ordnance Services report on the recovery operation noted that, 'As regards clothing, the BEF may be said to have arrived practically in rags, at least as regards the 'DYNAMO' groups',[75] a problem exacerbated at Army level because many soldiers left equipment behind in the Reception Areas creating a requirement for more issues from Command Ordnance Depots.[76] The regimental history of the Cameronians briefly described the process: 'On arrival at their destinations the troops were met and taken to camps, barracks or billets. Each man was given £1 pay[77] and refitted with essential clothing, kit and equipment.

70 The information in the table has been collated from details in TNA WO 197/134: Evacuation and Quartering of the BEF, para 6 and WOOH, *Quartering*, pp.18-19.

Table 19.3
Reception Areas – Home Commands

Command	Planned Personnel	Remarks
Aldershot	60,000	
Northern	40,000	Two divisional and one Corps Troops areas
Southern	150,000	Three divisional and one Corps Troops areas
Western	80,000	Two divisional and one Corps Troops areas
Total	330,000	Phase 2: one divisional area in Scottish Command

71 Rail movements at Dover Marine were complicated by the fact that trains could not easily be reversed into the platforms. This meant drawing the trains into the platform with a locomotive that then had to be released to shed after the train had departed. Tatlow, *Return from Dunkirk*. p.75. For a rail diagram, see, Richard Harman and Gerry Nichols, *Atlas of the Southern Railway* (Addlestone: Ian Allan, 2016), p.118, Map 86A – Dover Enlargements.

72 Railway operating out of Folkestone Harbour was constrained by the 1:30 gradient, which required the use of three shunting locomotives to haul the heavy troop trains out of the station to Folkestone Junction ready for dispatch. Ibid, p.65. For a rail diagram, see, Harman & Nichols, *Atlas of the Southern Railway*, p.117, Map 86 - Dover & Folkestone. The Harbour Branch closed in 2014 but the Folkestone Harbour Company is refurbishing the station as part of a wider development.

73 WOOH, *Movements*, p.105.

74 Signalman Yeomans related that after his various experiences in France and the English Channel, he detrained at Wool, to march the remaining three miles to Bovington Camp. JYIC 241099.

75 TNA WO 197/134: Evacuation from France and Quartering of the BEF – Activities of the Directorate of Ordnance Services in the Evacuation from France, para 8. In the first instance, Ordnance Services clothed all returning British soldiers and those Allied personnel that stayed in the UK, to home scale, less one suit of battle-dress and one shirt.

76 TNA WO 197/134: Evacuation from France and Quartering of the BEF - Activities of the Directorate of Ordnance Services in the Evacuation from France, para 3.

77 Using the RPI, this equates in 2018 to £53.64.

He remained in this centre for about twenty-four or forty-eight hours and was then directed to the place at which is Unit was to collect and reform.'[78]

Phase 2 was the restructuring process, in which ex-BEF soldiers were sent to Redistribution Areas.[79] These were areas allocated to divisions generated from the BEF's ORBAT.[80] This phase commenced on 30 May 1940 and involved quartering soldiers in barracks, temporary camps, some created from civilian facilities, and private houses. The soldiers of 2 Divisional Petrol Company (DPC) having passed through the Reception Area camp at Hereford were dispatched in details by scheduled rail services to Norton Tower to the North-West of Halifax[81] where they were billeted in homes and public houses, receiving a warm welcome from the local population[82] but creating considerable challenges for command, control, administration, and occasionally, for those residing in public houses, for discipline. This part of the operation was however, key, to regenerate coherent units, the members of which, in order to clear the SEP as quickly as possible were often sent far and wide across the Kingdom. The scribe of 1 Ordnance Field Park RAOC summarized the problem: 'Unit hopelessly split up and sent to various stations in England. Further recording of events impossible'.[83] For many units, the time in the Reorganization Area was one of mixed emotions. Soldiers were desperate for leave[84] but equally the chain of command was keen to commence the process of rehabilitation, an activity, which was partially based upon the delivery of equipment. In this respect, 2 DPC was relatively fortunate because soldiers, AFG 1098 equipment, rifles, clothing and webbing arrived, if sometimes in small quantities, on a daily basis.[85] A few requisitioned vehicles were also provided but on 20 June a large MT party departed for the vehicle depots at Feltham and Slough to collect a substantial issue of vehicles for the RASC components of 2nd Infantry Division.[86] On 22 June, having been reconstituted, 2 DPC moved to its allotted war station at Sledmere in East Yorkshire.

78 Barclay, *The History of the Cameronians (Scottish Rifles)*, Vol III, p.50.

79 Each Command prepared divisional and corps areas, based on the ORBAT of the BEF, to which soldiers would be redistributed from the Reception Areas. These were as follows: Southern (three divisional and one Corps Troops) Northern (two Divisional and one Corps Troops) Western (two divisional and one Corps Troops) and Scottish (one divisional). For further information, see, TNA WO 197/134: Evacuation and Quartering of the BEF, para 6 and WOOH, *Quartering*, pp 18-19.

80 Map 14: 14. UK – Post-evacuation Divisional Concentration & Deployment Areas.

81 WOOH, *Quartering* states that Northern Command was to plan on these areas being South of the Wash, but this was not the case as the line was Huddersfield-Hull.

82 TNA WO 167/212: 2 DPC RASC, WD, entries 2-6 June 1940.

83 TNA WO 1671192: 1 OFP RAOC, WD, 29 May 1940.

84 Acting GOC 2nd Division, Brigadier Findlay, Commander Divisional Royal Artillery, visited 2 DPC on 5 June and announced that All Ranks would be granted 10 days home leave as soon as possible, which greatly improved morale but only for 24 hours because the GOC, Major-General Irwin visited the next day to announce its cancellation 'for reasons sure to be appreciated', which probably related to a potential invasion. On a more positive note, there was free letter postage, half price tickets for the cinemas and buses, whilst in addition, a 72 hour leave pass was granted. TNA WO 167/212: 2 DPC RASC, WD, entries 5-6 June 1940.

85 TNA WO 167/212: 2 DPC RASC, WD, entries 8-19 June 1940.

86 TNA WO 167/212: 2 DPC RASC, WD, entries 20 June 1940. These vehicles included: 24 x ambulances, 10 x 3 ton (6x4) lorries, 64 x 30 cwt (4x4) trucks, 64 x 3 ton (4x4) lorries, 19 x 2 seat cars, 15 x 4 seat cars and 69 x motor-cycles. Of especial note were the 3 ton (4x4) lorries, which had entered mass production.

Soldiers who were unsure of their formation, were sent by Arm or Service to a Reorganization Area, an operation, which started on 8 June. In this respect, the RASC, operating its own mobilization centres was particularly well placed to ensure a timely flow of personnel to field units. Phase 2 placed a special burden on the RAOC and the NAAFI, for the provision of tentage but by 30 May, accommodation under canvas was available at Aldershot for 20,000 men and at Tidworth for 10,000.[87] These tented camps[88] were but a small proportion of the canvas requirement in July 1940, which the War Office estimated to be 412,000 bed-spaces,[89] although the requisitioning and enhancement of civilian buildings,[90] led to a substantial reduction of tented sites by December 1940.[91] Until units were issued with field catering equipment, the RASC was responsible for organizing 1st Line catering services.

No Written Instructions

The story of the BEF in most narratives, finishes on a railway train, 'somewhere in England' with exhausted but relieved soldiers leaning out of windows, smiling, waving and drinking tea but the engaging account of how the rail movement was planned and executed is rarely exposed. The reception and onward movement of the BEF was a complex and challenging operation, which involved a wide range of agencies, not least the War Office and the railways, and planning between these two organizations commenced formally on 21 May when representatives from the Directorate of Transportation (DGT) met with the Superintendent of Operations of the Southern Railway.[92] The railways were and still are, used to moving large numbers of people on a daily basis, so the potential demand to entrain 300,000 soldiers at the SEP with a maximum of 30,000 per day was less dramatic than it might first appear. In addition, the Big Four Railway Companies of the period, directed by the REC had considerable experience of the planning for, and execution of, military mobilization, the BEF's deployment to France and civilian evacuations.[93]

87 WOOH, *Quartering*, p.19.
88 Many soldiers felt psychologically uneasy in these camps, especially as much of the canvas was white. The regimental history of 9th Queen's Royal Lancers observed, 'we felt very vulnerable under our new white tents after the weeks of concealment in the woods of France'. Bright, *The Ninth Queen's Royal Lancers, 1936-1945*, p.23.
89 WOOH, *Quartering*, p.22.
90 Few new camps were constructed between May and December 1940 because it was much more effective to improve existing facilities. Thus, most of the available Nissen huts were used to enhance the capabilities of requisitioned sites. For example, a large country house with stables and outbuildings would be supplemented with 10-12 Nissen huts for additional accommodation and 2-3 for offices, stores and catering, thereby creating enough quartering for an infantry battalion. The greatest challenge was providing garaging, servicing facilities and hard-standing for MT.
91 In November 1940, there were 46,926 troops under 'permanent' canvas in the UK reducing to 9,141 by January 1941. Of these, soldiers serving with AA Command accounted for 19,539 and 8,598 respectively. WOOH, *Quartering*, p.23.
92 TNA WO 197/134: Evacuation from France and Quartering of the BEF - Activities of DGT in the Evacuation from France.
93 To support the civil evacuation in September 1939, the railway companies ran 3,823 trains, 1,577 of which, emanated from the London Civil Defence Area, to move 1,334,358 people. For details of train movement by area, Nock, *Britain's Railways at War: 1939-1945*, p.16.

The greatest difficulties they faced in planning for a possible recovery of the BEF, was confirmation of the ports that would be used, the DGT staff only suggesting that it could be any from Margate to Brighton,[94] whilst initially information on when the trains would be required, and the destinations, was even less defined. If there is one organization more focused on DQUAD than military logisticians it is the commercial railway and inevitably the railway HQs were hungry for information to enable work on the task to commence. Operation DYNAMO planning soon indicated however, that all the SEP plus Harwich would probably be the SPODs with Dover as the most important, although the number of trains run from each could not be planned in detail.[95] For the later evacuations South of the Somme, the key SPODs were Falmouth, Fowey, Southampton, Plymouth and Weymouth but Operations AERIAL and CYCLE created fewer problems for the railways because not only did they involve less troops but the planning and execution time-scales were longer.

To generate the lift required, the REC co-ordinated the provision of 186 train sets from the Big Four. Each set, held in a pool and capable of carrying 600 men, comprised 10-12 coaches, so the consist could be handled by any locomotive that was likely to draw it. The GWR provided 40 sets, the LMS 44, the LNER 47 and the Southern Railway, 55.[96] Initially, the hand-over of stock to the Southern Railway took place as follows: GWR at Salisbury, LMS at Kensington (Addison Road) and LNER stock at Banbury and Reading. As 80 percent of the soldiers were planned to move to areas within the territories of the Southern Railway and GWR, these two companies, and the former in particular, became the focus for the operation. The initial routing was kept as simple as possible:

Table 19.4
Operation DYNAMO – Train Routing[97]

SPOD	Route	Destination
Dover & Folkestone	Redhill – Kensington – Reading	Mainly Aldershot & Salisbury Plain
Margate & Ramsgate	Reading	Mainly Aldershot & Salisbury Plain
Southampton	Chichester then Salisbury	Mainly Salisbury Plain
Sussex Ports	Chichester then Salisbury	Mainly Salisbury Plain

To speed train working, the GWR ran some trains to Redhill Junction using its own locomotives; it was impossible to go further because route restrictions on SR lines in the South-East precluded their use. To simplify movement control, four Regulating Stations were selected, to which

94 The SPODs were identified as: Brighton, Dover, Eastbourne, Folkestone, Harwich, Hastings, Margate, Newhaven and Ramsgate. TNA WO 197/134: Evacuation from France and Quartering of the BEF – Activities of DST in the Evacuation from France.

95 The capture of Boulogne and Calais resulted in few troops landing at SPODs West of Folkestone, except casualties on hospital carriers evacuated to Newhaven.

96 Figures from Nock, *Britain's Railways at War: 1939-1945*, p.84.

97 Table collated from information in Tatlow, *Return from Dunkirk*, p.73.

trains from the ports would be directed, whilst destinations and supporting route information were confirmed. Under the supervision of the REC, the railways operated special control offices at Redhill, Reading, Banbury and Salisbury to enact this work. 572 trains[98] were run to support Operation DYNAMO,[99] with the points of departure as follows:

Table 19.5
Operation DYNAMO – Train Summary[100]

Port	Train Code	Special Trains	Ambulance Trains	Personnel	Remarks
Clacton		0		27*	*Local rail services
Dover	V	326	8	185,254*	*4,646 casualties
Folkestone	W	64		29,189	
Harwich		7		3,668	
Margate	M	75	21[101]	39,626	
Newhaven		2	17	3,523*	* 2,914 casualties
Ramsgate	R	82	1	39,665	
Sheerness	S	17		7,539	
Totals		573	47[102]	308,491	

The two busiest days were Friday 31 May, when 107 trains were run, evacuating 56,282 soldiers, and Saturday 1 June, when a total of 59,147 personnel[103] were moved from the ports to the Reception Areas, whilst the railways also ran trains to support civilian evacuations, a substantial additional task that is rarely exposed in the military histories.[104] The REC drew confidence from the fact that, there was no recorded loss or significant injury as a result of railway operations to support Operation DYNAMO in the UK; a remarkable achievement. Command and Control was a critical element of the operation and required the implementation of new chains of liaison, as well as the adoption of different operating mechanisms. Almost every aspect of

98 This may be compared with the running of 600 Special Trains in a 24 hour period to support Derby Day during the 1930s. The major difference was that DYNAMO ran for 9 days not one and the Southern Railway had a year to plan Derby Day. For additional examples of Specials, see, Bernard Darwin, *War on the Line, The Story of the Southern Railway in War-Time* (Waterloo: Southern Railway, 1946), p.24.

99 The Southern Railway ran 55 trains in support of pre-DYNAMO recovery operations.

100 Table collated from information in WOOH, *Movements*, p.105.

101 This figure is not confirmed but does corroborate the total figure of ambulance trains run; see fn 101 below.

102 Dunn, *MBOH, Emergency Medical Services*, Vol I, p.100 states that 47 ambulance trains moved 28,354 casualties.

103 Figures from Nock, *Britain's Railways at War: 1939-1945*, p.84.

104 On Sunday 2 June 1940, 60 trains supported civilian evacuation operations; 24 were run by the Southern Railway and 34 by the GWR.

P19.3 80 Years On. Headcorn Railway Station in 2020 looking East. The trains arriving from the South East Ports drew into the platform on the right, so soldiers could be offered fast food and tea. The clearance of the resulting rubbish was another logistic task; fast food litter is not a recent phenomenon. (Chris Farnham)

the operation was organized on the hoof, since there were no working timetables, and nearly all communication was conducted over the telephone, with written instructions being, for the most part, abandoned. Such was the efficiency and ability of the railways to keep pace with demand, one general was quoted as saying: "If only the Army could operate with as few written instructions as the Southern Railway does!"[105]

The 565 trains run in support of Operation DYNAMO, were not though, the whole story, there being a raft of supporting railway activity. Reciprocal movements of empty stock sets amounted to a similar figure, whilst at the end of the operation the pooled coaches had to be returned to the owning companies. To reduce light locomotive[106] working and to ensure the maximum availability of motive power,[107] locomotives were not returned to their home sheds at the end of

105 Darwin, *War on the Line*, p.25.

106 A locomotive moving without hauling wagons or coaches is defined as Light. The term is does not relate to the weight of the locomotive. Light locomotive movements require a train path.

107 Motive Power is the generic term for the mobile hauling power on a railway. Static power systems have included cables or gas pressure systems. Locomotives can be steam (coal or oil fired) diesel, diesel-

the roster. After concluding that the focal point of the operation would be Redhill Junction,[108] the Southern Operations staff, led by their Superintendent of Operations, Mr Wheeler, decided to centre the key logistic tasks of coaling and watering at Redhill Junction Yard. This in turn produced some interesting problems, not least of which, was the need for additional coal trains to service the bunkers, and wagons to collect 300 tons of ash. Approximately 450 loaded trains passed through Redhill Junction in nine days,[109] each of which, because of the layout of the site, required a second engine at the rear of the train.[110] Add to this the empty stock movements, special coal trains and shunting operations, it is easy to see how much of the railway operation to support Operation DYNAMO was hidden from the military planners' view. There was also the task of salvage and refuse collection from the *halte-repas* stations where the tracks were strewn with wax cups and grease-proof paper and the platforms piled with cardboard and wooden boxes.

A Word of Admiration

The rapid influx of 300,000 British troops and another 147,000 Allied personnel to the United Kingdom posed major challenges to the food services staff of the RASC. As the soldiers poured ashore from the evacuation ships, catering became a crucial activity because many of the troops had not consumed a substantial meal for several days. With the remit to ensure that the move of the BEF from the SEP was executed expeditiously, any plan to provide hot food on the dockside, or to halt trains for long periods for the purpose of victualling, would have created unacceptable risks and delays. Supplies & Transport (ST) 4, the Staff branch in the War Office, responsible for designing and issuing the food services plan, generated a simple but effective two-phase operation. The first part was buffet feeding at ports but with the provision that trains must not, under any circumstances, be delayed.[111] The second component was the 'feeding stations', an idea, which had been successfully enacted during the deployment of the BEF in France. 14 stations were designated as 'feeding halts' called *halte-repas*[112] and time was allocated in the rail schedule for the train to stop for a sufficient period for each soldier to be issued with a haversack ration. The typical meal consisted of sandwiches, containing meat, cheese or jam, a meat or fruit pie, a hard-boiled egg, fresh fruit, plus cigarettes and matches.[113] In some places, the local fare included rolls, sausages, jellied veal and sardines, with the food being carried on large wooden

electric or electric. Sections of the SR commuter network were electrified in 1940 but it was steam that was the mainstay of motive power during the operation.

108 For the junction diagram, see, Harman & Nichols, *Atlas of the Southern Railway*, p.89, Map 64A – Redhill & South Surrey Enlargements.

109 Tatlow, *Return from Dunkirk,* lists all the trains, which ran through Redhill Junction. The first was Dover to Fleet arriving Redhill, Monday 27 May at 0952 and departing 1003. The last, on Tuesday 4 June, ex-Folkestone to Tidworth, arrived at 1625 and departed at 1634. See, Appx 2, pp. 168-175.

110 Trains with a second locomotive coupled at the front are double-headed. Trains with a locomotive at the rear are banked. In both cases, the engine is defined as Assisting. See *Royal Corps of Transport Training*, Vol IV, *Transport Operations - Rail Transport*, p.79, para 380a.

111 TNA WO 197/134: Evacuation from France and Quartering of the BEF – Activities of DST in the Evacuation from France.

112 TNA WO 197/134: Evacuation from France and Quartering of the BEF – Activities of DST in the Evacuation from France.

113 TNA WO 197/134: Evacuation from France and Quartering of the BEF - Activities of DST in the Evacuation from France.

bakers' trays or pulled on platform trolleys. Water for tea was obtained from the water columns located at stations to fill locomotive tenders, with the tea served from large urns on the platforms. One little detail, and in logistics the devil is always in the detail, which could have been a show-stopper, was most fortuitously not overlooked; the provision of cups. Most of the troops had lost their utensils, but a thoughtful individual had arranged for the acquisition and distribution of wax-paper cups[114] and where no cups were available, the tea was often served in tins.

The Army contribution to catering at *halte-repas* was undertaken by staff and students from military catering schools[115] but they were ably assisted by many volunteers from numerous organizations,[116] their numbers swelled by the many house-wives living line-side, who, seeing the operation blossom at the bottom of their gardens, soon integrated themselves into the ORBAT. Whilst much of this was spontaneous, there had been precedent in early September 1939 during the planned much larger evacuation of children from the cities, involving the movement by rail in 3,823 trains of 1,334,358 people,[117] when many voluntary bodies had been involved in providing refreshments *en-route*. Sifting through the analysis of many campaigns however, it is difficult to find a finer example of 'Unity of Effort' from so many different organizations, with so little time to prepare and relatively few written orders. To assist this great endeavour, NAAFI provided 120,000 bags of fruit and chocolate, whilst many commercial companies also made valuable contributions, often in conjunction with public donations. At Addison Road and Paddock Wood, Horlicks of Slough issued supplies of malted milk, whilst at Basingstoke, where the official system was initially baulked by a funding problem, the publicly spirited citizens raised £500,[118] of which, the staff of the Thornycroft Works contributed £100; a major catering operation was then mounted, which included 100 ladies, the local fire brigade, Rotarians and church members.

Stations such as Basingstoke, Headcorn, Paddock Wood and Tonbridge were, for a short period, bereft of their commuters[119] and became places of frenetic military, catering and railway activity, the likes of which, have rarely been seen before or since.[120] The pressure the refreshment teams were under can be assessed from the timings allocated at a *halte-repas*; a train of 600 men would draw in, and there would be eight minutes in which to serve refreshments and the

114 These are seen in many of the contemporary photographs.

115 Six teams of instructors and students and supporting catering equipment were deployed. Four from the London School of Cookery and two from the Emergency Cookery Training Centre at Guildford. TNA WO 197/134: Evacuation from France and Quartering of the BEF - Activities of DST in the Evacuation from France.

116 These included the Women's Voluntary Service (WVS), the British Red Cross, the Salvation Army and the YMCA. Although there is no specific reference to them in the files consulted in the TNA, the catering staffs of the railway companies must have had an input to the operation.

117 R Bell CBE, *History of British Railways during the War 1939-1945* (London: The Railway Gazette, 1946), p.71.

118 Based on the RPI this equates to £26,820 in 2018.

119 Whilst not all passenger services were cancelled, there was inevitably disruption. Notices, which would be familiar to the 21st Century railway traveller appeared at many stations. The notices at Redhill read: 'Saturday 1st June. The train service between Redhill & Tonbridge & Redhill & Reading are [sic] cancelled. Buses will be provided between Redhill & Tonbridge Redhill & Guildford'.

120 A flavour of the occasion may be obtained by reading Darwin, *War on the Line*, pp.28-30 but the hive of activity at any one station must have been equalled by the departure of an estimated 40,000 people from York Station in the few hours following the Papal Visit in 1982.

haversack rations. As an example of those heady days in late May and early June 1940, the victuals at Headcorn Station[121] offer an interesting overview. The RASC provided some of the food, 19 cauldron cookers and 40 soldiers to cook and distribute the hot food, including beef spit-roasted in trenches, whilst local bakers produced 2,500 loaves daily but it was 50 determined and doughty ladies from Headcorn,[122] who, working in 8 hour shifts for 9 days, prepared the sandwiches in a barn at Rushford Manor.[123] The food was then carried across a field, now covered by the houses of Rushford Close to the Up Platform for distribution to the troops. Headcorn would appear to have missed out on the issue of wax-paper cups, so the equivalent of 100,000 cups of tea were offered to the troops in large tin cans. The final destination of this tea was also catered for, the LNER for example, erected temporary ablutions on the platforms at Leicester for the use of soldiers on the 242 troop trains, which halted there during the mid-summer of 1940.

In summary, a no more erudite, although not complete, conclusion to the dispersal operation can be found, than that written in *The Times* on Monday 3 June 1940:

> More than a word of admiration is due, not only to the staff work which has directed the miracle, but to the untiring civilian volunteers who have victualled and the railways which have transported the troops – especially the Southern Railway, which has conjured up at short notice a smooth and seemingly endless succession of trains and has lavished upon the emergency its great and peculiar experience in the handling of masses.[124]

One interesting food services challenge presented to the staff of ST 4, was the provision of rations for the 112,000 French troops brought to England. With a little ingenuity, a suitable ration was assembled with the exception of red wine. Not being experts in this area, ST 4 sought guidance from the War Office Wine Advisor,[125] who arranged for casks of a suitable vintage to be acquired from suppliers.

Operationally, it was fortunate that the *Luftwaffe* concentrated their aerial assault on the port of Dunkerque and the embarkation beaches: attacking the ports areas of Dover and Ramsgate and some of the key points on the railway system instead, could have caused great disruption to the operation. The coastal section between Dover and Folkestone, and other parts of the network, contained tunnels,[126] cuttings, embankments and

121 Headcorn Station on the South Eastern Railway route from London to Dover was opened in 1842. It is unlikely that any commuter offers a thought for those nine days in late May and early June 1940 when the village railway station was the scene of such historic drama.

122 In recognition of her work in organizing the refreshment at Headcorn, Mrs Joan Kempthorne was awarded the BEM.

123 The Manor House in the High Street is extant but sadly the barn has been replaced by housing of Rushford Close.

124 Nock, *Britain's Railways at War: 1939–1945*, p.87.

125 By custom, a member of the wine trade acted as the Honorary Advisor to the Director Supplies & Transport.

126 There were four major tunnels between Dover and Folkestone: Martello, Abbot's Cliff, Shakespeare and Arch Cliff.

sea-walls,[127] all of which were vulnerable to air delivered weapons, although free-fall bombs, which were the only type available in the summer of 1940, were not the most effective systems to attack precision targets. Nonetheless, a successful strike on a tunnel entrance could have closed a route,[128] causing significant interruption to the schedules. The production of contingency plans for road movement, to ensure access to the rest of the rail system, were therefore, wise. Low level strafing of troop trains had the potential to cause heavy casualties, and with these sorties being very difficult to intercept, might have meant a reversion to night movement only. With barely eight hours of darkness available, this would have had a massive impact on the clearance of troops from the ports.

The bombing of troop trains in France were infrequent events but potentially very damaging to morale and capability as was clearly exposed at Rennes on 17 June when there 177 British fatalities and many wounded.[129] Fortunately, the *Luftwaffe* operations staff had their minds focused on other matters and with events moving rapidly in France, were unable to seize the opportunity of creating or supporting this campaign.[130] Nonetheless, whilst the strategic position would have been unchanged by such action, the operational impact could have considerable. Unable to take trains from the ports, thousands of soldiers would have been camping out in gardens and fields with little equipment and even less sustenance. No doubt the redoubtable housewives of Kent and Sussex would have stepped forward with tea, sandwiches and plenty of spirit but the sight of the remnants of an evacuated Army littering England's green and pleasant land would not have raised morale. In this respect, the logistic capabilities of the Army and the Nation firmly demonstrated to its citizens that focused and constructive operations were being conducted. The soldiers of 9th Queen's Royal Lancers reflected upon a mix of emotions as they travelled by train from Plymouth to Warminster: 'All Ranks were pleased and surprised to see cheering crowds lining the railway almost without a break as long as it was daylight: we felt like heroes until we remembered we were part of a defeated army…'[131]

Recycling

There was more time to plan the recovery of the units returning by Operations AERIAL and CYCLE with the nine arrival ports spread from Liverpool in the North-West to Southampton on the South coast. The execution of the plan also had, generally, a more leisurely approach than that supporting Operation DYNAMO as the 9th Queen's Royal Lancers discovered:

127 For details of the engineering challenges involved in the construction of the line, see, C F Dendy-Marshall (Revised by R W Kidner), *History of The Southern Railway* (London: Ian Allan, 1988), pp.284-285.

128 Major track subsidence in the section between Abbot's Cliff and Shakespeare Tunnels, closed the route in the period 28 November 1939 - 7 January 1940.

129 TNA WO 361/114: Rennes Train Bombing, R Cas (Liverpool) typed note.

130 In the period Saturday 25 May-Tuesday 18 June 1940, the *Luftwaffe* mounted, mainly at night, a number of uncoordinated and sporadic raids with small numbers of aircraft. The targets, mostly in the South and East, were usually airfields or industrial areas, and although several residential properties were destroyed or damaged, the railway system was not the focus of attack. For a daily account of each raid, see, Winston G Ramsey (ed.), *The Blitz: Then and Now*, Vol 1 (London: Battle of Britain Prints International Limited, 1987), pp 96-98.

131 Bright, *The Ninth Queen's Royal Lancers, 1936-1945*, p.23.

> At dawn on 17th of June we steamed into Plymouth and dropped anchor. There was no one there to meet us at first, but later some ladies arrived and proceeded to prepare a canteen on the docks ... We sat on the docks all day waiting for a train, and the tea and refreshments served by the ladies' canteen were a boon to us all. Eventually at 8 pm a train arrived. We left at 9.45 and proceeded on our way to Warminster.[132]

The 10th Royal Hussars also had a civilian rather than military logistic welcome being supported by the City Fathers and the YMCA.[133] The experience of 157th Brigade, arriving at Southampton Docks from Cherbourg was rather different, the war diary recording: 'Complete and utter chaos reigned at Southampton as all units were muddled and included every unit in the BEF'.[134] The frustration with this reception soon boiled over into effectively a command revolt by the brigade HQ when the commander,[135] correctly identifying that, 'The main object appeared to be to get everybody into a train regardless of where it was going',[136] refused to comply with the order for the balance of the brigade to board a train for Bournemouth, when the rest of the formation had been dispatched to Bedford, resulting in a special train being provided.[137] Conceptually, the process was adapted from Operation DYNAMO to accept what were generally formed units, with formations and units passing through transit areas near the ports before onward moves by road and rail to assigned Reformation Areas.

Table 19.6
Operations AERIAL and CYCLE – Port and Transit Areas[138]

Transit Area	Supporting Areas	Personnel	Port Served	Remarks
Aintree	50th Division	15,000	Liverpool	
Plymouth	Launceston*	23,000	Falmouth Fowey Plymouth	* 23rd Division units
Tetbury	Bristol	5,000	Avonmouth	Mainly WMT
Southampton Transit Camp	Bournemouth* Southampton* Weymouth*	20,000	Poole Portsmouth Southampton Weymouth	* Billeting
Total		63,000		

132 Ibid, p.23.
133 Regimental Committee, *The 10th Royal Hussars in the Second World War*, p.7.
134 TNA WO 167/413: HQ 157th Brigade WD, entry 18 June 1940.
135 Brigadier (later Major-General) Sir John Emilius Laurie (1892-1983) DSO, late Seaforth Highlanders.
136 TNA WO 167/413: HQ 157th Brigade WD, entry 18 June 1940.
137 TNA WO 167/413: HQ 157th Brigade WD, entry 18 June 1940.
138 Table collated from information in TNA WO 197/105: Aerial Plan, 'Accommodation of Units evacuated from the BEF', War Office, DQMG Q.1/5539 dated 16 June 1940.

The remnants of 51st (Highland) Division evacuated under Operation CYCLE,[139] were to be located in Scottish Command in Ayrshire and Dumfries. The three divisions of the forming 2nd BEF evacuated under Operation AERIAL were each sent to a different Command. 1st Armoured Division was dispatched Longbridge Deverill, three miles South of Warminster, 1st (Canadian) to Aldershot Command and 52nd (Lowland) to Ely in Eastern Command.[140] Moving, tracking and reorganizing the myriad of logistic units that had formed the Base and the GLOC in France was a much more complex problem, neatly resolved by the simple but effective solution of grouping, as far as possible geographically, those units by technical task. Transportation units from the Royal Engineers were easy to assign. The Docks groups and stevedore battalions were allocated to Liverpool and ports on the South coast involved in the recovery operations, whilst for the railway units, all operating, construction and survey companies were dispatched to No 1 Railway Training Centre (RTC) at Longmoor[141] in Aldershot Command and the workshop companies and ambulance train maintenance sections No 2 RTC at Melbourne in Derbyshire in Northern Command.[142]

All the Ordnance units were sent to the Leicester area in Northern Command, including the personnel of the seven Base Ammunition Depots,[143] two Base Ordnance Depots, the Ordnance Workshops and the RAOC Port Detachments. The RASC Supply & Transport units, however, were spread across the Kingdom. 1 LOC Railhead Company was assigned to Sheffield and 2 LOC Railhead Company and 1 Heavy Repair Shop to Luton. 1 Bulk Petrol Company went to Barnard Castle and 3 Company to Swindon, although the field butchery and bakeries and the Supply Personnel companies were grouped in Wenvoe Camp,[144] five miles to the North of Barry in South Wales under Western Command.[145] Force K6 from the RIASC was dispatched to Shirley Common Camp on the Osmaston Estate near Ashbourne in Derbyshire,[146] whilst 29 Animal Transport Company was accommodated at Storey Castle Camp Aldershot.[147]

139 TNA WO 106/1739: Reports on Evacuation of British and French Troops in the Harve area.
140 TNA WO 197/105: Aerial Plan, 'Accommodation of Units evacuated from the BEF', War Office, DQMG Q.1/5539 dated 16 June 1940.
141 See, Ronald & Carter, *The Longmoor Military Railway,* pp.102-122 and David Ronald & Mike Christensen OBE, *The Longmoor Military Railway: A New History,* Vol 2: *World War Two and the Cold War Era* (Lydney: Lightmoor Press, 2013), pp.331-332.
142 TNA WO 197/105: Aerial Plan, 'Accommodation of Units evacuated from the BEF', War Office, DQMG Q.1/5539 dated 16 June 1940, Appx A, 'List of Units Allotted to Commands'.
143 1,2, 3, 4, 6, 21 and 22.
144 Wenvoe Camp is long gone but ground evidence remains.
145 TNA WO 197/105: Aerial Plan, 'Accommodation of Units evacuated from the BEF', War Office, DQMG Q.1/5539 dated 16 June 1940, Appx A, 'List of Units Allotted to Commands'.
146 Elements of K6 moved to Saint Austell Cornwall in October 1940, before the Indian Contingent as it was re-designated, moved to the Brecon Beacons and Snowdonia in mid-1941 to conduct mountain training and thence to Inverness-shire in Scotland in June 1942, supporting 52nd (Lowland) Division. The Indian Contingent returned to India between May 1943 and January 1944; the Force being disbanded in April 1944. For details of the Indian Contingent in UK, see, Hamish Johnston, 'A Corner of Pakistan in Scotland', *Highland Family History Society*, 2012 and Chris Kempton, *Force K6 The Indian Contingent: The RIASC Mule Companies in France & UK, 1939-1944*, (Gillingham: Chris Kempton, 2019).
147 TNA WO 197/105: Aerial Plan, 'Accommodation of Units evacuated from the BEF', War Office, DQMG Q.1/5539 dated 16 June 1940, Appx A, 'List of Units Allotted to Commands'.

There was a relatively small requirement for freight and vehicle movement because of the enormous losses of *materiel* in France. Of the 716 tanks sent to the BEF only 14[148] returned, so only a few rail wagons were required to move them. Units with WMT arriving at the Western Ports as part of Operation AERIAL were redeployed by road. Of the 109,000 tons of ammunition shipped to the BEF, 76,697 were expended, captured or destroyed, leaving only 32,303 tons to be returned to the UK,[149] some of which, was never unloaded from the exporting ships, which were turned around in French ports. This ammunition was moved by rail to Central Ammunition Depots[150] in the UK, the in-loading process[151] adding a significant activity to the receipt of ammunition from industry, and the out-loading of 18,000 tons of stocks to newly formed Operational Command Dumps, which were established as part of the developing anti-invasion plans.[152] In addition, work commenced on the construction of sixteen temporary Ammunition Sub-Depots (ASD) located across the country to in-load production from industry; six were opened in July 1940.[153] Each ASD was planned to store 20,000 tons of ammunition using 100-120 miles of mainly country roads and was served by at least three Ammunition Railheads. Inevitably, the ASDs became permanent, with holdings varying between 50,000 and 180,000 tons.[154]

A hidden activity but one which, was essential to the administration of the Army and the maintenance of morale, was the re-structuring of the BEF's Army postal system. The main burden was shouldered by the Home Postal Depot at Bournemouth, which became the focus for military postal activity in mid-1940. The task was enormous: enormous quantities of mail arrived from the General Post Office in UK, much of it linked to casualty correspondence, and all the post returned from France was also delivered to the Depot. With little information about the location of units, let alone individuals, the mail piled up, before being 'returned to sender',[155] although at some point in early June, the General Post Office was no longer accepting mail to soldiers serving in the BEF.[156] Time though, provided an answer. As clarification was received of formation and unit locations within the Redistribution Areas, postal personnel

148 For the issues relating to the variance of the figures, see the Conclusion, 'Reflection & Retrospect - Punishment of the Innocent?', fns 55 & 56.
149 The recovery of Gas Warfare munitions is explained in Chp 14, 'Operation FLANNELFOOT.'
150 Bramley and Corsham with Longtown under construction. Of the three, only Longtown remains operational.
151 This was a major task because the process involved accounting, inspecting, repairing, re-packing and storing a raft of ammunition natures.
152 See, Collier, BOH, *The Defence of the United Kingdom.*
153 The sites used corrugated iron sheds of 400 cubic feet capacity, which were emplaced on the verges of country roads and 30 foot strips of adjacent fields, although the sheds were also erected in woodland and country parks. Fernyhough & Harris, *History of the Royal Army Ordnance Corps, 1939-1945*, pp.448-450.
154 Ibid.
155 A letter dated 13 June 1940 from Kay Hind to her boy-friend, whom she married after the war, 5114497 Private Fred Gilbert of B Company, 8th Warwicks, was eventually returned to her in Coventry, marked 'missing' in manuscript and a stamp stating 'Addressee reported Prisoner of War' but it was not until February 1941 that his POW postcard dated 14 November 1940 reached her. Given that they both lived in Coventry, it was remarkable co-incidence that the date on the card was that of the Coventry bombing raid. Letters and card held by Elaine Schafer and Rosemary Duxbury.
156 Correspondence from Kay Hind dated 12 June 1940. Held by Elaine Schafer and Rosemary Duxbury.

P19.4 Missing - Reported Prisoner of War. One of the thousands of letters the Army Postal Service had to 'return to sender'. (Courtesy Elaine Schafer)

returning from France filtered into the Depot and were able to assist in redirecting mail, thereby restoring a semblance of order.

Lessons

The lessons of logistics arising from the reception and reorganization of the British Expeditionary Forces from France are varied but the most important one is that without National logistics the operation would have failed in time and space. A key component was the timely and accurate appreciation based upon the foundation of several sound assumptions by the War Office logisticians, which generated a number of important deductions that enabled the production of an effective plan. The use of the concept of DQUAD - Destination, Distance, Demand and Duration in the planning process, was certainly central to the effective resourcing of the operation, which was, for the most part, enacted through a process of what is now called Mission Command; few detailed orders were issued from the top, and Staff officers were rightly left free to co-ordinate the detail and cooperate with the railway authorities and civic agencies. Those participating in the operation were certainly integrated by an almost spontaneous 'Unity of Effort'[157] in a manner rarely seen before or since; most observers would describe it as the 'Dunkirk Spirit'. The plan had clarity with each phase having an obvious main effort.

The post–war monograph *Administrative Planning* published by the War Office in 1952, is clear about why the operations were successful:

> The plan itself bore the stamp and hall-mark of good planning - it was simple and flexible, and it made the utmost use of the resources available. Perhaps the speed at which it evolved was in some part responsible for the absence of any tendency to over-elaboration.'[158] There was certainly no opportunity to add, as Pooh Bah did, 'corroborative detail intended to give artistic verisimilitude to an otherwise bald and unconvincing narrative'.[159]

The foresight of the logistic Staffs enabled the necessary resources to be activated in sufficient time and given the initial paucity of information, they made economic use of the assets. Simplicity was the central element to the plan, and it was this, which generated the inherent flexibility that was so important in effectively conducting such a major and seemingly impossible operation. Close co-operation with the Royal Navy and the civil sector, particularly the railways and the voluntary agencies, was fundamental to the execution of the mission. None of these factors alone though, had sufficient weight to see the operation through to a successful conclusion, and had it not been for the character, courage, commitment, dedication, and initiative of the many who took part, the military position of the United Kingdom would have been much the poorer. Duty and Service were a vital component of logistics in 1940 as indeed they are now; we neglect such traditions at our peril.

157 *Army Doctrine Publication* Vol 2, *Command* (UK MOD, 1995), para 0213, states that unity of effort is a tenet of both Mission Command and the British doctrine for operations, providing a focus for separate but co-ordinated actions by subordinates. This certainly summarizes the recovery operations in May and June 1940.

158 TNA WO 277/1: Administrative Planning and Organization, 1939-1945 and WOOH, *Administrative Planning*, Colonel H W Wilson OBE TD (Comp.), (War Office 1952), p.5.

159 WOOH, *Administrative Planning*, p.172.

20

Reflection and Retrospect
Punishment of the Innocent?

Inquiry or Inquisition?

Well before the last ship carrying BEF men and material arrived in the UK, a series of reviews, reports and investigations at every level had been initiated into operations in France, with particular emphasis on Lessons Identified, the presence of an enemy only 22 miles from the English coast providing a very strong imperative to ensure this work was completed in an accurate and timely manner. The War Office work was embedded in the Bartholomew Report,[1] which interviewed 36 officers, 25 of whom were brigadier or above[2] and took written evidence and opinion from three more, one of whom was Major-General Bernard Montgomery. Only one of these officers held a logistics appointment, Lieutenant-General W G Lindsell, the BEF QMG, although through his rank and influence, logistic threads, with the exception of those issues appertaining solely to operations in the Base, were exposed. The effect of air attack

1 The Bartholomew Committee was chaired by General Sir William H Bartholomew GCB CMG DSO (1887-1962), late Royal Artillery and recently retired from the post of GOC Northern Command (1937-1940) before which, he was CGS India (1934-1937). There were four members, two major-generals, one of which was C C Walden, Director Military Training at the War Office, and two brigadiers. The Terms of Reference of the Bartholomew Committee were '1. To consider lessons of the recent campaign in Flanders which can be applied usefully to our present organization and training. 2. To suggest the modifications in our organization, training and equipment which should be made to meet the problems with which the British Army will be faced in the event of an attempted enemy invasion of this country'. TNA WO 106/1775: Bartholomew Committee - Report on lessons to be learnt from operations in Flanders; evidence, report and action arising.

2 One was a RAF officer, Air Vice-Marshal Charles Hubert Boulby Blount CB OBE MC (1893-1940) who commanded the BEF Air Component in France. Blount was commissioned into the Queen's (Royal West Surrey) Regiment in September 1913, transferring to the Royal Flying Corps in 1916 but not relinquishing his regimental commission until 1919 after receiving a permanent commission in the RAF. He held various senior air command and Staff appointments including Air Officer Commanding (AOC) 4 Bomber Group in 1938. As AOC 22 Army Co-operation Group, he was killed in an air crash on 23 October 1940 just after taking off from RAF Hendon on a flight to Belfast and he rests in the SW corner of Saint Mary the Virgin's Churchyard Essendon, Hertfordshire.

upon road and railway movement, whilst receiving mention, was deemed to have been of little significance,[3] although had the Committee interviewed those responsible for planning and executing these logistic activities, the report would surely have highlighted the good fortune that the BEF often had and the absolute importance of mitigation through active and passive air defence measures,[4] a point reinforced by many war diaries.

Whilst not part of the Bartholomew Final Report, the QMG authored a six-page resume entitled 'Movement and Maintenance in the BEF'[5] covering logistic operations in the period 3 September 1939 – 31 May 1940, which of course, omitted actions South of the Somme. The agile utilization of railheads at 'minor' stations to reduce enemy interest was however, definitively identified as a key mitigation in ensuring these important logistic nodes operated effectively in a hostile air environment.[6] The establishment of wireless links for Troop Carrying Companies with the assigned formations was another crucial lesson forged in the heat of the mobile battle,[7] although the provision of effective, resilient and agile communications systems was an issue that affected the whole of the BEF.[8] There was though, dissonance on logistic agility at the corps level. The Bartholomew Report suggested that an 'expert' committee examine the issue of the size, scope and shape of the corps' logistic capability, with a particular emphasis on the amount of WMT and the need for a mobile workshop.[9] The subject of 'dumping' also received scrutiny with the report supporting the GHQ Q Staff contention that it should be reduced to the minimum and the reserves held on ECM trains,[10] although during the campaign it had been the seven days of stocks dumped to the North of the River Somme that proved to be a game-changer for the survival of the BEF.[11] The creative tension generated by dumping programmes was an 'Old Chestnut' driven by concerns over losing stocks in a withdrawal or having insufficient transport to access them in an advance, the latter a particular problem during operations on the Western Front in the Hundred Days of 1918.[12] There had been concerns about the control of ammunition dumping in particular during the campaign and lessons were obviously been learned because a II Corps Operation Order of 23 May had specifically forbidden the practice.[13]

3 The significant impact of the flow of refugees however, upon operational, tactical and logistic movement was incisively articulated. TNA WO 106/1775: Bartholomew Committee Report, para 27, Refugees.
4 TNA WO 106/1775: Bartholomew Committee Report, para 10 a & b, Defence Against Air Attack.
5 TNA WO 197/112: 'Movement and Maintenance in the BEF' dated 22 June 1940.
6 TNA WO 106/1775: Bartholomew Committee Report, para 26, Railheads.
7 TNA WO 106/1775: Bartholomew Committee Report, para 31, Troop Carrying Companies.
8 For a penetrating analysis of this issue, see Smalley, *The British Expeditionary Force, 1939-40*, pp.84-140.
9 TNA WO 106/1775: Bartholomew Committee Report, para 29, Transport.
10 The Committee also identified that the 10 ton lorries operated by the LOC Railhead MT companies were too heavy for ECM road operations. TNA WO 106/1775: Bartholomew Committee Report, para 29a, Transport.
11 This point was firmly made by 2 Division CRASC, Lieutenant-Colonel C M C Luff in a manuscript POR held in TNA WO 167/210.
12 TNA WO 95/454/4: HQ Fourth Army, DDST, 'Notes on Conference at "Q" 6.45 pm, 28 August 1918'.
13 II Corps Operation Order 232005 May 1940, para 6, Ammunition in TNA CAB 44/67: The BEF in Belgium and Artois, 10 May - 3 June 1940.

A number of recommendations within the report, such as the introduction of new equipment[14] and the increase in the establishment of 3-inch mortars and carriers and the implementation of an anti-tank platoon in infantry battalions also had logistic implications, which whilst not immediately obvious, influenced the shape and size of RASC and RAOC capability, whilst the protection of logistic operations in the Base, the GLOC and Rear Corps Areas assumed a much greater operational and tactical significance that brought a step change in creating a culture of combat logistics, writ large in a plethora of revised doctrine, training directives and practical actions. *Army Training Memorandum* No 34 was explicit: 'Every unit of the Army, no matter how specialized, forms an integral part of the fighting machine as a whole, and must regard itself as a potential fighting instrument.[15] The RASC in particular was involved in several intense actions against German ground forces, including armour and were quick to recognize the significance of revitalizing unit combat capability[16] and the critical ability to operate at night.[17] At a rather different level, the Army Council decided that all regimental and Staff officers below the rank of brigadier must be trained to ride motor-cycles and that 'Brigadiers be prepared to ride a motor-cycle or be carried pillion'.[18] The RASC also identified the misuse of its motor-cycle Dispatch Riders allocated to the RA for ammunition supply duties for communication tasks between batteries and regimental HQs, thereby disrupting the delivery of gun munitions.[19] At a strategic level, the logistics piece was largely overlooked, the one focus in this arena being the losses of equipment, ammunition and stores, which attracted a significant amount of attention from both the Prime-Minister and the War Office, resulting in the formation of the Inter-Departmental Howard Committee[20] to report on the 'Evacuation of the BEF from French Ports', which focused upon ports to the South of the Somme. Whilst chaired by a retired Lieutenant-General,[21] the composition of the Committee was recognition that the evacuations involved not only the War Office but also the Admiralty, and equally importantly, the Ministry of Shipping, although the representatives of these two maritime departments did not attend until 1 October 1940.[22] The Terms of Reference (TOR) were very limited in time:

14 One key equipment not 'hastened into service' was the 6 pdr anti-tank gun, which was to have appreciable adverse operational and tactical impacts in future campaigns. TNA WO 106/1775: Bartholomew Committee Report, para 9d, Anti-tank weapons.

15 Army Council, *Army Training Memorandum* No 34, July 1940 (War Office, 1940), p.5, para 2, Protection in Rearward Areas.

16 General Staff, Royal Army Service Corps, Training Pamphlet No 1, Training System in War, Part III: Training of NCOs, pp.11-14.

17 Ibid, p.23-25, Appx G, Lessons from Experience from the RASC.

18 Army Council, *Army Training Memorandum* No 33, June 1940, para 10, Officers and Motor-Cycles, pp.10-11. How many accidents and injuries were caused by this decision would be an interesting area of research.

19 Army Council, *Army Training Memorandum* No 34, July 1940, Appx G, Lessons from Experience for the RASC, p.23.

20 For details of its work and outputs, see fns below.

21 Lieutenant-General Sir Geoffrey Weston Howard KCB CMG DSO (1876-1966). Commissioned into the Essex Regiment in 1897, Geoffrey Howard served in South Africa during the Second Boer War, being awarded the DSO in 1902. He commanded 145th Brigade in 1918 and was GOC 5th Division in Egypt before retiring in 1938.

22 The War Office representatives were Honorary Brigadier M H Dendy DSO MC (1885-1951), late RA and Colonel F Thornton who was posted on 8 October 1940 and not replaced. Rear-Admiral The Honourable C P Hermon-Heritage DSC represented the Admiralty and W G Hynard CB CBE,

> The lessons to be learned from the evacuation from the area south of the River Somme after the 10th June 1940, with special reference to the possibility of whether the evacuation of arms, equipment, vehicles and stores, both of the fighting formations and on the lines of Communication, could reasonably have been increased under existing circumstances, and to report.[23]

The Fall Guy

Given the dramatic events which were occurring, one might have thought the efforts of the Staff might have been better spent on anti-invasion or reconstitution planning but identifying key lessons from what was seen by some as more of a shambles than a success, demanded an appropriate investigation. The Committee thus proceeded with its work,[24] and fortunately for historians produced a comprehensive report given resources and time, although the pressure of events soon told on the members' time and energy, an issue compounded by the maritime officials only attending the later meetings and the colonel being posted, leaving only Lieutenant-General Howard and Brigadier Dendy to conduct the task. Surprisingly, the Committee pulled no punches, being highly critical of the War Office and HQ LOC, before placing culpability firmly on the shoulders of the GOC LOC, Lieutenant-General Karslake. The Committee's focus was the fact that he had failed to execute his instructions, namely: 'You will prepare plans … for the evacuation of personnel and important stores, to prevent them from falling into enemy hands'.[25] That plans were initiated and enacted is clear because despite all the chaos and confusion, significant stocks of material were evacuated to the UK, whilst considerable numbers of vehicles and stores reached the docks but were abandoned on the quayside. If the charge was based on the 'you will prepare plans …', then arguably the Committee was probably on strong grounds because it appears that Karslake had little, if any, positive influence on their development or execution, if only because of the many other distractions in which he was embroiled.[26] The instructions Karslake received on appointment were clear but the developing situation quickly overtook them and the logisticians and the Staff were never able to square the circle.

In general, the Staff were remarkably pro-active, but they and the logistic units were often thwarted by changes in strategic direction. Given a clear mission to evacuate and the provision of sufficient shipping, there is every probability that much larger quantities of *materiel* could have been returned to the UK, although labour and transportation[27] in France would probably

the Ministry of Shipping. Captain J C Masterman, later Chairman of the Twenty Committee co-ordinating the information being fed to the German intelligence agencies, was the Secretary.

23 TNA WO 33/2384: 'Report on the Committee on the Evacuation of the British Expeditionary Force from French Ports', hereafter, Howard Committee Report.

24 The Howard Committee interviewed or took written evidence from 53 officers, who, in contrast to the more senior ranks interviewed by the Bartholomew Committee, were generally ranked between colonel and major. TNA WO 33/2384: Howard Committee Report, Appx A.

25 TNA WO 33/2384: Howard Committee Report, para II, Command of Lines of Communication.

26 For an examination of the challenges Karslake faced, see the examination by his eldest son, Karslake, *1940: The Last Act*.

27 The decreasing out-turn of SNCF was noted by the Howard Committee. TNA WO 33/2384: Howard Committee Report, Appx B, Ammunition, Petrol, Ordnance Stores, Supplies, para 5b.

P20.1 Remembering the Logisticians 1999. 50th (Northumbrian) Division RASC 60th anniversary mobilization commemoration dinner invitation card. (Author)

have been the constraining factor; unequivocal missions, with a main effort, are essential to effective and successful logistic operations.[28] Lieutenant-General Brooke, recently returned from France as Commander of the 2nd BEF, highlighted the growing mania about the issue on 20 June: 'Apparently the fact that we did not get off more stores from Brest is now looming far larger than the fact that if I had followed out the Gov wishes at the start they would have lost both the Canadian and 52nd Divisions besides all stores and L of C personnel!'[29] Whatever the facts, the Howard Committee must though, have been alive to a bubbling witch's brew gently boiling a political hot potato and Karslake, an ex-India 'dugout'[30] was a convenient and expendable scapegoat. That he was never called to give evidence is perhaps an indicator of where the tide was flowing for him, yet it was the same stream that carried Brooke to a safe haven.[31]

Interestingly but perhaps not surprisingly, the Committee did not restrict its investigation to the dates enshrined in the TOR, stating that, 'Failure to make full use of the respite between May 20 and June 10 was the main cause for the abandonment of so much equipment'.[32] This comment not only had all the hall-marks of 20/20 vision but also the use of the term 'respite' gave the impression that the Base had few tasks to conduct when preparations were in train to continue to support the three corps in the BEF when the LOC was re-established. Once it was

28 Annex C to Chp 8, *Army Doctrine Publication*, Vol 2, *Command*, refers.
29 Danchev & Todman, *War Diaries, 1939-1945,* p.88, diary entry 20 June 1940.
30 'Dugout' was an Army term for a retired Regular officer mobilized from the Reserve to undertake activity duty. Whilst frequently applied to older officers, sometimes in a derogatory manner, 'dugout' referred to all officers in the category, with many bringing critical military experience and specific civilian professional and management expertise, to the Army and the BEF.
31 Lieutenant-General Sir Alan Brooke KCB DSO was interviewed by the Howard Committee. TNA WO 33/2384: Howard Committee Report, Appx A, Officers Interviewed by the Committee.
32 TNA WO 33/2384: Howard Committee Report, para IV, Salvage of Equipment.

clear that this plan would not mature, supporting the incoming 1st Armoured Division and then the formation of the 2nd BEF took priority, although under War Office direction some stocks were recovered to the UK. What the Committee failed, or perhaps chose not to grasp, was the dilemma the War Office presented Karslake. Even with crystal orders, a shortage of military and civilian labour and major interruption to rail movement, any withdrawal and evacuation was going to be difficult, but adding in reinforcement, without a clear military, rather than political mission, was asking too much. That there was confusion and hesitation is not in doubt; that there were good reasons for it are indisputable and the report at least recognized some of the difficulties they were facing, not least concern over the swift arrival of German forces, the effect of French armistice arrangements upon the BEF and the priority of 'Men over Material' in evacuation planning.

Whilst in some areas the Committee was unfair, it raised some interesting and relevant points. Although the report failed to mention it explicitly, the logisticians inability to have access to timely and credible intelligence prompted an associated comment: 'There was a tendency, both at Headquarters and at the ports, to pay too much regard to unauthenticated reports and rumours...........A robust determination not to be stampeded by unverified reports and hypothetical fears of disaster would have allowed more time for an orderly and successful evacuation'.[33] The Committee also believed that stock levels in France were, for the most part, far too high and for some commodities, one has to agree with them; neither was the support properly balanced. In May 1940, enormous resources were dedicated to storing, in-Theatre, 60 days rations for 400,000 men, whilst some key MT spares were dues out, a situation amply illustrated by the fact that on 30 April 1940, 1 Base Ordnance Depot had 16,000 indents unsatisfied and demands were arriving at the rate of 1400 per day.[34]

The failure to issue and execute a denial plan for the ammunition storage facilities, drew the attention of the Howard Committee, which placed the responsibility for this omission on the GOC of the Line of Communication, Lieutenant-General Karslake. The Committee concluded that: 'There was a lack of decision on the part of the GOC L of C on the policy of the destruction of ammunition left in the Depots, which resulted in many thousands of tons falling into the hands of the enemy',[35] although the logisticians were absolved by the Committee of any failure, the report noting. 'In the conditions existing it is not considered that more ammunition could have been evacuated to the UK, unless an earlier decision and more energetic steps had been taken to reduce the stocks in France'.[36] Given that replenishment to Theatre from UK could have been enacted in seven days, the plan to put the Base in France, with enormous quantities of resources and *materiel* held forward was almost certainly flawed. Concern about possible interruption of the Sea LOC appears to have had much to do with this and for ammunition, the shortage of storage space in the UK. Even though the BEF was originally deployed to engage

33 TNA WO 33/2384: Howard Committee Report, para III, The Evacuation.

34 WOOH, *Ordnance Services*, p.153.

35 TNA CAB 106/272: France and Flanders - Equipment Losses, War Officer Letter, Brigadier Latham to F W Deakin dated 18 September 1948, agrees with the Deakin figure of a loss of 7,000 tons. The Howard Committee however, estimated that ammunition abandoned to the enemy totalled 24,400 tons. TNA WO 33/2384: Howard Committee Report, Appx B, Ammunition, Petrol, Ordnance Stores, Supplies.

36 TNA WO 33/2384: Howard Committee Report, Appx B, Ammunition, Petrol, Ordnance Stores, Supplies.

in a defensive operation, the logistic support arrangements seem ponderous but when the plan changed to a failing encounter battle, it became positively unwieldy.

The Battle Goes On

There was continued discussion about the role of the railway in supporting operations in a manoeuvre environment but even in the Western Desert it proved indispensable to supporting major combat operations at scale. Adjustments were made to the position of forward railheads on the battlefield but replacing the railway with WMT imported so many challenges relating to supporting the additional vehicles, fuel, Equipment Support, trained MT manpower, road maintenance material and engineering resources that it was never a viable proposition. The experience in France for the provision of food services and Equipment Support resulted defined changes to the Army's logistic structure with the formation of the Army Catering Corps (ACC) in 1941 and the Royal Electrical & Mechanical Engineers (REME) in 1942, which withstood the test of time for 52 years in the case of the ACC[37] and is on-going for the REME.

The doctrinal debate relating to the RASC organizational arrangements for divisional support being based upon Commodity or Composite company structures rumbled on well after the evacuation from France, with both concepts having merits. The Commodity company had the advantages of operating the WMT more efficiently, had greater simplicity in the field, promoted particular expertise in the logistic spheres of ammunition, fuel and supply and enabled discreet capability to re-deploy at short notice.[38] The two limitations of the Commodity system were in resilience and flexibility. Should a Commodity company be destroyed or cut off from the division, there was an almost immediate reduction in capability, which was difficult to rapidly reconstitute. In addition, the Commodity arrangement could not support brigade group operations, which required a company arrangement containing all three RASC distribution capabilities, a point reinforced by the decision to form Composite companies to support the brigades rotating through Force W. Perforce of practical experience both systems were retained, a RASC Commission noting that, 'CsRASC[39] must be prepared to operate on either a composite or commodity basis as operational circumstances dictate'.[40]

At unit level, logistic commanders wrote Post Operational Reports, of varying quality, some of them focused on promoting the role of their units, and perhaps, thus themselves, but for the most part COs were focused on not repeating the failures in France, whilst ensuring that procedures and drills that had delivered logistic capability in combat were correctly understood and applied. One of the most prescient was by the commandant of the oldest technological logistic capability in the BEF, the Animal Transport Force K6, who in his first POR wrote, 'It is essential that a Comdr of an administrative Force should have up to date knowledge of

37 The ACC remained under the control of the RASC until 1 January 1965 when it became an independent Corps, becoming one of the Forming Corps of the Royal Logistic Corps (RLC) on 5 April 1993, which uses its motto. 'We Sustain'.
38 Document, nd but probably late 1945, held as Serial 9, 'The Operation of an Armoured and Infantry Division RASC' held in the RLC Museum.
39 Commanders Royal Army Service Corps.
40 RLC Museum, 'The Operation of an Armoured and Infantry Division RASC', p.48, para 2, Control & Operation.

modern strategy and tactics'.[41] Whether he was referring to his personal experience or the generic issue is impossible to define from the documents but his point was exceptionally well made. Logistics do not swim alone in the military pond and it was critical to military success in manoeuvre warfare that the logistic commander clearly comprehended the requirements of the combat forces and be capable of managing the resources in a dynamic operational environment.

Losses of *materiel* were substantial, the quantities perhaps only being occasionally exceeded by the amount of effort devoted to investigating the detail of the figures, an issue which remerged post-war, when research was on-going for Winston Churchill's volume *Their Finest Hour*.[42] The outfall of this work exposed the dissonance within the archival figures, the loss of wartime corporate memory and the location of pertinent documents. A War Office letter dated 18 September 1948 from Brigadier Harry Latham to F W Deakin, researching on behalf of Churchill, noted that, 'No figures were compiled by the War Office at the time, at any rate none can be found now'.[43] A particular point, and one that unmistakeably exposed the loss of corporate coherence was the loss of 90,000 rifles, which the War Office Ordnance Branch believed to be a 'pretty good guess', although in 1940, after an investigation at the behest of the Prime-Minster, losses were initially assessed to be 24,557, revised downwards to 6,152,[44] whilst another document states a loss of 180,000.[45] The inability to locate documents is lucidly illustrated by Brigadier Latham having to generate figures for artillery losses, including anti-tank guns, calculated from the BEF ORBAT, when the War Office had compiled working statistics in June 1940.[46]

WMT losses were enormous, with 84,427[47] of all types[48] being left in France, of which 52,859 were load-carriers in the 15 cwt – 10 ton range,[49] although many of these equipments were lost

41 Lieutenant-Colonel R W W Hills RIASC, HQ Force K6, 'Report on Operations in France' dated 8 June 1940, para, 35g.

42 Churchill, *Their Finest Hour*, p.125.

43 The former comment is patently incorrect because the documents rest in the TNA and it is quite clear that the War Office planning and logistic staffs were urgently seeking to establish ascertain equipment states. ACIGS (B) dated 5 June 1940, 'Estimated Losses of Main Types of Equipment' (SECRET) is held in TNA CAB 106/272: France and Flanders - Equipment Losses.

44 See, TNA PREM 3/183: Material lost in and evacuated from France, Letter Secretary of State for War (Anthony Eden) to Prime-Minister of July 1940 but nd.

45 TNA CAB 106/272: France and Flanders – Equipment Losses, 'Equipment Losses Sustained in the Evacuation of the BEF from France', nd but probably late 1940.

46 According to Latham's calculations, 1,812 artillery pieces and 324 light and heavy AA guns had been left in France. TNA CAB 106/272: France and Flanders – Equipment Losses, War Officer Letter, Brigadier Latham to F W Deakin dated 18 September 1948. ACIGS (B) dated 5 June 1940, 'Estimated Losses of Main Types of Equipment' (SECRET) held in TNA CAB 106/272: France and Flanders – Equipment Losses, lists 1,859 guns and 362 AA pieces. Farndale, *History of the Royal Regiment of Artillery: The Years of Defeat 1939-41*, p.264, Annex E, Table of Equipments Lost in France in June 1940, cites the total loss as 2,732 as follows: 1,954 tubes including anti-tank guns, plus another 518 destroyed in action or accidentally. AA gun losses are listed as 260. Annex E has no primary source references. Whilst Latham's total was 2,136, Churchill used the figure of 2,300.

47 WOOH, *Fighting, Support and Transport Vehicles*, Part II - *Unarmoured Vehicles*, p 63.

48 Of these, 20,475 were motorcycles. Ibid.

49 All figures calculated from tables in WOOH, *Fighting, Support and Transport Vehicles*, Part II, *Unarmoured Vehicles*, p.61.

as the BEF withdrew to the Channel coast.[50] One of the unforeseen advantages of these losses was the elimination, almost overnight, of the extensive type range of the 19,673 impressed 1-10 ton loading carrying vehicles and equipment transporters left in France,[51] along with the associated complex Equipment Support issues, although with new military production,[52] this ex-civilian fleet would, for the most part, eventually have been returned to the original owners, albeit not in pristine condition. This outcome created an opportunity to standardize equipment, although not creating the homogenous vehicle fleet that some experts sought and because of the experience of operations on the Continent, and the need to replace the losses, there was a view, quickly dispelled by the war in the Western Desert, that vehicles manufactured to civilian specification were acceptable to support manoeuvre warfare. The War Office selected the 3 ton lorry as the standard load-carrier, and although several different manufacturers produced their own type,[53] there were moves towards greater commonality. As the war moved into 1941, there was an increasing emphasis on the 4x4 vehicle but because many of the bodies built for the 6x4 system during the 1930s were still in use, this chassis continued in production until the end of the war.

Of the 716[54] tanks sent to the BEF only 14 returned, a staggering loss of 98 percent.[55] Whilst all the tanks in the BEF to the North of the Somme would have been lost, had more HETs been available to 1st Armoured Division, greater numbers could have been recovered from South of the River Somme. Whilst sources are at variance on the figures, [56] all those returned were

50 TNA CAB 106/272: France and Flanders – Equipment Losses, War Officer Letter, Brigadier Latham to F W Deakin dated 18 September 1948, summarized the losses as: 119,939 A, B and RASC vehicles, of which 2,481 were A. TNA CAB 106/272: France and Flanders – Equipment Losses, 'Equipment Losses Sustained in the Evacuation of the BEF from France' does not mention B vehicles but the A vehicle losses only total 1,298.

51 WOOH, *Fighting, Support and Transport Vehicles*, Part II, *Unarmoured Vehicles*, p.61, Appx B (1). Of this figure, 19,315 were in the 1-10 ton range, of which 14,009 were 3 ton 4x2 types, plus 358 transporters. Impressed vehicles, including motor-cycles, cars, ambulances, coaches, tractors and trailers, totalled 30,276.

52 In 1940, the total UK vehicle military production for the War Office and the Air Ministry of load-carriers, was 89,582 comprising 61,461 Lorries in excess of 1 ton and 28,121 x 15 cwt Trucks. Central Statistical Office, BOH *Statistical Digest of the War*, Table 127, Munitions, Wheeled Vehicles, p.149.

53 The five key vehicles, production numbers inclusive, were as follows:
Austin K3 (4x2): 17,000
Austin K5 (4x4): 12,280
Bedford QL (4x4): 52,248
Bedford OY (4x2): 72,385
Fordson WOT6 (4x4): 30,000

54 Of these, only 23 were the A12, the Infantry Tank Mark II.

55 TNA CAB 106/272: France and Flanders – Equipment Losses, 'Equipment Losses Sustained in the Evacuation of the BEF from France' lists only 450, 270 Cruisers and 180 Infantry. ACIGS (B) dated 5 June 1940, 'Estimated Losses of Main Types of Equipment' (SECRET) held in TNA CAB 106/272: France and Flanders – Equipment Losses, lists 475, 275 Light, 100 Cruiser and 100 Infantry. In November 1950, Director Royal Armoured Corps (Major-General N W Duncan CBE DSO) wrote to Major L F Ellis, the author of BOH, *The War in France and Flanders*, to confirm that the total numbers of tanks sent to France was 716, of which 22 had returned to the UK.

56 The published sources are certainly at variance. Ellis, BOH, *The War in France and Flanders*, p.327, states that a total of 22 tanks were recovered to UK, 13 x Mark VI and 9 Cruisers, figures which issued by DRAC in the War Office. A figure of 13 is quoted by Fletcher, *The Great Tank Scandal*, Part 1, p.34,

P20.2 Remembering the Logisticians 2019. The names of those logisticians who lost their lives during the campaign in Flanders and France and have no known graves, are remembered on the Dunkirk Memorial. (Author)

from 3rd Armoured Brigade evacuating through Cherbourg. The Evans Report,[57] written by the GOC 1st Armoured Division states that 14 x Cruisers and 12 x Mark VI were recovered

and includes 6 Mark VI and 7 Cruisers. A J Smithers, *Rude Mechanicals: An account of Tank Maturity during the Second World War* (London: Leo Cooper, 1987), p.51, gives a total of 26, 12 x Mark VI and 14 x A13s, all embarked at Cherbourg.

57 TNA WO 32/3932: 1st Armoured Division S/158/G dated 22 August 1940, pp.17-18.

through Cherbourg but the 11 x Dingo scout cars that reached the quayside were not, being, by some accounts, consigned to the harbour.[58] The failure to grasp the importance of the HET to delivering combat capability was a grave mistake,[59] and one that required the experience of the Western Desert[60] to reinforce,[61] although the failure to procure a HET for tank deployment and recovery is more understandable given the experience of the Great War and the expectation that tank railheads could be well forward.

The withdrawal, re-organization, reinforcement, support and evacuation of the BEF from France, was a tremendous feat of logistic planning and execution under extremely challenging conditions; it is not surprising therefore that mistakes were made, officers and soldiers found wanting and *materiel* lost. One of the logistic War Office histories written after the war took a surprisingly upbeat and pragmatic perspective of the experience, viewing the withdrawal from France as a learning opportunity precursor to the re-entry to the Continent in June 1944.[62]

> .... with the experience of six years of war it is an easy task to find errors and mistakes ... Mistakes were made and infallible systems found wanting as has happened in previous campaigns and will no doubt happen again. The misfortune of the BEF should therefore be remembered not as the military calamity that it undoubtedly was, but rather a heaven-sent opportunity to profit by the experience. Realistic administrative exercises in the British Army are regrettably conspicuous by their absence; if the battle of 1940 is viewed through exercise eyes it will be found that it was in effect one of the greatest administrative exercises of all time – expensive, no doubt, but it proved its value when, four years later, a new expeditionary force set foot upon the Continent.[63]

58 A document in the Tank Museum Library which is a 'Lecture (un-referenced and hand-written) on the Movement of 1 AD from Eng [land] to Somme, May 1940 and Lessons Learnt' states 12 x Cruisers, 12 Mark VI and 9 x Scout Cars.

59 The level of the failure is lucidly articulated by industrial production. Only five HETs were manufactured in UK in 1940, 41 in 1941 but 440 in 1942. Central Statistical Office, BOH, *Statistical Digest of the War*, Table 127, Munitions, Wheeled Vehicles, p.149.

60 Army Council, *Middle East Training Pamphlet*, Part 2, *Memorandum of Moves of Armoured Brigades or Regiments by RASC Transporters*, (War Office, 1943), IWM LBY 13/83

61 57/Vehs A880, Report on a visit to armoured formations in the Middle East, Feb-Mar 1941, cited in WOOH, *Fighting, Support and Transport Vehicles*, Part I, *Common Problems*, p.225.

62 Equally, although in different environments, the logisticians took their knowledge and experience to Malaya, Burma and North Africa. Malaya and North Africa await a logistic study of operations but Graham Dunlop, a retired Royal Marines officer, has written an outstanding analysis of logistics in Burma. *Military Economics: Culture and Logistics in the Burma Campaign, 1942-1945* (London: Pickering & Chatto, 2009).

63 WOOH, *Maintenance in the Field,* Vol 1, p 57.

Conclusion

For the most part, the BEF logistic structures stood the test of the French 'experience', although the shape, scope and size were adjusted to enhance effectiveness, agility and response. In this respect, culture was equally as important as systems. The BEF logisticians were cognizant that the expanding scale of the operation in France demanded consistent planning and sound preparation but were often pressed in the delivery of both by the dearth of resources to meet the demand especially across the GLOC where the jam was thinly spread. People were equally important as the culture and the systems, and in the logistic environment, the adage that 'a good planner is worth more than a good plan' remains as true now as it did in 1940. Whilst this approach reinforced that logistic coherency and effectiveness depended upon the concept of '*Le Diable dans les Detail*' equally, strong capable leadership made the difference between failure and success. The courage of logisticians was tested and sometimes found wanting but for every occasion of fragility, soldiers, Regular, Reserve, Militia and Volunteer, had stepped up to the plate with gallantry, determination and innovation to save the day, whether that was fighting the enemy or feeding their comrades. Their deeds, rapidly fading into the mists of time, are however, enshrined in stone by those who remained in France forever in 1940.

Often forgotten, the ability to deploy and sustain the Land and Air Forces in France was fundamentally underpinned by the logistic ability of the Merchant Marine to deliver the lift capacity and the RN, assisted by the RAF, to protect the passage. In this respect, after the initial deployment of the BEF, the demands of British naval and marine operations across the Globe constrained War Office plans to maintain the BEF solely through the French Western ports, prompting a reluctant General Staff and GHQ to engage in establishing an Advanced Base Area to reduce the requirements for RN escorts and logistic shipping lift. The reinforcement of, and evacuations from, the French North Channel Ports, firmly emphasized the significance of Britain's maritime strength, and sometimes limitations, to military operations on the Continent, the capabilities being even more apparent in supporting the North-West Expeditionary Force to Norway[1] and the evacuations from Western and Southern France. These were conducted over much greater distances and were maritime operations which, for the most part, the Germans were unable to prevent or effectively interdict.[2] The post-withdrawal attrition of shipping that had supported the BEF, through enemy action, navigational error and meteorological

1 Joseph Moritz, *Towards a Wider War, British Decision-Making and Military Effectiveness in Scandinavia, 1939-40* (Solihull: Helion, 2017).

2 Winser, *BEF Ships,* describes the types and numbers of ships taken up from trade to service the BEF's evacuation requirements.

conditions, was another unmistakeable and continuing reminder of the key and fundamental relationship between the Maritime and Land dimensions, the failure of which, for a nation deploying military forces beyond its shores, could have catastrophic results. In these respects, the key role of British salt-water capability in enabling the BEF to fight in France has been generally neglected, but sea-power in its broadest sense was as important to the BEF on the Continent as it was to the Eighth Army in North Africa or the Fourteenth Army in Burma.

The foundations of logistic support to the BEF were, given the circumstances, remarkably sound, although there was a high level of improvisation required. The structure though, failed not so much because of the rapidity of construction but because the architects failed to account for an intense storm, although a post-war official logistic history was surprisingly supportive of the planners and logisticians, observing: 'That the BEF was starved of the majority of the necessary modern weapons and stores of war was not the fault of the administrative staff in France, neither was it blameworthy that the principles upon which they had built up their organization were proved to be unsuited to 'blitzkreig' warfare'.[3] The importance of training across the logistic diaspora was writ large from the deployment to France and yet the burden was imposed upon the Army through rapid expansion, commanders and Staff as a body, being all too keenly aware of its significance. The Citizen Soldier brought however, enormous value to technical logistic areas, provided of course, the Army employed the individuals in the appropriate posts and was not inflexible in the manner, in which they were managed, mentored and encouraged. The lessons involving labour were understood, if not always deliverable, although the issues relating to enduring resilience and intelligent capability were an obvious experience from the time in France.

The logistic relationships with the Host Nation were vital to delivering combat capability and are undoubtedly worthy of a detailed study. Whilst inevitably there were frictions, some of which became more obvious as the Allied strategic position unravelled, the arrangements were built on solid foundations; had they not been, much of the BEF's logistic infrastructure and distribution capability would have failed to operate, with the relationship with the French National Railway, SNCF, being of especial importance. At the tactical level, there were spats about the allocation of real estate, BEF vehicles speeding in towns, ammunition and fuel stored in villages and the failure to follow Host Nation movement and logistic procedures but relations with the military and civil agencies in France were generally professional and cordial, although the unilateral denial operations involving the destruction of logistic stocks and facilities caused strong reactions from French military and civil authorities, a response British officers had increasingly to manage with sensitivity. Units certainly praised the industry and commitment of their French liaison officers and interpreters, who were assessed to have been essential to lubricating the interface with the complex components of the French logistic machinery.

The role of Viscount Gort in the logistic story deserves further analysis. His failure to inspect or visit any Base installation for which GHQ was responsible appears unprofessional from a 21st Century military perspective but may well have been the product of his military experience, doctrinal development and demanding responsibilities.[4] Whilst *Field Service Regulations* stated

3 WOOH, *Maintenance in the Field*, Vol 1, p.57.

4 Montgomery, never a great admirer of Gort's command qualities, commented that in being appointed as a C-in-C and an Army Commander, Gort was being asked to undertake the impossible. Colville, *Man of Valour*, p.191.

that the C-in-C was responsible for the in-Theatre maintenance of the Force in the Field, the regulations also noted that he and his Staff officers were only responsible for decisions on technical matters when the Head of a Service referred such issues or if the C-in-C or General Staff chose to interpose.[5] Unsurprisingly, the General Staff tended to avoid A&Q matters unless a crisis emerged and even then there was an understandable tendency to remain disengaged for fear of assuming responsibility for any perceived impending disaster. Whilst Gort had many tasks pressing upon his time, his interaction with logisticians and logistics appears to be have been infrequent at best, which may account at least partially for the sudden emergence of the petrol crisis in October 1939, the shortage of suitable clothing and the long running failure to grip at the highest level, the Equipment Support issues.

A key lesson from 1914, which itself was under-pinned by pre-Great War military assessments, was to retain the capability to withdraw along the GLOC. By creating a GLOC, which ran laterally across a potential German advance, created an in-built fragility, which was compounded by the Allied failure to maintain an effective strategic mobile reserve to mitigate the risks. It is certainly ironic that the man who took most of the blame for the failure to evacuate stocks from the Base, should have identified so incisively the vulnerabilities that the arrangement posed. The unravelling of the BEF's campaign in France created the one outcome that the BEF of 1914-1918 had fortuitously avoided, for it always retained access through its GLOC to the Channel ports, although in 1914 only timely decisions and some deft logistic foot-work enabled it to do so.[6]

From the BEF's perspective, its practitioners had only just started to get into their stride when the catastrophic arrival of the Germans on the Channel coast unbalanced the whole of the BEF's logistic lay-down. Had the Allies retained a powerful strategic reserve to counter-stroke the German penetration at Sedan, the outcome of the campaign, the Second World War and the 20th Century history of Europe could have been very different. Whilst the logisticians may still have been left out of the revised historiography, they would have been critical, as they were in 1914, to the BEF staying in the fight. It remains therefore, one of those frustrating historical 'ifs' as to the performance and effectiveness of the expanding BEF's logistic systems and how they would have developed to support the BEF in the field if the scenario had matured differently. What is not in doubt is that the BEF's logisticians were remarkably quick to learn and became masters of innovation especially when the chips were down, so the outcome in 1940 does not in any way change the conclusion that logistics of the BEF were indeed a 'Great Feat of Improvisation'.

5 Army Council, FSR, Vol I, *Organization and Administration*, p.9, Chp II, Command, Sect 6, para 3.

6 For an analysis, see, Maginniss, '*Muddling Through, Wully Robertson, agile operational logistics and the salvation of the British Expeditionary Force in 1914*', pp.145-170.

Bibliography

Primary Sources:

United Kingdom – The National Archives (UK TNA)

ADM 1/10494	Minelaying on the Rhine – Awards to Naval Expeditionary Force personnel.
ADM 179/158	Operation CYCLE.
ADM 234/360	Battle Summary No 41, The Evacuation from Dunkirk, Operation Dynamo, 26 May – 4 June 1940.
ADM 276/126	Operation CYCLE Reports.
AIR 2/5117	Chemical Warfare, Air Staff Policy.
AIR 2/5200	Air Ministry Bacteriological and Chemical Warfare.
AIR 2/6966	Explosion at 21 Maintenance Unit Fauld.
AIR 14/419	Smoke Curtain Installation, Technical Trials.
AIR 14/2735	Chemical Warfare Decontamination of SCIs.
AIR 19/523	Accidents at Explosive Depots Llanberis and Fauld.
AIR 24/680	HQ BAFF, Maintenance-Officer-in-Chief, Operational Record Book, October 1939 – June 1940.
AIR 27/1949	501 Squadron RAF, AASF, Operational Record Book, 1940.
AIR 29/780	4 Air Stores Park, AASF, War Diary, September 1939 – June 1940.
AIR 29/781	5 Air Stores Park, AASF, War Diary, September 1939 – June 1940.
AIR 29/990	28 Maintenance Unit, Operational Record Book.
AIR 29/1031	94 Maintenance Unit, Operational Record Book.
AIR 35/66	Aerodrome construction in France, Requirements and policy, 1939-1940.
AIR 35/115	Operational Roles of Aircraft.
AIR 35/123	Reserve stocks of aviation fuel, bombs and small arms ammunition, 1940.
AIR 35/125	Appointment of Maintenance Officer-In-Chief; Policy.
AIR 35/130	British Air Forces in France, Gas Policy.
AIR 35/131	British Air Forces in France, Holding of gas weapons.
AIR 35/244	AASF Operation Instruction No 7, Employment of AASF Bomber Units and Units of Bomber Command, which may be attached to AASF in event of an attempted land invasion by Germany dated 21 March 1940.
AIR 35/323	Haddock Force Operations.
AIR 35/336	Use of Air Transportation Service for evacuation of casualties.

AIR 35/352	67 Wing Operational Summaries 1940.
AIR 41/21	The Campaign in France and the Low Countries, September 1939 - June 1940, RAF Narrative (TOP SECRET) Air Historical Branch, 1944.
AVIA 15/254	Chemical Warfare: Research and Development, Reports on Gas Spraying Trials.
CAB 27/604	Royal Ordnance Factories – Miscellaneous Committees.
CAB 44/67	The BEF in Belgium and Artois, 10 May – 3 June 1940.
CAB 80/12/51	British Expeditionary Force: Instructions to General Brooke: memo by CIGS.
CAB 102/273	Munitions Factories – Location and Siting.
CAB 102/626	History of the Royal Filling Factory Swynnerton – Unpublished Narrative, D Mack.
CAB 102/627	Construction of Filling Factories - Unpublished Narrative, D Mack.
CAB 106/204	BEF Unit Narratives.
CAB 106/211	Notes on the 'Q' Organization of the BEF.
CAB 106/218	Plan W4: Notes on the preparation of the plan for the First Contingent of the British Field Force.
CAB 106/234	Saar Force – Ordnance Services.
CAB 106/235	BEF Ammunition Supply.
CAB 106/272	France and Flanders – Equipment Losses.
CAB 115/378	Evacuation of Personnel and Material from France.
CAB 120/247	British Expeditionary Force: Lord Gort's Despatches.
CAB 121/308	Royal Navy, Operation ROYAL MARINE, Proposals for laying mines in the River Rhine.
FO 371/63436	Dispatch of Shanghai Defence Force to Shanghai, 1927.
KV 2/443	Security Service: World War II, Renegades and Suspected Renegades, Chapple.
MAF 72/703	Protests against earmarking and impressments of food trade vehicles for War Office purposes.
PREM 3/183	Material lost in and evacuated from France.
SUPP 5/1260	Historical Notes on the Royal Ordnance Factories.
WO 32/3343	Underground Storage – Accommodation for Explosives.
WO 32/4612	Future Army Organization – 1935.
WO 32/9392	Operations of 1st Armoured Division in France.
WO 33/2384	Report of Committee on evacuation of British Expeditionary Force from French Ports.
WO 98/8/717	Victoria Cross details for Annand.
WO 106/1660	Report on the Transportation Service of the British Expeditionary Force.
WO 106/1739	Operation CYCLE - Evacuation Reports.
WO 106/1741	Bartholomew Committee – Report on lessons to be learnt from operations in Flanders: action arising from report.
WO 106/1775	Bartholomew Committee – Report on lessons to be learnt from operations in Flanders; evidence, report and action arising.
WO 106/1777	The British Front.
WO 163/49	OS Papers.

WO 163/415 Report of Committee on evacuation of British Expeditionary Force from French Ports.
WO 166/796 HQ 1st Armoured Division, GS, War Diary, September 1939 – April 1940.
WO 166/798 HQ 1st Armoured Division, AQ, War Diary, September 1939 – April 1940.
WO 166/799 1st Armoured Division, Support Group, War Diary, 1939 – 1941.
WO 166/804 1 Armoured Division Ammunition Sub-Park RASC, War Diary, 1939-1941.
WO 166/806 1 Armoured Division Divisional Troops Company RASC, War Diary, April 1940 – June 1941.
WO 166/809 1 Armoured Division, Reserve Supply Park RASC, War Diary, April 1940.
WO 166/4942 226 General Transport Company RASC, War Diary, July 1940 – December 1941.
WO 167/10 GHQ Quartermaster-General. Maintenance (Q).
WO 167/11 GHQ Adjutant-General, War Diary, September 1939 – April 1940.
WO 167/13 GHQ Major-General Royal Artillery, War Diary, September 1939 – June 1940.
WO 167/21 GHQ Staff Duties & Training, War Diary, September 1939 – April 1940.
WO 167/22 GHQ Director Ordnance Services, War Diary, September 1939 – April 1940.
WO 167/24 GHQ Commander Royal Army Service Corps, War Diary, 1 September 1939 – 31 May 1940.
WO 167/51 GHQ, Services, Transportation, War Diary, September 1939 – April 1940.
WO 167/56 Q Branch Line of Communication, War Diary, September 1939 – June 1940.
WO 167/57 Line of Communication – HQ 'Q' (M) Movement, War Diary, October – December 1939.
WO 167/93 1 Medical Base Sub–Area, War Diary, May 1940.
WO 167/122 2 Base Infantry Depot, War Diary, December – June 1940.
WO 167/124 I Corps, General Staff, War Diary, 1939 – 1940.
WO 167/129 I Corps, Commander Royal Engineers, War Diary, September 1939 – June 1940.
WO 167/159 II Corps Ammunition Park RASC, War Diary, September 1939 – June 1940.
WO 167/180 III Corps, Director Supply and Transport, War Diary, April 1940.
WO 167/205 HQ 2nd Division, Adjutant & Quartermaster, War Diary, September 1939 – April 1940.
WO 167/210 2 Division CRASC, War Diary, September 1939 – June 1940.
WO 167/212 2 Division Petrol Company RASC, War Diary, October 1939 – June 1940.
WO 167/215 2 Division Provost Company, War Diary, September 1939 – June 1940.
WO 167/224 3 Division Ammunition Company RASC, War Diary, September 1939 – April 1940.
WO 167/245 HQ 5th Division, A&Q, War Diary, December 1939 – April 1940.
WO 167/250 5 Division Ammunition Company RASC, War Diary, December 1939 – June 1940.

WO 167/251	5 Division Ammunition Company RASC, War Diary, 1939 – 1940.
WO 167/259	12 (Eastern) Division, CRASC, War Diary, May – June 1940.
WO 167/286	HQ 46th (North Midland & West Riding) Division, GS War Diary, May – June 1940.
WO 167/294	48 Division CRASC, War Diary, January – May 1940.
WO 167/297	48 Division Supply Column RASC, War Diary, December 1939 – May 1940.
WO 167/305	50 Division CRASC, War Diary, January – June 1940.
WO 167/315	HQ 51st (Highland) Division AQ, War Diary, May 1940.
WO 167/327	HQ 52nd (Lowland) Division AQ, War Diary, June 1940.
WO 167/330	52 Division CRASC, War Diary, June 1940.
WO 167/337	1 Armoured Division CRASC, War Diary, 1 May – 30 June 1940.
WO 167/342	1 Armoured Division Ammunition Sub-Park RASC, War Diary, May – June 1940.
WO 167/343	1 Armoured Division Petrol Sub-Park RASC, War Diary, May – June 1940.
WO 167/344	1 Armoured Division Provost Company RASC, War Diary, May – June 1940.
WO 167/345	1 Armoured Division Workshop RAOC, War Diary, April – July 1940.
WO 167/364	HQ 9th Infantry Brigade, War Diary, September 1939 – June 1940.
WO 167/413	HQ 157th Infantry Brigade, War Diary, June 1940.
WO 167/414	HQ 1st Army Tank Brigade, War Diary, May 1940.
WO 167/420	2 Armoured Brigade RASC Company, War Diary, May 1940.
WO 167/421	HQ 3rd Armoured Brigade, War Diary, May 1940.
WO 167/425	1 Anti-Aircraft Brigade Company RASC, War Diary, September 1939 – June 1940.
WO 167/446	10th Royal Hussars, War Diary, May 1940.
WO 167/468	7th Field Regiment RA, War Diary, September 1939 – May 1940.
WO 167/794	2nd Battalion Royal Norfolk Regiment, War Diary, September 1939 – June 1940.
WO 167/843	1st Battalion Royal Welch Fusiliers, War Diary, September 1939 – June 1940.
WO 167/857	GHQ Directorate Inland Water Transport, War Diary, January – April 1940.
WO 167/875	1 Docks Group RE, War Diary, September 1939 – June 1940.
WO 167/876	2 Docks Group RE, War Diary, September 1939 – June 1940.
WO 167/877	3 Docks Group RE, War Diary, December 1939 – May 1940.
WO 167/879	1 Railway Construction and Maintenance Group RE, War Diary, September 1939 – June 1940.
WO 167/880	2 Railway Construction and Maintenance Group RE, War Diary, September 1939 – June 1940.
WO 167/881	3 Railway Construction and Maintenance Group RE, War Diary, May – June 1940.
WO 167/906	8 Railway Construction & Operating Company RE, War Diary, September 1939 – April 1940.

WO 167/916 23 Field Company RE, War Diary, September 1939 – June 1940.
WO 167/918 29 Railway Survey Company RE, War Diary, September 1939 – June 1940.
WO 167/943 129 Forestry Company RE, War Diary, October 1939 – June 1940.
WO 167/944 135 Excavator Company RE, War Diary, September 1939 – May 1940.
WO 167/945 150 Railway Construction Company RE, War Diary, September 1939 – June 1940.
WO 167/946 151 Railway Construction Company RE, War Diary, September 1939 – June 1940.
WO 167/947 152 Railway Construction Company RE, War Diary, September 1939 – June 1940.
WO 167/948 153 Railway Operating Company RE, War Diary, February June 1940.
WO 167/949 154 Railway Operating Company RE, War Diary, September 1939 – June 1940.
WO 167/950 155 Railway Workshop Company RE, War Diary, January – May 1940.
WO 167/951 156 Transportation Stores Company RE, War Diary, September 1939 – June 1940.
WO 167/952 157 Railway Construction Company RE, War Diary, January – June 1940.
WO 167/953 158 Railway Construction Company RE, War Diary, February – June 1940.
WO 167/954 159 Railway Construction Company RE, War Diary, February – June 1940.
WO 167/955 161 Railway Construction Company RE, War Diary, May – July 1940.
WO 167/956 165 Railway Survey Company RE, War Diary, December 1939 – June 1940.
WO 167/960 190 Railway Operating Company RE, War Diary, April – June 1940.
WO 167/961 196 Transportation Stores Company RE, War Diary, April – May 1940.
WO 167/1076 GHQ, Supply Directorate (Petrol) RASC, War Diary, 1 September 1939 – 31 May 1940.
WO 167/1077 Line of Communication, Deputy Director Supply and Transport, War Diary, September 1930 – June 1940.
WO 167/1089 5 Reserve Motor Transport Company RASC, War Diary, March – June 1940.
WO 167/1091 7 Reserve Motor Transport Company RASC, War Diary, April – June 1940.
WO 167/1092 8 Reserve Motor Transport Company RASC, War Diary, April – June 1940.
WO 167/1096 2 Line of Communication MT Railhead Company RASC, War Diary, April – May 1940.
WO 167/1109 15 Troop Carrying Company RASC, War Diary, June 1940.
WO 167/1110 18 Troop Carrying Company RASC, War Diary, June 1940.
WO 167/1111 13 Troop Carrying Company RASC, War Diary, May 1940.
WO 167/1115 1 Base Supply Depot RASC, War Diary, September 1939 – May 1940.
WO 167/1119 1 Field Butchery RASC, War Diary, September 1939 – May 1940.
WO 167/1120 2 Field Butchery RASC, War Diary, September – April 1940.
WO 167/1121 3 Field Butchery RASC, War Diary, February – June 1940.

WO 167/1122	4 Field Butchery RASC, War Diary, February – June 1940.
WO 167/1123	1 Field Bakery RASC, War Diary, September 1939 – June 1940.
WO 167/1148	1 Petrol Depot RASC, War Diary, December 1939 – June 1940.
WO 167/1149	2 Petrol Depot RASC, War Diary, February – June 1940.
WO 167/1153	1 Motor Transport Vehicle Reserve Depot Depot, A Park, War Diary, 1939 – 1940.
WO 167/1155	1 Heavy Repair Shop RASC, War Diary, September 1939 – June 1940.
WO 167/1156	Advanced Motor Transport Stores Depot RASC, War Diary, September 1939 – June 1940.
WO 167/1157	Base Motor Transport Stores Depot, War Diary, September 1939 – June 1940.
WO 167/1158	1 Works Transport Company (76 Company) RASC, War Diary, October 1939 – March 1940.
WO 167/1168	1 Base Ordnance Depot RAOC, War Diary, September 1939 – June 1940.
WO 167/1169	2 Base Ordnance Depot RAOC, War Diary, September 1939 – April 1940.
WO 167/1175	1 Base Ammunition Depot RAOC, War Diary, 1939 – 1940.
WO 167/1176	2 Base Ammunition Depot RAOC, War Diary, September 1939 – May 1940.
WO 167/1177	3 Base Ammunition Depot RAOC, War Diary, November 1939 – February 1940.
WO 167/1178	4 Base Ammunition Depot RAOC, War Diary, January – May 1940.
WO 167/1179	5 Base Ammunition Depot (later 21 BAD) RAOC, War Diary, November 1939 – May 1940.
WO 167/1180	6 Base Ammunition Depot RAOC, War Diary, April – June 1940.
WO 167/1181	22 Base Ammunition Depot RAOC, War Diary, February – May 1940.
WO 167/1192	1 Ordnance Field Park RAOC, War Diary, September 1939 – May 1940.
WO 167/1193	Railhead Supply Ordnance RAOC, War Diary, September 1939 – April 1940.
WO 167/1194	2 Ordnance Field Park RAOC, War Diary, September 1939 – June 1940.
WO 167/1196	Advanced Ordnance Workshop RAOC, War Diary, September 1939 – June 1940.
WO 167/1201	2 Base Ordnance Workshop RAOC, War Diary, September 1939 – April 1940.
WO 167/1391	2 Mobile Bath Unit, War Diary, December 1939 – May 1940.
WO 167/1395	7 Mobile Bath Unit, War Diary, February – April 1940.
WO 167/1401	29 Mobile Bath Unit, War Diary, May – June 1940.
WO 167/1413	Beauman Division, Q, War Diary, June 1940.
WO 167/1422	Advanced Air Striking Force, Commander Royal Engineers, War Diary, September 1939 – December 1939.
WO 167/1423	Advanced Air Striking Force, Commander Royal Engineers (East), War Diary, January – April 1940.
WO 167/1424	Advanced Air Striking Force, Commander Royal Engineers (North), War Diary, January – June 1940.
WO 167/1425	Advanced Air Striking Force, Commander Royal Engineers (South), War Diary, January – April 1940.

WO 167/1428 82 Advanced Railhead Detachment RAOC, War Diary, 1939 – 1940.
WO 167/1433 Headquarters Force K6, Indian Contingent, War Diary, 1939 – 1940.
WO 167/1462 8 Field Hygiene Section RAMC, War Diary, December 1939 – April 1940.
WO 167/1719 Assistant Director Army Postal Services: Telegraph Survey, February 1940.
WO 177/14 Medical Services, QAIMNS, War Diaries, September 1939 – June 1940.
WO 189/4856 Porton Report, The laboratory preparation of Impregnate E (2.4 Dichlorophenyl benzoyl chloroimide).
WO 191/1 General Staff, Peacetime Operations Abroad, Shanghai Defence Force.
WO 193/712 Chemical Warfare – Offensive Policy.
WO 193/716 Despatch of Gas and Equipment to the BEF.
WO 193/717 Scale of Gas Attack to which the British Expeditionary Force may be subjected.
WO 193/721 Chemical Warfare, Strategy XIII: Gas Policy and Despatch of Supplies.
WO 193/723 Chemical Warfare – Intelligence.
WO 197/1 Movement Control Instruction Plan W4: movement of First Contingent of the Field Force and AASF to France.
WO 197/2 First Maintenance Project: Reception of Forces in France and system of maintenance in the initial stages.
WO 197/57 Forward Move of the BEF (Plan D) – Administrative instructions and correspondence.
WO 197/72 Appreciation of British retaliatory position in the event of Chemical Warfare.
WO 197/84 Preparations for demolition in Belgium and supply of explosives.
WO 197/86 Macforce – Operational Message and Notes.
WO 197/89 Evacuation of the Line of Communication.
WO 197/105 Aerial Plan – Accommodation of Units evacuated from the BEF.
WO 197/112 Movement and Maintenance in the BEF.
WO 197/115 Notes on the Operations in France between 10-31 May 1940 from a Movement Point of View.
WO 197/131 Evacuation of Marseilles Sub-Area.
WO 197/134 The Evacuation from France and the Quartering of the BEF after Dunkirk.
WO 208/3298 Escape and Evasion Reports.
WO 217/16 Private Diary of Lieutenant K R Gough RASC.
WO 222/1529 Aerial plan: reports.
WO 222/2137 Ambulance Trains during the Evacuation from France, 1940.
WO 277/1 Administrative Planning and Organization, 1939-1945.
WO 277/16 Morale of the Army.
WO 277/34 Air Support in the Battle of France.
WO 287/50 Impressment and collection of Mechanical Transport vehicles on mobilization.
WO 287/161 Regulations for the Storage, Transport, Maintenance and Disposal of Chemical Weapons.
WO 361/13 Evacuation of Dunkirk: losses on hospital carrier Maid of Kent, 21 May 1940.
WO 366/3 Historical Monographs Section: Production Costs and Staff Requirements.

WO 366/4	Official Histories and Monographs Policy.
WO 366/36	Ordnance Services: Appointment of an Author.
WO 366/43	Transportation: Revision of Draft Pages.
WO 366/44	Supplies & Transport: Progress and proof editing reports.
WO 366/45	Maintenance in the Field: Revision of Drafts.
WO 373/15/47	Recommendation for Award for Sanson, A N.
WO 373/16/259	Recommendation for Award for Keeble, R.
WO 373/16/410	Recommendation for Award for Wicks, R S.
WO 373/53/543	Recommendation for Award for FitzGerald, D J O.
WO 373/75/460	Recommendation for Award for Parminter, R H R.
WO 373/80/183	Recommendation for Award for Luff, C M C.
WO 373/81/26	Recommendation for Award for Langdon, C B.
ZLIB 29/455	Transportation on the Western Front (Text).

Imperial War Museum

Documents.10527	Private Papers of Major–General G S Szlumper CBE TD
Documents.21752	Private Papers of Major Michael Robbins.
Documents.6393	Private Papers of Brigadier James Whitehead.
GVS 3/1	Report on the Transportation Services of the British Expeditionary Force.
GVS 3/2	Notes of Director Railways, BEF, France.
LBY K.49621.	Private Papers of Brigadier R H R Parminter.

Tank Museum

Appendix U – 1st Armoured Division Organization: Mobilisation & Embarkation Numbers.

Lecture (un-referenced and hand-written) on the Movement of 1 AD from Eng [land] to Somme, May 1940 and Lessons Learnt.

Memorandum on the position regarding tanks in the BEF as known to the AFV Branch of GHQ, Cherwell Papers, G364/30.

Memorandum (un-referenced) Bulk Operational Holdings of Light and Cruiser Tanks – May/Jun 1940.

Readiness of 1 Armd Div for War, 79/Mob/3244 dated 15 Oct 39.

Report No 1 – Half yearly report on the progress of the Royal Armoured Corps – SD 7: September 1939 – June 1940.

Report of Operations of 1st Armoured Division in France (the Evans Report).

Report on the Technical Control of Tank Production, Cherwell Papers, G364/36.

Tank Production, SECRET, Cherwell Papers, G364/33.

The Crisis Formation of the Infantry Tank Squadron Placed Under Command of 1st Armoured Division, BEF, France, May – June 1940, R K Huggins, Unpublished.

Royal Logistic Corps Museum – Recent Official Logistic Publications

Air Publication 3000, *British Air Power Doctrine*, 3rd Edition, Directorate of Air Staff, UK Ministry of Defence, 1999.

Army Doctrine Publication, Vol. 1, *Operations*, HQDT/18/34/46, Army Code No 71565, UK Ministry of Defence, 1994.

Army Doctrine Publication, Vol. 2, *Command*, HQDT/18/34/51, Army Code No 71564, UK Ministry of Defence, 1995.

Army Doctrine Publication, Vol. 3, *Logistics*, DGD&D/18/34/63, Army Code No 71566, UK Ministry of Defence, 1996.

Army Field Manual, Vol. 1, *Combined Arms Operations*, Part 6, *Combat Service Support*, DGD&D 18/34/44, Army Code No 71344, UK Ministry of Defence, 1998.

Defence Council, *Administration in the Field, The Maintenance System for General War*, UK Ministry of Defence, 1975.

British Defence Doctrine, Joint Warfare Publication 0-01, UK Ministry of Defence, 1996.

Royal Corps of Transport Training, Vol. IV, *Transport Operations – Rail Transport*, A/26/GS Trg Publications/2921, Army Code No 70443, UK Ministry of Defence, 1975.

The Royal Logistic Corps, Vol. 1, Pamphlet 1, *Logistic Support Doctrine*, UK Ministry of Defence, 1997.

Official Military Publications

Admiralty, *British Merchant Vessels Lost or Damaged by Enemy Action during the Second World War* (London: HMSO, 1957).

Air Council, *Royal Air Force Pocket Book*, Air Publication 1081, Air Ministry, London: HMSO, 1937.

Air Council, *Royal Air Force War Manual*, Part II – *Organization and Administration*, Air Publication 1301, Air Ministry, 1939 (reprinted June 1940).

Army Council, *Army Training Memorandum*, 1939 – 1941, War Office.

Army Council, *Field Service Pocket Book*, 1938, War Office, London: HMSO, 1939 – 1940.

Army Council, *Field Service Regulations,* Vol. I, *Organization and Administration*, 26/Regulations/189, War Office, London: HMSO, 1930.

Army Council, *Field Service Regulations,* Vol. II, *Operations – General*, 26/Regulations/1468, War Office, London: HMSO, 1935.

Army Council, *Field Service Regulations,* Vol. III, *Operations – Higher Formations*, 26/Regulations/1803, War Office, London: HMSO, 1935.

Army Council, *Infantry Section Leading 1938*, 26 Manuals/1920, London: HMSO, 1938.

Army Council, *King's Regulations and Orders for the Army 1940*, War Office, London: HMSO, 1940.

Army Council, *Manual of Driving and Maintenance for Mechanical Vehicles (Wheeled)*, 1937, 26/Manuals/1472, War Office, London: HMSO, 1938.

Army Council, *Manual of Movement (War),* 26/Manuals/1297, War Office, London: HMSO, 1933.

Army Council, *Middle East Training Pamphlet*, Part 2, *Memorandum of Moves of Armoured Brigades or Regiments by RASC Transporters*, War Office, 1943.

Army Council, *Military Engineering*, Vol. VI, *Water Supply*, 30/War Office/8534, London: HMSO, 1922.

Army Council, *Military Engineering*, Vol. VIII, *Railways*, 26/Manuals/103, War Office, London: HMSO, 1929.

Army Council, *Military Engineering*, Vol. VII, *Accommodation and Installations*, 26/Manuals/1062, War Office, London: HMSO: 1934.
Army Council, *Military Engineering*, Vol. V, *Roads*, 26/Manuals/1061, War Office, 1935.
Army Council, *Ordnance Manual (War)*, War Office, HMSO, 1939.
Army Council, *Notes for the Guidance of Officer Mechanical Engineers*, RAOC, 1940.
Army Council, *Regulations for Army Ordnance Services*, Part 1, War Office, London: HMSO, 1937.
Army Council, *Regulations for the Auxiliary Territorial Service*, 1941, London: HMSO, 1941.
Army Council, *Regulations for the Equipment of the Army*, War Office, London: HMSO, 1940.
Army Council, *Regulations for Supply, Transport and Barrack Services*, 26/Regulations/2188, reprint of 1930 Edition with amendments 1-104, War Office, London: HMSO, 1943.
Army Council, *Royal Army Service Corps Training*, Vol. III, Supplies, War Office, London: HMSO, 1933.
Army Council, *The Royal Engineers Pocket Book*, 26/Manuals/1615, War Office, 1936.
Army Council, *Small Arms Training*, Vol. I, Pamphlet No 5, *Anti-Tank Rifle, 1942*, 26/GS Publications/702, War Office, 1942.
Army Council, *Supply Manual (War)*, War Office, HMSO, 1931.
Army Council, *The Employment of Air Forces with the Army in the Field*, 26/Manuals/1076, War Office, London: HMSO, 1932.
Army Council, *The Employment of Air Forces with the Army in the Field*, 26/Manuals/1869, War Office, London: HMSO, 1938.
Army Council Instructions, *Vocabulary of Army Ordnance Stores*, Section J2, *Portable Cookers*, 57/Vocabularly/382, War Office, 7 June 1939.

General Staff, *Notes on the French Army*, 1936 (amendments to 1940), War Office, HMSO, 1940.
General Staff, *Notes on the German Army*, War Office, HMSO, 1940.
General Staff, *Regulations for the Storage, Transport, Maintenance and Disposal of Chemical Weapons*, CONFIDENTIAL, 26/Regulations/2380, War Office, 1941.
General Staff, Royal Army Service Corps, Training Pamphlet No 1, *Training System in War*, Part III: *Training of NCOs*, War Office 1940.
General Staff, Royal Army Service Corps, Training Pamphlet No 1, *Training System in War*, Part IV: *Collective Training*, War Office 1940.
General Staff, *The Tactical and Technical Employment of Chemical Weapons*, Military Training Pamphlet No 32, Part I – *Chemical Warfare Units, Organization, Employment and Training*, 26/GS Pubns/308, War Office, April 1940.
General Staff, *The Tactical and Technical Employment of Chemical Weapons*, Military Training Pamphlet No 32, Part II – *The Projector*, 26/GS Pubns/363, War Office, July 1940.
General Staff, *The Tactical and Technical Employment of Chemical Weapons*, Military Training Pamphlet No 32, Part IV – *The Bulk Contamination Vehicle*, 26/GS Pubns/348, War Office, June 1940.
General Staff, *The Tactical and Technical Employment of Chemical Weapons*, Military Training Pamphlet No 32, Part V – *The Chemical Mine*, 26/GS Pubns/263, War Office, February 1940.

General Staff, *The Tactical and Technical Employment of Chemical Weapons*, Military Training Pamphlet No 32, Part VI – *Bombs, Ground, 6 lb*, 26/GS Pubns/289, War Office, March 1940.

Government of India Defence Department, *Frontier Warfare – India* (Army and Royal Air Force), MGS-M121 (N) 20000, New Delhi: Government of India Press, 1939.

Home Office, *Air Raid Precautions*, Handbook No 1, *Personal Protection Against Gas*, London: HMSO, 1938.

Indian Army Service Corps (IASC) *Manual* (War) Simla: Government of India Press, 1932.

Instructions as to the Conveyance of Explosive, Inflammable Liquid, Corrosive and Poisonous Chemical, Compressed or Liquefied Gases and other Dangerous Goods by Rail, Road or Water, London: Railway Executive Committee, 1939.

Quartermaster-General, *Notes on Military Railway Engineering*, Part I, *Survey*, War Office, 1940.

Quartermaster-General, *Notes on Military Railway Engineering*, Part II, *Engineering*, War Office, 1940.

Quartermaster-General, *Notes on Military Railway Engineering*, Part IV, *Operating*, War Office, 1942

War Office, *Textbook on Ammunition*, 26/Manuals/1543, HMSO, 1936.

Parliamentary Papers and Debates

Cmd 5104, *The General Annual Report on the British Army for the Year ending 30 September* 1935, London: HMSO, 1936.

Hansard, 16 March 1927, Vol. 203, c2112.

Armed Services Official Histories

Naval Staff History

BR 1736 (32), *Second World War*, Battle Summary No 41, *The Evacuation from Dunkirk, Operation Dynamo, 26 May – 4 June 1940*, TSD 64/48, Tactical and Staff Duties Division, Admiralty, 1949.

War Office Official History (WOOH) - Red Book Series

Army Council, *The Second World War, 1939-1945, Army*:

Administrative Planning, Colonel H W Wilson OBE TD, War Office, 1952.

Airborne Forces, Lieutenant-Colonel T B H Otway DSO, The Royal Ulster Rifles (Comp.), War Office, 1951.

Army Welfare, Brigadier M C Morgan CBE MC psc, War Office, 1953.

Fighting, Support and Transport Vehicles and the War Office Organization for their Provision, Part I, *Common Problems*, Major R Campagnac RASC & Major P E C Hayman, 15/19 KRH (Comp.s), War Office, 1951.
Fighting, Support and Transport Vehicles and the War Office Organization for their Provision, Part II, *Unarmoured Vehicles*, Major R Campagnac RASC & Major P E C Hayman, 15/19 KRH (Comp.s), War Office, 1951.
Manpower Problems, Major-General A J K Pigott CB CBE (Comp.), War Office, 1949.
Maintenance in the Field, Vol. I, *1939-1942*, Lieutenant-Colonel J A H Carter OBE KORR & Major D N Kann MBE RASC, War Office, 1952.
Military Engineering (Field), Major-General R P Pakenham-Walsh CB MC (Comp.), War Office, 1952.
Miscellaneous 'Q' Services, Brigadier A D Magnay CIE (Comp.), War Office, 1954.
Morale, Lieutenant-Colonel J H A Sparrow OBE (Comp.), War Office, 1949.
Movements, Major J B Higham RE & E A Knighton MBE (Comp.s), War Office, 1955.
Ordnance Services, Officers of the Ordnance Directorate, War Office, 1950.
Personnel Selection, Colonel B Ungerson CBE BSc (Comp.), War Office, 1953.
Quartering, Brigadier A D Magnay, War Office, 1949.
Royal Electrical and Mechanical Engineers, Vol. I, *Organization and Operations*, Major-General Sir E Bertram Rowcroft KBE CB (Comp.), War Office, 1951.
Signal Communications, Colonel T B Gravely OBE (comp.) War Office, 1950.
Special Weapons and Types of Warfare, Vol I, *Gas Warfare*, War Office, 1951, (SECRET).
Supplies and Transport, Vol. s I & II, Colonel D W Boileau late RASC, War Office, 1954.
The Auxiliary Territorial Service, Controller J M Cowper (Comp.), War Office, 1949.
Transportation, Brigadier R Micklem CMG CBE, War Office, 1950.
Works Services and Engineer Stores, Major-General A G B Buchanan MICE, War Office, 1953.

Air Ministry Official History (AMOH) - Blue Book Series

Air Ministry, *The Second World War, 1939-1945, Royal Air Force*:
Air Publication 3397 (CONFIDENTIAL downgraded UNCLASSIFIED, March 1966), *Maintenance*, CD 1131, Air Ministry, 1954.
Air Publication 3236, *Works*, Air Ministry, 1956.

Official Histories and Despatches

Crew, F A E, FRS, *Army Medical Services, Campaigns*, Vol. 1, London: HMSO, 1956.
Carter, G B, *Chemical and Biological Defence at Porton Down, 1916-2000*, London: The Stationary Office, 2000.
Central Statistical Office, *History of the Second World War, Statistical Digest of the War*, London: HMSO, 1951.
Collier, Basil, *History of the Second World War, The Defence of the United Kingdom*, London: HMSO, 1957.
Curry, John, *The Security Service, 1908-1945, The Official History*, London: The Public Record Office, 1999.

Derry, T K, *History of the Second World War: The Campaign in Norway*, London, HMSO, 1952.
Dunn, C D (ed.), *Medical History of the Second World War: Emergency Medical Services*, Vol. I, London: HMSO, 1952.

Edmonds, James, E, Brigadier-General Sir, CB CMG (Comp.) *History of the Great War, Military Operations, France and Belgium, 1916*, Vol. I, *Sir Douglas Haig's Command to the 1st July: Battle of the Somme*, London: Macmillan, 1932.
Ellis, L F, Major, *History of the Second World War, The War in France and Flanders, 1939-1940*, London: HMSO, 1953.

Gibbs, N H, *History of the Second World War, Grand Strategy*, Vol. I, *Rearmament Policy*, London: HMSO, 1976.

Henniker, A M, Colonel, CBE RE (Retired) (Comp.) *History of the Great War, Transportation on the Western Front, 1914-1918*, London: HMSO, 1937.
Hinsley, F H, et al, *History of the Second World War, British Intelligence in the Second World War*, Vol. I, London: HMSO, 1979 and Vol. 2, 1981.
Hornby, William, *History of the Second World War, Factories and Plant*, London: HMSO, 1958.

Indian General Staff, *The Third Afghan War, 1919, Official Account*, Calcutta: Government of India, 1926.
Indian General Staff, *Operations in Waziristan, 1919-1920* (2nd Edition), Delhi: Government Central Press, 1923.
Indian General Staff, *Official History of Operations on the NW Frontier of India 1936-37*, New Delhi: Government of India Press, 1943.
Indian General Staff, *Official History of Operations on the NW Frontier of India 1920-35*, New Delhi: Government of India Press, 1945.

Jones, H A, *History of the Great War, The War in the Air* Vol. VI, London: HMSO, 1937.

Mitchell, T J, Major, DSO MD RAMC and Smith, G M, Miss, MBE MA, *History of the Great War, Medical Services, Casualties and Medical Statistics of the Great War*, London: HMSO, 1931.
Mellor, W Franklin, (ed.), *Medical History of the Second World War, Casualties and Medical Statistics*, London: HMSO, 1972.
Miles, Wilfred, Captain, (Comp.) *History of the Great War, Military Operations, France and Belgium, 1916*, Vol. II, *2nd July 1916 to the End of the Battles of the Somme*, London: HMSO, 1938.

O'Brien, T H, *History of the Second World War, Civil Defence*, London: HMSO, 1955.

Parker, H M D, *History of the Second World War, Manpower, A Study of War-time Policy and Administration*, London: HMSO, 1957.
Payton-Smith, D J, *Oil, A Study in War-time Policy and Administration*, London: HMSO, 1971.

Playfair, I S O, Major-General, CB DSO MC, History of the Second World War (BOH) *The Mediterranean and Middle East*, Vol. I, *The Early Successes against Italy* (to May 1941), London: HMSO, 1954.
Postan, M M, *History of the Second World War, British War Production*, London: HMSO, 1952.

Rexford-Welch, S C, Squadron Leader, MA MRCS LRCP, RAF, *History of the Second World War, The Royal Air Force Medical Services*, Vol. 1, *Administration*, London: HMSO, 1954.
Roskill, S W, Captain DSC RN, *History of the Second World War, The War at Sea*, Vol. I, *The Defensive*, London: HMSO, 1954.
Ross, William F & Romanus, Charles F, *United States Army in World War II, The Quartermaster Corps: Operations in the War against Germany*, Office of the Chief of Military History, Washington: Department of the Army, 1965.

Savage, C I, *History of the Second World War, Inland Transport*, London: HMSO & Longmans, Green & Co, 1957.
Scott, J D, & Hughes, R, *The Administration of War Production*, London: HMSO, 1955.

Webster, Charles, Sir and Frankland, Noble, *History of the Second World War, The Strategic Air Offensive Against Germany, 1939-1945*, Vol. IV, London: HMSO, 1961.

Semi-Official Military Publications and Histories

Fletcher, David, *The Great Tank Scandal: British Armour in the Second World War*, Part 1, London: HMSO, 1989.
Fletcher, David, *Mechanized Force: British Tanks between the Wars*, London: HMSO, 1991.
Fletcher, David, *British Military Transport, 1829-1956*, London: The Stationery Office, 1998.

Harding-Newman, J C, Major-General, CB CMG, *Modern Military Administration, Organization and Transportation*, Aldershot: Gale and Polden, 1933.
Lindsell, W G, Colonel, DSO OBE MC psc RA, *A & Q, or Military Administration in War*, Aldershot: Gale & Polden, Third Edition, 1933.
Lindsell, W G, Sir, Major-General, DSO OBE MC idc psc, *Military Organization and Administration*, Aldershot: Gale & Polden, 23rd Edition, 1941.

Nicholls, T B, Lieutenant-Colonel, MB CHB RAMC (Retired), *Organization, Strategy and Tactics of the Army Medical Services in War*, 2nd Edition, London: Bailliere, Tindall & Cox, 1941.

Philson, Alan, *The British Army, 1939-1945, Tables of Organization and Equipment, British Expeditionary Force, Organization and Order of Battle, 10 May 1940*, (BEFORBAT) 6 Vol. s, Milton Keynes: Military Press, 2005-2007.

Tank Museum, *Data Book of Wheeled Vehicles, Army Transport, 1939-1945*, London: HMSO, 1983.

Ventham, Philip and Fletcher, David, *Moving the Guns: The Mechanization of the Royal Artillery 1854-1939*, London: HMSO, 1990.

Divisional, Regimental and Unit Histories

Aris, George, *The Fifth British Division, Being an account of the Journey and Battles of a Reserve Division in Europe, Africa and Asia*, London: The Fifth Division Benevolent Fund, 1959.

Barclay, C N, Brigadier, CBE DSO, *The History of the Cameronians (Scottish Rifles)*, Vol. III, London: Sifton Praed, nd but 1947.

Barclay, C N, Brigadier, CBE DSO, *The History of the Northumberland Fusiliers in the Second World War*, London: William Clowes, 1952.

Blake, George, *Mountain and Flood: The History of the 52nd (Lowland) Division, 1939-1946*, Glasgow: Jackson, Son & Co, 1950.

Blight, Gordon, Brigadier, *The History of the Berkshire Regiment, 1920-1947*, London & New York: Staples Press, 1953.

Bright, Joan, *The Story of an Armoured Regiment in Battle, 9th Queen's Royal Lancers, 1936-1945*, Aldershot: Gale & Polden, 1951.

Clay, Ewart W, Major, MBE, *The Path of the 50th: The Story of the 50th (Northumbrian) Division in the Second World War, 1939-1945*, Aldershot: Gale & Polden, 1950.

Courage, G, Major, DSO, *The History of the 15/19 The King's Royal Hussars, 1939-1945*, Aldershot: Gale & Polden, 1949.

Cucliffe, Marcus, *History of the Royal Warwickshire Regiment*, 1919-1945, London: William Clowes & Sons, 1956.

Ellis, L F, Major, CVO CBE DSO MC, *Welsh Guards at War*, Aldershot: Gale & Polden, 1946.

Erskine, David (Comp.), *The Scots Guards, 1919-1945*, London: William Clowes and Sons, 1955.

Farndale, Martin, General, Sir, KCB, *History of the Royal Regiment of Artillery: The Years of Defeat 1939-41*, London & Washington: Brasseys, 1996.

Ferguson, Bernard, *The Black Watch and the King's Enemies*, London: Collins, 1950.

Fernyhough, H A, Brigadier, CBE MC & Harris H E D, Major, *History of the Royal Army Ordnance Corps, 1939-1945*, London & Beccles: William Clowes, nd but 1967.

Forbes, A, Major-General, CB CMG, *A History of the Army Ordnance Services*, Vol. III, *The Great War*, London: The Medici Society, 1929.

Gunning, Hugh, Captain, *Borderers in Battle: The War Story of the King's Own Scottish Borderers, 1939-1945*, Berwick-upon-Tweed: The Regiment, 1948.

Guttery, D R, *The Queen's Own Worcestershire Hussars, 1922-1956*, Stourbridge: Mark & Moody, 1958.

Howard, Michael and Sparrow, John, *The Coldstream Guards, 1920-1946*, London, New York & Toronto: Oxford University Press, 1951.

Hughes, B P, Major General, CB CBE, (ed.), *History of the Royal Regiment of Artillery: Between the Wars, 1919-1939*, London & Washington: Brassey's (UK), 1992.

Jervois, W J, Brigadier, MC, *The History of the Northamptonshire Regiment, 1934-1948*, The Regimental History Committee, 1953.

Kemp P K, Lieutenant-Commander RN, *The History of the Norfolk Regiment*, Vol. III, *1919-1945*, Norwich: Regimental Association of The Royal Norfolk Regiment, 1953.

Kempton, Chris, *Locations of the Regiments of the British Army: 1st August 1914 and 1st September 1939*, Milton Keynes: The Military Press, 2006.

Kempton, Chris, *Force K6 The Indian Contingent: The RIASC Mule Companies in France & UK, 1939-1944*, Gillingham: Chris Kempton, 2019.

Kennedy, B B, Brigadier CBE & Tatman, J A, Colonel (Comp.s) *Craftsmen of the Army: The Story of the Royal Electrical and Mechanical Engineers*, London: Leo Cooper, 1970.

Liddell Hart, B H, Captain, *The Tanks: The History of the Royal Tank Regiment and its Predecessors*, Vol. Two, 1914-1939, London: Cassell, 1959.

Martin, T A, Colonel, MBE, *The Essex Regiment, 1929-1950*, The Essex Regiment Association, 1952.

Miller, Charles H, Major-General CB CBE DSO psc, *History of the 13th/18th Royal Hussars (Queen Mary's Own), 1922-1947*, London: Chisman, Bradshaw Ltd, 1949.

Morling, L F, Colonel, DSO OBE TD (Comp.), *Sussex Sappers, A History of the Sussex Volunteer and Territorial Army Royal Engineers from 1890 to 1967*, 208th Field Coy RE Committee, nd but 1973.

na, *A Short History of the 2nd Battalion Royal Fusiliers (City of London Regiment) during the First Year of the War*, Aldershot: Gale & Polden, 1941.

na, *The Story of 46 Division, 1939-1945*, Graz: Styria University Book Press, nd but c1946.

Nalder, R F H, Major-General, CB OBE, *The History of British Army Signals in the Second World War, General Survey*, London: Royal Signals Institution, 1953.

Nicolson, Nigel, Captain, MBE and Forbes, Patrick, *The Grenadier Guards in the War of 1939-1945*, Vol. I, *The Campaigns in North-West Europe*, Aldershot: Gale & Polden, 1949.

Nightingale, P R, Lieutenant Colonel, OBE, *The East Yorkshire Regiment (Duke of York's Own) in the War, 1939-45*, York & London: William Sessions Ltd, 1952.

Pakenham-Walsh, Major-General, R P, CB MC, *The History of the Corps of The Royal Engineers*, Vol. VIII, 1938-1948, Chatham: The Institution of Royal Engineers, 1958.

Parkinson, C Northcote, *Always a Fusilier: The War History of the Royal Fusiliers (City of London Regiment)*, London: Sampson Low, 1949.

Pile, Frederick, General, Sir, GCB DSO MC, *Ack-Ack: Britain's Defence Against Air Attack during the Second World War*, London: George G Harrap & Co, 1949.

Regimental Committee, *The 10th Royal Hussars in the Second World War*, Aldershot: Gale & Polden, 1948.

Regimental Committee, *The Story of the Royal Army Service Corps, 1939-1945*, Aldershot: Institution of the RASC, Bell & Sons, 1955.
Rhodes-Wood, E H, Major, A War History of the Royal Pioneer Corps, 1939-1945, Aldershot: Gale & Polden, 1960.
Riley, Jonathon, Lieutenant General, CB, DSO, Crocker, Peter, Lieutenant Colonel, & Sinnett, Richard, Lieutenant Colonel, *Regimental Records of the Royal Welch Fusiliers, Vol. IV, 1918-1945*, Part One, *November 1918 - May 1940*, Warwick: Helion, 2019.
Rissik, David, *The DLI at War: The History of the Durham Light Infantry, 1939-1945*, Durham: The Depot, nd but 1952.
Routledge, N W, Brigadier, OBE TD, *History of the Royal Regiment of Artillery, Anti-Aircraft Artillery 1914-1955*, London & New York: Brasseys (UK) 1994.

Salmond, J B, *The History of the 51st Highland Division*, Edinburgh & London: William Blackwood & Sons, 1953.
Sutton, John, Brigadier (ed.), *Wait for the Waggon: The Story of the Royal Corps of Transport and its Predecessors, 1794-1993* (Barnsley: Leo Cooper, 1998).

Townsend, C E C, Major (Retired) TD, *All Rank and No File: A History of the Engineer and Railway Staff Corps RE*, 1865-1965, London: The Engineer and Railway Staff Corps RE (TAVR), 1965.
Turpin, Patrick G, Major General, CB OBE MA FCIT, *The Turn of the Wheel: The History of the RASC 1919-1939*, Institution of the Royal Corps of Transport, Buckingham: Barracuda Books, 1988.

Williams, G, Colonel, OBE, *Citizen Soldiers of the Royal Engineers: Transportation & Movements and the Royal Army Service Corps, 1859-1965*, Institute of the Royal Corps of Transport, London & Southampton: The Camelot Press, nd but 1969.
Williamson, Hugh, *The Fourth Division, 1939-1945*, London: Newman Neame, 1951.
Wilson, Edward, *Press On Regardless: The Story of the Fifth Royal Tank Regiment in World War Two*, (Staplehurst: Spellmount, 2003).

Diaries & Memoirs

Danchev, Alex & Todman, Dan (eds), *War Diaries, 1939-1945, Field Marshal Lord Alanbrooke*, London: Weidenfeld & Nicolson, 2001.

Gilbert, Fred, *For You the War is Over* (Unpublished).
Gilbert, Fred, letters April – May 1940 (Courtesy of Elaine Schafer).
Gun Buster, *Return via Dunkirk*, London: Hodder & Stoughton, 1940.

Langley, J M, Lieutenant Colonel, MBE MC, *Fight Another Day*, London: Collins, 1974.

Macleod, Roderick, Colonel and Kelly, Denis (eds.), *The Ironside Diaries, 1937-1940*, London: Constable, 1962.
Minney, R J, *The Private Papers of Hore-Belisha*, London: Collins, 1950.

Montgomery, Viscount, KG, *The Memoirs of Field-Marshal Montgomery of Alamein*, London: Collins, 1958.

Inter-war Books

Bond, Brian, *France and Belgium, 1939-1940: The Politics and Strategy of the Second World War*, London: Harper Collins, 1975.
Bond, Brian, *British Military Policy Between the Two World Wars*, Oxford: Clarendon Press, 1980.
Brice, Martin H, *The Royal Navy and the Sino-Japanese Incident 1937-41*, London: Ian Allan, 1973.

Dennis, Peter, *Decision by Default: Peacetime Conscription and British Defence 1919-1939*, London: Routledge & Kegan Paul, 1972.
Dennis, Peter, *The Territorial Army, 1907-1940*, The Royal Historical Society, Woodbridge: The Boydell Press, 1987.

Edgerton, David, *Warfare State Britain 1920-1970*, Cambridge: Cambridge University Press, 2006.

Forczyk, Robert, *Case White: The Invasion of Poland, 1939*, Oxford: Osprey, 2019.
French, David, *Raising Churchill's Army: The British Army and the War against Germany, 1919-1945*, New York: Oxford University Press, 2000.

Higham, Robin, *Armed Forces in Peacetime, Britain, 1918-1940 a Case Study*, London: G T Foulis, 1962.
Howard, Michael, *The Continental Commitment: The Dilemma of British Defence Policy in the Era of Two World Wars*, London: Temple Smith, 1972.
Harris, J P, *Men, Ideas and Tanks: British military thought and armoured forces, 1903-1939*, Manchester: Manchester University Press, 1995.

Johnson, Gaynor, (ed.), *Locarno Revisited: European Diplomacy, 1920-1929*, London & New York: Routledge, 2004.

Kaufmann, J E, Kaufmann, H W, Jankovic-Potocnik, A & Lang, P, *The Maginot Line: History and Guide*, Barnsley: Pen & Sword, 2011.

Liddell-Hart, Basil, *The Defence of Britain*, London: Faber & Faber 1939.

Marks, Sally, *The Illusion of Peace: International Relations in Europe, 1918-1933*, Basingstoke: Palgrave Macmillan, 2003.
Morehead, Steven, *The British Defence of Egypt 1936-1940: Conflict and Crisis in the Eastern Mediterranean*, London & New York: Frank Cass, 2005.
Murray, Williamson, *The Change in the European Balance of Power, 1938-1939*, Yale: Yale University Press, 1975.

Noakes, Lucy, *Women in the British Army: War and the Gentler Sex, 1907-1948*, London & New York: Routledge, 2006.

Peden, G C, *British Rearmament and the Treasury, 1932-1939*, Edinburgh: Scottish Academic Press, 1979.

Portway, David, *Science and Mechanisation in Land Warfare*, Cambridge: W Heffer & Sons Ltd, 1938.

Robson, Brian, *Crisis on the Frontier: The Third Afghan War and the Campaigns in Waziristan, 1919-1920*, Staplehurst: Spellmount, 2004.

Salmon, Roger, *Everything Worked Like Clockwork: The Mechanization of the British Regular and Household Cavalry, 1918-1942*, Solihull: Helion, 2016.

Shay, Robert Paul Jr, *British Rearmament in the Thirties: Politics and Profits*, Guildford: Princeton University Press, 1977.

Wark, Wesley K, *The Ultimate Enemy: British Intelligence and Nazi Germany, 1933-1939*, London: I B Tauris, 1985.

Warren, Allan, *Waziristan: The Faqir of Ipi and the Indian Army, The North West Frontier Revolt of 1936-37*, Bangalore: Oxford University Press, 2000.

Winton, Harold R, *To Change an Army: General Sir John Burnett-Stuart and British Armoured Doctrine, 1927-1938*, Kansas: University of Kansas Press, 1988.

British Expeditionary Force & British Air Forces in France Books

Baughen, Greg, *The Fairey Battle, A Reassessment of its RAF Career* Stroud: Fonthill, 2017.

Bingham, Victor F, *Blitzed, The Battle of France, May-June 1940*, New Malden: Air Research Publications, 1990.

Blaxland, Gregory, *Destination Dunkirk: The Story of Gort's Army*, London: William Kimber, 1973.

Bond, Brian & Taylor, Michael (eds.), *The Battle for France and Flanders, Sixty Years On*, Barnsley: Leo Cooper, 2001.

Bond, Geoffrey, *Lancastria*, London: Oldbourne, 1959

Brazier, C C H, Brigadier, OBE, *XD Operations: Secret British Missions Denying Oil to the Nazis*, Barnsley: Pen & Sword, 2004.

Cornwell, Peter D, *The Battle of France, Then and Now: Six Nations Locked in Aerial Combat, September 1939 - June 1940* Old Harlow: Battle of Britain International, 2007.

Crabb, Brian James, *The Forgotten Tragedy: The Story of the Sinking of HMT Lancastria*, Donington: Shaun Tyas, 2002.

David, Saul, *Churchill's Sacrifice of the Highland Division, France 1940*, London & Washington: Brasseys 1994.

Fenby, Jonathan, *The Sinking of the Lancastria: Britain's Greatest Maritime Disaster and Churchill's Cover-Up*, London: Simon & Schuster, 2005.

Glover, Michael, *The Fight for the Channel Ports: A Study in Confusion*, London: Leo Cooper, 1985.

Jackson, Robert, *Air War over France, 1939-40*, London: Ian Allan, 1974.

Karslake, Basil, *1940: The Last Act: The Story of the British Forces in France after Dunkirk*, London: Leo Cooper, 1979.

Longden, Sean, *Dunkirk: The Men They Left Behind*, London: Constable, 2008.

Lynch, Tim, *Dunkirk 1940, Whereabouts Unknown: How Untrained Troops of the Labour Divisions were Sacrificed to Save an Army*, Stroud: Spellmount, 2010.

Nicholls, Mark & Washington, Linda (eds.) *Against All Odds: The British Army, 1939-1940*, London: National Army Museum, 1990.

Sebag-Montefiore, Hugh, *Dunkirk: Fight To the Last Man*, London: Viking, 2006.

Smalley, Edward, *The British Expeditionary Force, 1939-40*, Basingstoke: Palgrave-Macmillan, 2015.

Terraine, John, *Right of the Line, The Royal Air Force in the European War 1939-1945*, London: Hodder and Stoughton 1985.

Thurlow, Dave, *Building the Gort Line: The BEF and its Defences in France, 1939-40*, Warwick: Helion, 2019.

Logistics Books

Adkin, F J, *RAF Ground Support Equipment Since 1918*, Shrewsbury: Air Publishing, 1996.

Aves, William A T, *Supporting the British Expeditionary Force: The Royal Engineer Railway Units in France, 1939-1940*, Donington: Shaun Tyas, 2012.

Beith, John Hay, Major-General, CBE MC, *ROF, The Story of the Royal Ordnance Factories, 1939-1948*, London: HMSO: 1949.

Bell, R, CBE, *History of British Railways during the War 1939-1945*, London: The Railway Gazette, 1946.

Brooksbank, B W L, *London Main Line War Damage*, London: Capital Transport, 2007.

Bryan, Tim, *The Great Western at War 1939-1945*, Sparkford: Patrick Stephens Ltd, 1995.

Butler, Robert, *Richborough Port*, Ramsgate: Ramsgate Maritime Museum & East Kent Maritime Trust, 1999.

Coates, Robert, *Bedford to Berlin and Beyond, QL: The Forces Favourite 4x4*, Croydon: Fitzjames Press, 1994.

Cocroft, Wayne D, *Dangerous Energy: The Archaeology of Gunpowder and Military Explosives Manufacture*, Swindon: English Heritage, 2000.

Cole, Howard N, Lieutenant Colonel, OBE TD DL, *NAAFI in Uniform*, Aldershot: The Forces Press, 1982.

Cooke, R A, *Atlas of the Great Western Railway as at 1947* (Revised Edition), Didcot: Wild Swan Publications, 1997.

Cooper, Alan, Leggott, Peter & Sprenger, Cyril, *The Melbourne Military Railway, A History of the Railway Training Centre at Melbourne and King's Newton: 1939-1945*, Headington: Oakwood Press, 1990.

Croome, Desmond F, & Jackson, Alan, *Rails Through the Clay: A History of London's Tube Railways*, London: Capital Transport, 2nd Edition, 1993.

Crump, Norman, *By Rail to Victory: The Story of the LNER in Wartime*, London: The London & North Eastern Railway, 1947.

Darwin, Bernard, *War on the Line: The Story of the Southern Railway in War-Time*, Waterloo: The Southern Railway, 1946.

Dendy-Marshall, C F, (Revised by R W Kidner), *History of The Southern Railway*, London: Ian Allan, 1988.

Dinardo, R L, *Mechanized Juggernaut or Military Anachronism? Horses and the German Army of WWII*, Mechanicsburg: Stackpole Books, 2008.

Earnshaw, Alan, *Britain's Railways at War*, Penryn: Atlantic Publishing, 1995.

Evan, John, *Time Table for Victory: British Railways War History, 1939-45*, London: The British Railways, nd but 1947.

Frank, Reinhard, *Trucks of the Wehrmacht: German Vehicles in World War II*, Atglen PA: Schiffer Publishing Ltd, 1994.

Freathy, Les, *British Military Trucks of World War Two: Manufacturers, Types, Variants and Service of Trucks in British Army and Royal Air Force Service, 1939-1945*, Erlangen: Tankograd Publishing, 2013.

Georgano, G N, *World War Two Military Vehicles (Transport and Half-Tracks)*, London: Osprey Automotive, 1994.

Great Western Railway, Miscellaneous Instructions covering the Conveyance of Merchandise and Live Stock Traffic, Paddington: Great Western Railway, 1930.

Harman, Richard and Nichols, Gerry, *Atlas of the Southern Railway*, Addlestone: Ian Allan, 2016.

Jordan, Roger, *The World's Merchant Fleets 1939, The Particulars and Fates of 6,000 Ships*, Annapolis: Naval Institute Press, 1999.

Maginniss, Clem, *An Unappreciated Field of Endeavour: Logistics and the British Expeditionary Force on the Western Front, 1914-1918*, Warwick: Helion, 2018.

Marcosson, Issac F, *The Business of War*, London: John Lane, The Bodley Head, 1918.

McCamley, N J, *Secret Underground Cities*, Barnsley: Leo Cooper, 1998.

McCamley, Nick, *Subterranean Britain: Second World War Secret Bunkers*, Monkton Farleigh: Folly Books, 2010.

McCamley, Nick, *The Fauld Disaster, 27 November 1944*, Monkton Farleigh: Folly Books, 2015.

Mullay A J, *For the King's Service, Railway Ships at War*, Easingwold: Pendragon Publishing, 2008.

na, *The Railway Executive Committee and its Headquarters*, London: The Railway Gazette, 1944.
Nash, George C, *The LMS at War*, Euston: The London Midland & Scottish Railway, 1946.
Nevell, Mike, Roberts, John, & Smith, Jack, *A History of Royal Ordnance Factory, Chorley*, Lancaster: Carnegie Publishing, 1999.
Nock, O S, *Britain's Railways at War, 1939-1945*, London: Ian Allan, 1971.

O'Brien, Phillips Payson, *How the War was Won*, Cambridge: Cambridge University Press, 2015.

Plummer, Russell, *The Ships That Saved an Army: A Comprehensive Record of the 1,300 'Little Ships' of Dunkirk*, Wellingborough: Patrick Stephens Limited, 1990.

Robbins, R M, *190 in Persia, London:* Published Privately, *1951.*
Ronald D W & Carter, R J, *The Longmoor Military Railway*, Newton Abbot: David & Charles, 1974.
Ronald, David and Christensen, Mike, OBE, *The Longmoor Military Railway: A New History*, Vol. One: *1903-1939*, Lydney: Lightmoor Press, 2012.
Ronald, David and Christensen, Mike, OBE, *The Longmoor Military Railway: A New History*, Vol. Two: *World War Two and the Cold War Era*, Lydney: Lightmoor Press, 2013.

Shaw G C, Brevet Lieutenant-Colonel, *Supply in Modern War*, London: Faber & Faber, nd but 1938.
Smithers, A J, *Rude Mechanicals: An Account of Tank Maturity during the Second World War*, London: Leo Cooper, 1987.

Tapper, Oliver, *Armstrong-Whitworth Aircraft Since 1913*, London: Putnam, 1973.
Tatlow, Peter, *Return from Dunkirk: Railways to the Rescue, Operation Dynamo (1940)*, Usk: Oakwood Press, 2010.
Tuttle, William, G T, *Defense Logistics for the 21st Century*, Jr, Annapolis: Naval Institute Press, 2005.

Vanderveen, Bart, *Historic Military Vehicles Directory*, London: Battle of Britain International Prints Ltd, 1989.
Vollert, Jochen, *British Military Trucks in Wehrmacht Service*, Erlangen: Tankograd Publishing, 2012.
Winser, de S, John, *BEF Ships: Before at and after Dunkirk*, Gravesend: World Ship Society, 1999.

General Books

Addison, Paul and Crang, Jeremy A (eds.), *Listening to Britain, Home Intelligence Reports on Britain's Finest Hour, May-September 1940*, London: The Bodley Head, 2010.

Bigland, Eileen, *Britain's Other Army*, London: Nicholson & Watson, 1946.

Chamberlain, Peter and Doyle, Hilary, *Encyclopedia of German Tanks of World War Two*, London: Arms & Armour, 1999.

Chamberlain, Peter and Ellis, Chris, *British and American Tanks of World War Two*, London: Arms & Armour, 2000.

Churchill, Winston, S, *The Second World War*, Vol. II, *Their Finest Hour*, London: Cassell, 1949.

Colville, J R, *Man of Valour: Field-Marshal Gort VC*, London: Collins, 1972.

Eden, Phillip, *Great British Weather Disasters*, London: Continuum, 2008.

Egbert, Kieser, *Hitler On the Doorstep*, (translated by Helmut Bogler), London: Arms & Armour Press, 1997.

FitzGerald, Desmond, *Many Parts: The Life and Travels of a Soldier, Engineer and Arbitrator in Africa and Beyond*, London: Radcliffe Press, 2007.

Hamilton, Nigel, *Monty: The Making of a General 1887-1942*, London: Hamish Hamilton 1981.

Hamilton, Nigel, *The Full Monty: Montgomery of Alamein*, 1887-1942, London: Allen Lane, 2001.

Hawkins, Mac, *The Somerset & Dorset: Then and Now*, Wellingborough: Patrick Stephens Ltd, 1986.

Larn, Richard & Bridget, *Shipwreck Index of the British Isles*, Vol 3, *The East Coast*, London: Lloyd's Register of Shipping, 1998.

Larn, Richard & Bridget, *Shipwreck Index of the British Isles*, Vol 4, *Scotland*, London: Lloyd's Register of Shipping, 1998.

Longmate, Norman, *The Real Dad's Army, London:* Arrow Books, 1974.

Mackenzie, S P, *The Home Guard: A Political and Military History*, Oxford: Oxford University Press, 1995.

Mead, Richard, *General Boy: The Life of Lieutenant General Sir Frederick Browning*, Barnsley: Pen & Sword, 2010.

Moritz, Joseph, *Towards a Wider War: British Decision-Making and Military Effectiveness in Scandinavia, 1939-40*, Solihull: Helion, 2017.

na, *Britain's Modern Army*, London: Oldhams Press, 1941.

na, *The British Army in WWII*, London: Greenhill Books 1990.

Ramsey, Winston, G (ed.), *The Blitz: Then and Now*, Vol. 1, London: Battle of Britain Prints International Limited, 1987.

Street, A G, *From Dusk Till Dawn*, London: George Harrap & Co 1943.

Wavell, Archibald, *Generals and Generalship: The Lees Knowles Lectures Delivered at Trinity College Cambridge in 1939*, London: Macmillan, 1941.

Articles & Chapters

Bateman, Denis, C, 'Goodbye to Boots and Saddles, The Twilight of the British Cavalry', *British Army Review*, No 114, UK Ministry of Defence, December 1996, pp.75-89.

Bond, Brian, 'Dunkirk: Myths and Lessons', *The RUSI Journal*, Vol. 127, Issue 3, 1982, pp.3-8.

Burnett-Stuart, J, 'The Progress of Mechanisation', J, *Army Quarterly*, Vol. XVI, April 1928, pp.30-51.

Cameron, D C, Colonel, OBE RASC, 'The Supply of Mechanized Forces in the Field', *Royal United Services Institute*, Vol. LXXIV November 1929, No 496, pp.744-758.

Erskine, David, B, 'No Truce with Time …', *Tank Journal*, May 1990, pp.20-23.

Fletcher, David, 'The White Rhino's Baptism of Fire, 1st Armoured Division in France', 1940, *Military Illustrated 86*, July 1995, pp.36-38.

Hawes, Major General, L A, CBE DSO MC, 'The Story of the "W" Plan, The Move of Our Forces to France in 1939', *Army Quarterly*, July 1971, pp.445-456.

Johnston, Hamish, 'A Corner of Pakistan in Scotland', *Highland Family History Society*, 2012.

Lindsell, W G, Major (Temp. Lieutenant-Colonel), DSO OBE MC psc RA, 'Administrative Lessons of the Great War', *Journal of the Royal United Service Institution*, Vol. LXXI, February 1926, pp.712-719.

Lockhart, L K, Major MBE MC RA, 'Movement of a Division by Mechanical Transport', *The Army Quarterly*, Vol. XXXIV, April – July 1937, pp.98-106.

Mackenzie, E F W, Major, OBE MC RAMC, 'Report on a Series of Tests performed to ascertain the efficiency of the Ammonia Chlorine Treatment of Water applied by a Standardized Method', *Journal of the Royal Army Medical Corps*, Vol. LXVI, No 4, April 1936, pp.217-227.

Maginniss, C H, Major, 'The Most Unkindest Cut: The Impact of Manoeuvre Warfare upon Logistics in 1940', *British Army Review*, No 117, UK Ministry of Defence, December 1997, pp.16-29.

Maginniss, C H, Lieutenant Colonel, 'Hearts of Oak: The Stoneleigh Home Guard Platoon Group in the Defence of Middle England, 1940-1944', *British Army Review*, No 124, UK Ministry of Defence, Spring 2000, pp.61-71.

Maginniss, Clem, *An Unappreciated Field of Endeavour: Logistics and the British Expeditionary Force on the Western Front, 1914-1918*, (Warwick: Helion, 2018), Chapter 10, 'Four Wheels on My Wagon, The influence of Wheeled Motor Transport upon British Army operations on the Western Front, 1914-1918'.

Margry, Karel, 'Mustard Disaster at Bari', *After The Battle Magazine No 79*, London: Battle of Britain Prints International Ltd, 1993, pp.34-46.

Oliver, Hugh B, 'A Wartime Midlands Railway Branch', *Railway World*, December 1960, pp.376-381.

na, 'The Operations of the British Expeditionary Force in Belgium and Northern France', *The Journal of the Royal United Service Institution*, Vol. LXXXV, August 1940, No 539, pp.393-398.

Phillips, Christopher, 'Logistics and the BEF: The Development of Waterborne Transport on the Western Front, 1914-1916', *British Journal of Military History*, Vol 2, No 2 (2016).

Pyper, Alice, 'Manufacturing Munitions at Pembrey during the Two World Wars', *The Carmarthenshire Antiquary*, Vol. 53, 2017.

Reed, John, '21 Maintenance Unit RAF Fauld', *After The Battle Magazine No 18*, London: Battle of Britain Prints International Ltd, 1978, pp.35-40.

Shay, Robert Paul Jr, *British Rearmament in the Thirties, Politics and Profits* (Guildford: Princeton University Press, 1977), Chapter III, 'Industrial Mobilization for Rearmament'.

Sixsmith, E K G, Major General, CB CBE, 'The British Army in May 1940 - a comparison with the BEF 1914', *The RUSI Journal*, Vol. 127, Issue 3, 1992, pp.8-10.

Smalley, Edward, 'Discipline', *The British Expeditionary Force, 1939-40*, Basingstoke: Palgrave-Macmillan, 2015, pp.141-175.

Toler, T I J, Major, 'Poison Gas Manufacture in the UK', *After The Battle Magazine No 79*, London: Battle of Britain Prints International Ltd, 1993, pp.12-33.

Theses & Dissertations

Jones, Alexander, 'Pinchbeck Regulars? The Role and Organisation of the Territorial Army, 1919-1940' (Balliol College University of Oxford, PhD Thesis, 2016).

Maginniss, C H, 'Leadership, Propaganda and Popular Morale during the Battle of Britain', (University of Warwick, BA Dissertation, 1977).

Index

Notes:

1. Some terms, for example, BEF, GHQ, WMT, supply, dumps, movement and Base Area, which appear frequently throughout the text have been omitted from the Index unless they are linked to a specific reference.
2. Formations, Regiments, Corps and units are listed alphabetically and numerically, not by precedence. BEF Corps logistic units are identified thus eg II CAP rather than 2 CAP, to prevent confusion with Divisional elements.
3. There is no General Index; the subjects have been allocated in the manner of the time to G, Q and A. Locations in tables are not generally listed.

PEOPLE

PLACES

General

Belgium

France

United Kingdom

FORMATIONS & UNITS

British Expeditionary Forces

BEF Corps

Line of Communication

Divisions

Brigades

Armoured Units

Infantry Battalions

Royal Artillery

Railway & Docks Units - Royal Engineers

Medical Units

Miscellaneous

Production & Logistic Installations - United Kingdom

G - General Staff

Q - Quartermaster-General

A - Adjutant-General

Government & Commercial